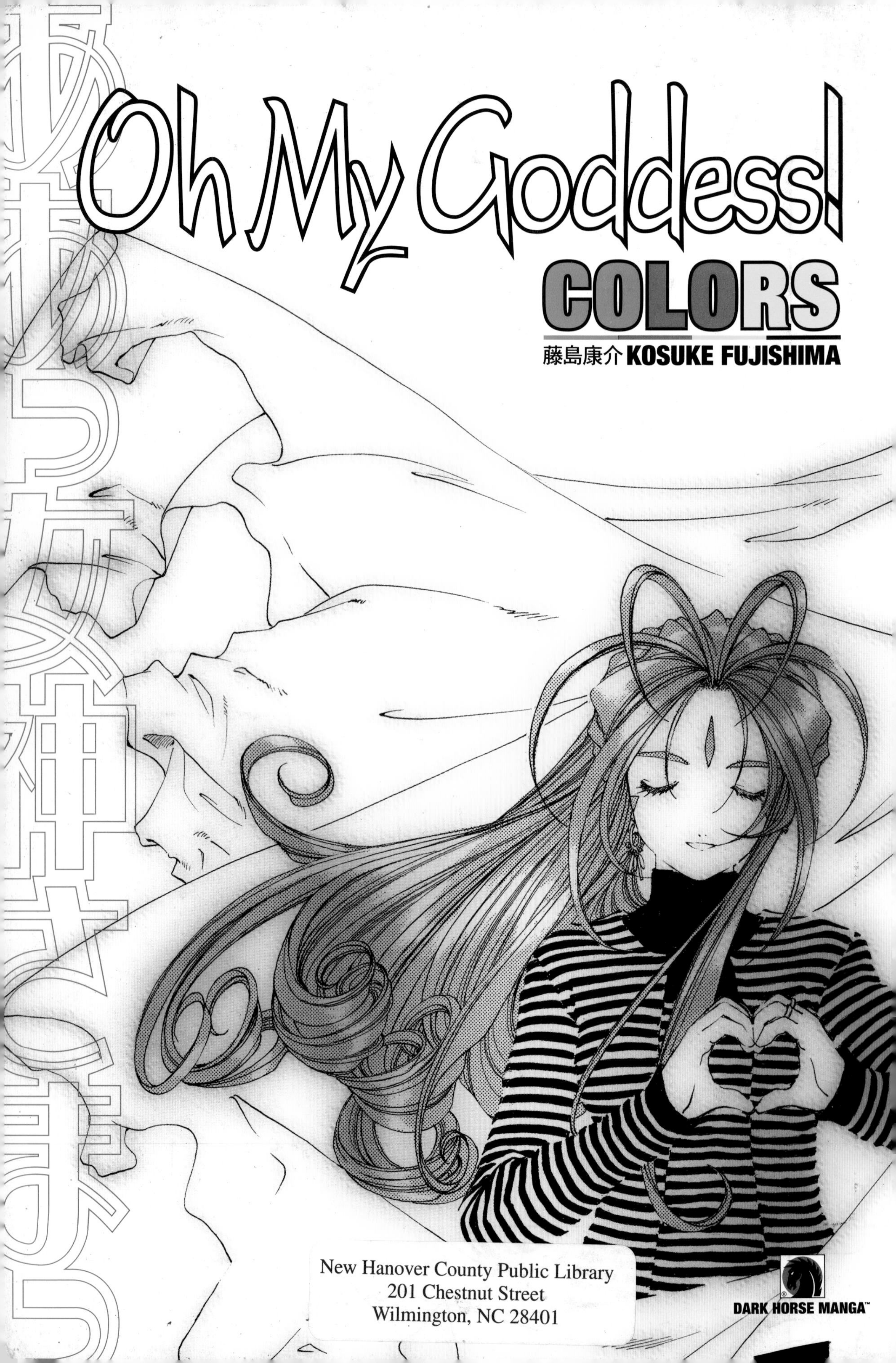
Oh My Goddess!
COLORS
藤島康介 KOSUKE FUJISHIMA
DARK HORSE MANGA™

OH MY GODDESS! COLORS **CONTENTS**

ALL-COLOR MANGA!

READINGS

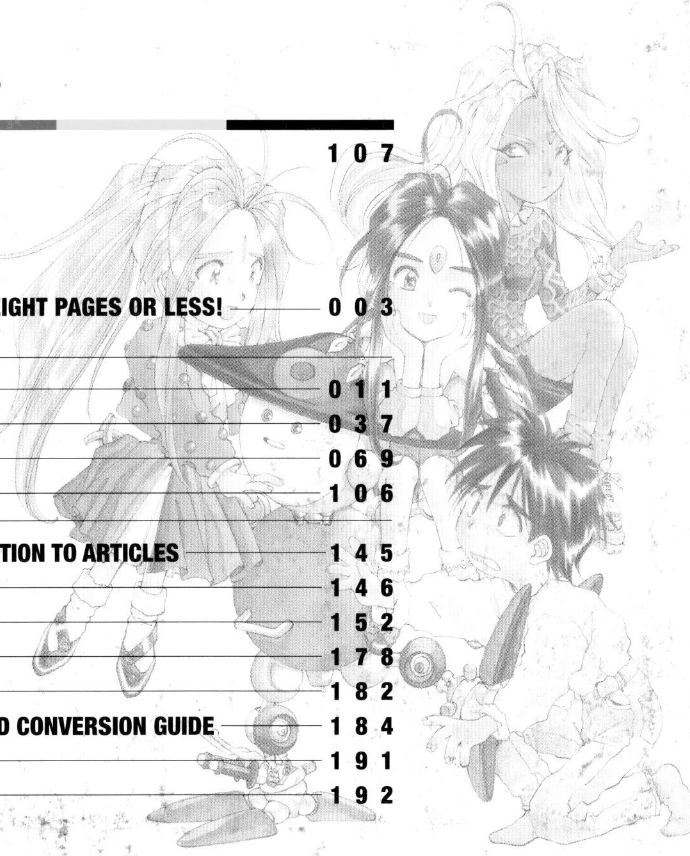

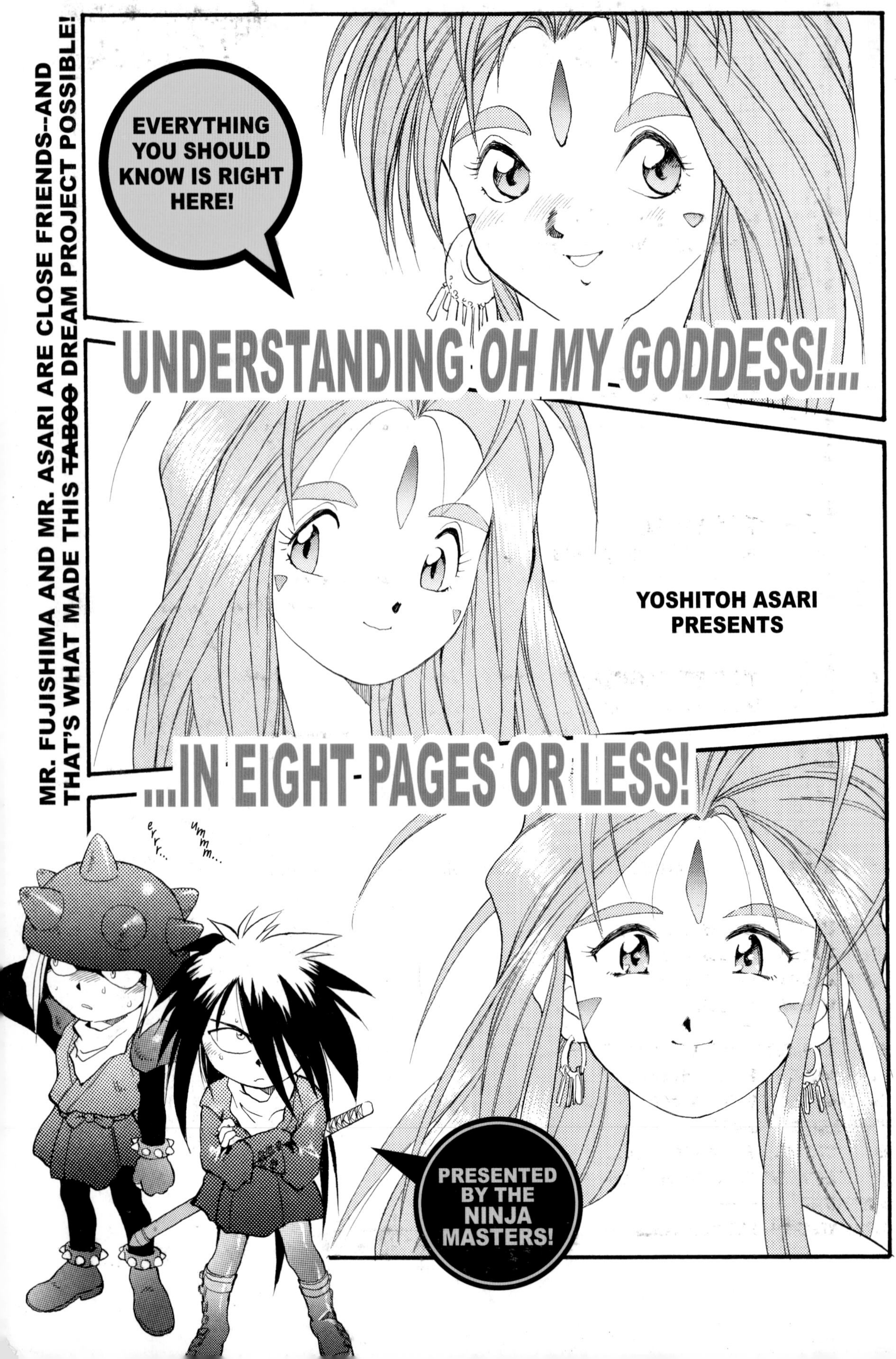
EVERYTHING YOU SHOULD KNOW IS RIGHT HERE!
UNDERSTANDING OH MY GODDESS!...
YOSHITOH ASARI PRESENTS
...IN EIGHT PAGES OR LESS!
umm...
errr...
PRESENTED BY THE NINJA MASTERS!
MR. FUJISHIMA AND MR. ASARI ARE CLOSE FRIENDS--AND THAT'S WHAT MADE THIS ~~TABOO~~ DREAM PROJECT POSSIBLE!

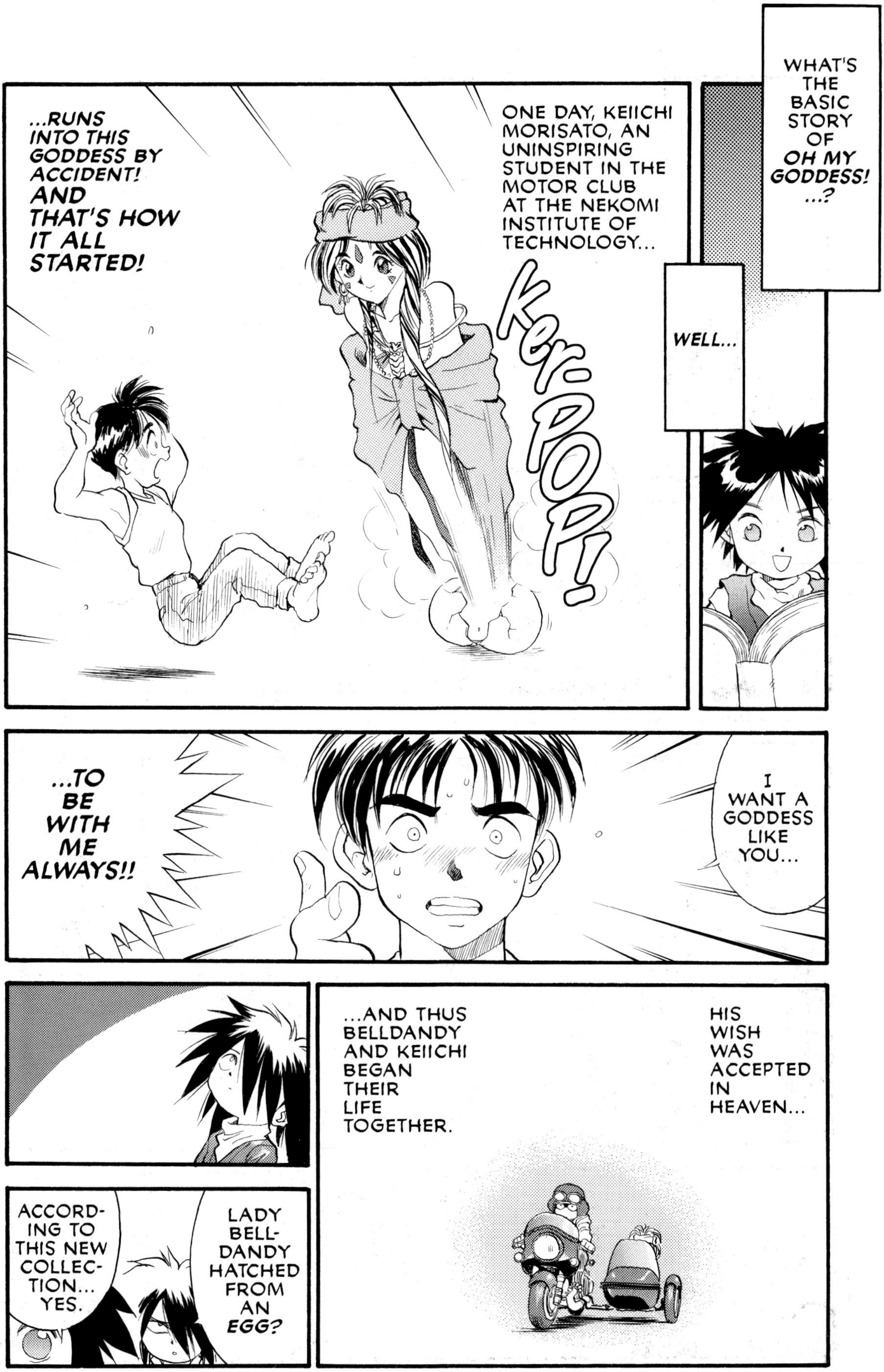

WHAT'S THE BASIC STORY OF OH MY GODDESS! ...?
WELL...
ONE DAY, KEIICHI MORISATO, AN UNINSPIRING STUDENT IN THE MOTOR CLUB AT THE NEKOMI INSTITUTE OF TECHNOLOGY...
KER-POP!
...RUNS INTO THIS GODDESS BY ACCIDENT! AND THAT'S HOW IT ALL STARTED!
I WANT A GODDESS LIKE YOU...
...TO BE WITH ME ALWAYS!!
HIS WISH WAS ACCEPTED IN HEAVEN...
...AND THUS BELLDANDY AND KEIICHI BEGAN THEIR LIFE TOGETHER.
LADY BELLDANDY HATCHED FROM AN EGG?
ACCORDING TO THIS NEW COLLECTION... YES.

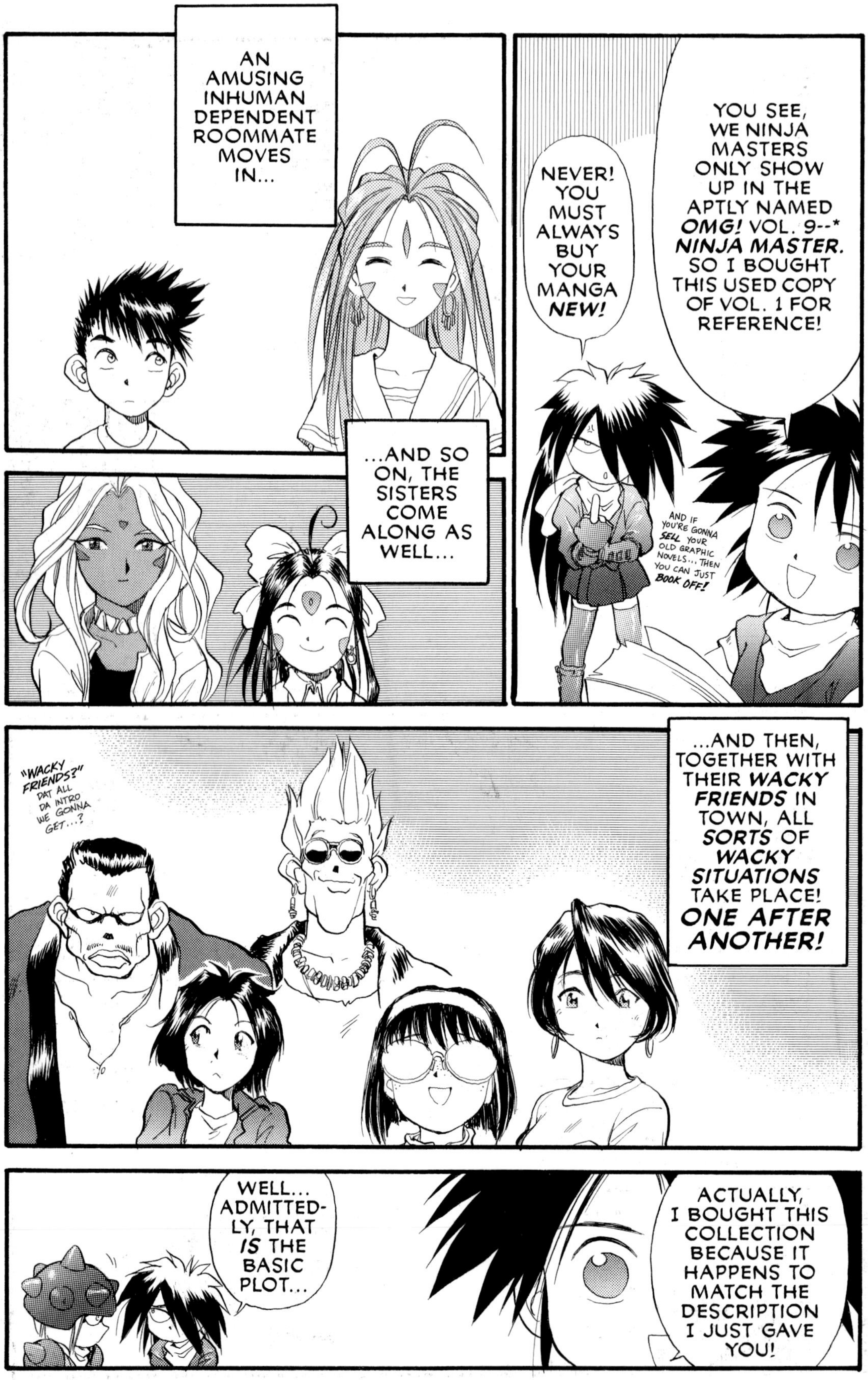
YOU SEE, WE NINJA MASTERS ONLY SHOW UP IN THE APTLY NAMED OMG! VOL. 9--* NINJA MASTER. SO I BOUGHT THIS USED COPY OF VOL. 1 FOR REFERENCE!
NEVER! YOU MUST ALWAYS BUY YOUR MANGA NEW!
AND IF YOU'RE GONNA SELL YOUR OLD GRAPHIC NOVELS... THEN YOU CAN JUST BOOK OFF!
AN AMUSING INHUMAN DEPENDENT ROOMMATE MOVES IN...
...AND SO ON, THE SISTERS COME ALONG AS WELL...
...AND THEN, TOGETHER WITH THEIR WACKY FRIENDS IN TOWN, ALL SORTS OF WACKY SITUATIONS TAKE PLACE! ONE AFTER ANOTHER!
"WACKY FRIENDS?" DAT ALL DA INTRO WE GONNA GET...?
ACTUALLY, I BOUGHT THIS COLLECTION BECAUSE IT HAPPENS TO MATCH THE DESCRIPTION I JUST GAVE YOU!
WELL... ADMITTED-LY, THAT IS THE BASIC PLOT...

*VOLUME 9 IN THE FLOPPED EDITION, THAT IS! VOLUMES 8-9 IN THE UNFLOPPED EDITION! SEE P.186

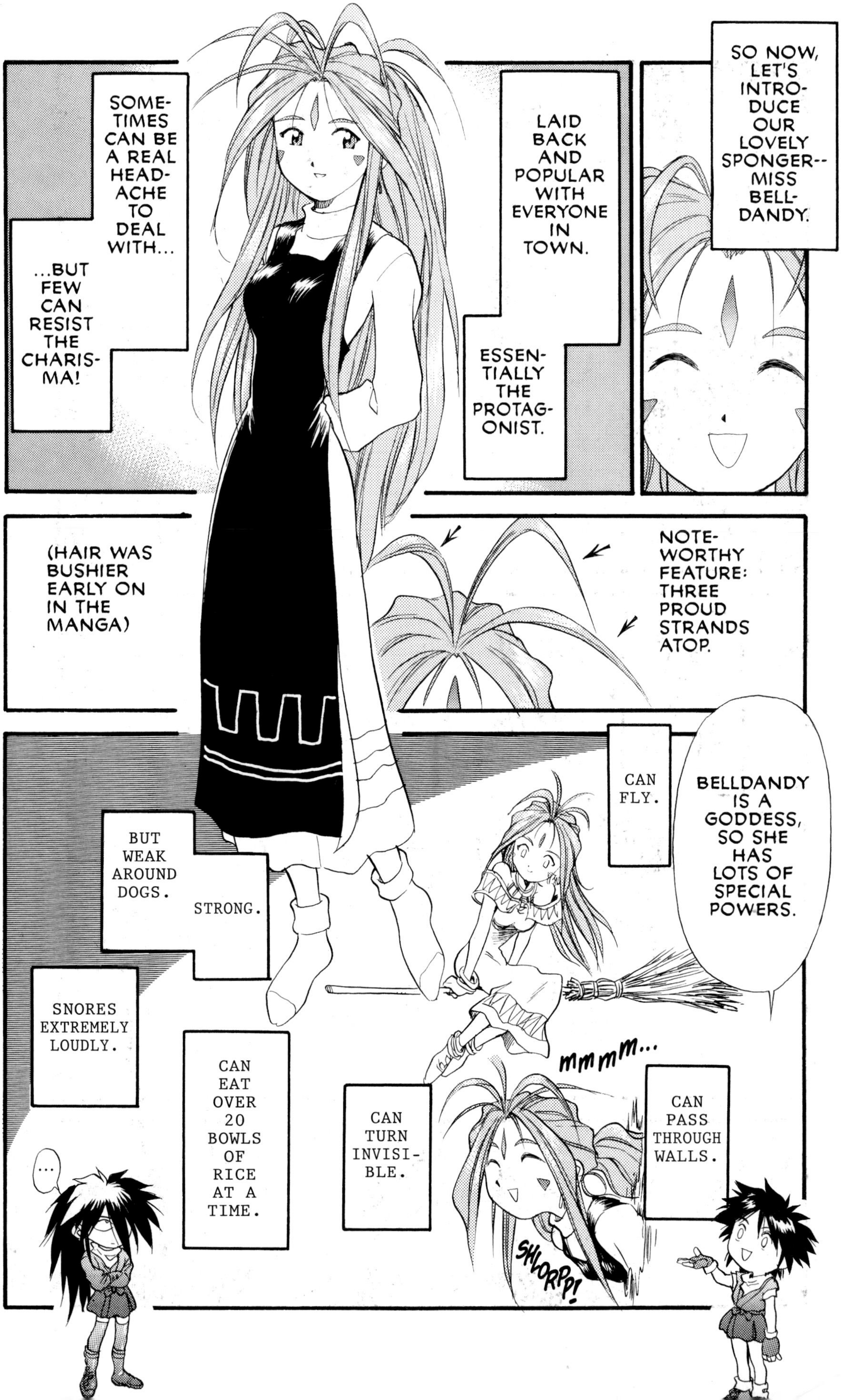
SO NOW, LET'S INTRO-DUCE OUR LOVELY SPONGER-- MISS BELL-DANDY.
LAID BACK AND POPULAR WITH EVERYONE IN TOWN.
ESSEN-TIALLY THE PROTAG-ONIST.
SOME-TIMES CAN BE A REAL HEAD-ACHE TO DEAL WITH...
...BUT FEW CAN RESIST THE CHARIS-MA!
NOTE-WORTHY FEATURE: THREE PROUD STRANDS ATOP.
(HAIR WAS BUSHIER EARLY ON IN THE MANGA)
BELLDANDY IS A GODDESS, SO SHE HAS LOTS OF SPECIAL POWERS.
CAN FLY.
STRONG.
BUT WEAK AROUND DOGS.
SNORES EXTREMELY LOUDLY.
CAN PASS THROUGH WALLS.
mmmm...
SHLORPP!
CAN TURN INVISI-BLE.
CAN EAT OVER 20 BOWLS OF RICE AT A TIME.
...

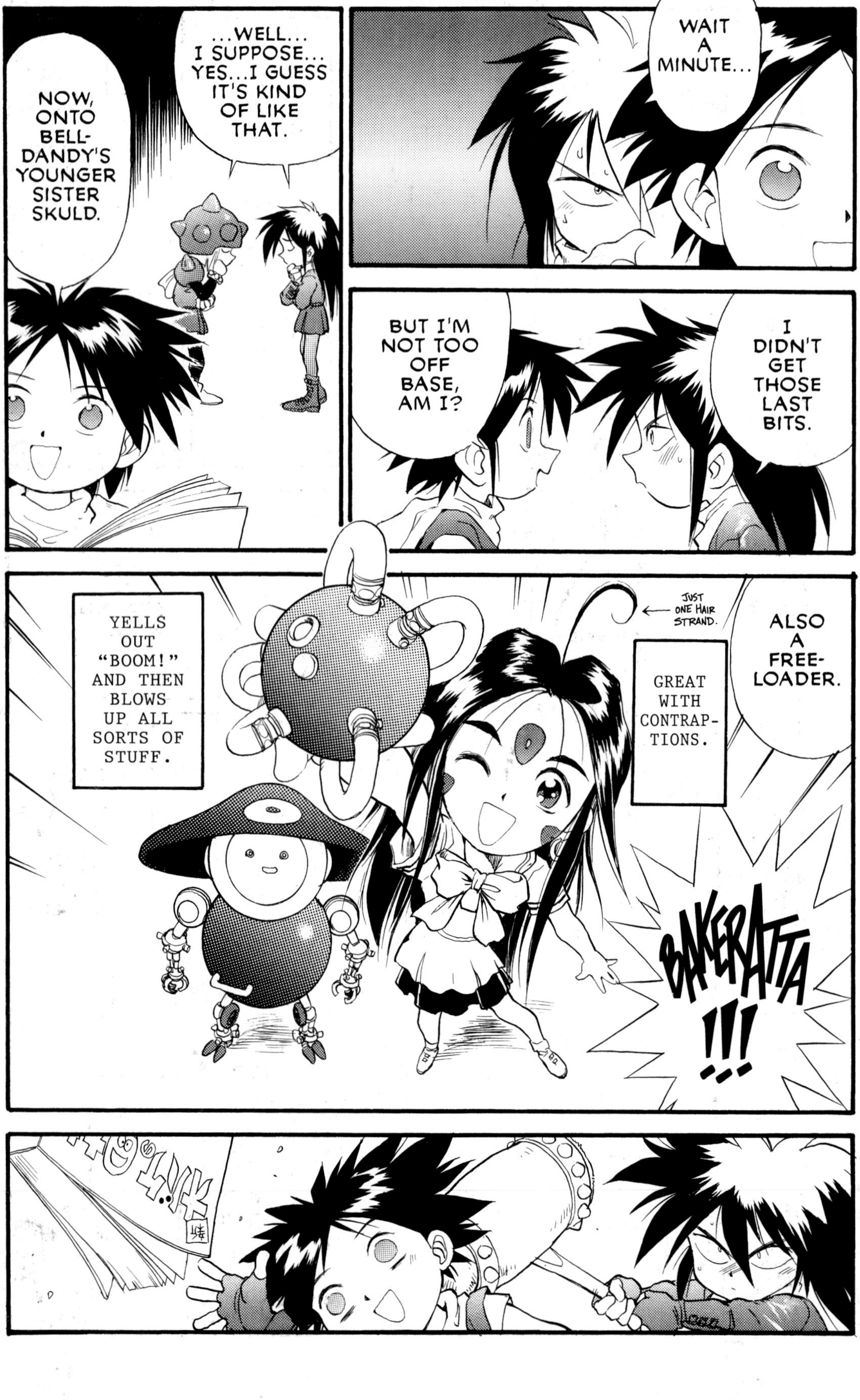
WAIT A MINUTE...
I DIDN'T GET THOSE LAST BITS.
BUT I'M NOT TOO OFF BASE, AM I?
...WELL... I SUPPOSE... YES...I GUESS IT'S KIND OF LIKE THAT.
NOW, ONTO BELL-DANDY'S YOUNGER SISTER SKULD.
ALSO A FREE-LOADER.
JUST ONE HAIR STRAND.
GREAT WITH CONTRAP-TIONS.
YELLS OUT "BOOM!" AND THEN BLOWS UP ALL SORTS OF STUFF.
BAKERATTA!!!

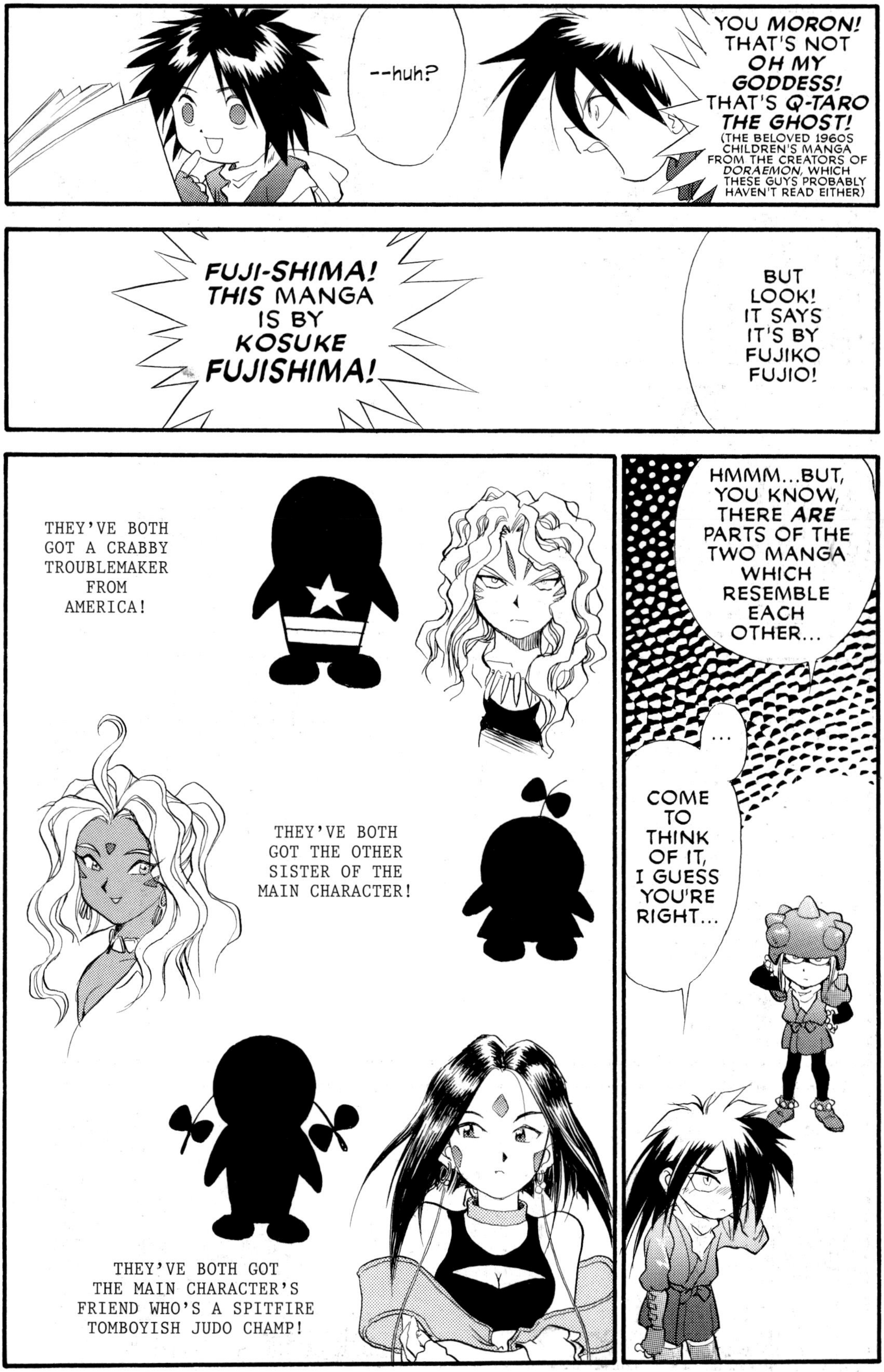
YOU MORON! THAT'S NOT OH MY GODDESS! THAT'S Q-TARO THE GHOST!
(THE BELOVED 1960S CHILDREN'S MANGA FROM THE CREATORS OF DORAEMON, WHICH THESE GUYS PROBABLY HAVEN'T READ EITHER)
--huh?
BUT LOOK! IT SAYS IT'S BY FUJIKO FUJIO!
FUJI-SHIMA! THIS MANGA IS BY KOSUKE FUJISHIMA!
HMMM...BUT, YOU KNOW, THERE ARE PARTS OF THE TWO MANGA WHICH RESEMBLE EACH OTHER...
...
COME TO THINK OF IT, I GUESS YOU'RE RIGHT...
THEY'VE BOTH GOT A CRABBY TROUBLEMAKER FROM AMERICA!
THEY'VE BOTH GOT THE OTHER SISTER OF THE MAIN CHARACTER!
THEY'VE BOTH GOT THE MAIN CHARACTER'S FRIEND WHO'S A SPITFIRE TOMBOYISH JUDO CHAMP!

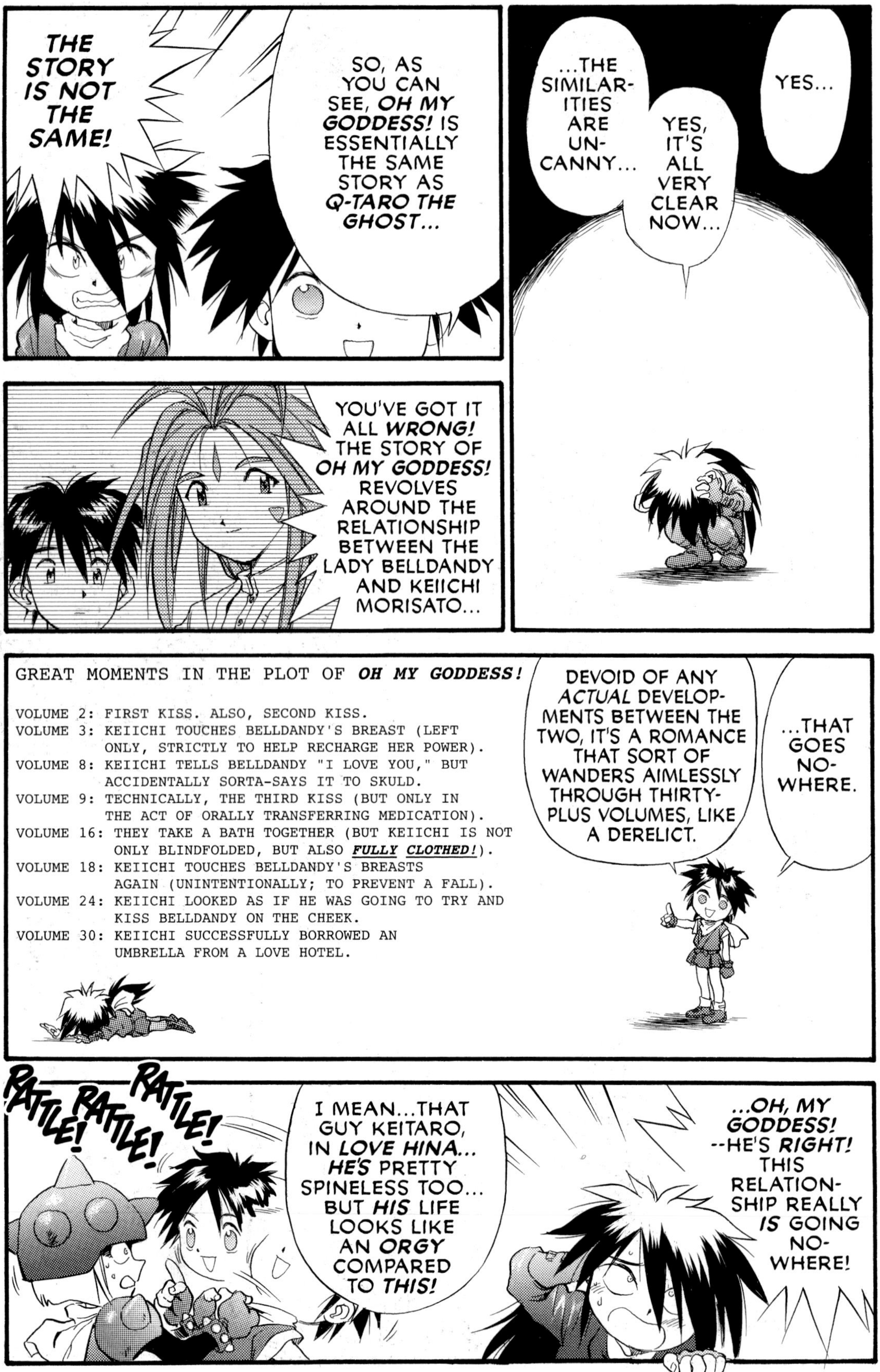

YES...
YES, IT'S ALL VERY CLEAR NOW...
...THE SIMILAR-ITIES ARE UN-CANNY...
SO, AS YOU CAN SEE, *OH MY GODDESS!* IS ESSENTIALLY THE SAME STORY AS *Q-TARO THE GHOST...*
THE STORY IS NOT THE SAME!
YOU'VE GOT IT ALL *WRONG!* THE STORY OF *OH MY GODDESS!* REVOLVES AROUND THE RELATIONSHIP BETWEEN THE LADY BELLDANDY AND KEIICHI MORISATO...
...THAT GOES NO-WHERE.
DEVOID OF ANY *ACTUAL* DEVELOP-MENTS BETWEEN THE TWO, IT'S A ROMANCE THAT SORT OF WANDERS AIMLESSLY THROUGH THIRTY-PLUS VOLUMES, LIKE A DERELICT.
GREAT MOMENTS IN THE PLOT OF ***OH MY GODDESS!***
VOLUME 2: FIRST KISS. ALSO, SECOND KISS.
VOLUME 3: KEIICHI TOUCHES BELLDANDY'S BREAST (LEFT ONLY, STRICTLY TO HELP RECHARGE HER POWER).
VOLUME 8: KEIICHI TELLS BELLDANDY "I LOVE YOU," BUT ACCIDENTALLY SORTA-SAYS IT TO SKULD.
VOLUME 9: TECHNICALLY, THE THIRD KISS (BUT ONLY IN THE ACT OF ORALLY TRANSFERRING MEDICATION).
VOLUME 16: THEY TAKE A BATH TOGETHER (BUT KEIICHI IS NOT ONLY BLINDFOLDED, BUT ALSO ***FULLY CLOTHED!***).
VOLUME 18: KEIICHI TOUCHES BELLDANDY'S BREASTS AGAIN (UNINTENTIONALLY; TO PREVENT A FALL).
VOLUME 24: KEIICHI LOOKED AS IF HE WAS GOING TO TRY AND KISS BELLDANDY ON THE CHEEK.
VOLUME 30: KEIICHI SUCCESSFULLY BORROWED AN UMBRELLA FROM A LOVE HOTEL.
...OH, MY GODDESS! --HE'S *RIGHT!* THIS RELATION-SHIP REALLY *IS* GOING NO-WHERE!
I MEAN...THAT GUY KEITARO, IN *LOVE HINA... HE'S* PRETTY SPINELESS TOO... BUT *HIS* LIFE LOOKS LIKE AN *ORGY* COMPARED TO *THIS!*
RATTLE!
RATTLE!
RATTLE!

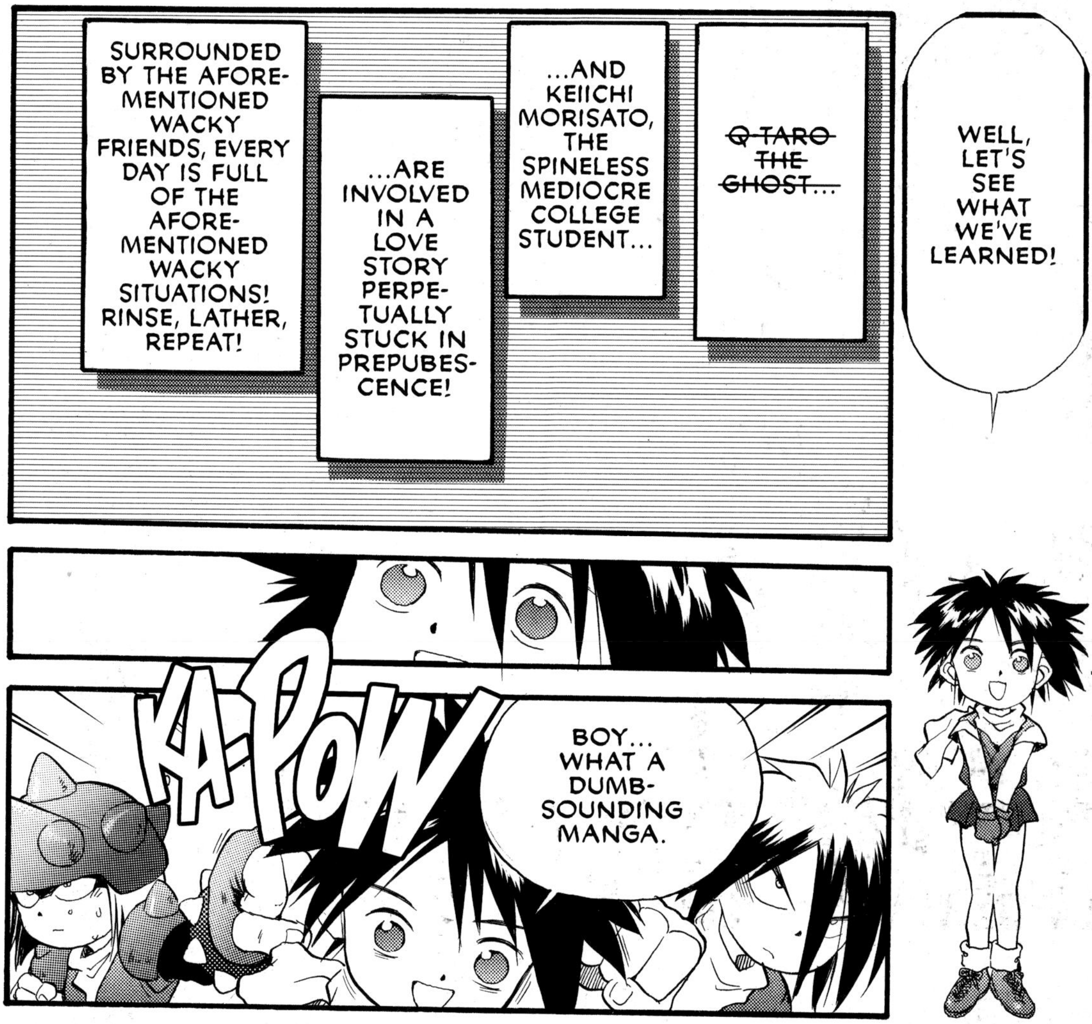
WELL, LET'S SEE WHAT WE'VE LEARNED!
~~Q TARO THE GHOST...~~
...AND KEIICHI MORISATO, THE SPINELESS MEDIOCRE COLLEGE STUDENT...
...ARE INVOLVED IN A LOVE STORY PERPETUALLY STUCK IN PREPUBESCENCE!
SURROUNDED BY THE AFOREMENTIONED WACKY FRIENDS, EVERY DAY IS FULL OF THE AFOREMENTIONED WACKY SITUATIONS! RINSE, LATHER, REPEAT!
KA-POW
BOY... WHAT A DUMB-SOUNDING MANGA.

NOW THAT YOU UNDERSTAND (MAYBE)...ENJOY THE REST OF ***OH MY GODDESS! COLORS!***

QUESTIONS FOR FURTHER READING:

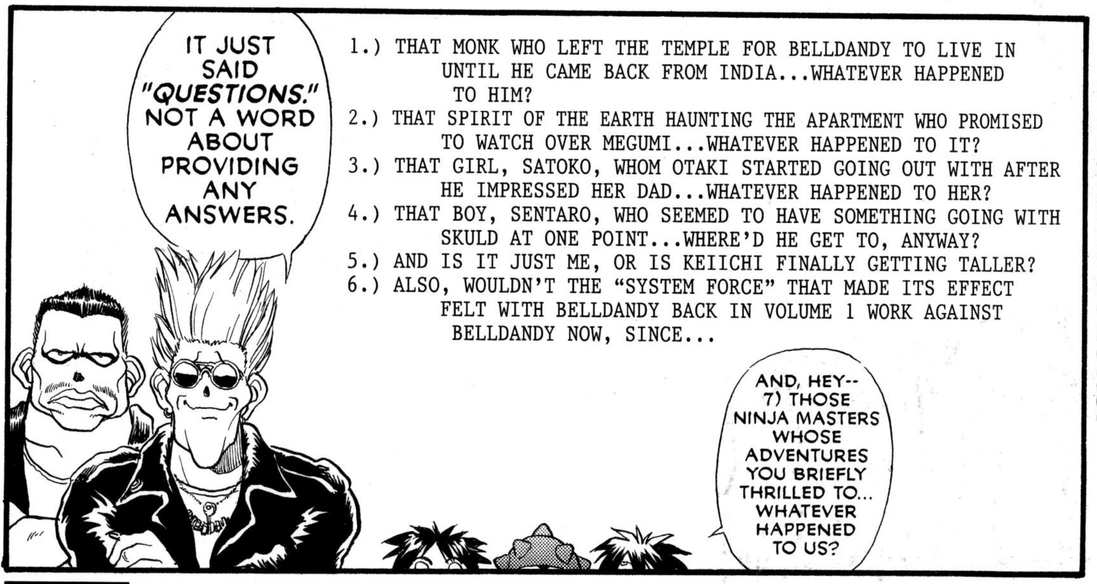

1.) THAT MONK WHO LEFT THE TEMPLE FOR BELLDANDY TO LIVE IN UNTIL HE CAME BACK FROM INDIA...WHATEVER HAPPENED TO HIM?
2.) THAT SPIRIT OF THE EARTH HAUNTING THE APARTMENT WHO PROMISED TO WATCH OVER MEGUMI...WHATEVER HAPPENED TO IT?
3.) THAT GIRL, SATOKO, WHOM OTAKI STARTED GOING OUT WITH AFTER HE IMPRESSED HER DAD...WHATEVER HAPPENED TO HER?
4.) THAT BOY, SENTARO, WHO SEEMED TO HAVE SOMETHING GOING WITH SKULD AT ONE POINT...WHERE'D HE GET TO, ANYWAY?
5.) AND IS IT JUST ME, OR IS KEIICHI FINALLY GETTING TALLER?
6.) ALSO, WOULDN'T THE "SYSTEM FORCE" THAT MADE ITS EFFECT FELT WITH BELLDANDY BACK IN VOLUME 1 WORK AGAINST BELLDANDY NOW, SINCE...

AND, HEY-- 7) THOSE NINJA MASTERS WHOSE ADVENTURES YOU BRIEFLY THRILLED TO... WHATEVER HAPPENED TO US?
IT JUST SAID *"QUESTIONS."* NOT A WORD ABOUT PROVIDING ANY ANSWERS.

END

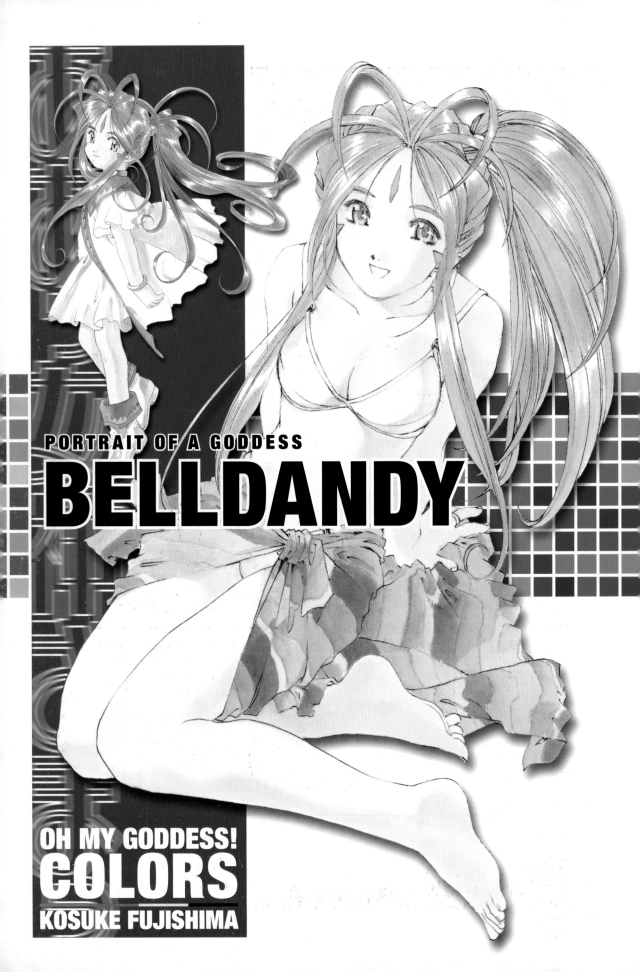

PORTRAIT OF A GODDESS

BELLDANDY

OH MY GODDESS!
COLORS
KOSUKE FUJISHIMA

PORTRAIT OF A GODDESS
BELLDANDY

PROFILE

Height:	165 cm (5'5")
Bust:	83 cm (32.7")
Waist:	57 cm (22.4")
Hips:	84 cm (33")
Place of birth:	Unclear
Age:	Unknown
Blood type:	Does she have one?
Favorite foods:	Black tea, chocolate
Favorite phrases:	"Thank you,"
	"Everybody get along"
Hobbies:	Knitting, embroidery,
	cooking, sunbathing

Goddess First-Class, Type 2, Unlimited. The Goddess realm has a licensing system, just like your DMV. Belldandy works for the Goddess Technical Help Line, which just sounds so fun when you hear it. Among the three goddess sisters, she is the Goddess of the Present.

In the course of her job, Belldandy came down to Earth to grant (technically, Heaven granted it; she just acts as the "antenna") college student Keiichi Morisato his wish, namely: "I want a goddess like you to be with me always." The new couple was immediately given the bum's rush by their dorm mates (the residence hall was men only) and they now live off campus in Tarikihongan Temple.

Goddesses like Bell-chan naturally lack some day-to-day knowledge of the human world. Sometimes, that's a relief. However, through attending the same school as Keiichi and living with him, Belldandy has also learned about the good side of humanity and its works.

Bell herself is limitlessly kind, strong in spirit, and filled with tenderness. You'd be justified in calling her the textbook example of a goddess. However, Bell's own life changed when she came in contact with Keiichi—her affection for him gave rise to feelings of jealousy, underscoring a side of her that seems like human weakness. The two of them are gradually (very gradually) becoming less like boyfriend and girlfriend, and more like husband and wife. We'll want to pay close attention to their relationship, especially on the off chance that they might move beyond the occasional kiss or touch.

Her hobbies are all relaxing ones, as you might expect. She is accompanied by the angel Holy Bell, who, as you also might expect, conveys the sound of pure bells ringing.

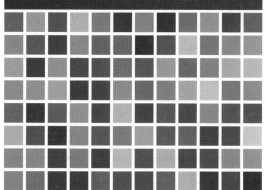

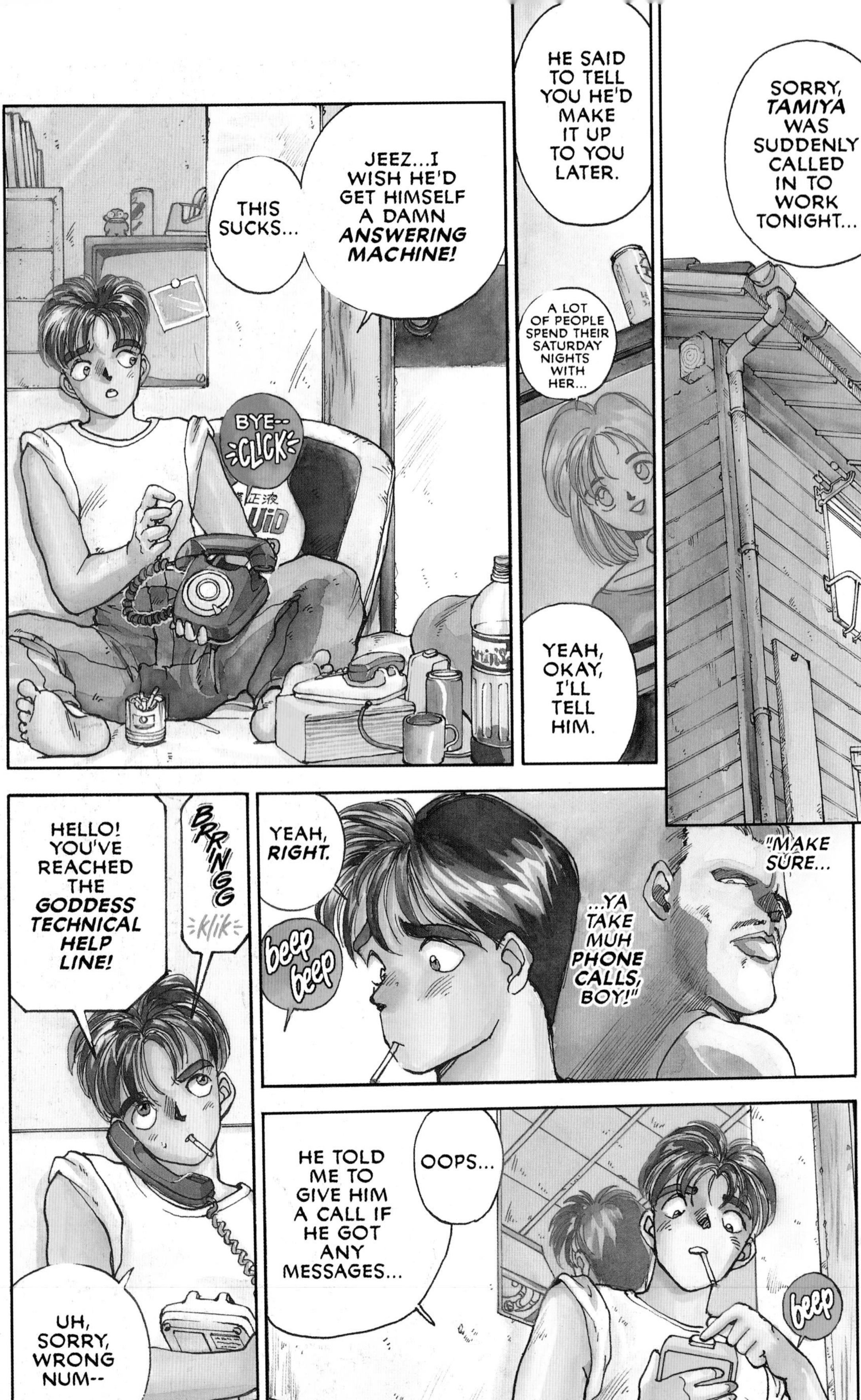
SORRY, *TAMIYA* WAS SUDDENLY CALLED IN TO WORK TONIGHT...
HE SAID TO TELL YOU HE'D MAKE IT UP TO YOU LATER.
A LOT OF PEOPLE SPEND THEIR SATURDAY NIGHTS WITH HER...
YEAH, OKAY, I'LL TELL HIM.
JEEZ...I WISH HE'D GET HIMSELF A DAMN *ANSWERING MACHINE!*
THIS SUCKS...
BYE--
CLICK
"MAKE SURE...
...YA TAKE MUH PHONE CALLS, BOY!"
YEAH, *RIGHT.*
beep beep
OOPS...
HE TOLD ME TO GIVE HIM A CALL IF HE GOT ANY MESSAGES...
beep
BRRINGG
HELLO! YOU'VE REACHED THE *GODDESS TECHNICAL HELP LINE!*
klik
UH, SORRY, WRONG NUM--

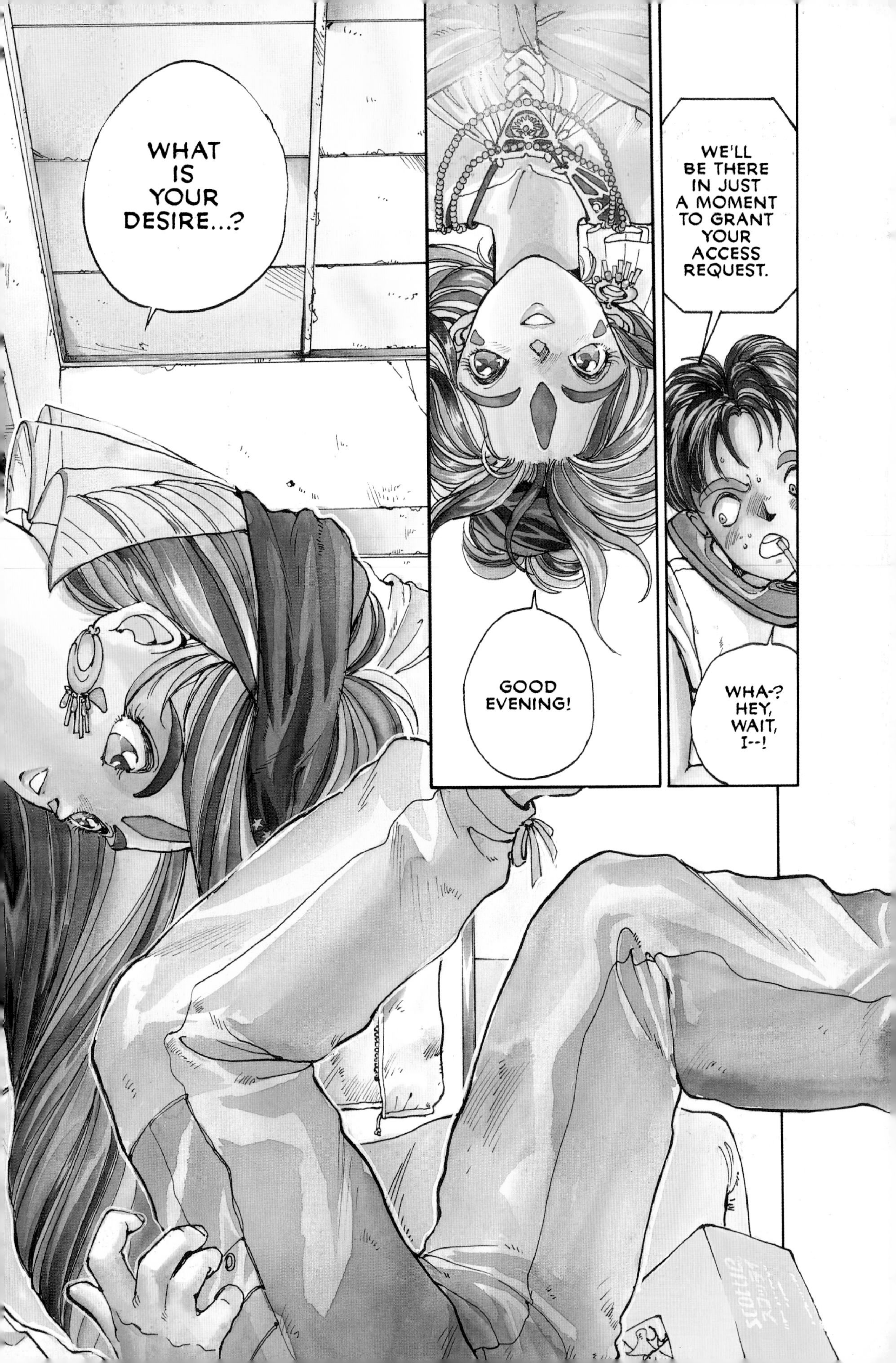
WE'LL BE THERE IN JUST A MOMENT TO GRANT YOUR ACCESS REQUEST.
WHA-? HEY, WAIT, I--!
GOOD EVENING!
WHAT IS YOUR DESIRE...?

TALE OF BELLDANDY:
The Number You Have Dialed Is Incorrect

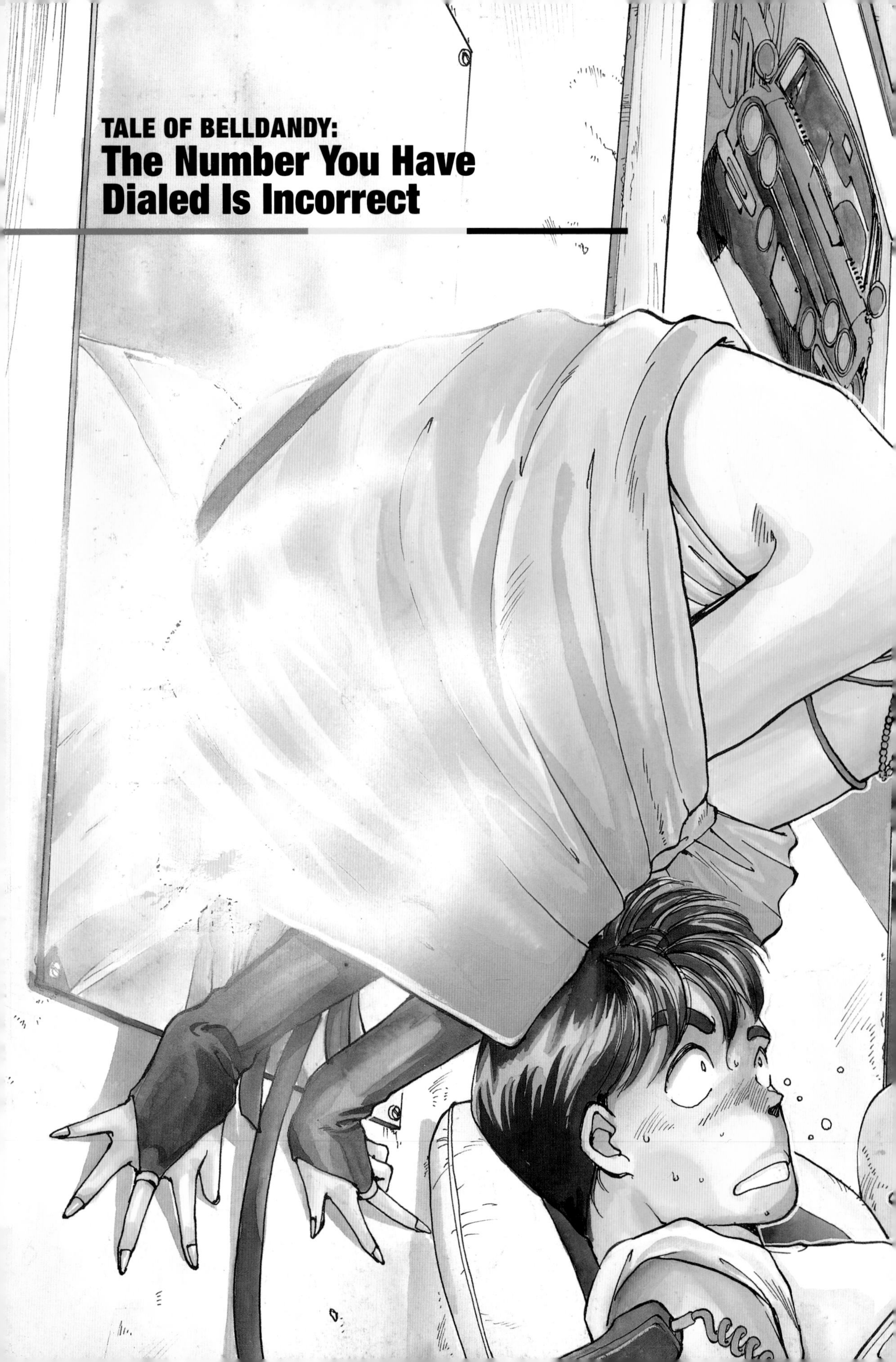

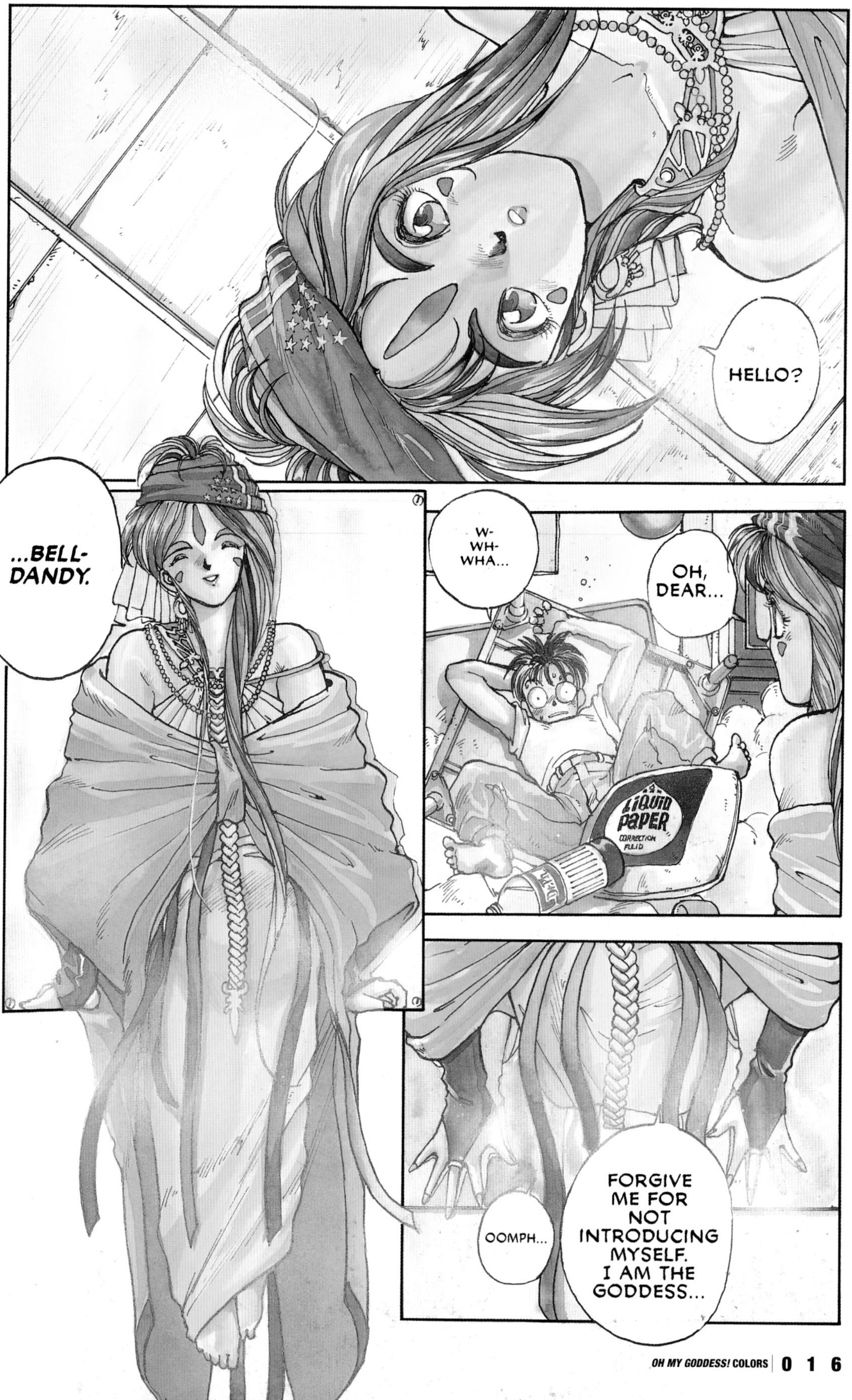
HELLO?
W-WH-WHA...
OH, DEAR...
FORGIVE ME FOR NOT INTRODUCING MYSELF. I AM THE GODDESS...
OOMPH...
...BELL-DANDY.
LIQUID PAPER
CORRECTION FLUID

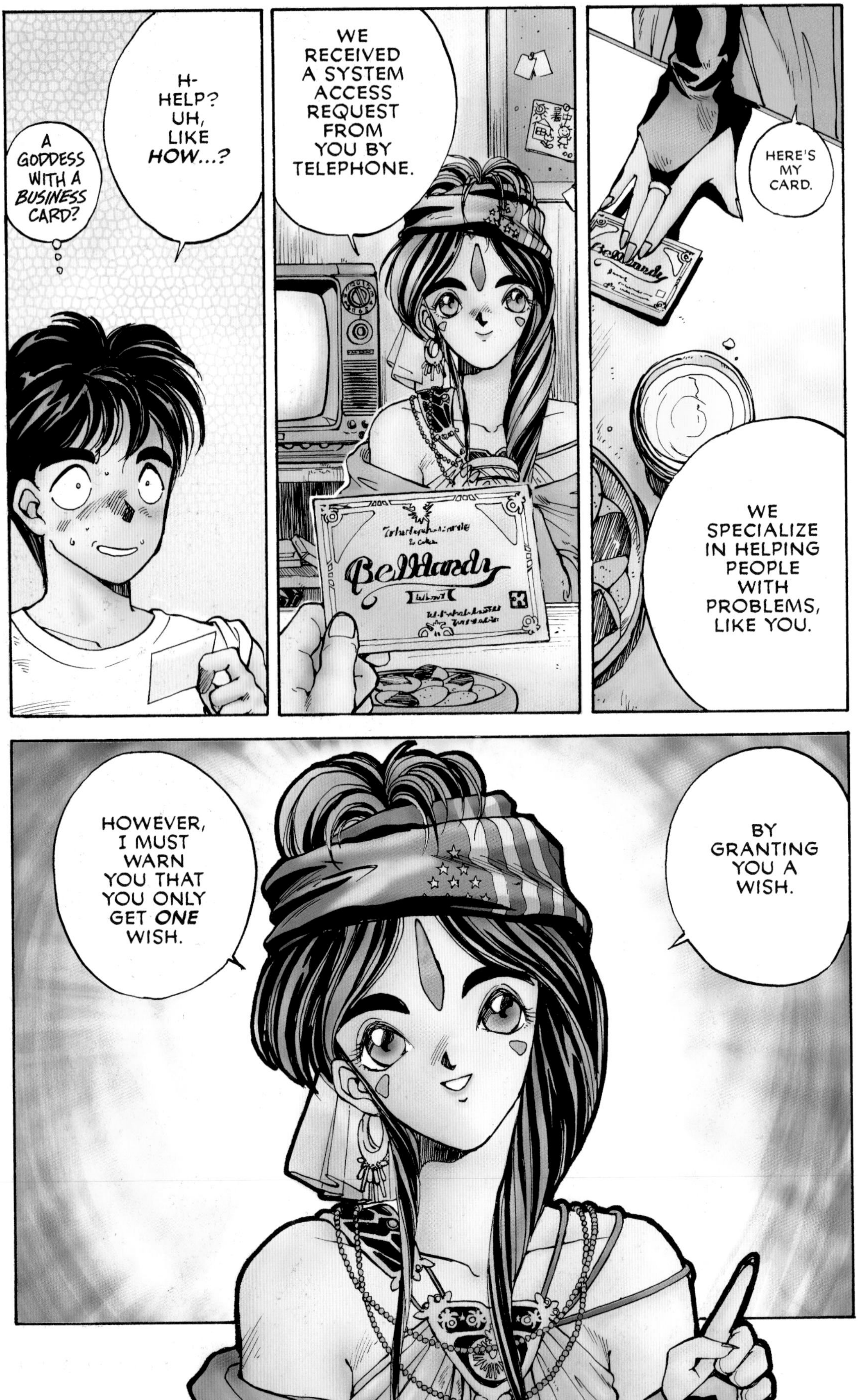
HERE'S MY CARD.
WE SPECIALIZE IN HELPING PEOPLE WITH PROBLEMS, LIKE YOU.
WE RECEIVED A SYSTEM ACCESS REQUEST FROM YOU BY TELEPHONE.
H-HELP? UH, LIKE *HOW*...?
A GODDESS WITH A *BUSINESS* CARD?
BY GRANTING YOU A WISH.
HOWEVER, I MUST WARN YOU THAT YOU ONLY GET *ONE* WISH.

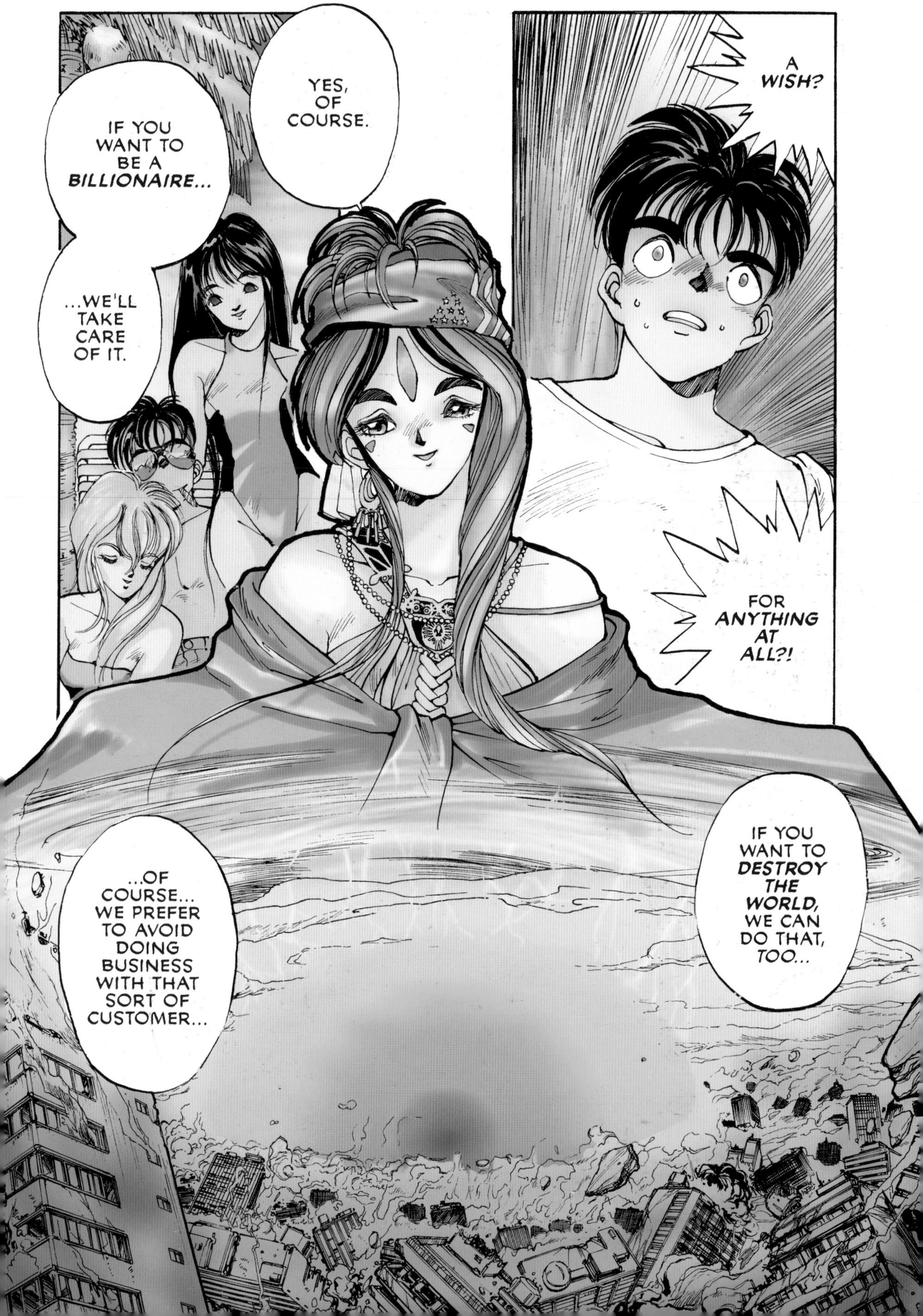
A *WISH?*
FOR *ANYTHING AT ALL?!*
YES, OF COURSE.
IF YOU WANT TO BE A *BILLIONAIRE...*
...WE'LL TAKE CARE OF IT.
IF YOU WANT TO *DESTROY THE WORLD,* WE CAN DO THAT, *TOO...*
...OF COURSE... WE PREFER TO AVOID DOING BUSINESS WITH THAT SORT OF CUSTOMER...

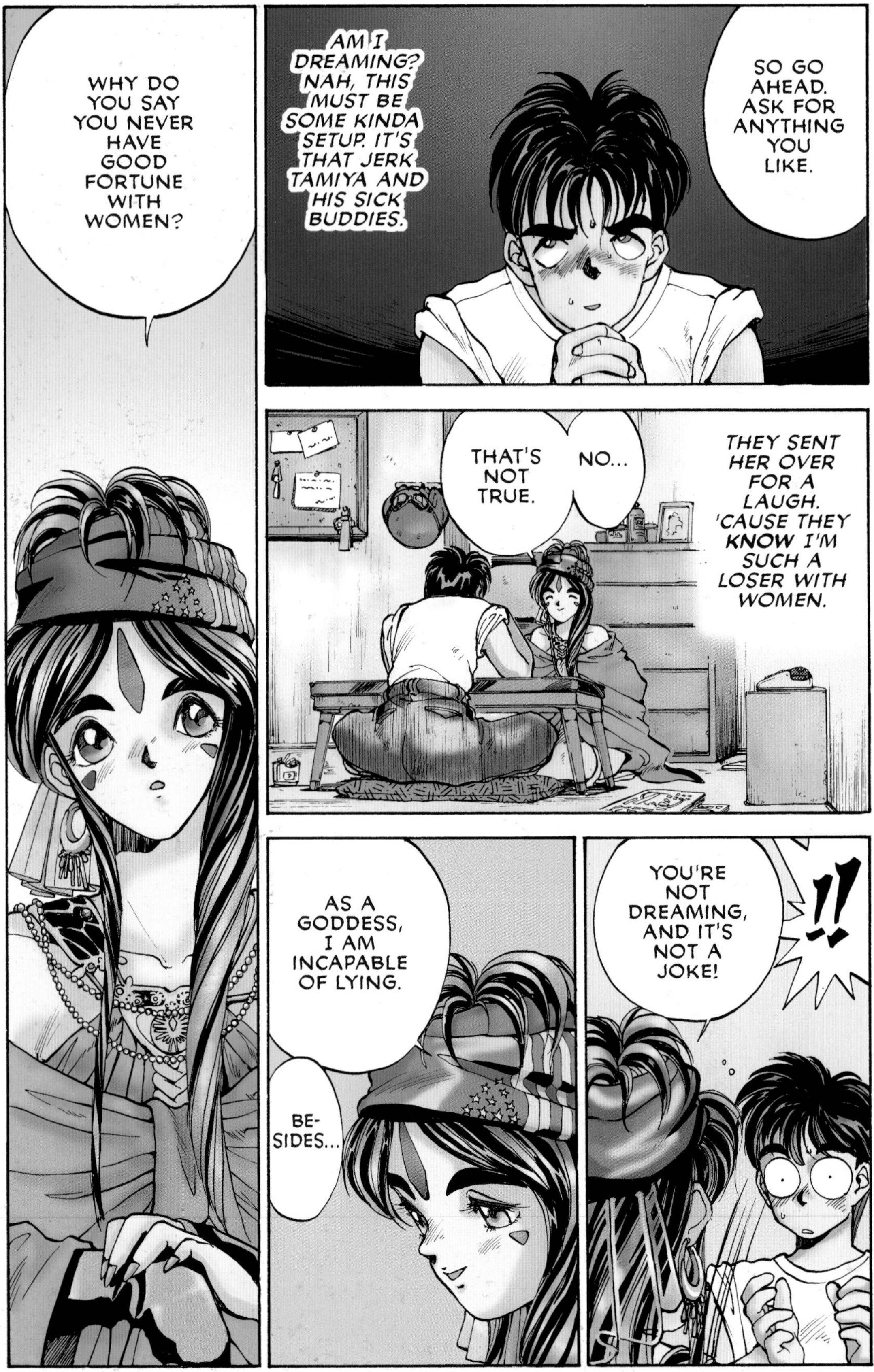
WHY DO YOU SAY YOU NEVER HAVE GOOD FORTUNE WITH WOMEN?
AM I DREAMING? NAH, THIS MUST BE SOME KINDA SETUP. IT'S THAT JERK TAMIYA AND HIS SICK BUDDIES.
SO GO AHEAD. ASK FOR ANYTHING YOU LIKE.
THAT'S NOT TRUE.
NO...
THEY SENT HER OVER FOR A LAUGH. 'CAUSE THEY *KNOW* I'M SUCH A LOSER WITH WOMEN.
AS A GODDESS, I AM INCAPABLE OF LYING.
BE-SIDES...
YOU'RE NOT DREAMING, AND IT'S NOT A JOKE!
!!

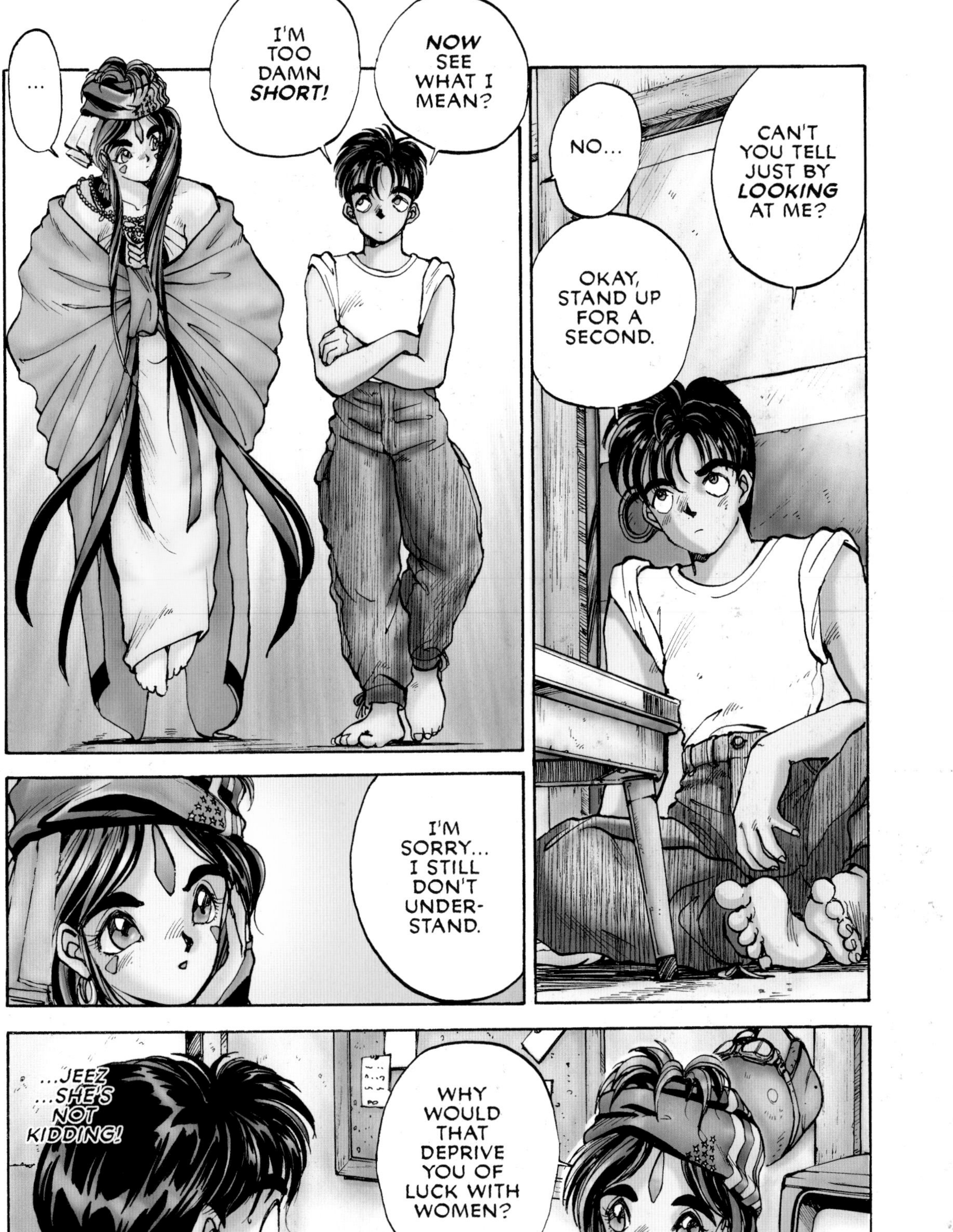
CAN'T YOU TELL JUST BY *LOOKING* AT ME?
NO...
OKAY, STAND UP FOR A SECOND.
NOW SEE WHAT I MEAN?
I'M TOO DAMN *SHORT!*
...
I'M SORRY... I STILL DON'T UNDER-STAND.
WHY WOULD THAT DEPRIVE YOU OF LUCK WITH WOMEN?
...JEEZ ...SHE'S NOT KIDDING!

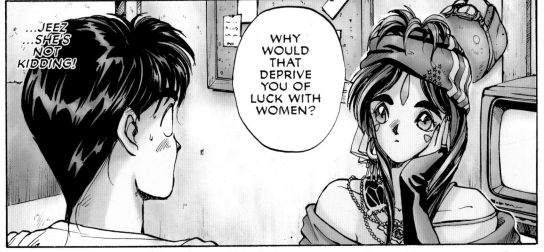

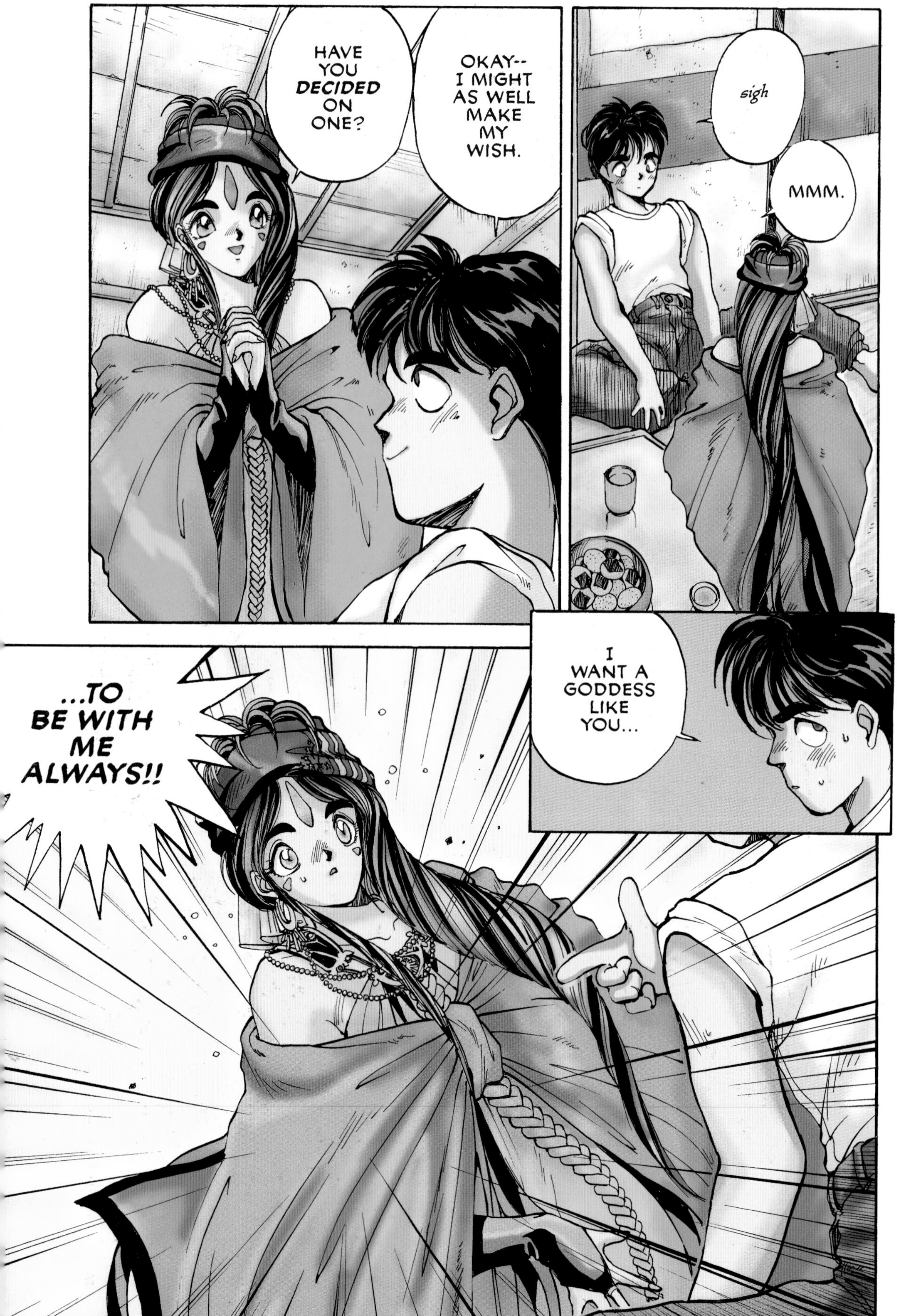
sigh
MMM.
OKAY-- I MIGHT AS WELL MAKE MY WISH.
HAVE YOU *DECIDED* ON ONE?
I WANT A GODDESS LIKE YOU...
...TO BE WITH ME ALWAYS!!

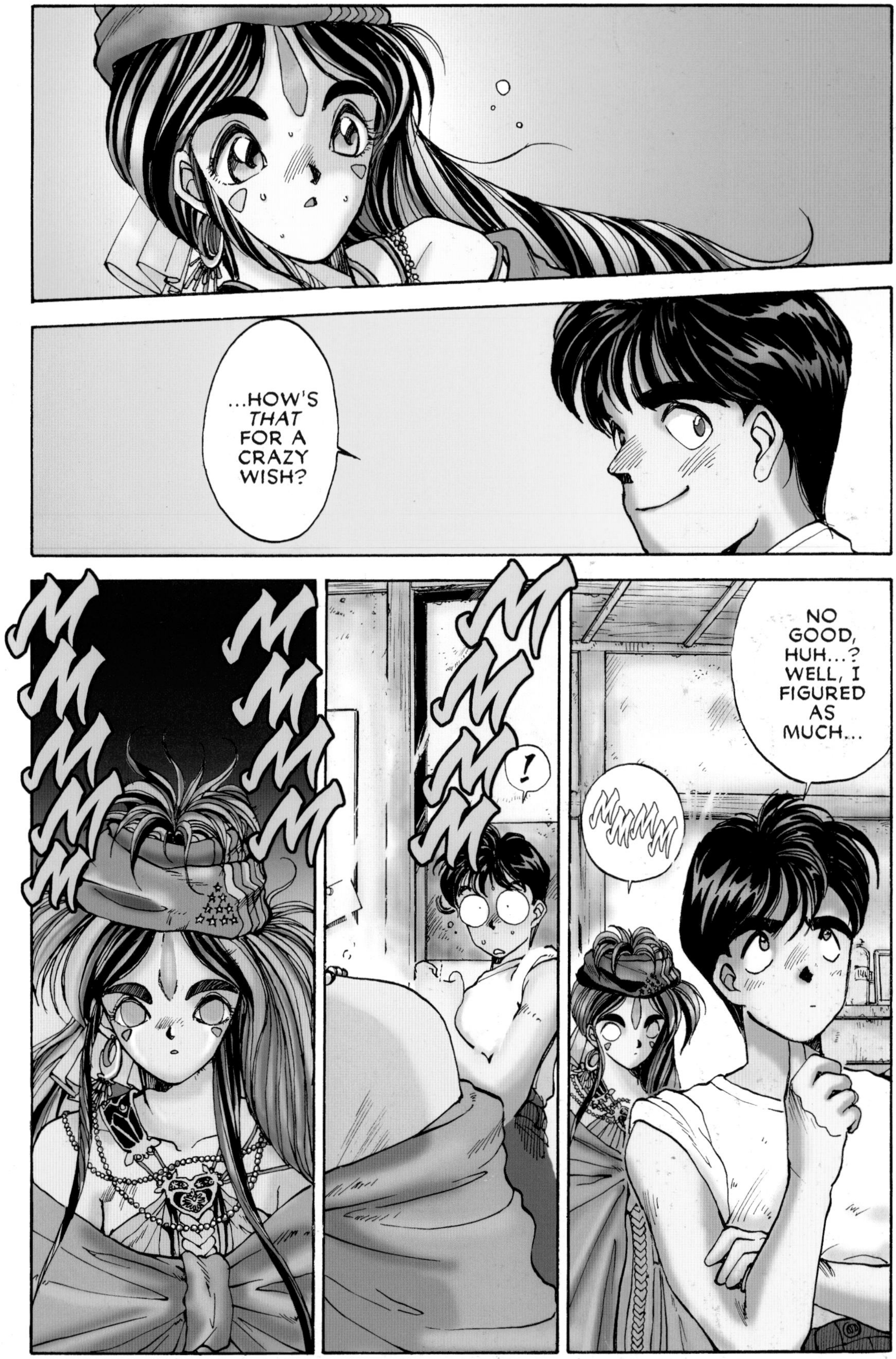
...HOW'S *THAT* FOR A CRAZY WISH?
NO GOOD, HUH...? WELL, I FIGURED AS MUCH...
MMMM
!

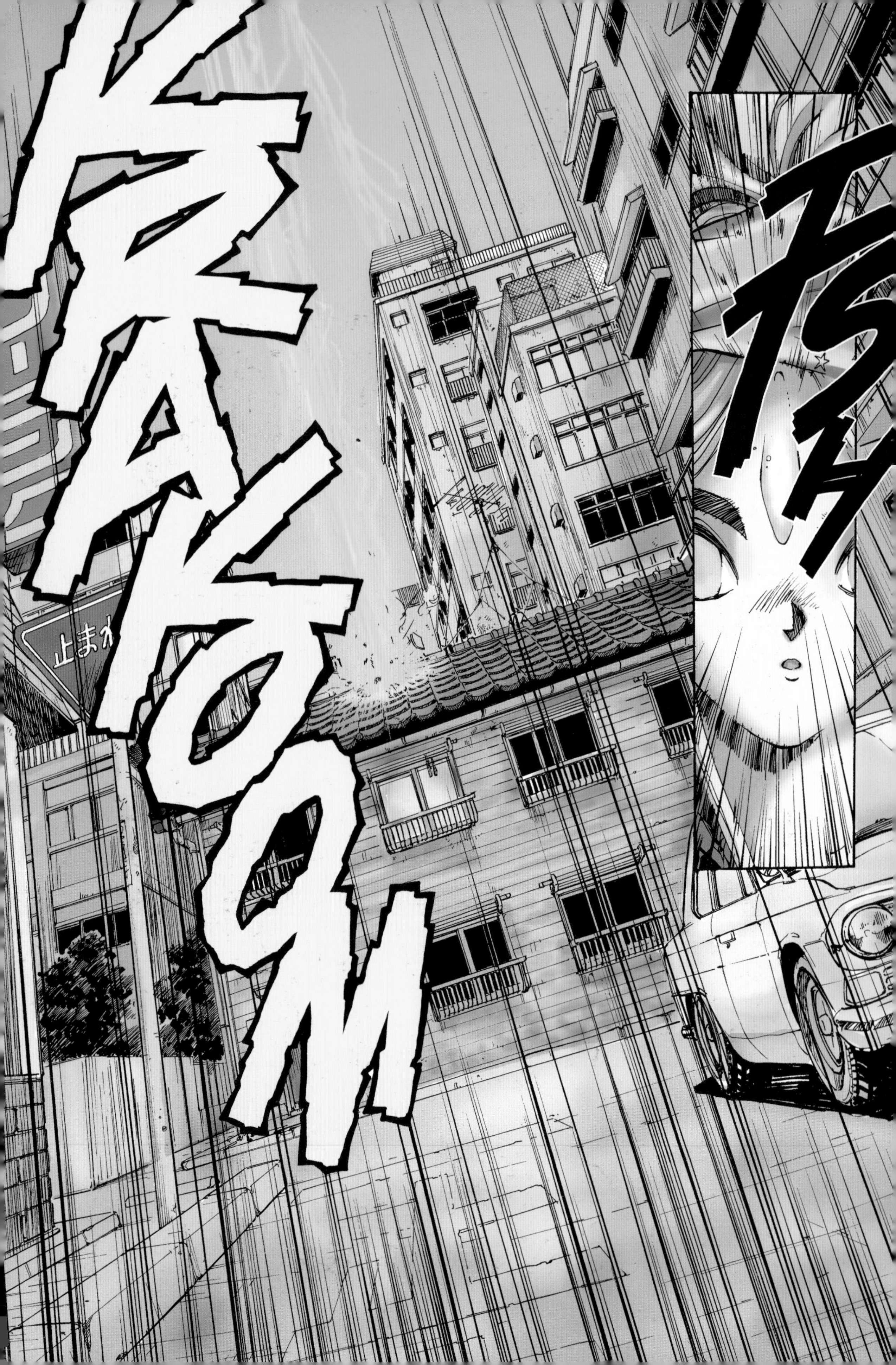
TSK
KRAKOOM

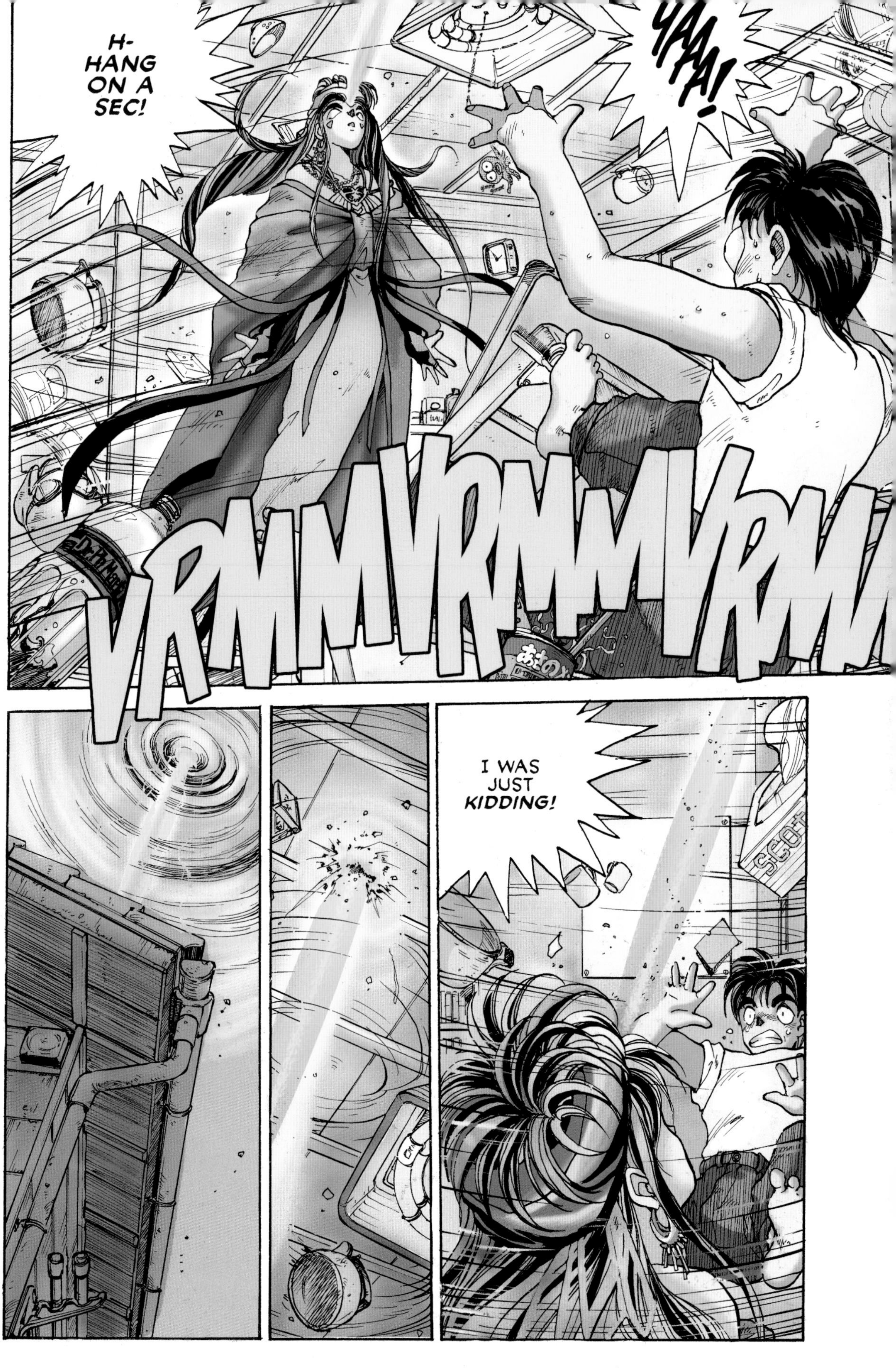
YAAAA!
H-HANG ON A SEC!
VRMMVRMMVRMM
I WAS JUST KIDDING!

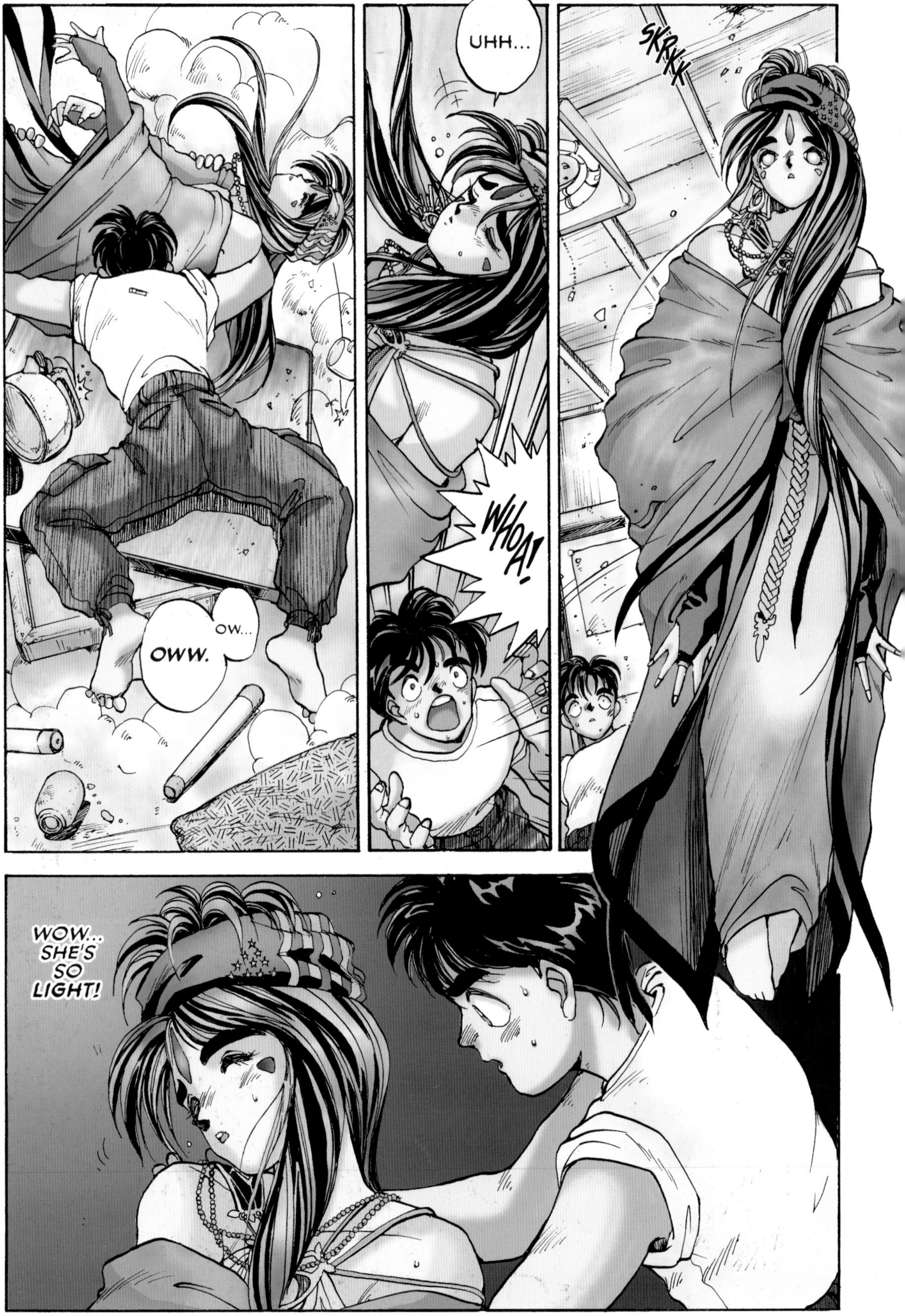
SKRKK
UHH...
WHOA!
OW...
OWW.
WOW... SHE'S SO LIGHT!

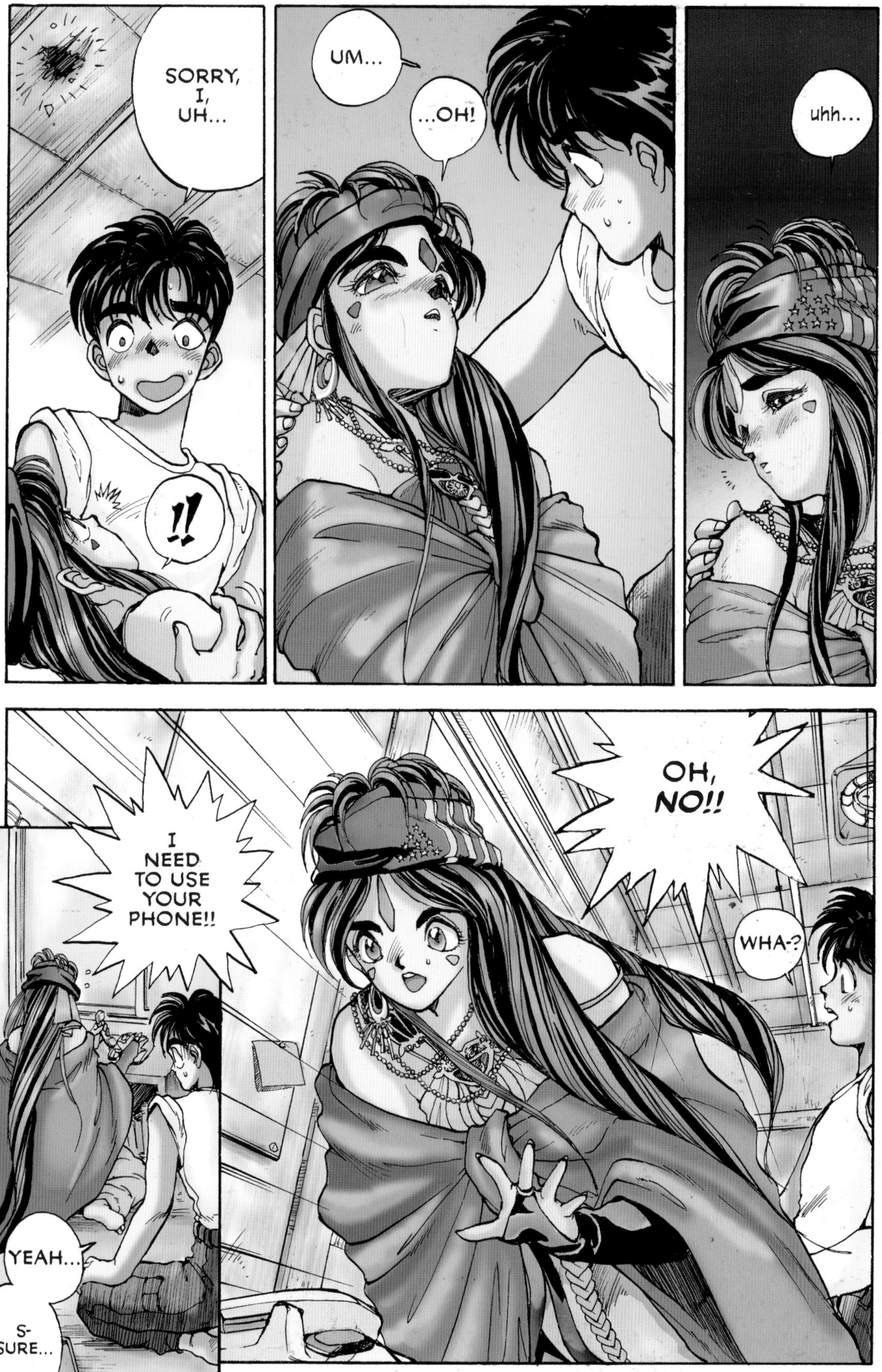
uhh...
UM...
...OH!
SORRY, I, UH...
!!
OH, NO!!
I NEED TO USE YOUR PHONE!!
WHA-?
YEAH...
S-SURE...

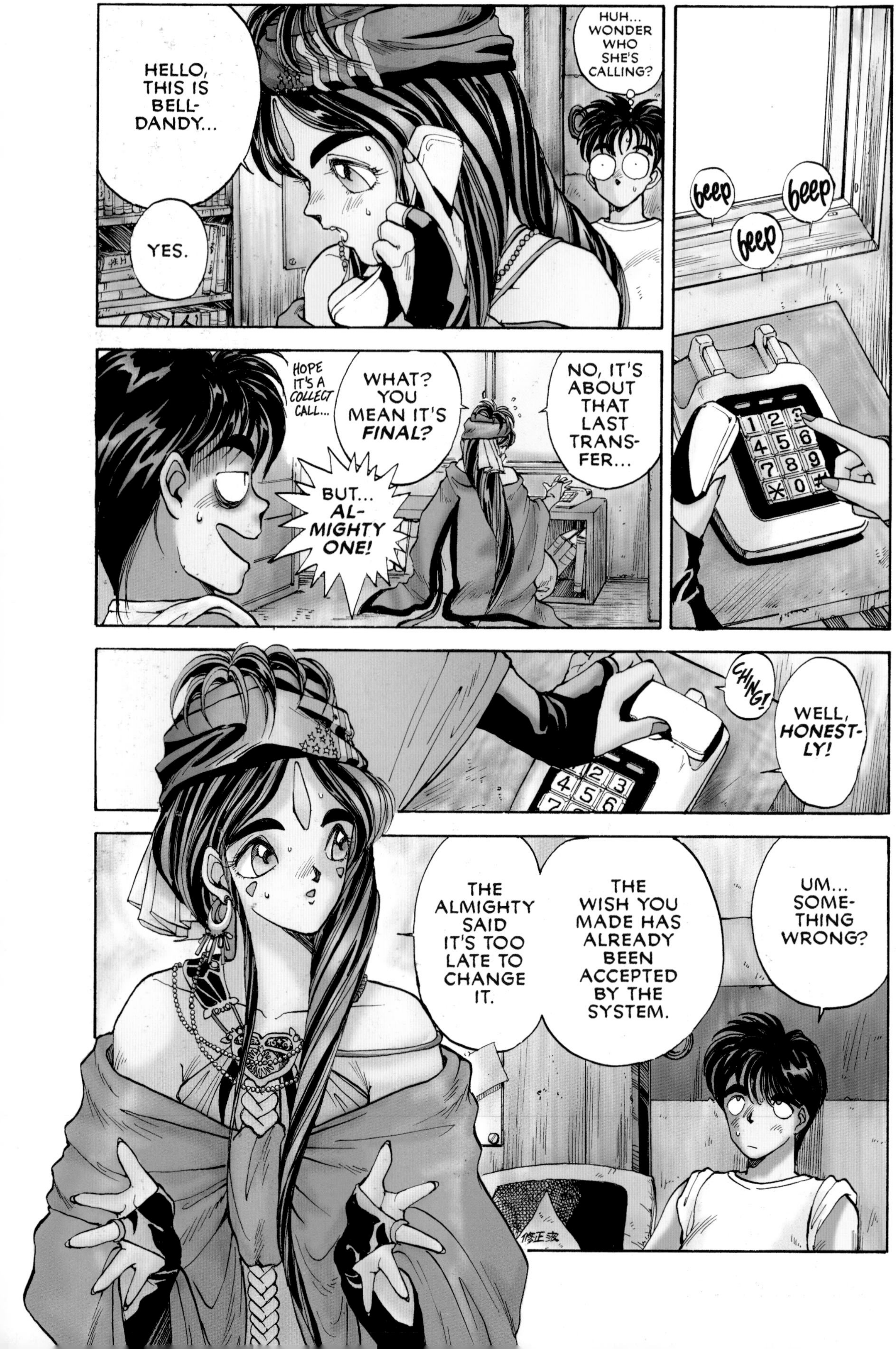
beep
beep
beep
HUH... WONDER WHO SHE'S CALLING?
HELLO, THIS IS BELL-DANDY...
YES.
NO, IT'S ABOUT THAT LAST TRANSFER...
WHAT? YOU MEAN IT'S *FINAL?*
HOPE IT'S A COLLECT CALL...
BUT... **ALMIGHTY ONE!**
CHING!
WELL, **HONESTLY!**
UM... SOMETHING WRONG?
THE WISH YOU MADE HAS ALREADY BEEN ACCEPTED BY THE SYSTEM.
THE ALMIGHTY SAID IT'S TOO LATE TO CHANGE IT.
修正液

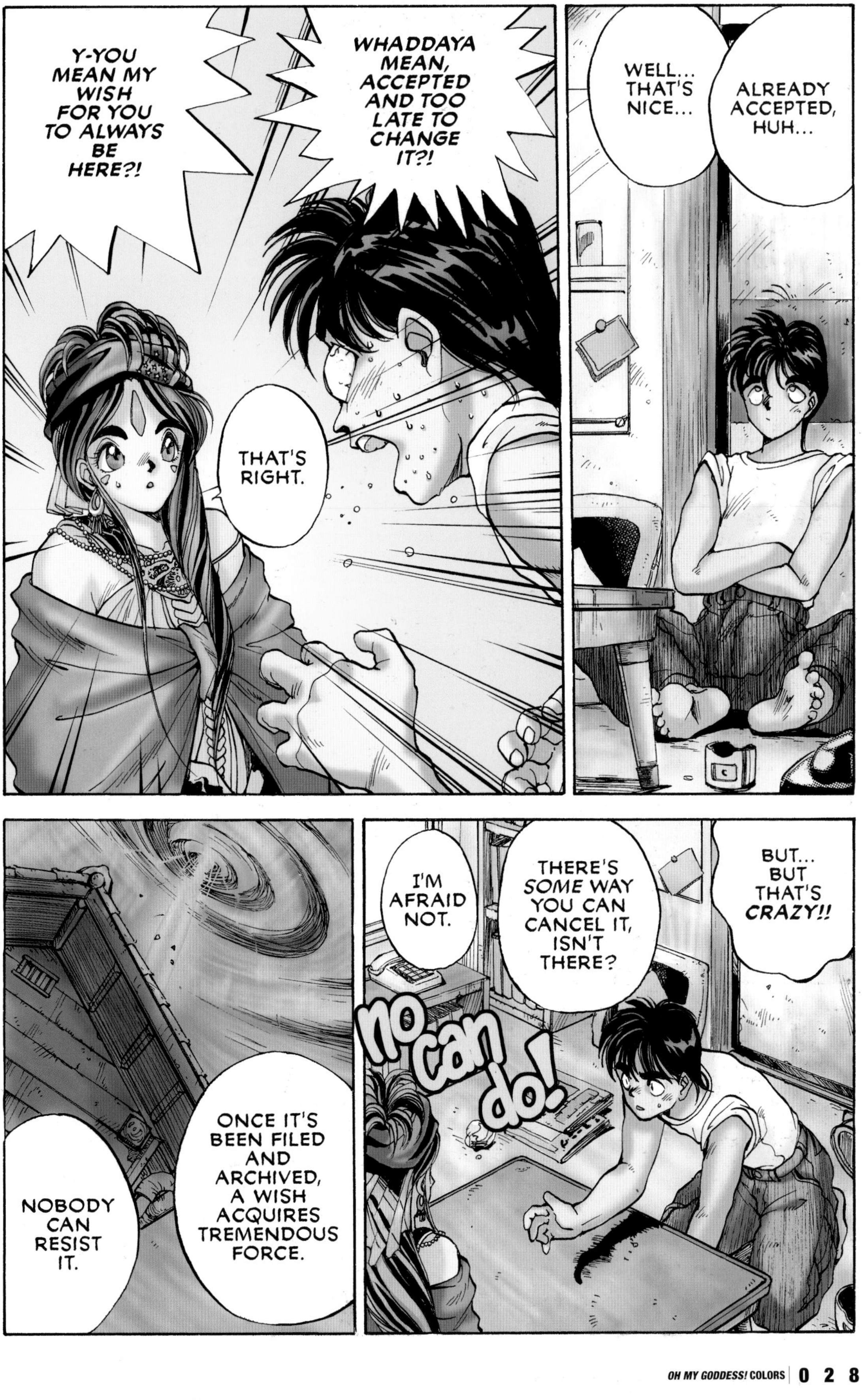
ALREADY ACCEPTED, HUH...
WELL... THAT'S NICE...
WHADDAYA MEAN, ACCEPTED AND TOO LATE TO CHANGE IT?!
Y-YOU MEAN MY WISH FOR YOU TO ALWAYS BE HERE?!
THAT'S RIGHT.
BUT... BUT THAT'S *CRAZY!!*
THERE'S *SOME* WAY YOU CAN CANCEL IT, ISN'T THERE?
I'M AFRAID NOT.
no can do!
ONCE IT'S BEEN FILED AND ARCHIVED, A WISH ACQUIRES TREMENDOUS FORCE.
NOBODY CAN RESIST IT.

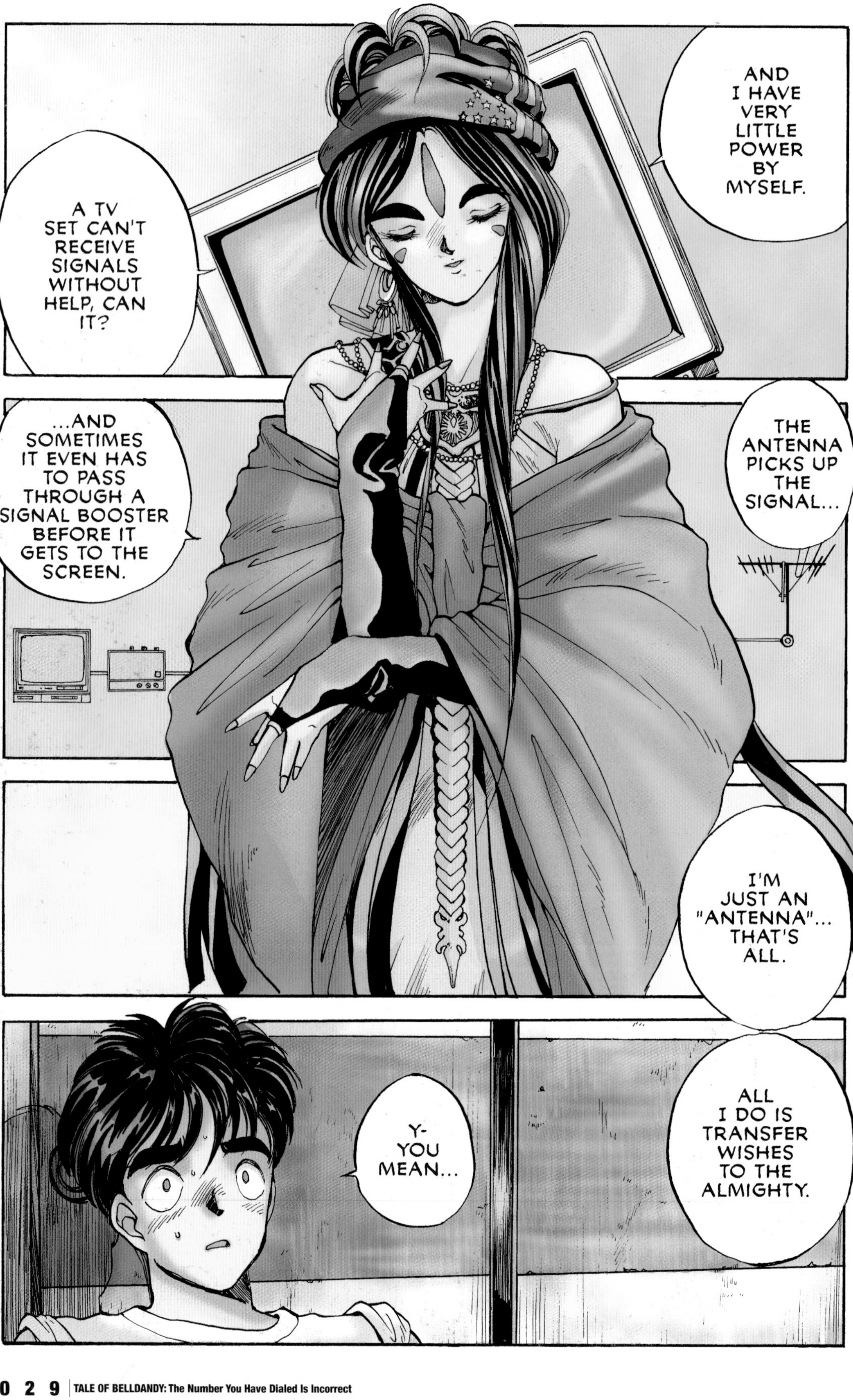
AND I HAVE VERY LITTLE POWER BY MYSELF.
A TV SET CAN'T RECEIVE SIGNALS WITHOUT HELP, CAN IT?
THE ANTENNA PICKS UP THE SIGNAL...
...AND SOMETIMES IT EVEN HAS TO PASS THROUGH A SIGNAL BOOSTER BEFORE IT GETS TO THE SCREEN.
I'M JUST AN "ANTENNA"... THAT'S ALL.
ALL I DO IS TRANSFER WISHES TO THE ALMIGHTY.
Y-YOU MEAN...

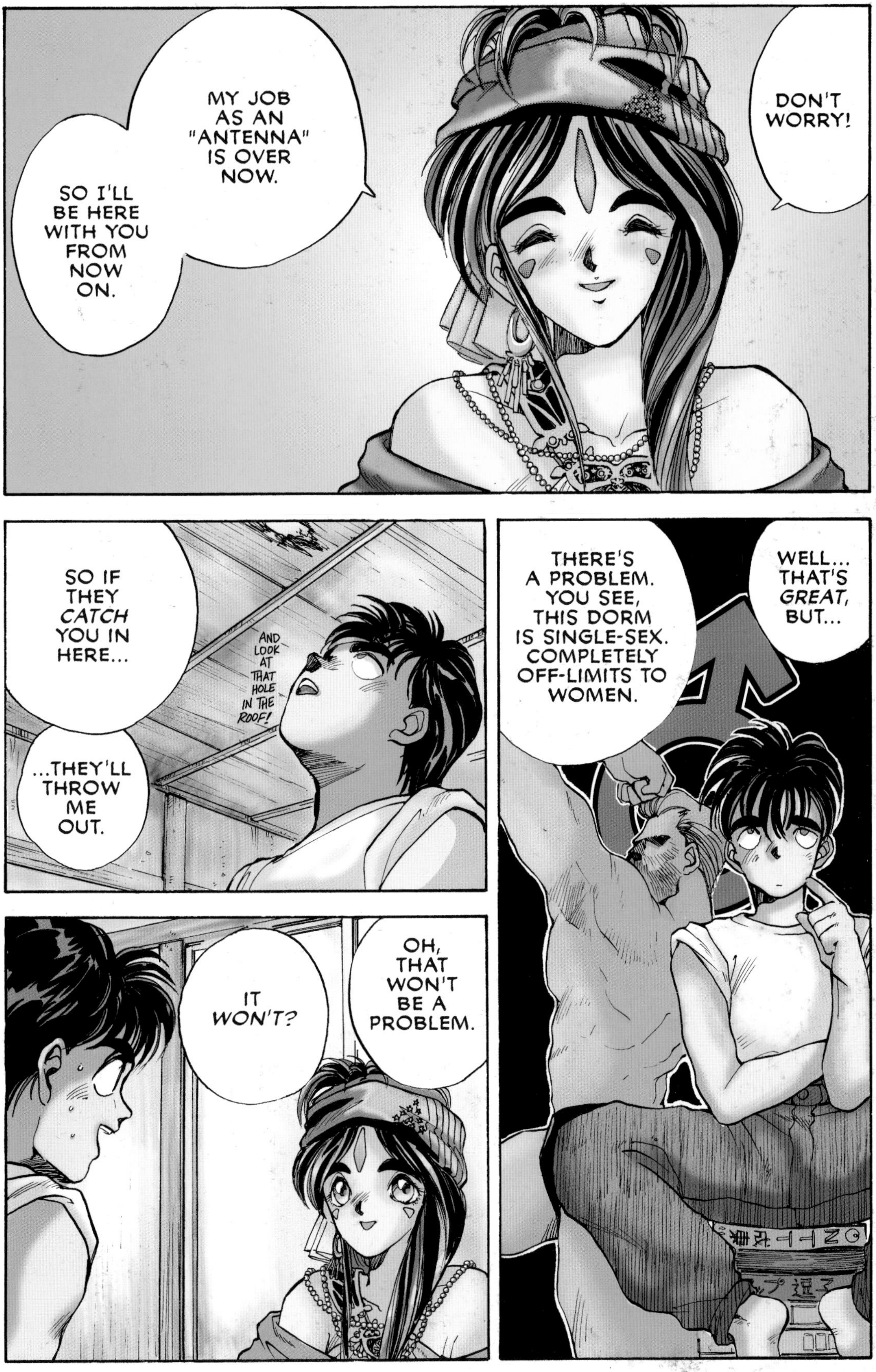
DON'T WORRY!
MY JOB AS AN "ANTENNA" IS OVER NOW.
SO I'LL BE HERE WITH YOU FROM NOW ON.
WELL... THAT'S GREAT, BUT...
THERE'S A PROBLEM. YOU SEE, THIS DORM IS SINGLE-SEX. COMPLETELY OFF-LIMITS TO WOMEN.
SO IF THEY CATCH YOU IN HERE...
AND LOOK AT THAT HOLE IN THE ROOF!
...THEY'LL THROW ME OUT.
OH, THAT WON'T BE A PROBLEM.
IT WON'T?

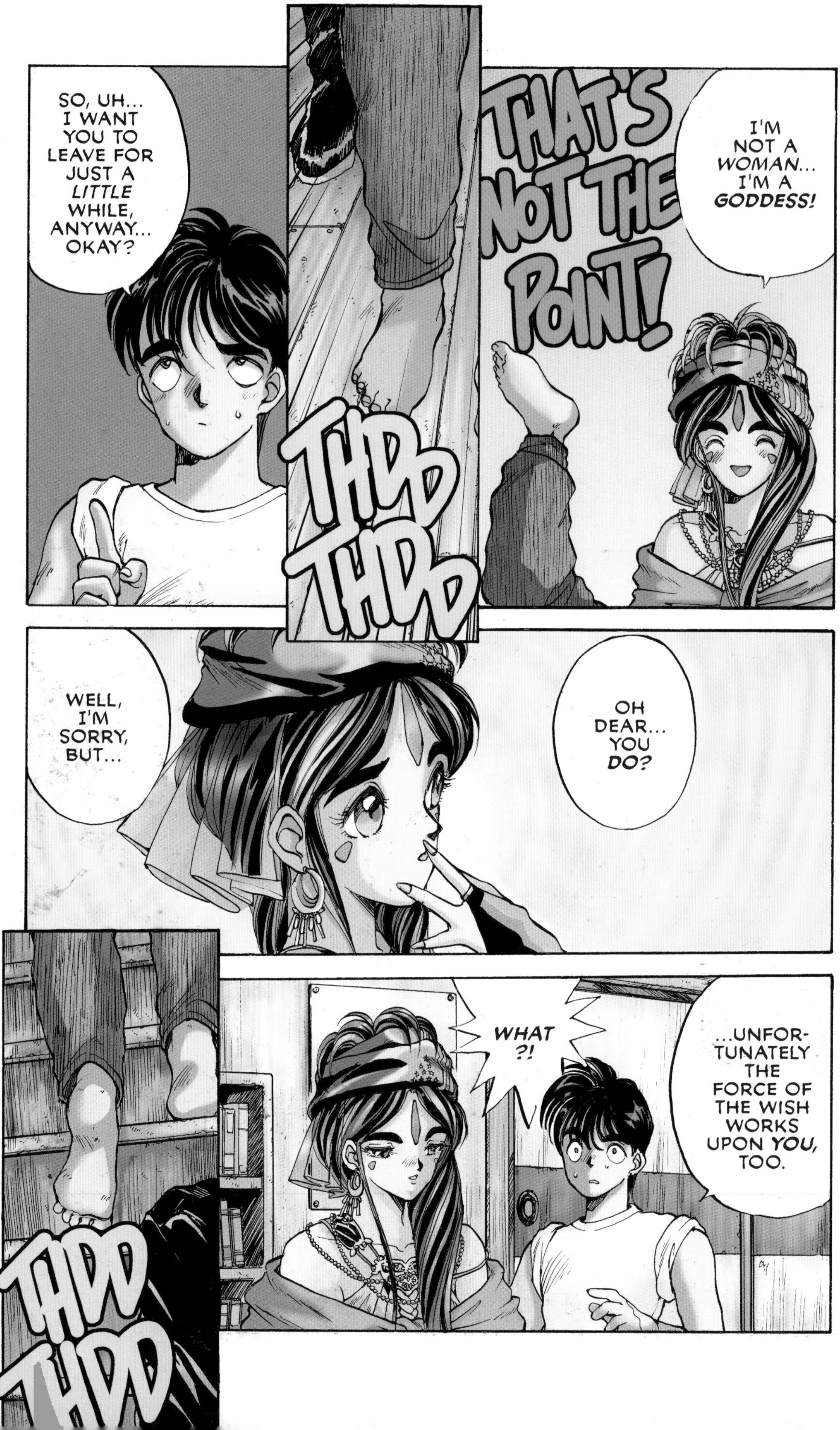
I'M NOT A *WOMAN*... I'M A ***GODDESS!***
THAT'S NOT THE POINT!
THDD THDD
SO, UH... I WANT YOU TO LEAVE FOR JUST A *LITTLE* WHILE, ANYWAY... OKAY?
OH DEAR... YOU ***DO?***
WELL, I'M SORRY, BUT...
...UNFORTUNATELY THE FORCE OF THE WISH WORKS UPON ***YOU,*** TOO.
WHAT ?!
THDD THDD

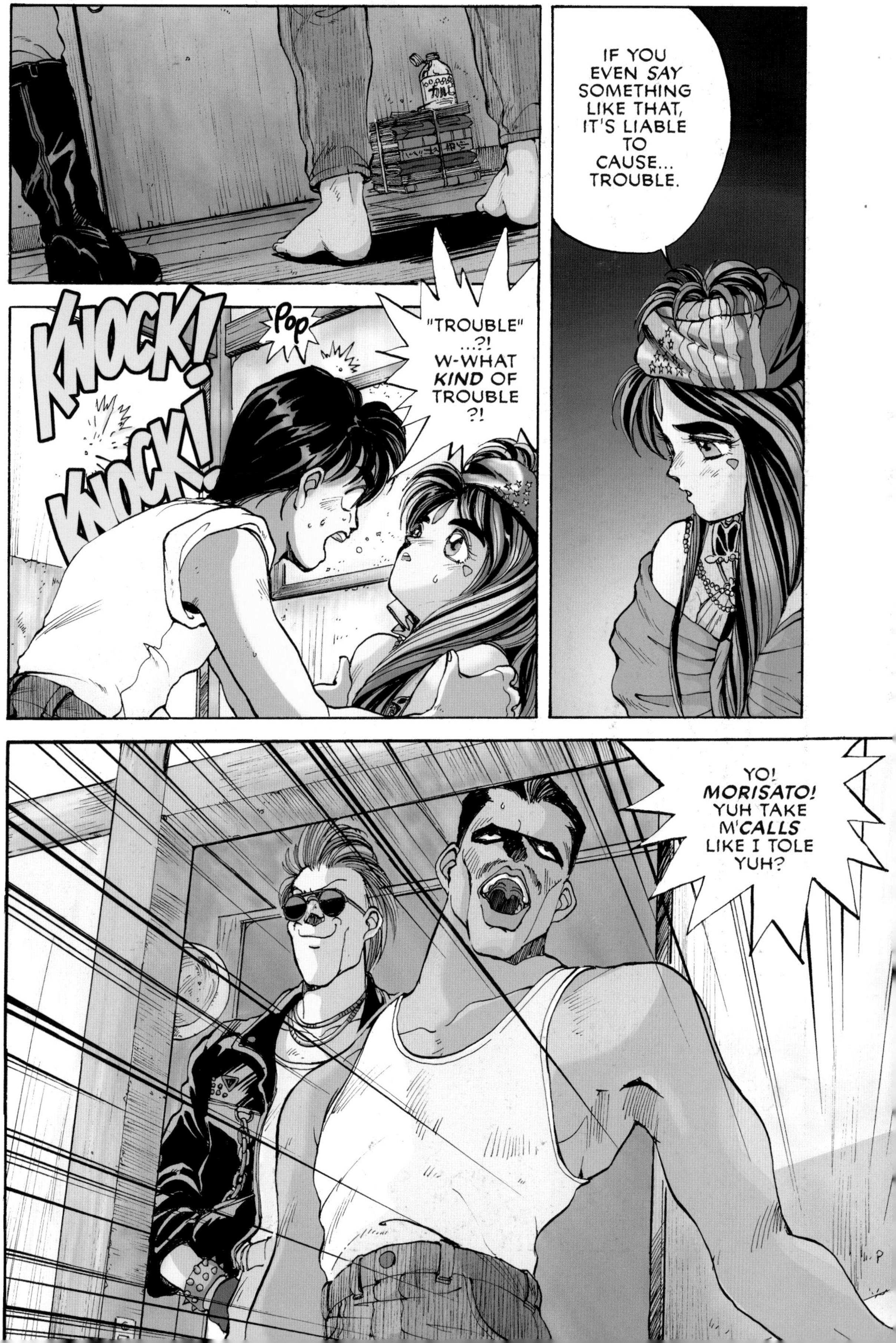
IF YOU EVEN *SAY* SOMETHING LIKE THAT, IT'S LIABLE TO CAUSE... TROUBLE.
"TROUBLE" ...?! W-WHAT *KIND* OF TROUBLE ?!
Pop
KNOCK!
KNOCK!
YO! ***MORISATO!*** YUH TAKE M'***CALLS*** LIKE I TOLE YUH?

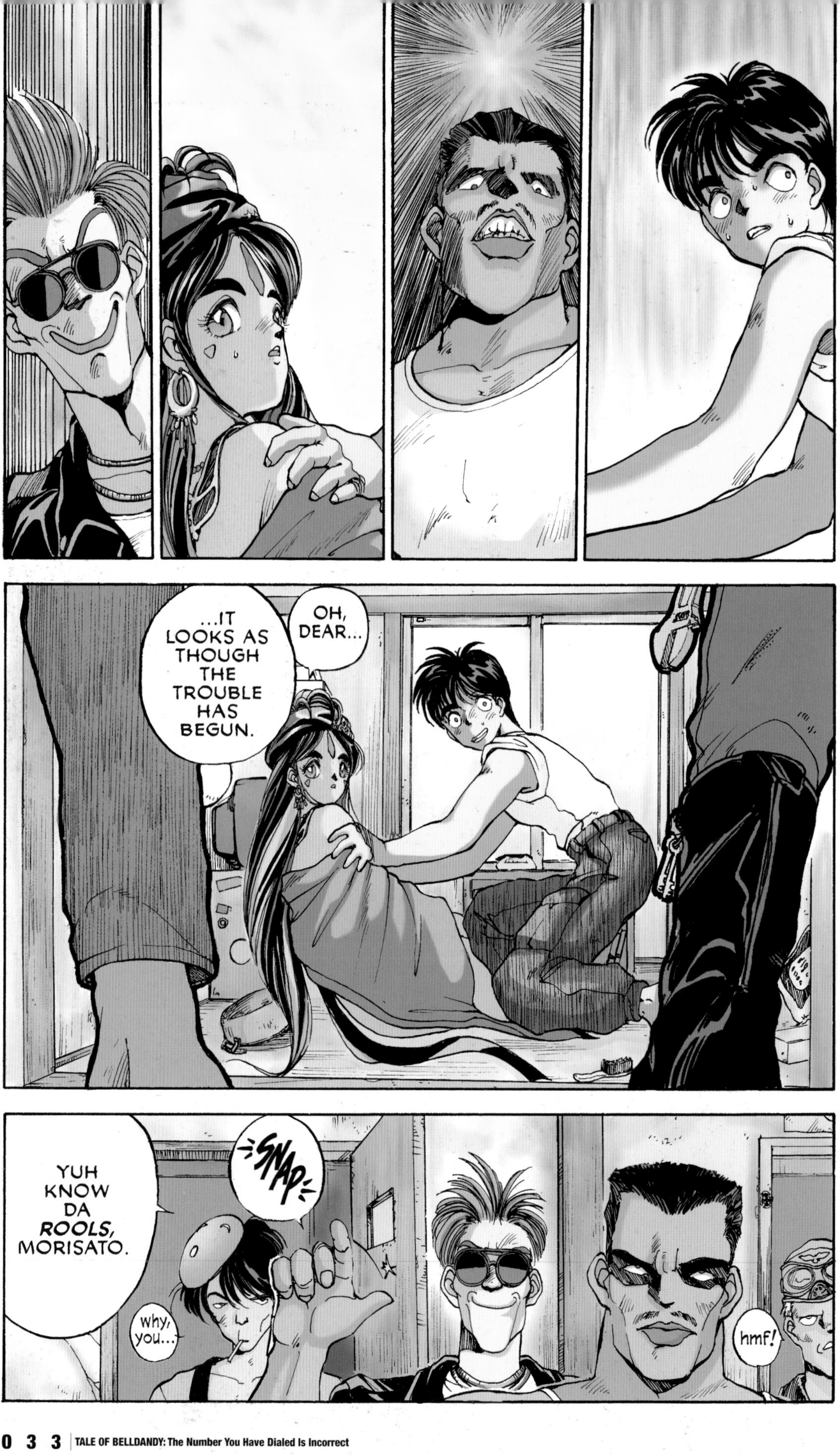
OH, DEAR...
...IT LOOKS AS THOUGH THE TROUBLE HAS BEGUN.
hmf!
SNAP
YUH KNOW DA *ROOLS,* MORISATO.
why, you...

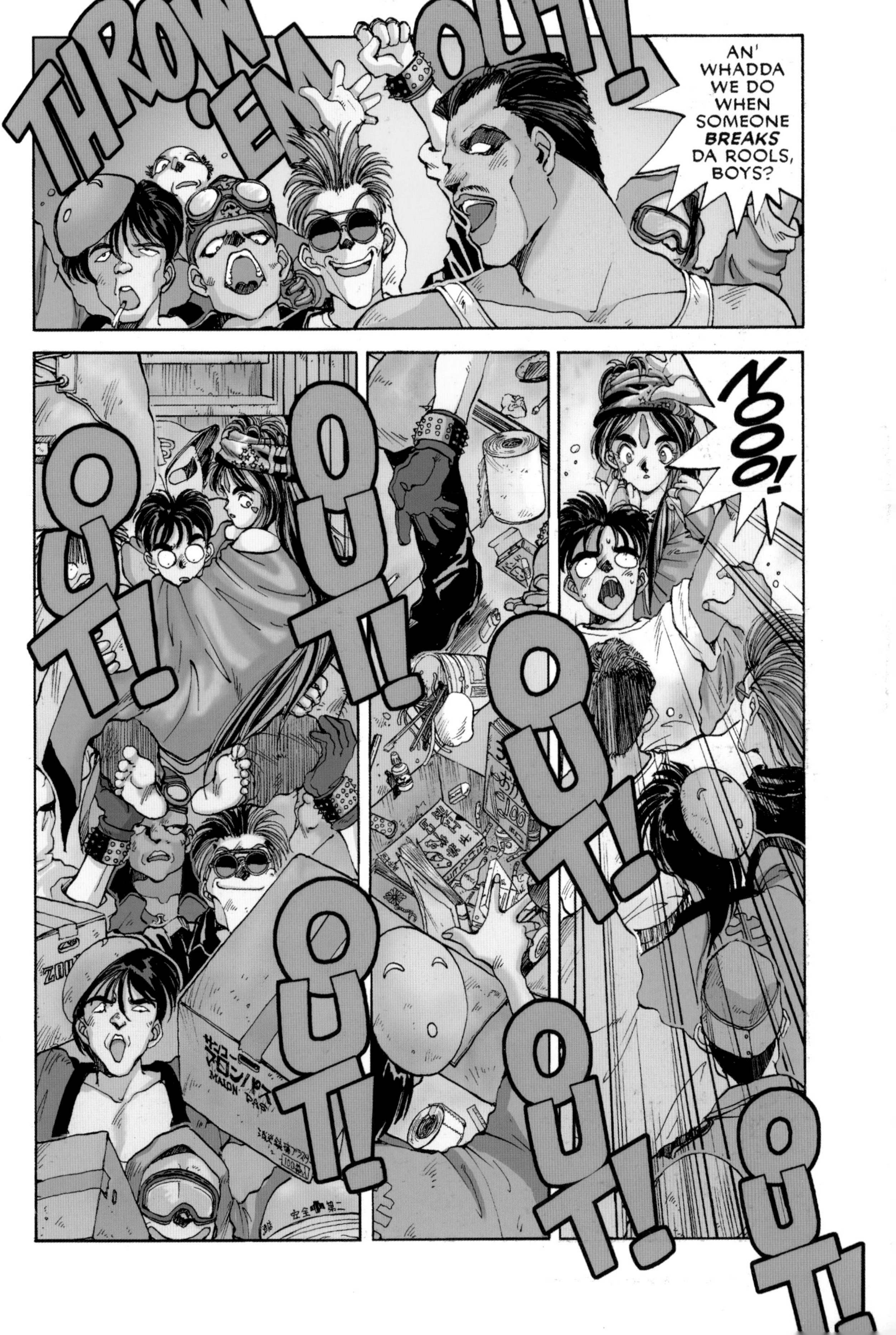
AN' WHADDA WE DO WHEN SOMEONE *BREAKS* DA ROOLS, BOYS?
THROW 'EM OUT!
NOOOO!
OUT!
OUT!
OUT!
OUT!
OUT!
OUT!

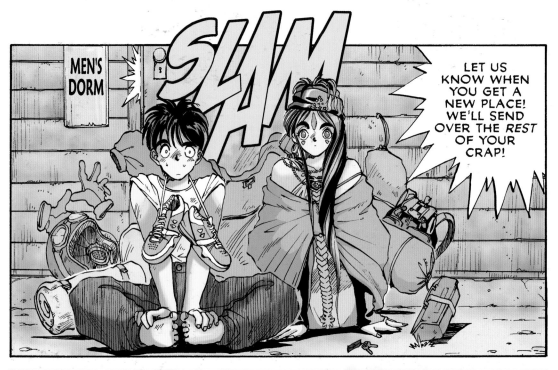

SLAM
LET US KNOW WHEN YOU GET A NEW PLACE! WE'LL SEND OVER THE *REST* OF YOUR CRAP!
MEN'S DORM
THAT'S THE FORCE OF YOUR WISH...
IT'LL START WORKING THAT WAY ANYTIME SOMETHING THREATENS TO SEPARATE US.
YEAH...? WELL, THIS TIME IT MIGHT NOT MAKE ANY DIFFER-ENCE.
?
THE SIDECAR ON MY BEEMER'S BUSTED, SO--
--huh?

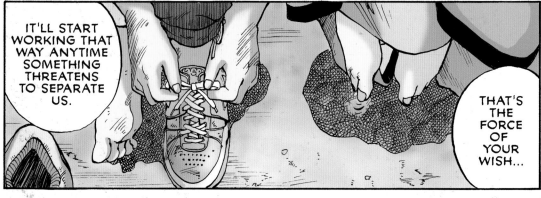

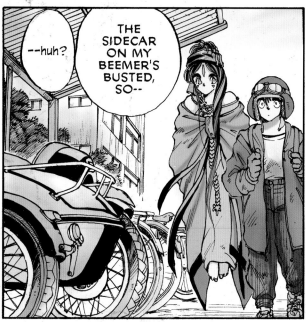

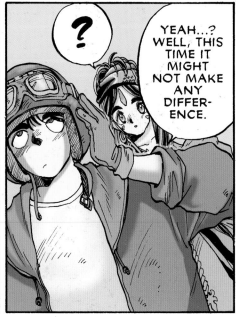

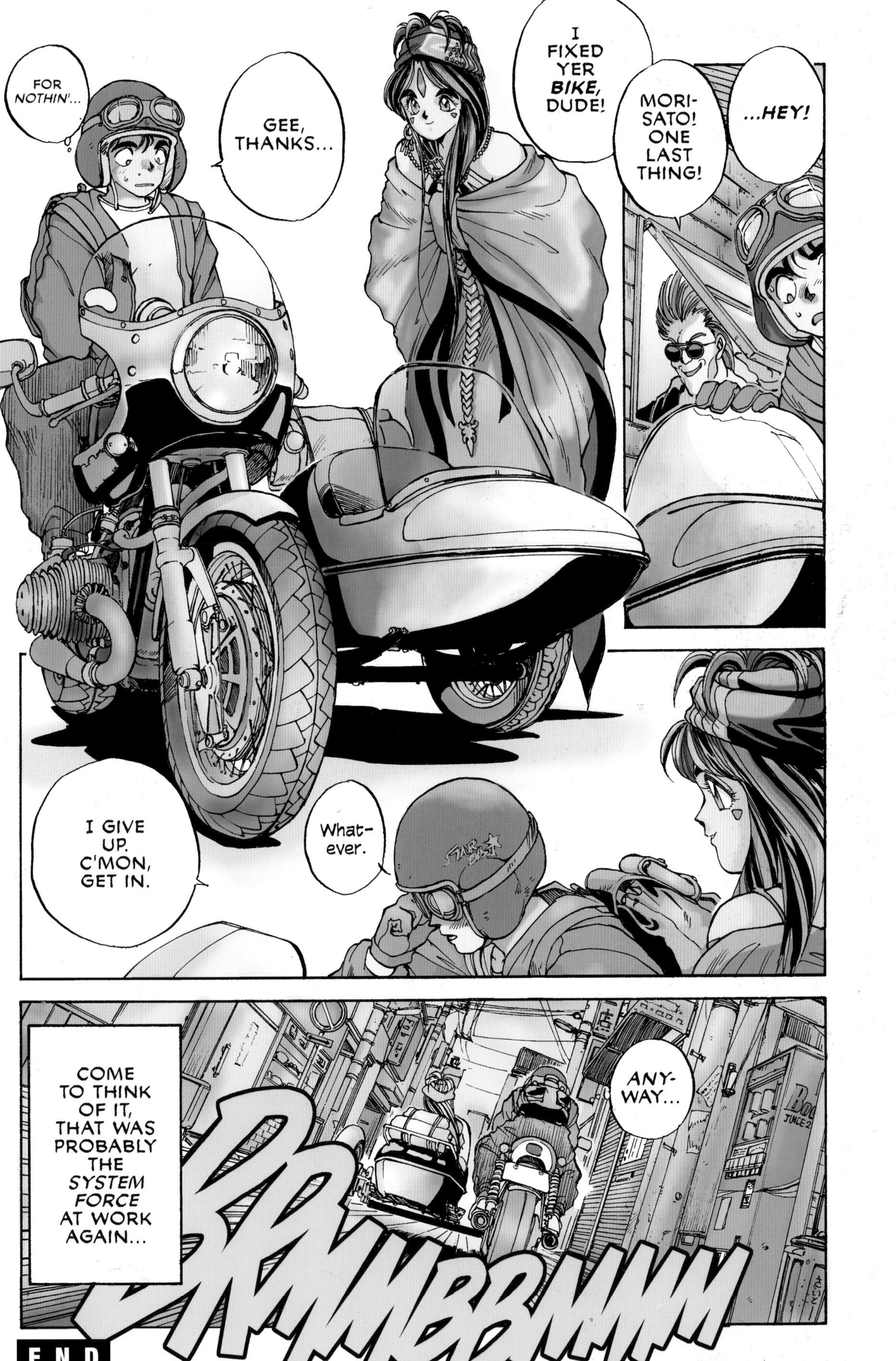
...HEY!
MORI-SATO! ONE LAST THING!
I FIXED YER BIKE, DUDE!
GEE, THANKS...
FOR NOTHIN'...
What-ever.
I GIVE UP. C'MON, GET IN.
ANY-WAY...
COME TO THINK OF IT, THAT WAS PROBABLY THE SYSTEM FORCE AT WORK AGAIN...
END

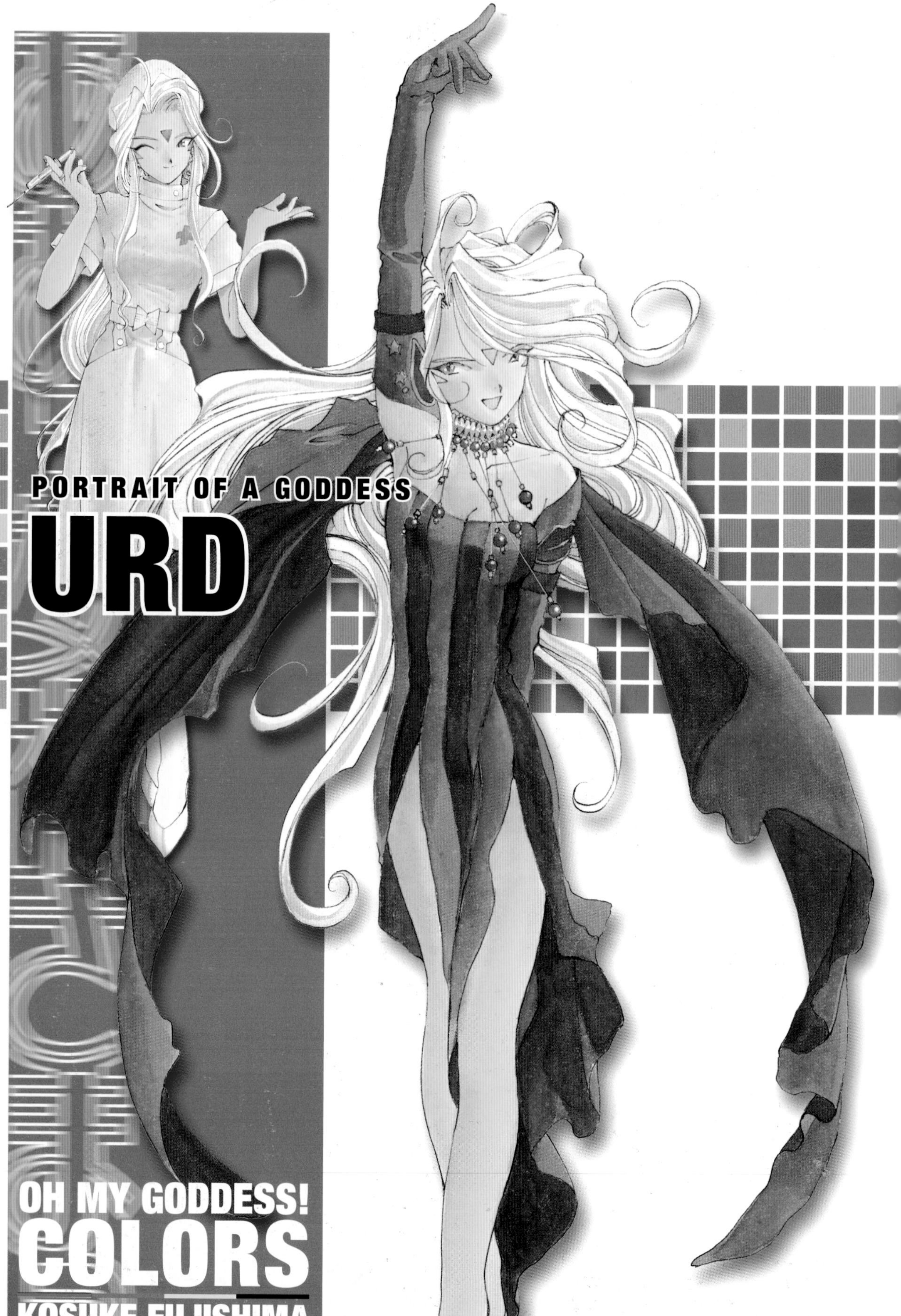
PORTRAIT OF A GODDESS
URD
OH MY GODDESS!
COLORS
KOSUKE FUJISHIMA

PORTRAIT OF A GODDESS
URD

PROFILE

Height:	170 cm (5'7")
Bust:	90 cm (35.4")
Waist:	60 cm (23.6")
Hips:	91 cm (35.8")
Place of birth:	Unclear
Age:	Unknown
Blood type:	Does she have one?
Favorite food:	Saké
	(up-market brands)
Favorite phrase:	"Consume by fire"
Hobbies:	Watching TV,
	drinking saké,
	concocting medicine

Goddess Second-Class, Type 1, Limited, with administrative restrictions. Half-demon on her mother's side; she, Belldandy, and Skuld (see below) share the same father. She is therefore Bell and Skuld's half-sister, but that technicality—while sometimes complicating the plot—has never lessened their fundamental love and concern for each other. The Goddess of the Past.

Urd is good at calling down the lightning. Incidentally, her energy is renewed by drinking saké—preferably, ones brewed only from the finest rice.

It certainly sounds impressive that Urd is the systems administrator of Yggdrasil, the heavenly computer. The reality is that she avoids work as much as possible, having fussed so much over Bell and Keiichi's tenuous (from her physical-minded perspective) relationship that she handed over most of the day-to-day duties of her job to her younger sister, Skuld. Urd would like to think of herself as the helping hand to shove the two of them "closer," but the reality (once more) is that her efforts fail. Heaven itself temporarily banned her for her egregious "violation of service terms."

Note that Urd is in fact good at her job and inspires great loyalty from her staff, but actually showing up to work at Yggdrasil requires, in her view, a "good reason"—for example, in Vol. 16, it took a direct summons from the Almighty and the threat of the total cessation of time on Earth.

Belldandy once said of Urd—and Goddesses First-Class, unlike Urd, don't lie—that she tends to think the end justifies the means, but she gets so wrapped up in the means that she forgets what the end even was. Very passionate, one could say. If Belldandy is the "rule-book" goddess, then Urd is the "throw-the-book-out-the-window" one.

Not surprisingly, Urd's own on-again, off-again boyfriend is Troubadour, the (rather handsome) spirit of the plum tree. However, when you look at their relationship as a love which comes like a storm and then departs again, you could say in its own way it is mature, and surprisingly pure.

Urd is accompanied by her angel, World of Elegance, who controls fire. Note that her first two hobbies go together, but her third one doesn't . . . which may be why it often leads to such spectacular results.

TALE OF URD:
Urd's Fantastic Adventure

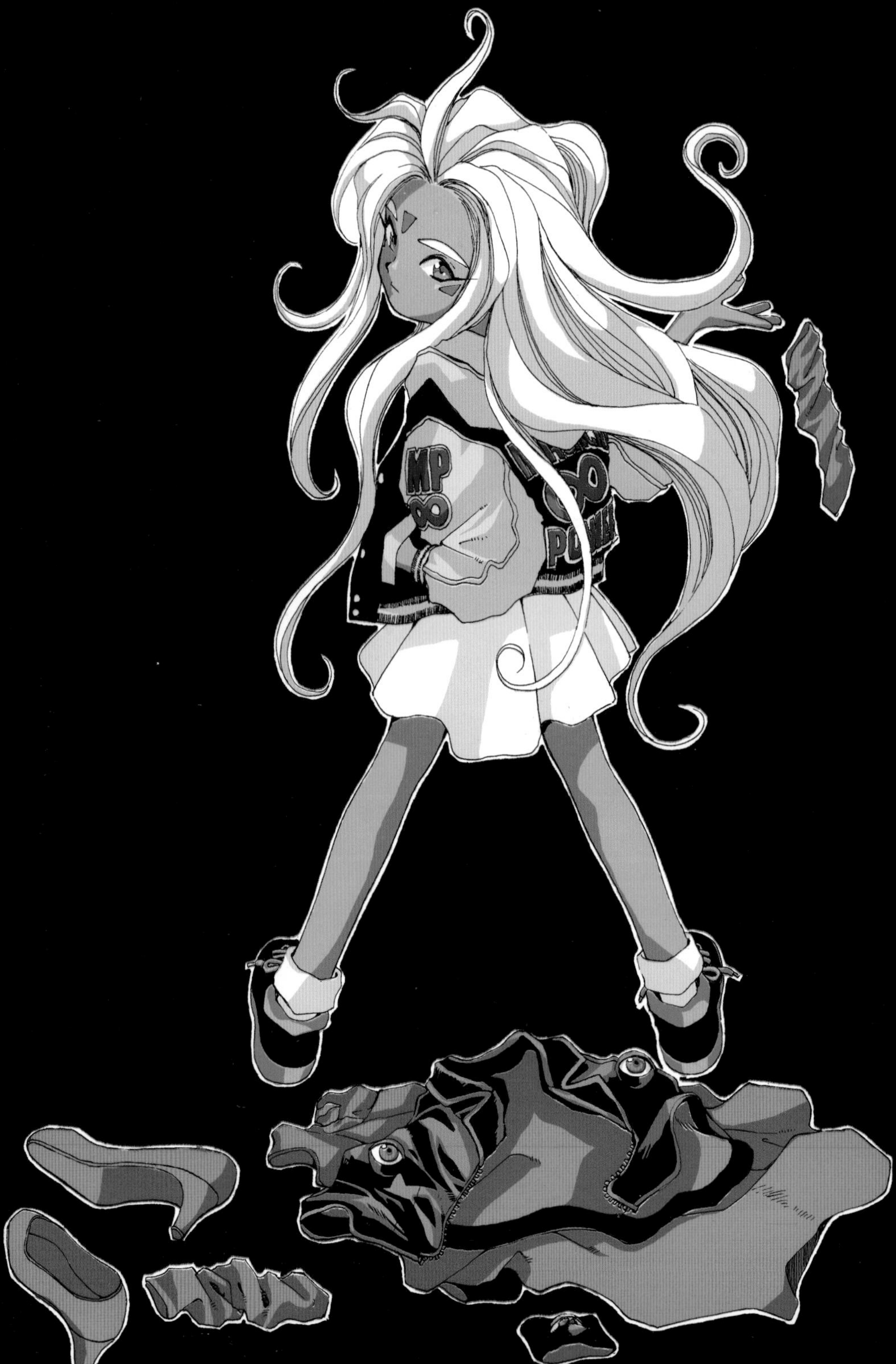
MP
POWER

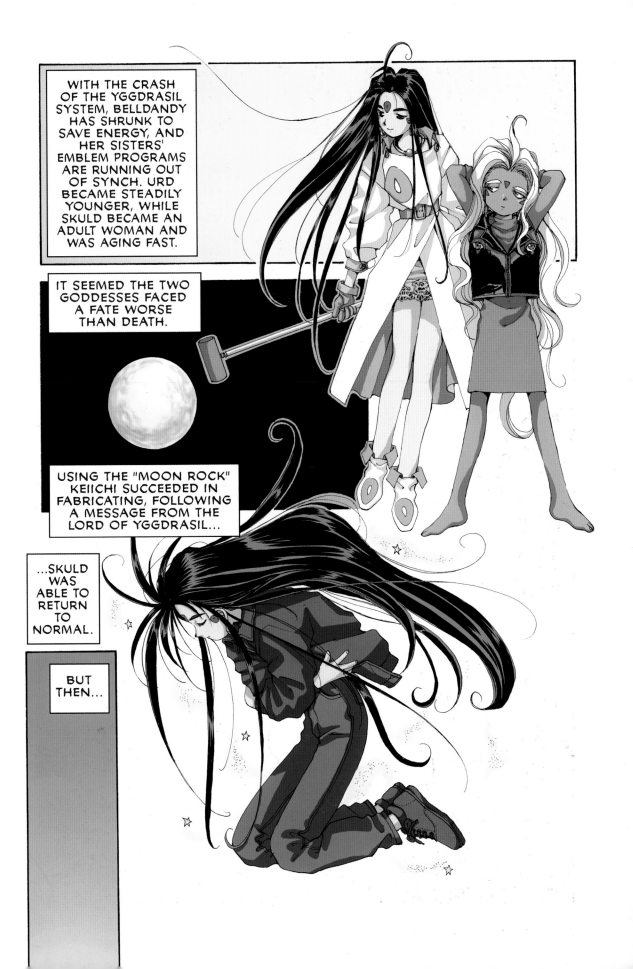

WITH THE CRASH OF THE YGGDRASIL SYSTEM, BELLDANDY HAS SHRUNK TO SAVE ENERGY, AND HER SISTERS' EMBLEM PROGRAMS ARE RUNNING OUT OF SYNCH. URD BECAME STEADILY YOUNGER, WHILE SKULD BECAME AN ADULT WOMAN AND WAS AGING FAST.

IT SEEMED THE TWO GODDESSES FACED A FATE WORSE THAN DEATH.

USING THE "MOON ROCK" KEIICHI SUCCEEDED IN FABRICATING, FOLLOWING A MESSAGE FROM THE LORD OF YGGDRASIL...

...SKULD WAS ABLE TO RETURN TO NORMAL.

BUT THEN...

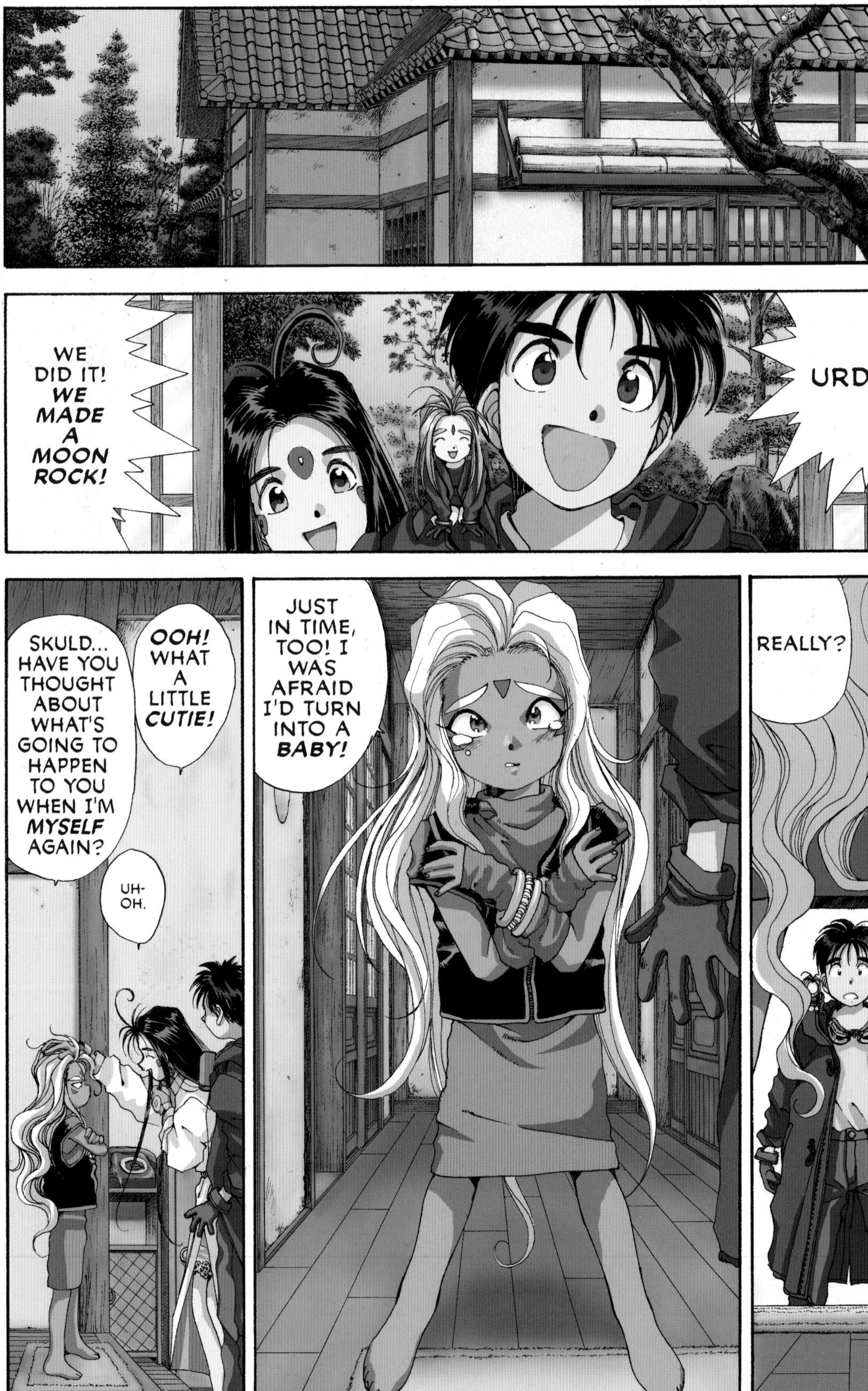
URD!
WE DID IT! WE MADE A MOON ROCK!
REALLY?
JUST IN TIME, TOO! I WAS AFRAID I'D TURN INTO A BABY!
OOH! WHAT A LITTLE CUTIE!
SKULD... HAVE YOU THOUGHT ABOUT WHAT'S GOING TO HAPPEN TO YOU WHEN I'M MYSELF AGAIN?
UH-OH.

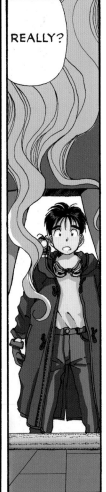

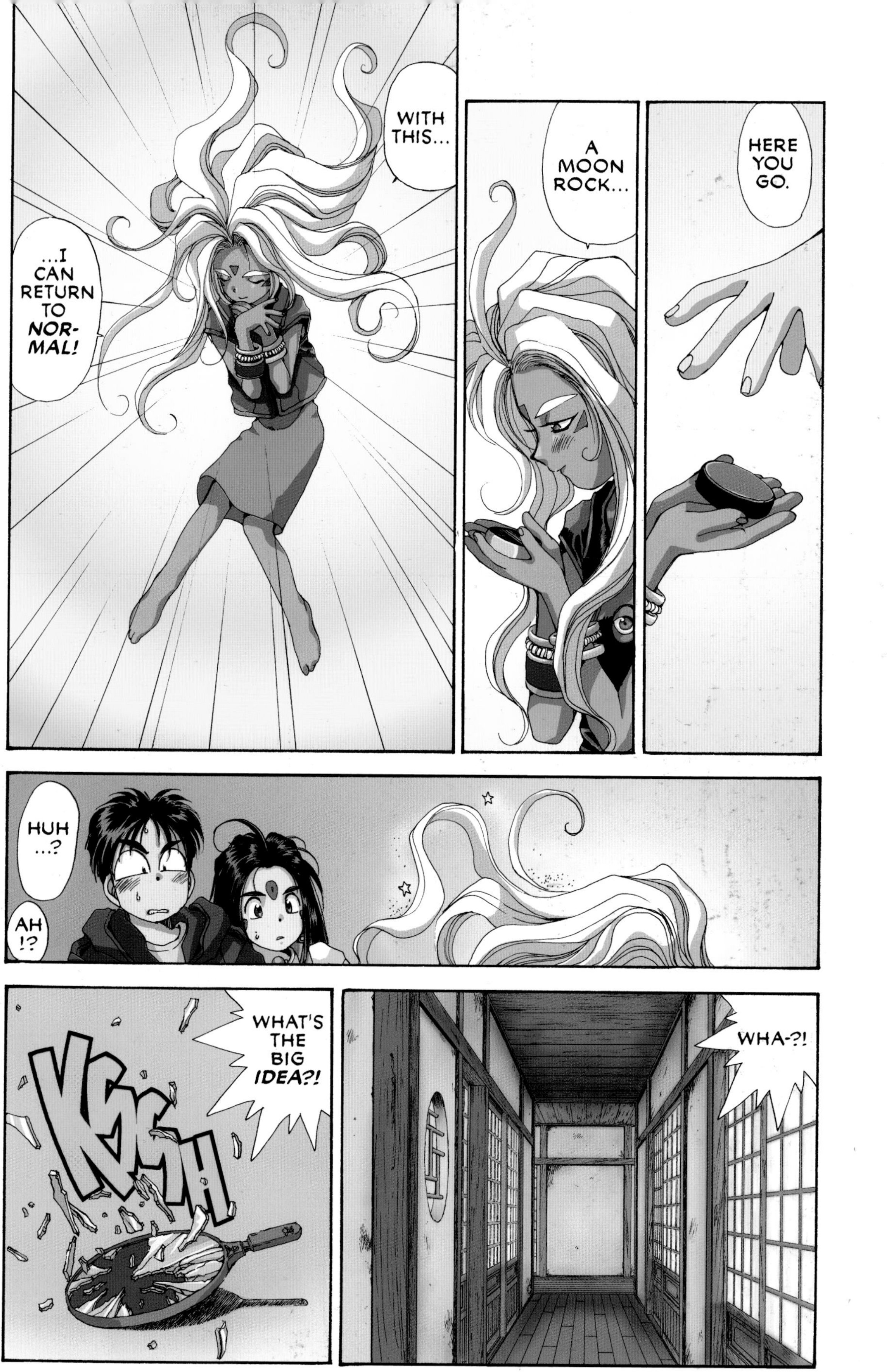
HERE YOU GO.
A MOON ROCK...
WITH THIS...
...I CAN RETURN TO *NORMAL!*
HUH ...?
AH !?
WHA-?!
WHAT'S THE BIG *IDEA?!*

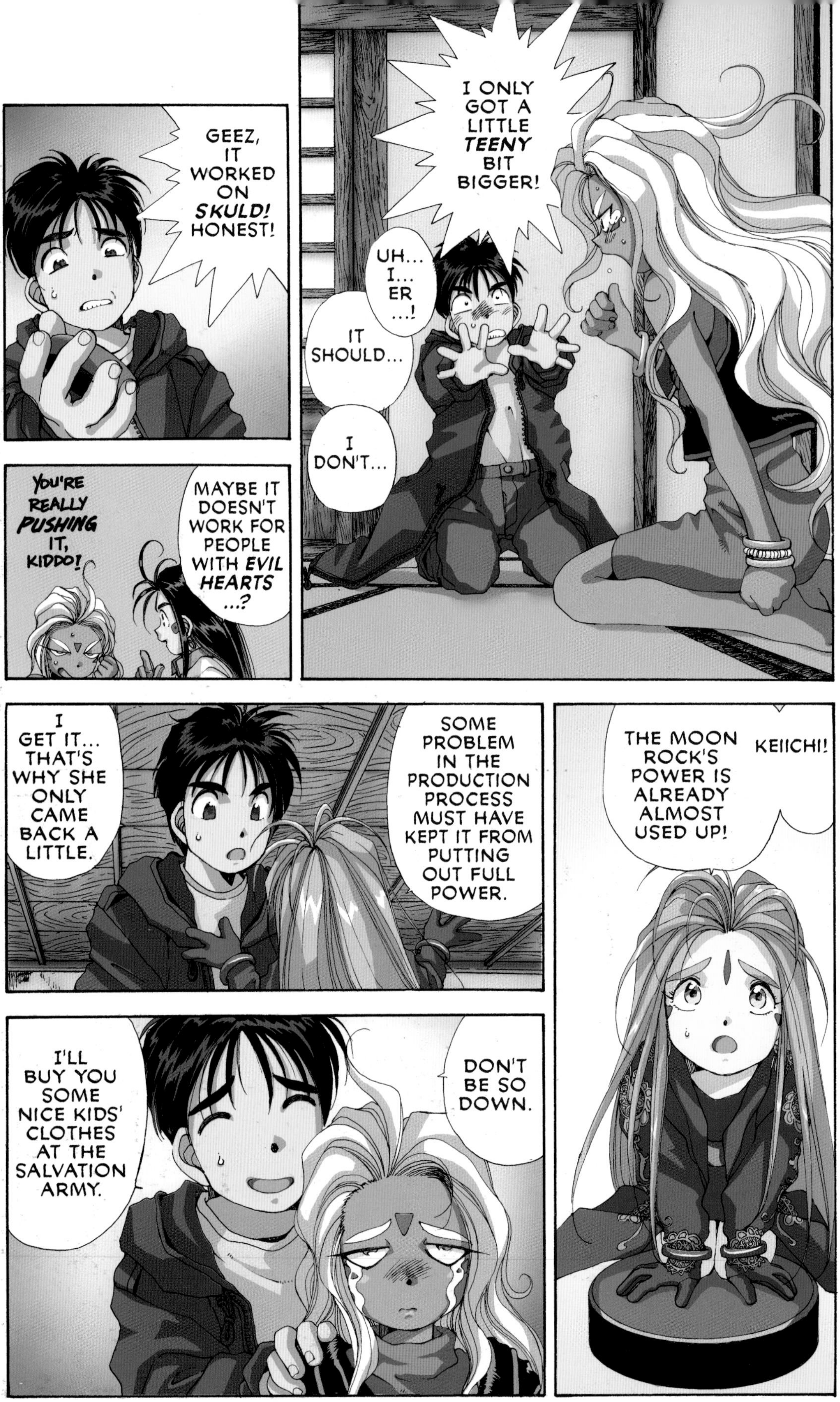
I ONLY GOT A LITTLE TEENY BIT BIGGER!
UH... I... ER ...!
IT SHOULD...
I DON'T...
GEEZ, IT WORKED ON SKULD! HONEST!
MAYBE IT DOESN'T WORK FOR PEOPLE WITH EVIL HEARTS ...?
YOU'RE REALLY PUSHING IT, KIDDO!
KEIICHI!
THE MOON ROCK'S POWER IS ALREADY ALMOST USED UP!
SOME PROBLEM IN THE PRODUCTION PROCESS MUST HAVE KEPT IT FROM PUTTING OUT FULL POWER.
I GET IT... THAT'S WHY SHE ONLY CAME BACK A LITTLE.
DON'T BE SO DOWN.
I'LL BUY YOU SOME NICE KIDS' CLOTHES AT THE SALVATION ARMY.

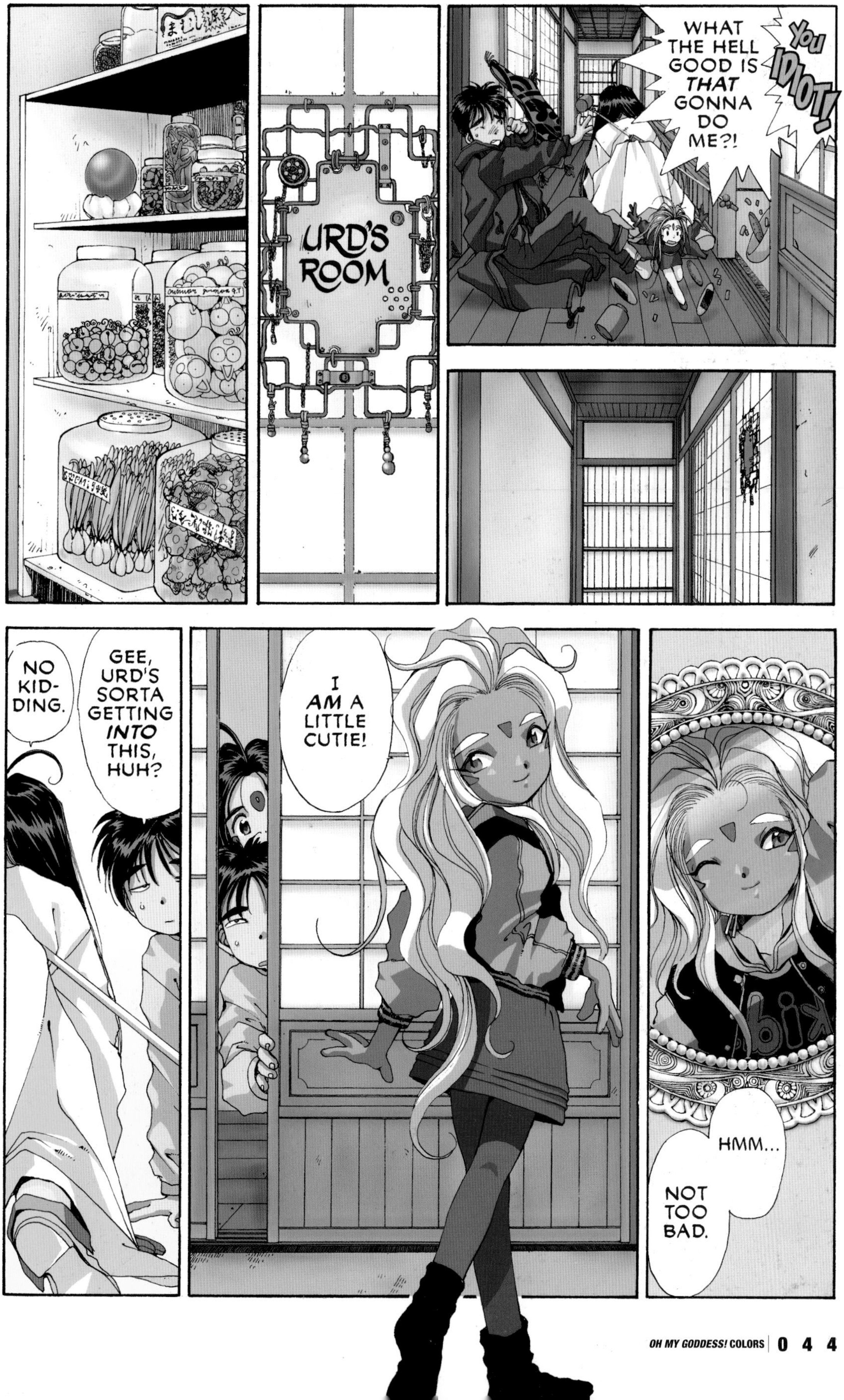
YOU IDIOT!
WHAT THE HELL GOOD IS *THAT* GONNA DO ME?!
URD'S ROOM
HMM... NOT TOO BAD.
I *AM* A LITTLE CUTIE!
GEE, URD'S SORTA GETTING *INTO* THIS, HUH?
NO KID-DING.

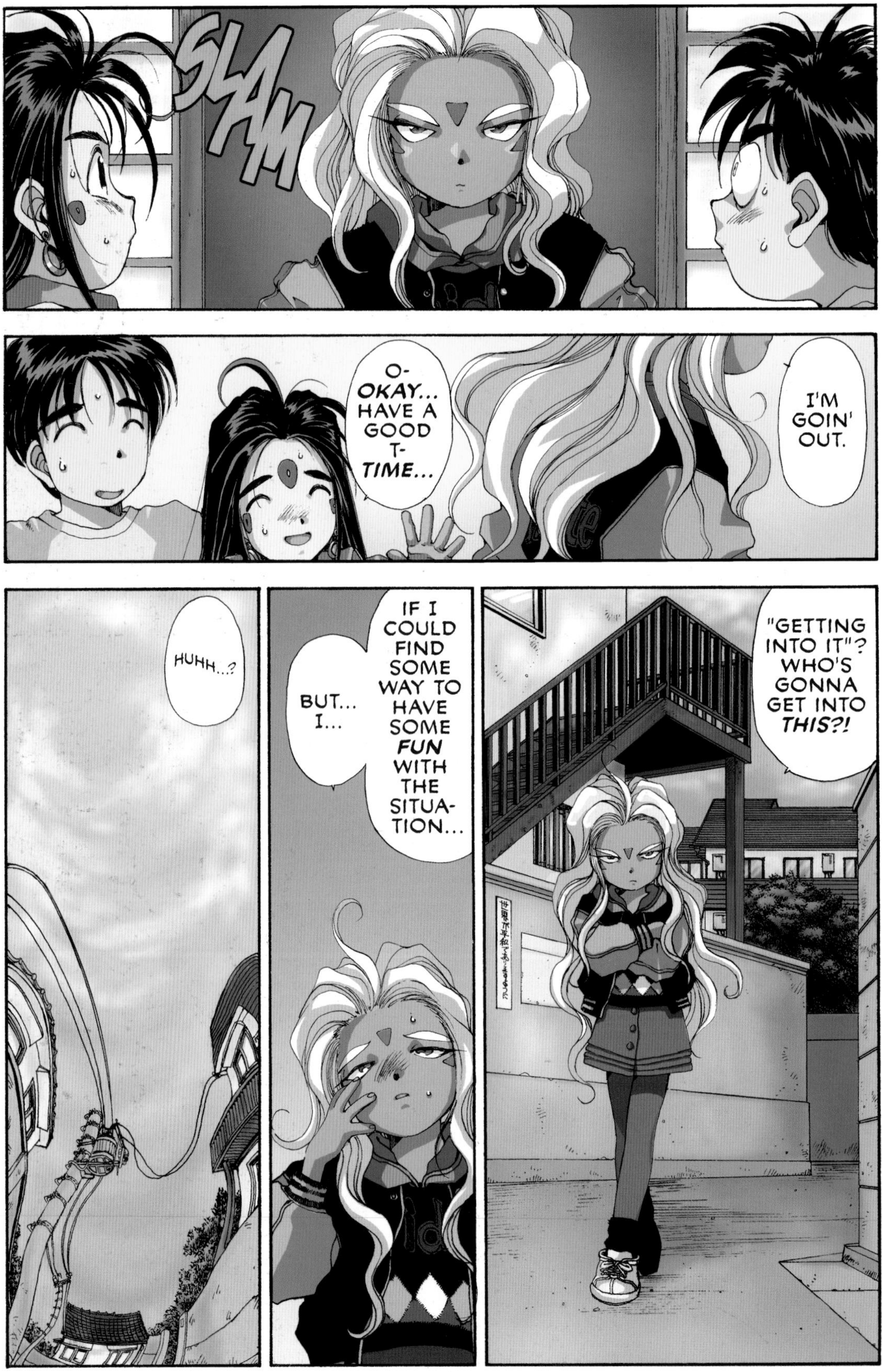
SLAM
I'M GOIN' OUT.
O-OKAY... HAVE A GOOD T-TIME...
"GETTING INTO IT"? WHO'S GONNA GET INTO THIS?!
IF I COULD FIND SOME WAY TO HAVE SOME FUN WITH THE SITUATION...
BUT... I...
HUHH...?

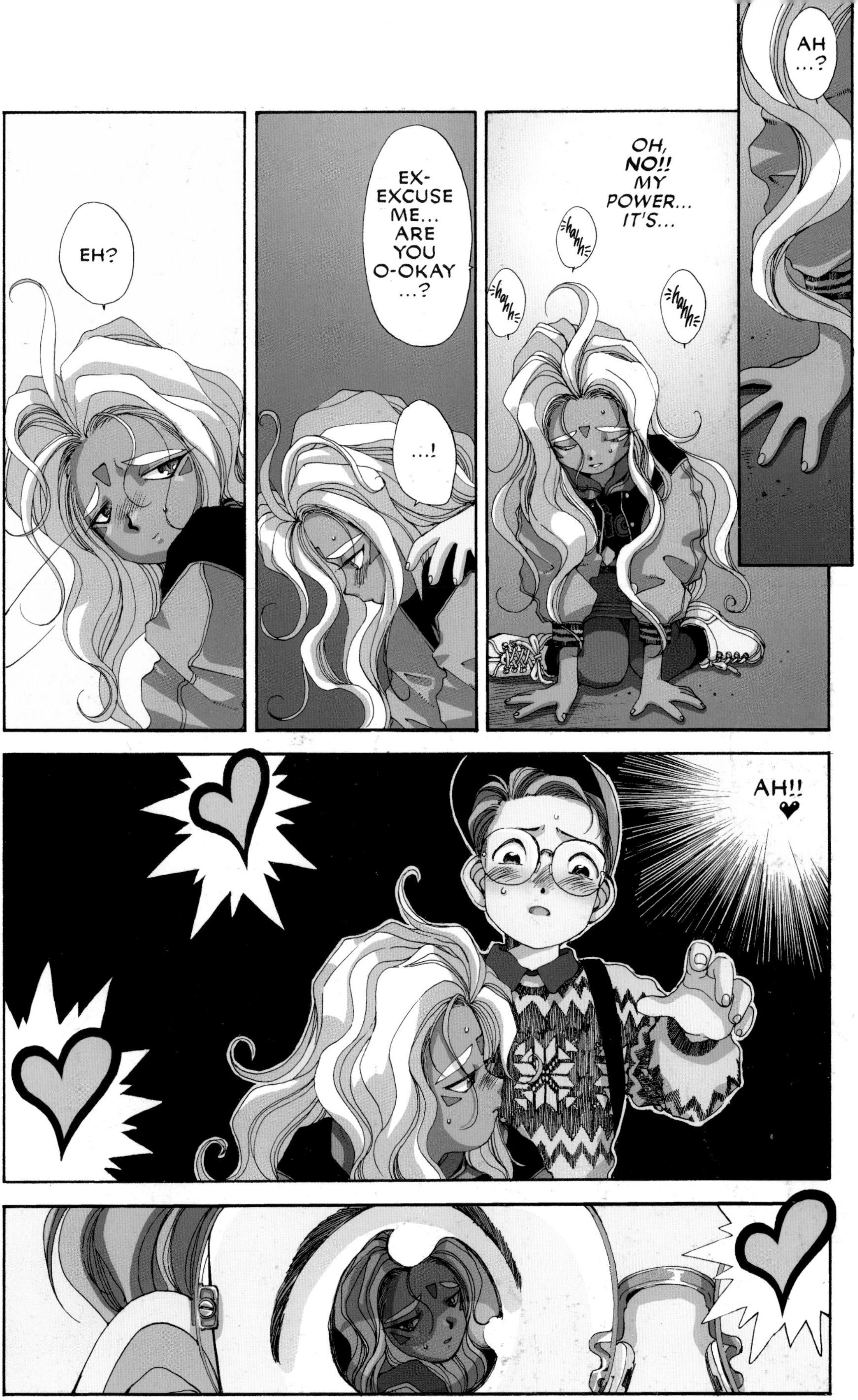
AH ...?
OH, NO!! MY POWER... IT'S...
hahh
hahh
hahh
EX- EXCUSE ME... ARE YOU O-OKAY ...?
...!
EH?
AH!! ♥

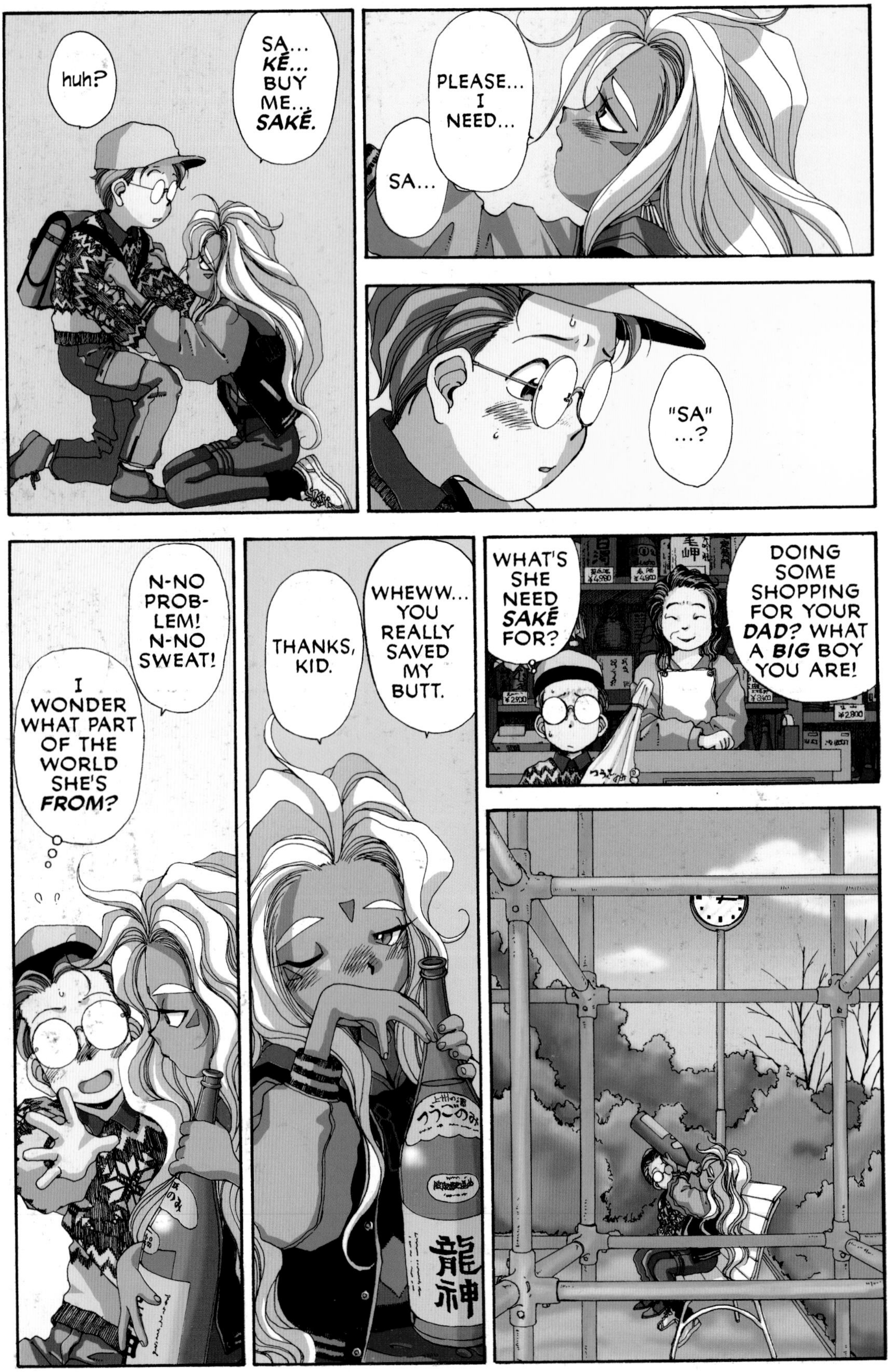
PLEASE... I NEED...
SA...
"SA" ...?
SA... KÉ... BUY ME... SAKÉ.
huh?
DOING SOME SHOPPING FOR YOUR DAD? WHAT A BIG BOY YOU ARE!
WHAT'S SHE NEED SAKÉ FOR?
WHEWW... YOU REALLY SAVED MY BUTT.
THANKS, KID.
龍神
N-NO PROB-LEM! N-NO SWEAT!
I WONDER WHAT PART OF THE WORLD SHE'S FROM?

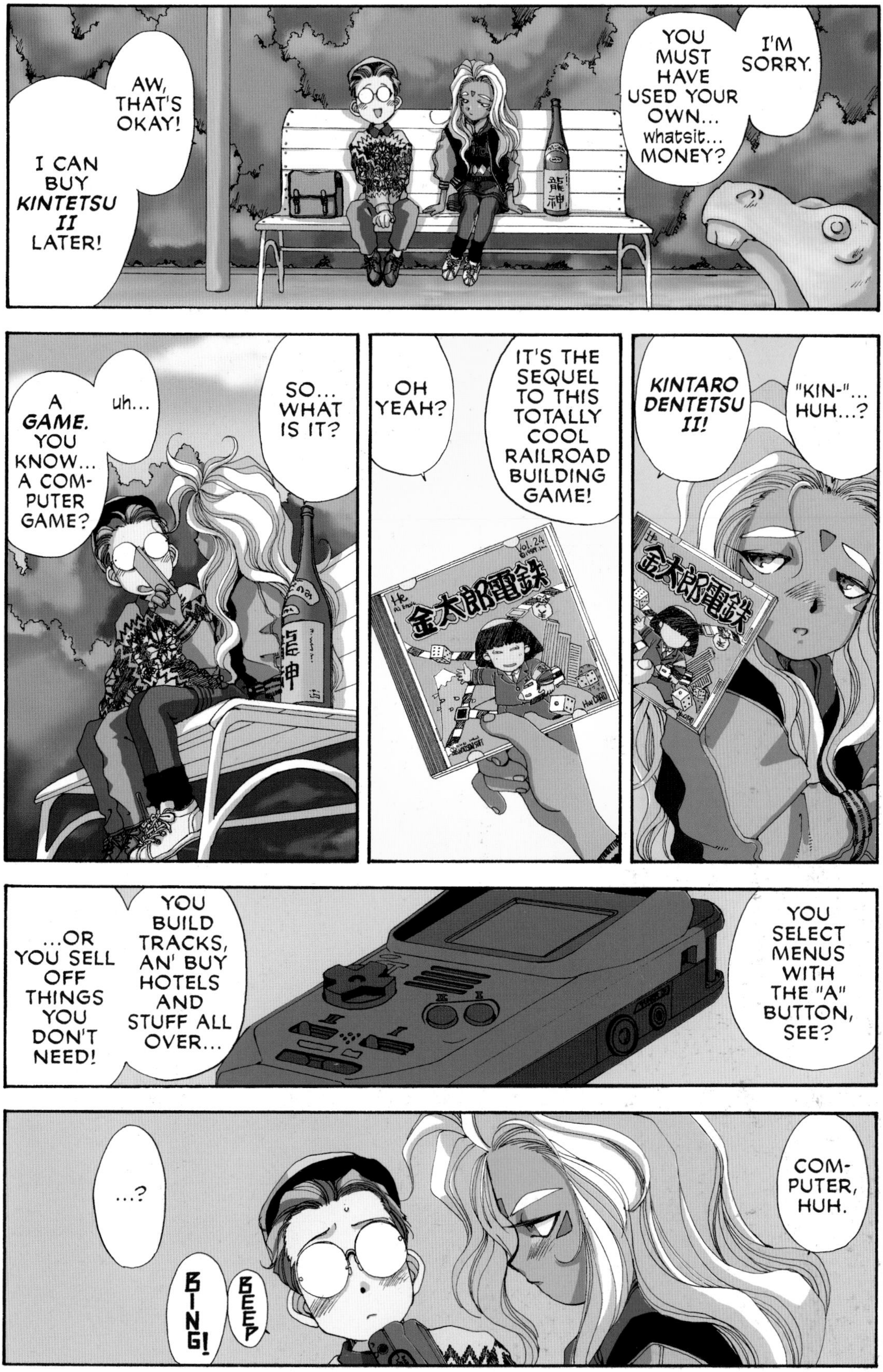

I'M SORRY.
YOU MUST HAVE USED YOUR OWN... whatsit... MONEY?
AW, THAT'S OKAY!
I CAN BUY *KINTETSU II* LATER!
"KIN-"... HUH...?
KINTARO DENTETSU II!
IT'S THE SEQUEL TO THIS TOTALLY COOL RAILROAD BUILDING GAME!
OH YEAH?
SO... WHAT IS IT?
uh...
A *GAME.* YOU KNOW... A COMPUTER GAME?
YOU SELECT MENUS WITH THE "A" BUTTON, SEE?
YOU BUILD TRACKS, AN' BUY HOTELS AND STUFF ALL OVER...
...OR YOU SELL OFF THINGS YOU DON'T NEED!
COMPUTER, HUH.
...?
BEEP
BING!

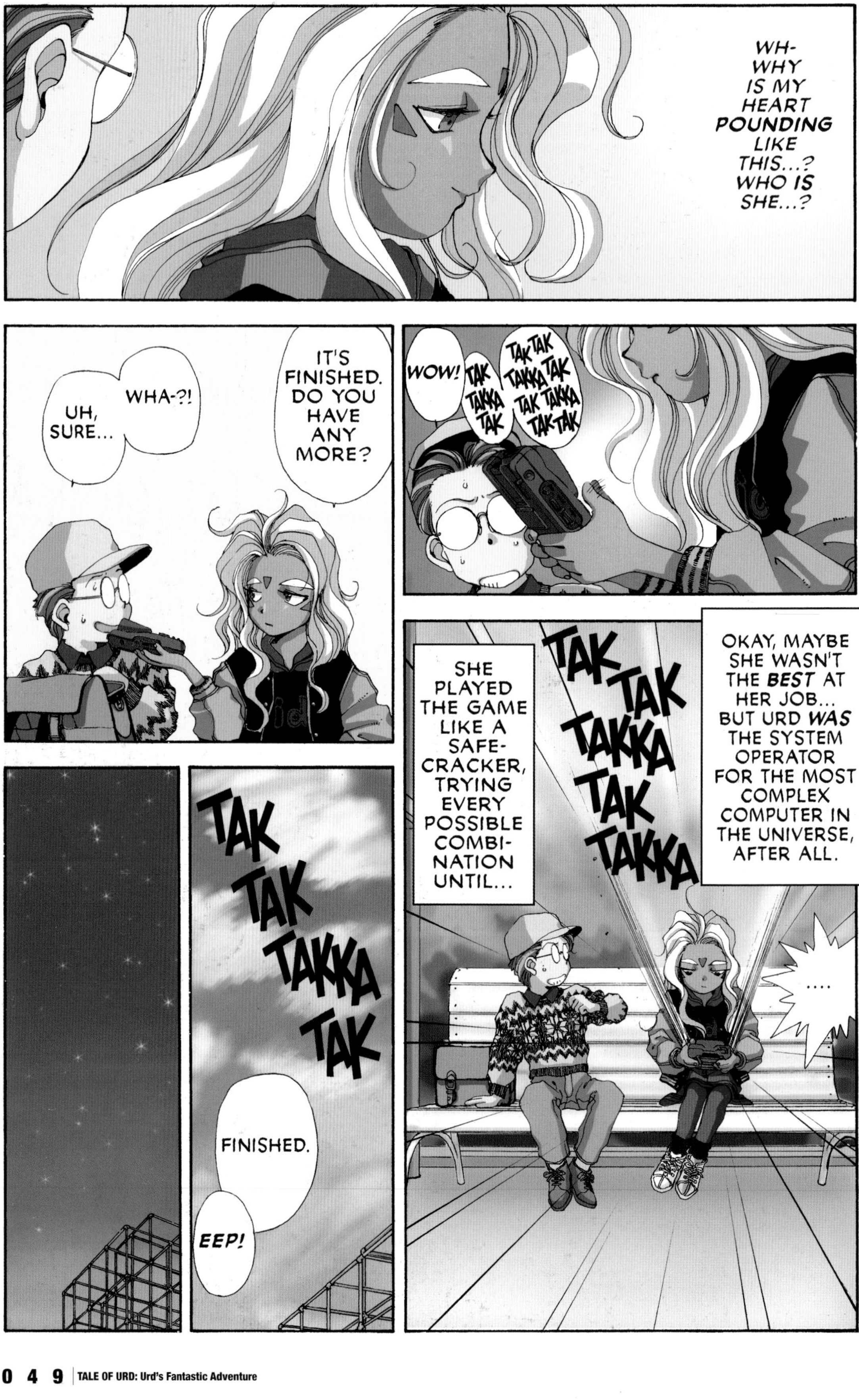
WH- WHY IS MY HEART POUNDING LIKE THIS...? WHO IS SHE...?
TAK TAK TAKKA TAK TAK TAKKA TAK-TAK
TAK TAKKA TAK
WOW!
IT'S FINISHED. DO YOU HAVE ANY MORE?
WHA-?!
UH, SURE...
OKAY, MAYBE SHE WASN'T THE BEST AT HER JOB... BUT URD WAS THE SYSTEM OPERATOR FOR THE MOST COMPLEX COMPUTER IN THE UNIVERSE, AFTER ALL.
TAK TAK TAKKA TAK TAKKA
SHE PLAYED THE GAME LIKE A SAFE-CRACKER, TRYING EVERY POSSIBLE COMBI-NATION UNTIL...
....
TAK TAK TAKKA TAK
FINISHED.
EEP!

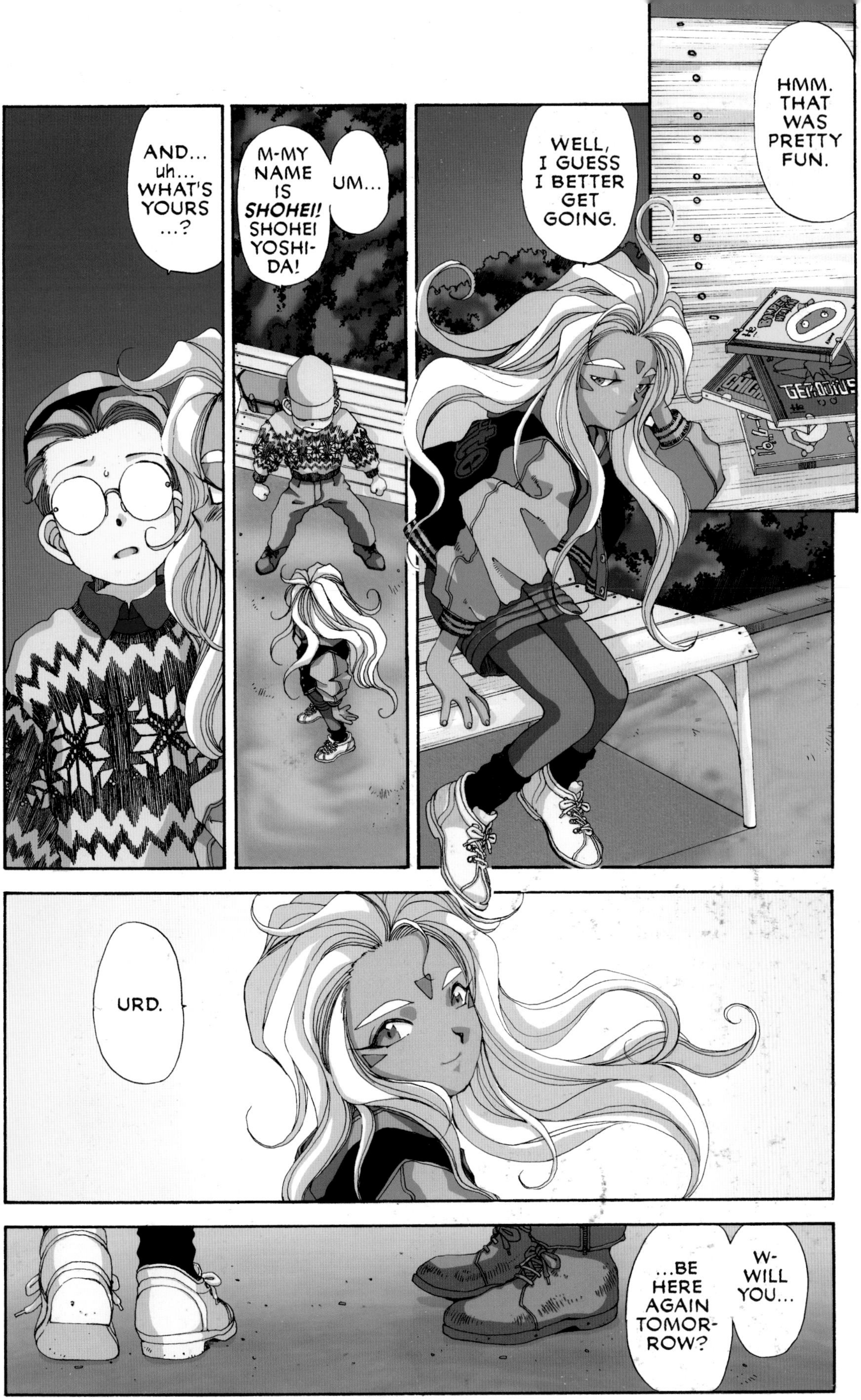
HMM. THAT WAS PRETTY FUN.
WELL, I GUESS I BETTER GET GOING.
UM...
M-MY NAME IS *SHOHEI!* SHOHEI YOSHI-DA!
AND... uh... WHAT'S YOURS ...?
URD.
W- WILL YOU...
...BE HERE AGAIN TOMOR-ROW?

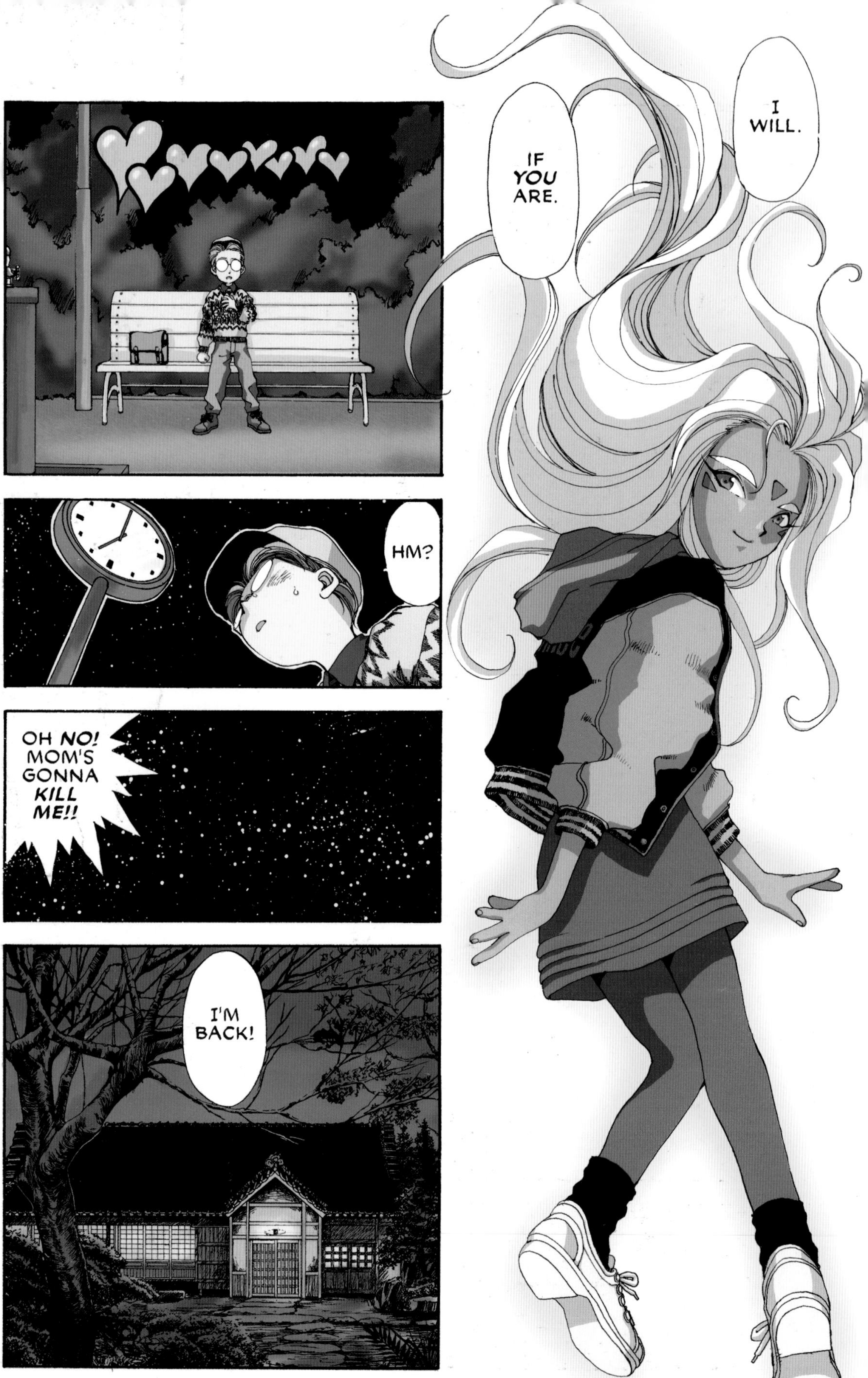
I WILL.
IF YOU ARE.
HM?
OH NO! MOM'S GONNA KILL ME!!
I'M BACK!

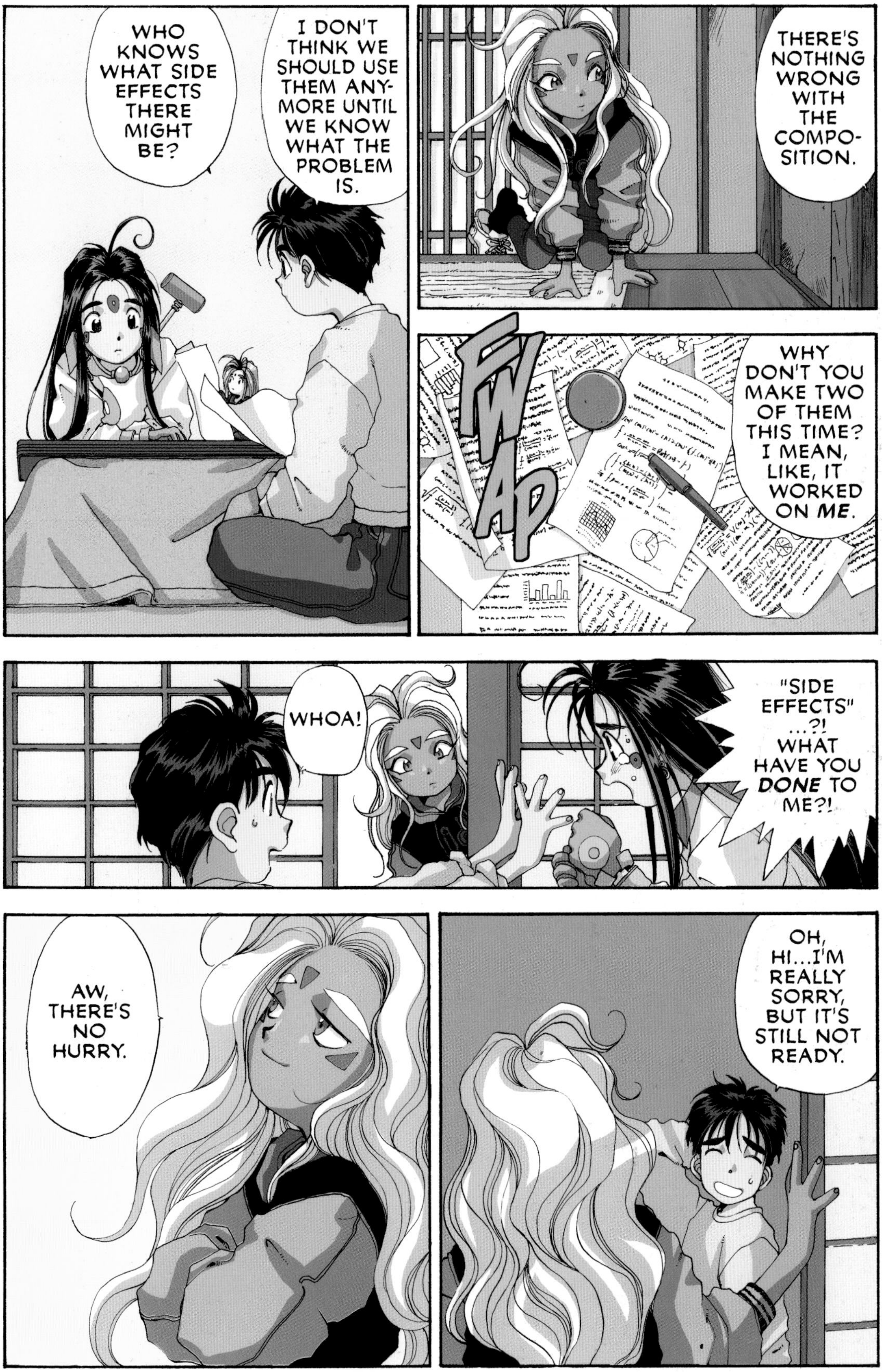
THERE'S NOTHING WRONG WITH THE COMPOSITION.
WHY DON'T YOU MAKE TWO OF THEM THIS TIME? I MEAN, LIKE, IT WORKED ON *ME*.
FWAP
I DON'T THINK WE SHOULD USE THEM ANYMORE UNTIL WE KNOW WHAT THE PROBLEM IS.
WHO KNOWS WHAT SIDE EFFECTS THERE MIGHT BE?
"SIDE EFFECTS" ...?! WHAT HAVE YOU *DONE* TO ME?!
WHOA!
OH, HI...I'M REALLY SORRY, BUT IT'S STILL NOT READY.
AW, THERE'S NO HURRY.

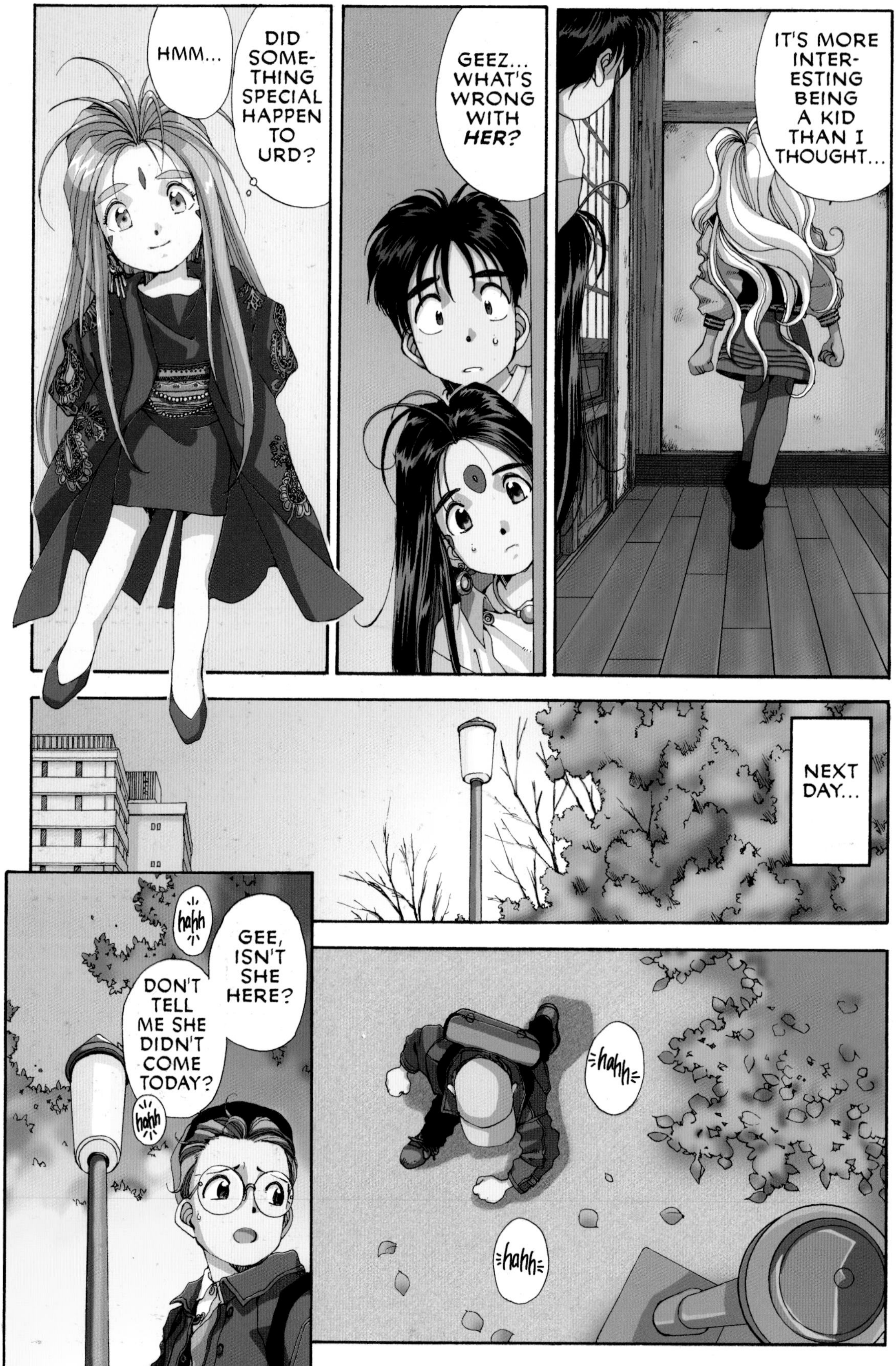
IT'S MORE INTER- ESTING BEING A KID THAN I THOUGHT...
GEEZ... WHAT'S WRONG WITH *HER?*
DID SOME- THING SPECIAL HAPPEN TO URD?
HMM...
NEXT DAY...
hahh
hahh
hahh
GEE, ISN'T SHE HERE?
DON'T TELL ME SHE DIDN'T COME TODAY?
hahh

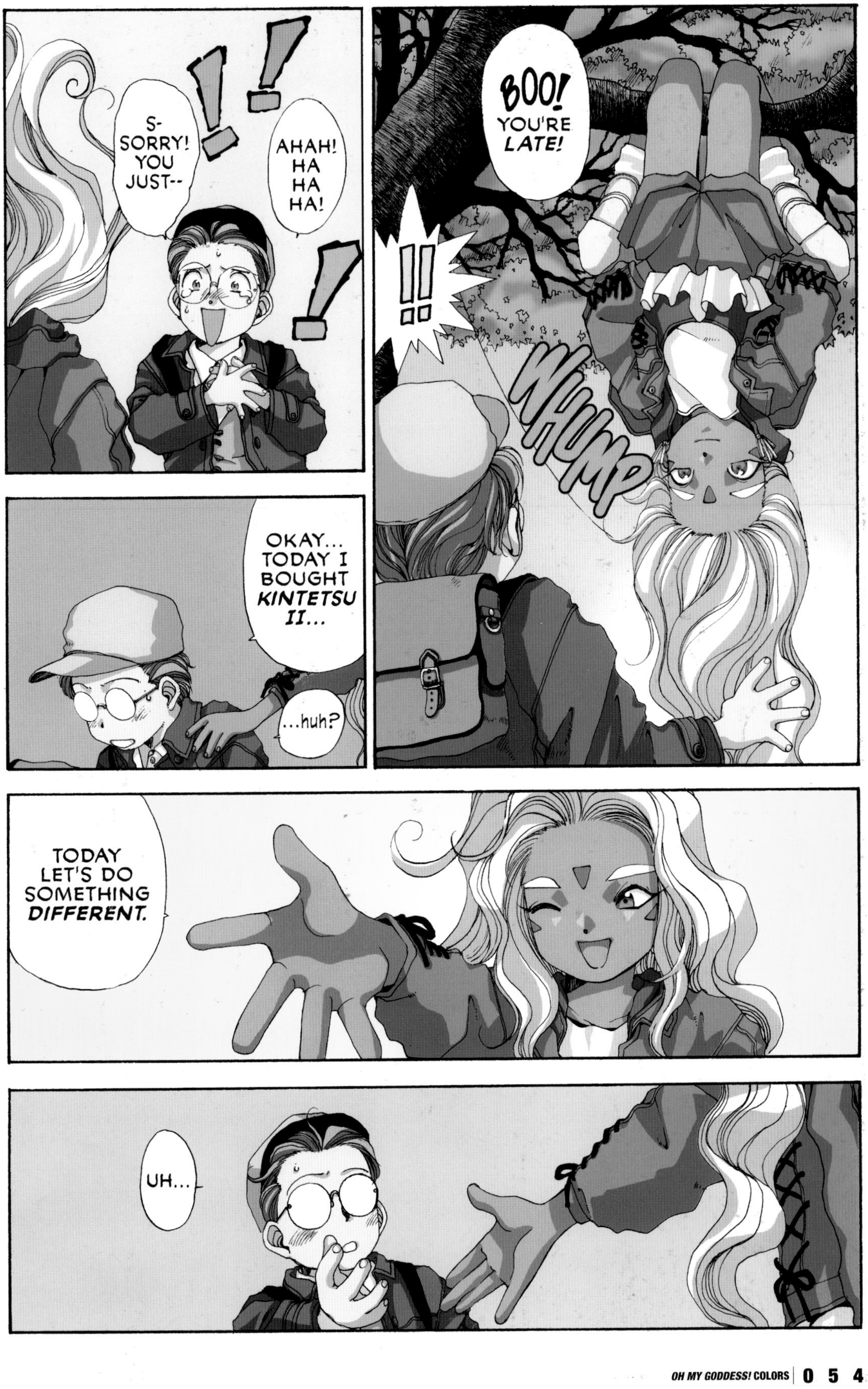
BOO! YOU'RE LATE!
!!!!
WHUMP
AHAH! HA HA HA!
S-SORRY! YOU JUST--
OKAY... TODAY I BOUGHT KINTETSU II...
...huh?
TODAY LET'S DO SOMETHING DIFFERENT.
UH...

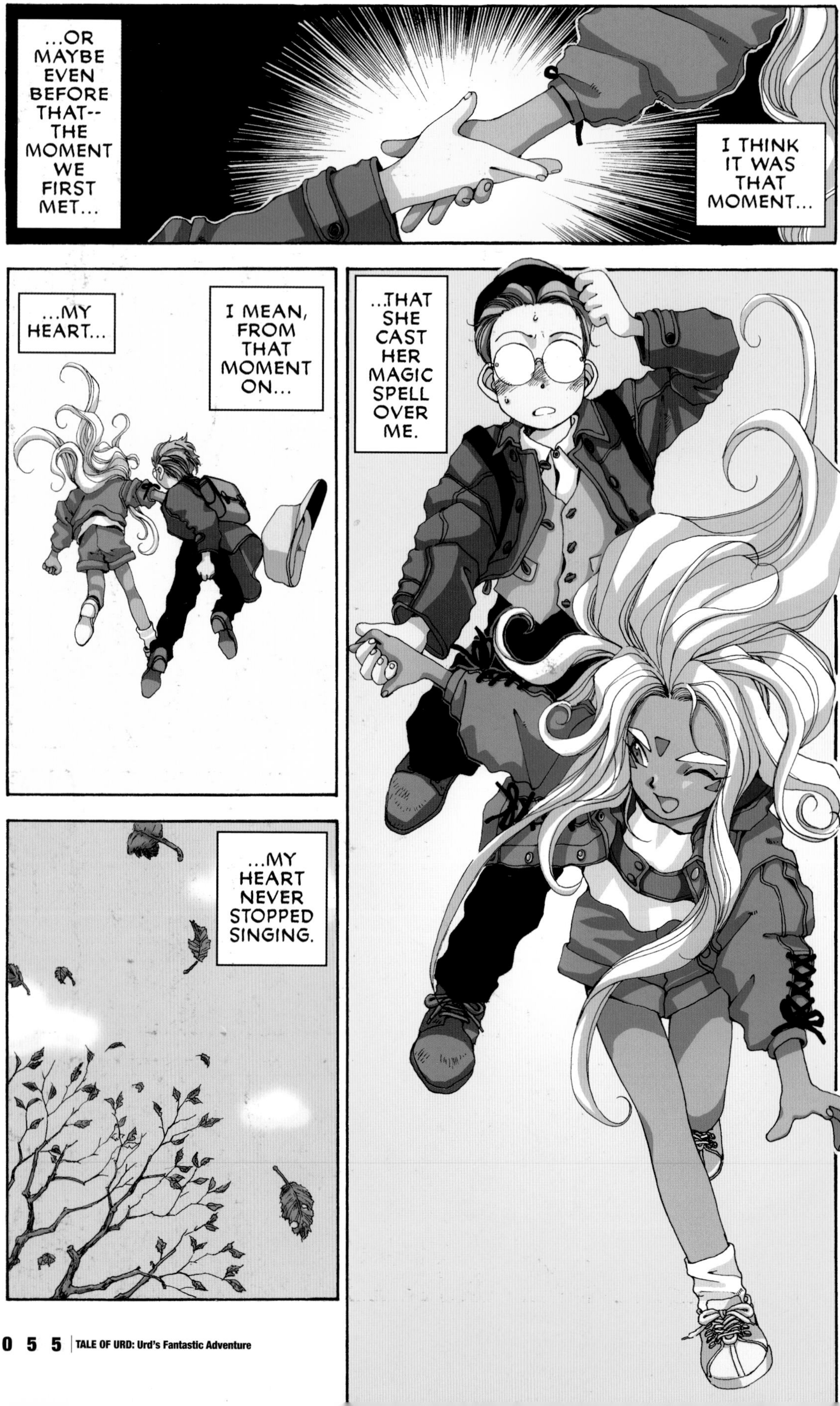
I THINK IT WAS THAT MOMENT...
...OR MAYBE EVEN BEFORE THAT-- THE MOMENT WE FIRST MET...
...THAT SHE CAST HER MAGIC SPELL OVER ME.
I MEAN, FROM THAT MOMENT ON...
...MY HEART...
...MY HEART NEVER STOPPED SINGING.

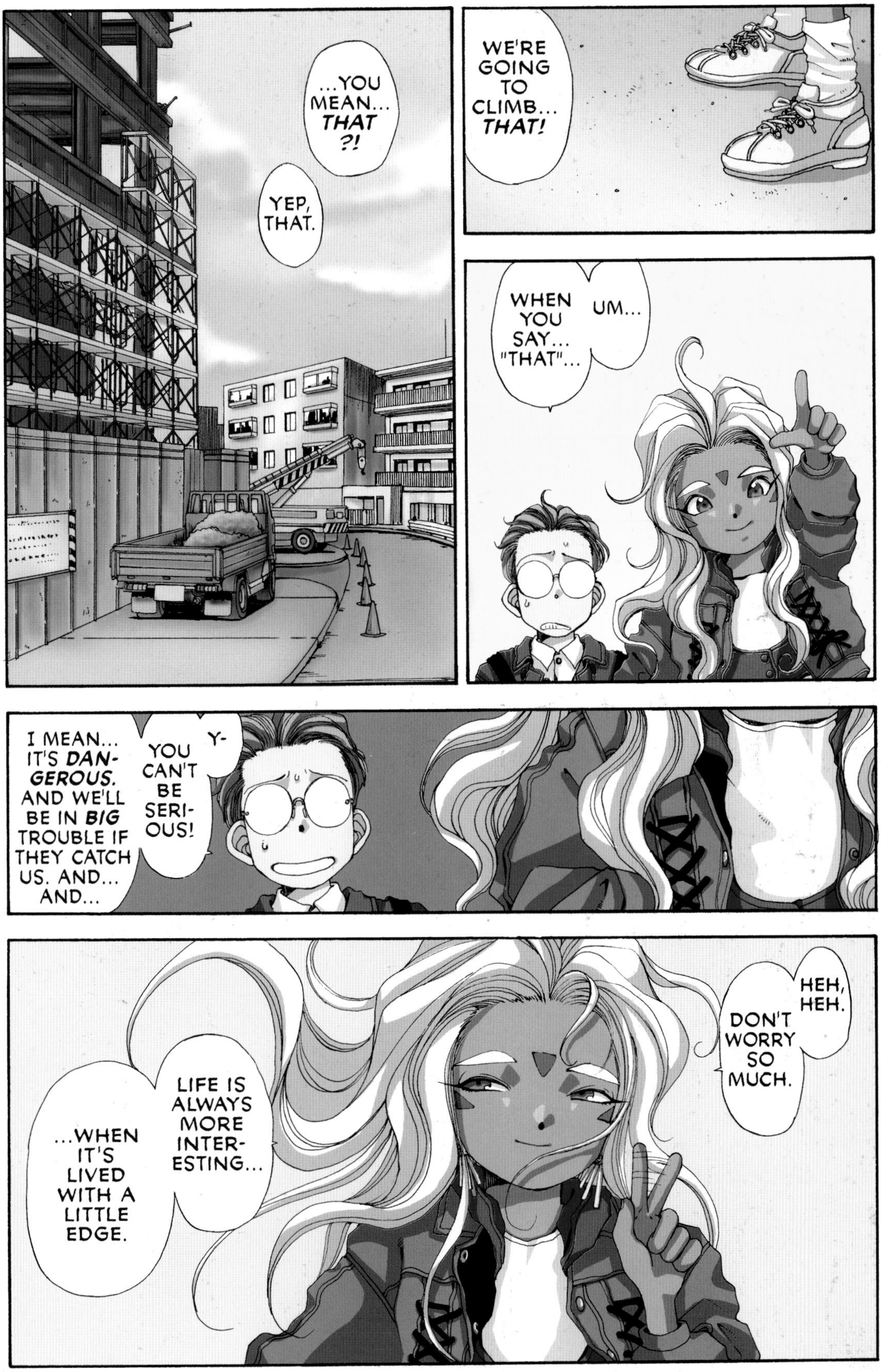
WE'RE GOING TO CLIMB... *THAT!*
UM...
WHEN YOU SAY... "THAT"...
...YOU MEAN... *THAT* ?!
YEP, THAT.
Y- YOU CAN'T BE SERI- OUS!
I MEAN... IT'S *DAN- GEROUS.* AND WE'LL BE IN *BIG* TROUBLE IF THEY CATCH US. AND... AND...
HEH, HEH. DON'T WORRY SO MUCH.
LIFE IS ALWAYS MORE INTER- ESTING...
...WHEN IT'S LIVED WITH A LITTLE EDGE.

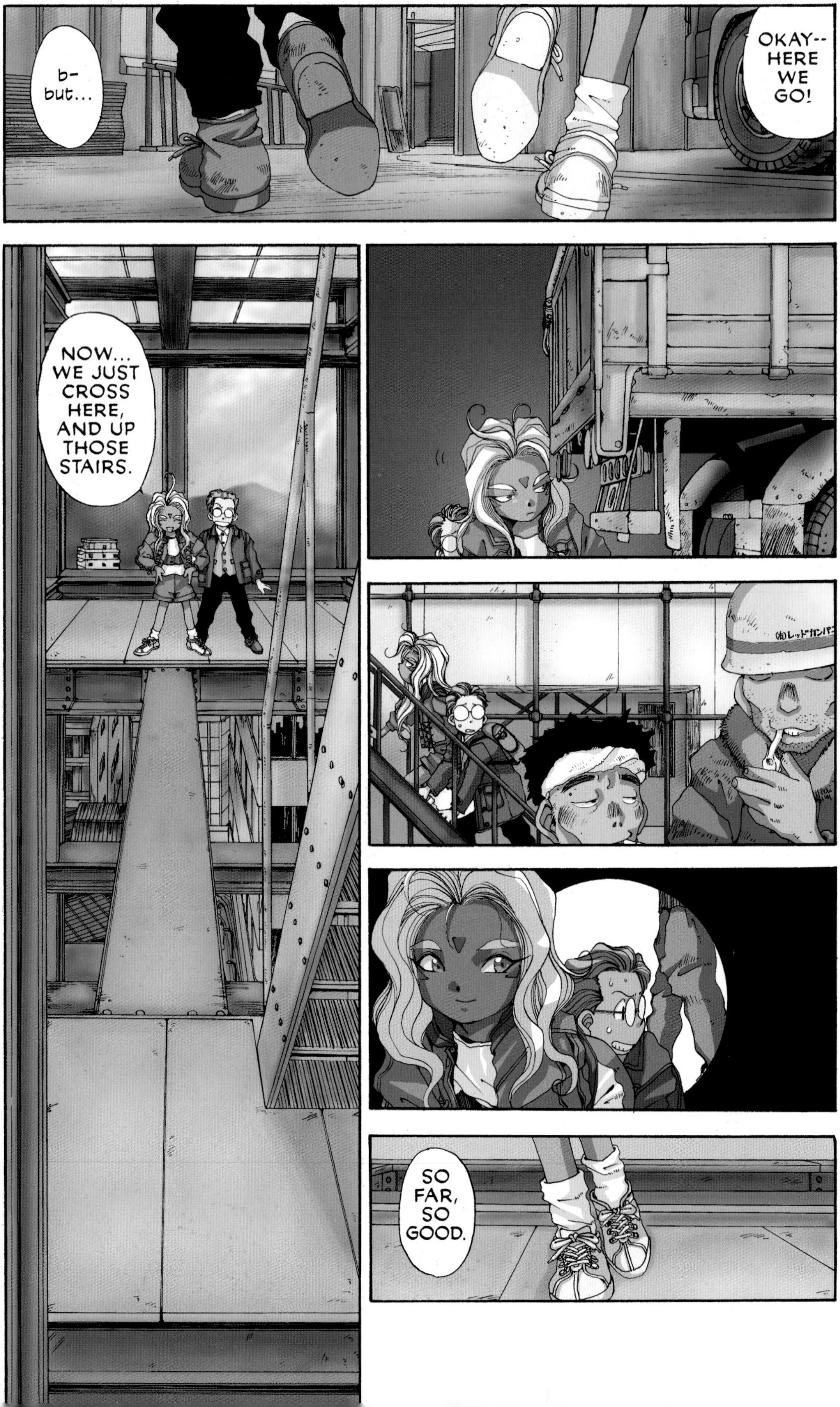
OKAY-- HERE WE GO!
b-but...
SO FAR, SO GOOD.
NOW... WE JUST CROSS HERE, AND UP THOSE STAIRS.

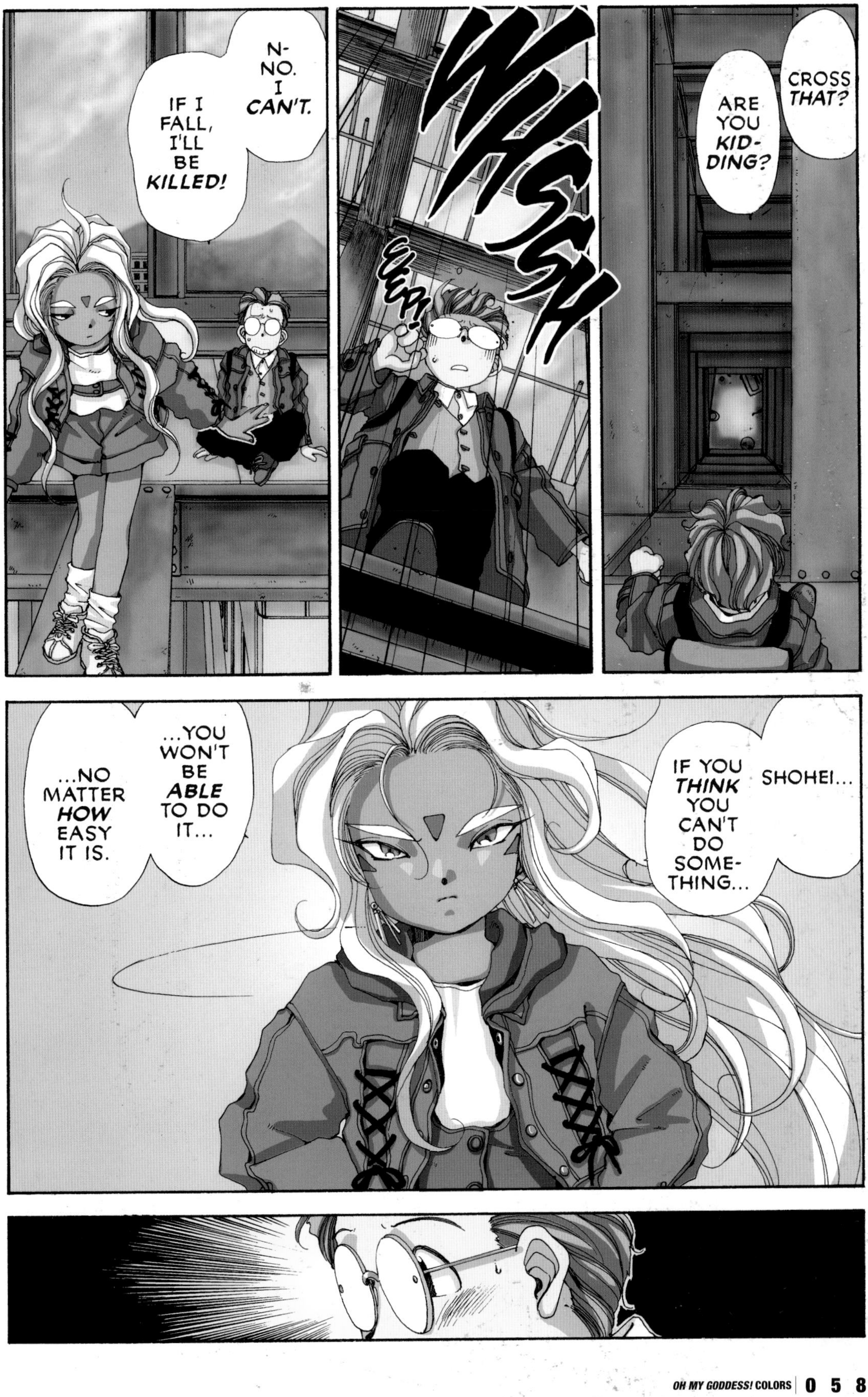
CROSS THAT?
ARE YOU KIDDING?
WHSSH
EEP!
N-NO. I CAN'T.
IF I FALL, I'LL BE KILLED!
SHOHEI...
IF YOU THINK YOU CAN'T DO SOMETHING...
...YOU WON'T BE ABLE TO DO IT...
...NO MATTER HOW EASY IT IS.

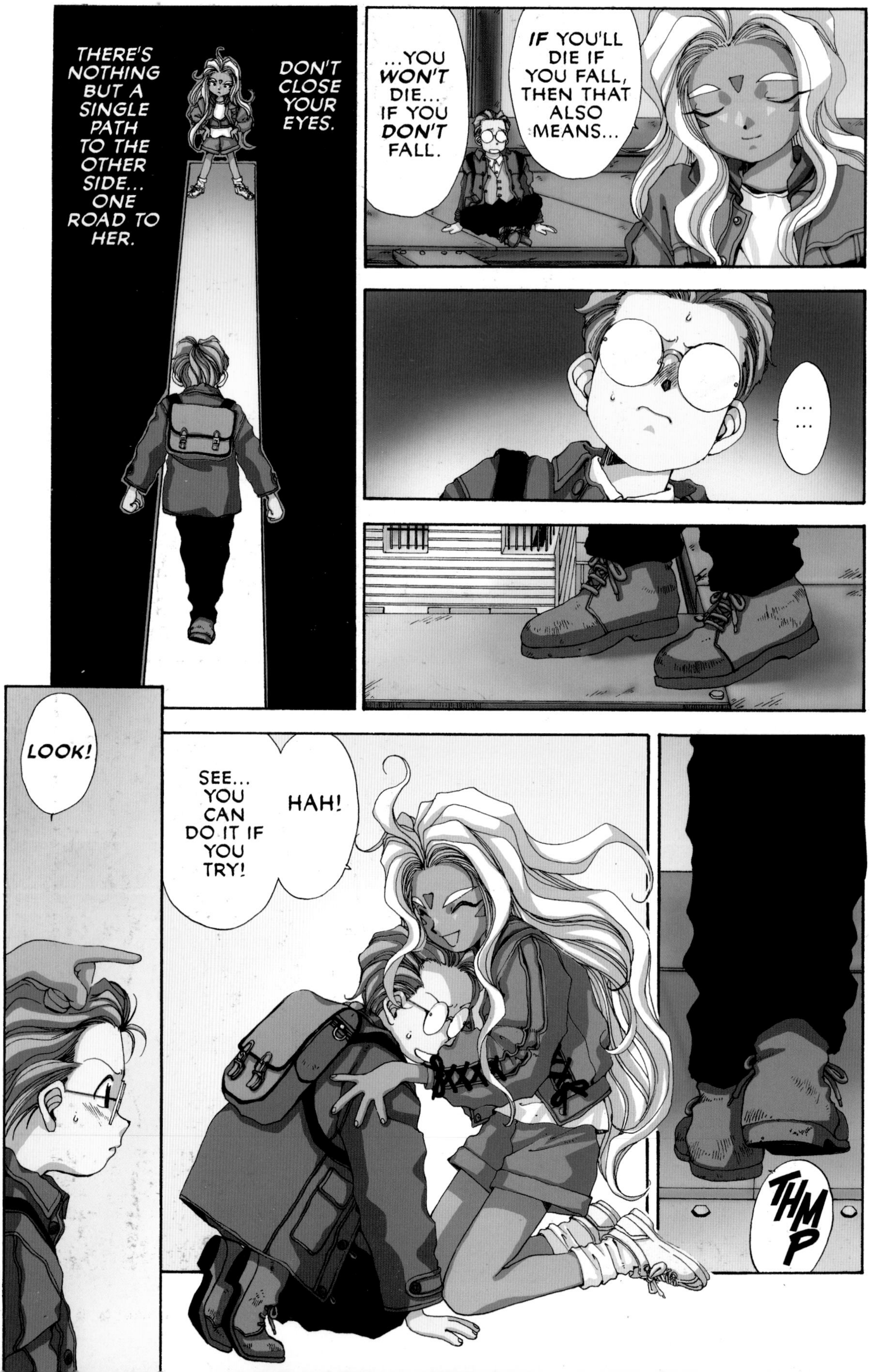
IF YOU'LL DIE IF YOU FALL, THEN THAT ALSO MEANS...
...YOU WON'T DIE... IF YOU DON'T FALL.
......
DON'T CLOSE YOUR EYES.
THERE'S NOTHING BUT A SINGLE PATH TO THE OTHER SIDE... ONE ROAD TO HER.
THMP
HAH!
SEE... YOU CAN DO IT IF YOU TRY!
LOOK!

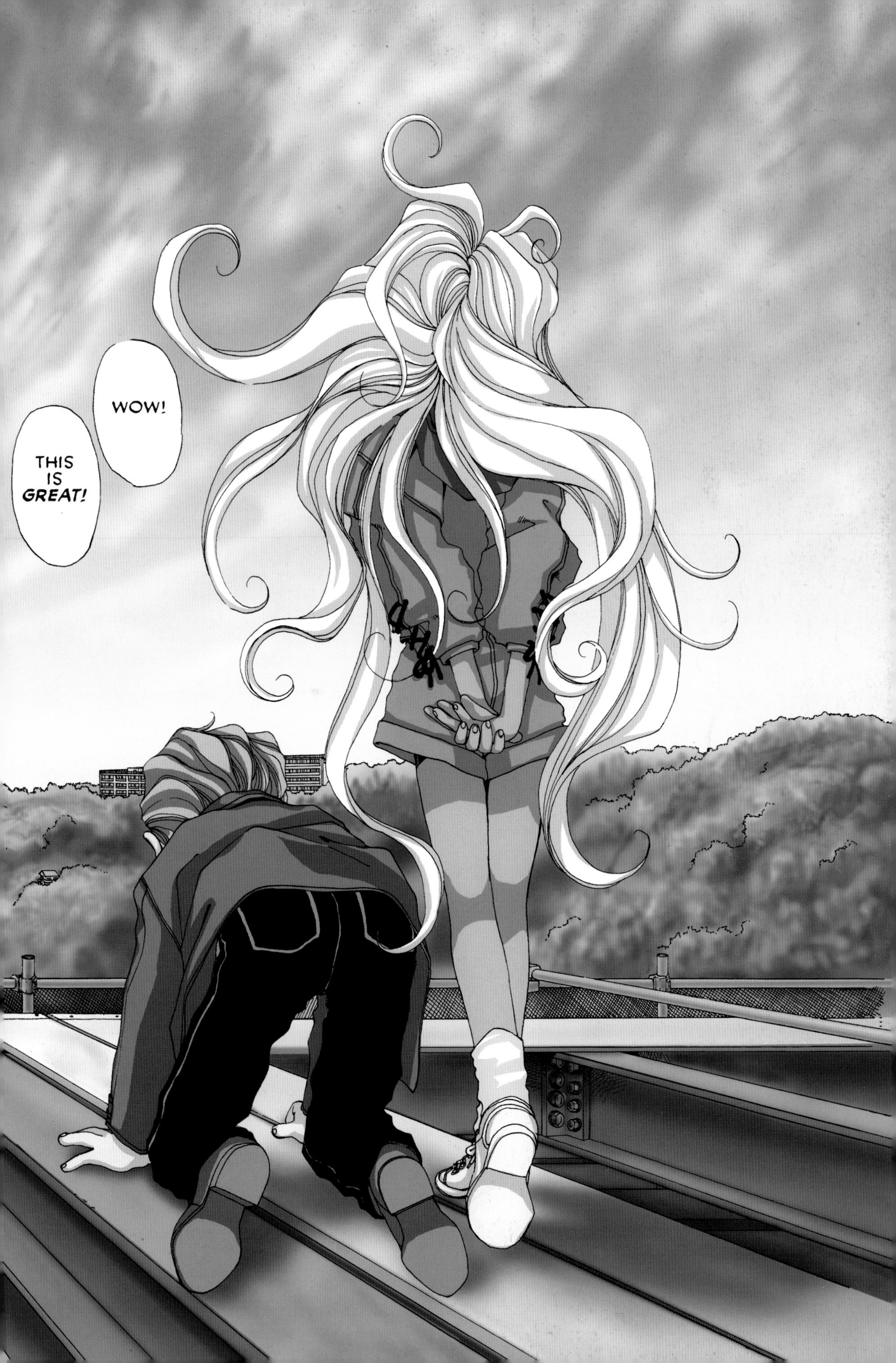
WOW!
THIS IS GREAT!

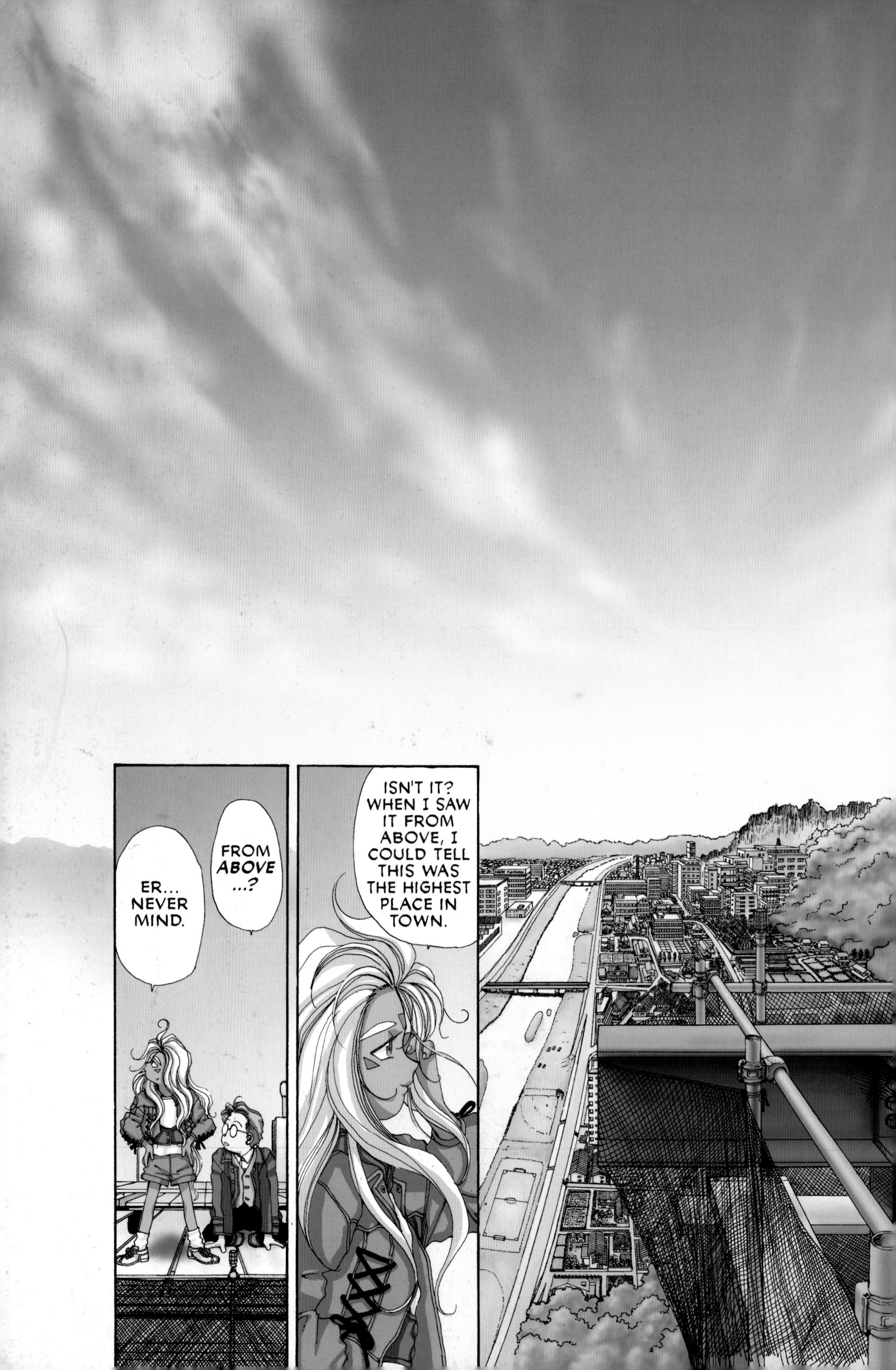

ISN'T IT? WHEN I SAW IT FROM ABOVE, I COULD TELL THIS WAS THE HIGHEST PLACE IN TOWN.
FROM *ABOVE* ...?
ER... NEVER MIND.

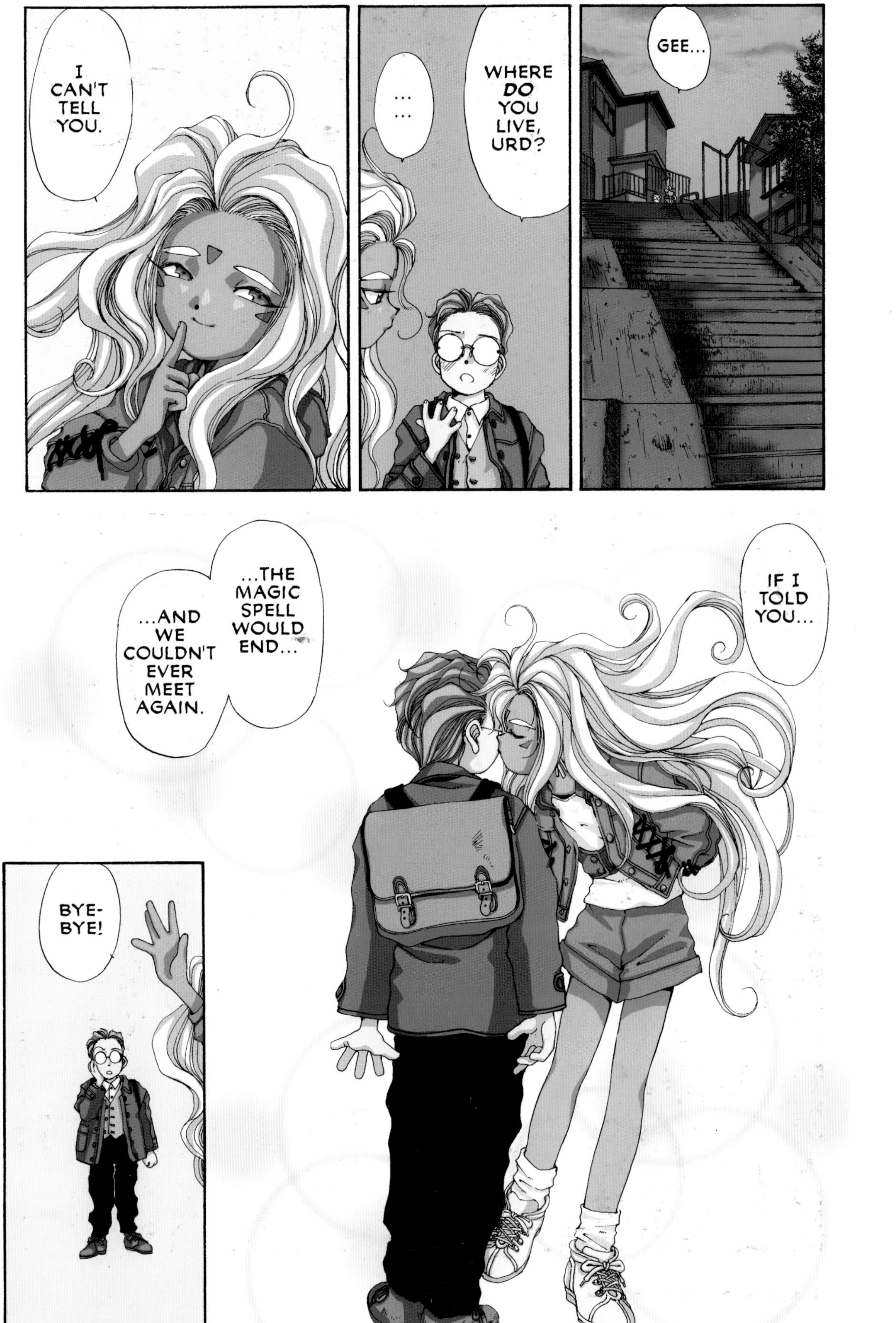
GEE...
WHERE *DO* YOU LIVE, URD?
... ...
I CAN'T TELL YOU.
IF I TOLD YOU...
...THE MAGIC SPELL WOULD END...
...AND WE COULDN'T EVER MEET AGAIN.
BYE-BYE!

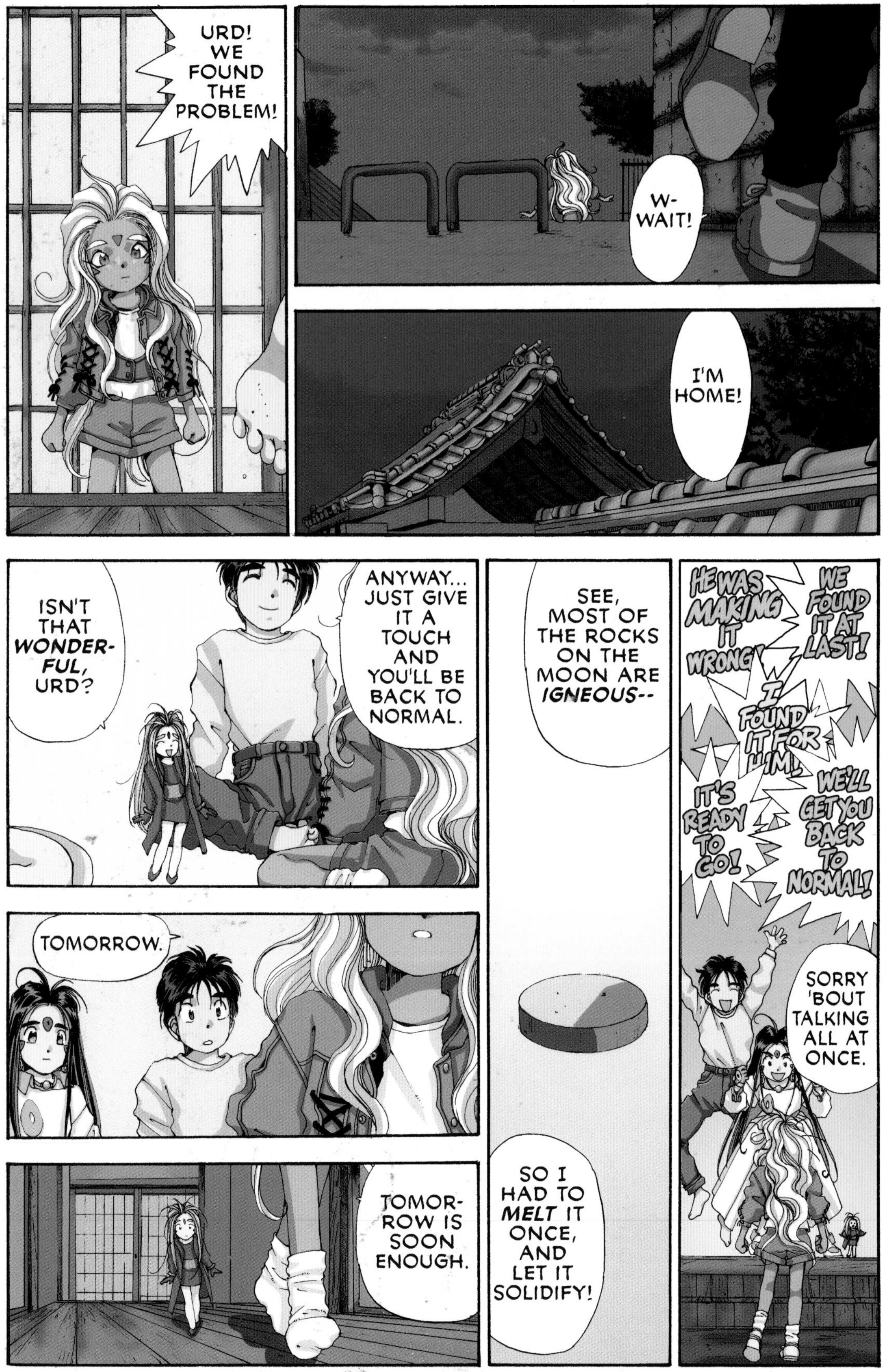

W-WAIT!
I'M HOME!
URD! WE FOUND THE PROBLEM!
WE FOUND IT AT LAST!
HE WAS MAKING IT WRONG!
I FOUND IT FOR HIM!
WE'LL GET YOU BACK TO NORMAL!
IT'S READY TO GO!
SORRY 'BOUT TALKING ALL AT ONCE.
SEE, MOST OF THE ROCKS ON THE MOON ARE *IGNEOUS*--
SO I HAD TO *MELT* IT ONCE, AND LET IT SOLIDIFY!
ANYWAY... JUST GIVE IT A TOUCH AND YOU'LL BE BACK TO NORMAL.
ISN'T THAT *WONDERFUL*, URD?
TOMORROW.
TOMORROW IS SOON ENOUGH.

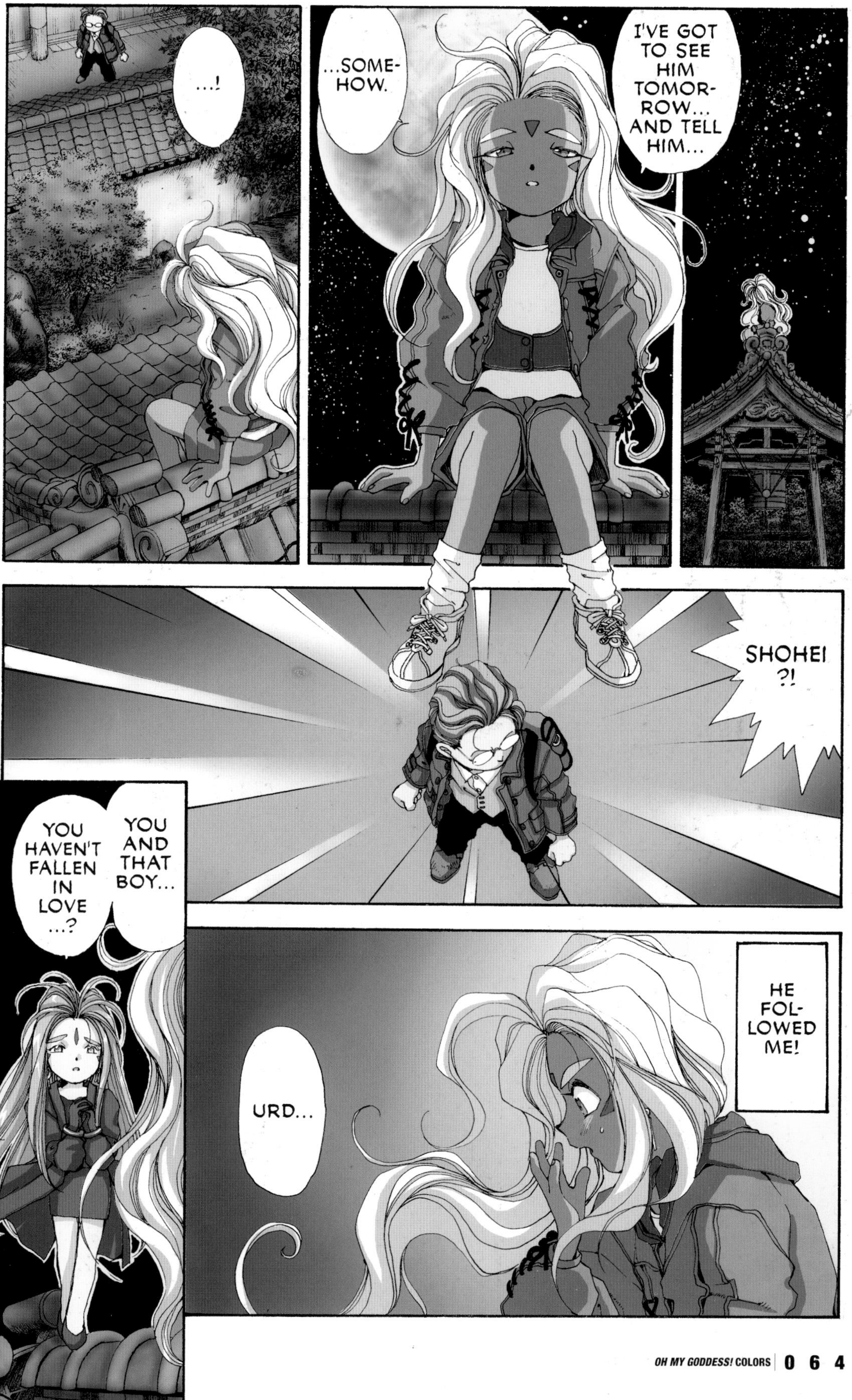
I'VE GOT TO SEE HIM TOMOR-ROW... AND TELL HIM...
...SOME-HOW.
...!
SHOHEI ?!
HE FOL-LOWED ME!
URD...
YOU AND THAT BOY...
YOU HAVEN'T FALLEN IN LOVE ...?

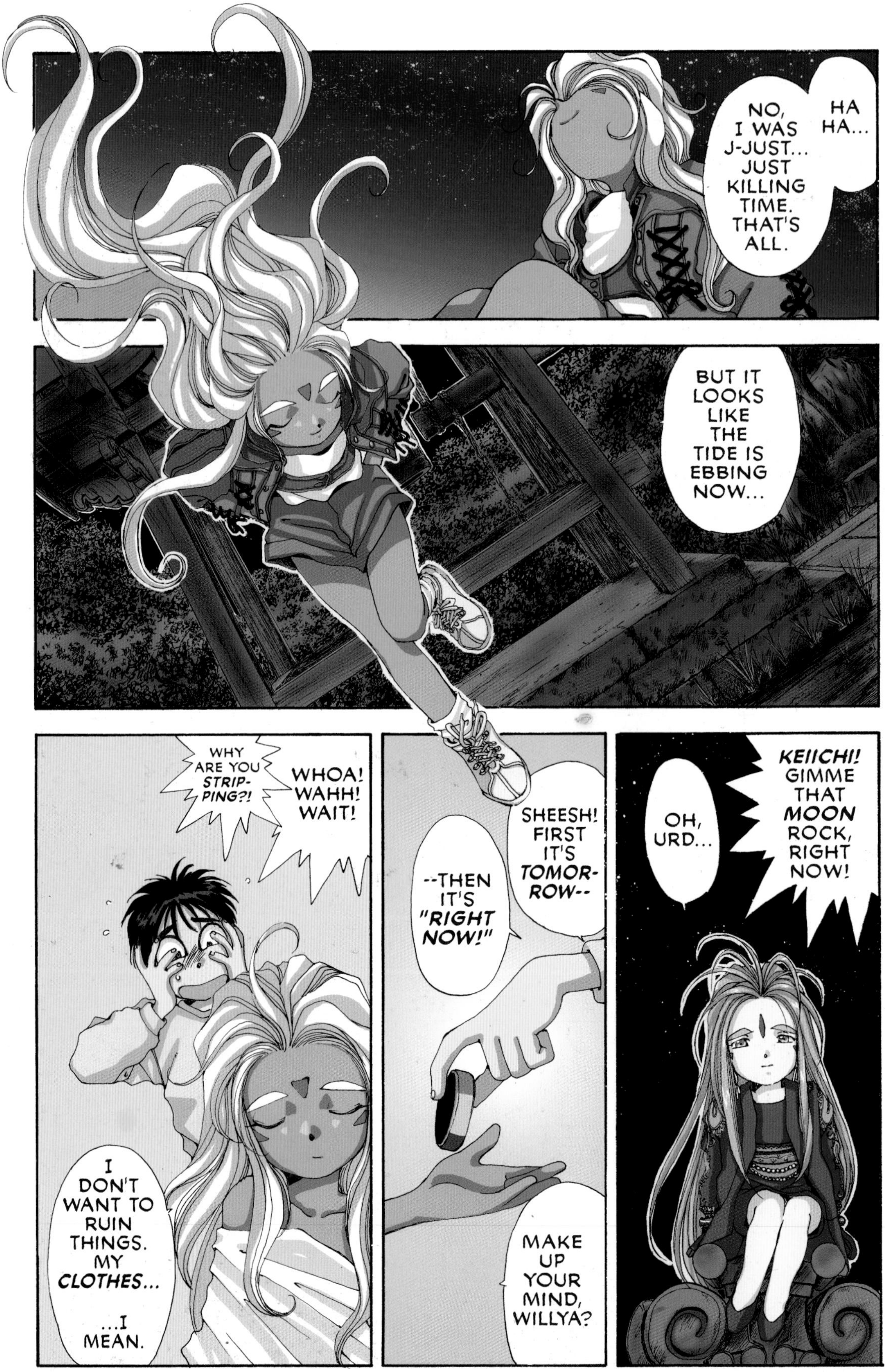
HA HA...
NO, I WAS J-JUST... JUST KILLING TIME. THAT'S ALL.
BUT IT LOOKS LIKE THE TIDE IS EBBING NOW...
KEIICHI! GIMME THAT MOON ROCK, RIGHT NOW!
OH, URD...
SHEESH! FIRST IT'S TOMORROW--
--THEN IT'S "RIGHT NOW!"
MAKE UP YOUR MIND, WILLYA?
WHOA! WAHH! WAIT!
WHY ARE YOU STRIPPING?!
I DON'T WANT TO RUIN THINGS. MY CLOTHES...
...I MEAN.

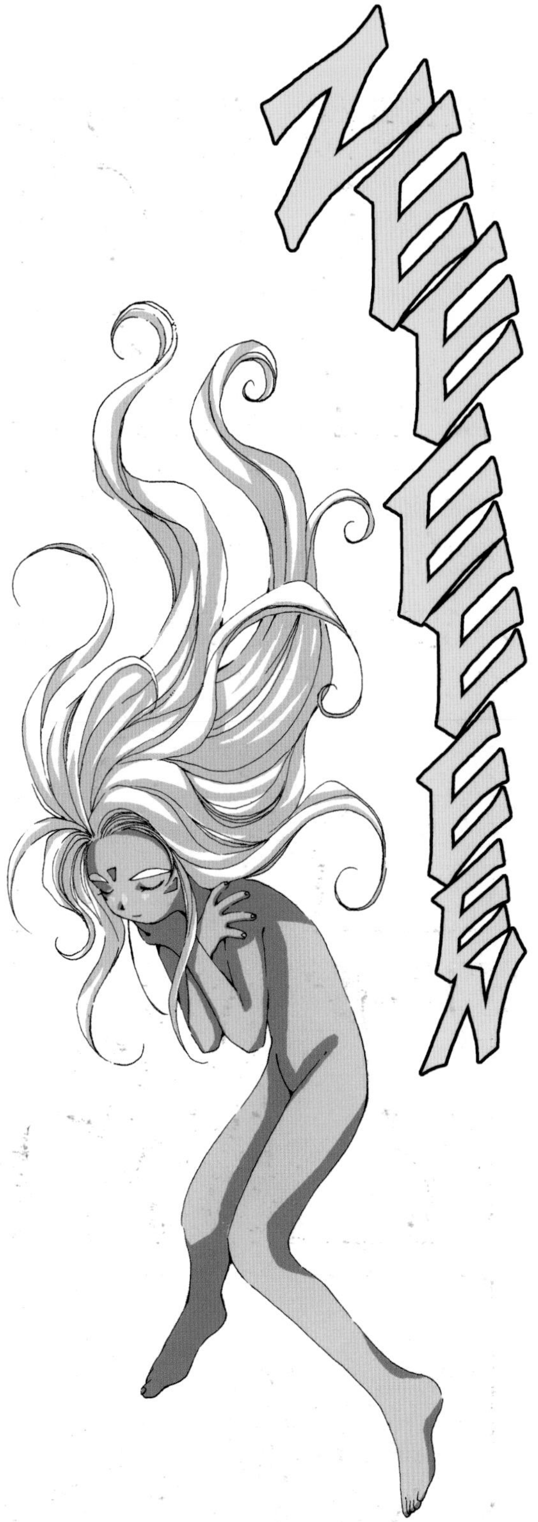
NEEEEEEEN

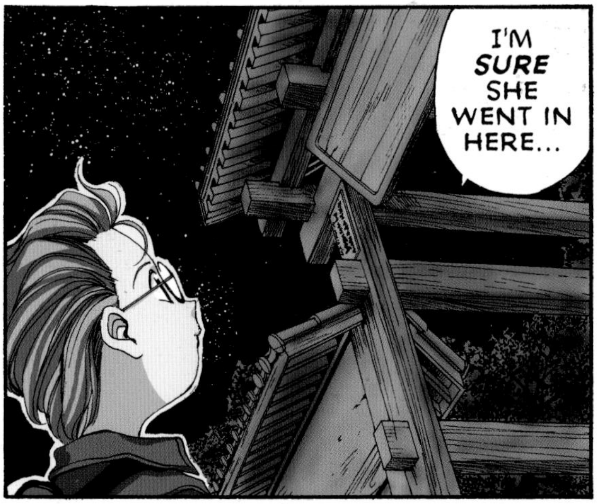
I'M *SURE* SHE WENT IN HERE...

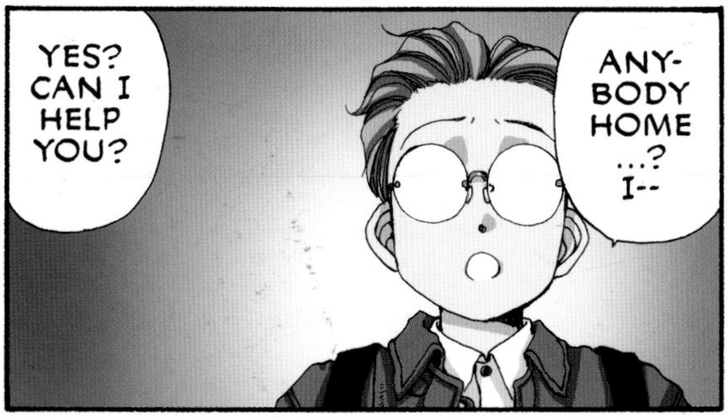
ANY-BODY HOME ...? I--
YES? CAN I HELP YOU?

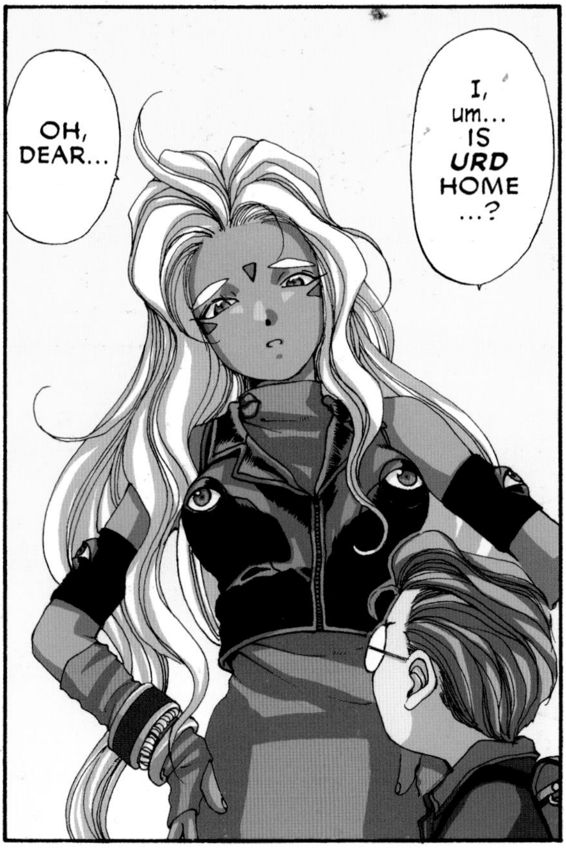
I, um... IS *URD* HOME ...?
OH, DEAR...

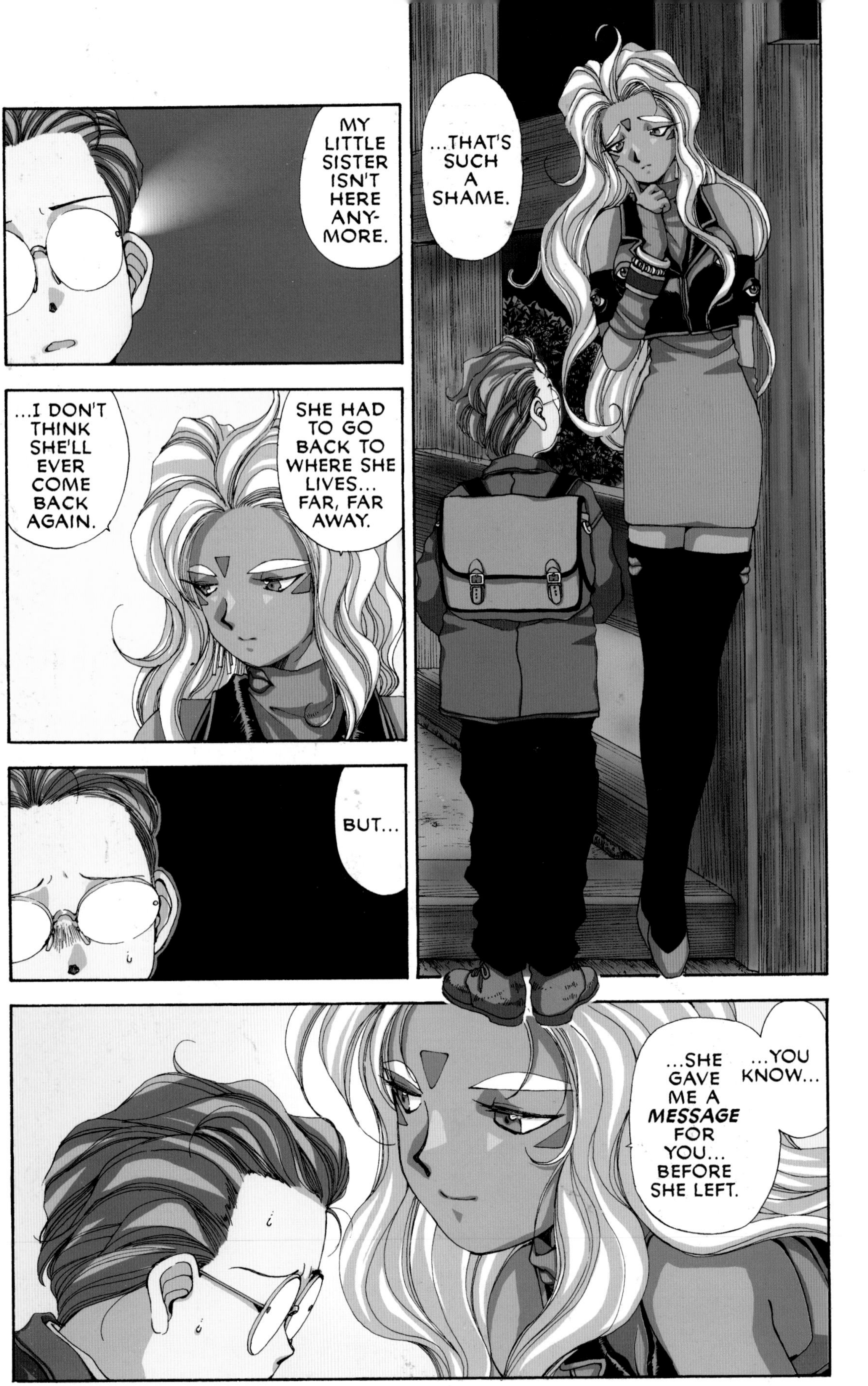
...THAT'S SUCH A SHAME.
MY LITTLE SISTER ISN'T HERE ANYMORE.
SHE HAD TO GO BACK TO WHERE SHE LIVES... FAR, FAR AWAY.
...I DON'T THINK SHE'LL EVER COME BACK AGAIN.
BUT...
...YOU KNOW...
...SHE GAVE ME A *MESSAGE* FOR YOU... BEFORE SHE LEFT.

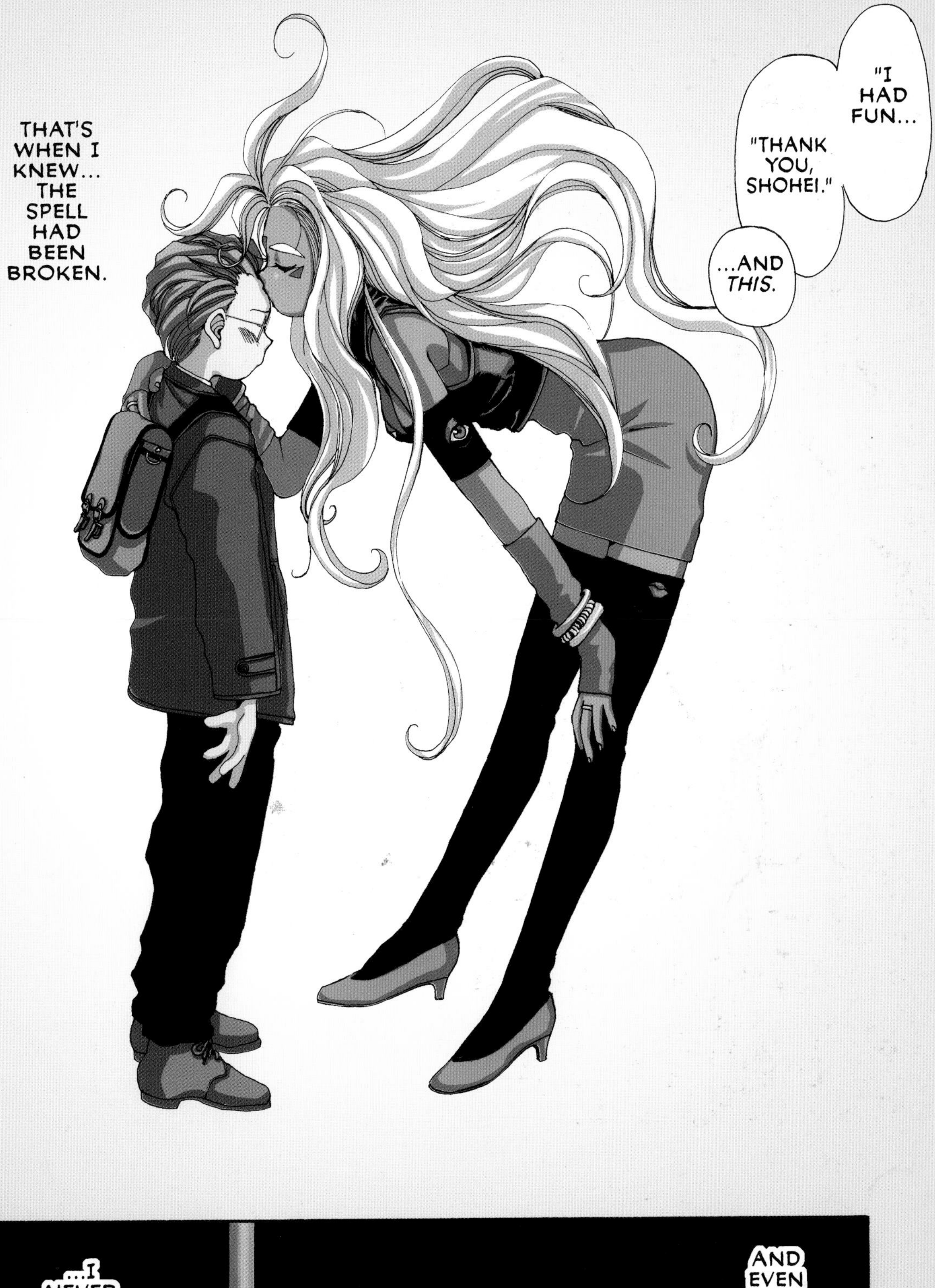
"I HAD FUN...
"THANK YOU, SHOHEI."
...AND *THIS.*
THAT'S WHEN I KNEW... THE SPELL HAD BEEN BROKEN.

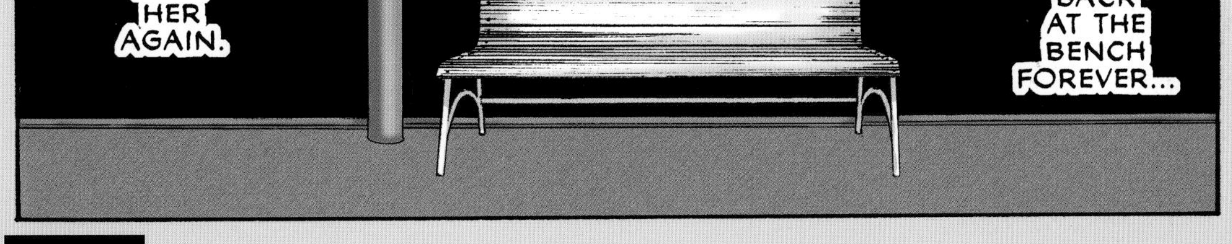
AND EVEN IF I WAITED BACK AT THE BENCH FOREVER...
...I NEVER WOULD MEET HER AGAIN.

END

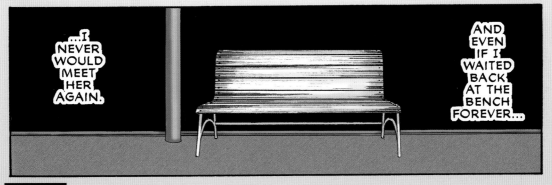

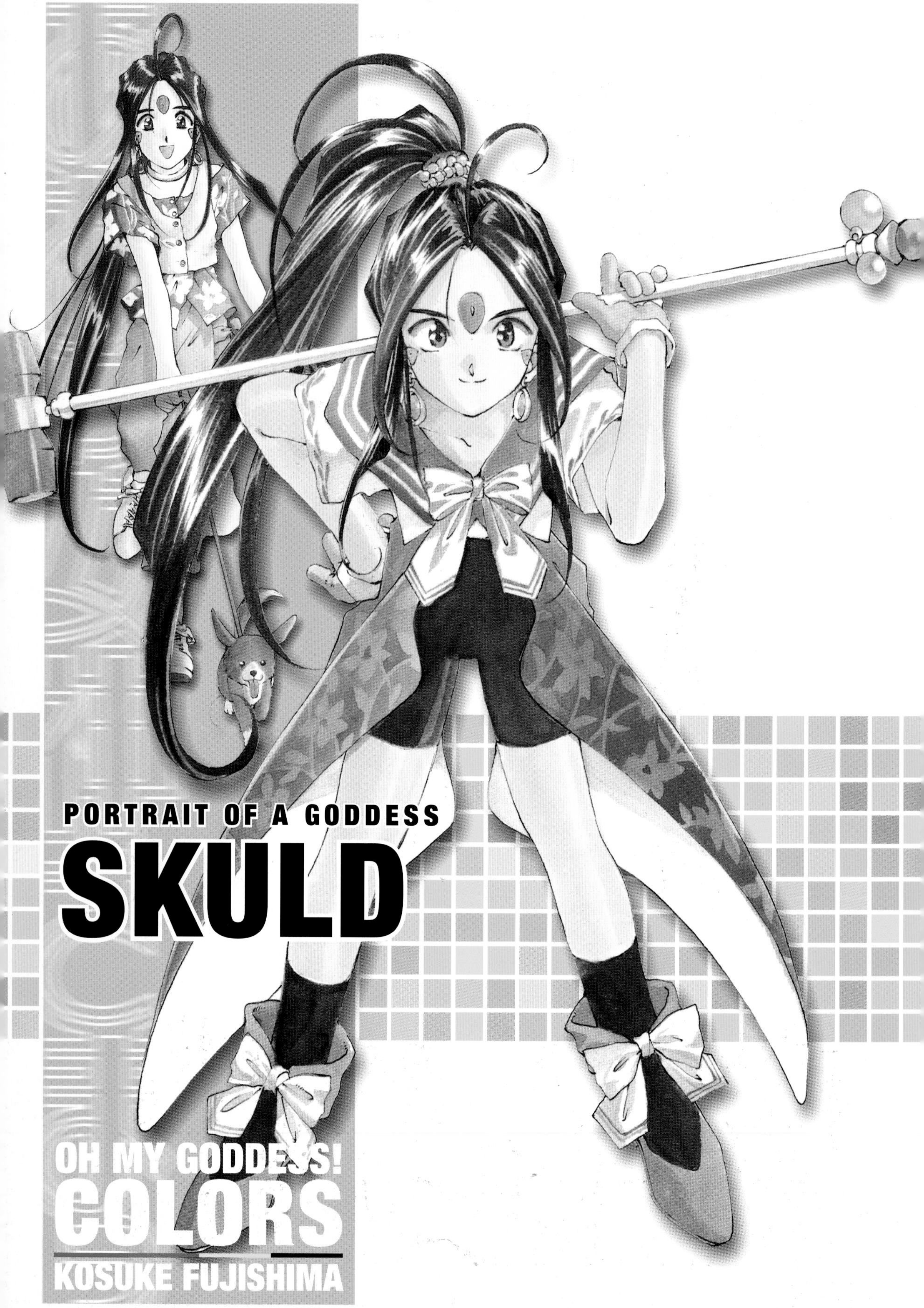

PORTRAIT OF A GODDESS

SKULD

OH MY GODDESS!
COLORS

KOSUKE FUJISHIMA

PORTRAIT OF A GODDESS
SKULD

PROFILE

Height:	**150 cm (4'11")**
Bust:	**None of your business**
Waist:	**A secret**
Hips:	**I'm not telling**
Place of birth:	**Unclear**
Age:	**Unknown**
Blood type:	**Does she have one?**
Favorite food:	**Ice cream**
Favorite phrases:	**"Perfect,"**
	"Functional beauty"
Hobbies:	**Assembling machines,**
	disassembling machines

Goddess Second-Class, Type 1, Limited—although she has so little power at her age that she hardly merits restrictions. She was eventually able to conjure just one trick: the ability to physically stamp on faces and objects the words which people say—what use is that? As befits the youngest sister of the trio (she and Bell both had the same mother), she is the Goddess of the Future. Incidentally, when she overuses her powers, she eats ice cream to replenish her vital goddess nutrients.

After Urd left her in charge of the Yggdrasil System, Skuld found that bugs were multiplying out of control inside it. Chasing them all the way to Earth, she emerged here first into Urd's bath, and then into Keiichi's teacup (as Bell moves through mirrors and Urd through the TV, Skuld gates through the dimensions via hot water—preferably not too hot; she found the tea uncomfort-able, as did, suddenly, Keiichi).

Skuld's still at the age where you want to dote on her, but she's adoring, jealous, and protective of Belldandy all at once, which occasionally manifests itself in hostility for the person now most close to Bell: Keiichi. Skuld's also always fighting with Urd, who treats her (appropriately) like a child—although Urd's own maturity level is somewhat open to debate.

If Belldandy is the textbook goddess and Urd chucked hers out, then maybe Skuld is the one who hasn't finished reading it yet. Yet living with her sisters and Keiichi on Earth is definitely help-ing her to grow up as well. After a brief sort-of crush on Keiichi, she met a boy of her own (also briefly, but who knows?).

Skuld was accompanied by the transcendently adorable angel, Noble Scarlet—yet unfortunately it was still too immature to emerge again from its egg. Yet its time came around, too.

Skuld's hobbies revolve entirely around engineering and me-chanics; her ideal in design is a device that proves both func-tional and beautiful (note: not "useful" or "sensible"). She's very proud of Banpei, the robot she built to guard the goddesses' household.

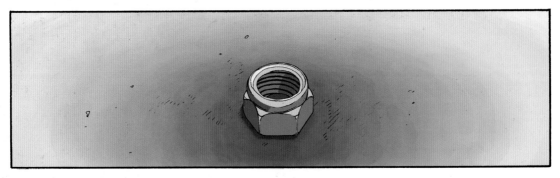

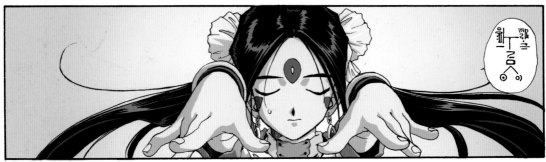

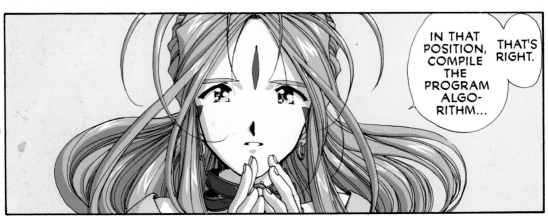

THAT'S RIGHT.
IN THAT POSITION, COMPILE THE PROGRAM ALGORITHM...
FOCUS NOT ON THE OBJECT, BUT *INSIDE.*
CONCENTRATE YOUR CONSCIOUSNESS.
THE ALGORITHM IS JUST A GUIDE.
WHAT SPRINGS UP FROM *WITHIN...*

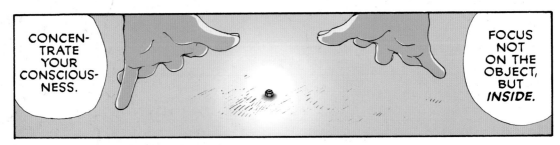

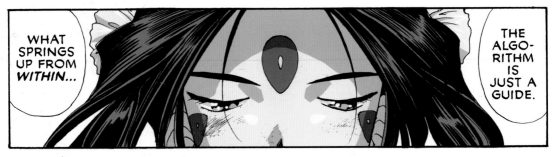

TALE OF SKULD:
Crazy Little Thing Called Love

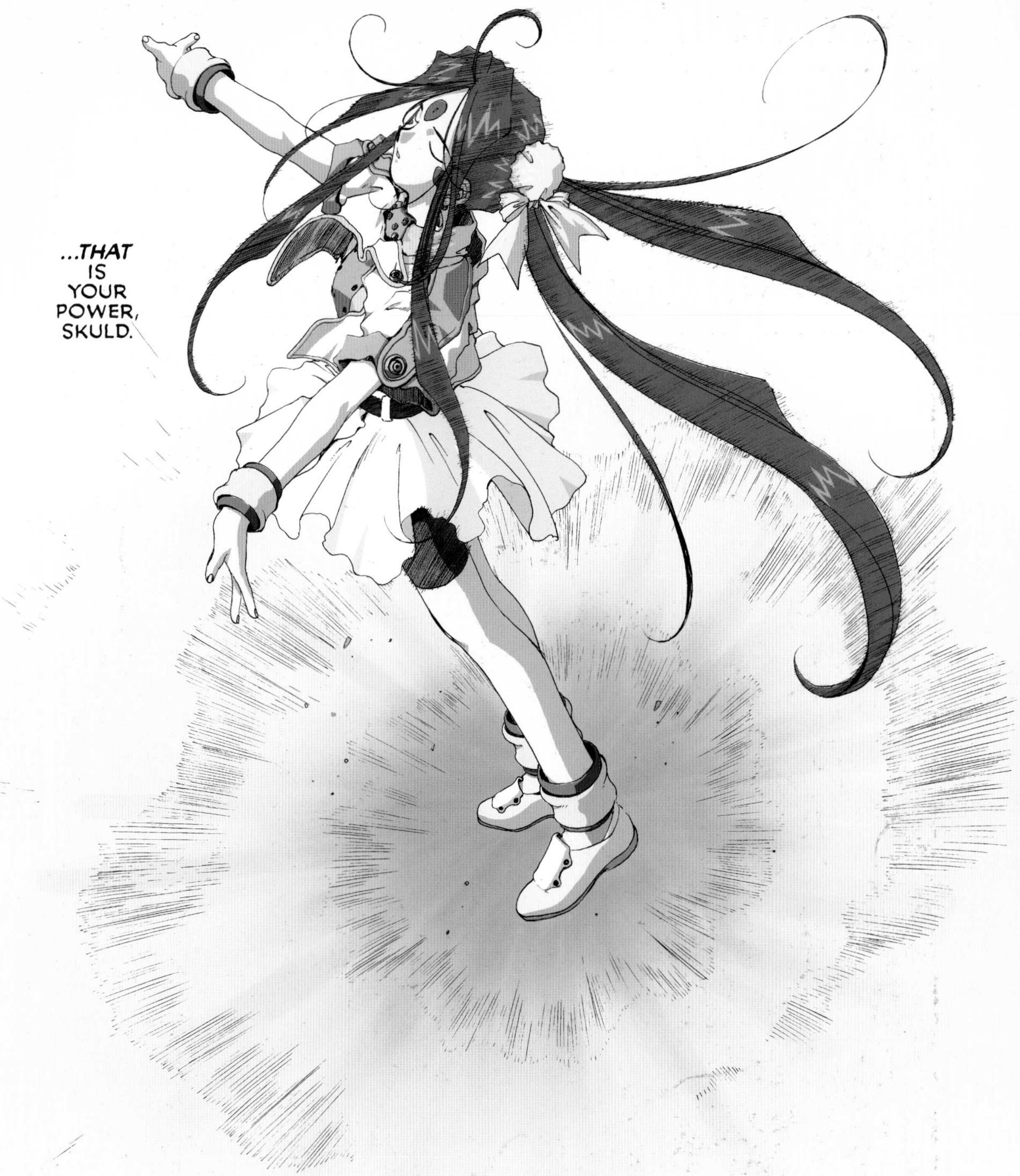
...THAT IS YOUR POWER, SKULD.

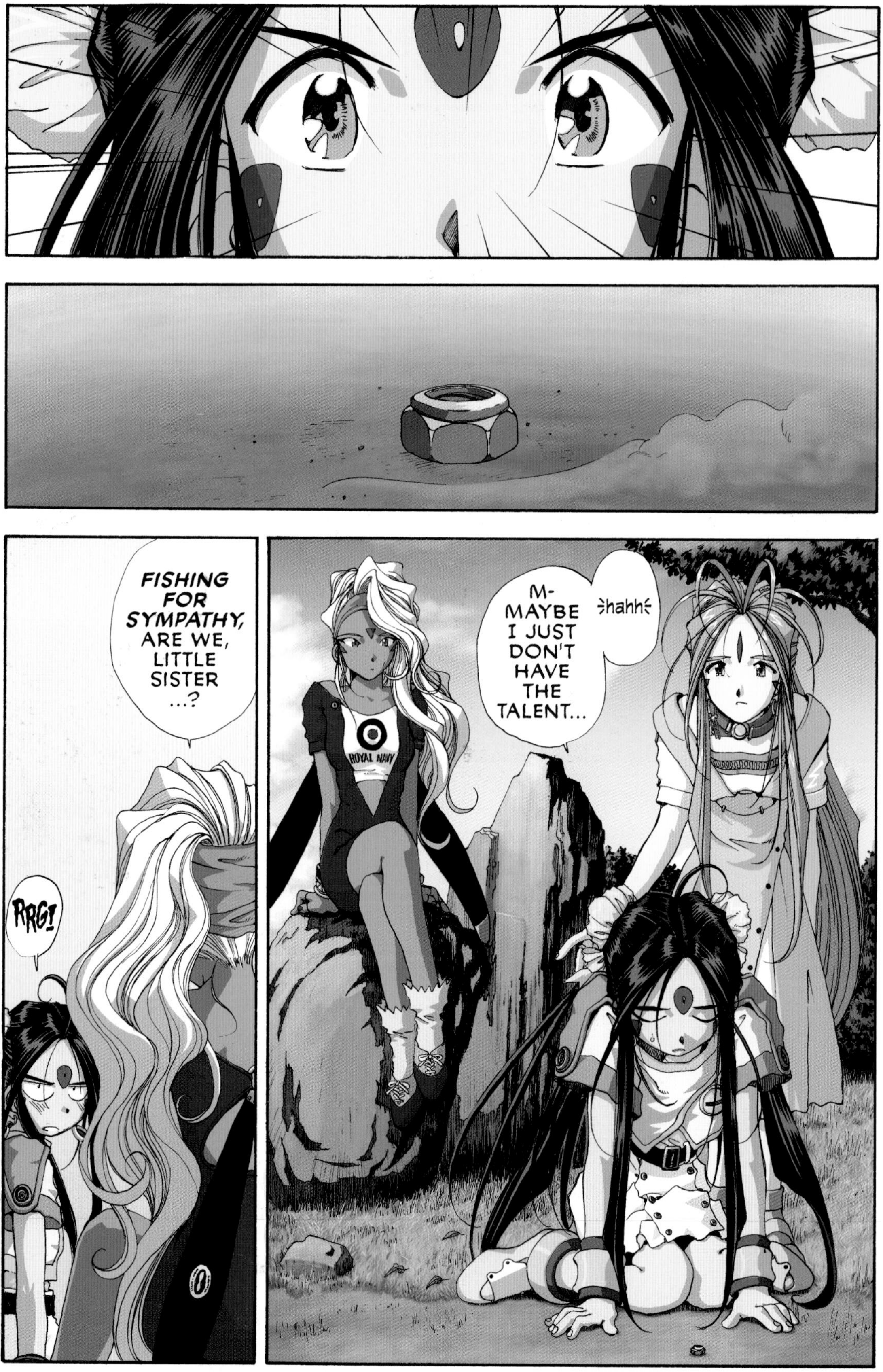

ꟷhahhꟷ
M-MAYBE I JUST DON'T HAVE THE TALENT...
ROYAL NAVY
FISHING FOR SYMPATHY, ARE WE, LITTLE SISTER ...?
RRG!

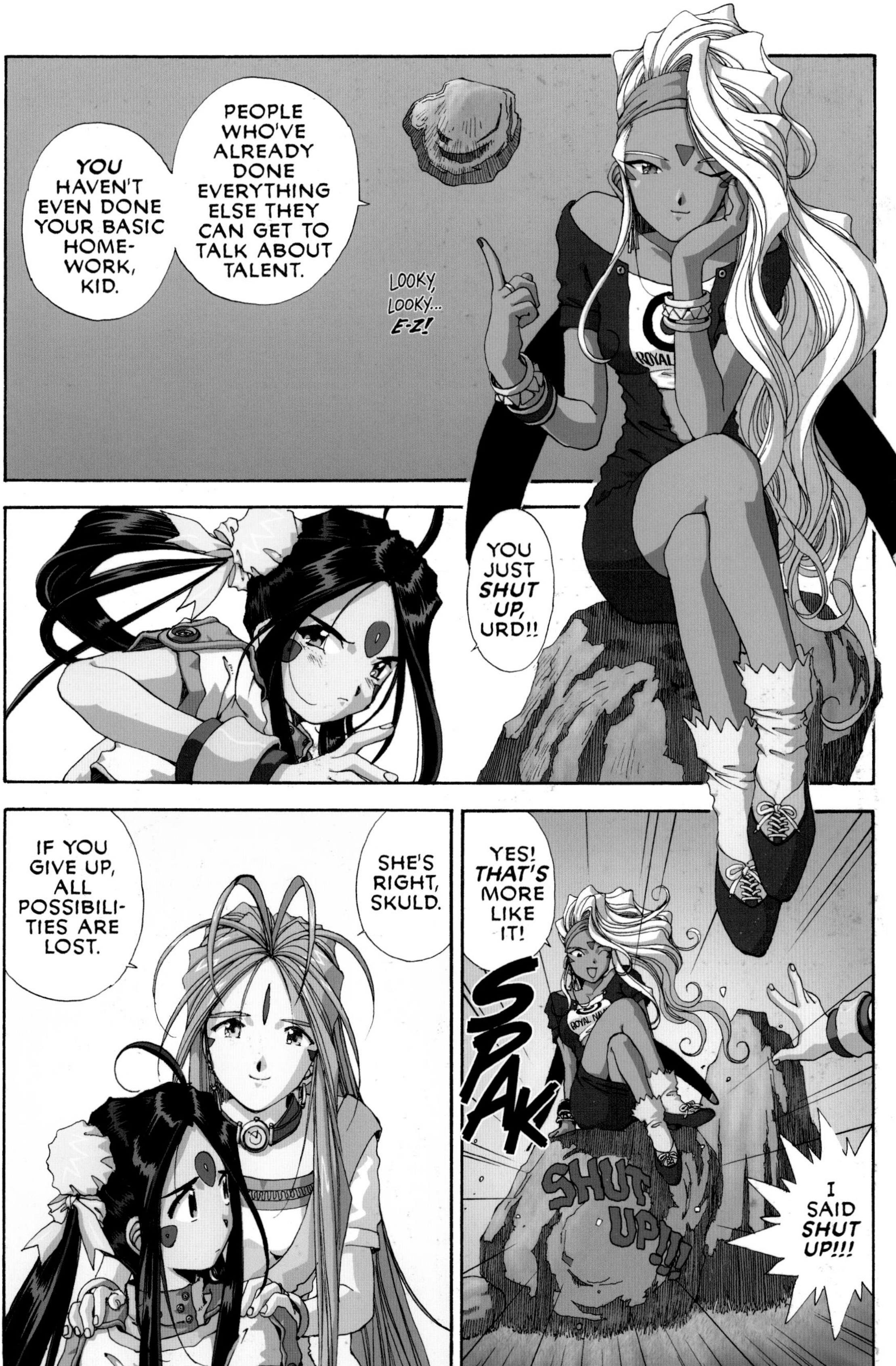
PEOPLE WHO'VE ALREADY DONE EVERYTHING ELSE THEY CAN GET TO TALK ABOUT TALENT.
YOU HAVEN'T EVEN DONE YOUR BASIC HOME-WORK, KID.
LOOKY, LOOKY... E-Z!
YOU JUST SHUT UP, URD!!
YES! THAT'S MORE LIKE IT!
SPAK
SHUT UP!!!
I SAID SHUT UP!!!
SHE'S RIGHT, SKULD.
IF YOU GIVE UP, ALL POSSIBILI-TIES ARE LOST.

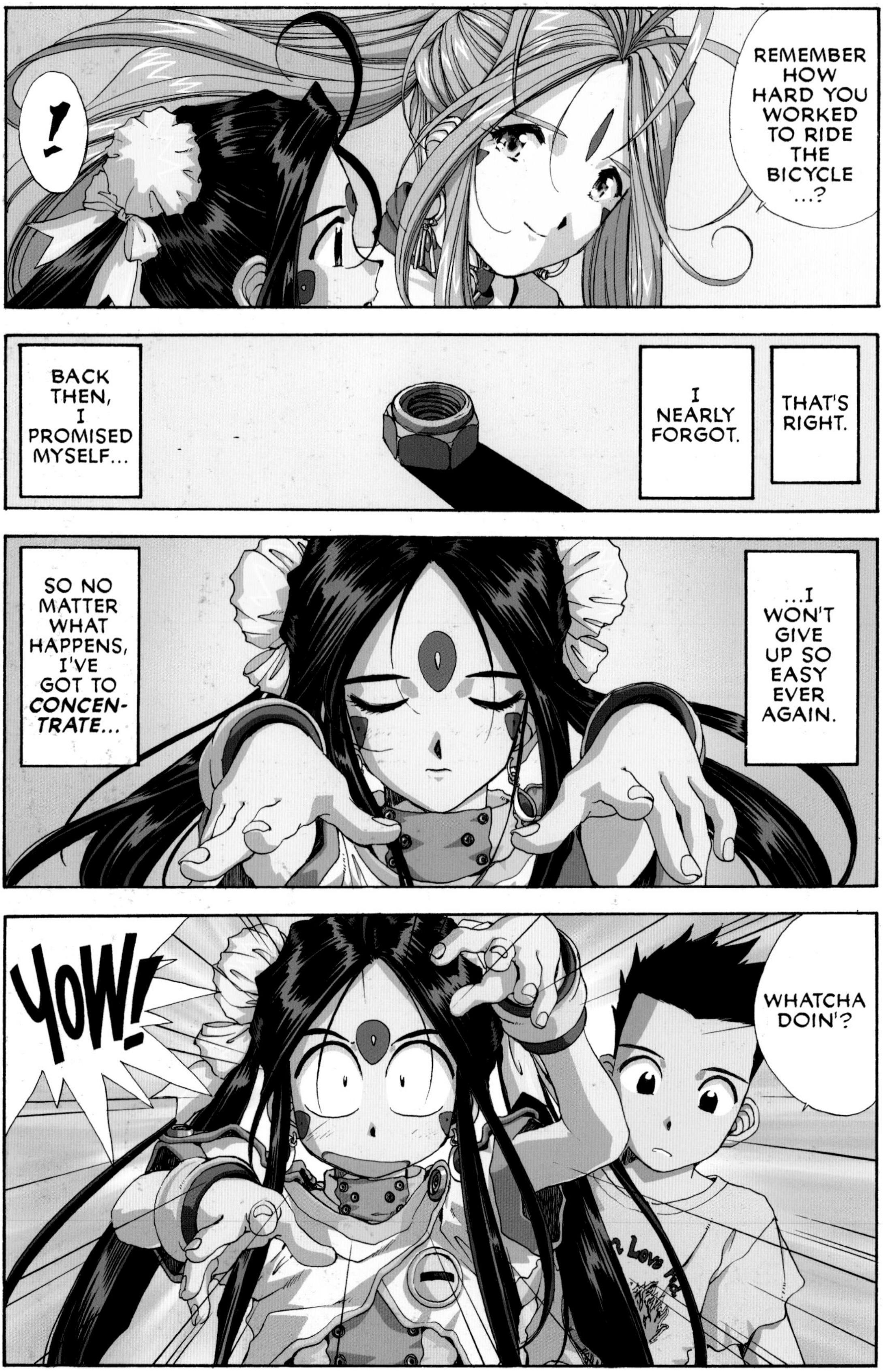
REMEMBER HOW HARD YOU WORKED TO RIDE THE BICYCLE ...?
!
THAT'S RIGHT.
I NEARLY FORGOT.
BACK THEN, I PROMISED MYSELF...
...I WON'T GIVE UP SO EASY EVER AGAIN.
SO NO MATTER WHAT HAPPENS, I'VE GOT TO *CONCEN-TRATE...*
WHATCHA DOIN'?
YOW!!

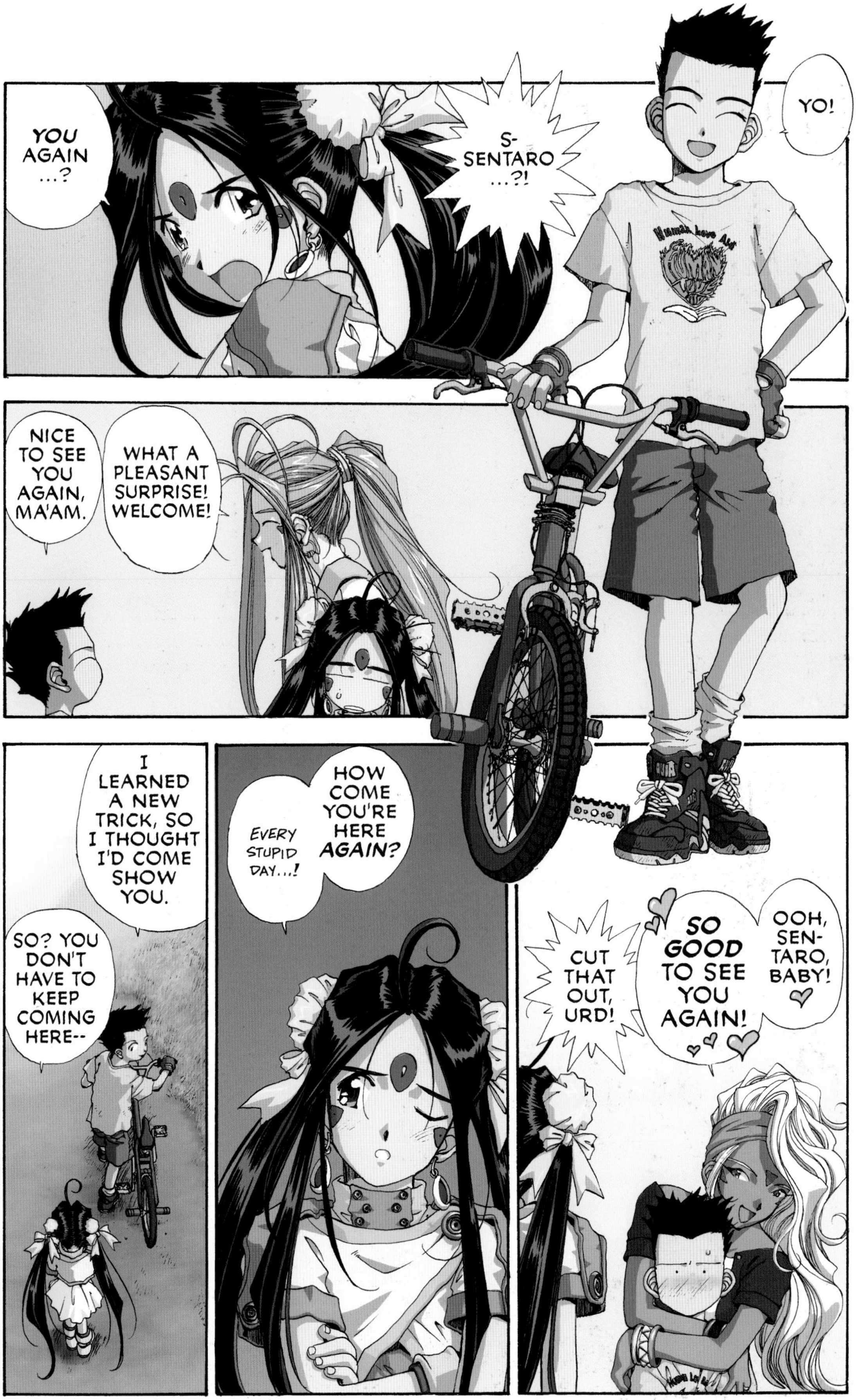
YO!
S-SENTARO...?!
YOU AGAIN...?
WHAT A PLEASANT SURPRISE! WELCOME!
NICE TO SEE YOU AGAIN, MA'AM.
OOH, SEN-TARO, BABY!
SO GOOD TO SEE YOU AGAIN!
CUT THAT OUT, URD!
HOW COME YOU'RE HERE AGAIN?
EVERY STUPID DAY...!
I LEARNED A NEW TRICK, SO I THOUGHT I'D COME SHOW YOU.
SO? YOU DON'T HAVE TO KEEP COMING HERE--

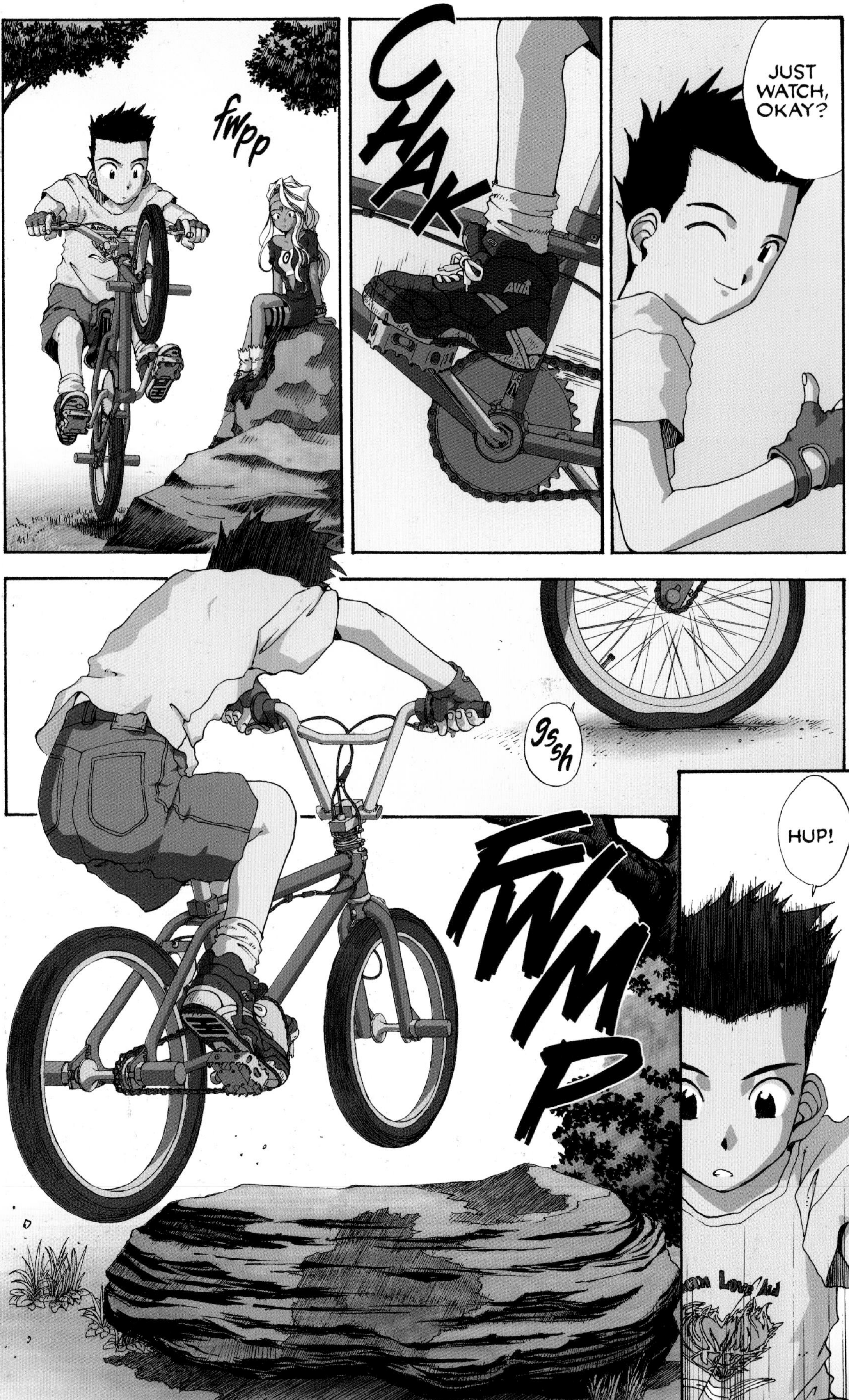
JUST WATCH, OKAY?
CHAK
fwpp
gssh
HUP!
FWMP

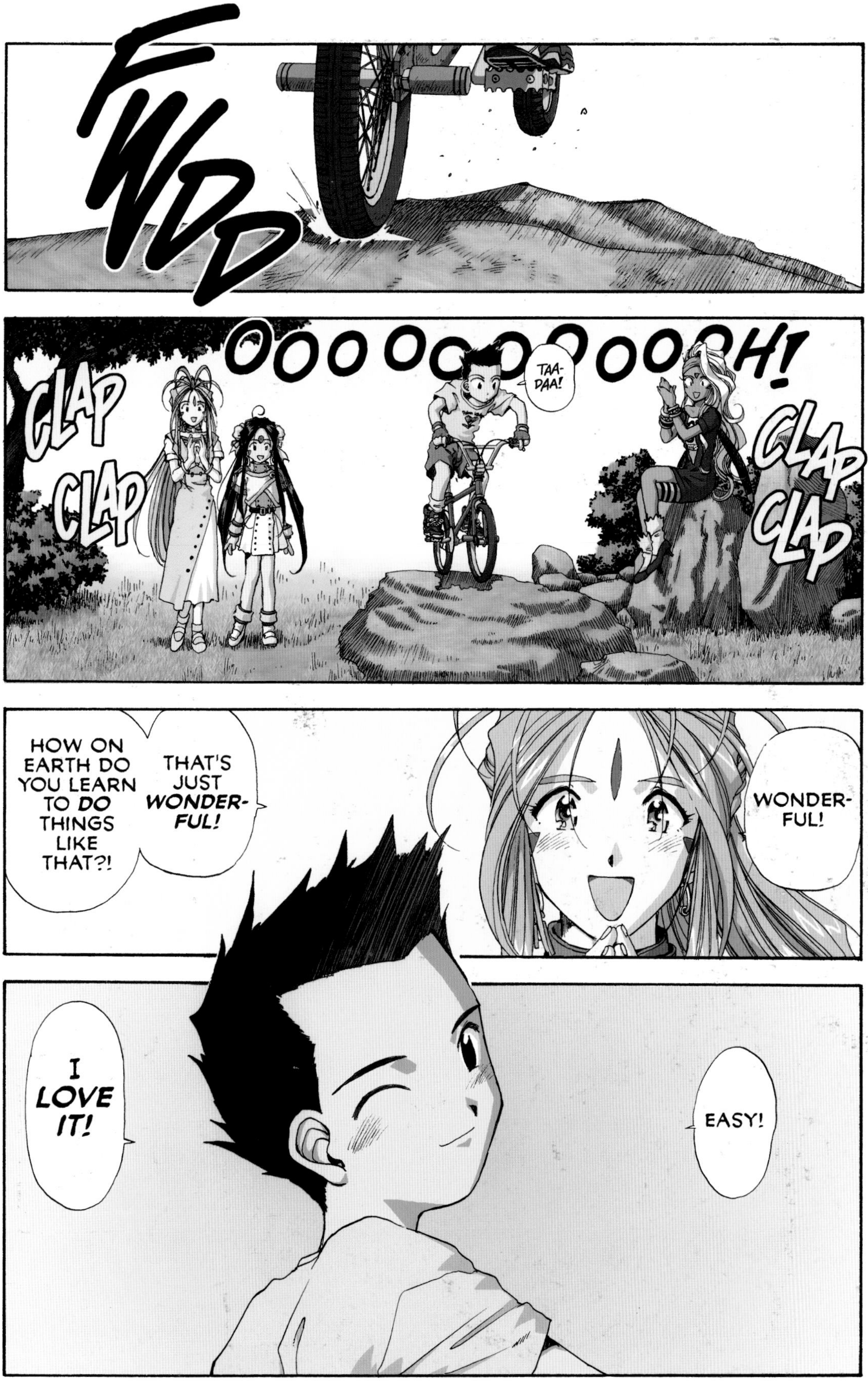

FWDD
CLAP CLAP
OOOOOOOOOOH!
TAA-DAA!
CLAP CLAP
WONDER-FUL!
THAT'S JUST WONDERFUL!
HOW ON EARTH DO YOU LEARN TO DO THINGS LIKE THAT?!
EASY!
I LOVE IT!

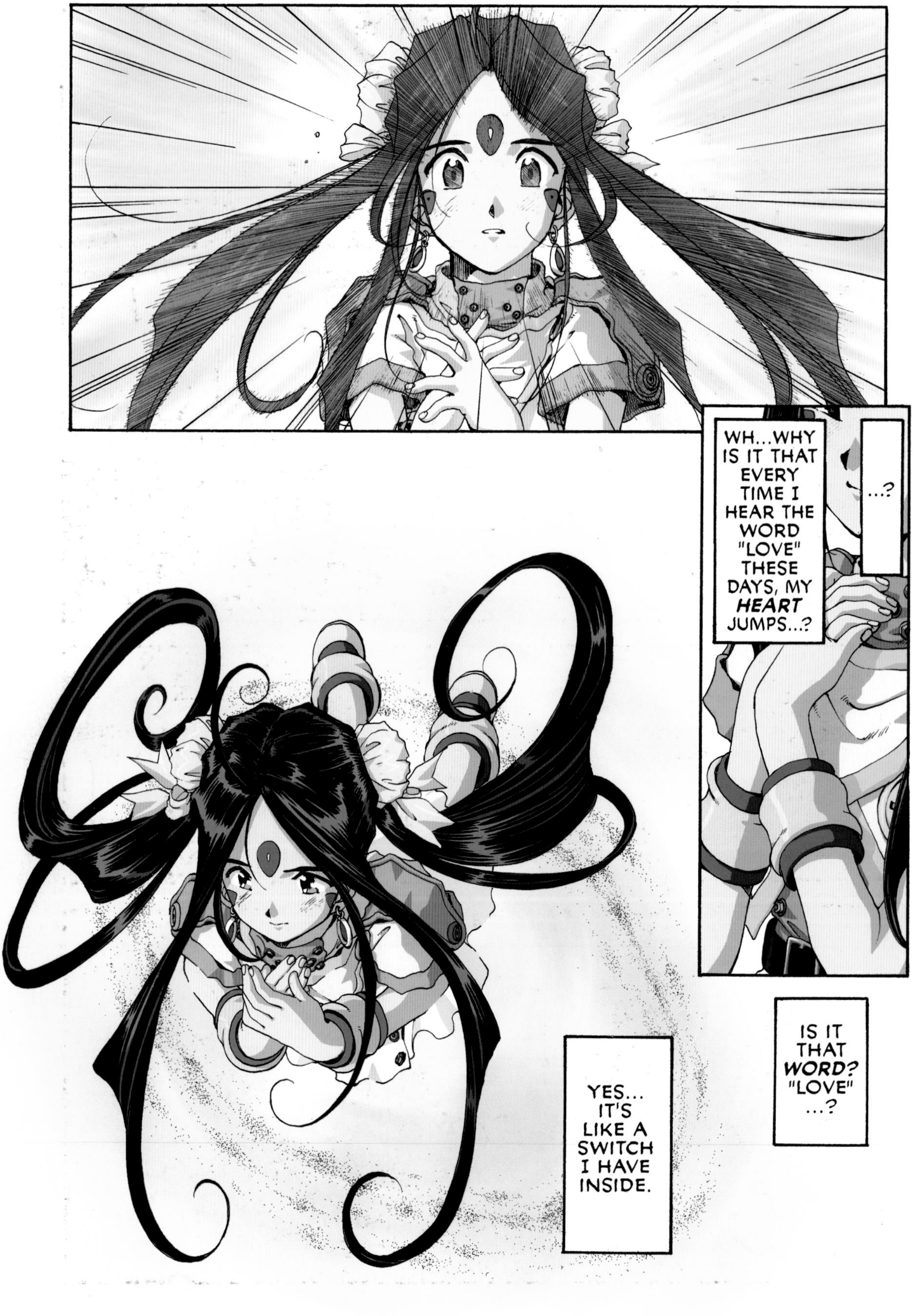
...?
WH...WHY IS IT THAT EVERY TIME I HEAR THE WORD "LOVE" THESE DAYS, MY ***HEART*** JUMPS...?
IS IT THAT ***WORD?*** "LOVE" ...?
YES... IT'S LIKE A SWITCH I HAVE INSIDE.

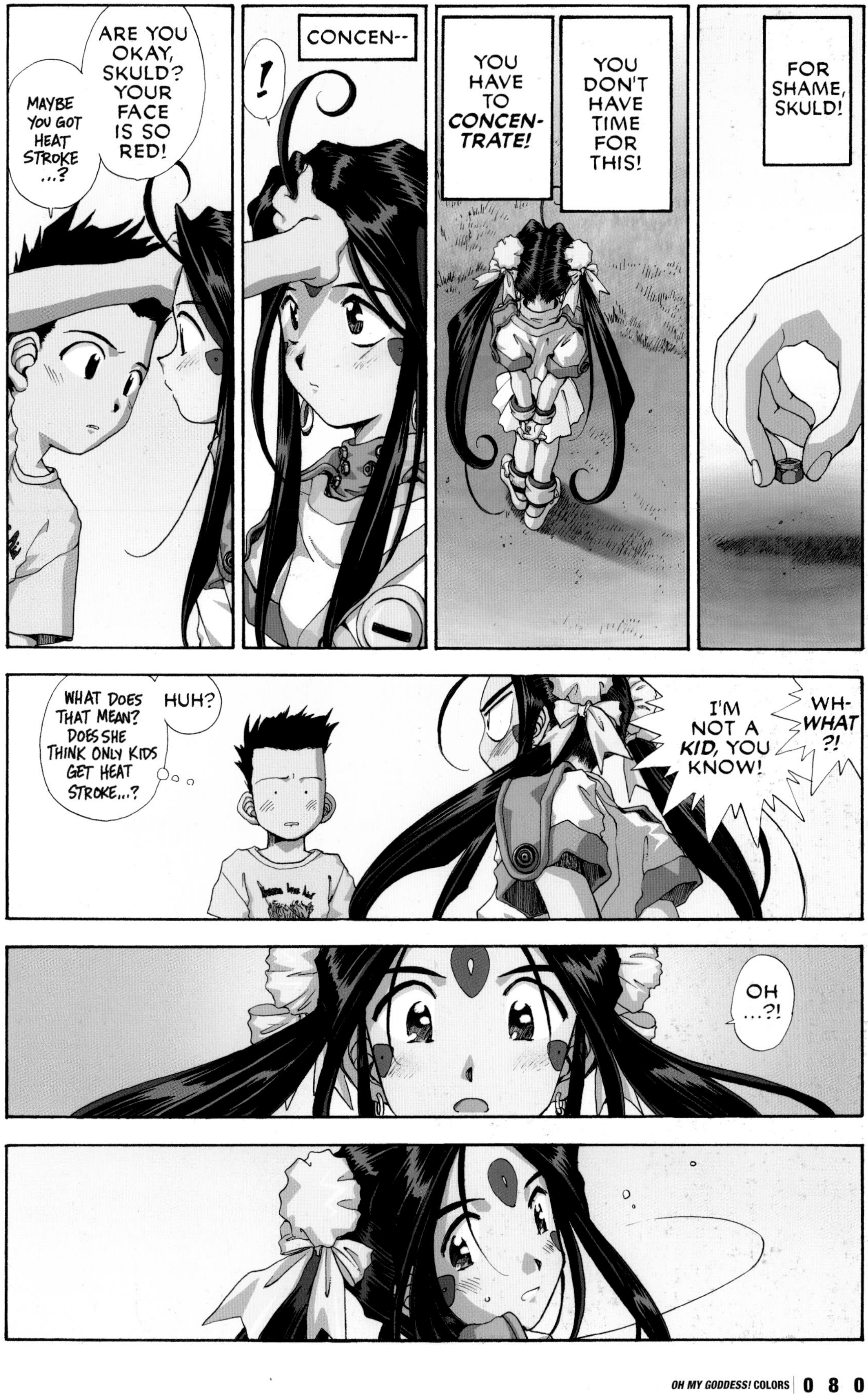
FOR SHAME, SKULD!
YOU DON'T HAVE TIME FOR THIS!
YOU HAVE TO *CONCENTRATE!*
CONCEN--
!
ARE YOU OKAY, SKULD? YOUR FACE IS SO RED!
MAYBE YOU GOT HEAT STROKE ...?
WH- *WHAT* ?!
I'M NOT A *KID*, YOU KNOW!
HUH?
WHAT DOES THAT MEAN? DOES SHE THINK ONLY KIDS GET HEAT STROKE...?
OH ...?!

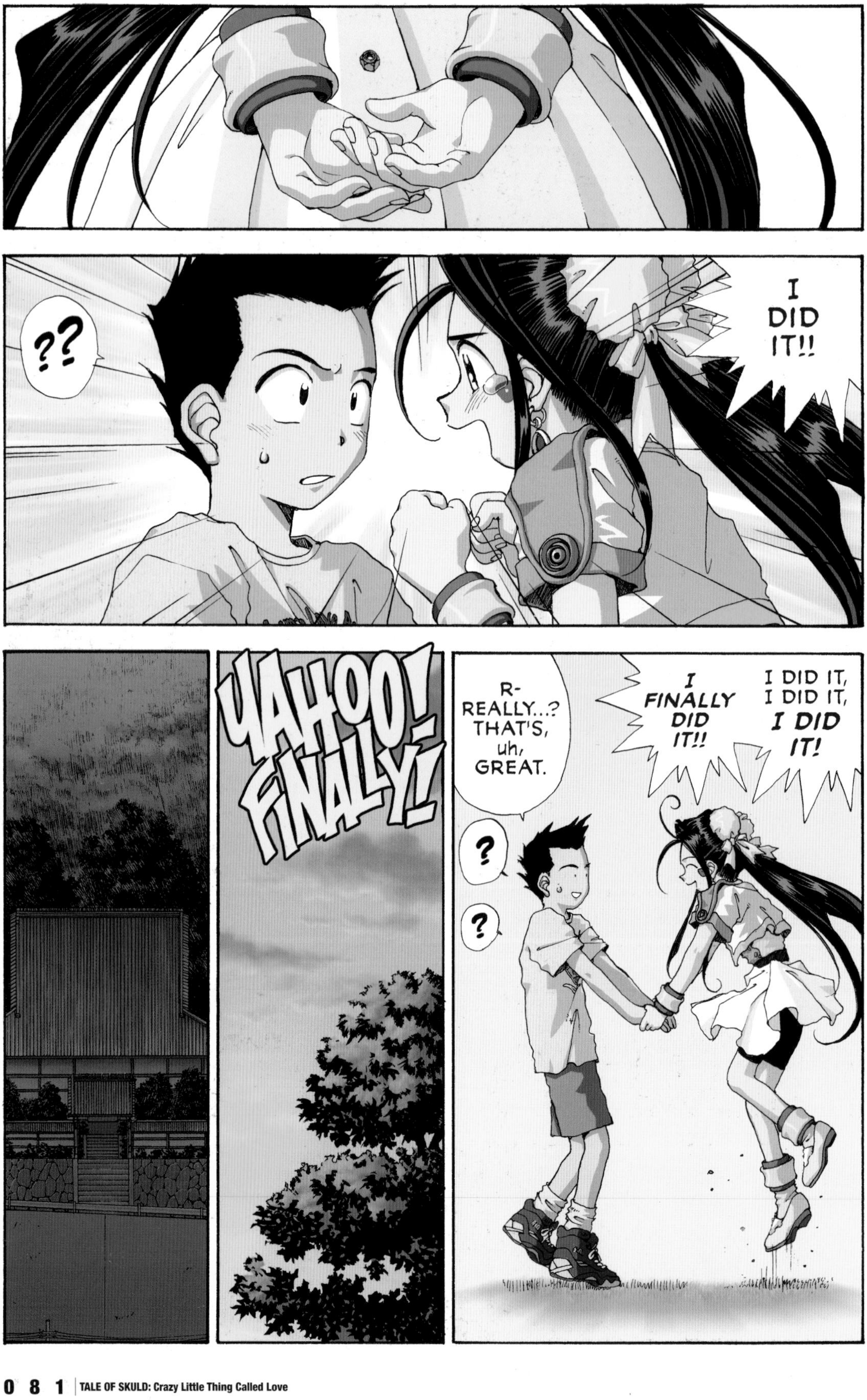
I DID IT!!
??
I DID IT, I DID IT, I DID IT!
I FINALLY DID IT!!
R-REALLY...? THAT'S, uh, GREAT.
?
?
YAHOO! FINALLY!

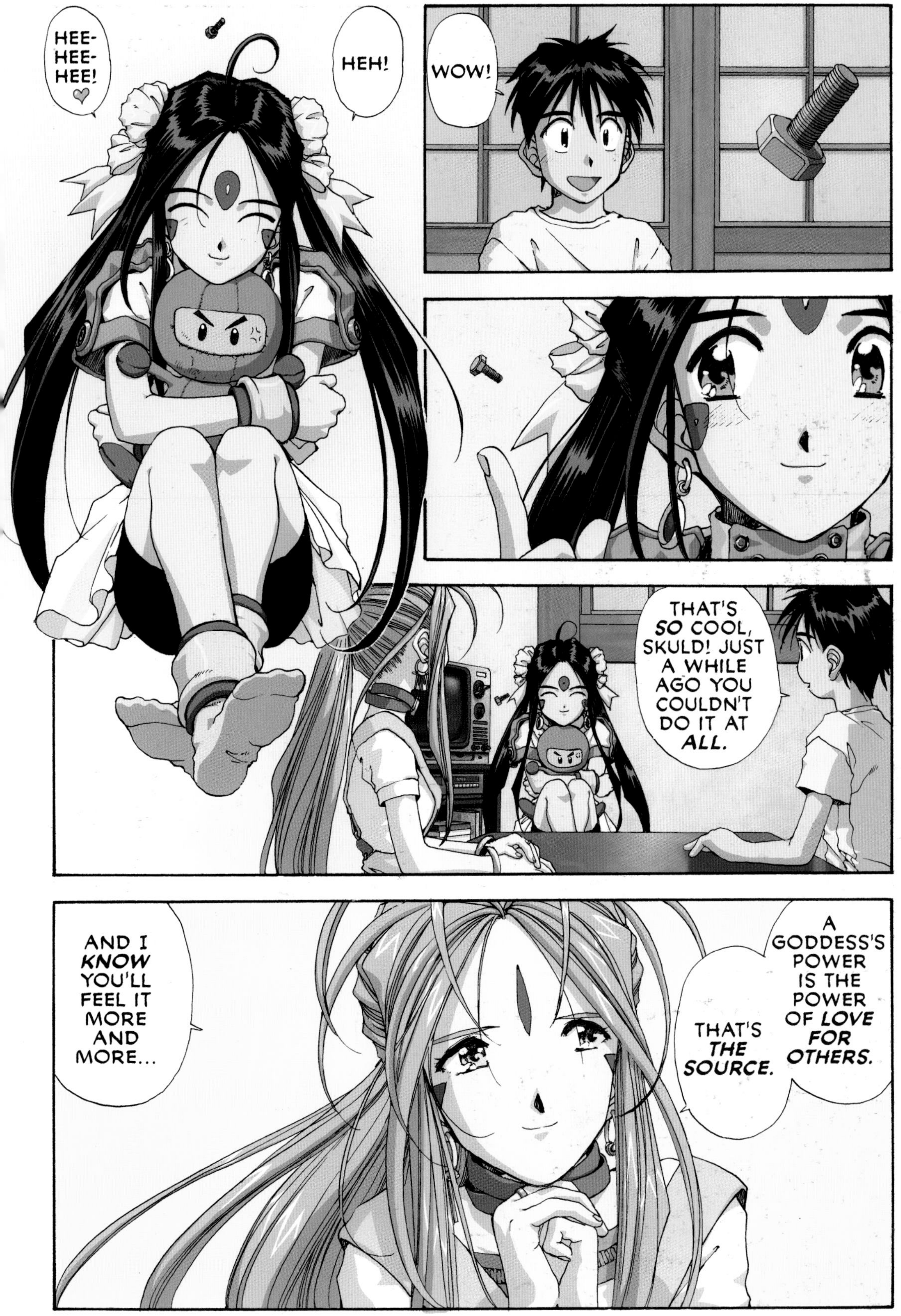
WOW!
HEH!
HEE-HEE-HEE! ♥
THAT'S *SO* COOL, SKULD! JUST A WHILE AGO YOU COULDN'T DO IT AT ***ALL.***
A GODDESS'S POWER IS THE POWER OF ***LOVE FOR OTHERS.***
THAT'S ***THE SOURCE.***
AND I ***KNOW*** YOU'LL FEEL IT MORE AND MORE...

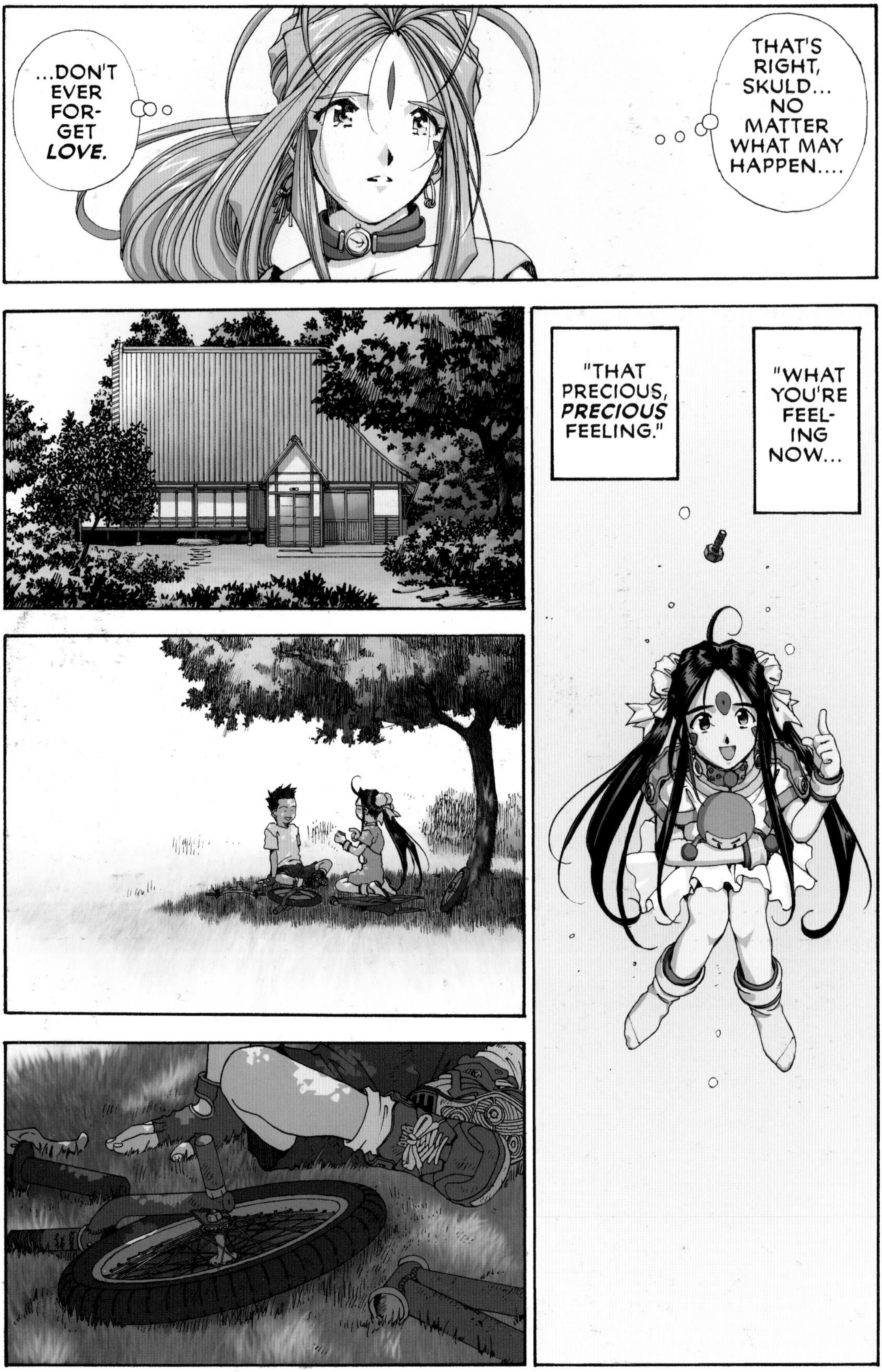
THAT'S RIGHT, SKULD... NO MATTER WHAT MAY HAPPEN....
...DON'T EVER FOR-GET *LOVE.*
"WHAT YOU'RE FEEL-ING NOW...
"THAT PRECIOUS, *PRECIOUS* FEELING."

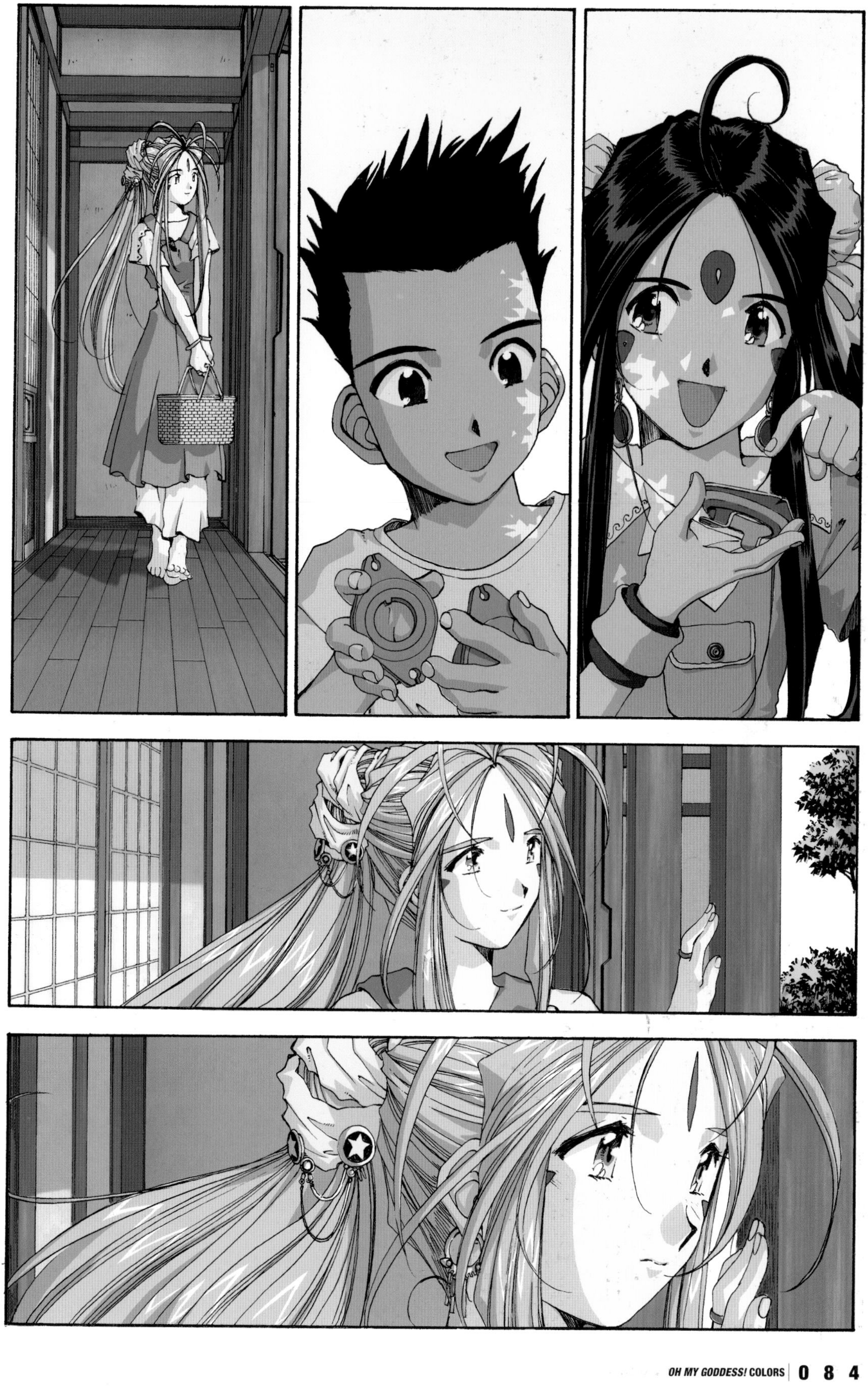

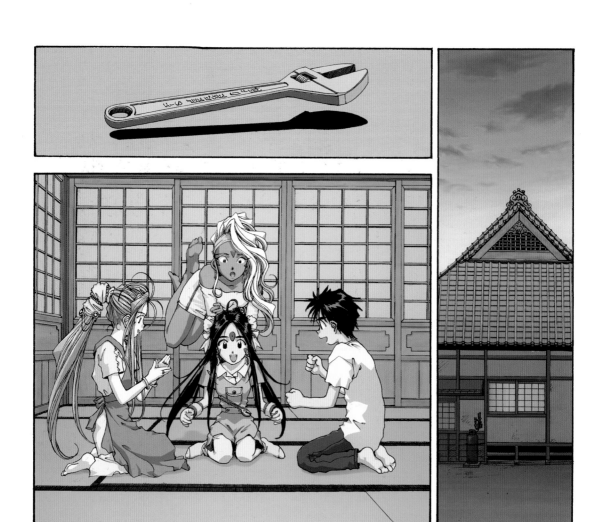

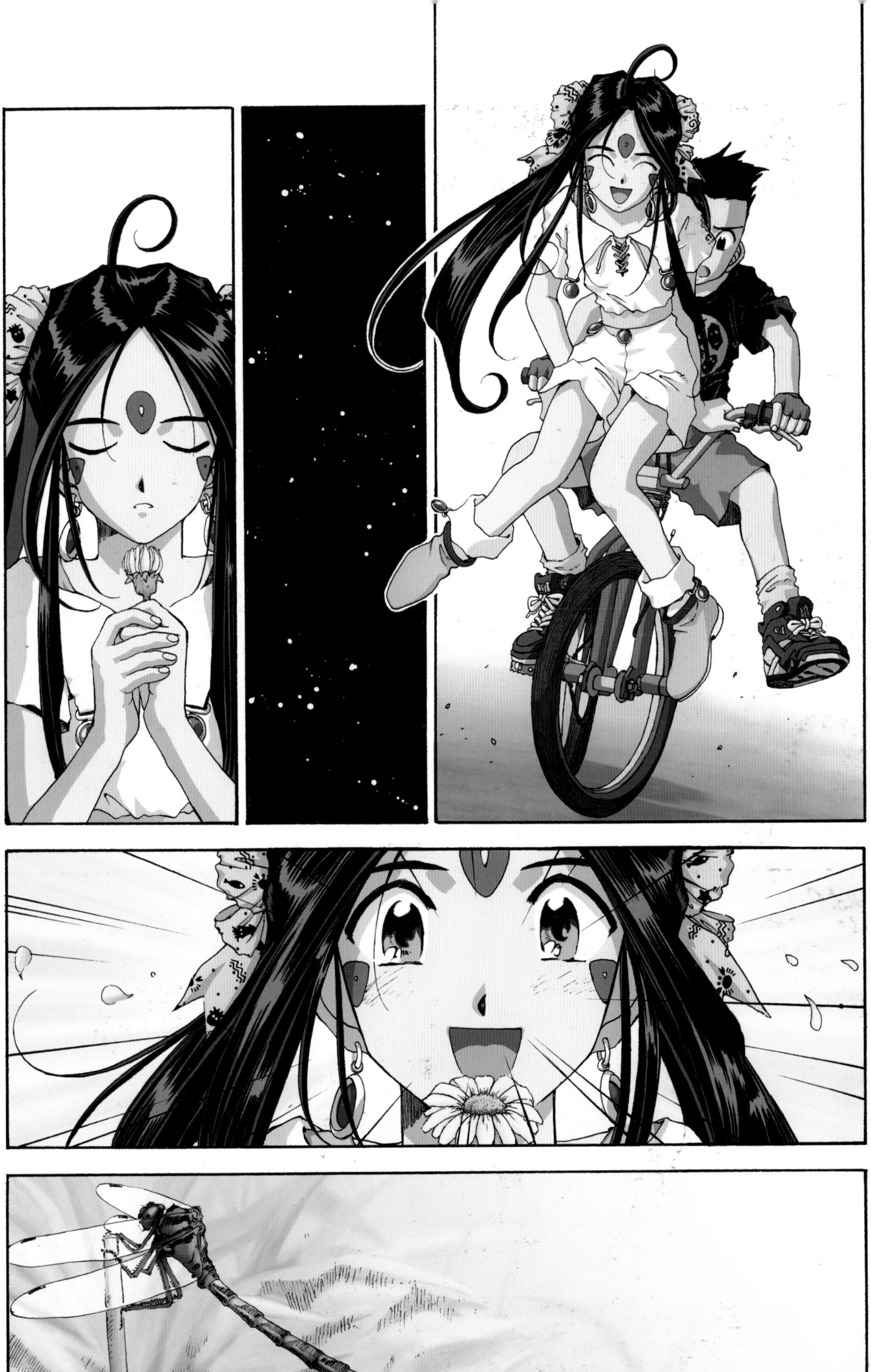

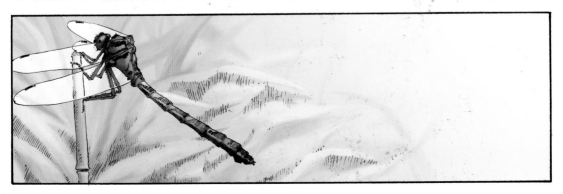

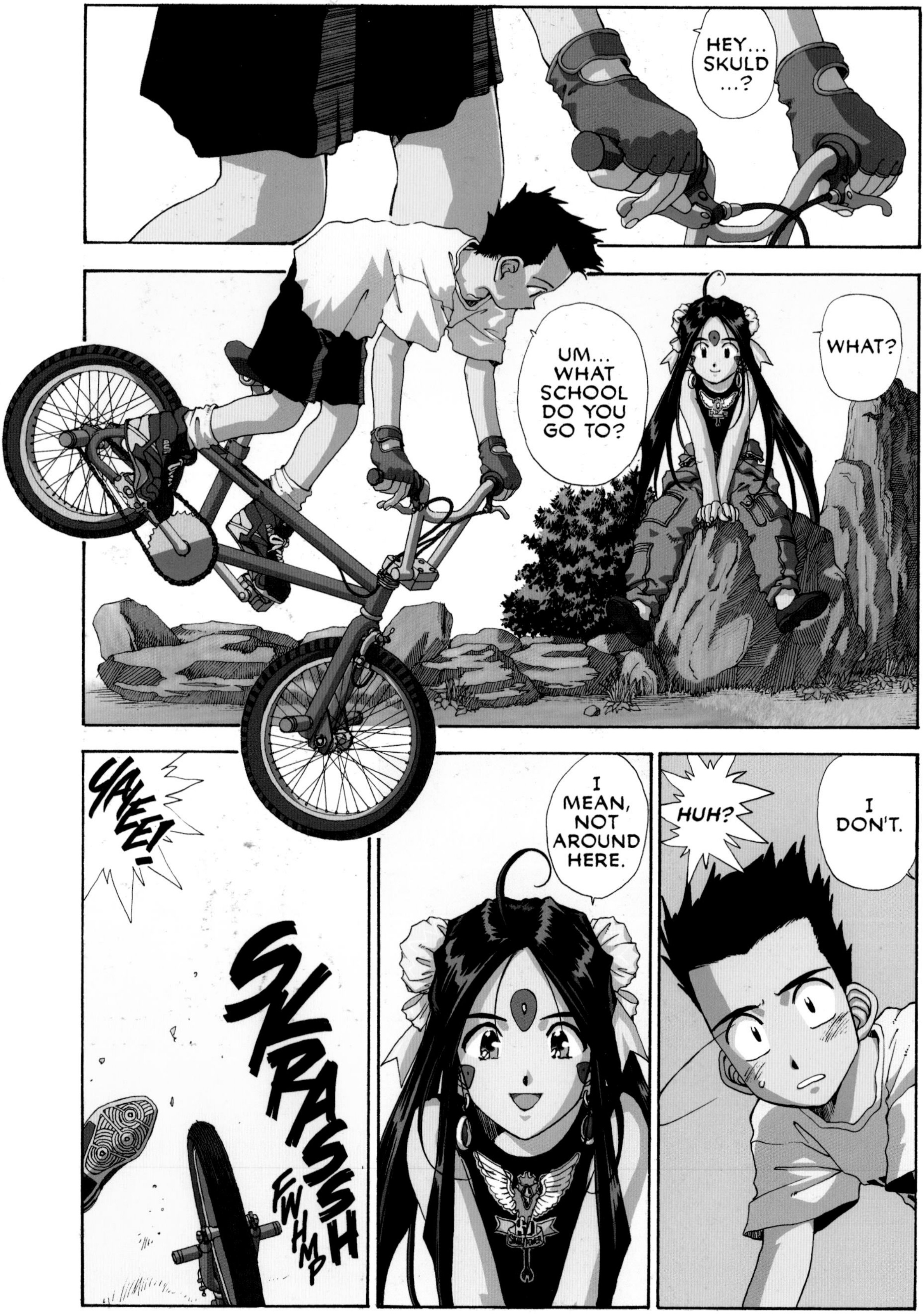
HEY... SKULD ...?
WHAT?
UM... WHAT SCHOOL DO YOU GO TO?
I DON'T.
HUH?
I MEAN, NOT AROUND HERE.
YAEEE!
SKRASSH
FWHMP

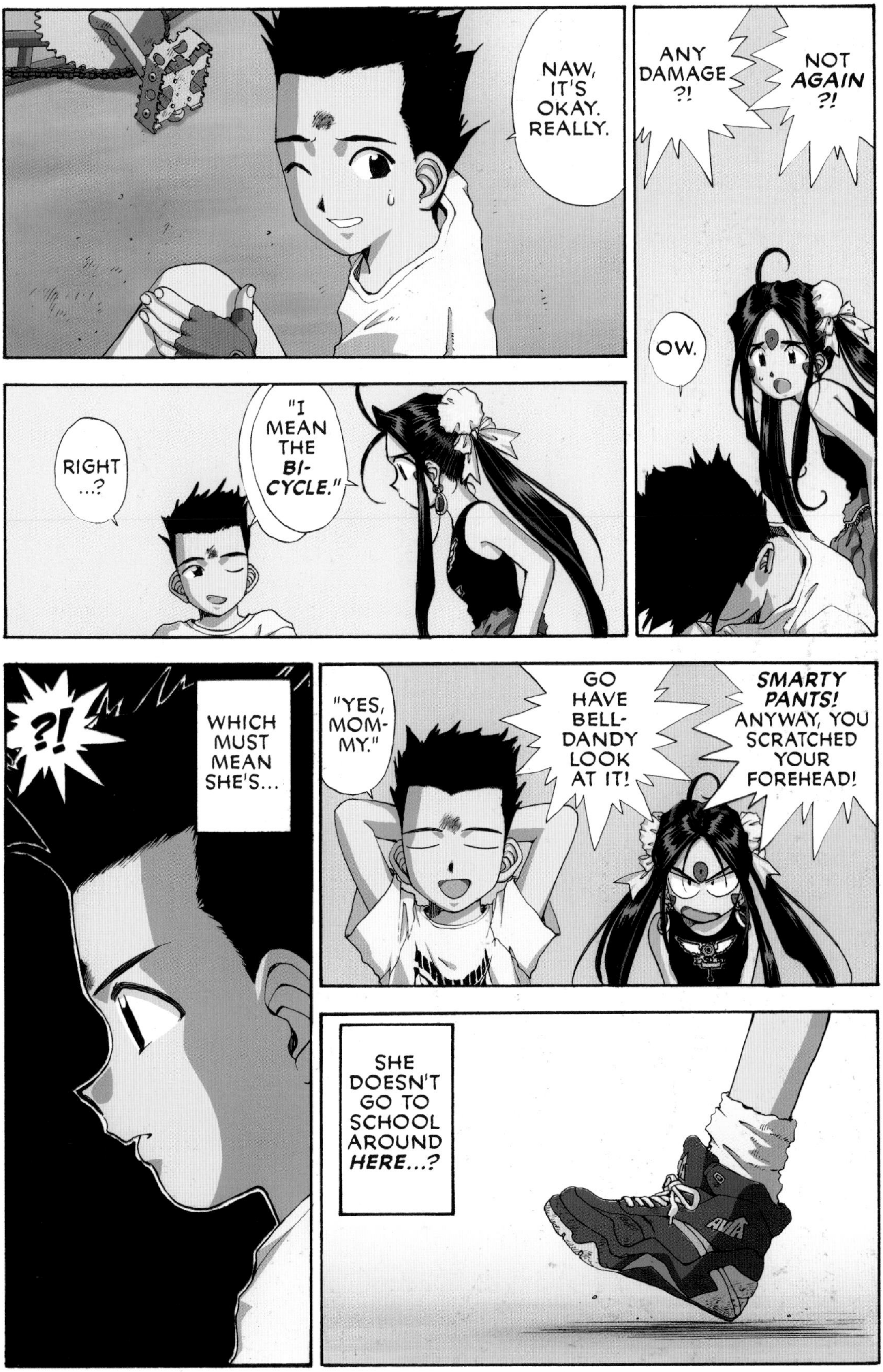
NOT AGAIN?!
ANY DAMAGE?!
OW.
NAW, IT'S OKAY. REALLY.
"I MEAN THE BI-CYCLE."
RIGHT...?
SMARTY PANTS! ANYWAY, YOU SCRATCHED YOUR FOREHEAD!
GO HAVE BELL-DANDY LOOK AT IT!
"YES, MOM-MY."
SHE DOESN'T GO TO SCHOOL AROUND HERE...?
?!
WHICH MUST MEAN SHE'S...

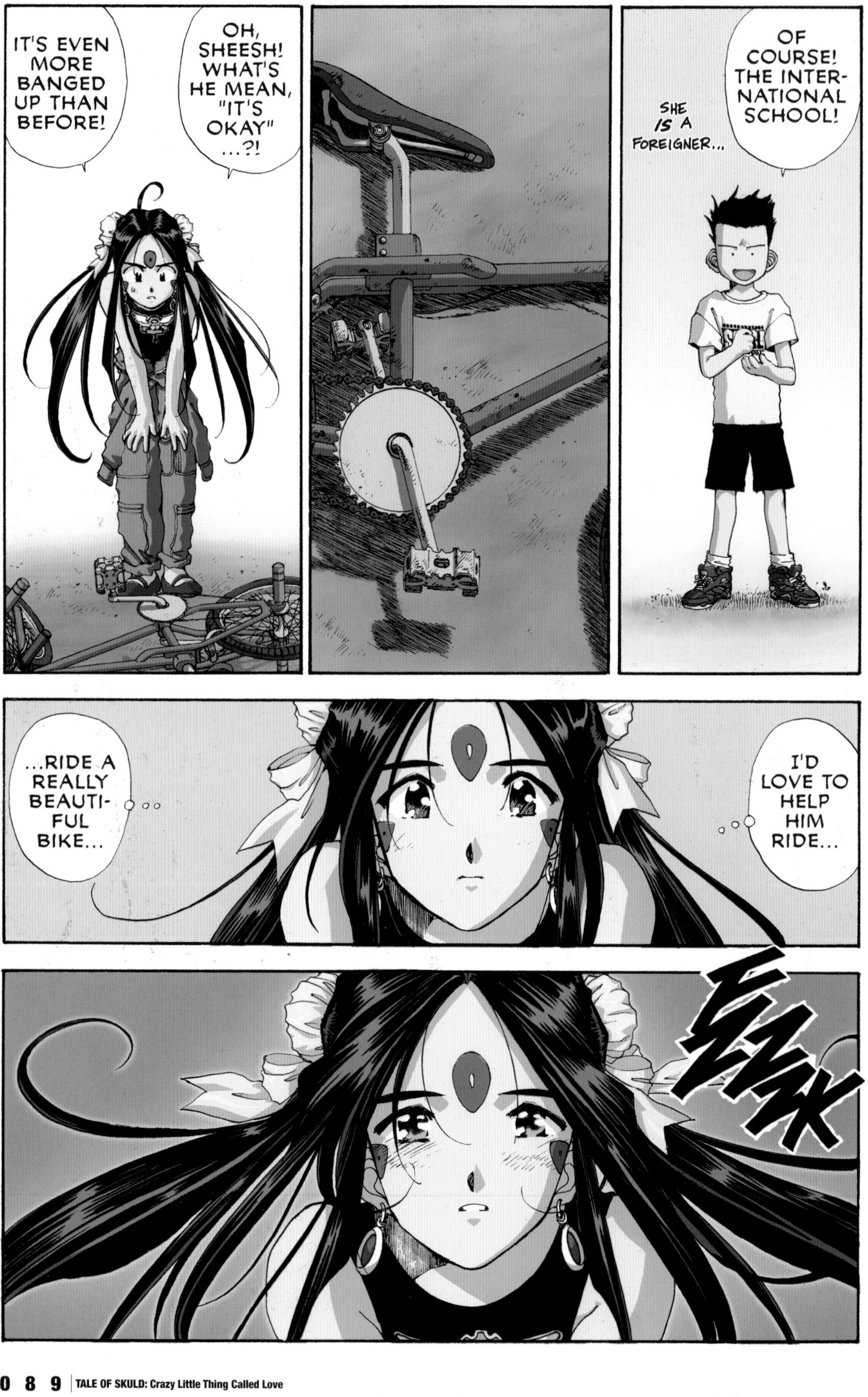
OF COURSE! THE INTER-NATIONAL SCHOOL!
SHE IS A FOREIGNER...
OH, SHEESH! WHAT'S HE MEAN, "IT'S OKAY" ...?!
IT'S EVEN MORE BANGED UP THAN BEFORE!
I'D LOVE TO HELP HIM RIDE...
...RIDE A REALLY BEAUTI-FUL BIKE...

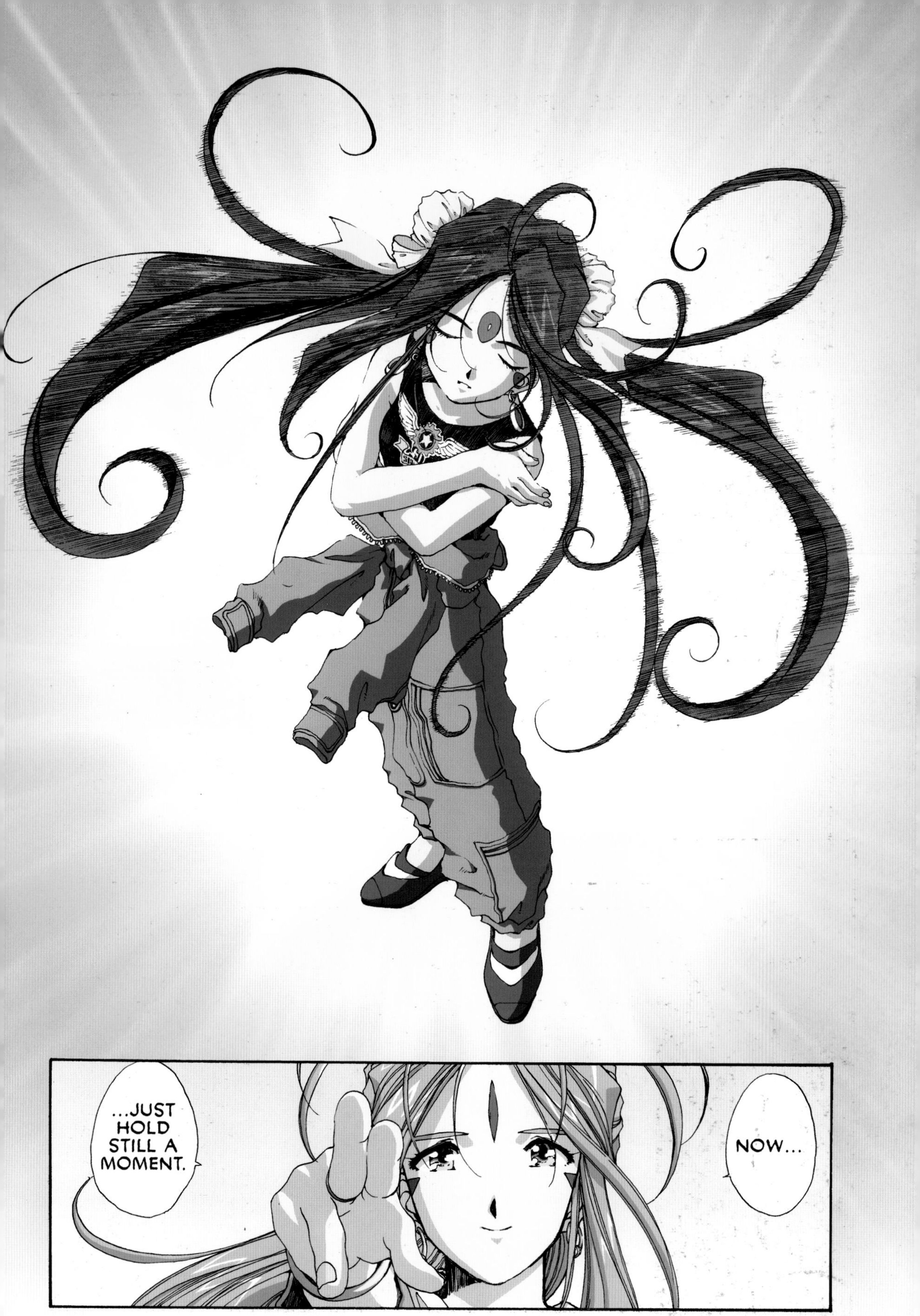
NOW...
...JUST HOLD STILL A MOMENT.

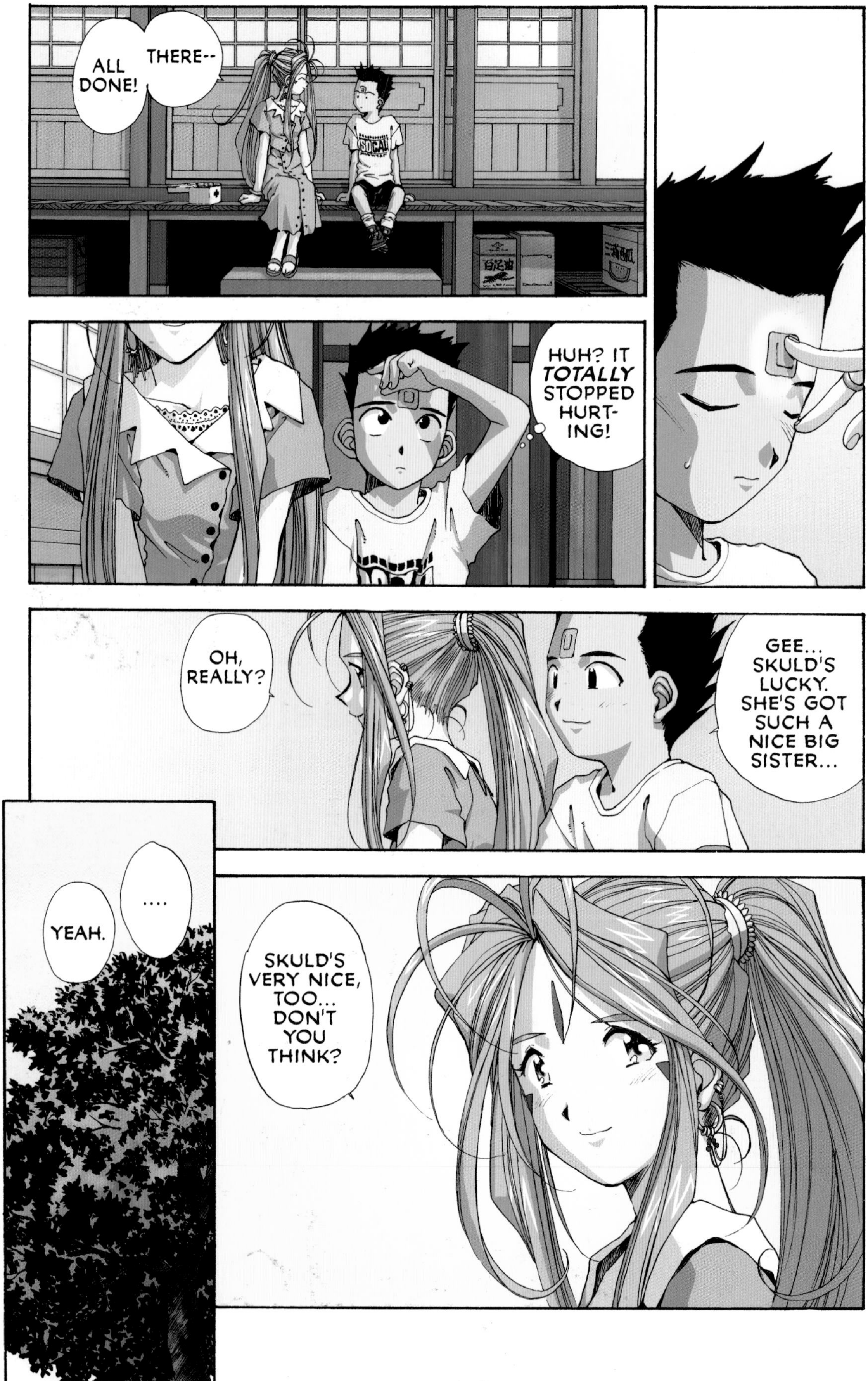
THERE--
ALL DONE!
HUH? IT *TOTALLY* STOPPED HURT-ING!
GEE... SKULD'S LUCKY. SHE'S GOT SUCH A NICE BIG SISTER...
OH, REALLY?
SKULD'S VERY NICE, TOO... DON'T YOU THINK?
....
YEAH.

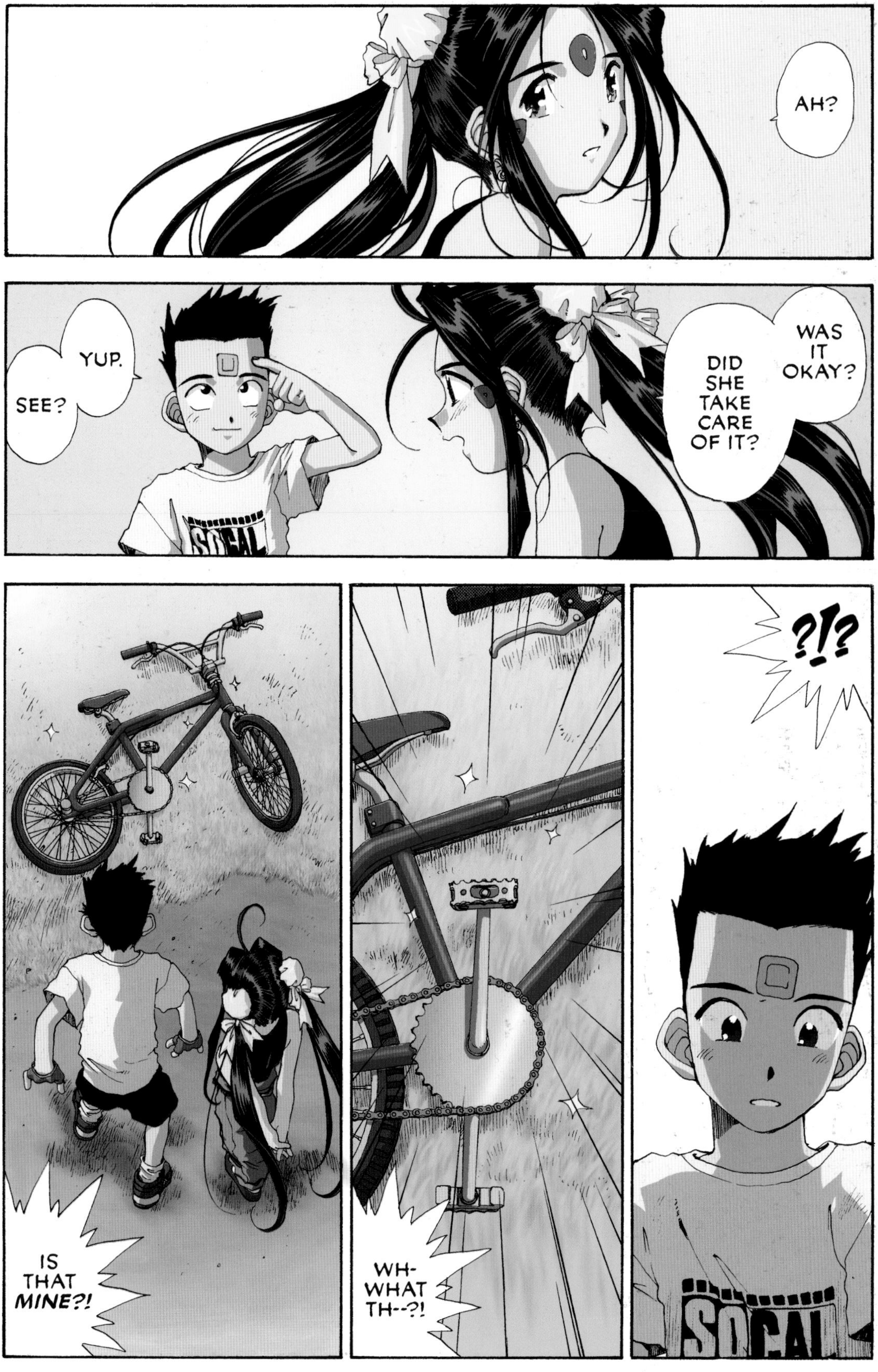
AH?
WAS IT OKAY?
DID SHE TAKE CARE OF IT?
YUP.
SEE?
?!?
WH- WHAT TH--?!
IS THAT *MINE?!*

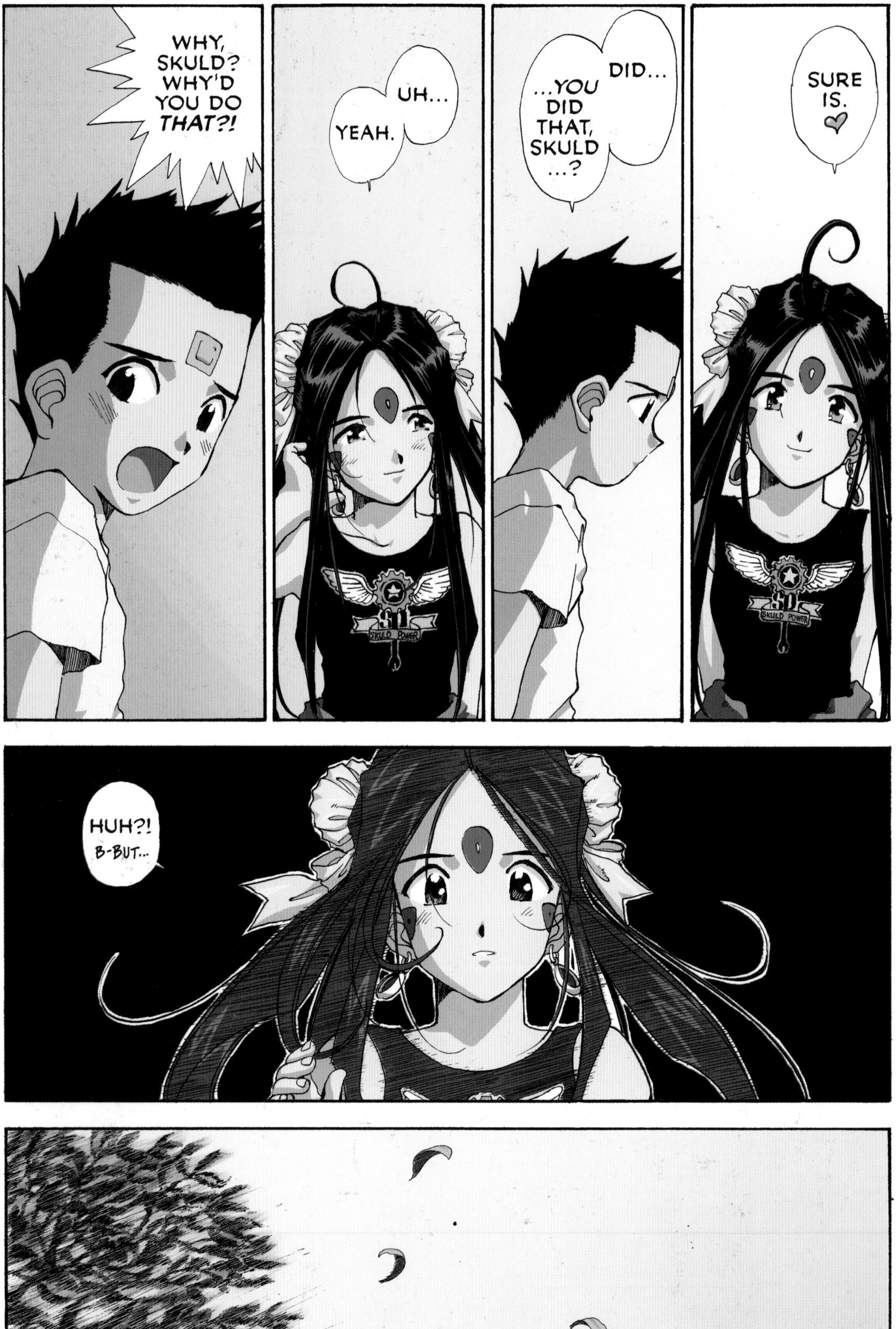
WHY, SKULD? WHY'D YOU DO THAT?!
UH...
YEAH.
DID...
...YOU DID THAT, SKULD ...?
SURE IS. ♥
HUH?! B-BUT...

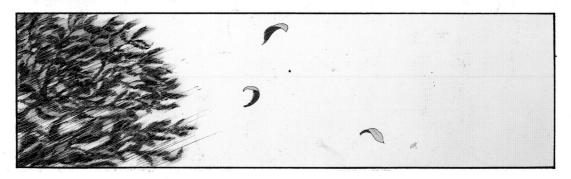

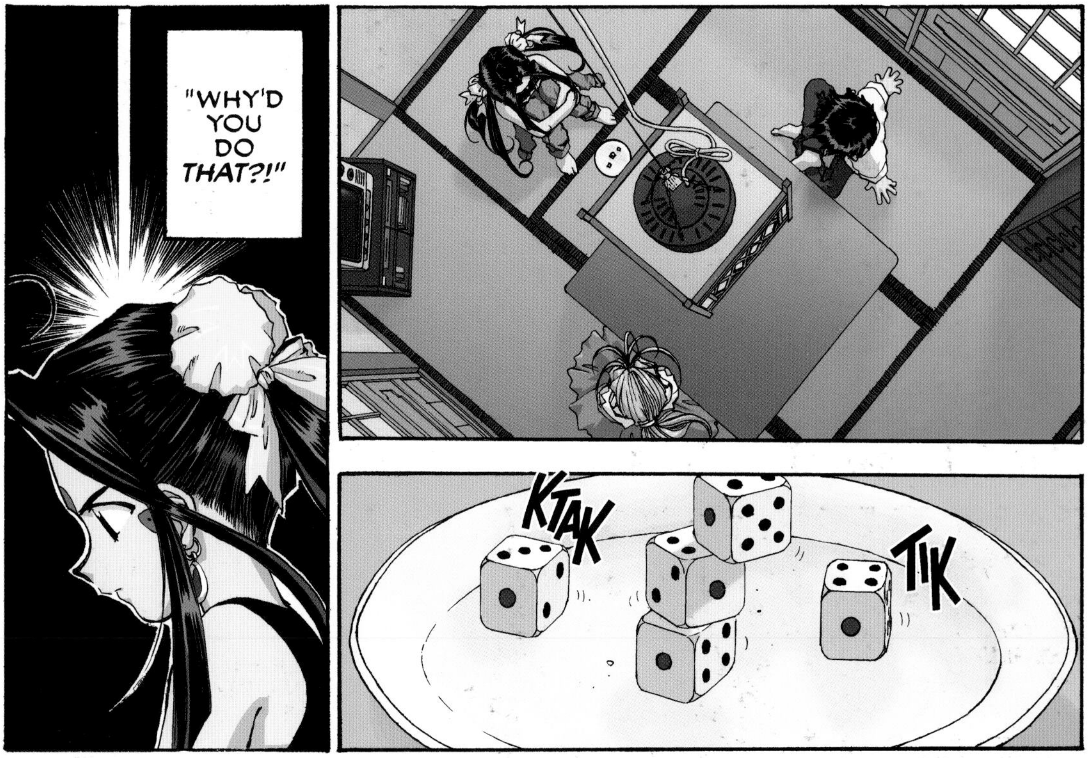
KTAK
TIK
"WHY'D YOU DO *THAT?!*"

SPECIAL TRAINING TO CONTROL HER POWER--SHE HAS TO LINE UP ALL THE NUMBERS ON THE DICE. ▲

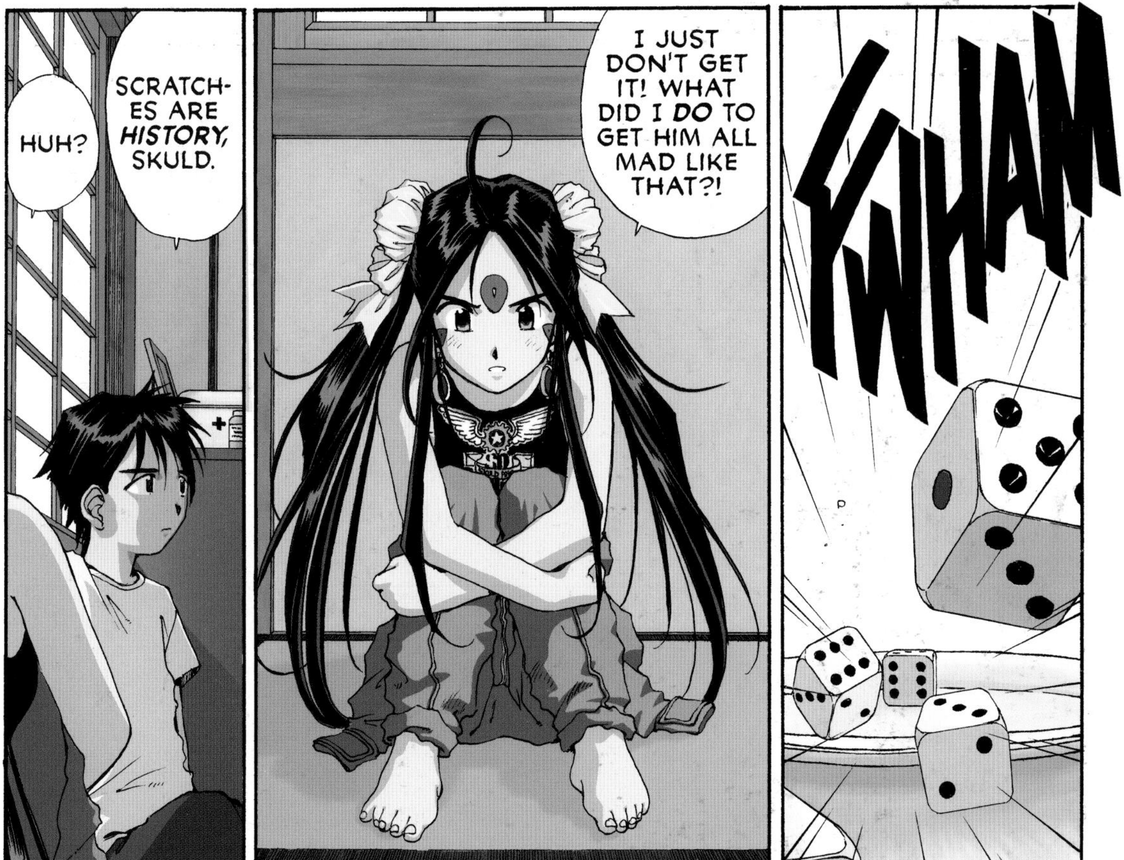
WHAM
I JUST DON'T GET IT! WHAT DID I *DO* TO GET HIM ALL MAD LIKE THAT?!
SCRATCH-ES ARE *HISTORY,* SKULD.
HUH?

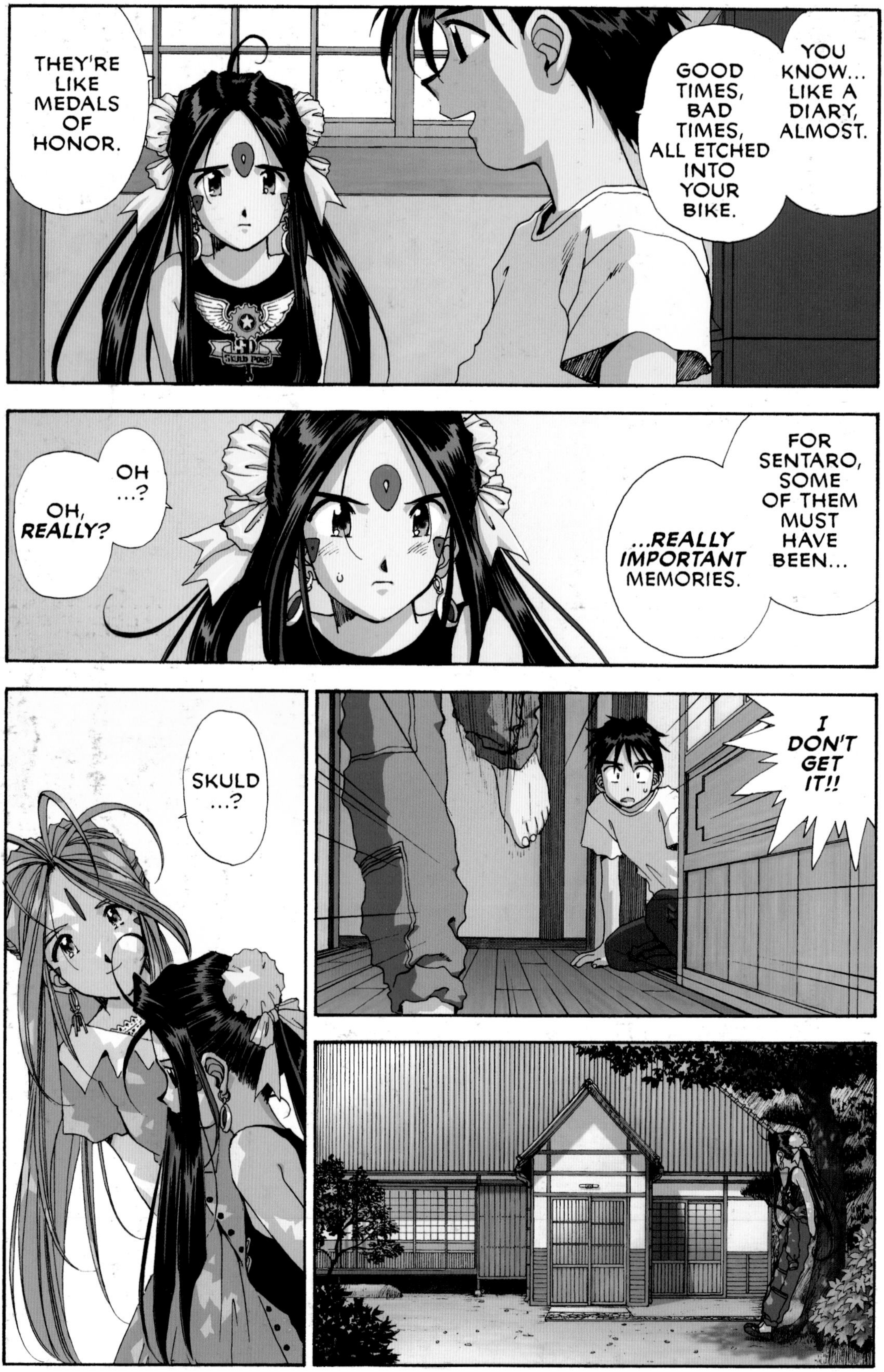
YOU KNOW... LIKE A DIARY, ALMOST.
GOOD TIMES, BAD TIMES, ALL ETCHED INTO YOUR BIKE.
THEY'RE LIKE MEDALS OF HONOR.
FOR SENTARO, SOME OF THEM MUST HAVE BEEN...
...*REALLY IMPORTANT* MEMORIES.
OH ...?
OH, *REALLY?*
I DON'T GET IT!!
SKULD ...?

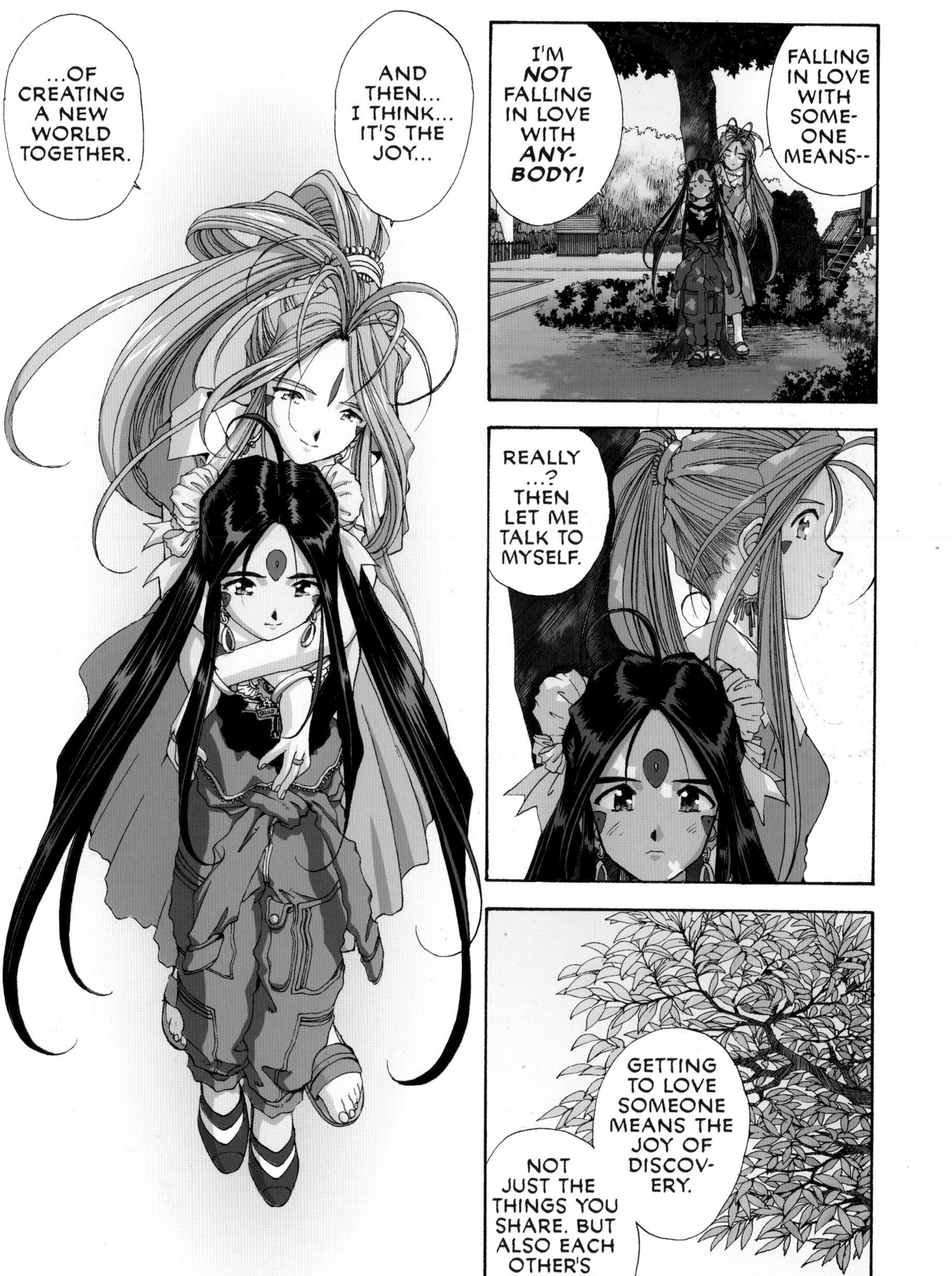
FALLING IN LOVE WITH SOME-ONE MEANS--
I'M *NOT* FALLING IN LOVE WITH *ANY-BODY!*
REALLY ...? THEN LET ME TALK TO MYSELF.
GETTING TO LOVE SOMEONE MEANS THE JOY OF DISCOV-ERY.
NOT JUST THE THINGS YOU SHARE. BUT ALSO EACH OTHER'S NEW AND DIFFERENT FEELINGS.
AND THEN... I THINK... IT'S THE JOY...
...OF CREATING A NEW WORLD TOGETHER.

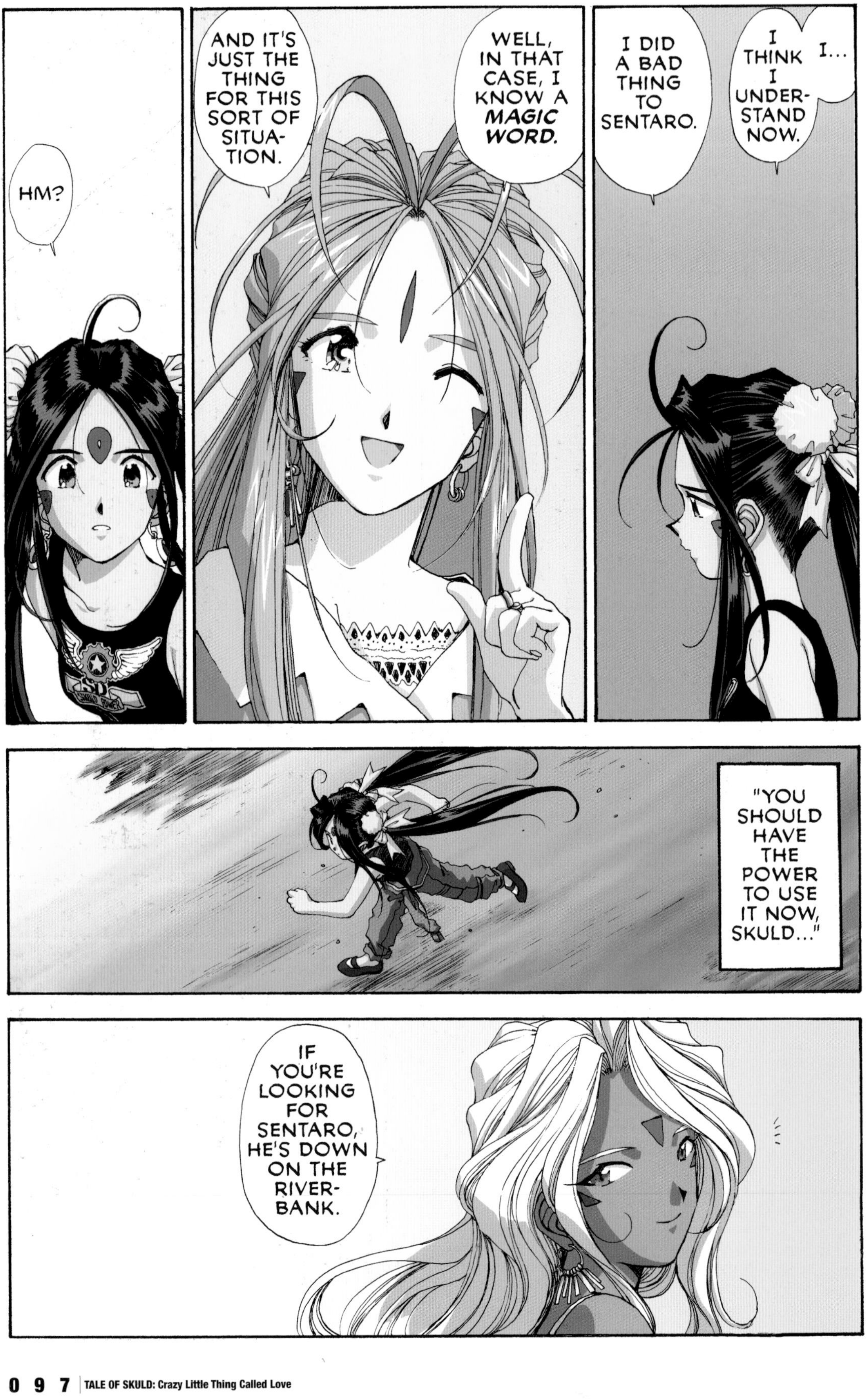
I...
I THINK I UNDER-STAND NOW.
I DID A BAD THING TO SENTARO.
WELL, IN THAT CASE, I KNOW A *MAGIC WORD.*
AND IT'S JUST THE THING FOR THIS SORT OF SITUA-TION.
HM?
"YOU SHOULD HAVE THE POWER TO USE IT NOW, SKULD..."
IF YOU'RE LOOKING FOR SENTARO, HE'S DOWN ON THE RIVER-BANK.

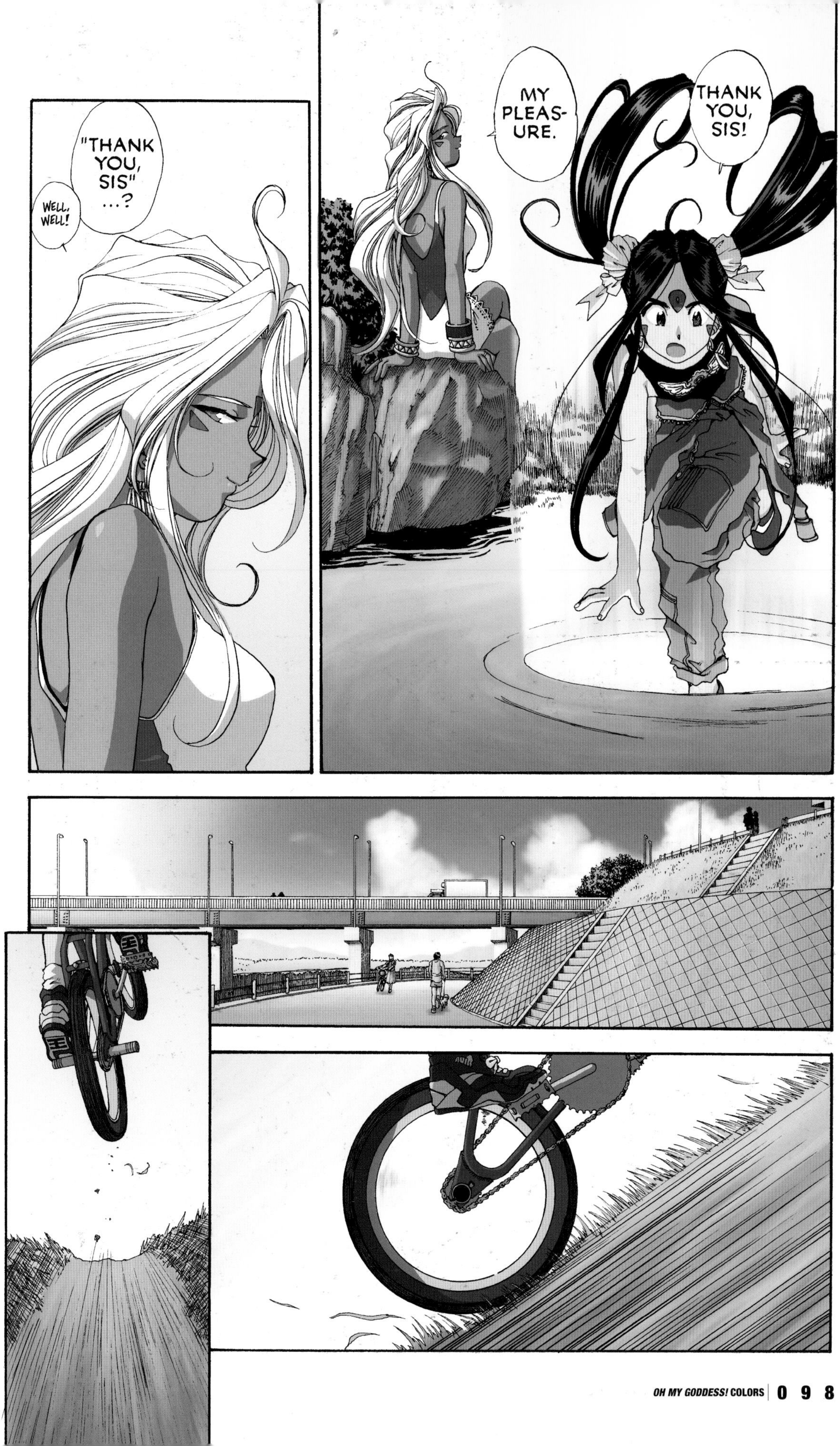
THANK YOU, SIS!
MY PLEAS-URE.
"THANK YOU, SIS" ...?
WELL, WELL!

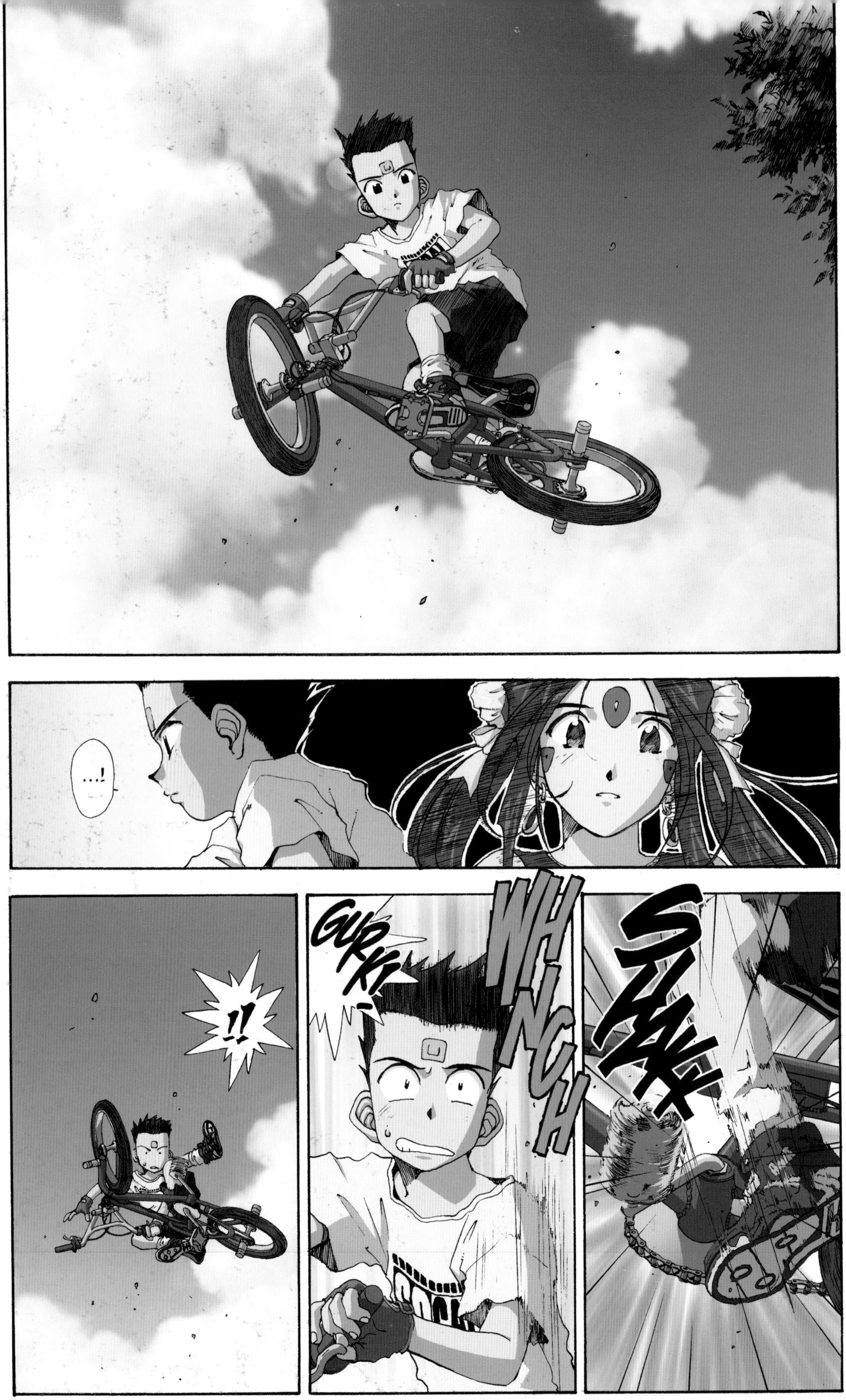

...!
SHWAKK
WHNCH
GURK!-
!!

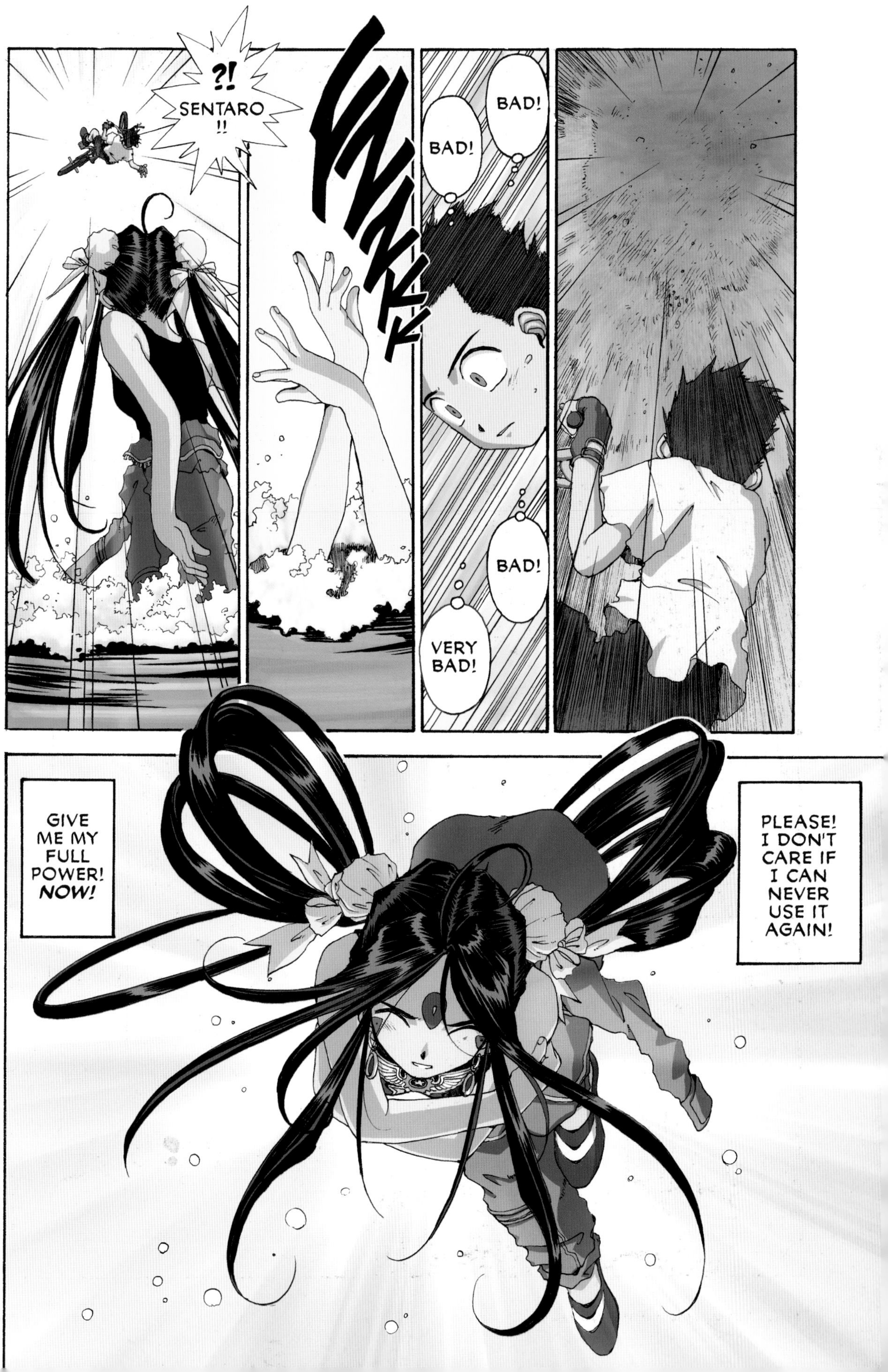
BAD!
BAD!
BAD!
VERY BAD!
?! SENTARO !!
PLEASE! I DON'T CARE IF I CAN NEVER USE IT AGAIN!
GIVE ME MY FULL POWER! *NOW!*

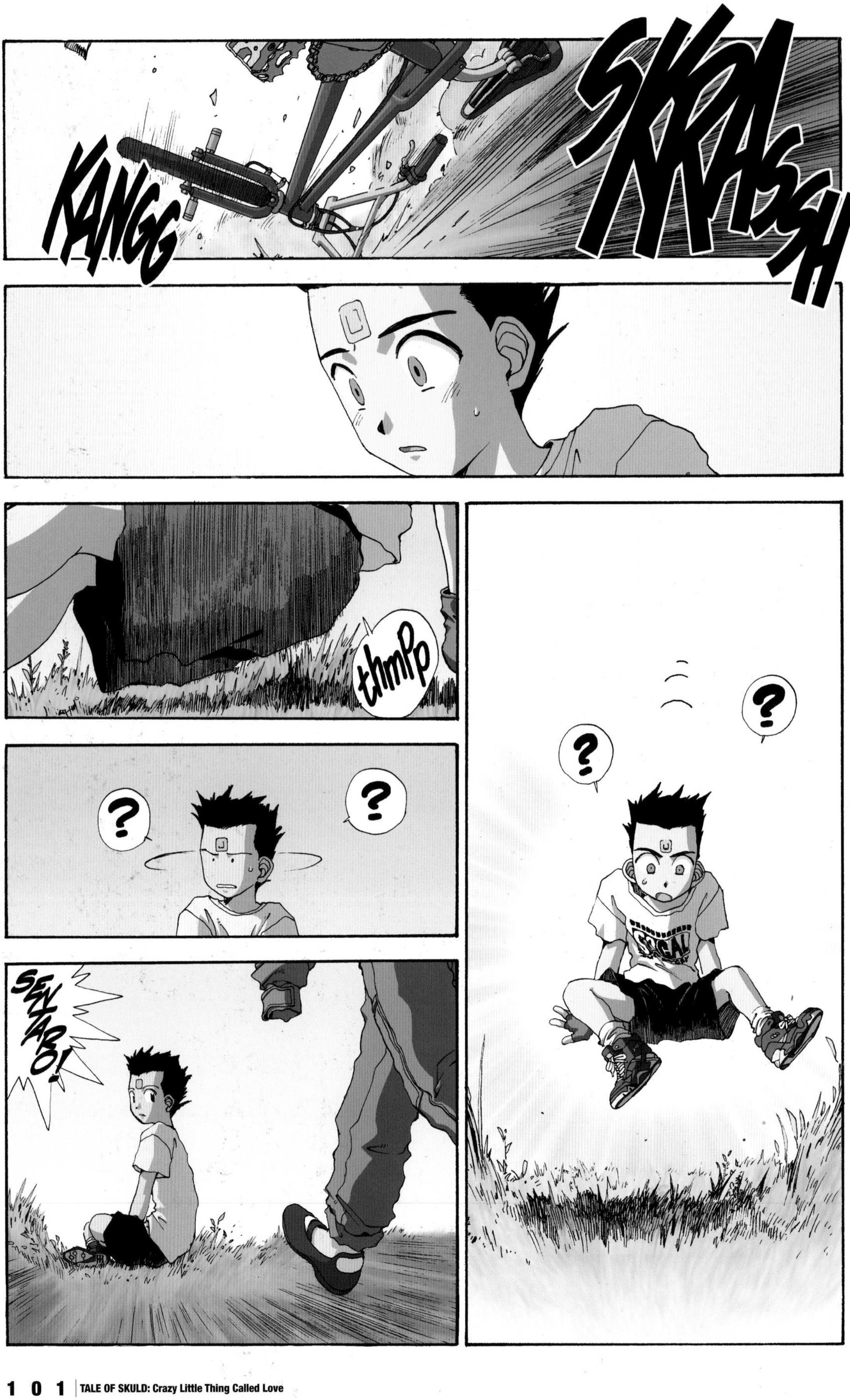
SKRASSH
KANGG
?
?
thmpp
?
?
SENTARO!

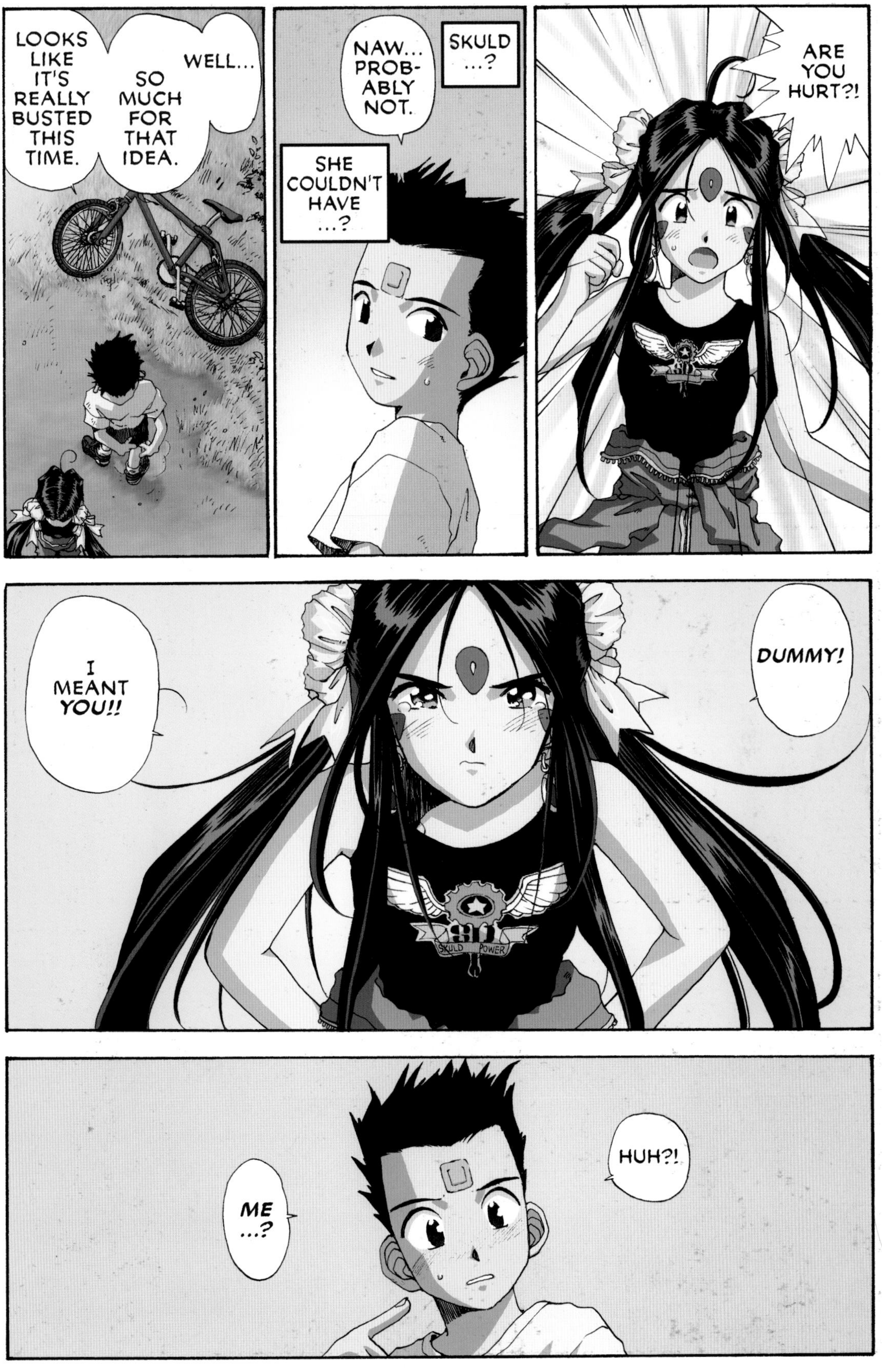
ARE YOU HURT?!
SKULD ...?
NAW... PROB-ABLY NOT.
SHE COULDN'T HAVE ...?
WELL... SO MUCH FOR THAT IDEA.
LOOKS LIKE IT'S REALLY BUSTED THIS TIME.
DUMMY!
I MEANT *YOU!!*
HUH?!
ME ...?

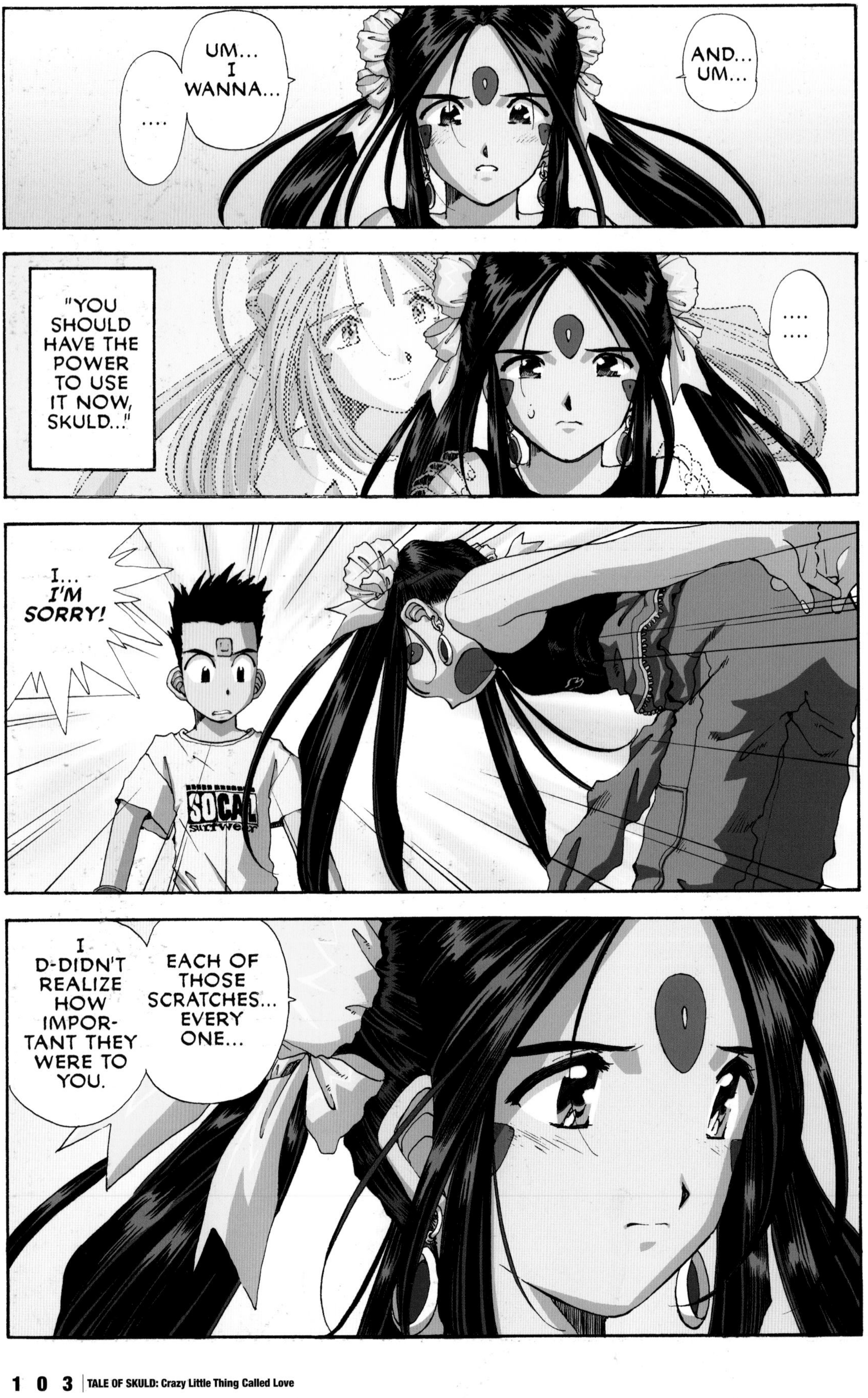
AND... UM...
UM... I WANNA...
....
....
....
"YOU SHOULD HAVE THE POWER TO USE IT NOW, SKULD..."
I... *I'M SORRY!*
EACH OF THOSE SCRATCHES... EVERY ONE...
I D-DIDN'T REALIZE HOW IMPOR-TANT THEY WERE TO YOU.

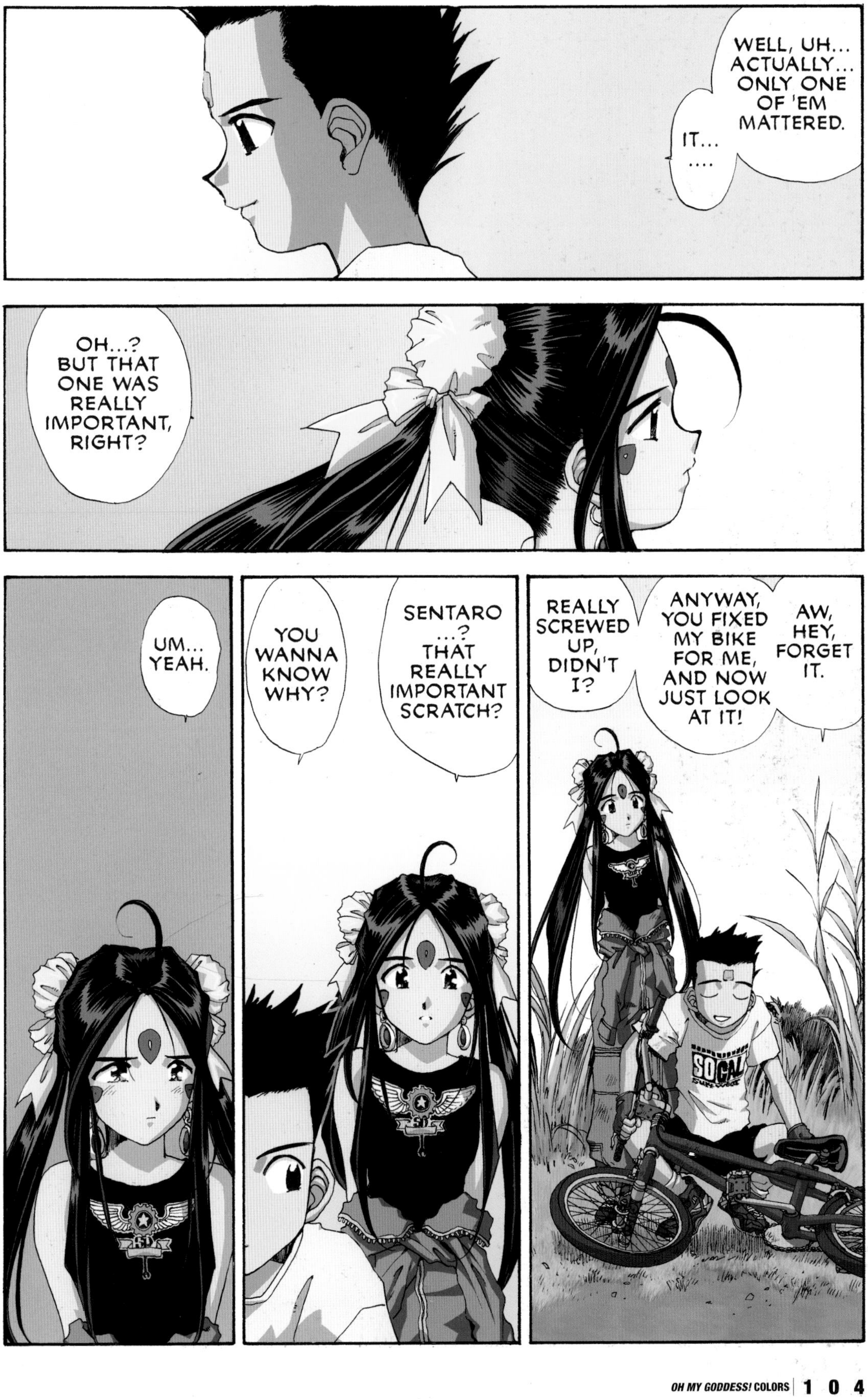
WELL, UH... ACTUALLY... ONLY ONE OF 'EM MATTERED.
IT... ....
OH...? BUT THAT ONE WAS REALLY IMPORTANT, RIGHT?
AW, HEY, FORGET IT.
ANYWAY, YOU FIXED MY BIKE FOR ME, AND NOW JUST LOOK AT IT!
REALLY SCREWED UP, DIDN'T I?
SENTARO ...? THAT REALLY IMPORTANT SCRATCH?
YOU WANNA KNOW WHY?
UM... YEAH.

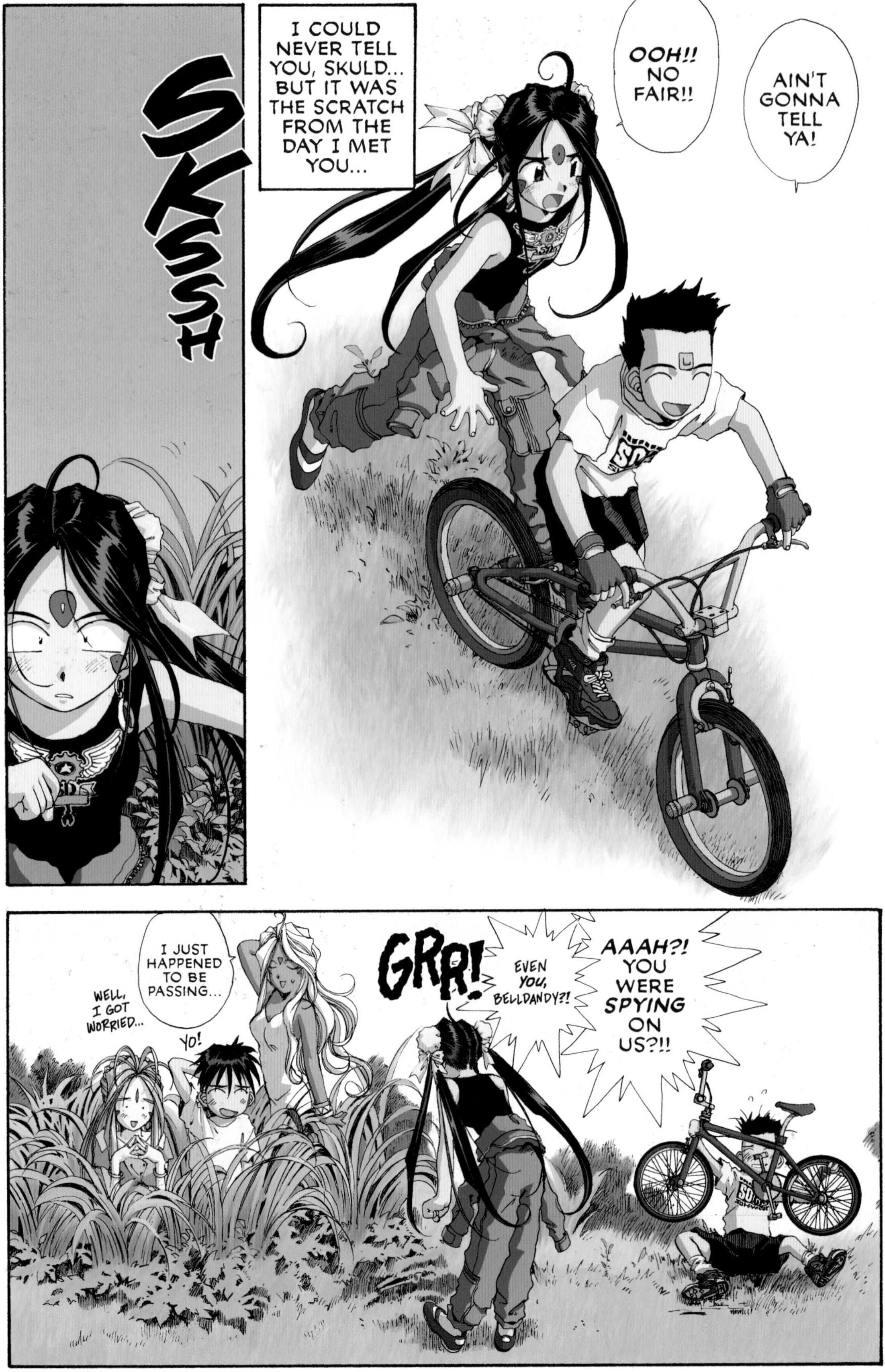
AIN'T GONNA TELL YA!
OOH!! NO FAIR!!
I COULD NEVER TELL YOU, SKULD... BUT IT WAS THE SCRATCH FROM THE DAY I MET YOU...
SKSSH
AAAH?! YOU WERE SPYING ON US?!!
EVEN YOU, BELLDANDY?!
GRR!
I JUST HAPPENED TO BE PASSING...
YO!
WELL, I GOT WORRIED...

END

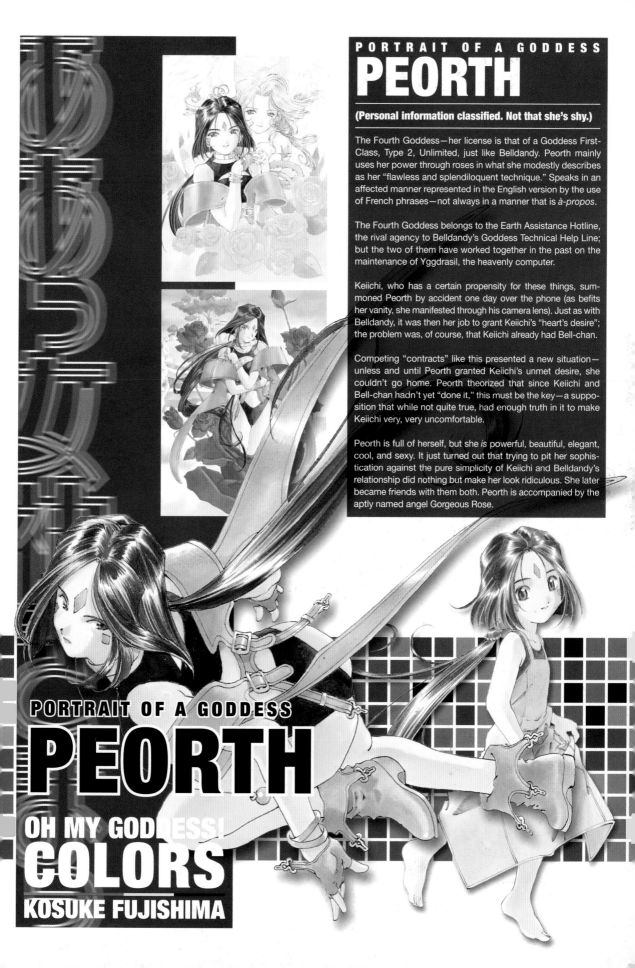

PORTRAIT OF A GODDESS

PEORTH

(Personal information classified. Not that she's shy.)

The Fourth Goddess—her license is that of a Goddess First-Class, Type 2, Unlimited, just like Belldandy. Peorth mainly uses her power through roses in what she modestly describes as her "flawless and splendiloquent technique." Speaks in an affected manner represented in the English version by the use of French phrases—not always in a manner that is *à-propos*.

The Fourth Goddess belongs to the Earth Assistance Hotline, the rival agency to Belldandy's Goddess Technical Help Line; but the two of them have worked together in the past on the maintenance of Yggdrasil, the heavenly computer.

Keiichi, who has a certain propensity for these things, summoned Peorth by accident one day over the phone (as befits her vanity, she manifested through his camera lens). Just as with Belldandy, it was then her job to grant Keiichi's "heart's desire"; the problem was, of course, that Keiichi already had Bell-chan.

Competing "contracts" like this presented a new situation—unless and until Peorth granted Keiichi's unmet desire, she couldn't go home. Peorth theorized that since Keiichi and Bell-chan hadn't yet "done it," this must be the key—a supposition that while not quite true, had enough truth in it to make Keiichi very, very uncomfortable.

Peorth is full of herself, but she *is* powerful, beautiful, elegant, cool, and sexy. It just turned out that trying to pit her sophistication against the pure simplicity of Keiichi and Belldandy's relationship did nothing but make her look ridiculous. She later became friends with them both. Peorth is accompanied by the aptly named angel Gorgeous Rose.

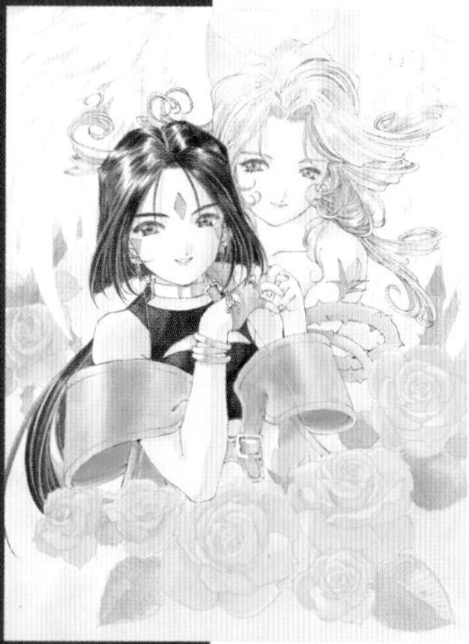

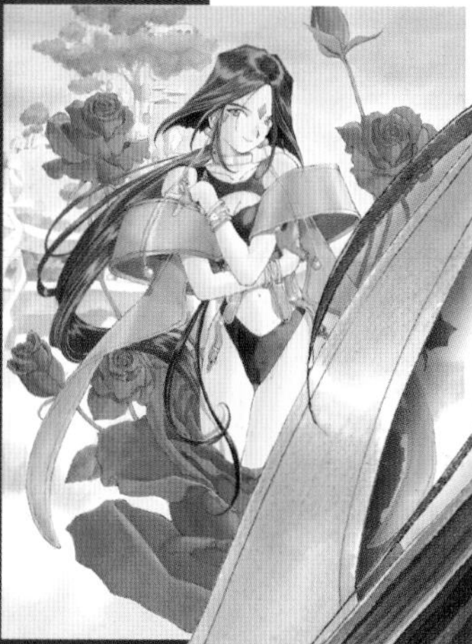

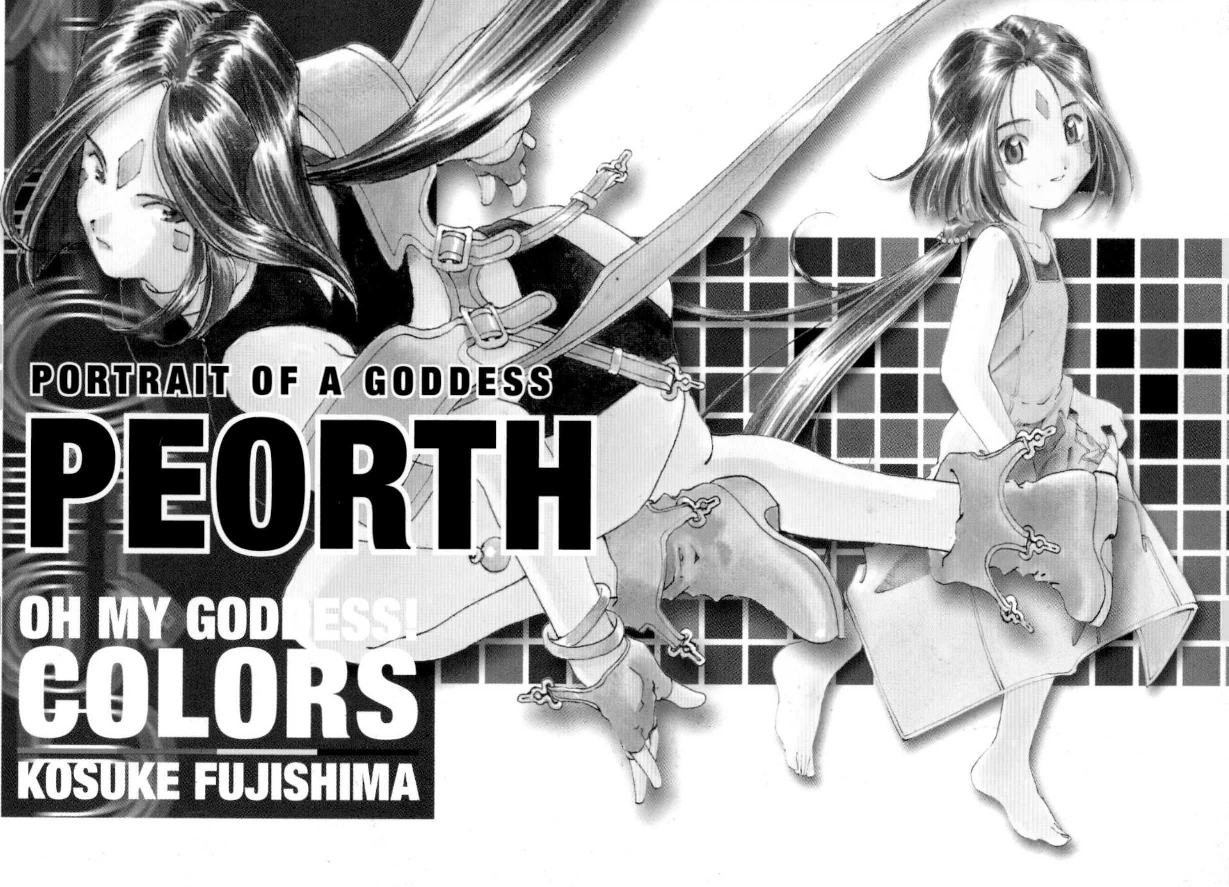

PORTRAIT OF A GODDESS

PEORTH

OH MY GODDESS! COLORS

KOSUKE FUJISHIMA

TALE OF PEORTH:
Are You Being Served?

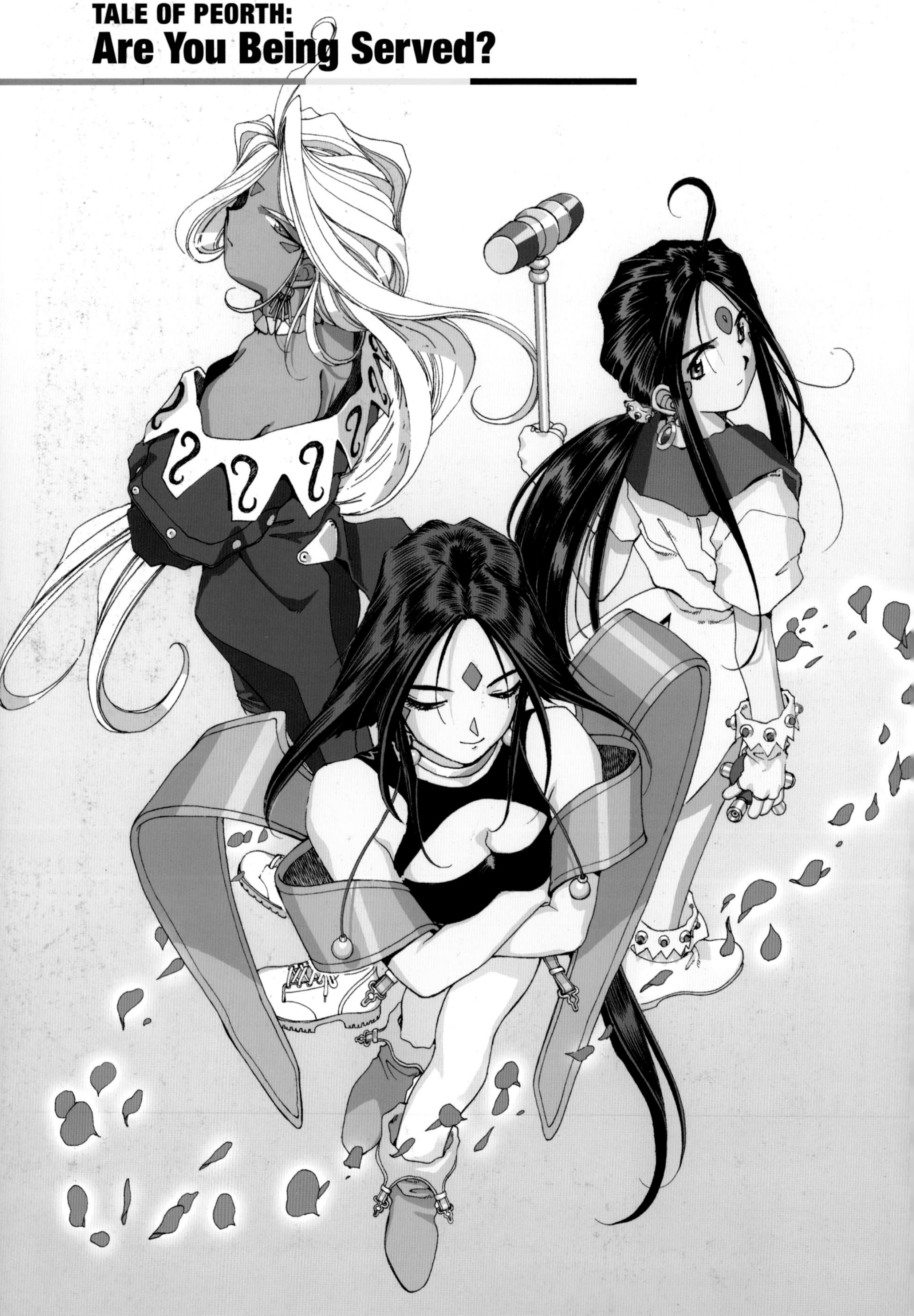

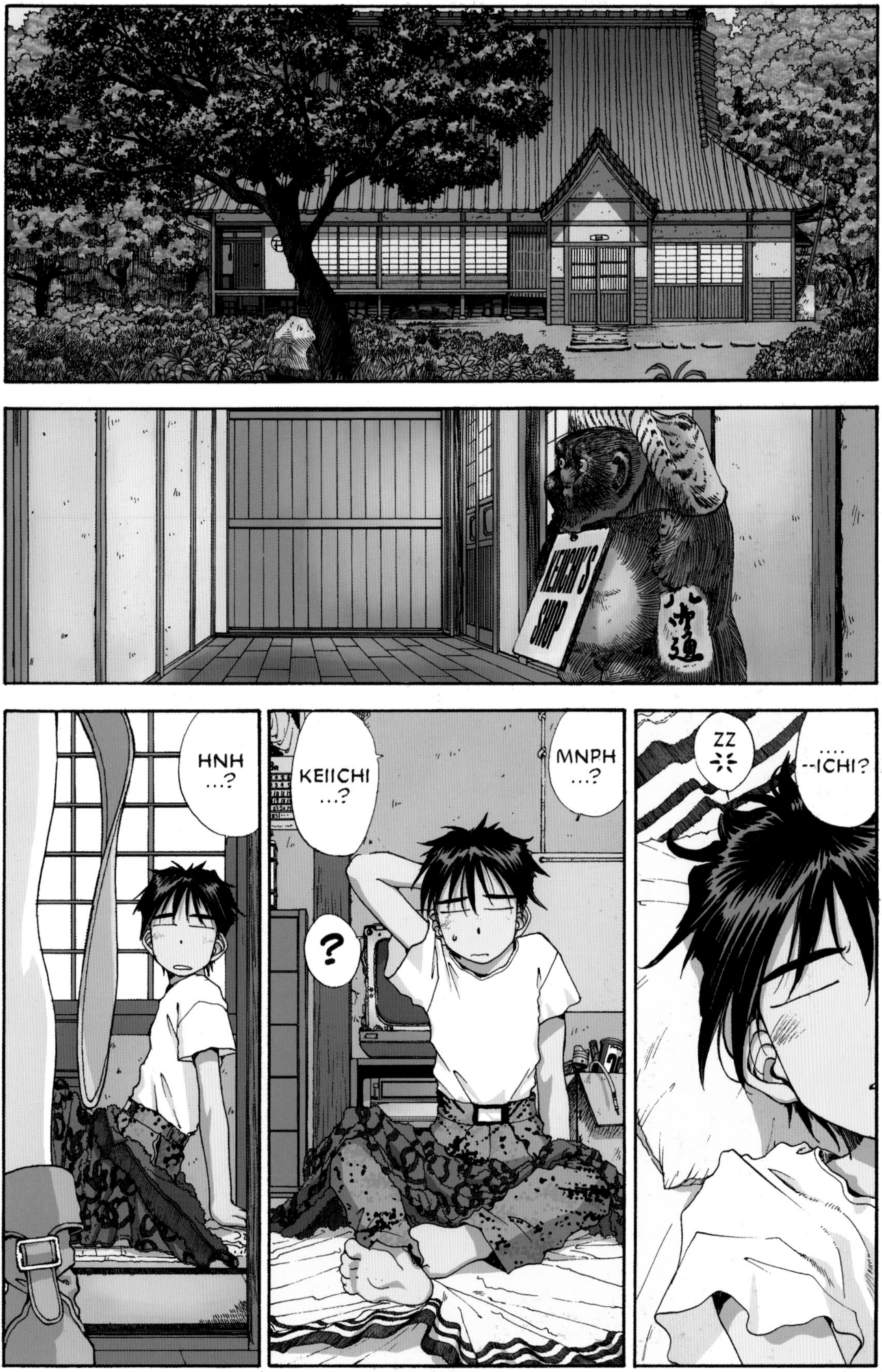
KEIICHI'S SHOP
....
--ICHI?
ZZ
MNPH ...?
KEIICHI ...?
?
HNH ...?

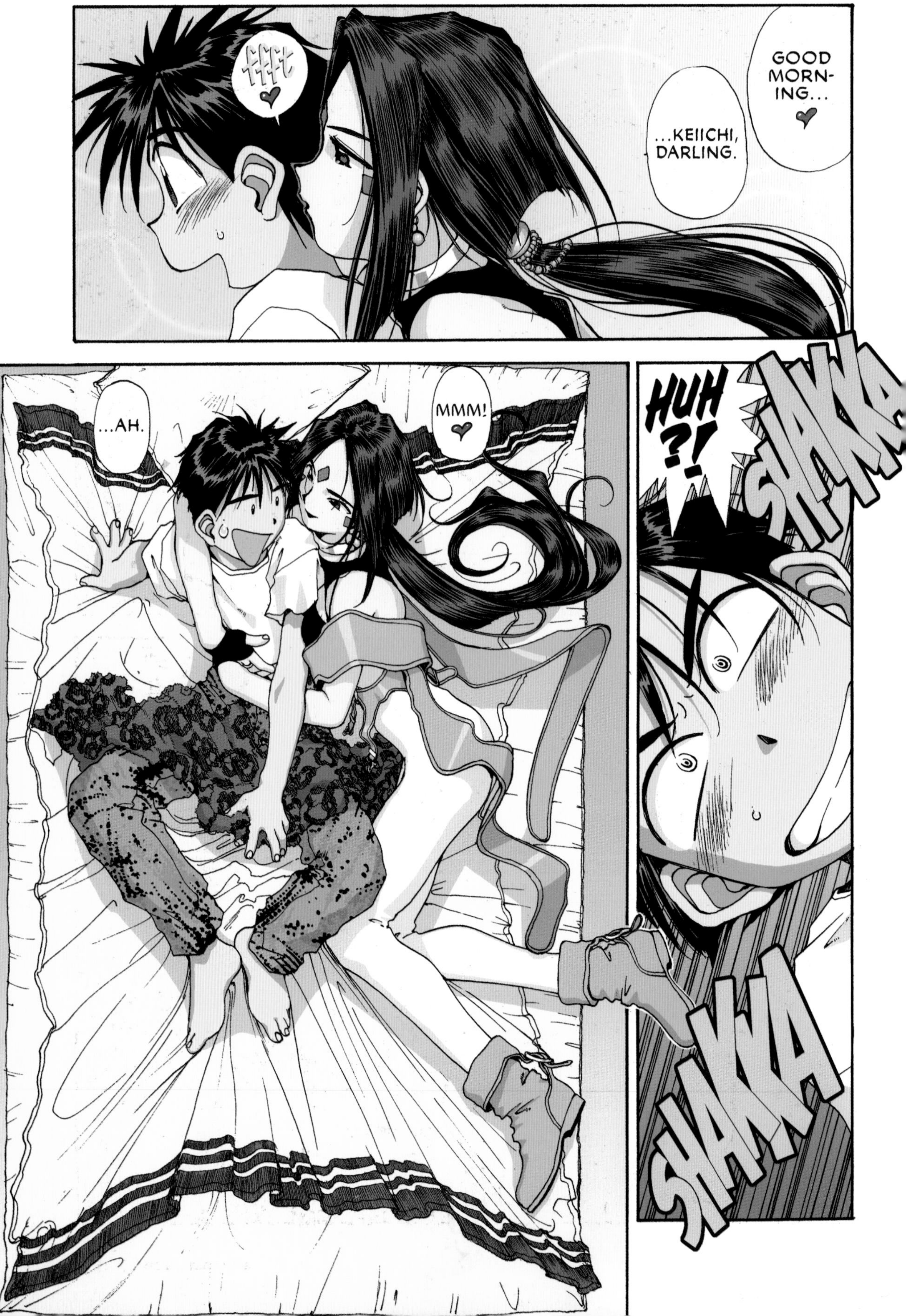
GOOD MORNING-ING... ♥
...KEIICHI, DARLING.
ffft ♥
SHAKA
HUH ?!
SHAKA
MMM! ♥
...AH.

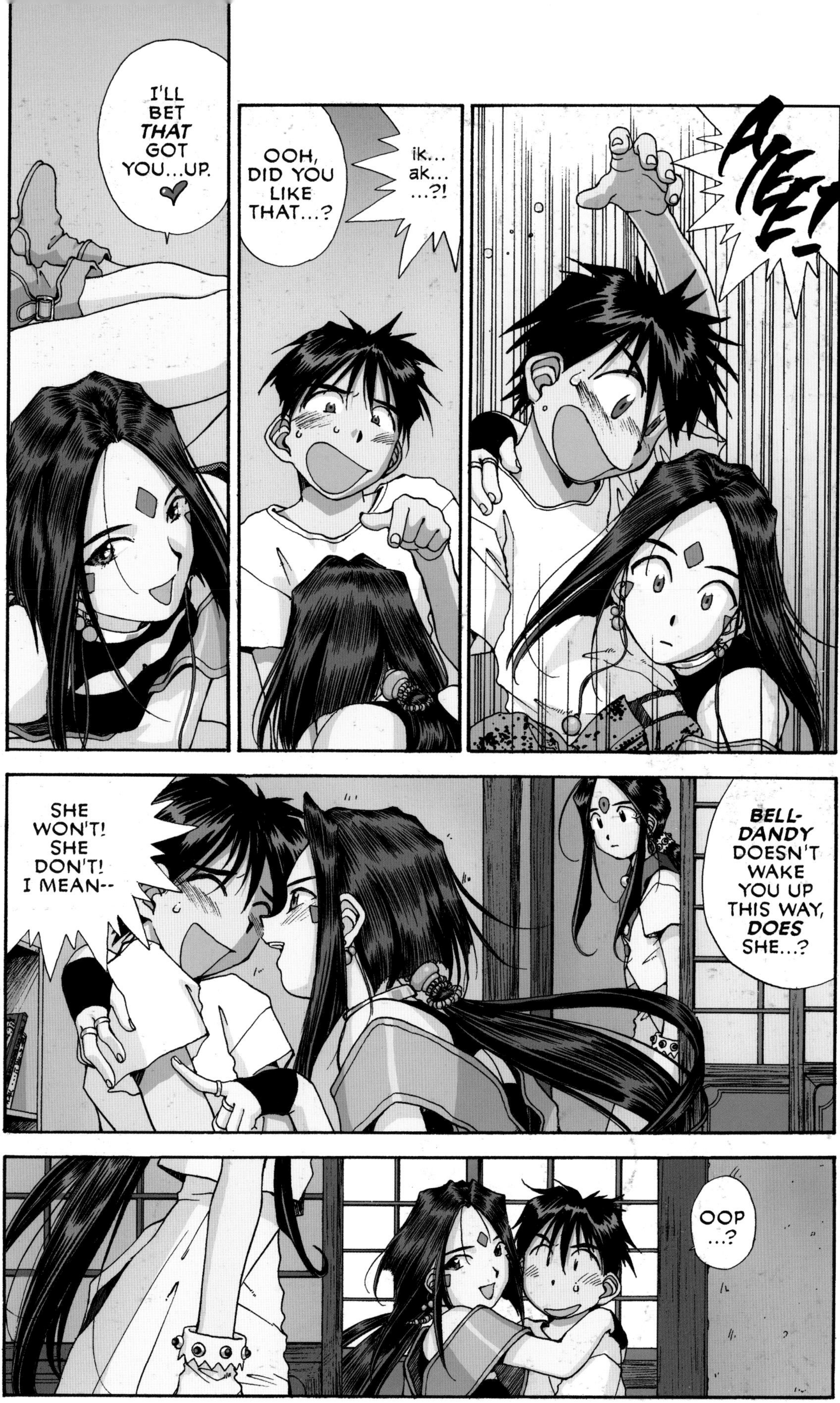
AIEEE!
ik... ak... ...?!
OOH, DID YOU LIKE THAT...?
I'LL BET *THAT* GOT YOU...UP.
BELL-DANDY DOESN'T WAKE YOU UP THIS WAY, *DOES* SHE...?
SHE WON'T! SHE DON'T! I MEAN--
OOP ...?

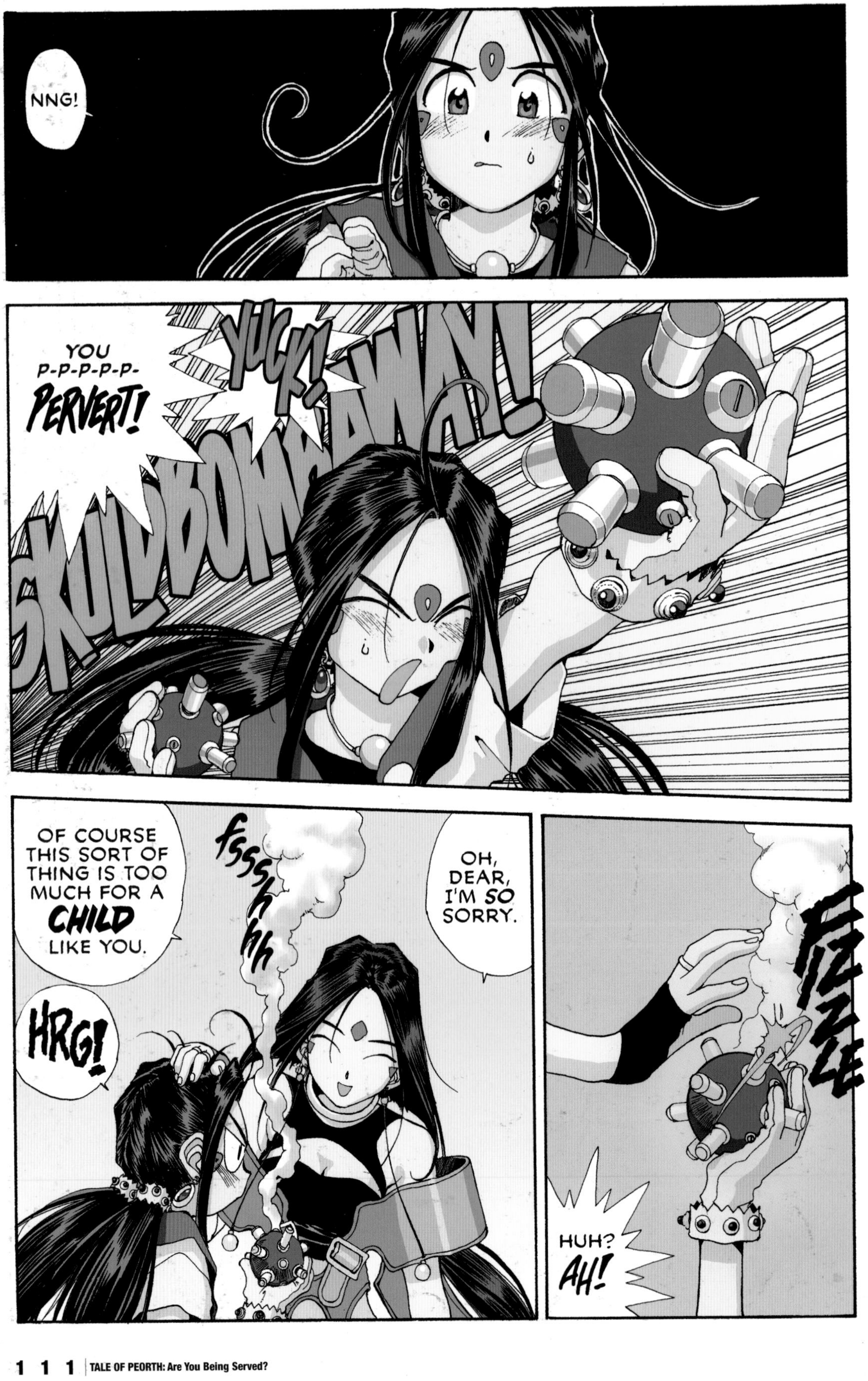
NNG!
YUCK!
SKULDBOMBAWAY!
YOU P-P-P-P-P- PERVERT!
FIZZLE
HUH? AH!
OH, DEAR, I'M SO SORRY.
fssshhh
OF COURSE THIS SORT OF THING IS TOO MUCH FOR A CHILD LIKE YOU.
HRG!

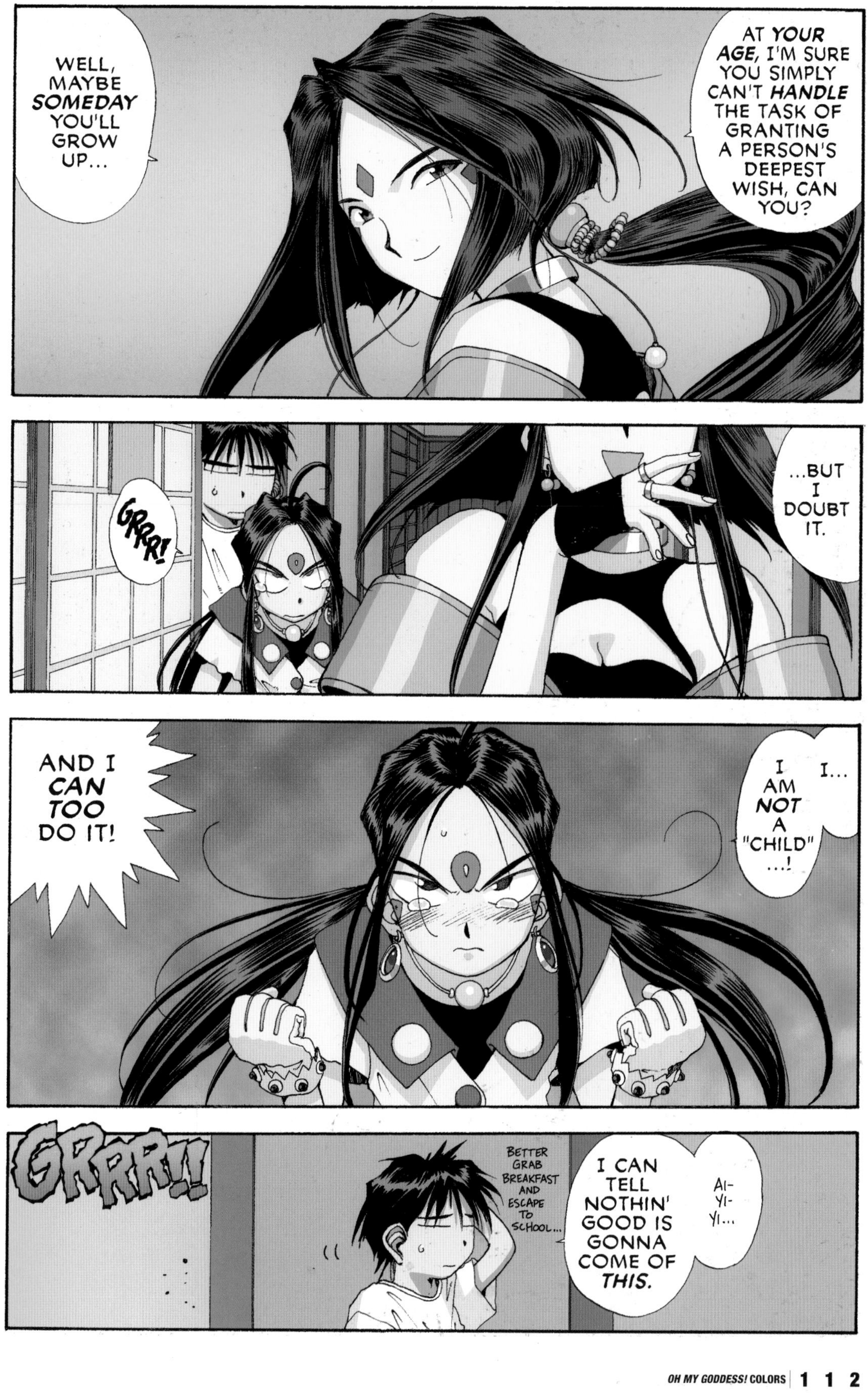
AT YOUR AGE, I'M SURE YOU SIMPLY CAN'T HANDLE THE TASK OF GRANTING A PERSON'S DEEPEST WISH, CAN YOU?
WELL, MAYBE SOMEDAY YOU'LL GROW UP...
...BUT I DOUBT IT.
GRRR!
I...
I AM NOT A "CHILD" ...!
AND I CAN TOO DO IT!
AI-YI-YI...
I CAN TELL NOTHIN' GOOD IS GONNA COME OF THIS.
BETTER GRAB BREAKFAST AND ESCAPE TO SCHOOL...
GRRR!!

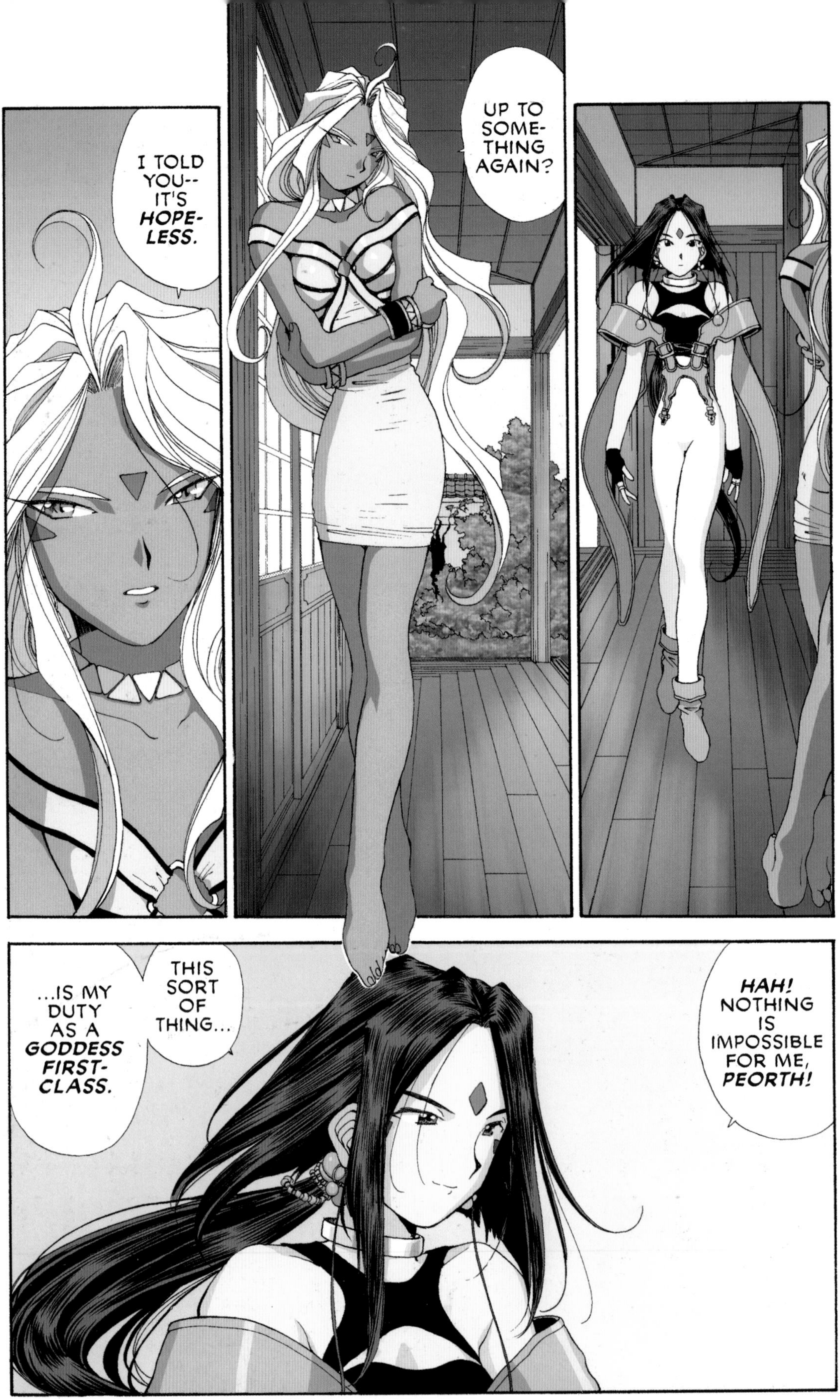
UP TO SOMETHING AGAIN?
I TOLD YOU-- IT'S *HOPELESS.*
HAH! NOTHING IS IMPOSSIBLE FOR ME, *PEORTH!*
THIS SORT OF THING...
...IS MY DUTY AS A *GODDESS FIRST-CLASS.*

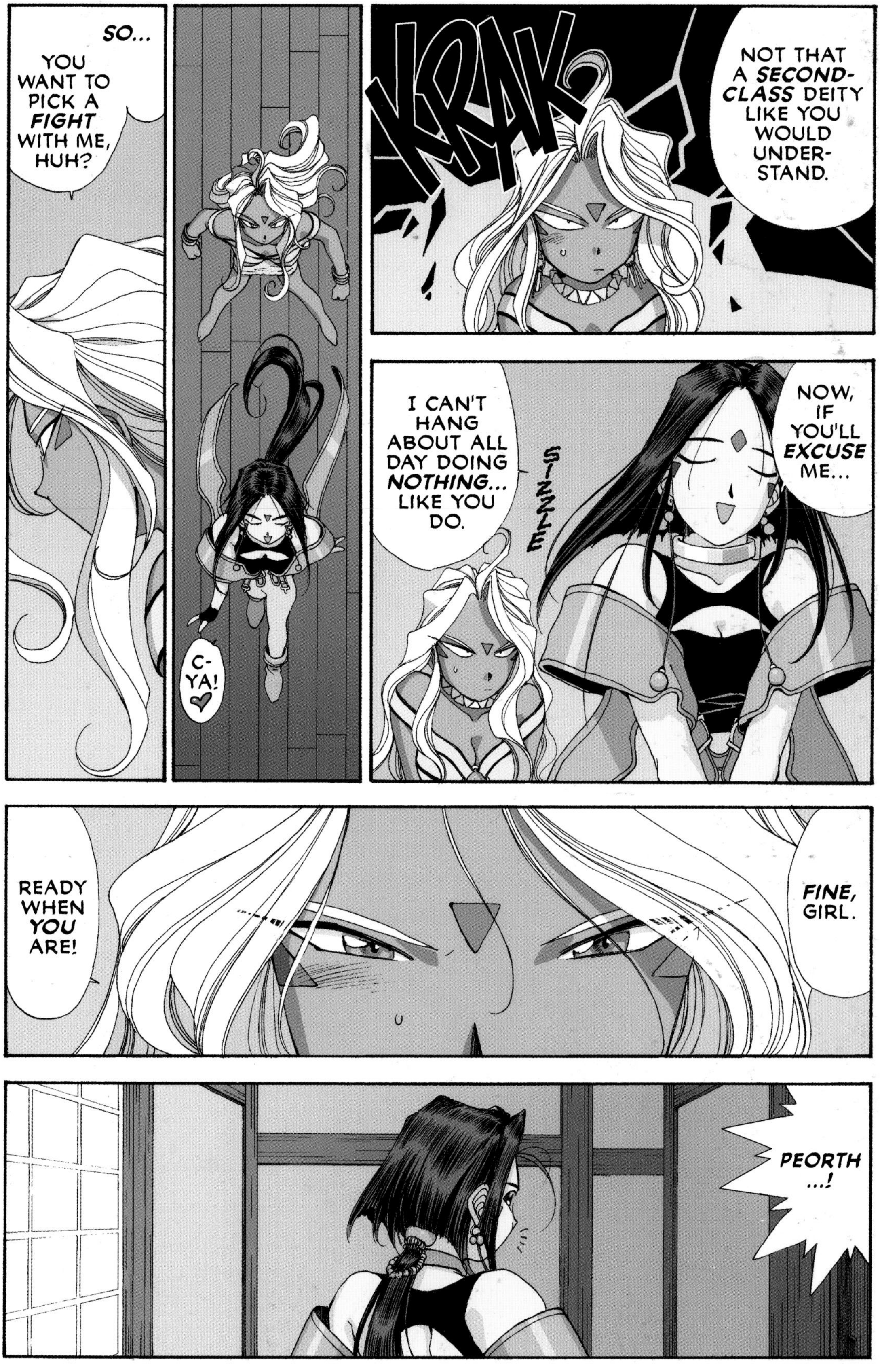
NOT THAT A SECOND-CLASS DEITY LIKE YOU WOULD UNDERSTAND.
KRAK
NOW, IF YOU'LL EXCUSE ME...
I CAN'T HANG ABOUT ALL DAY DOING NOTHING... LIKE YOU DO.
SIZZLE
C-YA! ♥
SO...
YOU WANT TO PICK A FIGHT WITH ME, HUH?
FINE, GIRL.
READY WHEN YOU ARE!
PEORTH ...!

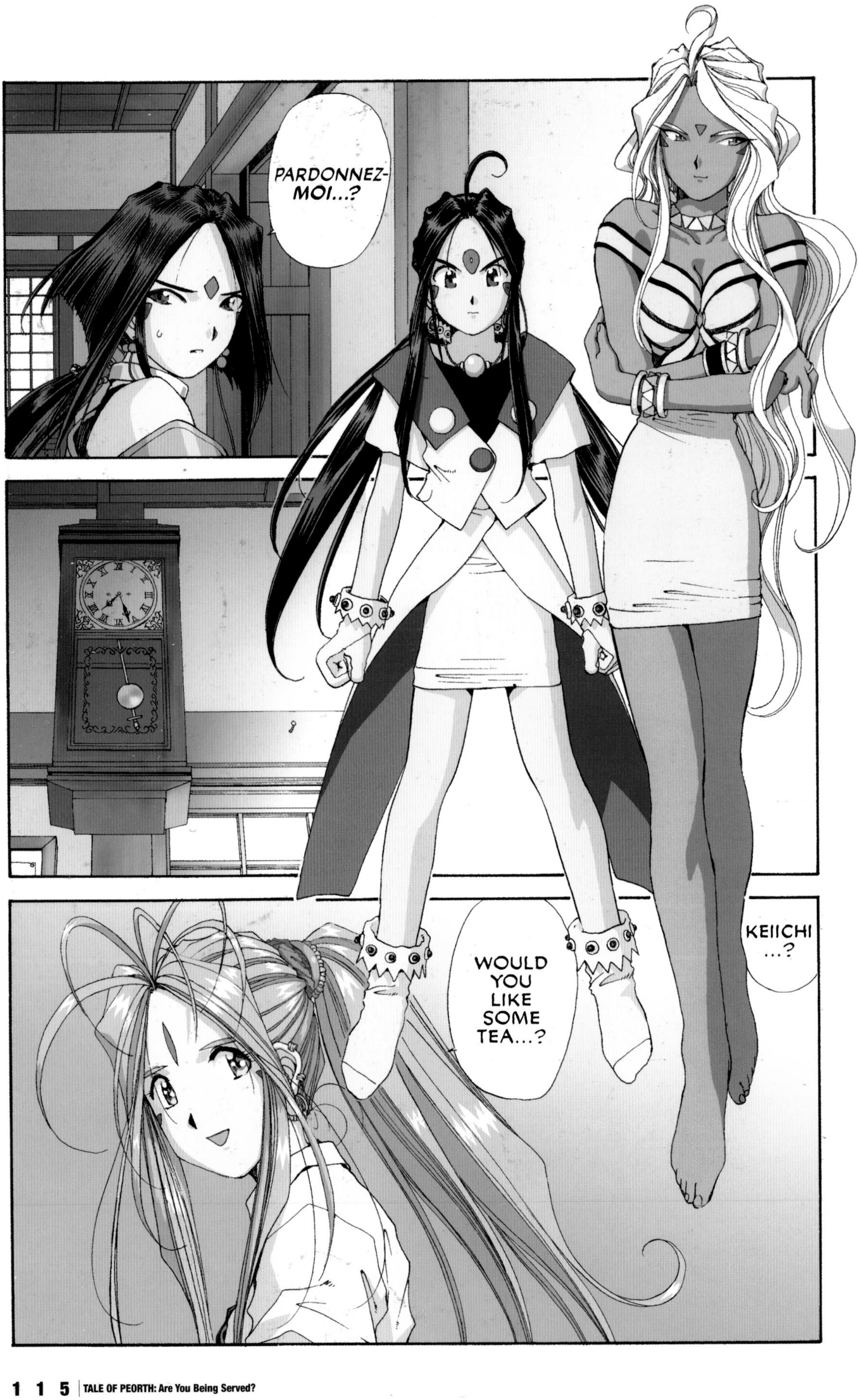
PARDONNEZ-MOI...?
KEIICHI ...?
WOULD YOU LIKE SOME TEA...?

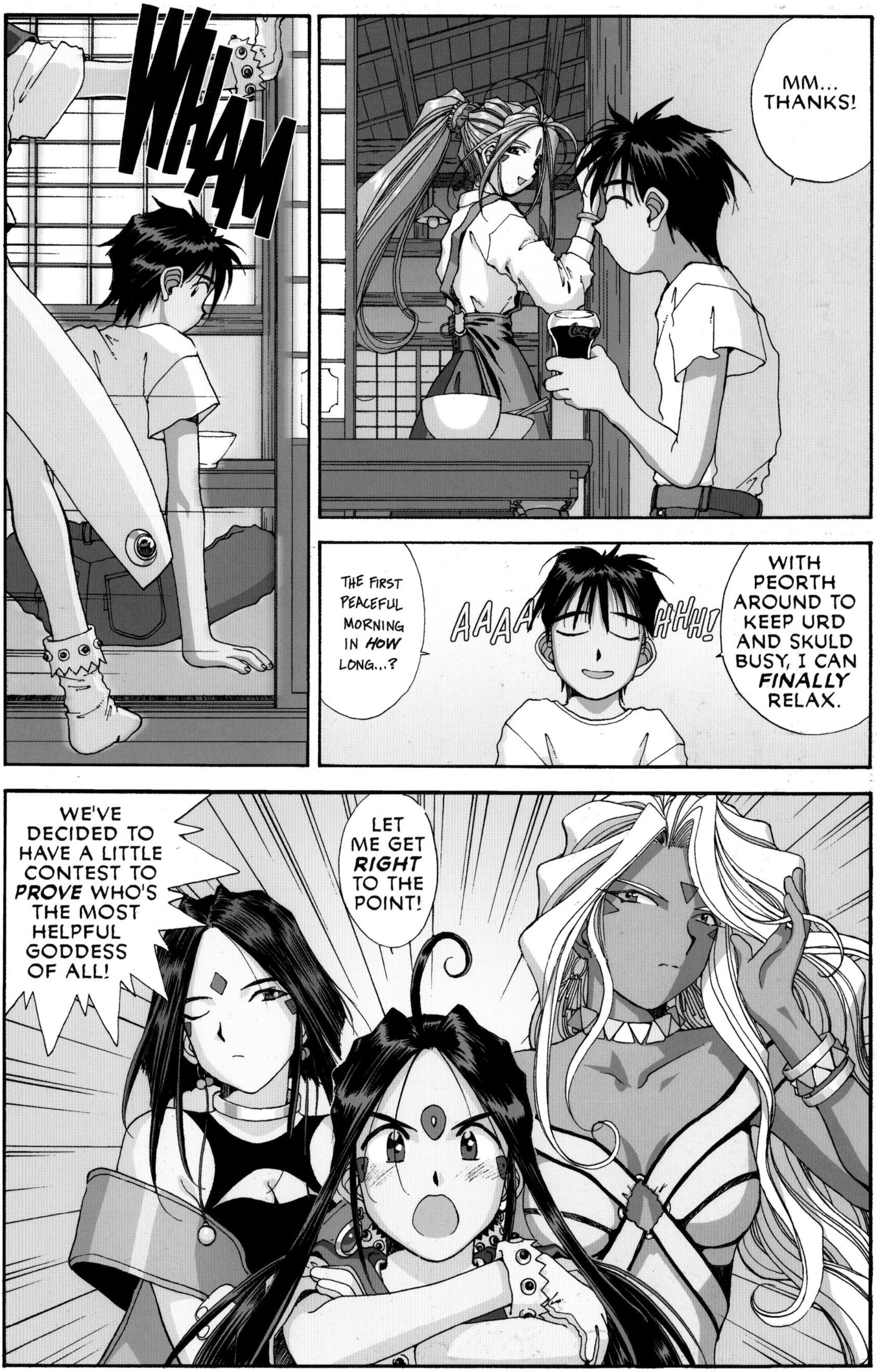
MM... THANKS!
WITH PEORTH AROUND TO KEEP URD AND SKULD BUSY, I CAN FINALLY RELAX.
AAAAHHH!
THE FIRST PEACEFUL MORNING IN HOW LONG...?
WHAM
LET ME GET RIGHT TO THE POINT!
WE'VE DECIDED TO HAVE A LITTLE CONTEST TO PROVE WHO'S THE MOST HELPFUL GODDESS OF ALL!

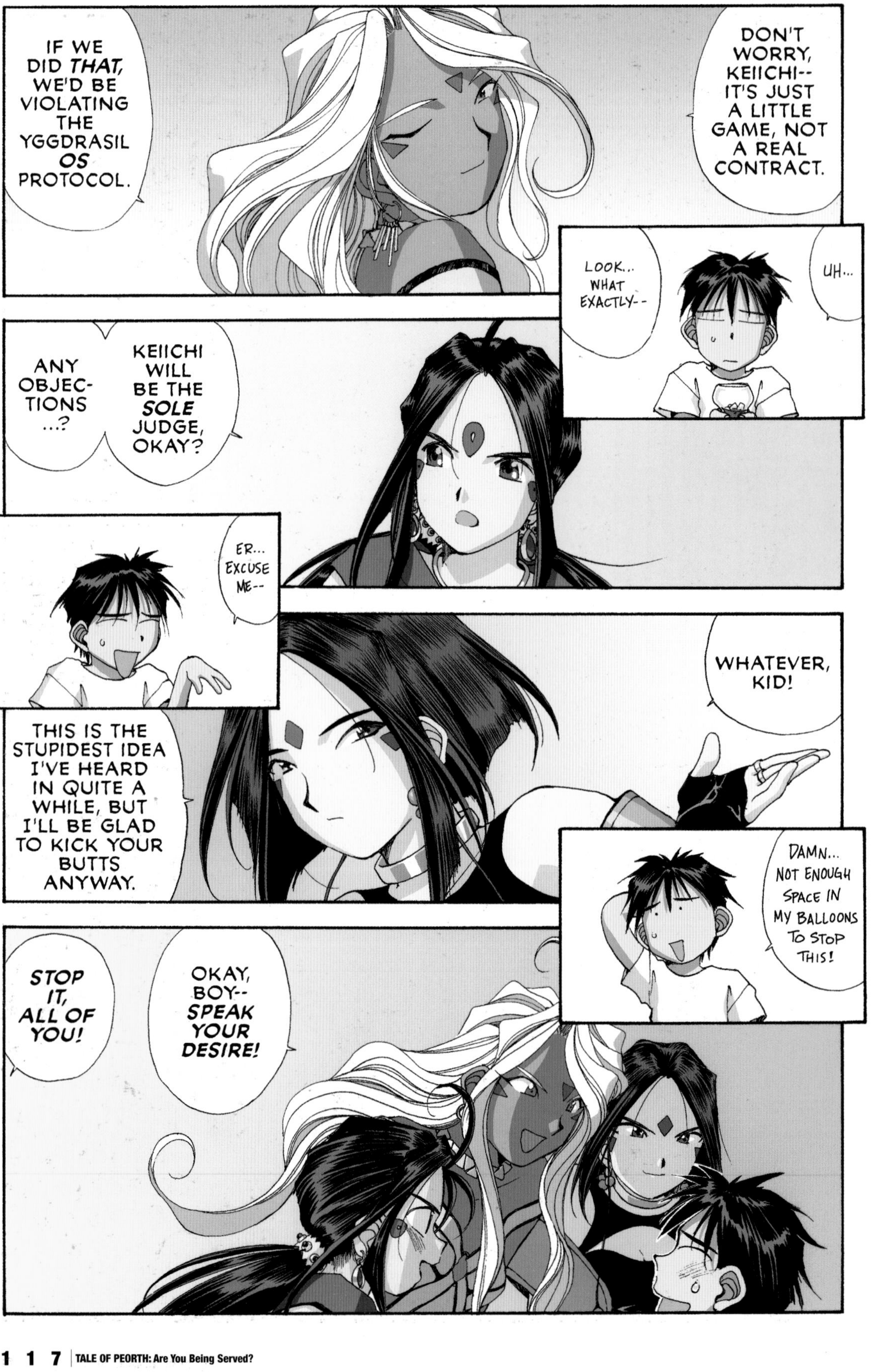
DON'T WORRY, KEIICHI-- IT'S JUST A LITTLE GAME, NOT A REAL CONTRACT.
IF WE DID *THAT*, WE'D BE VIOLATING THE YGGDRASIL *OS* PROTOCOL.
UH...
LOOK... WHAT EXACTLY--
KEIICHI WILL BE THE *SOLE* JUDGE, OKAY?
ANY OBJECTIONS ...?
ER... EXCUSE ME--
WHATEVER, KID!
THIS IS THE STUPIDEST IDEA I'VE HEARD IN QUITE A WHILE, BUT I'LL BE GLAD TO KICK YOUR BUTTS ANYWAY.
DAMN... NOT ENOUGH SPACE IN MY BALLOONS TO STOP THIS!
OKAY, BOY-- *SPEAK YOUR DESIRE!*
STOP IT, ALL OF YOU!

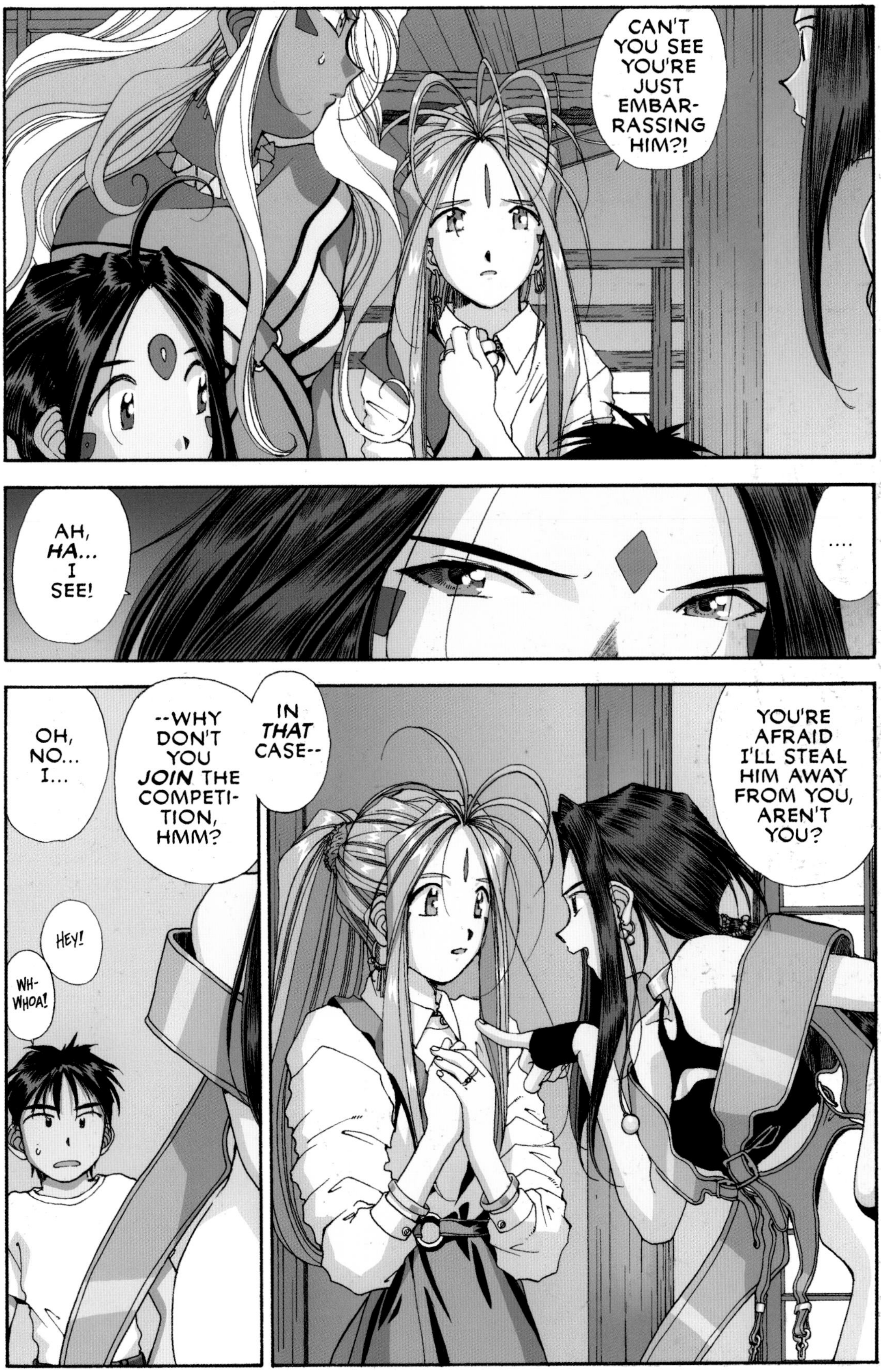
CAN'T YOU SEE YOU'RE JUST EMBARRASSING HIM?!
....
AH, *HA...* I SEE!
YOU'RE AFRAID I'LL STEAL HIM AWAY FROM YOU, AREN'T YOU?
IN *THAT* CASE--
--WHY DON'T YOU *JOIN* THE COMPETITION, HMM?
OH, NO... I...
HEY!
WH-WHOA!

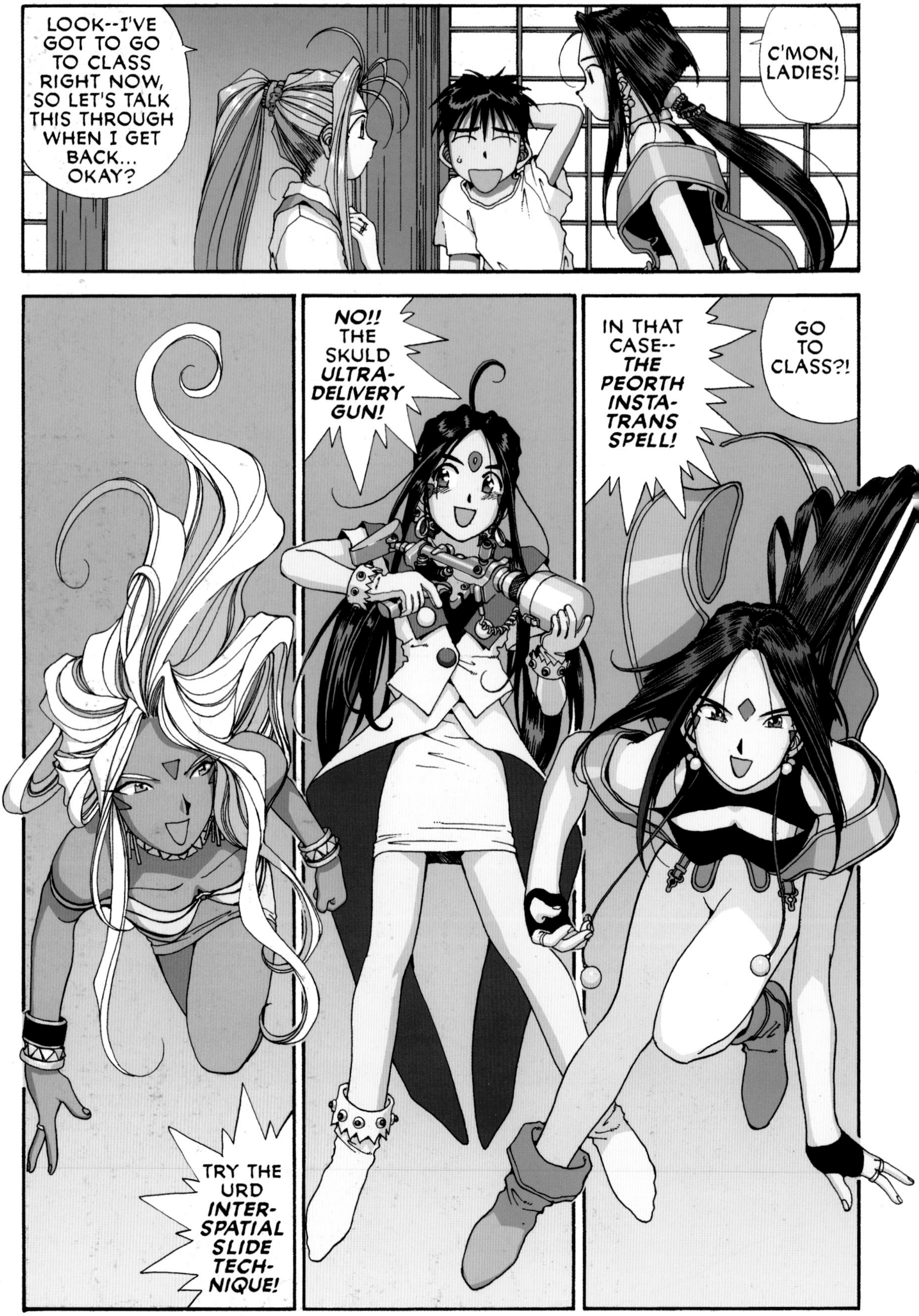
C'MON, LADIES!
LOOK--I'VE GOT TO GO TO CLASS RIGHT NOW, SO LET'S TALK THIS THROUGH WHEN I GET BACK... OKAY?
GO TO CLASS?!
IN THAT CASE-- THE PEORTH INSTA-TRANS SPELL!
NO!! THE SKULD ULTRA-DELIVERY GUN!
TRY THE URD INTER-SPATIAL SLIDE TECHNIQUE!

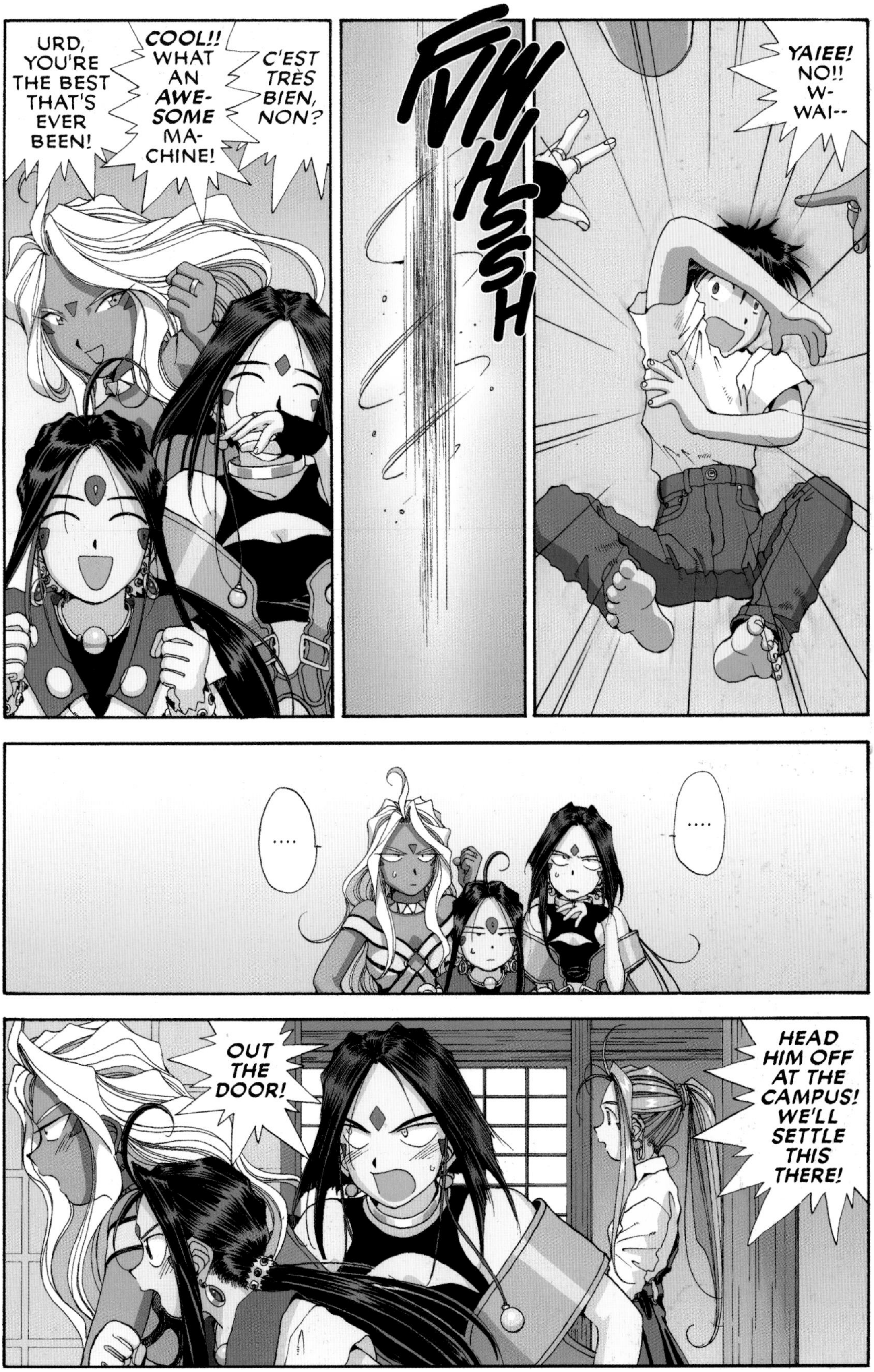
YAIEE! NO!! W-WAI--
FWHSSH
C'EST TRÈS BIEN, NON?
COOL!! WHAT AN AWESOME MACHINE!
URD, YOU'RE THE BEST THAT'S EVER BEEN!
....
....
HEAD HIM OFF AT THE CAMPUS! WE'LL SETTLE THIS THERE!
OUT THE DOOR!

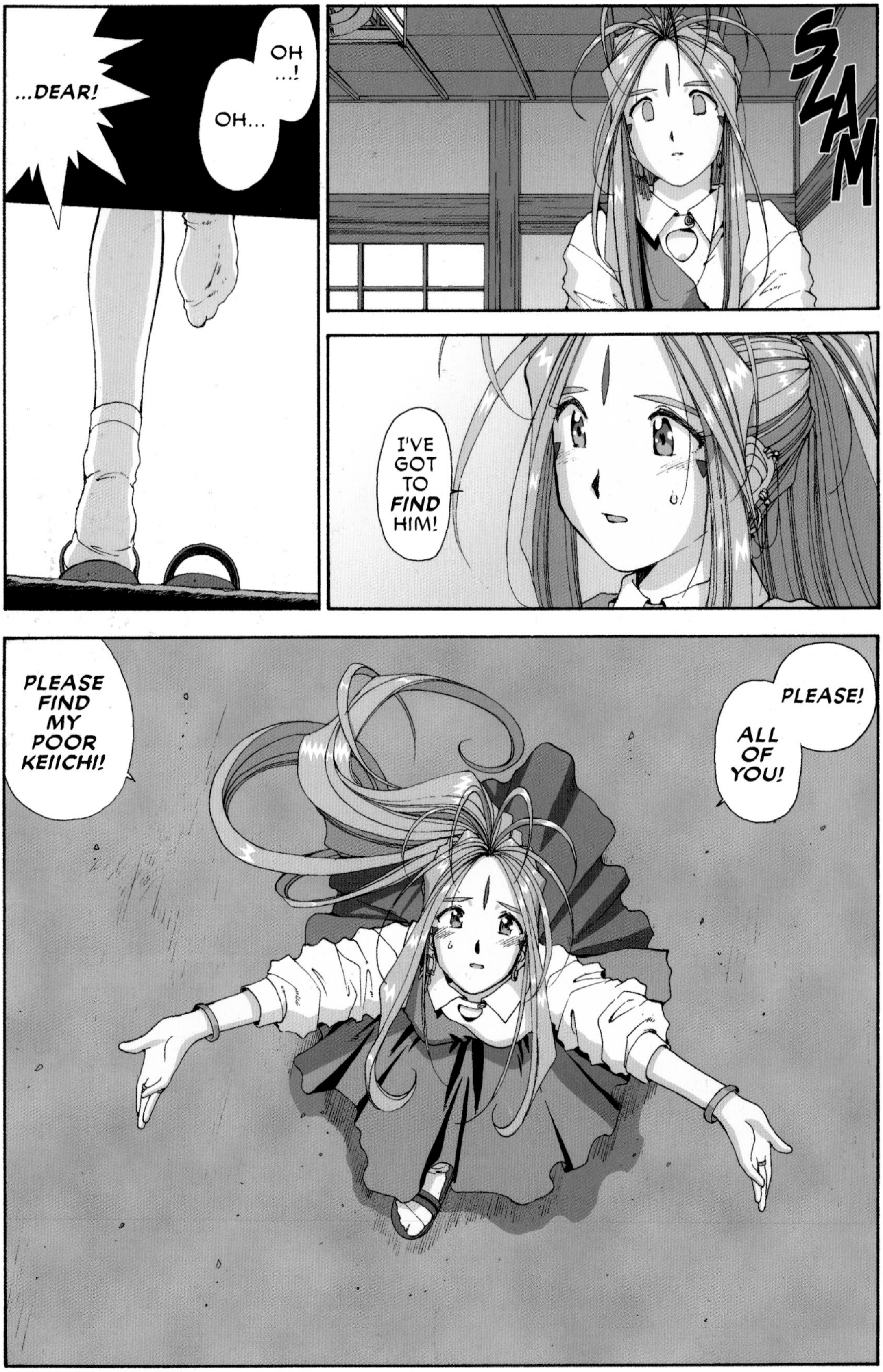
SLAM
I'VE GOT TO FIND HIM!
OH ...!
OH...
...DEAR!
PLEASE!
ALL OF YOU!
PLEASE FIND MY POOR KEIICHI!

PLEASE!

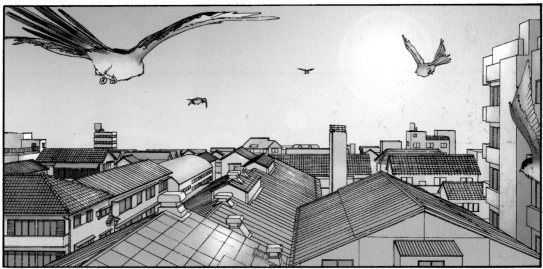

N.I.T....

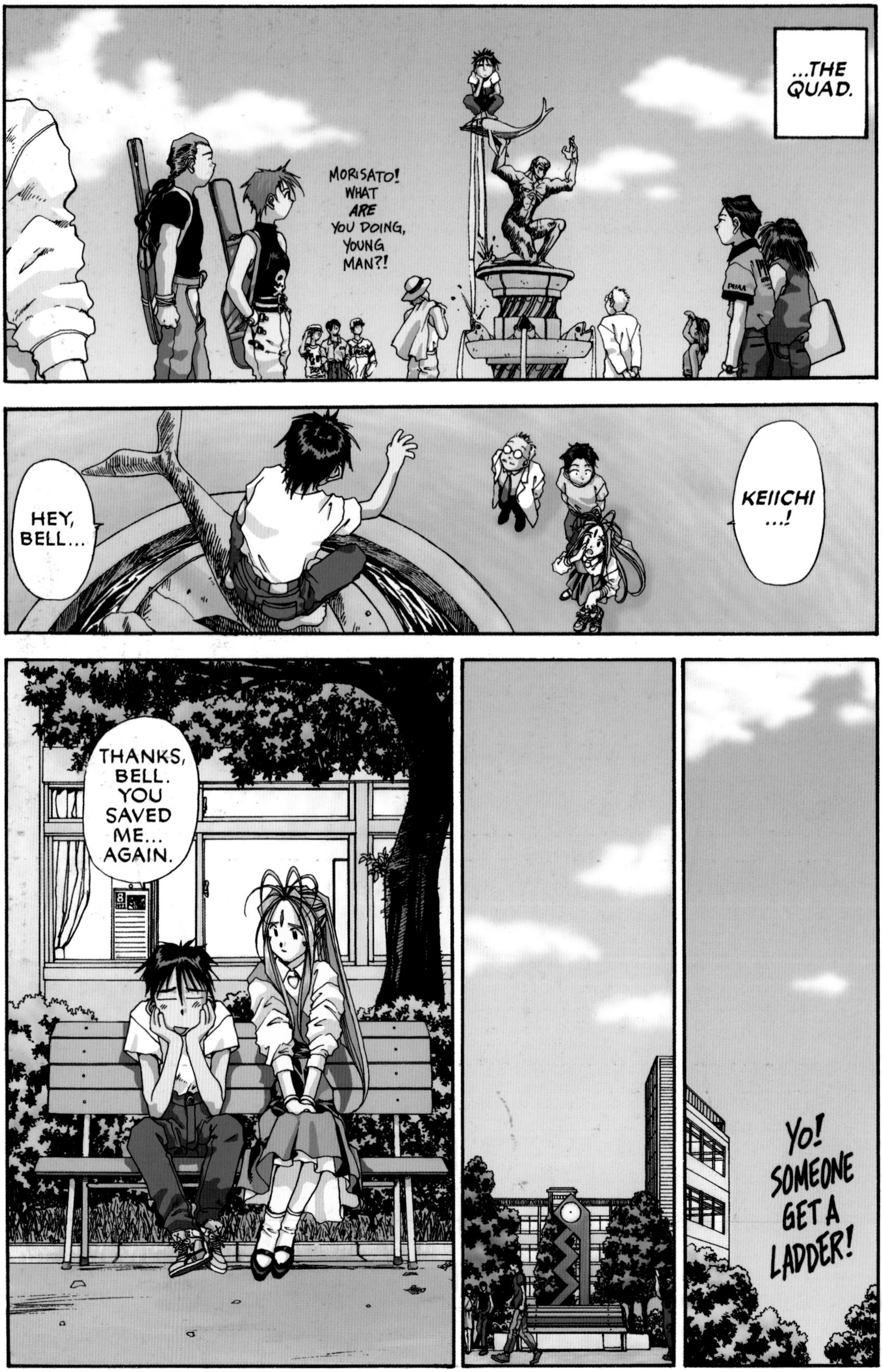
...THE QUAD.
MORISATO! WHAT ARE YOU DOING, YOUNG MAN?!
KEIICHI ...!
HEY, BELL...
YO! SOMEONE GET A LADDER!
THANKS, BELL. YOU SAVED ME... AGAIN.

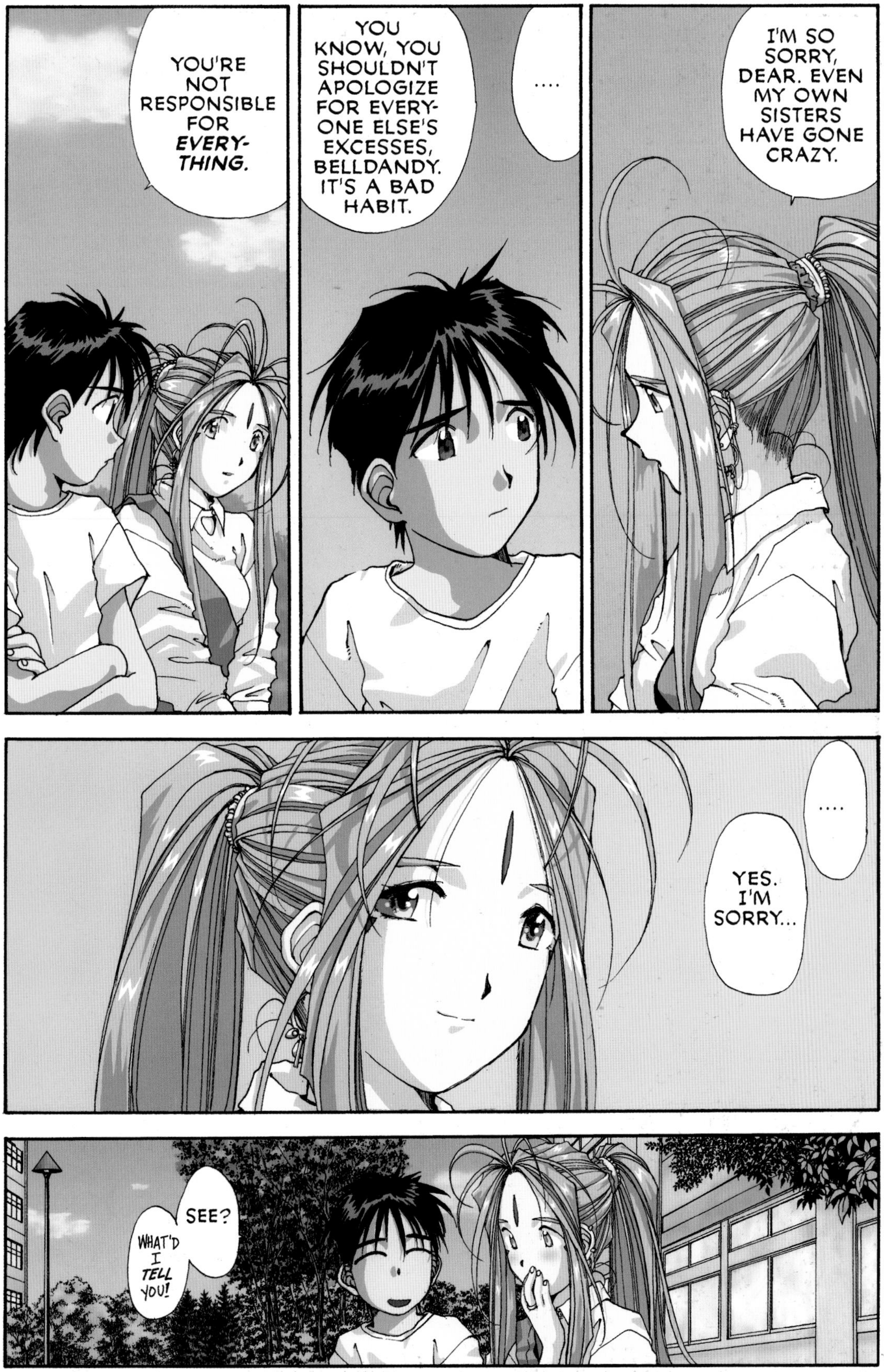
I'M SO SORRY, DEAR. EVEN MY OWN SISTERS HAVE GONE CRAZY.
....
YOU KNOW, YOU SHOULDN'T APOLOGIZE FOR EVERYONE ELSE'S EXCESSES, BELLDANDY. IT'S A BAD HABIT.
YOU'RE NOT RESPONSIBLE FOR *EVERYTHING.*
....
YES. I'M SORRY...
SEE?
WHAT'D I *TELL* YOU!

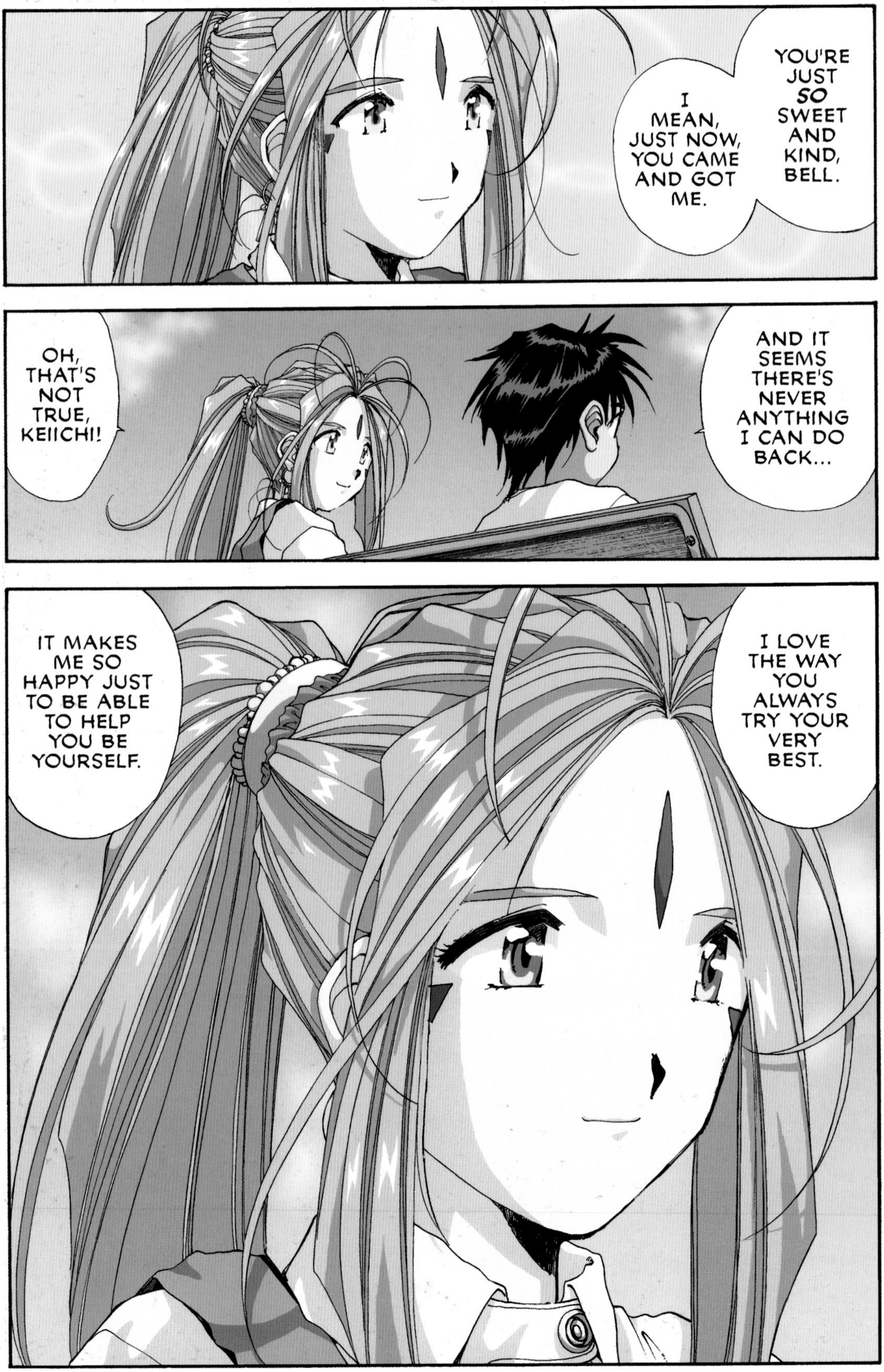
YOU'RE JUST *SO* SWEET AND KIND, BELL.
I MEAN, JUST NOW, YOU CAME AND GOT ME.
AND IT SEEMS THERE'S NEVER ANYTHING I CAN DO BACK...
OH, THAT'S NOT TRUE, KEIICHI!
I LOVE THE WAY YOU ALWAYS TRY YOUR VERY BEST.
IT MAKES ME SO HAPPY JUST TO BE ABLE TO HELP YOU BE YOURSELF.

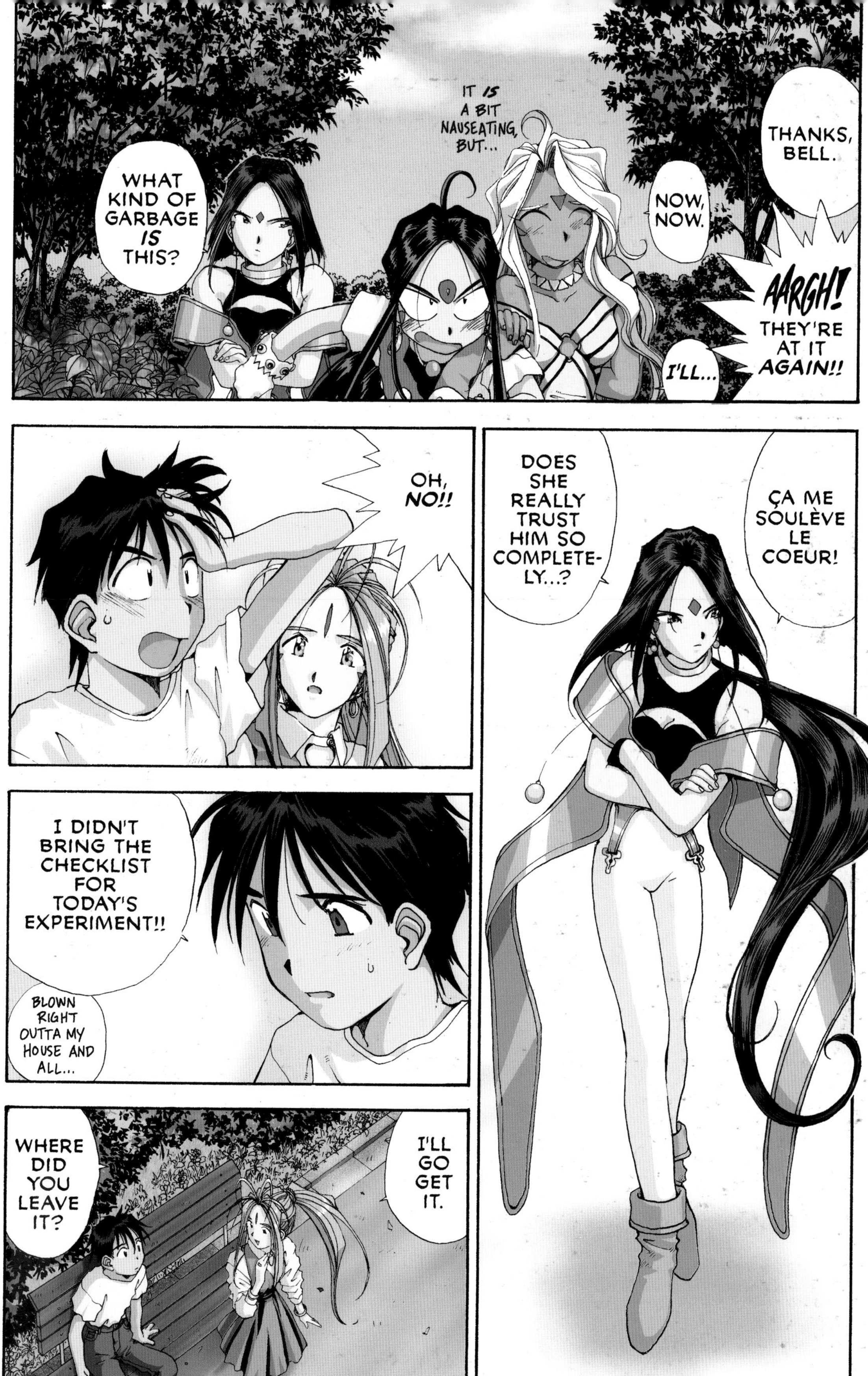
THANKS, BELL.
AARGH! THEY'RE AT IT AGAIN!!
IT IS A BIT NAUSEATING, BUT...
NOW, NOW.
I'LL...
WHAT KIND OF GARBAGE IS THIS?
ÇA ME SOULÈVE LE COEUR!
DOES SHE REALLY TRUST HIM SO COMPLETE-LY...?
OH, NO!!
I DIDN'T BRING THE CHECKLIST FOR TODAY'S EXPERIMENT!!
BLOWN RIGHT OUTTA MY HOUSE AND ALL...
I'LL GO GET IT.
WHERE DID YOU LEAVE IT?

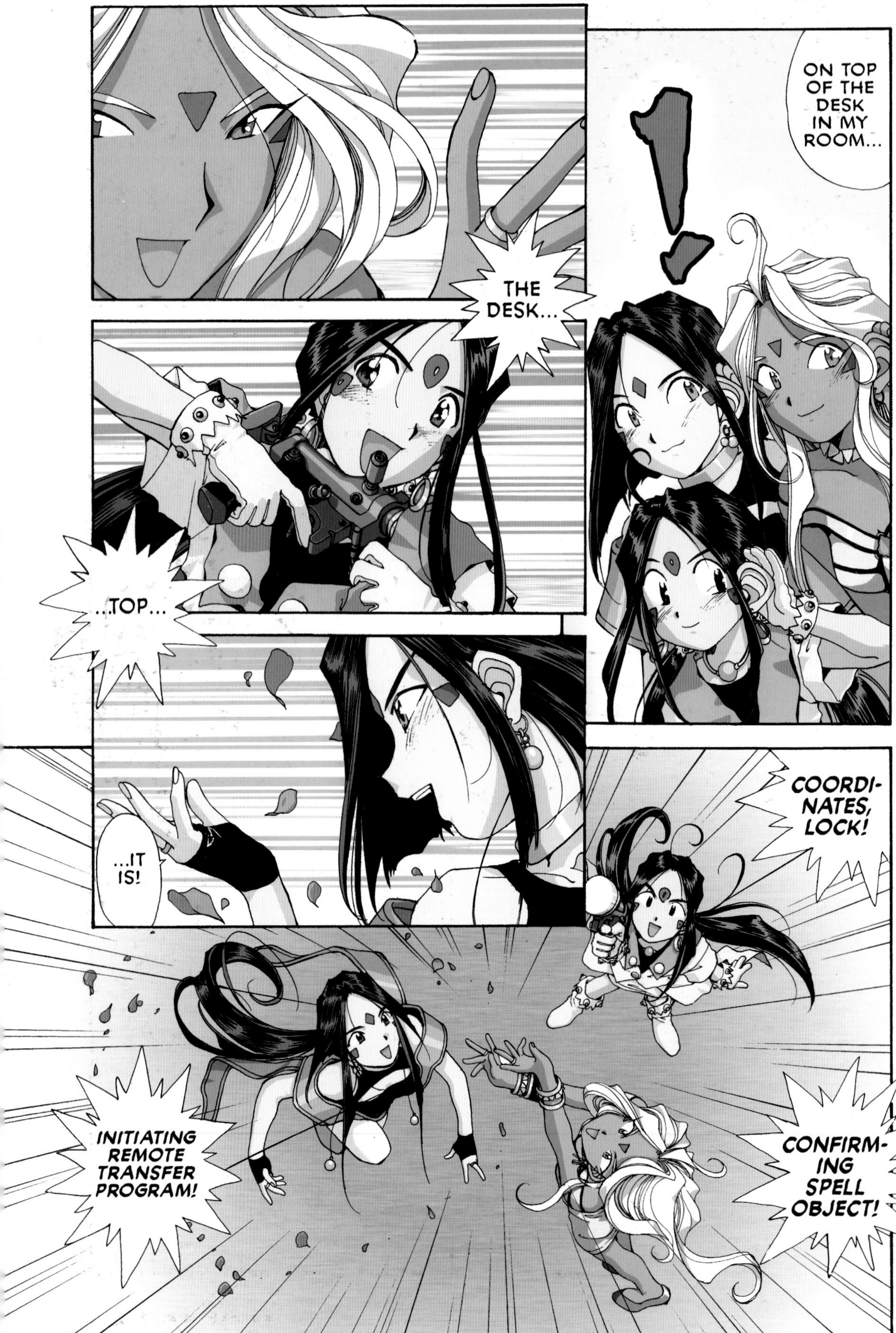
ON TOP OF THE DESK IN MY ROOM...
THE DESK...
...TOP...
...IT IS!
COORDI-NATES, LOCK!
CONFIRM-ING SPELL OBJECT!
INITIATING REMOTE TRANSFER PROGRAM!

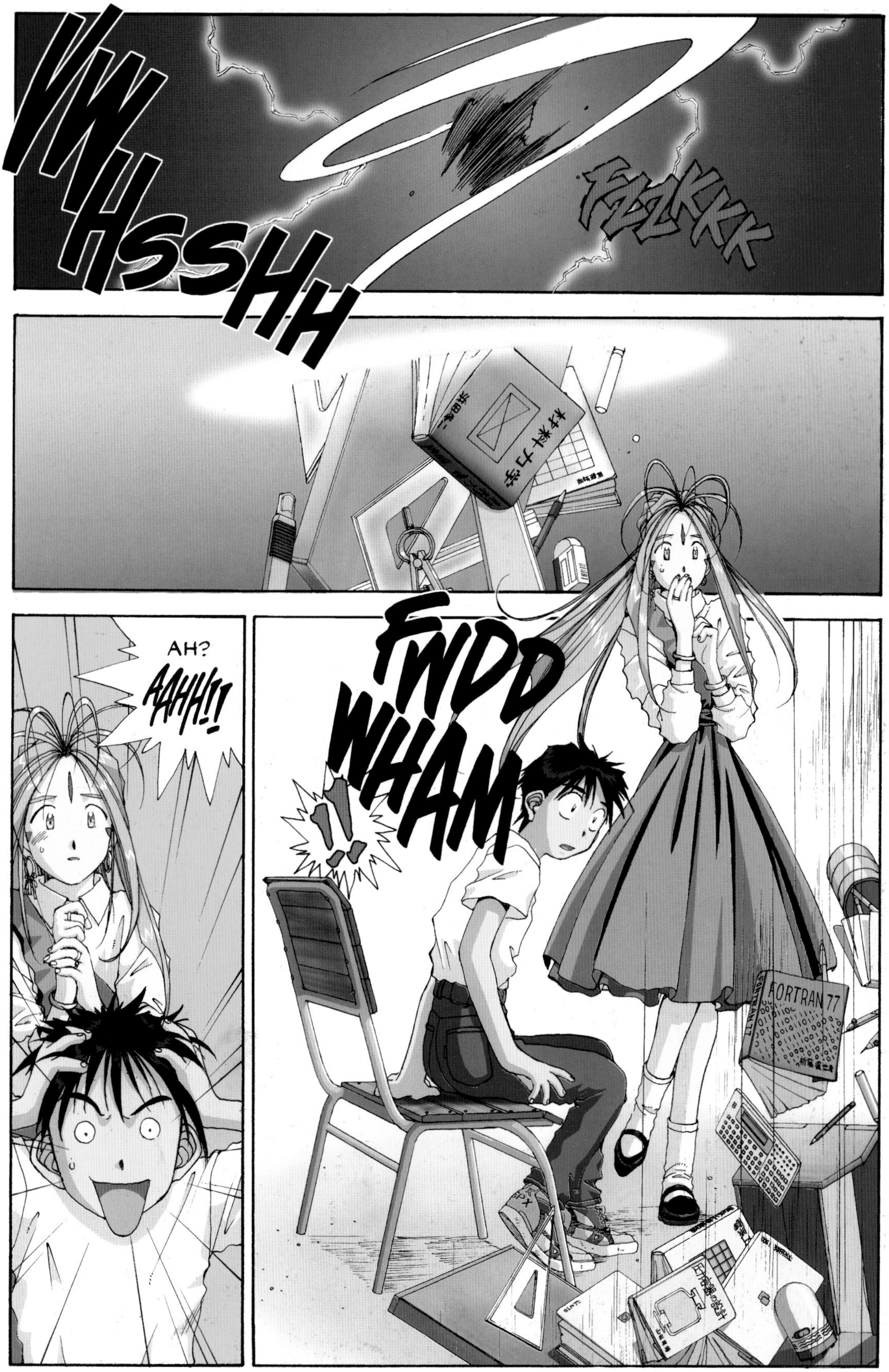
VWHSSHH
FZZKKK
FWDD
WHAM
FORTRAN 77
AH?
AAHH!!

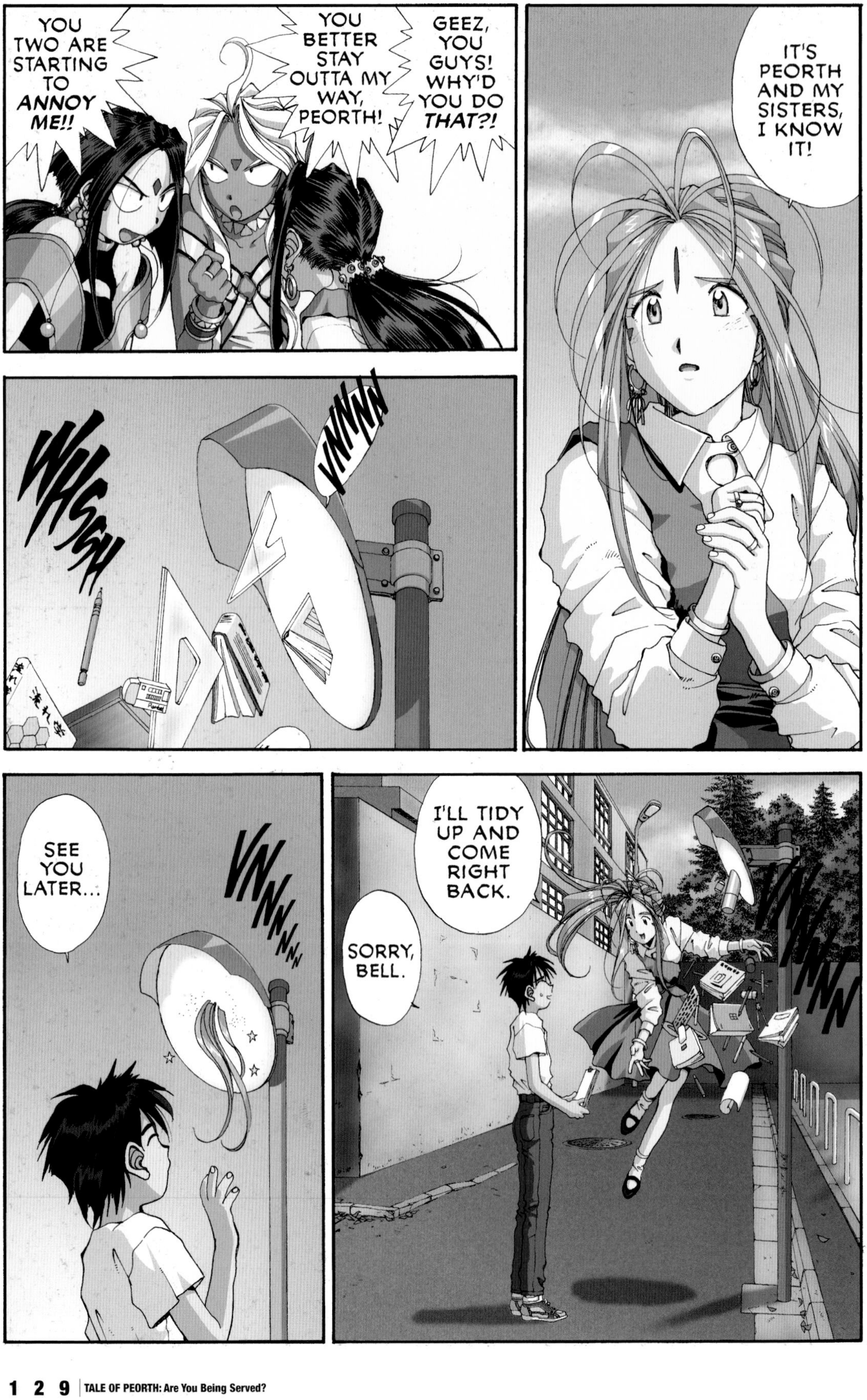
IT'S PEORTH AND MY SISTERS, I KNOW IT!
GEEZ, YOU GUYS! WHY'D YOU DO THAT?!
YOU BETTER STAY OUTTA MY WAY, PEORTH!
YOU TWO ARE STARTING TO ANNOY ME!!
VNNNN
I'LL TIDY UP AND COME RIGHT BACK.
SORRY, BELL.
SEE YOU LATER...

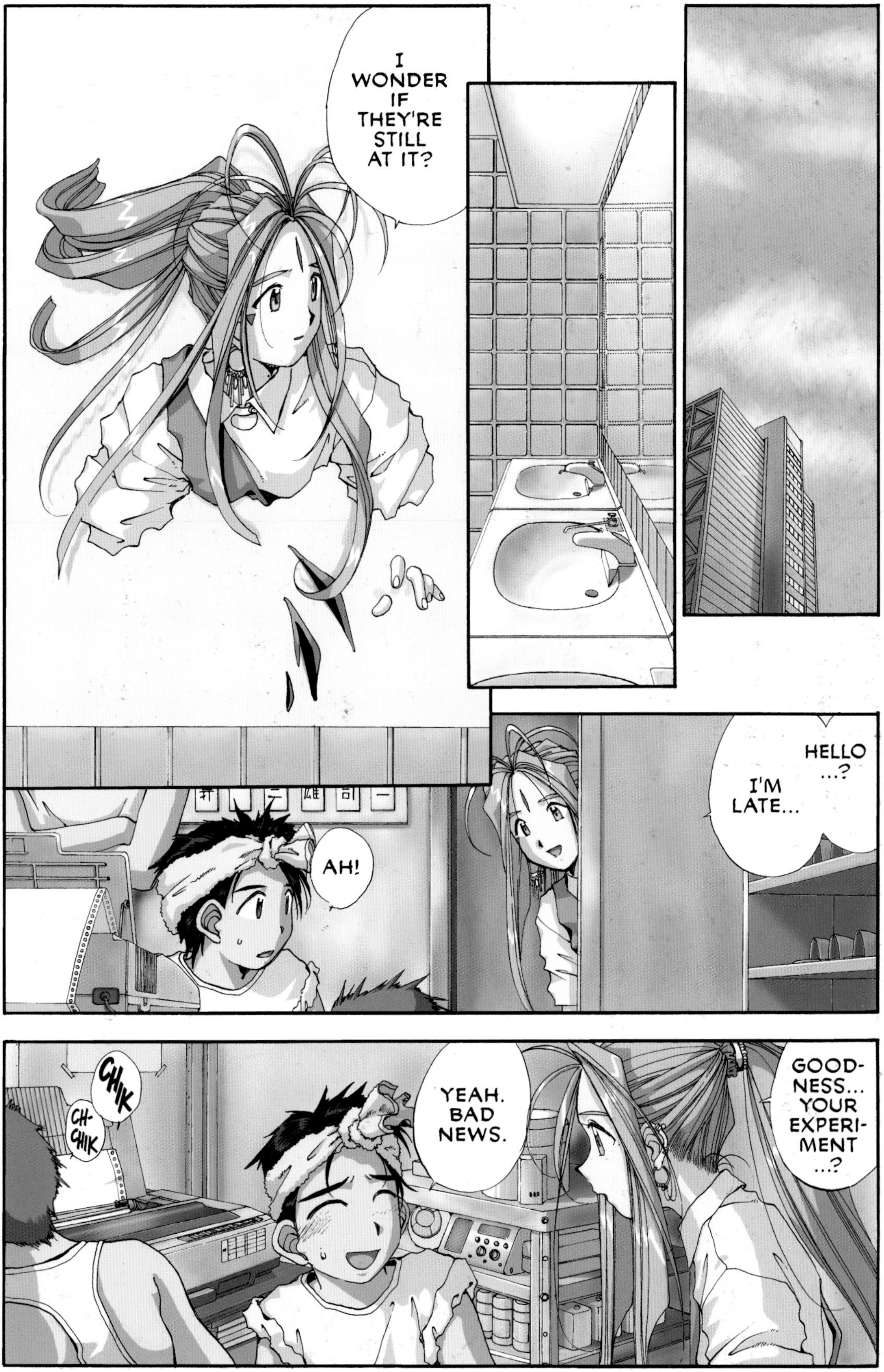
I WONDER IF THEY'RE STILL AT IT?
HELLO ...? I'M LATE...
AH!
GOOD-NESS... YOUR EXPERI-MENT ...?
YEAH. BAD NEWS.
CHIK
CH-CHIK

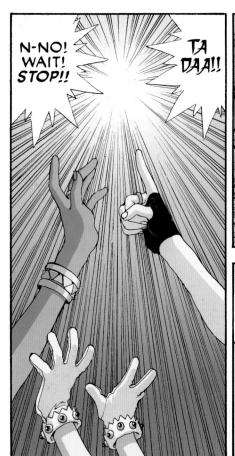

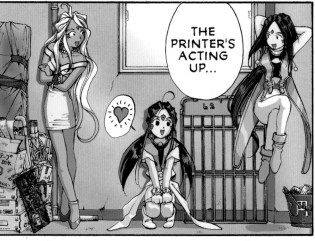

THE PRINTER'S ACTING UP...
MACHINE PROB-LEMS! LEAVE IT TO ME!
NO WAY, SIS! ME, TOO!
TA DAA!!
N-NO! WAIT! STOP!!
CH-CHIK
CH-CHIK
CHIK
HUH...? IT'S WORK-ING...?
ZREEE
ZREEE
ZREEEE
!!

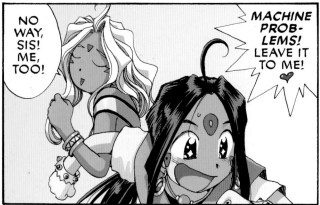

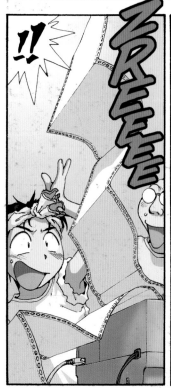

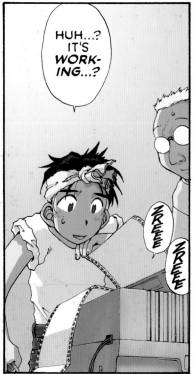

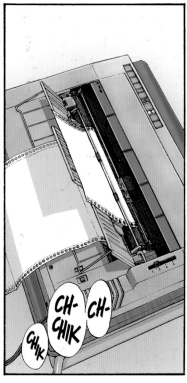

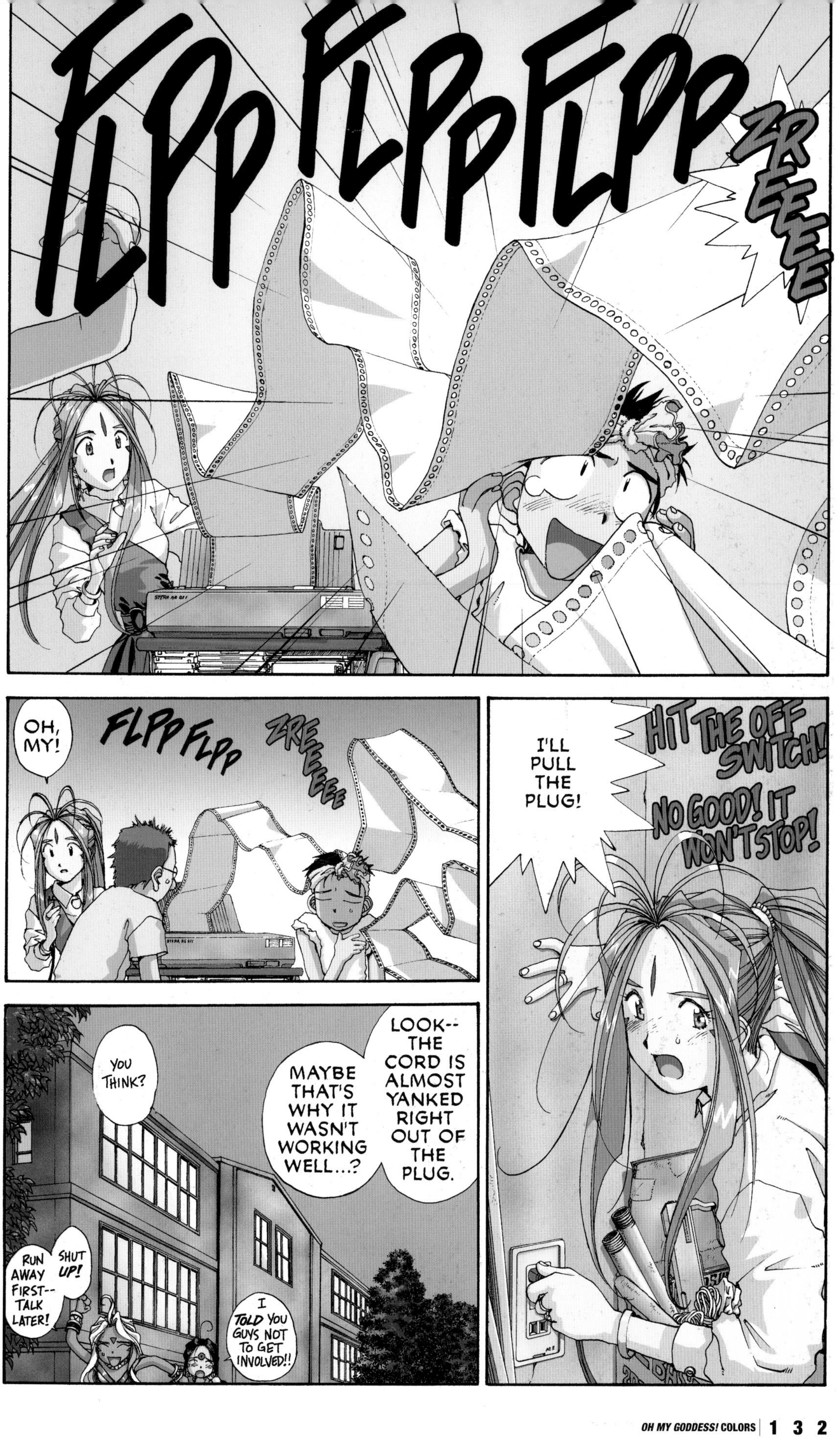
FLPP FLPP FLPP
ZREEEEE
HIT THE OFF SWITCH!
NO GOOD! IT WON'T STOP!
I'LL PULL THE PLUG!
OH, MY!
FLPP FLPP
ZREEEEE
LOOK-- THE CORD IS ALMOST YANKED RIGHT OUT OF THE PLUG.
MAYBE THAT'S WHY IT WASN'T WORKING WELL...?
YOU THINK?
I *TOLD* YOU GUYS NOT TO GET INVOLVED!!
SHUT *UP!*
RUN AWAY FIRST-- TALK LATER!

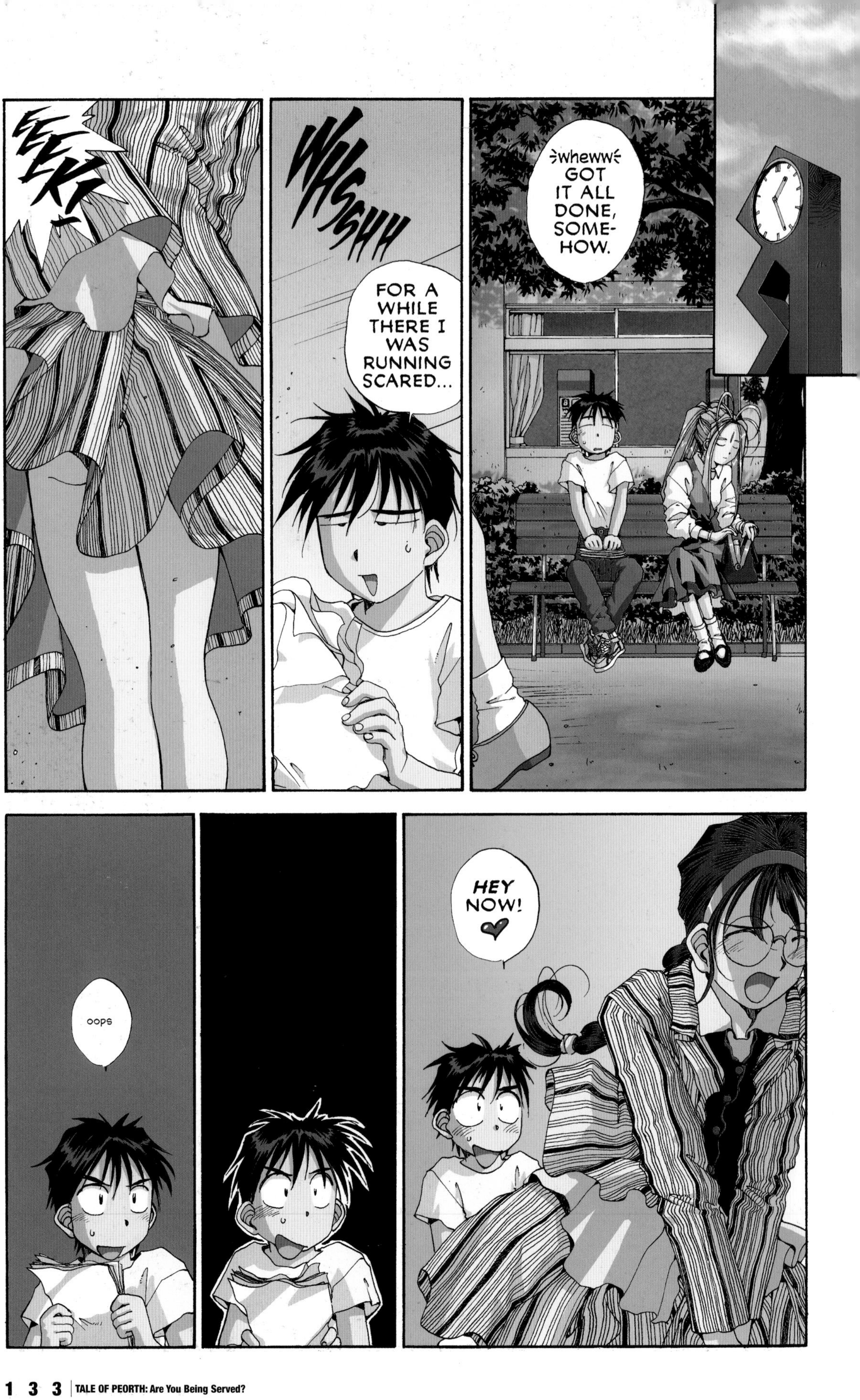

≶wheww≶ GOT IT ALL DONE, SOME-HOW.
WHSSHH
FOR A WHILE THERE I WAS RUNNING SCARED...
EEEK!
HEY NOW! ♥
oops

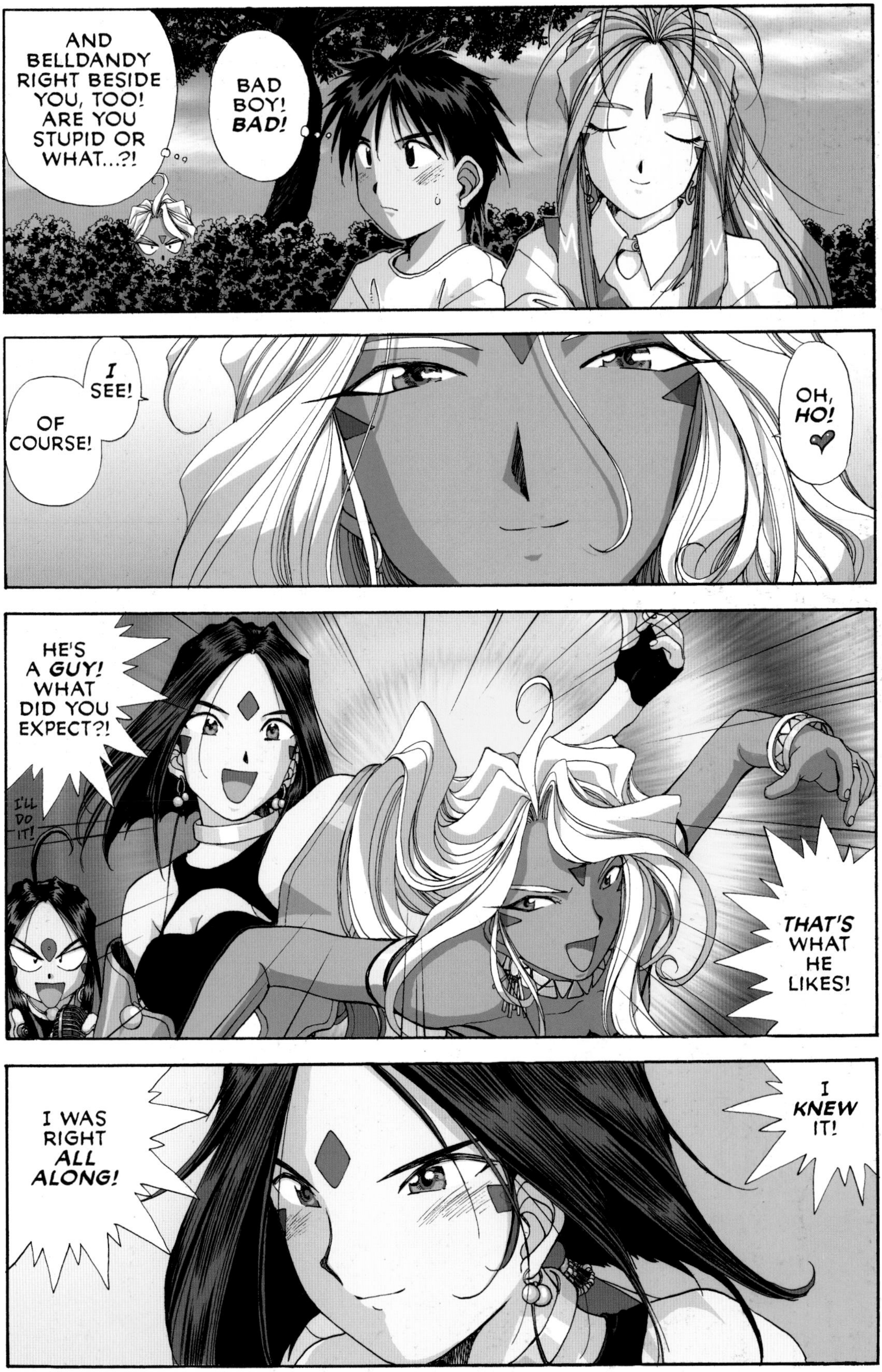
BAD BOY! BAD!
AND BELLDANDY RIGHT BESIDE YOU, TOO! ARE YOU STUPID OR WHAT...?!
OH, HO! ♥
I SEE!
OF COURSE!
HE'S A GUY! WHAT DID YOU EXPECT?!
THAT'S WHAT HE LIKES!
I'LL DO IT!
I KNEW IT!
I WAS RIGHT ALL ALONG!

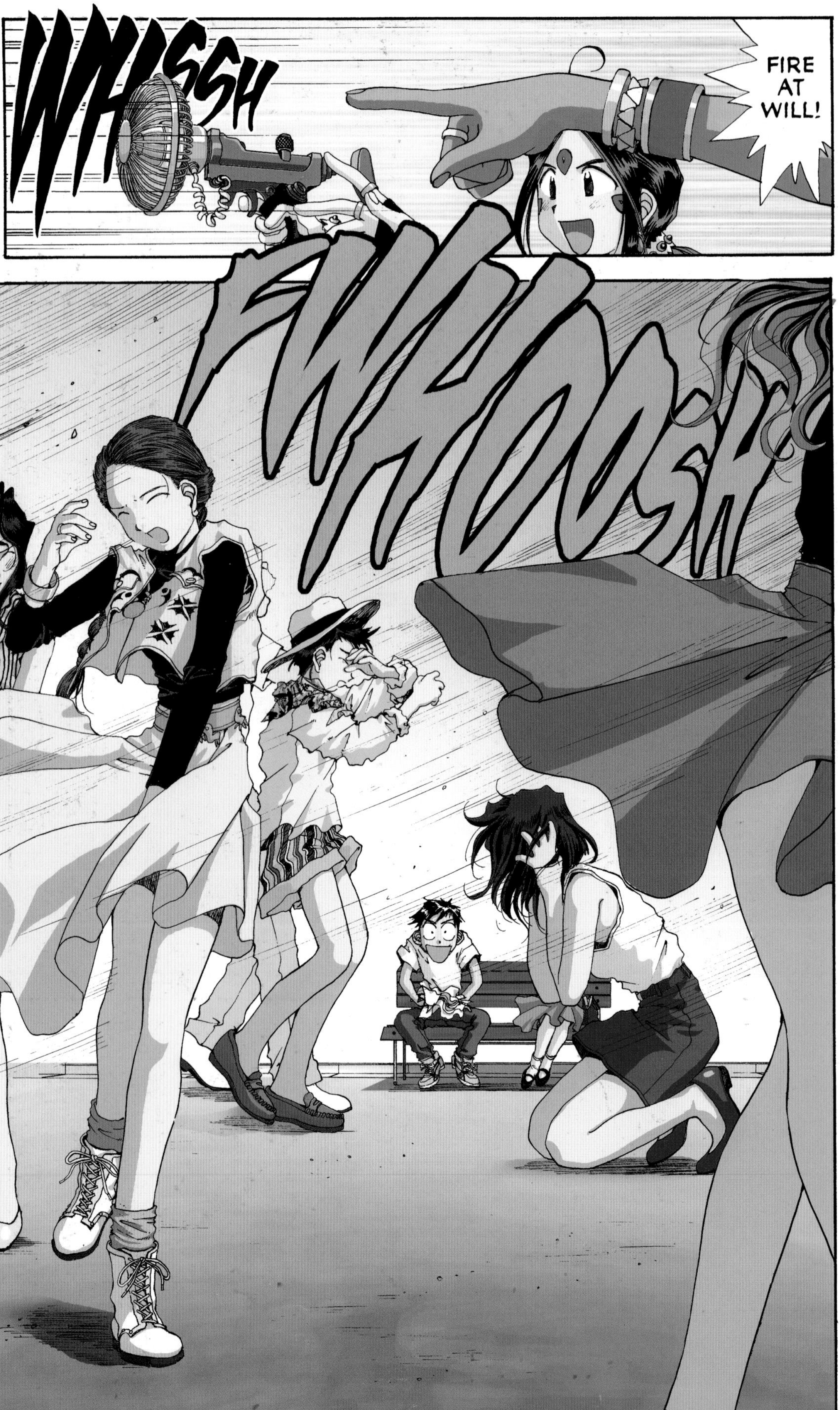
FIRE AT WILL!
WHISSH
FWHOOSH

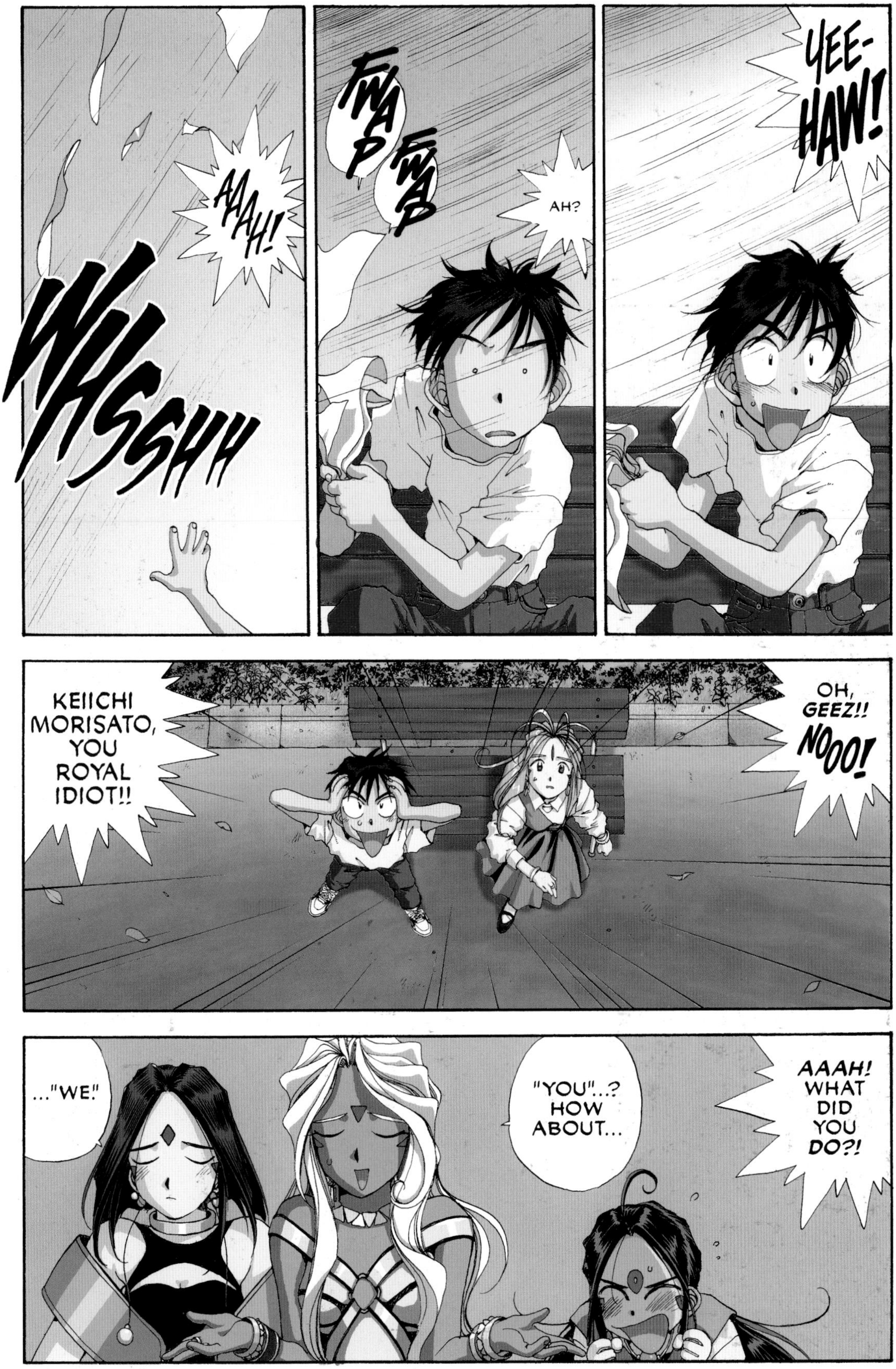

YEE-HAW!
FWAP
FWAP
AH?
AAAH!
WHSSHH
OH, GEEZ!! NOOO!
KEIICHI MORISATO, YOU ROYAL IDIOT!!
AAAH! WHAT DID YOU DO?!
"YOU"...? HOW ABOUT...
..."WE."

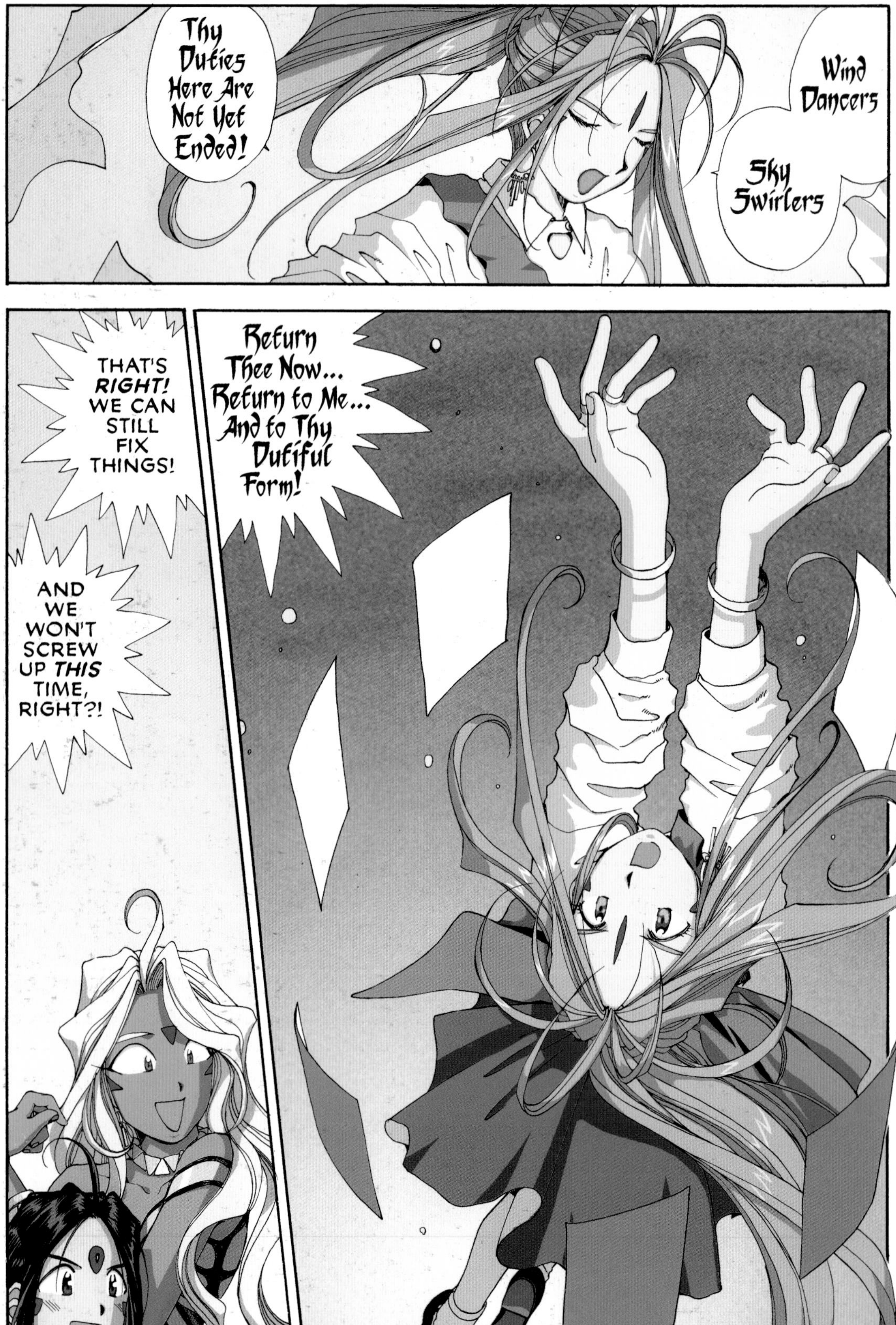
Wind Dancers
Sky Swirlers
Thy Duties Here Are Not Yet Ended!
Return Thee Now... Return to Me... And to Thy Dutiful Form!
THAT'S *RIGHT!* WE CAN STILL FIX THINGS!
AND WE WON'T SCREW UP *THIS* TIME, RIGHT?!

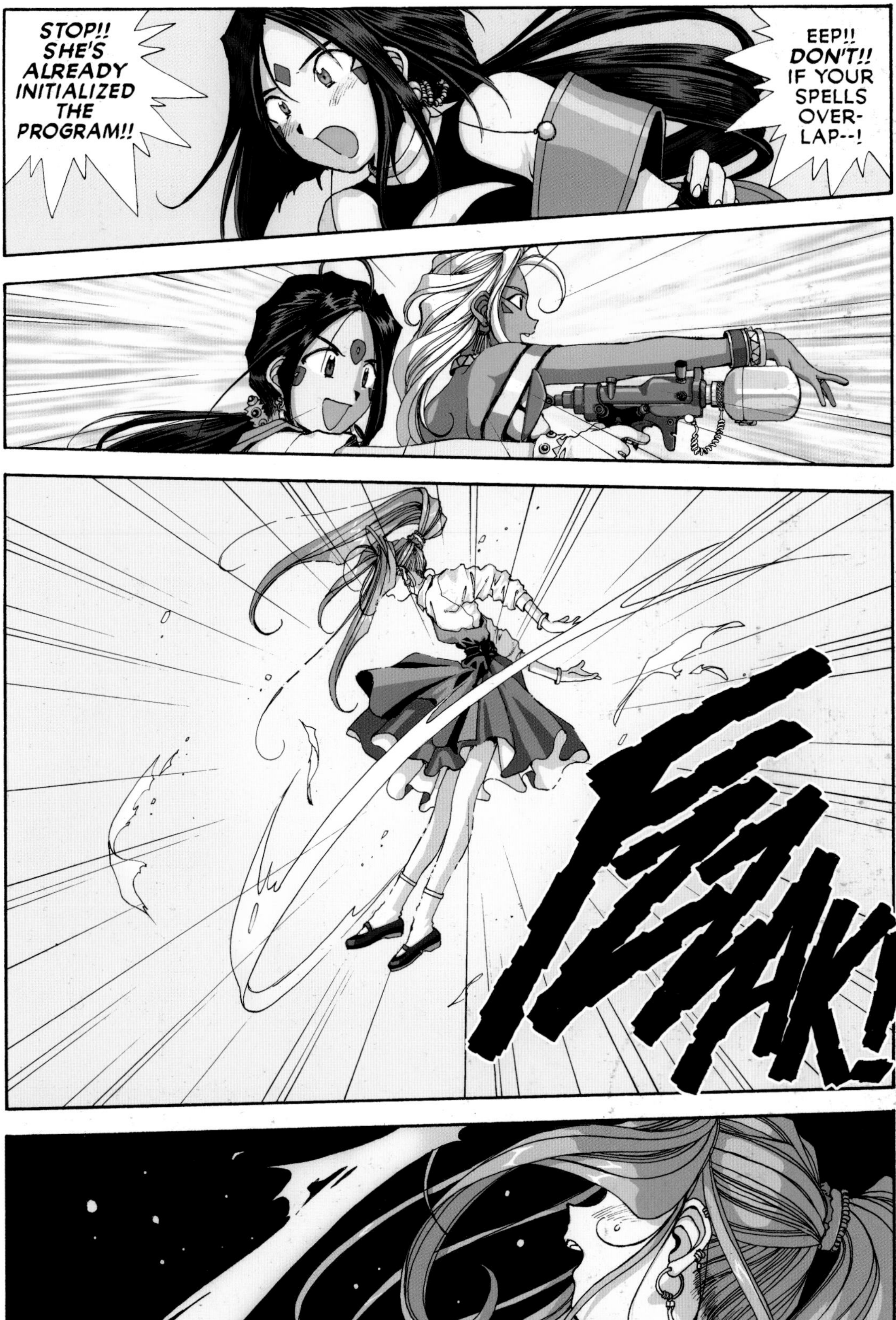
EEP!! DON'T!! IF YOUR SPELLS OVER-LAP--!
STOP!! SHE'S ALREADY INITIALIZED THE PROGRAM!!
FZAK!

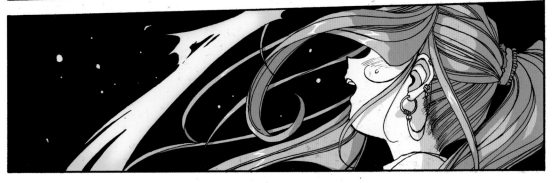

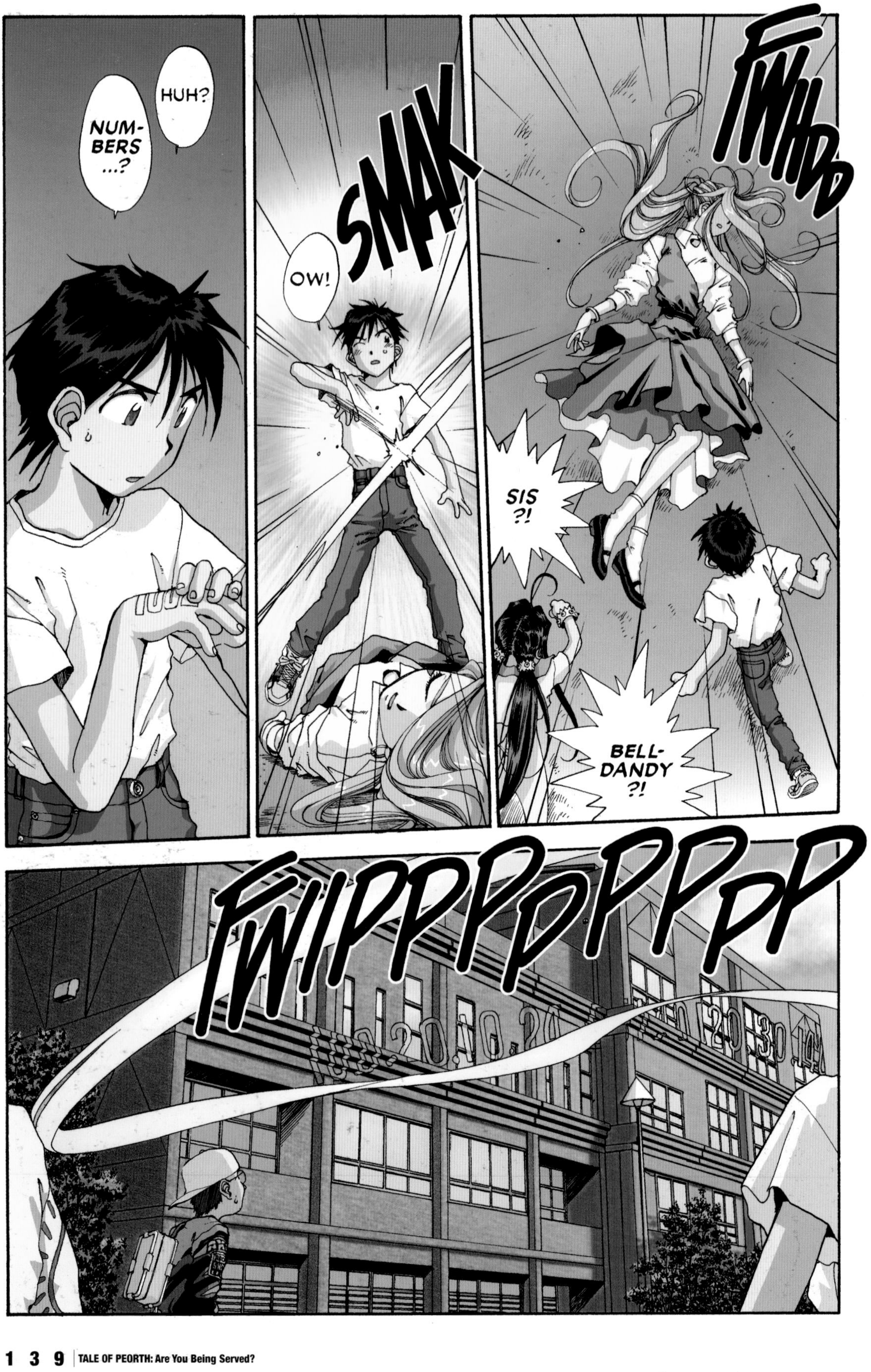
FWHOO
SIS ?!
BELL-DANDY ?!
SMAK
OW!
HUH?
NUM-BERS ...?
FWIPPPPPPPPP

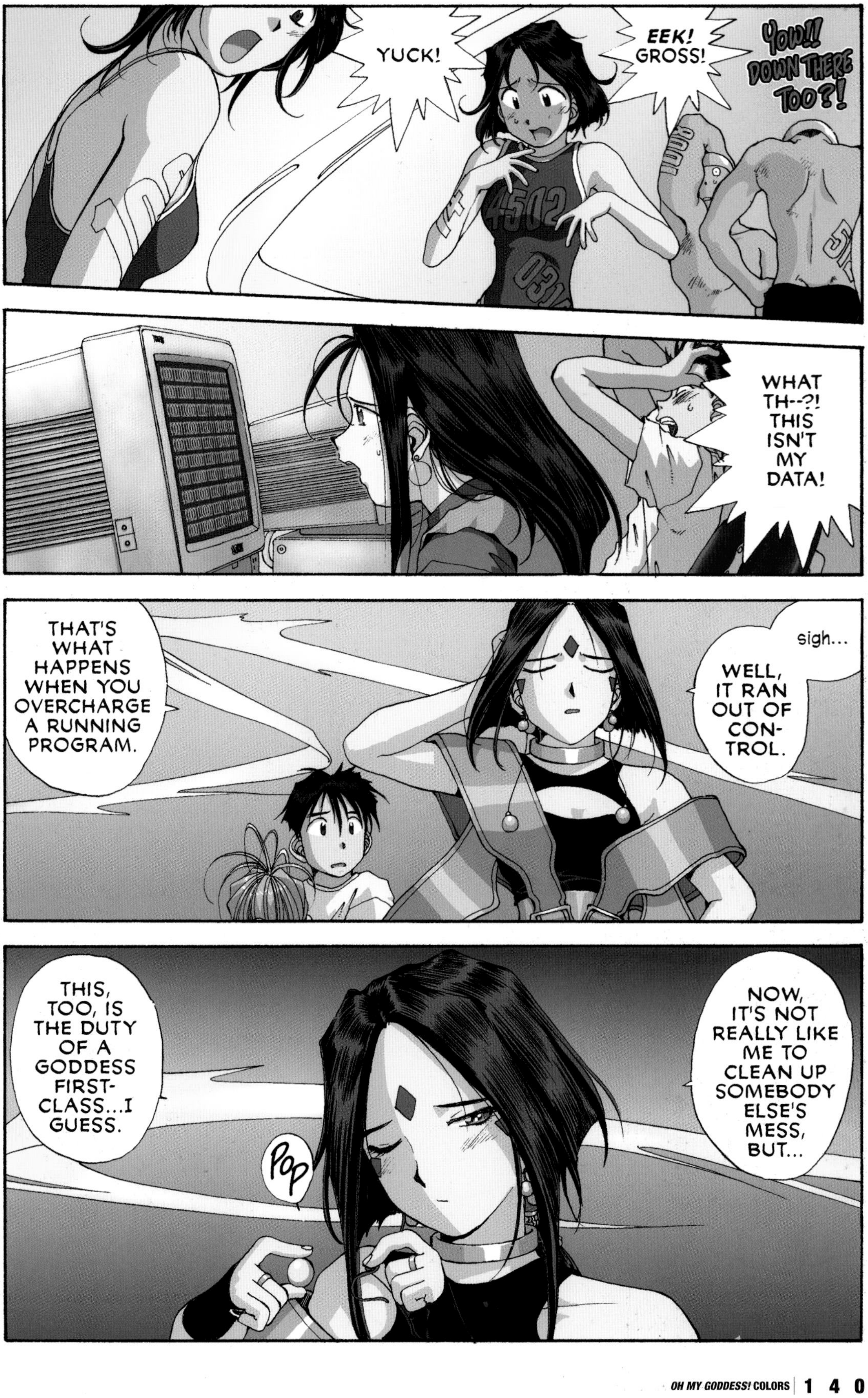
YOW!! DOWN THERE TOO?!
EEK! GROSS!
YUCK!
WHAT TH--?! THIS ISN'T MY DATA!
sigh...
WELL, IT RAN OUT OF CON-TROL.
THAT'S WHAT HAPPENS WHEN YOU OVERCHARGE A RUNNING PROGRAM.
NOW, IT'S NOT REALLY LIKE ME TO CLEAN UP SOMEBODY ELSE'S MESS, BUT...
THIS, TOO, IS THE DUTY OF A GODDESS FIRST-CLASS...I GUESS.
POP

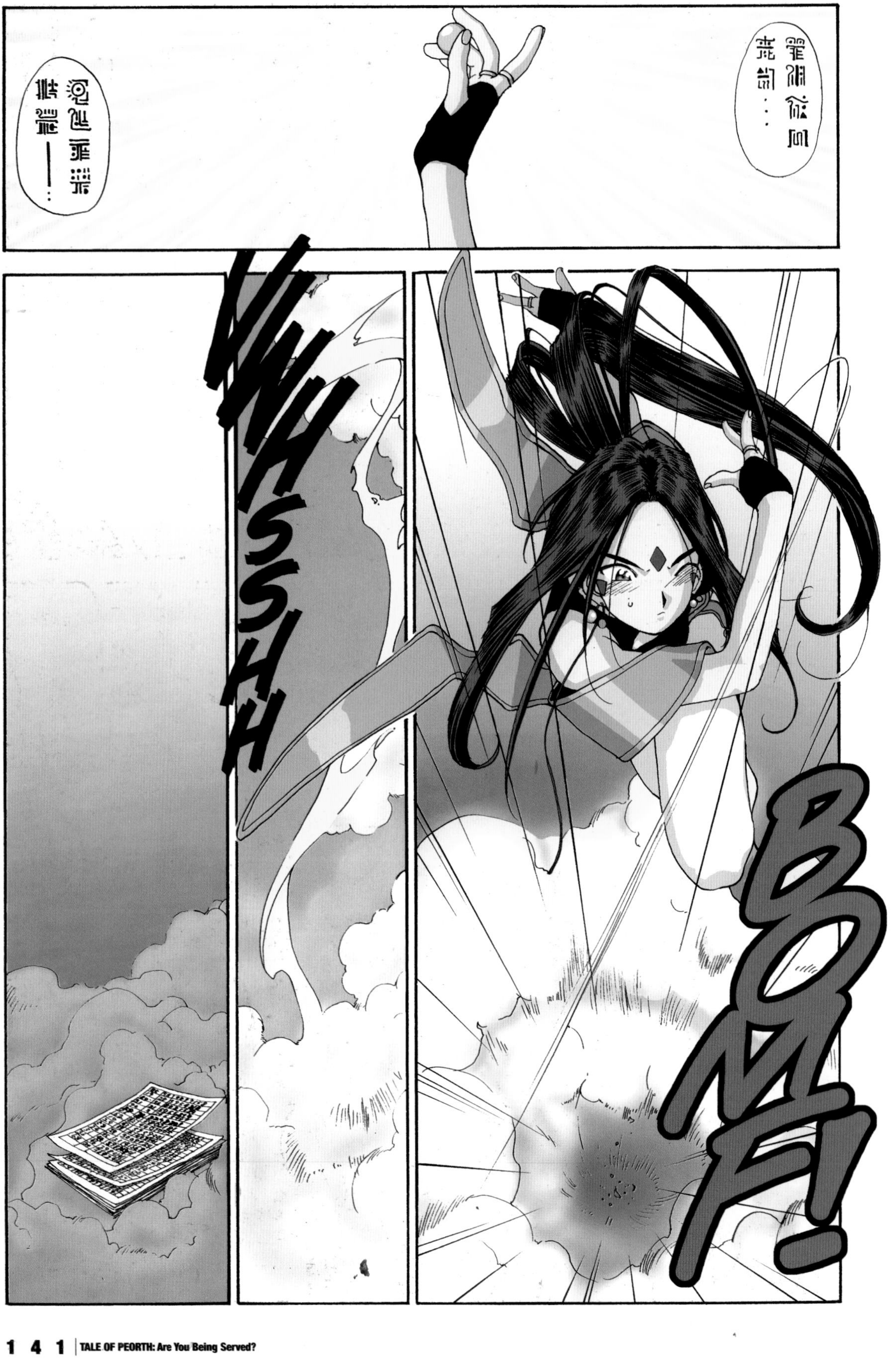
BOMF!
WHISSHH

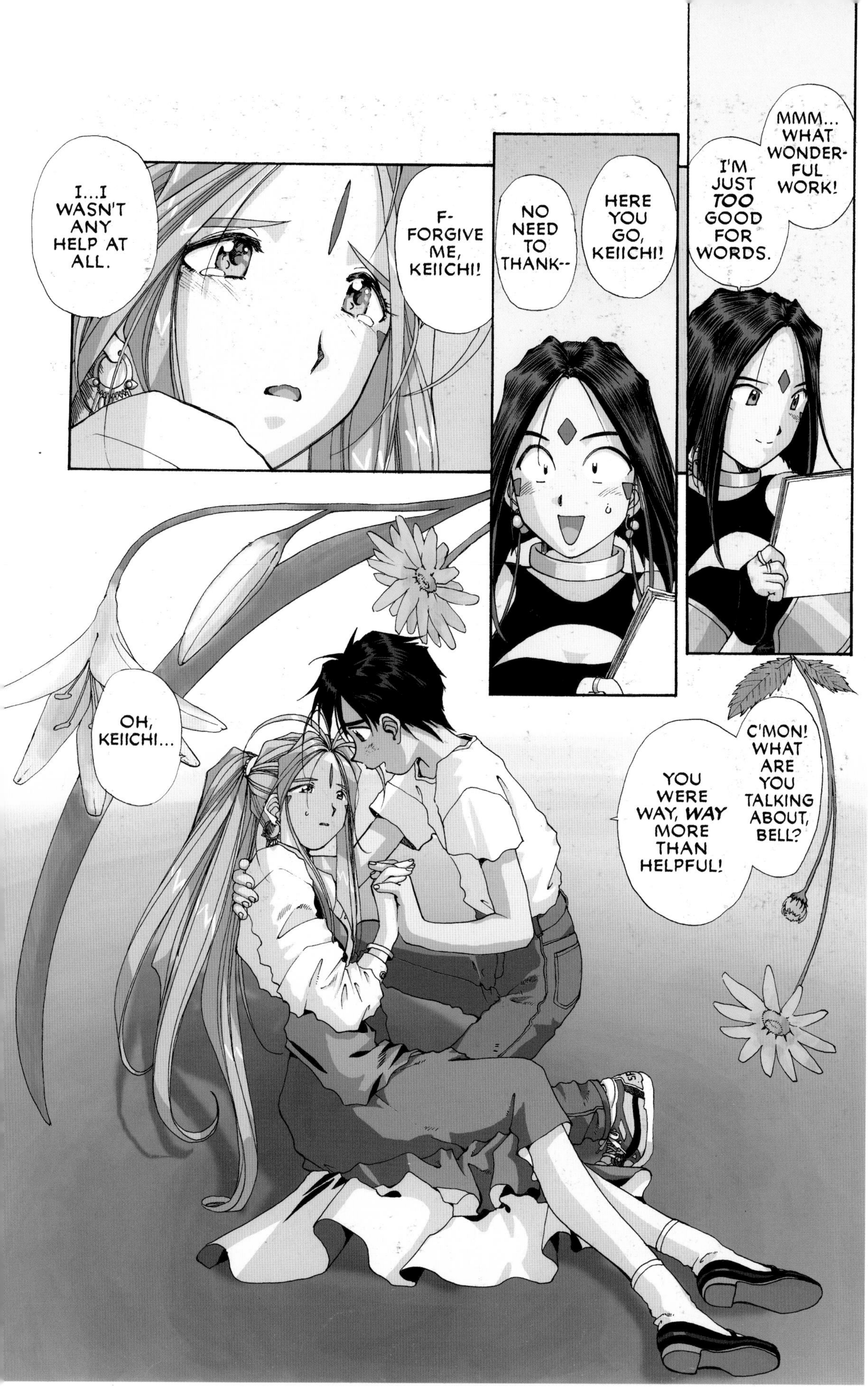
MMM... WHAT WONDERFUL WORK!
I'M JUST *TOO* GOOD FOR WORDS.
HERE YOU GO, KEIICHI!
NO NEED TO THANK--
F-FORGIVE ME, KEIICHI!
I...I WASN'T ANY HELP AT ALL.
C'MON! WHAT ARE YOU TALKING ABOUT, BELL?
YOU WERE WAY, ***WAY*** MORE THAN HELPFUL!
OH, KEIICHI...

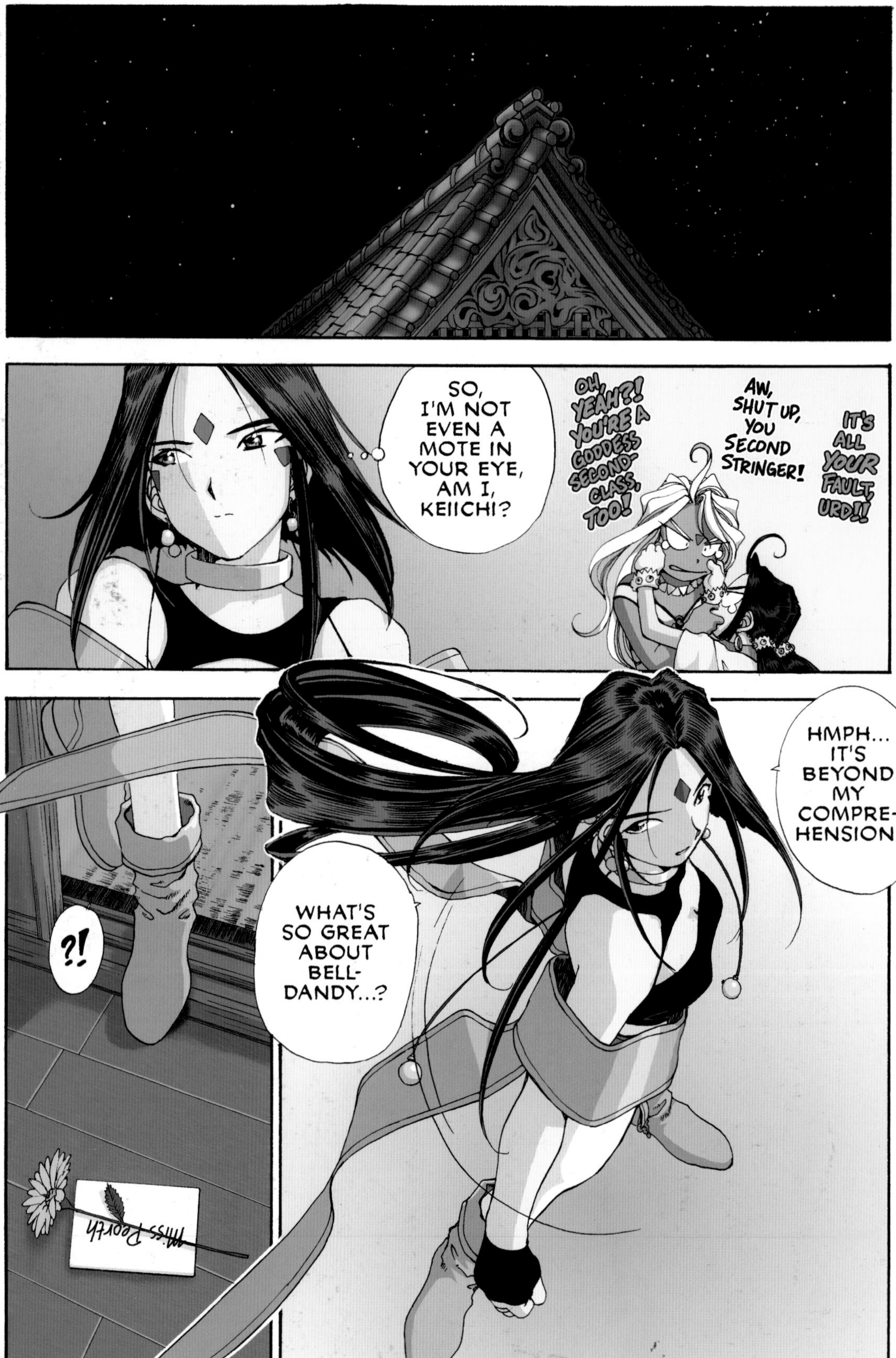
IT'S ALL YOUR FAULT, URD!!
AW, SHUT UP, YOU SECOND STRINGER!
OH, YEAH?! YOU'RE A GODDESS SECOND-CLASS, TOO!
SO, I'M NOT EVEN A MOTE IN YOUR EYE, AM I, KEIICHI?
HMPH... IT'S BEYOND MY COMPREHENSION!
WHAT'S SO GREAT ABOUT BELL-DANDY...?
?!
Miss Peorth

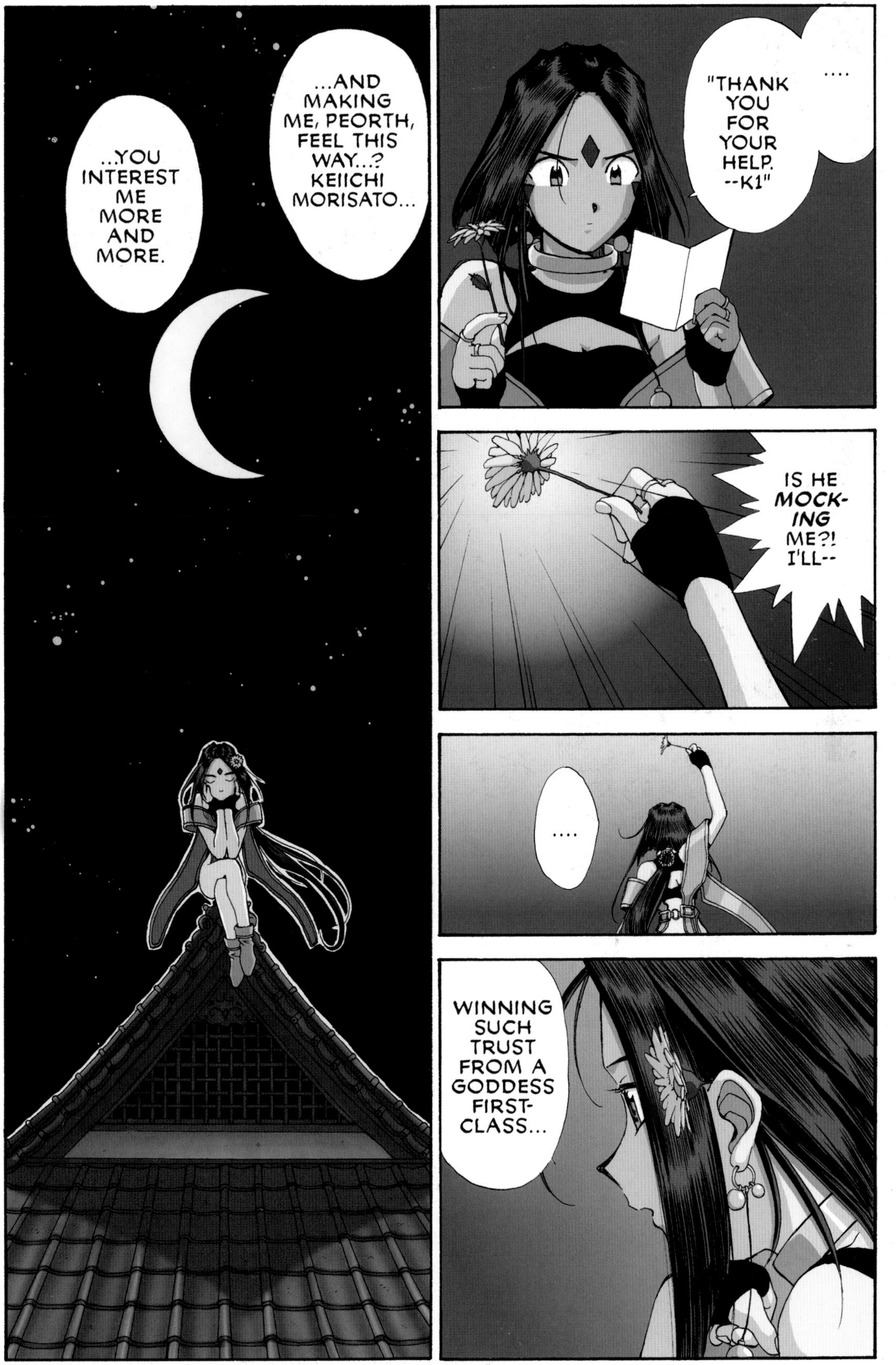
....
"THANK YOU FOR YOUR HELP. --K1"
IS HE *MOCKING* ME?! I'LL--
....
WINNING SUCH TRUST FROM A GODDESS FIRST-CLASS...
...AND MAKING ME, PEORTH, FEEL THIS WAY...? KEIICHI MORISATO...
...YOU INTEREST ME MORE AND MORE.

END

ああっ女神さまっ

Oh My Goddess!

MONOCHROME

藤島康介 **KOSUKE FUJISHIMA**

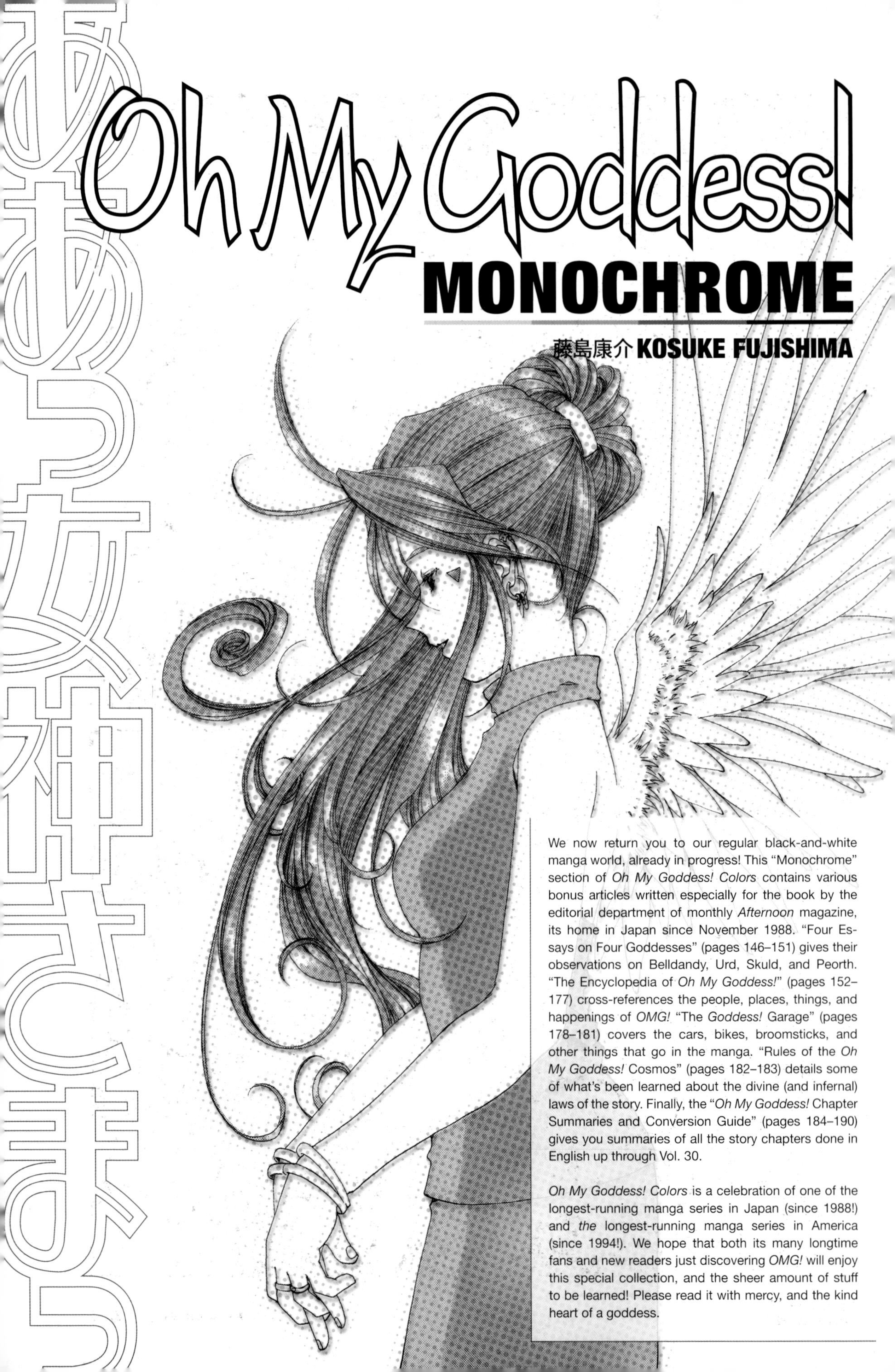

We now return you to our regular black-and-white manga world, already in progress! This "Monochrome" section of *Oh My Goddess! Colors* contains various bonus articles written especially for the book by the editorial department of monthly *Afternoon* magazine, its home in Japan since November 1988. "Four Essays on Four Goddesses" (pages 146–151) gives their observations on Belldandy, Urd, Skuld, and Peorth. "The Encyclopedia of *Oh My Goddess!*" (pages 152–177) cross-references the people, places, things, and happenings of *OMG!* "The *Goddess!* Garage" (pages 178–181) covers the cars, bikes, broomsticks, and other things that go in the manga. "Rules of the *Oh My Goddess!* Cosmos" (pages 182–183) details some of what's been learned about the divine (and infernal) laws of the story. Finally, the "*Oh My Goddess!* Chapter Summaries and Conversion Guide" (pages 184–190) gives you summaries of all the story chapters done in English up through Vol. 30.

Oh My Goddess! Colors is a celebration of one of the longest-running manga series in Japan (since 1988!) and *the* longest-running manga series in America (since 1994!). We hope that both its many longtime fans and new readers just discovering *OMG!* will enjoy this special collection, and the sheer amount of stuff to be learned! Please read it with mercy, and the kind heart of a goddess.

Four Essays on Four Goddesses

First: Belldandy and the System Force

A long, long time ago—no, that's not right, time just runs at a different speed in this manga—there was a college called the Nekomi Institute of Technology, and a young freshman named Keiichi Morisato, sometimes known as just "K1" (*ichi* means "one"). He was pretty good at his course work, especially auto and motorcycle mechanics. But he was a little shorter than normal, and so perhaps you could say he wasn't a hit with the ladies. He also didn't know the extent of the true goodness that was inside him.

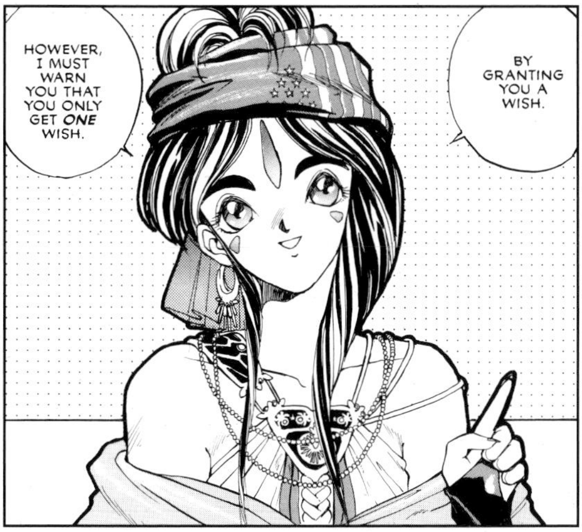
BY GRANTING YOU A WISH.
HOWEVER, I MUST WARN YOU THAT YOU ONLY GET *ONE* WISH.

N.I.T. is far away from K1's hometown of Kushiro in Hokkaido, so naturally he lived on campus. In an all-male dorm, to be exact, and, of course, this being an engineering school, there was regrettably still something of a gender imbalance. You get the feeling that it's not so much that Keiichi was *unpopular* with women, as that he didn't get as many chances as a more typical student might to meet up.

Be that as it may, one Saturday night something happens. Maybe it's just the strange encounters underclassmen often have; maybe it's because his *sempai* (upperclassman), the hulking, semihuman Tamiya, makes him stay in and take his phone messages; maybe (and this feels like the most likely explanation) it's a consequence of his troublesome, purehearted nature.

While shrewdly unraveling the mysteries of a touch-tone phone, Keiichi endeavors to reach Tamiya and pass along a message from a friend. But instead he reaches a kindly, beautiful, and unquestionably female voice which says:

"Hello! You've reached the Goddess Technical Help Line!"

It takes Keiichi about a tenth of a second to realize he has reached a wrong number.

"We'll be there in just a moment to grant your access request."

"Wha-? Hey, wait, I--!" Keiichi breaks out into a sweat, just in time for the beautiful owner of the beautiful voice to come into his bedroom—through the mirror on the wall. It's enough to make anyone freeze up in fear and wonder, but the mysterious female sets down her business card politely and introduces herself. "I am the Goddess Belldandy . . . We specialize in helping people with problems, like you." "H-help?" stutters Keiichi. "Uh, like ***how . . . ?***"

Well, now! At the words "by granting you a wish," wild images of money, women, and world destruction fill the air, but K1 stops to think it over and figures this exceedingly generous offer is all some sort of prank by his upperclassmen, mocking the fact that he's such a loser. But Belldandy says that as a goddess, she's incapable of lying. And when Bell-chan asks him why he thinks he's unlucky that way, K1 reels in shock again—*did she just read his mind?*

So he asks her to stand up for a moment and says he's just too damn short (Bell-chan *does* seem taller than he is; Keiichi hasn't noticed that this is because she's floating above the ground), but Belldandy still doesn't understand what being short has to do with it. He can tell she's serious, and not making fun of him . . . and that alone makes him a little happy. Feeling that it might still be just a prank, he relaxes and makes his wish . . .

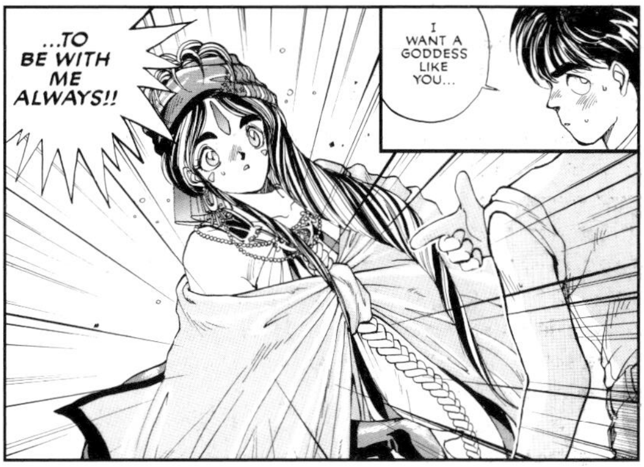
I WANT A GODDESS LIKE YOU...
...TO BE WITH ME ALWAYS!!

Any doubts that Belldandy is who she claims to be are literally blown aside as the room starts to shake and she ascends to the ceiling. Even as Keiichi protests that he was only kidding, a bolt from heaven lances down through the roof of the dorm to ground itself on the strange, spindle-shaped mark upon Belldandy's forehead. Then the rumbling skies close again, and the exhausted goddess drops straight back down, into Keiichi's arms—knocking him to the floor, despite the lightness of her body (real smooth, K1).

When she awakens a few moments later, Bell-chan sees what she thinks is Keiichi's kindly, concerned face (actually, it's a frightened, timid face, afraid Bell will think he tried some monkey business while she was passed out). And then Belldandy makes a mad dash—for the phone that started all this—

"What? You mean it's ***final?*** But . . . ***Almighty one!***"

—but, kidding or not, Keiichi's wish indeed went through, and, having been filed and archived, Bell explains, it has now acquired a tremendous "System Force" that cannot be resisted by the parties involved. "I'll be here with you from now on," she says with a smile.

The first thought which occurs to Keiichi is that the dorm is men only.

"I'm not a *woman* . . . I'm a ***goddess!***" she says with another smile.

What's that sound of feet stomping up the stairs? Why,

it's Tamiya and the upperclassmen, none too pleased at the sight of Keiichi desperately pleading with a beautiful girl, his hands upon her shoulders. Thanks to quick teamwork by his dorm mates, K1 and Belldandy are hustled down the stairs and dumped on the pavement faster than you can say "notice of eviction." Bell interprets this ruthless application of dorm rules as the influence of the System Force keeping them together—if one has to go, they both have to go. And keep going, as sempai Otaki has (in further evidence of the System Force's effect) unexpectedly fixed the sidecar on Keiichi's motorcycle.

"Whatever," he says, and the two of them hit the road, not even knowing where they're going to stay the night. The next display of Belldandy's power comes as people on the street start to gawk at her lavish robes and headband. As K1 flinches in fear (and fascination, as her old clothes momentarily vanish), Bell's previous attire is replaced with a more normal late-eighties student ensemble, complete with a "GODDESS" designer label. "I just dismantled matter at the atomic level and rearranged it a little," she says, with, of course, a smile.

But Belldandy can't use her power more than two or three times a day without falling asleep, and after a few more misadventures trying to find shelter, she passes out, prompting a panicked Keiichi to pull over next to a Buddhist temple. Carrying her under its gate in the rain, he's soon fast asleep as well.

The two awaken in a bedroom, lying on the same futon, a concept which causes Keiichi to panic once again with a high-pitched, girlish shriek, which in turn causes the head priest to burst in and beat him about the head with a baton, apologizing to Bell for inadvertently placing this lecher in the same room with her. As the burly monk starts to haul away K1's stricken form, a quick explanation from Belldandy is necessary to save him from yet further chastisement, if not further embarrassment.

Apologizing for the error, the priest lets the two of them stay at his temple, Tarikihongan—as long as they do odd jobs, and, of course, practice their meditation (this earns Keiichi another four whacks for insufficient poise). But after witnessing Belldandy's effortless skill at tasks, her discipline in the lotus posture, and even the Buddha-like sign on her forehead, the priest jumps to an even bigger conclusion, departing the temple with a letter left behind for "The Lady Belldandy":

You have awakened me to my spiritual imperfection. I have set forth for India to study the true Buddhism as you yourself have so clearly done. I know it is presumptuous of me, but please use the temple as you wish until I return.

Well, not quite—although Belldandy *is* a goddess, so perhaps she is closer to Nirvana than most (the Buddha once said that even gods and goddesses need enlightenment). But that was how Keiichi and Bell came to live off campus in a Buddhist temple. Could it have been the System Force at work again?

What do you think?

Second: The Descent of Urd
(May Contain Adult Themes)

This tall woman you are about to meet, with the long white hair, and long brown body, is Urd-sama—Belldandy's older sister. Do not neglect to add the respectful *sama* after her name, for she is someone to be always feared, and sometimes respected.

By the time she comes down to Earth, Keiichi and Belldandy are beginning to care for each other in a normal relationship (kinda), despite incidents involving Sayoko, Megumi, Otaki, and the ever-beneficent Tamiya (see the section "Encyclopedia of *Oh My Goddess!*" on pages 152–177 for details—*why* are there problems wherever Keiichi goes?).

Urd (sorry—Urd-*sama*) is unsatisfied with their progress, however, and being (probably) much more experienced than either one of them, knowing all the tricks and traps of love, she decides the way the couple is coming along is *much* too slow for her. So one day, while Bell-chan is out shopping, Keiichi just happens to receive a mysterious video in the mail entitled *I'll Show You Everything*. Keiichi once again thinks that his sempai are behind this (he should have started to suspect he's just a goddess magnet), but as a healthy young man he can't pass up the chance to watch the video before Belldandy gets back. If you are under eighteen years of age, you do not need to know why.

But more fool him (if that were possible). Just as Bell enters our world through mirrors, Urd (let's just drop the *sama* from here on) enters it, appropriately enough, through the idiot box—the TV. First her lovely feet, then the elegant curve of her calves, then her firm, gleaming thighs . . . and then . . . and then she falls out of the screen, knocking K1 cold with a demure knee to the face.

It is more or less at that moment that Belldandy's gentle voice is heard in the hall outside: "**Keiichi . . . ! Are you home?**" Urd panics—proof enough that she knows Belldandy well. Popping the video out of the deck (it's evidence), she uses

HEY.

COULD I SCRUB YOUR BACK ...?

sorcery to wind herself into the tatami floor. Fortunately, Bell's own power allows her to rewind K1's groggy memories, and what she sees inside the last few minutes of his head is—sure enough, her big sister.

Perceiving that the jig is up, Urd re-emerges from the floor (between Keiichi's legs), and claims that she's just come down to Earth to recharge Belldandy's System Force (abandoning her post as system administrator of Yggdrasil, the main computer in Heaven, and leaving the job to Skuld—see below!). But Bell-chan also knows her sister well; too well to accept that's the whole story. At this point Urd freely admits she's been spying on (and recording) Bell and K1, and then proceeds to play back the scanty highlights of

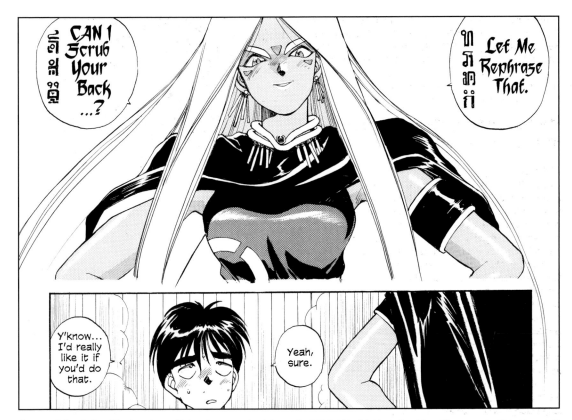

Let Me Rephrase That.
Can I Scrub Your Back ...?
Yeah, sure.
Y'know... I'd really like it if you'd do that.

the couple's relationship thus far—offering her expert advice to help move things along for the two of them.

The next thing Keiichi knows, the gentle Belldandy is shouting that she wants the recording, sending a bolt of lightning straight in Urd's direction—which Urd deflects onto K1, probably not on purpose.

Later on, Keiichi is trying to recover in a nice peaceful bathtub, but he can't help but reflect on how gorgeous Bell's big sister is. These are dangerous thoughts indeed, for Urd, as if summoned, enters the bathroom and asks as seen above:

Determined that she has the obligation to teach Keiichi everything about women (in order to move him along with Belldandy, she tells herself—but she seems to be enjoying it, too), Urd repeats the command, a bit more *sorcery*-fully this time . . .

Keiichi is about to give in to her mystical temptation, but manages to resist—what saves the boy is an image in his head of how Belldandy would look upon his surrender. He sits back in the bath . . . then gets back out of the tub, as Urd cranks up her spell to full power. Keiichi hesitates yet again . . . at which point Urd can no longer deal with his indecision and blasts him senseless with a lightning bolt.

That evening, Belldandy attends to his wishy-washy wounds while trying to explain to Keiichi about Urd: "My sister tends to think the end justifies the means. But then she gets so wrapped up in the ***means*** she forgets what the ***end*** was. Urd is very . . . ***passionate*** . . . about ***everything*** she does." Bell also mentions that Urd is much more powerful than she, and is surprised K1 was able to resist her. "I just kept weighing the pull of her ***tremendous power*** . . . against how mad you'd look," he replies. Belldandy gives him a hug, saying, "*Really?* Am I really that scary?" She seems happy to find out that Keiichi is thinking about her. They are about to kiss each other for the first time (in a while), but Urd is peeking. Love is not easy, is it?

Urd isn't the type to throw in the towel so easily, though. After checking that Belldandy is sound asleep, she tiptoes into K1's bedroom (naturally, they sleep in separate rooms . . .), and tries to appeal to him with logic.

Her seven-point argument runs something like this: 1) Belldandy received only a certain amount of System Force energy when she came down from Heaven, so 2) eventually her internal power will run out, and 3) she will have to return to Heaven, because 4) Keiichi's wish contract wasn't properly uploaded in the first place, owing to 5) the heavenly computer, Yggdrasil, requiring a biometric signature. However, 6) fortunately, Urd is herself a remote terminal, connected directly to Yggdrasil, so the whole problem can be solved if Keiichi will just 7) make love to her immediately.

Now, Belldandy told K1 when they first met that, as a goddess, she's incapable of lying. Under the influence of Urd's spell (which one?) he moves closer, believing he must do it for Bell-chan . . .

Belldandy bursts in, and Keiichi immediately explains Urd's theory. "Do you *ever* stop lying?" Bell says to her older sister. Yes, although Urd *is* more powerful than Bell, she's still only a Goddess Second-Class, Type 1, Limited, with administrative restrictions . . . precisely *because* she's such a "liar, liar, pants on fire." It's Goddesses *First*-Class who are incapable of lying—it's one of the qualifications.

The unrepentant Urd smirks that her fibs are worth it, "to get you two closer together," at which point it looks like another magical battle between Bell and her is in the offing—until lightning straight from Heaven shuts Urd down. Glyphs

burned upon the floor proclaim a "RECENT SYSTEM CRASH DUE TO VIOLATION OF SERVICE TERMS BY USER GODDESS SECOND CLASS (LIMITED) URD" and that she is "HEREBY ***BANNED FROM HEAVEN*** UNTIL FURTHER NOTICE."

So, it seems like a second goddess is going to be hanging around the place a while longer. What are Belldandy and Keiichi going to do? Nothing, as usual.

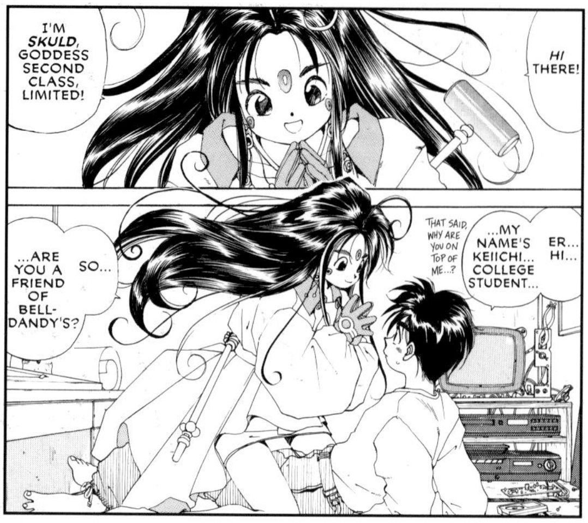
HI THERE!
I'M *SKULD*, GODDESS SECOND CLASS, LIMITED!
ER... HI...
...MY NAME'S KEIICHI... COLLEGE STUDENT...
THAT SAID, WHY ARE YOU ON TOP OF ME...?
SO...
...ARE YOU A FRIEND OF BELL-DANDY'S?

Third: Skuld Asks, "So . . . Are You a Friend of Belldandy's?"

Well, they're going to have even less time to themselves, that's for sure. But at least you never run out of excitement when Urd is around. The demon Mara (First-Class, Unlimited) drops in, while the Nekomi Motor Club enters a race whose wager is a new clubhouse. Throughout all of this, Belldandy and Keiichi *do* manage to grow closer—without the help of Urd, whose methods really are too forceful for the two of them.

One day, Urd finds herself in a hot bath that's not so relaxing, when a rambunctious young girl bursts from the surface of the water, floats about in midair for a moment, looks around, sees Urd, and then vanishes back the way she came.

Yes, it's she, Belldandy's *younger* sister, Skuld, the third goddess. As Belldandy enters this world through mirrors, and Urd through the TV, Skuld does so through water. Bursting out again, this time through K1's steaming teacup, she knocks the boy to the floor, and cheerfully informs him who she is.

Urd then jumps right out of the teacup as well (apparently, she can do that) and goes after Skuld. The two don't seem to get along. As soon as Belldandy comes home, Skuld runs away to her side. When Urd asks why *she* doesn't get a hug, Skuld lists Urd's faults as follows:

A) arrogant, B) violent, C) selfish, and D) stupid. By contrast, Skuld likes the fact Belldandy is I) honest, II) unselfish, III) gentle, and IV) pure.

Skuld is, of course, correct, but just as she's finished explaining that she came to Earth to bring Bell-chan back home, Sleipnir, the great white-maned, eight-legged divine steed, rises from the floor, an incident which prompts Skuld to put on a pair of glasses, an act that makes visible to her an eight-legged *rabbit*, which without delay she slams flat with a sledgehammer, causing it to vanish, along with Sleipnir.

That "rabbit" was what a bug in the Yggdrasil System looks like, and Skuld's job is to debug it. As usual, Keiichi is at the center of the disturbance, so he asks Belldandy to explain the problem, and she does so with clarity. "You see, bugs are proliferating out of control in the Yggdrasil System metaprogram. Without constant debugging, they'll go into a loop state, in which the bugs will endlessly reproduce themselves. And if *that* happens, a quasi-differential will occur between the existence probabilities of normally equivalent spaces, causing fluctuations in the locus of space 'a,' or the complete disappearance of space 'b,' for example. Or an entirely different space, 'c,' may suddenly materialize"—like space in the form of great white-maned, eight-legged divine steeds, for example. Or Keiichi might suddenly fly off—as he then proceeds to

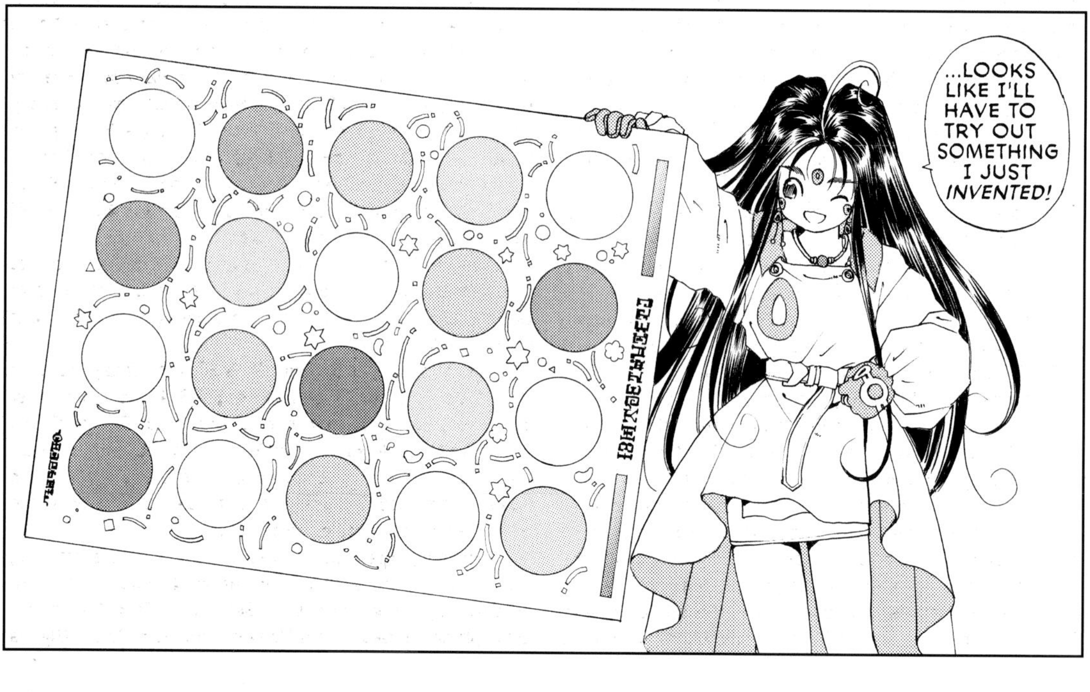
...LOOKS LIKE I'LL HAVE TO TRY OUT SOMETHING I JUST *INVENTED!*

do at that very moment—prompting further speculation from Belldandy and Skuld that he might rematerialize at ten thousand meters up, or inside the core of a nuclear reactor.

Not to worry; he didn't go far—he simply rematerializes inside the bathtub, to which Urd had returned during the explanation. Keiichi is not totally unhappy with these troubles.

But why *do* these things always happen to him? Skuld speculates that his being too close to her sisters creates a kind of singularity. Bell-chan realizes if they can't come up with a working debugging program soon, they'll be chin deep in rabbit-bugs. K1 tries to cheer Skuld up by saying this kind of weirdness is an everyday thing around here, but Skuld retorts, "Don't treat me like a little kid, okay?" She has both a tear and a smile as she says this—so she still is a kid, after all.

Urd, who is taller and older but not necessarily any more mature, just tries to blow up all the bugs at once with a lightning bolt. Make that "twice," as all her attack does is double the number of bugs . . .

rightful heiress to the manifestation of the prophesied Lord of Terror. When Urd's demon personality is awakened, the entire universe is in danger, and in the end its salvation comes down to Bell's love for Keiichi.

There is a certain goddess in Heaven whose concern is not love, but something not quite the same—desire. She is also just a little narcissistic. Although if you were her, perhaps you would be more than a little.

On the temple veranda, Keiichi and Belldandy are looking at some new photos of her he's taken, using a camera his sister Megumi was kind enough to sell him (he reflects on how she could have just *given* it to him). As Bell-chan leans on him for a better view, his heart starts to beat faster; she's so close, he can feel her sweet warmth—in other words, their love still exists in a divine form, one perfect, unsullied; i.e., Platonic. Urd passes by, looks at the photos, and gives compliments to Keiichi. He tells her that the cameraman is very good, but Urd says it's due to love, not talent.

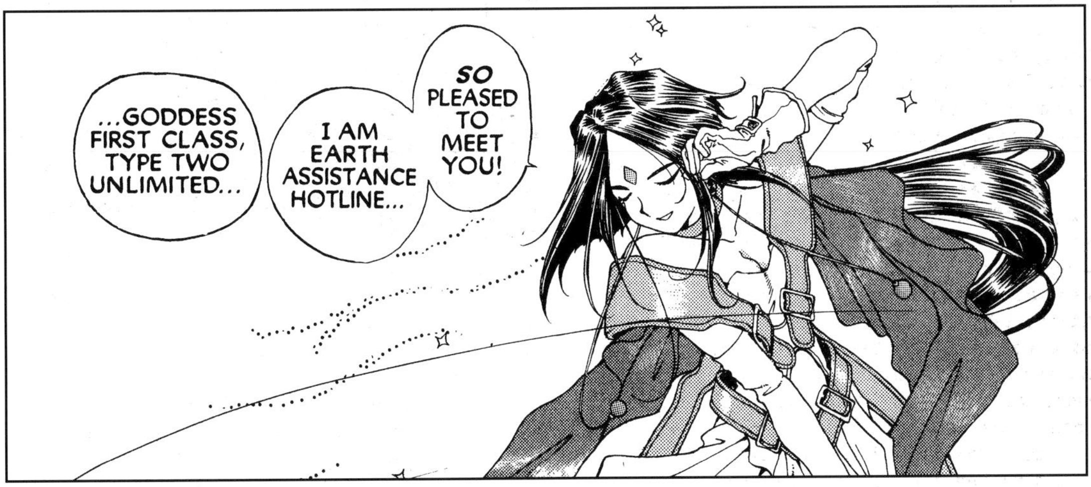

SO PLEASED TO MEET YOU!
I AM EARTH ASSISTANCE HOTLINE...
...GODDESS FIRST CLASS, TYPE TWO UNLIMITED...

. . . and open a giant hole under Keiichi's feet, leading to an ominous-looking alternate reality. As Bell grabs his hand, she tries to apologize, but Keiichi tells her, "If this is the price I have to pay for living with a goddess, it's a ***bargain!***"

Skuld doesn't like the sound of that, and blasts him out of the hole with a grenade. "You're a nice guy and all . . . but I don't want you touching my sister." Is she somehow feeling envious of Belldandy? "I wasn't going to resort to *this*," says Skuld, "but . . ."

The *n*-dimensional game of Twister® blasts the bugs away temporarily, but Skuld theorizes they will continue to multiply unless both her sisters come home. Urd scoffs, "I don't remember raising you to come running to your big sisters every time something goes *wrong!*" Skuld counter-scoffs, "I don't remember being raised by you, ***period!***"

Lightning meets grenade, and what do you know—the bugs are back.

Fourth: Peorth—Belldandy's Archrival (Wannabe)

The bug problem gets resolved . . . eventually . . . but now Skuld, too, has moved into the temple, and the next complication to arise is the biggest yet: Urd's heritage. Urd isn't quite Belldandy and Skuld's sister; she's their half-sister. On her mother's side, she's not a god, but a demon. And Urd is the

At least no one can deny K1 has a talent for *trouble*, and, of course, in his case it can often take as little as just one phone call—like the one he tries to make now to Megumi about how well the pictures turned out. Instead he hears on the other end, with a remarkable sense of déjà vu, "Yes, yes, yes, yes, ***yes***, my dear! Earth Assistance Hotline here! I've been absolutely ***dying*** for your call. In fact, I think I'll come and take care of you ***on-site!***"

As Keiichi stands there frozen (also a Keiichi specialty), a ray of light shoots forth from his camera lens to the ceiling. And descending in its beam, striking a lovely pose, is the Fourth Goddess, Peorth.

Keiichi tells Peorth, "Actually, I'm sort of full up on goddesses right now."

The aforementioned heavenly surfeit arrive one by one in the room, much to the surprise of Peorth, who had no idea whatsoever this Earthling was living with them. Belldandy's friendly greeting she recoils from, icily noting that they work for rival agencies, and she has been "properly summoned . . . by ***that boy!***" This startles Bell, too—could it mean that she is not enough for him?

Well, in any case, you know the rules—all Keiichi has to do is name his wish, and her mission here will be accomplished. She tries to get him to confess his heart's desire . . . but claims to already know what it is. Keiichi speaks it aloud: "Please go home, Peorth."

One magical storm of painfully thorny roses later (for Peorth is mistress of the roses), and K1 is reminded not to mock a goddess. Peorth decides to look a little deeper into this matter, telling her fellow beings that they all appear to be stuck here "because this spineless wimp can't make up his mind." "No," says Belldandy, "I've contracted . . . with Keiichi." When Peorth wants to know why the contract hasn't been fulfilled after all this time, Keiichi whispers in her ear what it was he asked Belldandy . . .

. . . and the elegant Peorth bursts into diaphragm-gripping laughter: "No way *that* would go through, right?! *HA! HA!*"

One confirmation check with the Lord on High later, everyone tries to calm down with a nice cup of tea. Peorth says there are no regulations governing a case like this, where two goddess contracts overlap with the same client. Moreover, her personal pride won't permit her to return until she grants Keiichi's wish. "And therefore—until you speak your *heart's desire*, Keiichi, *I am staying*. Your *true* wish, you understand? The one in the very depths of your heart and soul . . ."

Belldandy looks more worried than ever. "What's she talking about?" wonders K1. " 'Heart's desire' . . . ?" He reassures Bell that he'll wish for some stupid little thing to make her go away, and puts his hand on her shoulder . . . and shivers to think about how soft and smooth her skin is . . .

In his room, Keiichi tries to come up with some quick, yet suitable, wishes, such as 1) "Write my term paper," 2) "Fix my CD player," and 3) "Give Schwantz racing number 34." But somehow he senses none of these will satisfy *Peorth*. And while she's waiting, she demonstrates her "service" by cooking up a sumptuous magical banquet for K1 of dishes so good, they insist that they be eaten . . . no, they really insist. As the pile of delicacies begins to shove itself down Keiichi's throat, Urd points out to Peorth the heartfelt look on Bell's face in the photo Keiichi took of her, suggesting if Peorth thinks she can come between the couple, she had better think again.

Peorth doesn't buy it—she believes Keiichi's call must have gone through to her for a logical reason: because the original contractor, Belldandy, isn't fulfilling her duty.

Taking a bath, Keiichi is still trying to figure out what his wish should be. He's up to 4) "Turn our bathtub into a hot spring," when Peorth walks in, wearing only a towel. "That doesn't exactly qualify as your 'heart's desire,' does it . . . ?" she asks as he shrieks (one more thing he's good at). Peorth leaps into the tub, offering to scrub his back, and perhaps elsewhere. When she's finished exfoliating him, he admits to himself it did feel a *little* good . . . and in a lower voice, well, okay, to be honest, **real** good.

Peorth is waiting for him in ambush again outside the bathroom, and magically changes his T-shirt and baggy pants for a pink brushed-silk robe with lace trim, which for some reason she thinks will impress girls. The final trap awaits him in his bedroom—

—which Peorth has redecorated into a boudoir worthy of Louis XIV, his humble futon now a gilded mattress upon which lies Peorth in sheer lingerie, spritzing herself with perfume and cupping a goblet of fine liqueur. An ordinary man would just melt down right there—but Keiichi is *not* like ordinary men!

He runs away, and hides in Belldandy's room.

Keiichi tells Bell-chan that it's been hard for him to figure out what to ask Peorth. Belldandy is quiet for a moment, and, seeming to work up courage, says to him, "What you asked me for . . . back at the beginning . . . was it the right thing . . . ?"

"Huh . . . ? That's a funny thing to ask . . . after all this time . . . Maybe it sounded like a joke or something . . . but at that moment, there wasn't anything else in my mind. It was what I really wanted . . . from the bottom of my heart. And *that's* why my wish was granted. I'm sure of it."

Peorth keeps waiting in the bedroom—and waiting. Eventually, after a lot of how-de-doo, high jinks, and rigmarole (see *Colors'* fourth story, "Are You Being Served?" for a few of the details), she realizes Urd was right about Bell and K1, and takes off. But she does still drop by every once in a while . . .

Fifth: Sorry.

There's a Fifth Goddess, too, and we don't mean to shortchange her. But always leave them hungry for more, we say. You'll have to read about Lind in the next section!

THE ENCYCLOPEDIA OF

OH MY GODDESS!

A Look at Goddess Terminology

女神用語の 基礎知識

The "Encyclopedia of *Oh My Goddess!*" section lists people, places, and things both important and trivial in the *OMG!* saga thus far. But because *Oh My Goddess!* has a long history in the U.S., it might be a good idea to take a moment to explain it.

Although this special *Oh My Goddess! Colors* book is printed in Japanese reading order, right-to-left, two-thirds of the stories referred to in this encyclopedia are available from Dark Horse in their older, left-to-right format. This is simply because *Oh My Goddess!* is Dark Horse's longest-running title (since 1994!) and during most of that time, the industry standard in the U.S. was to publish manga left-to-right. So you may see two different English versions of *Oh My Goddess!* around—the newer, right-to-left format, and the older, left-to-right format.

How can you tell which version you're dealing with? If you've got it, of course, you can see what direction it reads; the flopped (i.e. left-to-right) editions also had larger page sizes (about 6" by 8"—the same format as Dark Horse's *Blade of the Immortal*). But if you only see it listed online or in a catalog, there are other ways to tell. First of all, if the volume number is 21 or higher, it's unflopped. If the volume number is lower, check to see if the volume has a title name, such as *Wrong Number*, *Ninja Master*, etc. If it does, it's flopped—the unflopped editions *only* have volume numbers, never volume titles. Another way to tell is that the unflopped volumes all cost US$10.95, whereas the flopped versions had varying cover prices.

The way listings are given in this encyclopedia section is designed to help you look them up in either version, where applicable.

In left-to-right format, Dark Horse has previously released nineteen volumes of *Oh My Goddess!*: Vol. 1: *Wrong Number*; Vol. 2: *Leader of the Pack*; Vol. 3: *Final Exam*; Vol. 4: *Love Potion No. 9*; Vol. 5: *Sympathy for the Devil*; Vol. 6: *Terrible Master Urd*; Vol. 7: *The Queen of Vengeance*; Vol. 8: *Mara Strikes Back!*; Vol. 9: *Ninja Master*; Vol. 10: *Miss Keiichi*; Vol. 11: *The Devil in Miss Urd*; Vol. 12: *The Fourth Goddess*; Vol. 13: *Childhood's End*; Vol. 14: *Queen Sayoko*; Vol. 15: *Hand in Hand*; Vol. 16: *Mystery Child*; Vol. 17: *Traveler*; Vol. 18: *The Phantom Racer*; and Vol. 19/20: *Sora Unchained* (see note on page 189). In this encyclopedia, you will sometimes see references to the way something was done in the "original English version"; this will always refer to the older, flopped version, whose translation sometimes differed from the current, unflopped version.

The switch to right-to-left, that is, to Japanese style, came with Vol. 21 (July 2005) which picked up the story where Vol. 19/20: *Sora Unchained* left off. In December 2005, Dark Horse also went back to the beginning of the series and began to release "early" as well as "ongoing" volumes in right-to-left format starting with Vol. 1. Every two months, DH switches off. By the time *Colors* is released, we should be up to Vol. 31 and Vol. 11, respectively. If you're a new reader and don't want to wait for the right-to-left versions to "catch up" with the older, you may wish to consider checking out those previously released flopped versions, which are still available and are of excellent quality!

Oh My Goddess! has fans both old and new, so these entries are marked in a way to be useful to both. Each entry is listed three ways to help you reference it. For example, the entry **Abacus** is listed as being found in "*Terrible Master Urd*, Chapter 39, Vol. 6." So this means the abacus reference appears (generally, this means *first* appears) in Chapter 39 of *Oh My Goddess!*, which is found in *Terrible Master Urd* in the old version, and is found in Vol. 6 in the new version. By contrast, an entry such as that for **Ahem Bug** only says "Chapter 177, Vol. 28," because all volumes from 21 on have no volume titles, and only ever appeared in an unflopped version. For a complete chapter-by-chapter breakdown of the two versions, please see pages 184–190.

Of course, during the next few years, Dark Horse will continue to rerelease previously flopped portions of the *Oh My Godddess!* story as unflopped editions, until eventually you should be able to get the entire series in unflopped format.

These encyclopedia entries were compiled by the staff of *Afternoon*, the Japanese magazine that is home to *Oh My Goddess!*, with additions by the editor of the English-language edition. Many fans, of course, have conducted their own analysis of the people, places, and things of the *OMG!* saga, so even this encyclopedia is unlikely to be completely comprehensive (or free of contradiction or even error); however, hopefully everyone will find new viewpoints here and there within.

The current editor of the English-language *Oh My Goddess!* would like to emphasize that his intention is to illustrate the differences (when they occur) between the original Japanese version, the original English version, and the current English version, not to criticize them. One also has to be wary of the limitations of what a character "literally" said in the original Japanese—it is often assumed this must, naturally, be closer to the "intended meaning." But this is not necessarily the case, as anyone will realize when thinking about English words and phrases that don't make "literal" sense, yet are understood by native English speakers.

The current English version, despite being in some ways "closer" to the Japanese original, has idiosyncracies of its own (and no doubt, mistakes of the editor's own—see the entry for **Ugo Ugo Ruga**); furthermore, the current English version only exists because the excellent original English version kept its readership for eleven years, a success found well before the "manga boom." The current English version is not only based on it, but is made possible in the first place by it.

Many definitions also contain within them terms that have their own entries elsewhere in the encyclopedia, but some entries also specifically point to a cross-reference. These are marked by a ➔ arrow. Entries with a ⇔ refer to an antonym to that entry.

A

Abacus (*Terrible Master Urd*, Chapter 39, Vol. 6)
Manual counting aid using beads strung along wires on a wooden frame; known in both ancient Rome and China, it is still used today in some parts of the world for business and education; in Japan the abacus is called a *soroban*, and is used for teaching mathematics in the third and fourth grade. Skuld was forced to make do with one to help her design the ten-dimensional scythe/toad/rice cooker.

Absolute Good Fortune Spell (*Traveler*, Chapter 102, Vol. 17)
An amulet Urd wore on her right hand (or in the original English version, her left hand ^_^) in order to win the rock-paper-scissors game against Skuld—though, in fact, both of them lost. ➔ **Hyper Dexterity Glove**

Aerodynamics 101 (*Hand in Hand*, Chapter 86, Vol. 15)
A popular class held at the Inokuradai Campus of the Nekomi Institute of Technology, six kilometers from the main campus via a long, winding mountain road. Taught Wednesdays by popular lecturer Professor Kurihara, attendance is limited to the first thirty students to arrive, turning the route each time into an impromptu racing circuit. ➔ **Queen, The**

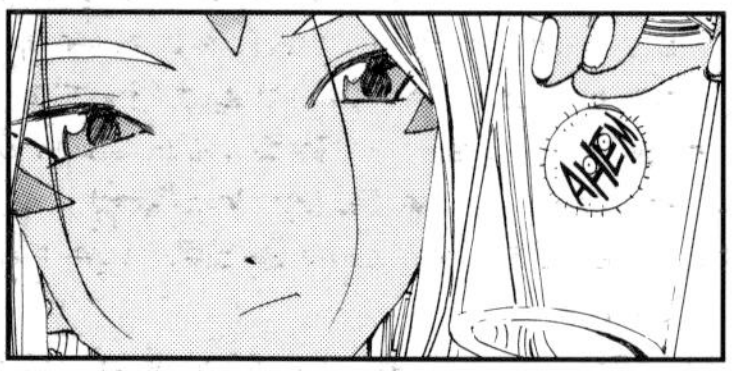
AHEM

Ahem Bug (Chapter 177, Vol. 28)
In the original Japanese, the *gohon* bug, from the Japanese manga sound FX for a deep cough; a small magical creature that infected Belldandy, giving her laryngitis. Urd sucked it out of her with a kiss, a procedure that certainly got Keiichi's undivided attention.

Ah, My Lady Belldandy! (*Queen Sayoko*, Chapter 80, Vol. 14)
Internal cry of Stringfellow, the flying broom, who fell in love with Belldandy as a result of being lent to her by Urd. A play on the manga's Japanese title.

Airbug and Spiralee (*Sora Unchained*, Chapter 120, Vol. 19)
The "spirits of air and pressure" which Belldandy summons up in order to stop the Racing Board mini go-kart that gets out of Hasegawa's control.

Almighty, The (*Wrong Number*, Chapter 1, Vol. 1)
Ruler of the heavenly realm, as Hild is ruler of the demon realm. Although often used in the original English-language version of the manga, the term "Almighty" has been de-emphasized in the unflopped version in favor of titles such as "Lord," "Heavenly One," or "Mighty One," in part because he does not seem to literally be almighty (as evidenced by the conflict with the demons), and because this term is not used in the original Japanese. His title in the original manga, *Kami-sama*, is simply a respectful way of saying "God," (as the *megami-sama* in the manga's Japanese title, *Aa Megami-sama*, is simply a respectful way of saying "Goddess"). Yet in English, this word, used by itself, suggests an image of the monotheistic God of the Abrahamic religions, which the character in *Oh My Goddess!* does not resemble; rather, he is more like the ruler, and possibly sire, among a pantheon of lesser gods, comparable to Odin in Norse religion (from which many of the characters in *OMG!* take their names). Hild's conversation with Belldandy in Vol. 22, Chapter 136, can be interpreted to suggest that he is the common father Belldandy, Urd, and Skuld share, although this is open to debate. Interestingly, although there *was* an entry for "Hild" in the original Japanese version of this encyclopedia, there was no corresponding one for "Kami-sama"; this entry therefore is written from the perspective of the English-language editor.

Almond Pocky (*The Queen of Vengeance*, Chapter 43, Vol. 7)
The pretzel chocolate snack shared by Keiichi and Belldandy when she ate it and came under the influence of the Super High Grade Love Seed. The English-language editor notes that the first time he ever saw a stick of Almond Pocky, he thought it was regular Pocky which had somehow melted and reformed, having no idea as yet there were other varieties. He had just received his first stick the night before from Richard Kim, who in the 1990s was largely responsible for bringing Pocky to American anime conventions, like a wandering missionary carrying an unholy book.

α–707 (*Hand in Hand*, Chapter 89, Vol. 15)
Inspired (!) by the device Mara used to maintain Sayoko's Castle, Skuld built this magical amplifier (stripping Keiichi's home electronics to do so), pronounced "Alpha-707," in hopes of increasing her power to the point where she could control her beloved angel, Noble Scarlet, then confined to its egg. Keiichi accidentally switched it on, but before Skuld had hooked up its control circuit, so it could be said there was plenty of blame to go around.

Alternative Energy Source (*Wrong Number*, Chapter 3, Vol. 1)
The goddesses receive a certain flow of power from Heaven, but should that flow be interrupted, or used too much within a short time, each has an individual way of "recharging." In Belldandy's case, for example, it is sleep or "hibernation" (sleep mode, as it were?); in Urd's, saké; and in Skuld's, ice cream. It is noted that Skuld can easily consume two liters of ice cream a day, a remarkable achievement for her size; whereas Urd can easily consume 1.8 liters of saké a day—even more remarkable considering that saké is 40 proof.

Amphibian Stalker (*Sora Unchained*, Chapter 128, Vol. 20)
Skuld's favorite TV program, which she fought with Urd over the right to watch in an elaborate battle stretching over two chapters. Original name of the show was *Doobutsu Chikyuu Kikoo*, or "Animals of the Earth." ➔ ***When Plants Attack***

An Donutko (*The Fourth Goddess*, Chapter 69, Vol. 12)
"Jelly Donut Girl" in the English version, which is what it means. Partner of Kanpanman.

Angels (*The Fourth Goddess*, Chapter 71, Vol. 12)
Companions that exist inside the goddesses, sharing their feelings and perceptions; they can be summoned forth from their bodies at need to help or protect them. An angel becomes part of a goddess when she swallows its egg; it then develops within, acquiring her personality, even reflecting her soul. They are not physically "born," but emerge when ready from the back of the goddess. However, this process requires that the goddess has sufficient personal energy (and personal need) to sustain her angel; if not, the angel may have to return to its egg state. It even proved possible in an emergency for a human such as Keiichi to sustain an angel temporarily; Lind said in his case, it was because he himself was supported by the love of so many goddesses. ➔ **Cool Mint, Die Wespe der Blauen Lanze, Gorgeous Rose, Holy Bell, Noble Scarlet, Spear Mint, World of Elegance**

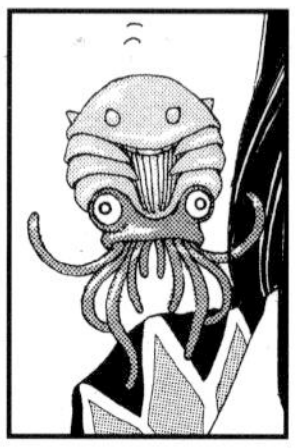

Anki (*Childhood's End*, Chapter 75, Vol. 13)
A tentacled demon that gets its energy through devouring people's ability to trust and believe. Urd had received an anki's egg by mistake (she had ordered an angel's egg), and the hatched anki then attached itself to Sayoko.

Antidote Amulet (*Love Potion No. 9*, Chapter 25, Vol. 4)
Counteracts the effect of a love potion; Belldandy was seen holding one at the end of an incident where Urd had accidentally imbibed such a potion and declared her love for Keiichi. ➔ **Love Seed**

Anti-force Shield (*Ninja Master*, Chapter 51, Vol. 8)
The shield Belldandy used to protect Skuld from the Arrow of Lost Love fired by Urd, who believed her younger sister had become dangerously infatuated with Keiichi.

Anti-Mara Mode Emergency Program (*The Devil in Miss Urd*, Chapter 63, Vol. 11)
An attack method using Banpei's head-mounted speaker to blast praise-and-worship music against the hard-rocking demon Mara.

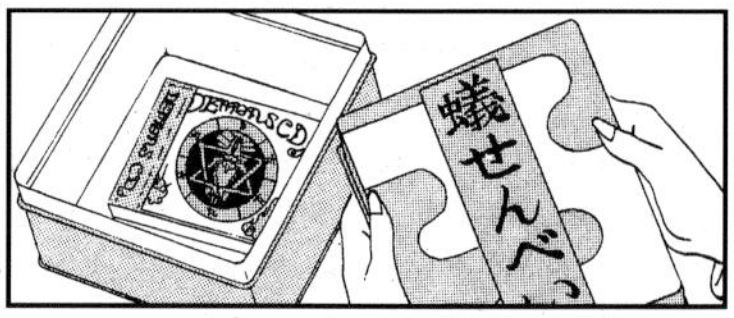

Ant Sembei (*Love Potion No. 9*, Chapter 27, Vol. 4)
The label on a tin cracker box (presumably, once filled with ant-flavored crackers) used to seal away the Demons CD.

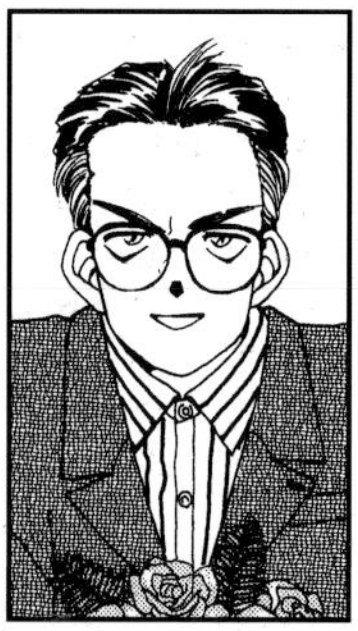

Aoshima, Toshiyuki (*Final Exam*, Chapter 20, Vol. 3)
Campus rich dude and Sayoko Mishima's cousin; wealthy young heir to the Aoshima Group. We first meet him as a freshman at Nekomi Tech, majoring in telecommunications. He tries to impress Belldandy with his Ferrari GTO and fine clothing.

Aoyama-sempai (*Wrong Number,* Chapter 1, Vol. 1)
One of *Oh My Goddess!*'s greatest mysteries, right up there with the fate of the monk who left Tarikihongan Temple in the care of Belldandy. Aoyama is mentioned in the very first line of the manga (see p. 013, panel 1)—in the original Japanese version, that is. The reference to "Aoyama" being called in to work suddenly was changed to "Tamiya" being called in to work suddenly in the English version—possibly because "Aoyama" is never mentioned or identified again, and the page seems to imply the reference is supposed to be the same guy later identified as "Tamiya." There have been two general theories: 1) Mr. Fujishima had originally intended Tamiya to be named Aoyama; and 2) Aoyama is one of the other upperclassmen who return to the dorm that evening, some of whom remain unnamed. The original Japanese entry for Aoyama in this encyclopedia section supports the second theory, explaining that he was "*one of* [emphasis added—CGH] the upperclassmen Keiichi house-sat for. He appears in name only, but Keiichi came to meet Belldandy as a result of him, so he's sort of like a Cupid." ➔ **Goddess Technical Help Line**

Art Club (*Leader of the Pack,* Chapter 10, Vol. 2)
The club Sayoko Mishima belongs to (association with some kind of activity club is as strong a feature of Japanese school life as American, if not stronger). This is where Sayoko plotted to embarrass Keiichi and Belldandy by tricking them into posing as nude models.

Artist's Betamax (*Terrible Master Urd*, Chapter 38, Vol. 6)
Skuld claimed that among the consequences of Urd becoming the Lord of Terror was that the "artist's Betamax"—presumably, meaning Kosuke Fujishima's—broke. Note that although Urd originally manifested herself through a VHS tape in the manga, when this scene was later portrayed in anime (in both the 1994 OAV and 2005 TV episode), it was through a Betamax tape, despite the fact the Beta home-video format declined rapidly after the mid-1980s.

Asari, Yoshitoh (*Oh My Goddess! Colors*)
Writer and artist of *Colors*'s introductory comic "Understanding *Oh My Goddess!* . . . In Eight Pages or Less," Mr. Asari is also the creator of one of *OMG!*'s neighbor manga in *Afternoon* magazine, *LuCuLuCu*. It's a bit like *OMG!*, except it's a cute *devil* girl who moves in with a schoolboy short on cash. It seems the underworld is so full of sinners it's running out of room, and the infernal powers have decided if the "other side" isn't doing enough to keep people out of Hell, they've got to come to Earth themselves, and teach humans how to be better people! The brilliant but *outré* Mr. Asari (he is rumored to have shaved his head and grown a beard as a tribute to Slayer's Kerry King) is a prolific manga artist in Japan, with such works as *Space Family Carl Vinson*, *WAHHAMAN* (also previously in *Afternoon*), and the educational *Manga Science* series, but is probably best known to English-speaking fans, however, as the person who designed the Angels Sachiel, Samshel, and Zeruel in *Neon Genesis Evangelion*.

Assistant A (*The Phantom Racer*, Chapter 114, Vol. 19)
The name Dr. Moreau gave to a stray student named Keiichi Morisato, drafting him into helping him test his Autonomous Bipedal Walking Machine.

B

Baka (*Ninja Master*, Chapter 51, Vol. 8)
The word Skuld hurled at Urd upon using her power for the very first time, with the result it became temporarily imprinted onto her big sister's face. Meaning "fool" or "idiot," it is sometimes thrown around by foreign fans just as carelessly—think of Susie from *Genshiken*, *Oh My Goddess!*'s neighbor in *Afternoon* magazine—but has nevertheless become part of the international otaku creole, and hence its translation as "fool" in the original English version of the manga is now simply given as "baka." Its use by otaku is actually something of a revival of *baka,* at least in the English-speaking world, as a June 1945 *TIME* article notes that U.S. soldiers were using the term "baka bomb" to refer to the *Jinrai*, a kind of rocket-powered kamikaze plane that would decades later be portrayed in the anime *The Cockpit*.

Balance Ball (*Sympathy for the Devil*, Chapter 28, Vol. 4)
Crystal ball-like device used by the demoness Mara. It can make visible the emotional balance present in a person's heart, thus making it possible to see if one's words and actions are tipping it one way or another. Mara hoped to use it, through Sayoko, to break up Keiichi and Belldandy.

Bandage Tornado (*Queen Sayoko*, Chapter 82, Vol. 14)
In the original English version, the "Ace Bandage Tornado"; one of Urd's themed attacks when forced to play a nasty nurse in a game of "Human *Virtua Fighter*."

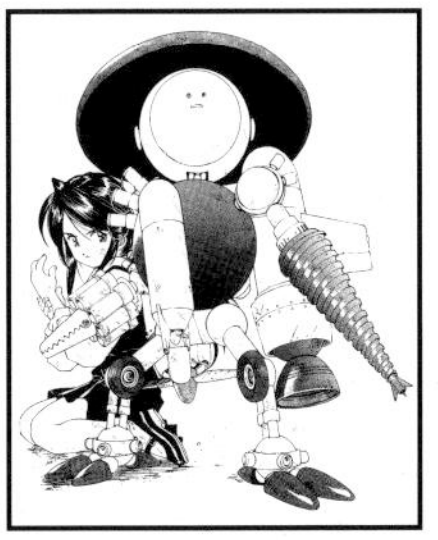

Banpei-kun (*Mara Strikes Back*, Chapter 46, Vol. 7)
Originally known as Mini-Banpei RX, Skuld developed this robot to guard against the attacks of the demonness Mara; appropriately enough, *banpei* is a traditional word for a guard or sentinel; his "headgear" is an imitation of the sloping straw hat worn in the samurai era. Banpei took up so much power, however, that every time he was activated, the fuses would blow—until Belldandy magically assembled a "booster circuit" for him. This led Banpei to develop emotions (first directed at Belldandy), and he gradually assumed the role of a guardian of the Tarikihongan Temple against all strangers, demonic or otherwise. Skuld has frequently modified him with accessory parts, including drills, jets, caterpillar tracks, and even cooking gear. Note that Skuld later applied the term "Mini-Banpei" not to her original robot, but to dozens of smaller, foot-high versions of him she made. The original usage of "Mini" probably meant in comparison to a normal adult human being (i.e., a real *banpei*).

Banshee's Tears (*The Queen of Vengeance*, Chapter 43, Vol. 7)
Urd's secret ingredient for her Ultra High-Grade Love Seeds (referred to as a "super-deluxe love potion" the first time they appear in the English version; the Seeds of Love appear again in *The Fourth Goddess*) to inspire Belldandy to get passionate with K1. ➔ **Pakdortamya X-20 Extract, Soup of a Jack o' Lantern**

Basic Matter Separator (*Hand in Hand*, Chapter 91, Vol. 16)
Device by which Skuld proposed to separate Keiichi's hand from Belldandy's, locked together by enchantment. The Basic Matter Separator sounds fancy, but it's actually just her traditional folding pocket knife, a style of blade called *higonokami* in Japanese; in the original manga, Skuld referred to the "gadget" as her *kuukan setsudan higonokami-kun*, or "Good Ol' Space-Cutting Higonokami."

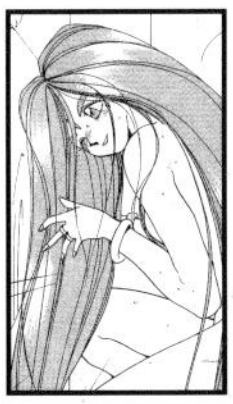

Bathing (*Love Potion No. 9*, Chapter 21, Vol. 3)
A favorite activity of Belldandy's, upon which Toshiyuki Aoshima peeped in. He was *supposed* to videotape her to "collect evidence" helpful in breaking up her and Keiichi's relationship, but found himself seized by a heartfelt prayer of gratitude that he had been able to witness this sight, so that Sayoko had to yank the camcorder out of his hands raised to heaven.

Believing Is the Best Magic (*Sora Unchained*, Chapter 127, Vol. 20)
In the original Japanese, *saikyoo mahoo ni atai suru*; literally, "as good as the best magic"—this was Keiichi's response to Belldandy saying, "You always have a chance as long as you never think you don't . . . that's how Keiichi and I win."

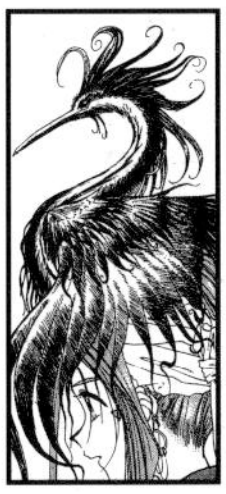

Bennu Bird (*The Fourth Goddess*, Chapter 71, Vol. 12)
A sacred creature with the power to show "the skein of time unwoven." Known as a "Vanir bird" in the original English version, after the Vanir, one of the two groups of gods within Norse mythology. Peorth summoned it to reveal an incident from the past which she regarded as a terrible crime against her by Belldandy, but which Bell-chan herself could not remember.

Bicycle Lessons (*Childhood's End*, Chapter 73, Vol. 13)
Skuld, who had a hard time understanding the unimproved technological simplicity of a bicycle, also could not understand at first why Belldandy wouldn't use her magic to help her learn how to ride. A bet with Urd had triggered the whole affair. ➔ **Three Laps around Town by Tricycle**

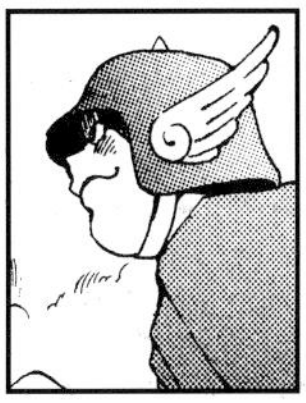

Big Z (*Mara Strikes Back*, Chapter 46, Vol. 7)
A TV anime show Urd's crazy about; the hero becomes a giant when he receives an injection. Note this joke pre-dates the anime series *The Big O* by several years; rather, it is a reference to the 1964 anime show *Big X*, based on the Osamu Tezuka manga of the same name. ➔ **Giant X**

BIOS (Chapter 133, Vol. 21)
Standing for "Basic Input/Output System," or, alternately, "Basic Integrated Operating System." This is the most fundamental software within a personal computer, the means by which it first "boots up" when started. Keiichi's tweaking of Chihiro's BIOS to speed up her computer gave Belldandy a crucial insight as to why she and her sisters had been unable to return Peorth to her original size.

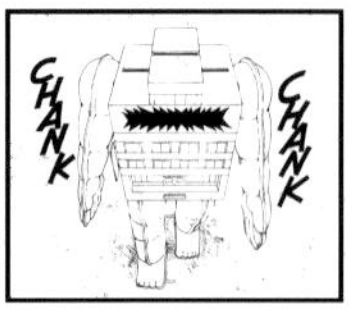
CHANK
CHANK

Black Silver (*The Phantom Racer*, Chapter 116, Vol. 19)
Name of a two-legged toy robot found in Dr. Moreau's lab. Taken together with the super high-tech appearance of the 'bot, it is obvious Fujishima-san named it for Black Silver, another menacing invention of the mad Dr. Kishiwada, hero of Tony Takezaki's (*Space Pinchy*, *Daigassaku*) manga *The Scientific Love of Dr. Kishiwada*, which was a neighbor of *Oh My Goddess!* in *Afternoon* magazine. Note that the robot was nameless in the original English version of this story.

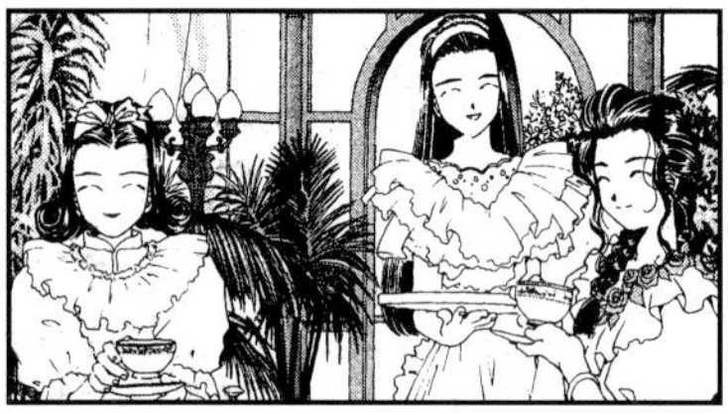

Black Tea Brand Guessing Game (*Queen Sayoko*, Chapter 82, Vol. 14)
The sinister-sounding Black Tea Club (called simply "The Tea Club" in the original Japanese version) challenged Belldandy to guess the provenance of various teas, as one of the tests to pass in Sayoko's castle. A bit of a walkover, it would seem, for the cuppa-loving goddess; unfortunately, their true intention was to drug her unconscious.

Blue No. 6 (*Ninja Master*, Chapter 50, Vol. 8)
Name of a marine upgrade Skuld made for Banpei-kun to function as a jet-ski/submersible, all under her remote control . . . while Keiichi is riding on top. Most likely a reference to the original 1960s manga *Blue Submarine No. 6* by Satoru Ozawa, as this *OMG!* story pre-dated the better-known 1999 Mahiro Maeda (director of the *Gankutsuou* TV series) anime version by several years. Called the "Banpei Deep-Six" in the original English version.

BMW 535i (*Wrong Number*, Chapter 5, Vol. 1)
Sayoko Mishima's car when we first meet her; she had to give it to a friend after losing a bet that she could make a "fawning slave of that wimp" Keiichi, but not before the System Force had reduced its engine to a heap of slag.

Book of World Inventions (*Ninja Master*, Chapter 53, Vol. 9)
In Japanese, *Sekai Hatsumei Gijiroku*—in the original English version, the show title was given as *Beyond 3000*. Skuld had previously planned to watch this tech-y show at 5:30 p.m., and thus had to join the channel fight with Urd against Kodama and Hikari when the mini-ninja ended up hijacking the frequencies. ➔ ***Nimpu Kamuri Gaiden*, Holmes**

Boopie-chan (*Sympathy for the Devil*, Chapter 31, Vol. 5)
A TV puppet called simply "Boopie" in the original English version; quite possibly the same individual seen as a groaning spirit in Chapter 2—although the name was spelled differently on that occasion ("Poopie"; literally *puupii*; it's the "u" in Japanese that has the "ooh" vowel sound; whereas the value of "o" is "oh"); puppets have notoriously bad pronunciation. Name of the doll that appeared in the TV show Urd was watching. ➔ **Garrickson-kun**

Booster Demons (*Sympathy for the Devil*, Chapter 31, Vol. 5)
Octopoid hench-creatures grown in a vat by Mara in a scheme to magnify her powers and infiltrate the Tarikihongan Temple to switch Belldandy's chocolate valentine for Mara's ethos-switching variety. Not quite as bright as their mistress. ➔ **Sudaru**

Breast Missiles (*Traveler*, Chapter 102, Vol. 17)
The Welcome Robot believed she was equipped with these, but they're actually just plug covers for power and data. For more information, please see ➔ **Rocket Punch**

Bundled Hand Grenades (*Terrible Master Urd*, Chapter 38, Vol. 6)
Apparently keeping it under her loose-fitting dress, Skuld produced this device (unusually for one of her gadgets, it has no special name; the original Japanese version of the manga just had a footnote below the panel saying "bundled hand grenades") to hurl at the Lord of Terror. Made of several Skuld Bombs bundled onto a throwing handle, it is perhaps modeled on the German *Geballte Ladung* of WWII, which similarly took a standard "potato masher" grenade and wired six additional warheads around the main one, in an attempt to give an infantryman something that could disable a tank.

C

Call Us *"Mama Dear"* (Chapter 138, Vol. 22)
In the original Japanese, *Okaasan-tte Yonde*; for Urd to address her as "Mama Dear" was Hild's fallback condition for returning Peorth to normal. Urd declined to honor the request, out of 1) fear that feeling love for her mother might tip her over to her demon half; and 2) the argument that to do so would be conduct "unbecoming to a goddess." Therefore, in the original Japanese, Urd instead called her not *okaasan* but *okachimenko*, "ugly woman," whereas in the English edition Urd began to say "Mama dear" but decided "*M*aybe not." ➔ **Condition, Kid Peorth**

Campus Queen Contest (*Final Exam*, Chapter 15, Vol. 2)
So far in the story, we've seen mention of two Campus Queen contests at Nekomi Tech. The first one, in Chapter 15, was sponsored by the Motor Club, who wanted go beyond mere beauty into evaluating the contestants' skill as gearheads. Belldandy won the contest (even though Urd competed as well!); in the original Japanese of Chapter 81, Sayoko is seen looking at a poster that features Belldandy as last year's winner, and mentions that the next contest, then seeking entrants, is now in charge of the no doubt more professional "Campus Queen Contest Executive Committee."

Can Any Light Exist Without the Darkness? (*The Devil in Miss Urd*, Chapter 64, Vol. 11)
In the original Japanese, *yaminashi de sonzai dekiru hikari wa ariemasuka?* A rhetorical question Urd asks Belldandy; the "light" in this case being her goddess side, and the "darkness" her demon side. Having been born half of each, Urd could not continue to exist were her demon nature to destroy itself.
➔ **Monopolar Demon Personality**

Carpenter from Hell (*Sora Unchained*, Chapter 123, Vol. 20)
Hasegawa's latest nickname (?), after having been known previously as the "Chef Assassin" and the "Director of Death." A member of the Motor Club muttered this phrase when the head of her hammer flew off the handle while helping to prepare for the Director Race.

Carpenters, The (*Traveler*, Chapter 109, Vol. 18)
A brother-sister duo, Richard and Karen Carpenter were one of the best-selling pop groups of the early 1970s. In the original Japanese version of Vol. 18, three of their singles were played: "Sing," "Top of the World," and "Only Yesterday." Karen Carpenter's death at thirty-two from complications of anorexia put their musical legacy in a bittersweet perspective. Her brother endowed the Richard and Karen Carpenter Performing Arts Center at Cal State Long Beach in her memory; the English version of Hiroyuki Okiura's anime film *Jin-Roh* had its U.S. premiere at the Carpenter Center in 2001. Due to licensing difficulties with the Carpenters' single, *OMG!* fan Matthew Sweet graciously permitted his songs to be used instead.
➔ ***Millennium Blues***

Catalyst (*Love Potion No. 9*, Chapter 26, Vol. 4)
Demons are summoned and sealed using paired magical objects; in the case of Mara, the catalysts were a two-CD set. ➔ **Gods CD, Demons CD**

Channel Fight (*Sora Unchained*, Chapter 128, Vol. 20)
Urd and Skuld's beloved pastime of playing games of skill or chance over who has the right to watch what channel on TV, despite the fact they could easily each watch a TV of their own. Winning the fight is of more importance.

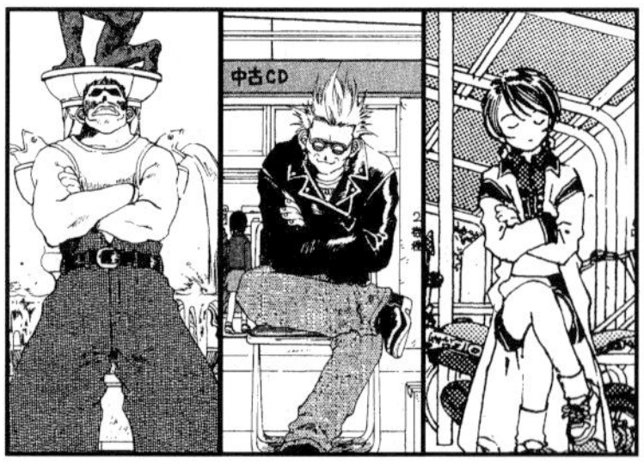
中古CD

Checkpoints 1–3 (*Sora Unchained*, Chapter 124, Vol. 20)
Under the rules of the Director Race, Sora and Keiichi had to chickkety-check themselves without wrickkety-wrecking themselves past three checkpoints, receiving a stamp at each as proof: Checkpoint 1 was administered by Tamiya at the campus fountain; Checkpoint 2 was administered by Otaki in front of the student co-op; and Checkpoint 3 was administered by Chihiro in the bicycle lot.

Chicken Diver (*Queen Sayoko*, Chapter 82, Vol. 14)
In the original Japanese, *Chikin Daibingu* (i.e., "Chicken Diving"); in the original English edition, "Killer Chicken Kick"—a special attack used by Froghorn Leghorn during the Human Virtua Fight.
➔ **Gigaton Wing Punch**

Chihiro (*Childhood's End*, Chapter 76, Vol. 13)
Unlike many characters in *OMG!*, she is better known by her first name (her last name is "Fujimi"). The first director of the NIT Motor Club, she effectively founded the organization by taking over and restructuring its immediate predecessor, the Nekomi Tech Automobile Club. Tamiya and Otaki were both (and still are) in love with her, but Chihiro felt it was her duty to choose the good of the club over love. After graduation, she joined the racing team of a leading motorcycle manufacturer, and eventually started her own cycle shop, Whirlwind, but still maintains an affection for her old outfit. Chihiro instantly respected Keiichi as club director the day they met for his belief that it's a sufficient motive to do a project because it's fun, for she had expressed the same sentiment in her day. This doesn't stop her from exploiting him just the littlest bit when he comes to work for Whirlwind, but hey, he needed the job.

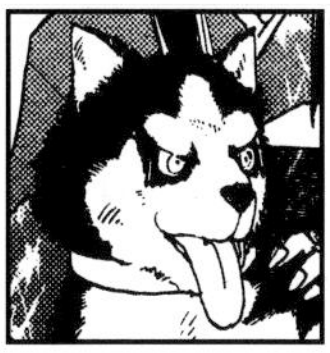

Chobi (*Leader of the Pack*, Chapter 18, Vol. 3)
Although apparently not mentioned in the story itself, this was 1) the name of the dog which gave friendly chase to a terrified Otaki during the New Year's Life Suguroku Special game; and 2) apparently belonged to Risa-chan, the neighbor from across the street.

Cold! Okazaki Beer (*Love Potion No. 9*, Chapter 26, Vol. 4)
In the original Japanese, *Tsumetai! Okazaki Beer*—the brand Tamiya threw at Mara when he inadvertently (how else?) summoned her forth. Limited local production?

Community Service Mark I (*Mara Strikes Back*, Chapter 47, Vol. 7)
In the original English version, "Labors of Love Mark One." Skuld devised this "super-deluxe" set of attachments for Banpei to allow him to do various chores around the temple. As in *Gilbert Ratchet*, it has an unfortunate risk of going destructively into reverse.

Condition (Chapter 135, Vol. 21)
As a condition for helping to return Kid Peorth to her original state, Hild suggested that Urd "defect" to the demon realm. When Urd flatly said no, Hild changed the condition to honoring an unspecified "itsy-bitsy, teeny-tiny li'l favor," which Urd also declined when the time came.

Consume by Fire! (*Hand in Hand*, Chapter 89, Vol. 15)
The words of elemental fire magic spoken by Urd after resummoning her angel, World of Elegance. Note this English phrase was used in the original Japanese version, pronounced *konshuumu bai faiaa*. ➔ **Fire Elemental Magic**

Cool Mint (Chapter 156, Vol. 25)
One of Lind's twin binary angels; she has blue eyes, and her single wing on the right-hand side of her body. ➔ **Ice Blade**

Crowd Vector Confusion Hell (*Ninja Master*, Chapter 51, Vol. 8)
This is the literal meaning of the original Japanese *hitogomi bekutoru midare jigoku*; in the English version, it is rendered more poetically as the "Mosh Pit Hell Spell." Takes the normal vectors of human crowd movement and, adding a "tad of power," deflects them so as to crush together a designated point; in this case, the bodies of Skuld and Keiichi.

Cultured Body (*The Devil in Miss Urd*, Chapter 61, Vol. 10)
Soulless clone grown (i.e., cultured) of Urd by Mara, created from a hair of the goddess filched by Senbei at the Itoh Hot Springs Resort.

Cursed Headphones (*Sympathy for the Devil*, Chapter 28, Vol. 4)
Magic spell used on more than one occasion by Mara against Urd, and vice versa. Mara can be made to perform an irresistible dance by headphones playing hard rock, whereas Urd can be bored to sleep by those playing *enka* music (traditional Japanese ballads).

Curtain of Roses (*Ninja Master*, Chapter 52, Vol. 8)
In the original Japanese, *higi baragakure*, or "Secret Weapon Hiding Rose." Kodama used this ninja technique to escape after framing Urd for smashing up Skuld's workshop. Note that unlike Peorth's rose combat, Kodama only requires the petals. ➔ **Peorth Rose Storm Attack, Peorth Wafting Rose Attack**

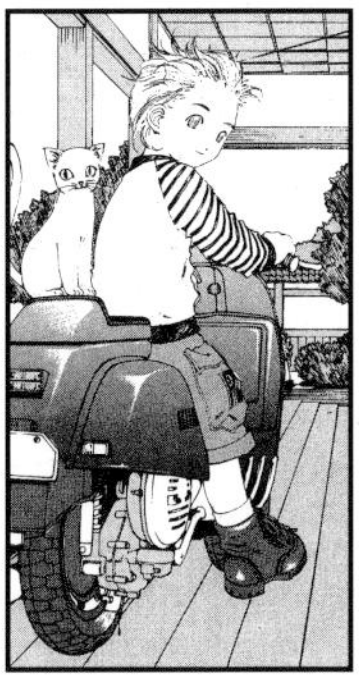

Cutest Boy ♥, Cutest Bike ♥, and Cutest Cat ♥ (Chapter 140, Vol. 22)
Three of Chihiro's favorite things, an illusion induced by Mara around the Goddess Catcher to lure her into kissing it and being thence trapped within. A play on the "Three Treasures," the ancient heirlooms of sword, mirror, and jewel held by the Japanese Imperial Household.

D

Daikokuya (*The Devil in Miss Urd*, Chapter 60, Vol. 10)
Traditional inn Keiichi and crew stayed at after mysteriously winning (i.e., as part of a sinister plot) a vacation trip to the Itoh Hot Springs. Venue of the Karaoke Match.

Day-After Hair Pack Treatment: For Damaged Hair (*Sympathy for the Devil*, Chapter 32, Vol. 5)
In the original Japanese, *Dei Afutaa Heaa Pakku Toriitomento Boro Boro Taipu*, this personal care product is visible just to the left of Urd's lovely foot as she steps into the bath in panel 1, page 35. Urd is shown in the next three panels working her hands through her hair, raising the intriguing question—do the extra-long coifs favored by the goddess sisters require a high level of maintenance?

Death God Director Hasegawa (*Sora Unchained*, Chapter 121, Vol. 20)
In the original Japanese, *Shinigami Buchoo Hasegawa*; Sora Hasegawa acquired this unfortunate nickname through the fact every club throughout her school years to have her as a director disbanded shortly thereafter. It was for this reason she wished not to be named the new director of the N.I.T. Motor Club. Called "Director Sora, Angel of Death" in the original English version.

Demon Office (*Love Potion No. 9*, Chapter 26, Vol. 4)
In Japanese, it has the very businesslike sound of *Akuma Jimusho*; this is why Hild's (see below) title was translated as "CEO." Although rarely referred to, this is the infernal agency that Mara works for; needless to say, it is the direct enemy of such celestial concerns as Belldandy's Goddess Technical Help Line.

Demon Personality (*The Devil in Miss Urd*, Chapter 64, Vol. 11)
A reference to the unusual case of Urd, who as half goddess and half demon, can theoretically be split into two separate personas, each containing one aspect of her personality; in this case, the evil half.
⇔ **Goddess Personality**

Demon Realm (*Mystery Child*, Chapter 101, Vol. 17)
Also called the "infernal realm," or the "realms below," it is, naturally, the homeland of the demons, as the heavenly realm is that of the gods. The original term used in the Japanese manga, *makai*, means "demon world," and is not the same term usually used in Japanese to evoke "hell," which is *jigoku*. Whereas we have seen much of the heavens in *OMG!*, we've seen relatively little of the demon realm. Interestingly, it is portrayed not as a subterranean place of flames, but as a futuristic city sitting under the skies (of Heaven?). Please see the separate section "Rules of the *Oh My Goddess!* Cosmos" for more details.
⇔ **Heavenly Realm**

Demon Urd (*The Devil in Miss Urd*, Chapter 62, Vol. 10)
Not to be confused with the Demon Personality within it, this was a clone of Urd (cultured by Mara from a strand of her hair) into which the Demon Personality was physically transferred via the Personality Separation Precipitator Urn.
⇔ **Goddess Urd**

Demon Urd and Keiichi's Kiss (*The Devil in Miss Urd*, Chapter 62, Vol. 10)
The evil plan adopted by Mara for how to use the Demon Urd: Demon Urd tricked Keiichi into kissing her in order to break up his contract with Belldandy. "Adopted," because Mara originally *had* no plan; when the captive Urd theorized that this was what Mara intended to do, it gave the empty-headed demon the idea.

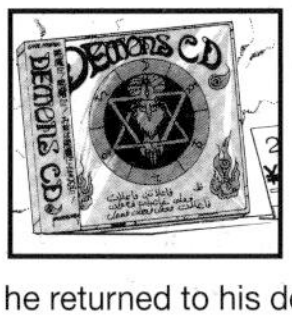
Demons CD

Demons CD (*Love Potion No. 9*, Chapter 26, Vol. 4)
One of the double-CD set (*Gods & Demons*) Tamiya bought, mysteriously attracted to its power, not realizing until he returned to his dorm that he doesn't own a CD player. Has the power to summon demons . . . such as Mara, of course. ➔ **Gods CD**

Demon's Dance Premium Saké (*The Queen of Vengeance*, Chapter 41, Vol. 6)
Tengu no Hana Dai-Ginjoo in the original Japanese; literally "Tengu's Dance Great Choice." The *tengu* is a creature in Japanese folklore, often portrayed with a long nose, and variously translated as a ghost, demon, or goblin—"demon" was chosen here for the sake of euphony. Keiichi's favorite brand, and quite expensive, none of which stopped Urd from emptying his supply.

Deportation Gate (*Mara Strikes Back!*, Chapter 47, Vol. 7)
Also known as the "Return Gate" in the original English version of the manga, this cosmic gateway is a procedure by which the goddesses' lord can forcibly repatriate one of them to Heaven.

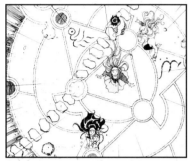

Deportation Gate Destruction Mandala (*Mara Strikes Back!*, Chapter 47, Vol. 7)
When Banpei dropped a stone in the Ultimate Magical Warding Mandala, its new geometry caused the mandala to destroy the Deportation Gate in midoperation, thus permitting Urd to stay on Earth under Article 25, Section 16.

Depth Bomb Descent (*Ninja Master*, Chapter 52, Vol. 8)
Name of spell Urd invoked against Skuld's Magical Bomb. In Japanese, *Bakurai Koorin*; note that the kanji in *bakurai* separately mean "Burst Lightning," evocative of Urd's lightning powers, but together they form the technical term for a depth bomb. In the original English version, this line was rendered varyingly as "Lightning, heed the call of Urd!" or "Urd Bolt, strike!"

Die Wespe der Blauen Lanze (Chapter 187, Vol. 29)
Meaning "Wasp of the Blue Lance" in German (continuing Velsper's trend of associating himself with German names; see **Glühende Herz**), this was the name Velsper decided to give the familiar that Hild had originally implanted in Belldandy back in Vol. 25, in hopes of controlling her. On the contrary, Belldandy's influence turned the familiar angelic, but the being's mixed nature caused a series of ongoing crises. Keiichi bore the familiar for a time (Belldandy explained its affection for him by the fact he always regarded it as an angel) but this irregular arrangement was unstable, and he and Urd convinced Velsper to accept it.

Director Candy (*Sora Unchained*, Chapter 119, Vol. 19)
A sugar-candy cone whose string Hasegawa successfully picks as part of a *kujibiki* (random drawing—the same *kujibiki* as in the meta-awful series *Kujibiki Unbalance*) to decide who will become the next director of the Motor Club, succeeding Keiichi.

Director Race (*Sora Unchained*, Chapter 119, Vol. 19)
A race to determine whether or not the still-dithering Sora Hasegawa would, in fact, succeed Keiichi as Motor Club director, in compliance with the Club Article 26, Clause 5 (see "Rules of the *Oh My Goddess!* Cosmos"). The race requires having to pass three checkpoints on campus—drivers being free to choose any route between them—and then returning first to the goal line in the parking lot. For the terrible truth behind the true purpose of this race, please see ➜ **Power Board, Racing Board**

Disenchanter (Chapter 130, Vol. 21)
In the original Japanese, *Gejutsushi*; one of the people or groups (together with the Spell Research Institute and the Supreme Spell Conservatory) from whom Peorth sought aid to return to her adult body after Velsper reduced her physically to a kid. This was rendered "spell analysts" in the English edition, but in retrospect the original is much cooler, and would make a great title for an Outrageous Cherry album.

Dobon (*The Fourth Goddess*, Chapter 69, Vol. 12)
Name of Skuld's favorite shojo magazine. A play on the real shojo magazine *Ribon*, published by Shueisha. *Ribon* manga released in the U.S. so far include such titles as *GALS!*, *Kodocha, Ultra Maniac,* and *Marmalade Boy.* Although Peorth thought *Dobon's* view of relationships was "dopey," she decided to base her plan to win Keiichi's heart on the stories she read in the magazine, and eventually became so addicted to it she stole Skuld's entire collection.
➜ *Ohashi Inn 202*

Doggie Keiichi (*Queen Sayoko*, Chapter 84, Vol. 15)
Caught in a trap while storming Sayoko's castle, Keiichi had his Skuld Will Wave Wall Shielded Ribbon Cable, Mark 1 removed and consequently fell under the campuswide mind-control rays of Queen Sayoko, whom it pleased to dress him up like a dog.

Don't Call Me Father! (Chapter 143, Vol. 23)
Phrase, with punch accompaniment, uttered by Keima toward Keiichi. Although Keima is in fact Keiichi and Megumi's father, he holds up a family rule that everyone should go by first names rather than addressing each other as relatives.

Dorm Renovation (*Traveler*, Chapter 105, Vol. 18)
The reason why a large number of his fellow students, led by the persuasive Tamiya, asked to store their belongings with Keiichi at Tarikihongan. Even the spacious temple interior proved inadequate to the task, leading directly to the Infinite Tea Room incident.

Drag Queen Keiichi (*Final Exam*, Chapter 19, Vol. 3)
In the original Japanese, *Josoo no Keiichi*—the nickname he acquired on campus after an unfortunate incident where his seniors, always looking out for his welfare, dressed him up as a woman during a cram session, leaving him no time to change before the exam.

Dr. Moreau (*The Phantom Racer*, Chapter 114, Vol. 19)
Nickname for one of Keiichi's more crazed professors, after his real name Professor (Koichi) Morozumi. It's a reference to Jules Verne's mad scientist of the same name. Obsessed with building an Autonomous Bipedal Walking Machine (an achievement later made in real life by Honda, with their ASIMO robot).

Dynamite Baseball Brothers (*Miss Keiichi*, Chapter 58, Vol. 10)
A masked Otaki and Tamiya don this *nom de guerre* to help out Megumi—short two players—in her match against the NIT Baseball Club. You would have to be a complete moron not to see it's Otaki and Tamiya, but everyone humors them, and presumably humors them again when they both strike out.

E

Earth Assistance Hotline (*The Fourth Goddess*, Chapter 66, Vol. 11)
Peorth's agency; a competitor to Belldandy's Goddess Technical Help Line.

Earth Spirit, Third Class (*Leader of the Pack*, Chapter 9, Vol. 1)
The reason why no one had rented the too-good-to-be-true apartment Megumi Morisato wanted to move into near campus: it was haunted by this local nature spirit, trapped there by the construction of the building. Belldandy reenergized it, enabling the spirit to leave, but as a favor to her it assumed the form of a live-in guardian to watch over Megumi as a rat.

Easy Seals (*The Devil in Miss Urd*, Chapter 62, Vol. 10)
Known as "Simple Seals" in the original English version of the manga. Mara ends up helping the Demon Urd seal away Belldandy after being told that it was easy to break it open—the truth is, however, that no one can break it, except for the Demon Urd . . . and the Goddess Urd.

Eater of Angels (Chapter 155, Vol. 24)
In Japanese, *Tenshigui*—a creature ordinarily kept under observation at the Magical Creatures Research Center in Heaven. It lures angels to emerge from their companion goddesses by imitating the distress cry of a fellow angel, leaving

the goddesses comatose. Its theft prompts Lind to travel to Earth to track it down, not realizing that she herself is carrying it as part of a plot by Hild.

Economy Run (*Sympathy for the Devil*, Chapter 30, Vol. 4)
An invitation to this event—intended for their campus rival the Four Wheels Club—was delivered by mistake to the N.I.T. Motor Club instead. In this type of race, the winner is the team whose vehicle uses the least fuel over a fixed distance and time. ➜ **N.I.T. Four Wheels Club**

Emotion Circuit (*The Devil in Miss Urd*, Chapter 65, Vol. 11)
A classic concept in SF robotics (although emotions in humans are also understood as a circuit from a neuroanatomical perspective), this is a wiring or pathway that enables emotional response. Banpei showed his first evidence for this function in Chapter 46, when, shortly after his construction by Skuld, Belldandy's installation of a booster circuit created a sort of "compassion feedback," whereby Banpei responded by feeling protective and caring toward Belldandy. This phenomenon vanished after his batteries went dead, but returned in Chapter 65, to cause Skuld grave concern; it was revealed that she deliberately tried to keep emotions out of Banpei's makeup from fear they might override his self-preservation instinct. ➜ **Sigel**

Engine No. 1 (*Childhood's End*, Chapter 73, Vol. 13)
The name Sentaro gave Skuld as he helped to keep her bicycle steady, standing on the back axle and leaning over her as she rode. ➜ **Bicycle Lessons**

Enka (*Sympathy for the Devil*, Chapter 28, Vol. 4)
A style of music that is one of Urd's weaknesses, making her fall asleep whenever she hears it. Although compared to polka music in the original English version of the manga, *enka* is perhaps better compared to traditional American honky-tonk music in theme (loneliness, lost love, drinking, hardship), if not instrumentation (as enka contains both elements of Western ballad singing with traditional Japanese instruments such as the *shamisen*). The fact that it makes Urd fall asleep is probably meant to reflect the fact enka is rarely popular among young people in Japan. ➜ **Rock**

Eumaniienmai ♥ (*Sora Unchained*, Chapter 119, Vol. 19)
Mysterious words Sora Hasegawa uttered when she was eating the Director Candy (simply written as "nmm ymm ymmm?" in the original English version of the manga). She was probably, however, trying to say *Belldandy-sempai*—"sempai" being an honorific (of the same kind as "-san" or "-chan") used to refer to someone with a certain seniority over you in a group, such as a school, company, or (in this case) club. It is often translated in English as "Senior," and as such might be phrased before rather than after the name—so "Senior Belldandy."

Everybody's Tea Room (*Queen Sayoko*, Chapter 79, Vol. 14)
Belldandy's private room at Tarikihongan; although her gracious and hospitable nature means it often serves as the general living room. Note that the carved wooden sign on the door is bilingual even in the original Japanese manga, with the "Everybody's" part in Japanese *hiragana*, and "Tea Room" in English. ➜ **Keiichi's Shop, Skuld Labs, Urd's Room**

Explosion Grass (*The Devil in Miss Urd*, Chapter 60, Vol. 10)
Dangerous, yet presumably decorative element simultaneously added to floral bouquets sent by Urd to Mara (and by Mara to Urd) on an occasion when they were trying to make up their previous friendship. It is said to be similar to flowers such as balsam or jewelweed which scatter their seeds up to several meters, but more shrapnel-like in effect. Referred to as "blast flowers" in the original English version of the manga.

Exorcism and Annihilation (*Ninja Master*, Chapter 53, Vol. 9)
An incantation used by Belldandy in a last-ditch effort to save Keiichi from a swarm of ninja; Urd calls it "the most powerful of all purification spells" and remarks that its use took such energy, it almost cost Bell her life. Note that this is a translation of the original Japanese *hama mekkyaku*, both words of which have strong Shinto associations; the kanji in *hama* are taken from *hamayumi*, the traditional bow and arrow sent as a gift to boy children to symbolically shoot evil spirits; this link with protecting males (there is a corresponding charm, the *hagoita*, a wooden shuttlecock paddle, to protect girl children) perhaps explains its choice by Belldandy.

F

Familiar (Chapter 158, Vol. 25)
In black magic, a familiar is a creature that assists a sorcerer to work evil; Hild so names the spirits by which she proposes to turn the goddesses demonic—implanting familiars in them once their angels are removed. The plan seriously backfires, though, as her test subject, Belldandy, instead turns the familiar angelic! ➜ **Die Wespe der Blauen Lanze**

Fenrir Wolf (*Terrible Master Urd*, Chapter 37, Vol. 6)
The *Oh My Goddess!* universe has a number of motifs related to Norse mythology, in which the Fenrir Wolf is the child of the malevolent trickster god, Loki. During the advent of the Lord of Terror, the possessed Urd summoned Fenrir forth to wreak havoc—its appearance well befitted the legend that during the apocalypse, the wolf would have grown to such great size that its open jaws would touch both ground and sky. Fenrir was in fact the form in which the Ultimate Destruction Program embodied itself for a time, before it transferred itself to the Midgard Serpent. ➜ **Midgard Serpent**

Ferrari 288GTO (*Final Exam*, Chapter 20, Vol. 3)
An icon among high-end sports cars of the 1980s, most students of the era could only experience the 288GTO through wall posters (usually juxtaposed with the curves of a reclining woman and a champagne bottle and the unlikely slogan "DECISIONS"), but Aoshima, coming from a rich family, had one to drive around. Keiichi could not resist his offer of borrowing it for a test drive, during which time Aoshima's flunkies sabotaged his bike—allowing Aoshima to conveniently suggest giving Belldandy a "ride home" in that very same GTO.

Fire Elemental Magic (*Hand in Hand*, Chapter 89, Vol. 15)
The elemental force associated with Urd. Belldandy's Wind Elemental Magic was useless as a counter when Skuld trapped herself within a feedback loop of her own Water Elemental Magic, making it necessary that Urd invoke her Angel, World of Elegance, for the first time in years, to give her the strength to free Skuld. Urd in fact often seems to favor lightning spells, although perhaps this is a metaphoric aspect of fire. ➜ **Water Elemental Magic, Wind Elemental Magic**

500 Yen per Hour (*Hand in Hand*, Chapter 91, Vol. 16)
The amount Chihiro offered Belldandy to assist with odd jobs at Whirlwind (in the original English version, the sum is described simply as "minimum wage.") When the offer coincides with Bell and Keiichi finally being able to separate their magically joined hands, Chihiro looks upon her sudden joy with the mistaken thought, "Maybe I could have gotten her for 400."

Flash Burst Thunder Attack Bullet (*The Devil in Miss Urd*, Chapter 63, Vol. 11)
Two levels more powerful than the Depth Bomb Descent; used by the Goddess Urd against the Demon Urd. In the original English version, it is referred to as the "Super-Bolt Lightning Ball."

Flavor Emperor Gold 200 (*Mara Strikes Back!*, Chapter 49, Vol. 8)
Supposedly taste-enhancing tablets Urd gave to Sora Hasegawa, in order to help her improve her truly awful cooking. While it "makes your meal a feast you'll never forget," Urd neglected to mention that it works as, you guessed it, a love potion. Called "Emperor of Flavor Gold Two-Hundred" in the original English version. Six of one . . .

Floppy Disk (*Terrible Master Urd*, Chapter 39, Vol. 6)
Skuld tricked the Ultimate Destruction Program into transferring itself from Keiichi onto a floppy disk (so called because although it was encased in a rigid, square plastic shell, the magnetic disk within was indeed thin and flexible). The 3.5" model of these disks, which could in theory store up to 1.47 megabytes each, were the most common form of portable storage for personal computers from the mid-eighties through the mid-nineties, until replaced by the CD-ROM. However, strictly speaking, the disk used by Skuld was a 2.8" by 3" 128K unit salvaged from a Nintendo Famicom Disk System (never released in the U.S.).

Forced Alliance (*Sora Unchained*, Chapter 125, Vol. 20)
In the original Japanese, *kyoosei teki ni mikata ni naru* ("forcibly making an ally"); this was part of the phrase said alluringly by Urd right

before planting a surprise kiss on Keiichi's lips. The issue at hand was his refusal as a matter of honor to accept help from the other goddesses in the Director Race against Hasegawa, even though she herself was receiving aid from Belldandy. Urd decided to help him anyway by slipping the Guts Accelerator down his throat during the kiss. In the original English edition, Urd said, "You don't have to accept my help . . . but you're gonna get it!" ➔ **Guts Accelerator**

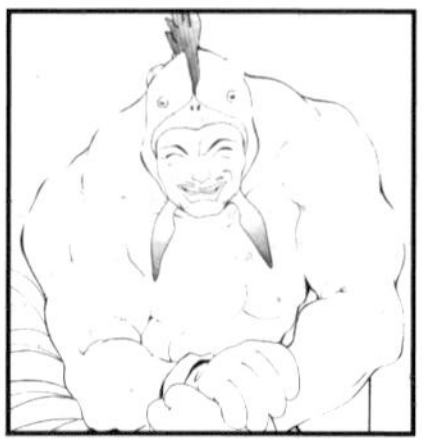

Froghorn Leghorn (*Queen Sayoko*, Chapter 82, Vol. 14) Ohnishi's stage name for the human version of *Virtua Fighter* he was drafted into as one of the games in Sayoko's castle. The original Japanese name was *Hakushoku Reguhoon Ohnishi*, or "White-Colored Leghorn Ohnishi." *Hakushoku Reguhoon* is the Japanese name for the important agricultural chicken variety known in English-speaking countries as the "Single Comb White," a fact that a small yet distinct portion of the editor hates himself for taking a half-hour to confirm. The fighter who fought against Urd during the Human Virtua Fight. ➔ **Urd the Nightingale**

Furisode (*Final Exam*, Chapter 18, Vol. 3)
The beautiful kimono with the floor-length sleeves Belldandy and Urd wore for the New Year's party (portrayed in lovely color on pages 28–29 of the unflopped edition) are *furisode*, the most formal and expensive style of kimono. According to Dark Horse's Riko Frohnmayer (who, like many Japanese women, first wore one for her *shiki-jitsu*, the coming-of-age ceremony of full legal adulthood, considered to be twenty in Japan) they can cost anywhere from US$1,000 up to US$20,000, depending on label and workmanship—considering how short of money Keiichi's household is, it's a good thing Belldandy can conjure up clothing.

G

Galant GTO MR (*Final Exam*, Chapter 17, Vol. 3)
The car Keiichi "borrowed" from a freshman in the Motor Club for his date with Belldandy at the Hotel Koenig. It was a rare example of the *sempai/kohai* relationship—where younger students do favors for older ones, receiving mentoring in return—working out in Keiichi's favor for a change; consider his usual relations with Tamiya and Otaki. An early 1970s vehicle, the Mitsubishi Galant GTO MR was somewhat inspired by the great American muscle cars of the period (the kind seen in *Death Proof*).

Game Match (*The Devil in Miss Urd*, Chapter 60, Vol. 10)
Second of the three matches Urd and Mara fought against each other during their truce (from *actual* fighting) at the Daikokuya Inn. The game in this case was a countertop version of the Atari classic, *Breakout*. Urd won the match. ➔ **Karaoke Match, Ping-Pong Match**

Gamerabbit (*Final Exam*, Chapter 16, Vol. 2)
To help earn money to buy a ring for Belldandy, Keiichi briefly took on the humiliating part-time job of dressing up in a department store as "Gamerabbit," a portmanteau of "rabbit" and "Gamera," the famous flying giant-turtle monster of Japanese film.

Ganbare Gen-san (*Terrible Master Urd*, Chapter 37, Vol. 6)
"Ganbare!" meaning roughly "keep it up!" is a traditional word used to cheer someone on in Japan; "Gen-san" is a person's name. This was what Skuld called the optical illusion projector (known as "Mr. Opto" in the original English-language version) she employed to help trap the Fenrir Wolf. The gadget was possibly so called after the Kikkoman-brand saké of the same name, which might no doubt also induce you to see things that aren't there.

Gan-chan (*Adventures of the Mini-Goddesses*, Chapter 67, Vol. 11)
After being rebuked by Urd for declaring he was henceforth to be named not "Mr. Rat," but "Mitsuo Iwata," the rodent premiered this new nickname. As Urd's outrage was based on the impudence of him giving himself a last name, "Gan-chan" either makes fun of her, or tries to play it safe, by cutting the last name "Iwata" in half—it uses the same character as the "Iwa" in "Iwata," except this kanji is read *gan* when used by itself. *Gan* usually means "stone," by the way, and *Iwata* can have the same meaning as the English last name "Stonefield," or the German "Steinfeld." ➔ **Iwata, Mitsuo**

Garm (*Miss Keiichi*, Chapter 57, Vol. 9)
Dread watchdog of Nibelheim, the Land of the Dead in the Norse mythology that influences the *Oh My Goddess!* cosmos. Amateur exorcist Shiho Sakakibara accidentally summoned him while trying to conjure Kundali instead.

Garrickson-kun (*Sympathy for the Devil*, Chapter 31, Vol. 5)
A TV puppet called "Garkson" in the original English version; quite possibly the same individual seen as a groaning spirit in Chapter 2—although the name was spelled differently on that occasion ("Garikin"); puppets have notoriously bad pronunciation. ➔ **Boopie-chan**

Ghost of the Pass (*The Phantom Racer*, Chapter 110, Vol. 18)
Spectral, riderless Honda NS400R that challenges drivers on the mountain pass leading to Nekomi Tech's Inokuradai Campus. The bike had been Chihiro's, lost five years ago in an accident when it flew off a cliff.

Giant X (*The Fourth Goddess*, Chapter 68, Vol. 12)
While poking around Urd's pills, hoping to find her "Seeds of Love," Peorth first comes across her "super growth potion, Giant X," possibly a reference to the plot gimmick of Urd's beloved anime series, *Big Z*—although "Giant X" was also the pseudonymous company name of Gainax (also friends of Kosuke Fujishima) in their 1991 *Otaku no Video*.

Gift Shop Karin (*Queen Sayoko*, Chapter 80, Vol. 14)
The store where Belldandy purchased a decorative cover (?) for Stringfellow, the flying broom, when she went shopping with "him" and Keiichi.

Gigaton Wing Punch (*Queen Sayoko*, Chapter 82, Vol. 14)
Special attack used by White-Colored Leghorn Ohnishi, AKA Froghorn Leghorn, during the Human Virtua Fight. It's just like an ordinary punch, except you do it while shouting "Gigaton Wing Punch!" and then get your clock cleaned by Urd. ➔ **Chicken Diver**

Glühende Herz (Chapter 180, Vol. 28) Meaning "Glowing Heart" in German, this is the name of Velsper's beloved former flying broom—now in the custody of the mistress of all demons, Hild. Although classed as a broom, it resembles more a sort of high-tech jet spear, emblazoned with a hexagram symbolizing black magic. The eight-time racing champion of the demon world, Glühende Herz excels on short courses, a fact Belldandy is able to use to her competitive advantage.

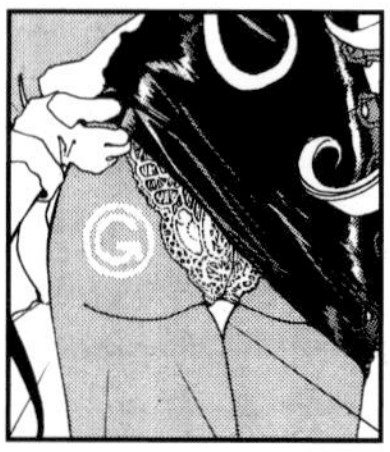

G Mark, The (*The Devil in Miss Urd*, Chapter 63, Vol. 11)
Stamp cleverly placed on the Goddess Urd's rear in order to distinguish her from the otherwise identically appearing Demon Urd.

Goddess Catcher (Chapter 139, Vol. 22)
Teapot-shaped miscellaneous magic item made for Mara by her demonic rat flunkies; any goddess (or, for that matter, mortal) touching their lips to its spout will be sucked inside. Those thus trapped can only be released by adding hot water to the pot, and rubbing it three times.

Goddess Personality (*The Devil in Miss Urd*, Chapter 64, Vol. 11)
A reference to the unusual case of Urd, who as half Goddess and half Demon, can theoretically be split into two separate personas, each containing one aspect of her personality; in this case, the good half. ⇔ **Demon Personality**

Goddess Song (Chapter 131, Vol. 21)
Belldandy attempted to restore Kid Peorth to her normal body by means of a song made of compressed spell commands. Frequency shifts from note to note execute the spell subroutines; if a single note is off pitch in the thirty-minute song, the entire song fails.

Goddess Symbol (Chapter 188, Vol. 29) An ornate calligraphic sigil, specific to each individual goddess, that expresses such information as her name, class, power, affiliation, and predilictions. A Goddess Symbol calls for great precision to express its meaning properly.

Goddess Technical Help Line (*Wrong Number*, Chapter 1, Vol. 1)
In the original Japanese, *O-tasuke Megami Jimusho*, more literally "Goddess Assistance Office," and the job Belldandy was working at in the heavenly realm whereby she met Keiichi. The job itself involved helping "people with problems" by granting them one wish; Keiichi's fateful wish, of course, was that a goddess like Belldandy be with him always.

Goddess Urd (*The Devil in Miss Urd*, Chapter 63, Vol. 11)
After Mara separated Urd's Goddess and Demon personalities, transferring the latter to a clone

grown from Urd's hair, the former remained within Urd's original body, making her frighteningly thoughtful and considerate. ⇔ **Demon Urd**

Gods CD (*Love Potion No. 9*, Chapter 26, Vol. 4)
One of the double-CD set (*Gods & Demons*) Tamiya bought, mysteriously attracted to its power, not realizing until he returned to his dorm that he doesn't own a CD player. Has the power to bind demons . . . such as Mara, of course.

Going Steady for Dummies (*Wrong Number*, Chapter 7, Vol. 1)
Romance advice manual that Keiichi bought, in hopes of speeding up his relationship with Belldandy. Interestingly, the title of it in the original Japanese was also in English: *Sutedii Atakku Mesoddo*, the Japanese way of writing "Steady Attack Method."

Golden Bush Warbler (*Love Potion No. 9*, Chapter 25, Vol. 4)
Object quested for by Urd's former boyfriend Troubadour, who left her to embark upon the search. He felt it was one of those man's-gotta-do type situations, even though he's technically not a man, but a plum tree spirit. ➔ **Scroll of Golden Verse**

Golden Empire (*Love Potion No. 9*, Chapter 26, Vol. 4)
One of the CDs on display next to the *Gods & Demons* double-disc set. Mysteriously, seems to contain Aztec glyphs.

Golden Hammer Competition (*Love Potion No. 9*, Chapter 22, Vol. 3)
An intercollegiate racing match involving a preliminary, qualifying go-kart event, and a final timed rally under varying terrain. The winning team receives a trophy in the shape of a golden hammer, as well as prize money, but the victorious N.I.T. received only the hammer, the money being withheld to defray their snacks and drinks bill. ➔ **LAIT**

Golden Reggae Hits (*Love Potion No. 9*, Chapter 27, Vol. 4)
The younger generation, which knows music only as an efreet-like spirit on computer files, may never understand the bitter disappointment of finding a long-sought CD case, only to find the wrong disc inside, as Mara did when the *Demons* case she thought would free her was revealed to actually contain the steel-drum sounds of *Golden Reggae Hits* (called *Best of Reggae King* in the original Japanese version). ➔ **Demons CD, Gods CD**

Gomorrah, Yuki (*The Queen of Vengeance*, Chapter 41, Vol. 6)
Business name of the robed, hooded president of the Fortune-Telling Subcommittee of the N.I.T. Mystery Club. Yuki read Keiichi (without being asked) his "secrets" (actually, just the stuff she already knew about him), but ended up being used as a conduit by the Almighty to convey information about an Alternative Energy Source for the goddesses.

Good-Luck Charms (*Sympathy for the Devil*, Chapter 29, Vol. 4)
One of Mara's weaknesses; examples include *hamaya* arrows and *tanuki* statues. She is allergic to their touch, and the effect on her may drain her energy, or even her memory. ➔ **Rock**

Gorgeous Rose (*The Fourth Goddess*, Chapter 71, Vol. 12)
Name of Peorth's angel; called "La Rose Magnifique" when first introduced in the original English version of the manga. The angel's form is wound with flowering rose vines—thorned, of course.

Gooten (*The Devil in Miss Urd*, Chapter 65, Vol. 11)
The name of the Chinese restaurant (meaning "Rumbling Skies") from which the Urd's-Skin-Covered Banpei-kun rescued a cat when the building caught fire. In the original English version of the manga, it was called "Emmy's Chinese Restaurant."

Grandma's Bag of Tricks: Diagonal 45-Degree Chop! (*Traveler*, Chapter 102, Vol. 17)
The special technique (i.e., smacking it with the edge of her hand) Urd proposed to use on Banpei when he was malfunctioning, perhaps based on the theory it works for TVs. Known as "Auntie Urd's Home Cure! The Forty-Five Degree Chop!!" in the original English version of the manga.

Guts Accelerator (*Sora Unchained*, Chapter 126, Vol. 20)
Although called the "Chutzpah Hammer" in the original English version of the manga, it was literally the English words *Gattsu Akuserareetaa* in Japanese; Urd administered this preparation (by mouth, via a kiss) to Keiichi to make him focused and shameless during the Director Race.

H

Hakko Girl (*The Queen of Vengeance*, Chapter 41, Vol. 6)
In the original Japanese version of Vol. 6 (the reference was in panel 5, the last caption), Urd, having shrunk to the body of a child, was referred to as being a *hakko no shojo*, or "Hakko Girl." This is a play on words—*shojo* means "girl," but depending on the kanji used, *hakko* can mean either "misfortune" or "fermentation," a reference to Urd's Alternative Energy Source, saké.

Hakozaki, Tsutomu (*Queen Sayoko*, Chapter 79, Vol. 14)
Name of the boy who earned second place in the BMX race that Sentaro won. A fairly obscure trivia question, you'll admit.

Half Goddess/Half Demon (*The Devil in Miss Urd*, Chapter 61, Vol. 10)
Urd's father was godly, but her mother was a demon, giving her an inherent hybrid nature, although it is important to note that Urd takes great pride in her legal status as a goddess and worries about tilting over to her "demon side." Urd claims to Mara that not even the ruler of Heaven himself was able to spiritually separate out the two sides of her nature—although that doesn't stop Mara from attempting it with another harebrained gadget.

Half Goddess/Half Demon Seal Earring Program (*The Devil in Miss Urd*, Chapter 63, Vol. 11)
As noted in Chapter 36, Vol. 5, a Goddess First-Class, such as Belldandy, wears a seal earring as a safety device to restrict her power. Although Urd is legally a Goddess Second-Class due to her habitual lying, she apparently wears one as well (Belldandy remarked in Chapter 14, Vol. 2, that Urd is "far more powerful" than herself). It is suggested that Mara placed a copy of the original

Urd's program on the ear of her all-demonic Urd clone, not realizing until later the program would crash due to incompatible "hardware"—i.e., it was written for an Urd that is half goddess and half demon. ➔ **Separation of Goddess/Demon Personalities**

Hana to Ume (Chapter 140, Vol. 22)
A shojo magazine Skuld loves to read. *Hana to Ume* means "Flowers and Plums" (actually, an *ume* is a Japanese apricot, but it's traditionally translated as "plum"). This is a play on the real-life shojo magazine *Hana to Yume*, which means "Flowers and Dreams." A number of manga from *Hana to Yume* have been published in English, including Kaori Yuki's *Angel Sanctuary* and Natsuki Takaya's *Fruits Basket*. ➔ **Dobon**

Hand-Knit Sweater (*The Queen of Vengeance*, Chapter 44, Vol. 7)
As the name implies, it was a sweater Belldandy made for Keiichi by hand; however, it also became a symbol of Belldandy's belief that knitting is an exercise in contemplation as well as simply construction. The sweater took on further meaning for Sayoko, who had stolen it before it could be given to Keiichi. Originally, she had been jealous of Belldandy only because she drew attention away from her previous position as "campus queen," but the sweater made Sayoko realize she was also jealous of the kind of love Belldandy and Keiichi have. In the end, she couldn't bring herself to destroy the sweater, the symbol of that love.

Happy Badge (Chapter 188, Vol. 29) Magical measuring device cooked up by Peorth for Keiichi to wear during Urd's final qualifying problem to achieve First-Class Goddess status. The badge has an expressionless face when the wearer is emotionally neutral, an unhappy face when the wearer is sad, and an ecstatic expression at "happiness quotient 500." It was Urd's task to get Keiichi to that level by six o'clock the following evening . . .

Happy Family Planning (*Ninja Master*, Chapter 51, Vol. 8)
Condoms the old coot at the Kasugano Pharmacy assumed Keiichi needed because he "seemed so nervous." He ended up slipping them into Keiichi's bag anyway as a freebie. Literally "Bright Family Planning" (*Akarui Kazoku Keikaku*). Called *Cupid Thins* in the original English version.

Hasegawa, Sora (*Mara Strikes Back*, Chapter 45, Vol. 7)
A member of the N.I.T. Motor Club, and eventually its director; drives a Fiat 500. A cute *meganekko* (girl wearing glasses), Hasegawa is younger than Keiichi, but, because of her small stature, is frequently mistaken for being even younger than that. Has a quite unrequited crush on Toshiyuki Aoshima.

Hasegawa, the Chef Assassin (*Mara Strikes Back*, Chapter 49, Vol. 8)
In the original Japanese, *Satsujin Shefu Hasegawa*—the rather unkind nickname given to Sora Hasegawa since her grade-school days, owing to her poor marks in home economics.

Hashimoto (*Queen Sayoko*, Chapter 82, Vol. 14)
Apparent leader of the Chemistry Club; one of many to fall under the control of Sayoko's Mind Force Field.

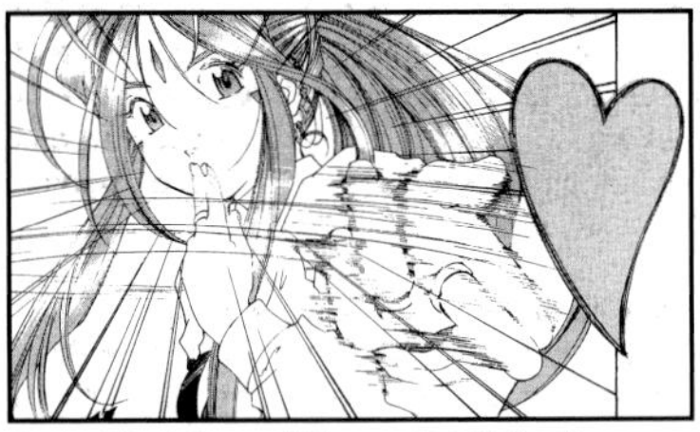

Heart Kiss Throw (Chapter 136, Vol. 22)
The kiss Belldandy threw to save Keiichi from the Spade Kiss Throw of Hild.

Heavenly Realm (*Leader of the Pack*, Chapter 13, Vol. 2)
Also called "the Heavens" or simply "Heaven," although the use of the latter is somewhat problematical in the English edition of *Oh My Goddess!*, as the original term used in the Japanese manga, *tenkai*, means "heaven world" and is not the same term used in Japanese to evoke "heaven," which is usually just *ten*, or *tengoku* ("Kingdom of Heaven"). The heavenly realm is typically (as might be expected) portrayed as if one were looking up towards it in the sky (compare with downward-looking portrayal of the demon realm), and as having an architecture of organic-looking spires and helix-shaped bridges. A recent depiction (Chapter 189, Vol. 30) showed it as three massive cones edged by wooded terraces, each surmounted by a single tree. This is perhaps linked to the image of Yggdrasil, which in the Norse religion is the World Tree that forms the axis of the various realms of existence; the computer system in Heaven that performs a similar cosmic function is named for this tree. The heavenly realm is evidently populated by many other youthful-appearing goddesses, and perhaps gods as well (as seen in Chapter 189) and is of course the home of the goddesses Belldandy, Urd, Skuld, Peorth, and Lind, as well as the figure sometimes called "the Almighty" in the English version of the manga. Velsper's memories (if they are to be relied upon) showed a somewhat different side of Heaven in Vol. 28, Chapter 181, as he recalled racing through a region of it containing a stone bridge over a chasm, with a steepled building visible above, and folkloric-looking inhabitants such as a goat-headed centaur, a winged leprechaun, and a Little Bo Peep-like figure. Please see the separate section "Rules of the *Oh My Goddess!* Cosmos" for more details. ➔ **Demon Realm**

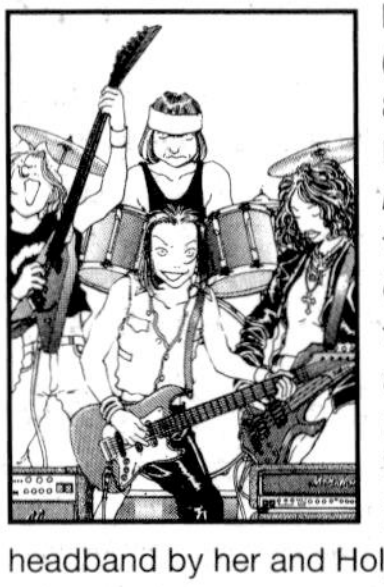

Heavy Metal Troop (*Queen Sayoko*, Chapter 83, Vol. 15)
In the original Japanese, *Hebii Metaru Butai*—this four-man headbanger contingent attempted to block Belldandy's attempt to find Keiichi inside Sayoko's Mind Force Field, but were knocked boot over headband by her and Holy Bell.

Hell of Burning Muscles (*Queen Sayoko*, Chapter 81, Vol. 14)
Tamiya and Otaki, likewise under Sayoko's mind control, attempted this maneuver (referred to as "Da Fiery Hell Uv Muscle Heat!" in the original English version of the manga) to stop Keiichi from entering. It consisted of the two of them catching Keiichi's body between their two large, buff, sweaty ones, and squeezing.

Hell of Explosion and Flame (*The Devil in Miss Urd*, Chapter 60, Vol. 10)
In the original English version of the manga, "Hellfire Thunder Blast!!"—the spell Mara invoked against Urd's Lightning Summons (called "Lightning Strike" in the original English version) after they had reached a bit of an impasse in their karaoke competition.

Help! Banpei!!! (*The Phantom Racer*, Chapter 116, Vol. 19)
In the original Japanese, *Tasukete Banpei!*—the cry Sigel (at the time, still known only as "Robo-chan") made in hopes that Banpei would rescue her from Dr. Moreau, although it really was her last resort, and she really hated to do it.

Heven Eleven (*Final Exam*, Chapter 16, Vol. 2)
The convenience store Keiichi worked at part time in order to earn enough money to buy Belldandy a ring. Note that it is not spelled "Heaven," but rather like "Seven," except with an "H."

Hiding Technique (*The Phantom Racer*, Chapter 115, Vol. 19)
In the original Japanese, *kakuremi no jutsu*—Robo-chan's profoundly ineffective approach (among other things, she cries it out at the top of her little mechanical lungs—in the original English version of the manga, she shouted "Last resort!" at this moment; but see above) of trying to conceal herself from Banpei, and later Dr. Moreau, by jumping on top of Keiichi's head.

High Sensitivity Sound Collection Sensor (*Sora Unchained*, Chapter 128, Vol. 20)
In the original Japanese, *kookando shuuon sensaa*—in the original English version, referred to as the "Skuld" Neko Sound Amplifier "Version 1.2," owing to their *nekomimi*, or "cat ears," appearance. In fact, when Skuld dons both these and the accompanying Noise Silencing Shoes, she is said to be "in a catgirl cosplay state." ➔ **Noise Silencing Shoes**

Highway Star (*The Devil in Miss Urd*, Chapter 60, Vol. 10)
The first track on Deep Purple's famous 1972 album *Machine Head* (you know, the one "Smoke on the Water" comes from). Well-known in Japan, Katsuhiro Otomo named one of his early short manga stories after the song; Urd does it on karaoke in the original Japanese version of the manga, and subsequently drunkenly mangles it in the unflopped English version during her karaoke battle with Mara (the flopped English version had them face off against each other with an odd medley of tunes, including the Bee Gees, the Village People, The Police, Soundgarden, Stone Temple Pilots, and Matthew Sweet; to be fair, some of these artists are likely to be found on Japanese karaoke machines as well ^_^).

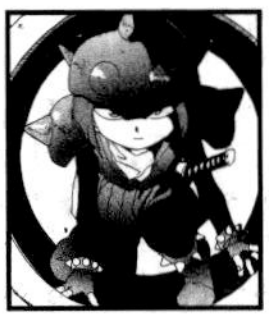

Hikari (*Ninja Master*, Chapter 53, Vol. 9)
Known as "Lightning Hikari," she is one of the three Ninja Masters. Hikari is an *oi-shinobi*, a ninja who hunts other ninja that have violated their code—in this case, Kodama. Before she was transmuted into a ninja, her original form was that of a roof rat (*Rattus rattus*). Hikari is named for the second-fastest of the three train services on the famous Tokaido Shinkansen bullet train route between Tokyo and Osaka. ➔ **Kodama, Senrigan the Peeping Tomboy**

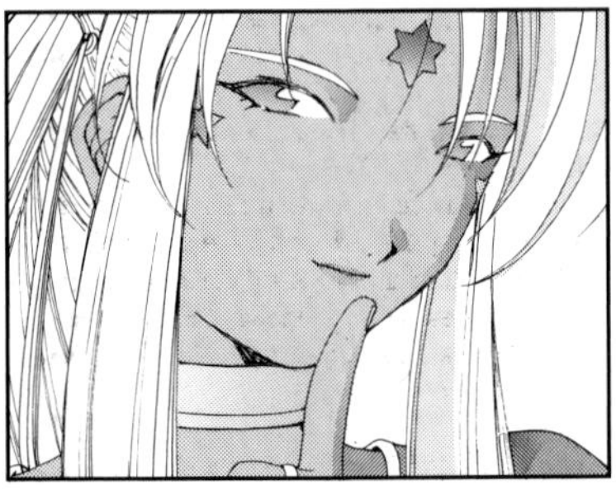

Hild (Chapter 134, Vol. 21)
The Great CEO of the demon realm—in Japanese, *Dai-Makai-Cho*; the term "CEO" was used in English, as *cho* has a very business-executive sound to it—and Urd's mother, although not that of Skuld and Belldandy (they all share the same father, however; Hild's conversation with Belldandy in Vol. 22, Chapter 136, can be interpreted to suggest the Almighty is this father, although this is open to debate. She is, naturally, Mara and Velsper's boss, as she is leader of all demons. Hild appears to love her daughter, and has a certain respect for Belldandy—but that does not temper her ruthlessness as a competitor in the cosmic rivalry between her side and that of the goddesses. For her own part, Urd says that she "must not" love her mother, as she believes this will tip her spirit over to her demon side—although Belldandy seemed to suggest to her that this would not necessarily be the case. While she is of nurturing motherly proportions, Hild often chooses to appear in the body of a young girl, or even in a tiny *chibi* form, which she claims is herself "at one-millionth power."

Hill Climb (*Miss Keiichi*, Chapter 56, Vol. 9)
Although some motorcycle races called "hill climbs" involve uphill courses on paved roads, Keiichi participated in a specialized form of hill climb where specially modified off-road bikes attempt to scale a 70- or even 80-degree slope in a single, high-speed charge.

Holmes (*Ninja Master*, Chapter 53, Vol. 9)
A favorite TV show of Urd (possibly *Meitantei Holmes*, the 1984–85 animated version of Sherlock Holmes co-directed by Hayao Miyazaki, released in English as *Sherlock Hound*); she missed it when she lost a viewing-rights fight to the ninja Kodama and Hikari. ➔ ***Ninpu Kamuri Gaiden***

Holy Bell (*The Fourth Goddess*, Chapter 71, Vol. 12)
Belldandy's angel; we first see her invoked on the solemn occasion of a tickling match between Holy Bell and Peorth's angel Gorgeous Rose during the first round of the Triple Challenge of the Goddesses. Holy Bell was called "Blessèd Bell" when introduced in the original English version of the manga.

Holy Storm (*Queen Sayoko*, Chapter 83, Vol. 15)
Magical attack used by Belldandy through her

angel Holy Bell to defeat the abovementioned rockers of the Heavy Metal Troop.

Holy Wind Press (*Queen Sayoko*, Chapter 81, Vol. 14)
In the original Japanese, "Wind Breath" (the English phrase was used, pronounced *uindo buresu*). Belldandy used this technique to bust Keiichi out from the Hell of Burning Muscles. The English version of the attack perhaps took its name from the fact it was assisted by Holy Bell; Skuld commented that Belldandy ordinarily never uses attack spells, and that it seemed to reflect genuine anger.

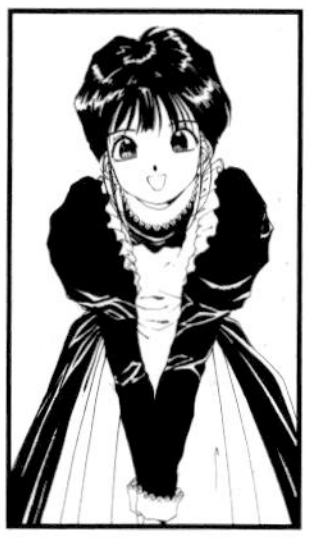

Honda, Chieko (*Mara Strikes Back*, Chapter 48, Vol. 8)
Temporary housekeeper of the Honda Lodge; this attractive young girl in an old-fashioned maid's outfit makes little secret of the fact she's actually been waiting there since the 1930s for the return of Keiichi's grandfather, Hotaru-no-suke, whom he resembles at that age. Belldandy realizes Chieko is long dead, but has become a *shinnentai*—not an incorporeal ghost, but a physical manifestation of her unfulfilled desire.

Honda Lodge (*Mara Strikes Back*, Chapter 48, Vol. 8)
An old-fashioned mountain resort hotel run by a friend of Keiichi's grandfather, enabling the N.I.T. Motor Club to get cheap rooms there for their second weeklong "Summer Endurance Training Camp" (the first one having been at a beach resort, as seen in *Leader of the Pack*, Chapter 13, Vol. 2).

Honey Zerion (*The Queen of Vengeance*, Chapter 43, Vol. 7)
One of Urd's carefully inventoried magical ingredients, used in her alchemical concoctions. The name is a direct reference to Episode 8 of the 1966 TV series *Ultra Q*, "The Fear of Sweet Honey," in which a researcher accidentally develops a nutritive chemical, "Honey Zerion," that makes animals enormous.

Hoshimaru (*Sora Unchained*, Chapter 125, Vol. 20)
When Keiichi appeared a bit hesitant to take a shortcut through the girls' locker room in the Director Race, Urd offered to give him a disguise, whipping out a mask resembling Hoshimaru—yes, *that* Hoshimaru, from the manga *Shadow Star*, which, like *Oh My Goddess!*, first ran in Kodansha's *Afternoon* magazine.

Hotel Koenig (*Final Exam*, Chapter 17, Vol. 3)
With a little help (i.e., the conjuring of an awe-inspiring heavenly vortex) from Belldandy, Keiichi won dinner and accommodations for two at the swank Hotel Koenig in a game at the Nekomi Merchants' Association Year-End Festival. He was looking forward to a romantic evening with Belldandy, but between Sayoko and Urd, who were also in attendance, he was lucky to get out of the dining room intact.

Hotel LaForte (Chapter 191, Vol. 30)
A local love hotel (see **Hotel Magic 3** below) in Nekomi, right across the street from the Nakata Pharmacy. In a sign of how far their relationship has come in the one hundred and seventy-one chapters since Keiichi helped rescue Bell from a love hotel, this time he actually considered asking her to go into one with him. Considered, and chickened out.

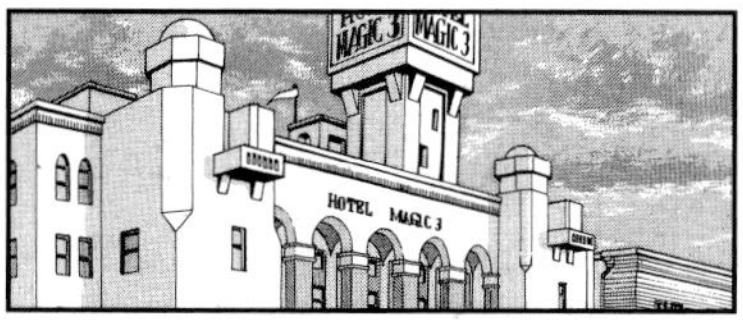

Hotel Magic 3 (*Final Exam*, Chapter 20, Vol. 3)
A love hotel off the coast road outside of Nekomi, where, as the euphemism suggests, couples get together for an evening or just an hour. The difference between them and the American concept of the "no-tell motel" is that Japanese love hotels tend to be well kept, and boast individual decorative themes, often quite lavish and tasteless ones. Aoshima tricked Belldandy into checking into one with him; although she seemed to know what kind of place it was, she nevertheless bade that Aoshima be borne away on a whirlwind to "contemplate his error" in being so pushy.

Human Virtua Fight (*Queen Sayoko*, Chapter 82, Vol. 14)
One of the elimination contests ordained by Queen Sayoko, it's a live-action video game where the players, using magical joysticks and buttons, control actual fighters in an actual ring *as if* they were game characters. Note that although the game is clearly a satire of the popular 1993 Sega fighting game *Virtua Fighter*, it is spelled differently in the original Japanese. Note also that in the fight, Keiichi "plays" Urd, whose voice actor in the anime version of *Oh My Goddess!*, Yumi Tohma, would in fact end up playing Pai Chan in 2007's *Virtua Fighter 5*.

Hyakume-chan (*Sympathy for the Devil*, Chapter 33, Vol. 5)
Although only called a "neutrino counter" in the English version of the manga, the original Japanese nickname of Skuld's, well, neutrino counter, was *Hyakume-chan*, meaning "A Hundred Eyes." **➔ Ms. Paku-Paku Bug Man**

Hyper Dexterity Glove (*Traveler*, Chapter 102, Vol. 17)
In the original Japanese, *koosoku enzan guroobu*—in the original English version, referred to as the "Hyper-Processor Glove." *Enzan* can be translated as "calculator," but Dark Horse's Director of Asian Licensing, Michael Gombos, points out that the same kanji used here for *enzan* are also used in the Japanese edition of *Warhammer Fantasy Roleplay* to describe gauntlets that enhance dexterity. Skuld employed this gadget against Urd's Absolute Good Fortune Spell in a game of rock-paper-scissors to win a Channel Fight. **➔ Absolute Good Fortune Spell**

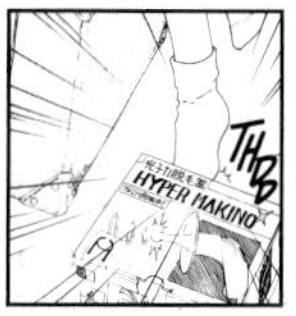
HYPER MAKINO

Hyper Makino (*Traveler*, Chapter 106, Vol. 18)
A photon-powered depilation device; one among the many chattels dumped off at Tarikihongan for storage by Keiichi's former dorm mates when their residence hall was under renovation (the irony of their having thrown out *Keiichi's* possessions, as well as Keiichi, in the very first chapter was presumably lost on them). Belldandy happened to trip on the Hyper Makino—a simple but disturbing proof that she had lost her powers.

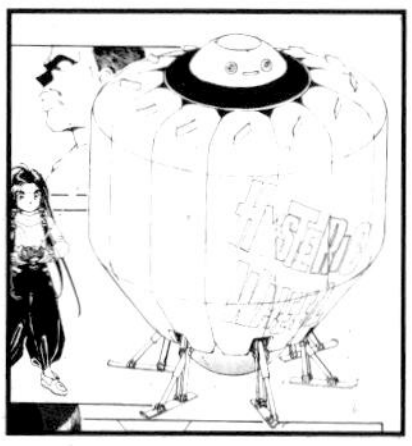

Hysteric Wheel #1 (*The Queen of Vengeance*, Chapter 40, Vol. 6)
Skuld created this machine for the Robot Battle; despite its name, it had the shape of a rapidly rotating upright cylinder, rather than a wheel. Since the object of the Robot Battle was to collect the largest number of empty oil drums set up in a ring, Skuld designed the Hysteric Wheel to capture them rapidly and *en masse*, sucking them in through curved outer doors in a manner not unlike a cyclone. It worked well, until her rival Megumi employed an unexpected tactic. **➔ Pot Shaker Dragon**

I

Ice Blade (Chapter 162, Vol. 25)
Magical beam of cold used by Cool Mint to freeze the Eater of Angels.

Idaten-kun (*Queen Sayoko*, Chapter 80, Vol. 14)
An optional part Skuld offers to attach to Stringfellow, who wishes to become human. Not referred to by name in the original English version of the manga, it is apparently a pair of mechanical legs. *Idaten* is the Japanese name for Skanda, a heroic guardian figure in Buddhism, said in legend to be both a great runner and warrior. Stringfellow, however, being a broom, was looking for something a bit more profound then bolted-on attachments.

I'll Show You Everything (*Leader of the Pack*, Chapter 14, Vol. 2)
The name of a mysterious video tape mailed to Keiichi with no return address; he leapt to the conclusion it was an adult video sent by Tamiya and Otaki, and, Belldandy being out shopping, he immediately popped it in the VCR. Within seconds Urd made her premiere into the story by emerging from the screen and accidentally kneeing him in the head, a harbinger of sensations to come.

Imai, Takami (*Wrong Number*, Chapter 1, Vol. 1)
The upperclassman with the mask atop his head in Chapter 1 of *Oh My Goddess!* (page 033, panel 6 in *OMG! Colors*)—but never named until Chapter 78! Although he helped to eject Keiichi from the dorm for the offense of bringing a girl into it, Imai later charitably tries to help him get a job at Wyvern. In a piquant irony, it is later revealed his true motivation was the hope that some of Keiichi's well-known female company would visit the all-male job site.

Imperial Model Club Research Center (*Queen Sayoko*, Chapter 83, Vol. 15)
Apparently one of the many campus clubs at Nekomi Tech; under the influence of Sayoko's Mind Force Field, they planned to make a 1:1 scale silicone figurine of the unconscious Belldandy. While they were fighting over who got to perform the task of applying the mold-release lubricant to her body, Mara appeared, reviving her while knocking them out.

Inanimate Spirits (*The Phantom Racer*, Chapter 117, Vol. 19)
In Japanese, *inochi naki tamashii*—Belldandy uses this phrase to describe the expressive and "almost alive" bikes Keiichi fixes. The remark prompted them to discuss how and in what way such "life" differed from that of Banpei and Robo-chan. **➔ Sigel**

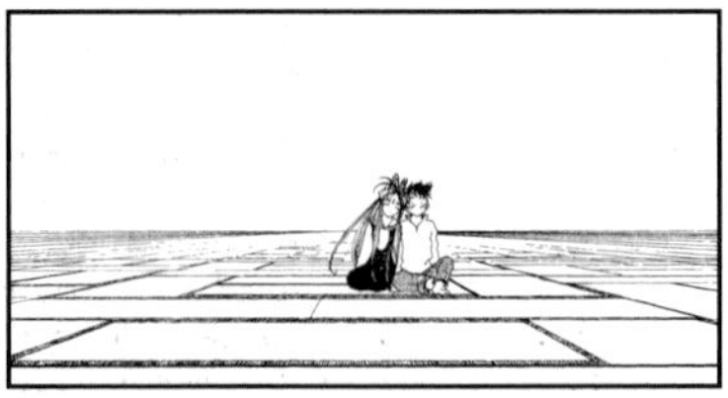

Infinite Tea Room (*Traveler*, Chapter 106, Vol. 18)
Having a sudden need for more storage space (see **Hyper Makino**, above), Keiichi attempted to work the controls of the Space Doubler, which Skuld had already used to square the previous volume of the tea room, only to increase its size to *infinite*—and, all locations on an infinite plane being the perceived center, he and Belldandy had no way to leave the now-vast room. **➔ Schrödinger's Whale**

Inokuradai Campus (*Hand in Hand*, Chapter 86, Vol. 15)
Satellite campus of Nekomi Tech. Site of the popular seminar Aerodynamics 101; the winding six-kilometer mountain road leading there later became the site of the Parent-Child Showdown.

Insta-Trans Spell (*The Fourth Goddess*, Chapter 67, Vol. 11)
In the original Japanese, *shunkan idoo hoojutsu*, literally "instantaneous transport magic." Peorth's method to get Keiichi to class during the "Who's the Most Helpful Goddess?" contest. **➔ Interspatial Slide Technique, Ultra-Delivery Gun**

Interspatial Slide Technique (*The Fourth Goddess*, Chapter 67, Vol. 11)
In the original Japanese, *kuukan suraido hoo*, literally "space slide method." Urd's method to get Keiichi to class during the "Who's the Most Helpful Goddess" contest. **➔ Insta-Trans Spell, Ultra-Delivery Gun**

Iron Ball Batting (*Miss Keiichi*, Chapter 58, Vol. 10)
Special practice Urd made Keiichi go through for the game between the Baseball Club and Softball Club, apparently inspired by the savage training methods she saw in classic 1970s sports anime. **➔ Thousand-Ball Burning Fielding Training**

Iron Sand Doll (*Ninja Master*, Chapter 50, Vol. 8)
Magnetically controlled metallic robot girl Skuld arranged for Keiichi to meet on the beach in a scheme to break him and Belldandy apart. Aside from her massive weight, Keiichi began to notice the way his motorcycle keys flew out of his pocket and stuck to her forehead.

Itadaki (Chapter 143, Vol. 23)
Name of the traditional Japanese sweet shop where Keima bought *yokan* (a jellied dessert made with sweetened red bean paste) for Takano. *Itadaki* by itself means "the summit," but is also related to the words for "gift" and the phrase *itadakimasu*, said in thanks when one partakes of food.

Itoh Hot Springs (*The Devil in Miss Urd*, Chapter 60, Vol. 10)
Resort town at which Keiichi and crew vacationed after mysteriously winning (i.e., as part of a sinister plot) a trip there. Site of the Daikokuya Inn, subsequent host to the Karaoke Match.

I've Turned into a Girl! (*Miss Keiichi*, Chapter 54, Vol. 9)
In the original Japanese, *Onna ni Natte Shimatta!*—the heartfelt cry of Keiichi after his experimentation with Urd's drugs (testing to see if they were safe medicine for Belldandy) turned him into, well, a girl.

I Want a Goddess Like You to Be with Me Always! (*Wrong Number,* Chapter 1, Vol. 1)
The fateful wish—in the original Japanese, *kimi no yoona megami ni zutto soba ni ite hoshii!*—Keiichi uttered to Belldandy, when she offered to grant him any one thing he desired. It is noted by the Japanese editors that he was half joking at the time, but the wish was formally accepted.

Iwata, Mitsuo (*Adventures of the Mini-Goddesses*, Chapter 62, Vol. 10)
Japanese voice actor (*seiyuu*) for "Gan-chan," the anime version of Mr. Rat, AKA "Ratty," in the *Mini-Goddess* strips. Urd reacted with outrage at Mr. Rat's declaration that he was henceforth to be known as "Mitsuo Iwata," as apparently even the goddesses don't get to have last names.

I Wonder If It's Not Sadder That We Leave You Behind? (Chapter 132, Vol. 21)
In the original Japanese, *hontoo ni kanashii no wa kimitachi nokosarete iku mono nanja nai no ka?*—Keiichi said this in answer to Kid Peorth after she acknowledged that, Belldandy being an immortal goddess and Keiichi a human being, "it is your destiny to be together for the rest of *your* life . . . but not hers." Keiichi speculated that the goddesses must have had to say goodbye countless times over their existence; Peorth said in reply that she finally understood why Belldandy loved him so much, and told him to remember "the people we goddesses love, live forever in our hearts."

J

Jealousy Storm (*The Fourth Goddess*, Chapter 72, Vol. 12)
The phenomenon is alluded to in Chapter 57, but named for the first time (the English phrase is used, pronounced *jerashii sutoomu*) in Chapter 72. Despite Belldandy's own personal self-control and discipline, feelings of jealousy weaken the effect of the power seal Belldandy wears as her left earring—very likely because her assignment on Earth is centered around being with Keiichi. In theory this could cause her power to go wild, raising the prospect of a "Jealousy Storm." **➔ Remote Body Control**

K

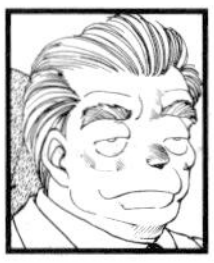

Kakuta (*Wrong Number*, Chapter 4, Vol. 1)
"Doc" Kakuta is an N.I.T. professor and pioneer in ceramic engine design. His lab was the first class on campus that Belldandy ever attended, effectively emptying out the lecture of Kakuta's rival, Professor Ozawa (Kakuta lets his students call him "Doc" or just "Kakuta," but Ozawa definitely insists on being listed under *Professor* Ozawa). Under the influence of the Love Seeds in Chapter 25, Urd briefly attempted to seduce him, an experience Kakuta said made him feel young again "for about ten seconds."

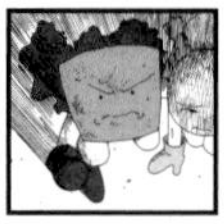

Kanpanman (*The Fourth Goddess*, Chapter 69, Vol. 12)
The main character of the movie Keiichi and Peorth watched together on their date, using the free tickets Belldandy got for renewing her newspaper subscription (such premiums are not uncommon in Japan). Called "Chocolate Man" in the original English version; however, *kanpan* is a cracker or biscuit that keeps for a long time and is often used in Japanese earthquake survival kits. It is therefore a cruel play on *Anpanman*, a real anime about a hero who is a bun filled with bean jam, something, by contrast, kids in Japan might actually like to eat. A measure of the popularity of this concept may be found in the detail that Takashi Yanase, creator of *Anpanman*, was among the top ten manga artists in 2004 in terms of income tax paid. **➔ An Donutko**

Karaoke Match (*The Devil in Miss Urd*, Chapter 60, Vol. 10)
Third of the three matches Urd and Mara fought against each other during their truce (from *actual* fighting) at the Daikokuya Inn. Unfortunately for the cause of peace, they tied. **➔ Game Match, Ping-Pong Match**

Kasugano Pharmacy (*Ninja Master*, Chapter 51, Vol. 8)
Keiichi's local pharmacy. Thinking that Skuld had been "acting funny" lately, Keiichi thoughtfully went there and bought her a pack of Zofi. The store's name is said to have nothing to do with Kasuga no Tsubone, influential nanny of Iemitsu Tokugawa, who was played by Yuki Matsushita in the 2004 Fuji TV series *Ooku Dai-ishou*. Called more simply *U-Buy Drug* in the original English version. **➔ Happy Family Planning, Zofi**

Katagai Beach (*Leader of the Pack*, Chapter 13, Vol. 2)
Site of the N.I.T. Motor Club's annual four-day retreat. Tamiya arranged the booking together with the Art Club, in order to get the group rate and improve the retreat's "gender balance."

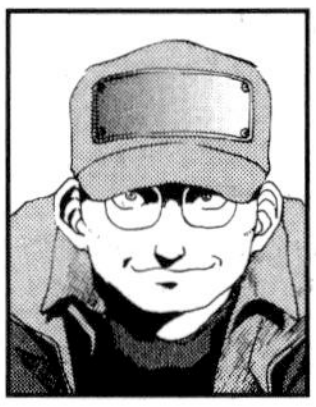

Kawabata (*Queen Sayoko*, Chapter 82, Vol. 14)
Keiichi's opposing player in the Human Virtua Fight; apparently selected by Sayoko because he was a member of the N.I.T. Game Club. Known as Johji "Joystick Jockey" Kawabata in the original English edition of the manga. **➔ Froghorn Leghorn**

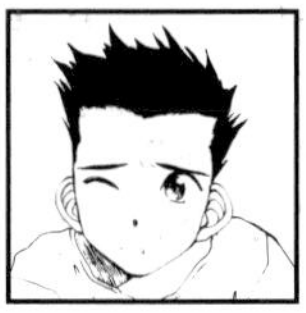

Kawanishi, Sentaro (*Childhood's End*, Chapter 73, Vol. 13)
A BMX champ who helped Skuld realize how fun it was to ride a bike. Skuld's sweet but half-grown angel Noble Scarlet innocently tried to push the two of them together, which caused Skuld some distress, as she had little experience with romance. Skuld and

Sentaro seem to have been getting along well as of Chapter 79, but as Yoshitoh Asari points out, we haven't seen much of him since . . . ➔ **Engine No. 1, Bicycle Lessons**

Keiichi's Shop (*Ninja Master*, Chapter 52, Vol. 8) Keiichi's private room at Tarikihongan, where he usually did his school studies and design work for the Motor Club. ➔ **Everybody's Tea Room, Skuld Labs, Urd's Room**

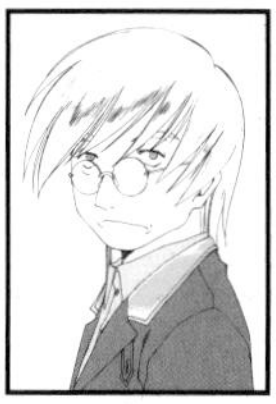

Keima (Chapter 142, Vol. 23) Keiichi and Megumi's mysteriously aged-appearing father; although evidently quite skilled at motorcycle repair as well as racing, he is a glass artist by profession, and lives in remote Kushiro Prefecture in Hokkaido—almost the northernmost part of Japan—with his wife Takano. He insists everyone in their family call each other by their first name, as words like "dad," "sis," "mom," or "son" are mere "job descriptions," that "denigrate the individual." He also develops an allergic reaction and runs away when any woman, excepting Takano or Megumi, gets within one meter of him; Belldandy was the first other woman able to get so close, a fact that intrigued Takano rather than made her jealous. ➔ ***Don't Call Me Father!***

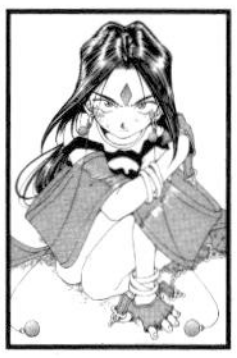

Kid Peorth (*Mystery Child*, Chapter 98, Vol. 17) Not an outlaw of the Old West, but the child form to which Peorth was reduced by Velsper's use of a program from Yggdrasil that can rewind a person in time; Peorth consequently lost not only much of her height, but most of her power. She remained in this state until cured by Hild in Vol. 22.

Kinsui (*Hand in Hand*, Chapter 90, Vol. 15) Meaning "Golden Water," it's the name of an expensive brand of saké. It was found empty after the opening party for Whirlwind, but who drank it?

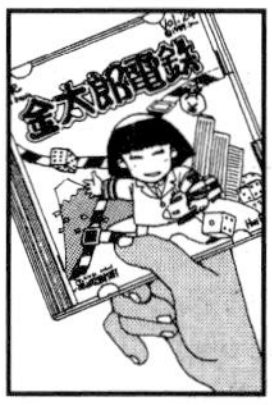
金太郎電鉄

Kintetsu (Kintaro Electric Railway) II (*The Queen of Vengeance*, Chapter 42, Vol. 6) Name of game software Shohei Yoshida was planning to buy, but he romantically spent the money on booze for Urd instead. A parody of the real game *Momotaro Dentetsu*.

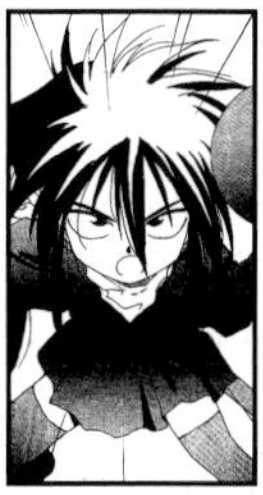

Kodama (*Ninja Master*, Chapter 52, Vol. 8) One of the three Ninja Masters that Mara created; before she was transmuted into a ninja, her original form was that of a Norway rat (*Rattus norvegicus*), in which she had a friendship with Hikari that "transcended the bounds of sub-species." Although Kodama carries a seemingly impossible load of concealed weaponry, she also used feminine wiles in attempting to seduce Keiichi, claiming she was "the fourth goddess" (fortunately for her, this was before Peorth showed up). Kodama is named for the third-fastest of the three train services on the famous Tokaido Shinkansen bullet train route between Tokyo and Osaka. ➔ **Hikari, Senrigan the Peeping Tomboy**

Kondo (*Sora Unchained*, Chapter 119, Vol. 19) Goateed, mustachioed, begoggled member of the N.I.T. Motor Club, habitually wearing a *yukata* (light robe); adamantly opposed to Hasegawa becoming director. The other members of the club at this time (although the manga did not put faces to names) were Ishii, Miwa, and Kawada.

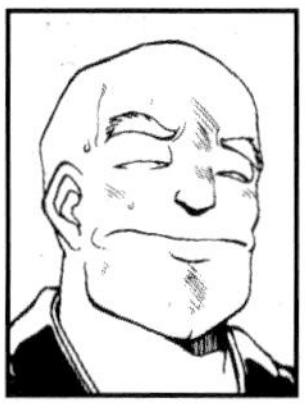

Koshian (*Wrong Number*, Chapter 3, Vol. 1) A Buddhist priest, formerly in charge of the Tarikihongan Temple. He at first granted Keiichi and Belldandy temporary shelter there in exchange for chores; later, he believed that Belldandy's general awesomeness (and the mark on her forehead) revealed her to be a *bodhisattva*—an enlightened person who works for the enlightenment of others. He promptly turned Tarikihongan over to Belldandy in a note that said he intended to travel to India to study "the true Buddhism, as you yourself have so clearly done," and Belldandy and her companions have lived there ever since. Will Koshian ever return, perhaps at the end of the story? ^_^

Kumada, Sachiyo (*Final Exam*, Chapter 15, Vol. 2) Participant in the N.I.T Motor Club's Campus Queen contest, introduced before Sayoko, Urd, and Belldandy; although she is apparently never seen, the looks on the glazed eyes and upturned, open mouths of the men in the audience suggest she is a powerful sight.

Kundali (*Miss Keiichi*, Chapter 57, Vol. 9) In Tantric Buddhism (which greatly influenced Buddhism in Japan through the work of the famed ninth-century proselytizer, Kukai) Kundali is one of the five *Godai-Myo-o*, or Wisdom Kings, that in turn each protect one of the five embodiments of the Buddha. Shiho Sakakibara tried to summon him, but instead ended up evoking the Norse monster Garm, thus getting her mythologies wrong by about five thousand miles.

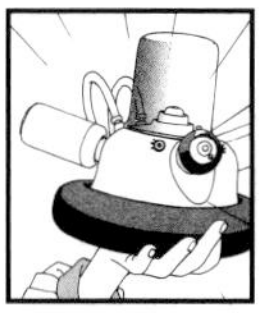

Kyupon Inhaler Z (*The Queen of Vengeance*, Chapter 43, Vol. 7) Vacuum unit by which Skuld attempted to recover a potion of Urd's that she had spilled. The results were a bit low, leading Skuld to try to make up the deficit by pouring in bits of this and that.

L

LAIT (*Love Potion No. 9*, Chapter 22, Vol. 3) The (fictitious) Los Angeles Institute of Technology, probably based on the real Cal Tech, which, it is important to note, is not in Los Angeles, but the very different town of Pasadena. At the Golden Hammer Competition, the LAIT team was the chief rival of the Nekomi Tech Motor Club. Considering the meaning of the word in French, the editor now groans in retrospect at the joke Mr. Fujishima *probably* intended by having it stretched across Diana Lockheed's generously filled tank top.

Laplacian Demon's Stone (*Final Exam*, Chapter 18, Vol. 3) A magical "gaff" (cheating method or device) that Urd uses to control the spin of the wheel in the Life Sugoroku Special game. It is named for the astronomer and researcher in probability theory Pierre-Simon Laplace (1749–1827), although the actual demon within doesn't resemble him. For more information, please see the notes for 41.1.2 in the back of *Oh My Goddess!* Vol. 3, or the reader comments on same in the note for 45.5 in the back of Vol. 5. ➔ **Life Sugoroku Special, Maxwell's Demon Stone**

Last Rhumba, The (*The Fourth Goddess*, Chapter 69, Vol. 12) The film Peorth *wanted* to go see with Keiichi—figuring it was a good date movie—although they (and everyone else tagging along) ended up seeing a children's film instead. Directed by "Lyme Patton" and starring "Kyle Krankan" and "Marilyn Casalle," the film is perhaps named for the subtitle of Track 5 on Jean Michel Jarre's 1981 electronic album *Magnetic Fields.* ➔ **Kanpanman**

Law of Conservation of Happiness (*Mara Strikes Back*, Chapter 45, Vol. 7) According to Senbei, God of Poverty and Disaster, the volume of happiness in the universe is finite, and when Senbei causes misfortune in others, that lost happiness is "conserved" by being transferred to Senbei himself. The theory is flawed, however, as Belldandy is capable of creating new happiness where none existed previously. As is often the case in *Oh My Goddess!*, the "Law" is a play on a real concept in physics; in this case, the law of conservation of energy in thermodynamics.

Lesser Ritual of the Hexagram (*Miss Keiichi*, Chapter 57, Vol. 9) A magical (or "magickal," as he would have spelled it) rite devised by Aleister Crowley, through which Shiho Sakakibara attempts to banish Keiichi's "evil spirits" in the original Japanese version of the manga, and in the unflopped English version. For what it is worth, her posture is off, as her left arm should have been at her side. Perhaps this explains why she ends up summoning Garm instead; of course, Shiho's whole approach to exorcism could be politely called syncretic. In the flopped English version of the manga, Shiho recites from the *Egyptian Book of the Dead*, in particular a passage in the same form used by Philip Glass in his *Funeral of Amenhotep III*. It should be noted that both rites evoked figures from ancient Egyptian religion.

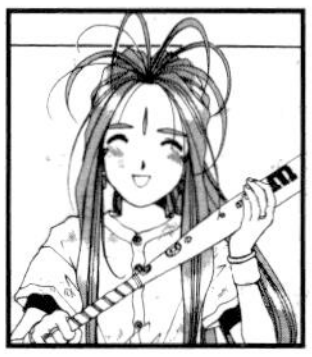

Let's Have It Bat! (*Miss Keiichi*, Chapter 58, Vol. 10) In the original Japanese, *baaaatto akaruku yarimashoo*; this was Belldandy's effort at cheering up the softball team with a joke. Her drawn-out pronunciation of "bat," as in the softball bat she was holding, made it sound a little like the English word bright; whereas *akaruku* means "brightly." In the original English version, this was just rendered as "Let's see a happy smile!" with Keiichi gulping at her as she says this, gripping a bat in her hands; in the unflopped edition it was rendered as "We need to win bat-ly!" Belldandy is kind, beautiful, and courageous, which may explain why she doesn't make much of a comedian. ➔ ***Won't Have Mitts!***

Life Sugoroku Special (*Final Exam*, Chapter 18, Vol. 3)
A fun but terrible game that makes everything happening on the board come true. *Sugoroku* means "a pair of sixes," as in dice. It's traditional during New Year's parties in Japan to play such games, which is why Urd hauls it out on that occasion; also, in hopes of embarrassing everybody. Sugoroku originally referred to two traditional types of board game—one like backgammon, and the other like what is known in the United States as "Chutes and Ladders" (more commonly in the rest of the world, "Snakes and Ladders"). Urd's version is a play on a meaning sugoroku developed in Japan after 1988, when the Takara toy corporation (called "Dakara" here) produced a Japanese version of Milton Bradley's The Game of Life, which became a tremendous hit in Japan. It uses no dice, but rather Life's traditional spinning wheel—thus taking sugoroku one step further from its origins. ➔ **Furisode**

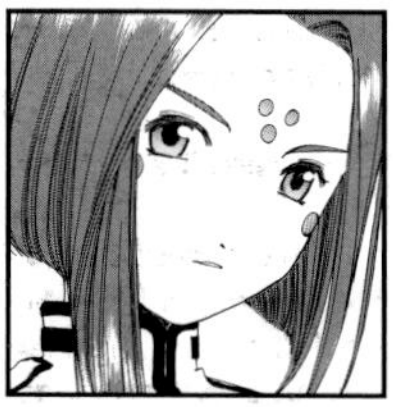

Lind (Chapter 155, Vol. 24)
The Fifth Goddess, Lind is serious and even stern by nature—not at all like the fun-loving Belldandy, Urd, Skuld, and Peorth. But she is of a different order from them: the combat section of the goddesses, known as the Valkyries. A legendary figure in Heaven known as "The Fighting Wings" and the "Goddess of the Ax" owing to her long, pole arm–like weapon. Lind's other nicknames are "One-Winged Lind" and "Lind of the Binary Angel"—a reference to the fact she has two angels, not one—each with but a single wing, and neither of whom have ever manifested at the same time—their not having met a source of sorrow to Lind, for whom angels are as important as any goddess. Although Lind takes joy in hand-to-hand combat, she is also a calm, methodical tactician possessing insight into the personality of others, and who comes up with the unexpected plan that saves her fellow goddesses. ➔ **Cool Mint, Spear Mint**

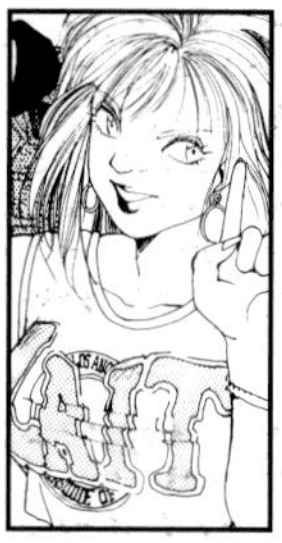

Lockheed, Diana (*Love Potion No. 9*, Chapter 22, Vol. 3)
The female half of the LAIT racing team. She is the All USA Kart (i.e., go-kart) Champ. Blond and large-breasted, as many female Americans tend to be in manga; *OMG!*'s magazine-mate *Genshiken* was progressive by manga standards, in suggesting some Americans may also be blond and small-breasted. ➔ **Golden Hammer Competition; Proter, David**

Lord of Terror (*Terrible Master Urd*, Chapter 34, Vol. 5)
According to a prophecy quoted to Belldandy by the Almighty, the Lord of Terror is a being whose advent on Earth will bring madness to humanity, rock the globe on its axis, rend it asunder, and "after seven days of fire, all shall be destroyed." Although the Almighty had sealed the Lord away in the past, he informs Belldandy (much to her shock) that Urd, due to her mixed blood, is the one in whom the Lord would be incarnated should he ever break free. Mara, who had been attempting to summon this very being using the Urn of Mao Za Haxon, was also a bit surprised to find out it was Urd, although she cites another prophecy that the Lord will be "bronze of skin." This is perhaps related to interpretations of supposed prophecies by the sixteenth-century apothecary Nostradamus, particularly quatrains II.41 ("the great star for seven days will burn") and X.72 ("from the sky will come a great king of terror"). The truth is somewhat more complicated; Urd is not the Lord of Terror herself, but only the first embodiment to bear that name; the true identity of the Lord is not a person, but a thing: the Ultimate Destruction Program. ➔ **Ultimate Destruction Program, Urn of Mao Za Haxon**

Love Drop (*The Fourth Goddess*, Chapter 68, Vol. 12)
The "improved" version of the Love Seed (below), modified by Peorth, in order to "cure" his *fukansho*—meaning "frigidity" or "prudishness," although in Japanese this has connotations of apathy or indifference to sexual obligations, rather than moral objections to it; in the original English version, Peorth was motivated out of a concern for Keiichi being "monogamous." In any case, the Love Drop had the actual effect of making *everyone else* fall for Keiichi—Urd, Skuld, his sister Megumi . . . In the original English version of the manga, it was referred to as the "Crystal Teardrop of Love."

Love Seed (*Love Potion Vol. 9*, Chapter 25, Vol. 4)
A pill concentrate formulated by Urd, and then dropped by her into a thermos of tea to make a love potion. Urd's aim was to get Keiichi to drink it, and thus "encourage" him to accelerate his relationship with Belldandy.

Lucky Star (*Leader of the Pack*, Chapter 12, Vol. 2)
Not the recent anime and manga series that threatens to reveal terrible things about the state of modern fans, but a concept Belldandy discusses with Keiichi: that individuals have lucky (or unlucky) stars, and that when they are directly overhead, good or bad fortune follows for them in a deterministic fashion rather than by chance, the end of a causal chain of decisions (the Japanese editors explain this means one's daily behavior). Hence calling such a star "Lucky" seems somewhat contentious; for more information, please see ⇔ **Unlucky Star**

M

Mabudachi Song, The (*The Devil in Miss Urd*, Chapter 60, Vol. 10)
Pretty little ditty that Belldandy made Urd and Mara duet as punishment when they broke their truce. *Mabudachi* is a somewhat masculine, slangy way of saying "best friends" that first arose in the early 1980s, by combining *mabui*, which has the sense of "good, great, for real" with *tomodachi*, friends.

Mach Engine (*Miss Keiichi*, Chapter 56, Vol. 9)
In both English versions of the manga, this famed Kawasaki motorcycle engine is referred to by the nickname its model IV-H2 earned in the early 1970s, the "Widowmaker," as it had power and speed previously unheard of in a two-stroke engine. The Mach series included the 250 Mach I, 350 Mach II, and the 750 Mach IV, but the best known would be 500 H1 (Mach III). It was this engine that the N.I.T. Motor Club used in the bike they assembled for the Hill Climb race. ➔ **Pokke**

Machiner (Chapter 174, Vol. 27)
A strange race of purely mechanical beings, varying greatly in size, moving about on anything from servo-powered legs to jet engines. They showed up without warning one night at Whirlwind for repairs, startling Keiichi, but not Belldandy, who seemed already familiar with them, explaining blithely to Keiichi that "if you tilt the world's axis just a little, you'd find it's filled with other races humans just aren't aware of." Machiners seem able to speak human languages, but with their sentences oddly jumbled. As magic doesn't work well on Machiners, it was Keiichi who used his mechanical skills to help them out. ➔ **Ou Pyuru Kyuin, Pi Pu Pii Gaa**

Magical Mai (*Wrong Number*, Chapter 2, Vol. 1)
Name of Sada's apparent favorite anime; the full title of the series appears to be *Magical Superstar Magical Mai*, therefore presumably making it even more magical. For more information, please see the notes in Vol. 1 of the manga, particularly for 34.6 and 45.1.

Makuhari Messe (*Terrible Master Urd*, Chapter 37, Vol. 6)
A major seaside convention center in Chiba Prefecture, Japan, not far from Tokyo Disneyland. This is where the Fenrir Wolf, embodiment of the Ultimate Destruction Program, first manifested itself; not inappropriately, it was also the venue for two sold-out shows of Rage Against The Machine during their 2007–2008 reunion tour. "Makuhari" is a traditional name for the area, whereas "Messe" is a Japanese loanword from German with several meanings—although originally in German it referred to a mass (in the sense of the religious gathering), it later came to also connote gatherings of people for trade or festivals, and it is this sense of *messe*, pronounced "mess-seh," that is used in Japanese.

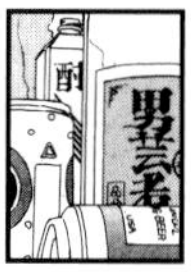

Male Geisha (*Hand in Hand*, Chapter 90, Vol. 15)
In Japanese, *Otoko Geisha*; the brand on a bottle of sake spotted at Whirlwind's opening party. Empty, of course.

Mandrake Root (*The Queen of Vengeance*, Chapter 43, Vol. 7)
One of Urd's many secret ingredients for her Ultra High-Grade Love Seeds (also referred to as a "love potion" in the original English version). Note that when Urd was forced in Vol. 24, Chapter 155, to turn over some mandrake she had bought to Lind, the Fifth Goddess commented, "I'm appalled you buy that stuff."

Mankind's Dream (*The Phantom Racer*, Chapter 115, Vol. 19)
Dr. Moreau utters this phrase (in the original Japanese, *Jinrui no yume*) after seeing Banpei walk casually past—the bipedal locomotion of a robot being a goal he had worked on for years in vain. In full, he declares mankind's dream to be the making of an artificial human, capable of walking, talking, laughing, smiling, and (after getting socked by Sigel for undue scientific curiosity) rocket-punching.

Man on Stage, A (*The Fourth Goddess*, Chapter 70, Vol. 12)
In the original Japanese, *Otoko no hanamichi*, which literally means "The Flower Path of a Man." *Hanamichi*, "flower path," is a term from Japanese

theater. Originally referring to a catwalk or runway leading out into the audience, where an actor could receive flowers after a performance, it has come to be used also as the spot where a particularly dramatic or memorable moment might be staged, allowing it to happen closer to the audience. Otaki suggested he and Tamiya sing *Otoko no hanamichi* to commemorate Tamiya's resolve to win the heart of Peorth. Neither "flower path," nor "catwalk," nor "runway" seems to quite suggest the manliness of the moment, so the unflopped English edition uses the less exact "A Man on Stage." The original English edition of the manga—perhaps understandably given the translation difficulty—simply had Tamiya sing Percy Sledge's "When a Man Loves a Woman," admittedly one of the manliest love songs ever written. ➔ ***Measure of a Man, The*; *What a Man's Gotta Do***

Mara (*Love Potion No. 9*, Chapter 26, Vol. 4)
A Demon First-Class, Unlimited License, Mara—perhaps fortunately for the goddesses—is the top operative at the Demon Office, thus making her in one sense Belldandy's chief competitor, despite the fact the two have known each other since childhood (the first time encountered in the story, the somewhat hair-metal-looking Mara managed to convince the somewhat gullible Kei-chan that she was a he, and Belldandy was "his" fiancée). Mara's job is to expand the market share of the infernal realm vs. the divine by tracking down people such as Keiichi who have made contracts with goddesses, and getting them to sign pacts with demons instead—a sort of cosmic refinancing scheme with all eternity to pay.

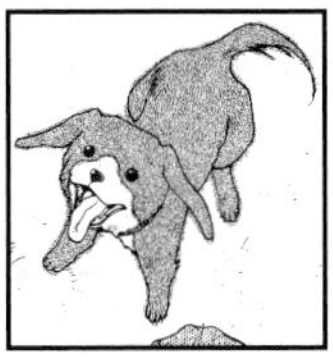

Marone (*Miss Keiichi*, Chapter 59, Vol. 10)
Pronounced "Mah-rohhh-neh" (just as with the name of artist Adrian Tomine, Japanese names don't have silent *e*'s at the end), with a long middle syllable, this is the real name of the stray puppy Megumi found and brought to Tarikihongan; although Belldandy, Skuld, and Urd preferred the names "Assam," "Pliers," and "Penicillin," respectively. The original English version of the manga used the spelling "Marron." ➔ **Nihonmaru**

Matchless G50 (Chapter 142, Vol. 23)
The motorcycle Keima rode all the way to N.I.T. from Kushiro. Made by Matchless, a now-defunct British bike company, the 350 cc G50 came out in 1960, and hence was as much as four decades old. Chihiro was amazed that Keima would ride the bike (the G50 was designed for racing, not touring) such a long way, to which Keima replied, "We all used to ride these . . . today's bikes are . . . comfy."

Maxwell's Demon Stone (*Love Potion No. 9*, Chapter 21, Vol. 3)
Similar in concept to the Laplacian Demon's Stone—although why it isn't called the Maxwellian Demon's Stone, or the former called the Laplace's Demon Stone, is unknown. Belldandy seemed to carry it as a charm on her earring, casting it into the straw of a flying broom (is it Stringfellow?) at need. Named for James Clerk Maxwell, the most important physicist of the nineteenth century, it separates out fast air molecules from slow ones, thus building energized (heated) air to provide thrust for the broom. For more information, please see the notes for 120.6 in the back of *Oh My Goddess!* Vol. 3, or the reader comments on same in the note for 121.2 in the back of Vol. 5.

Mazda T2000 (*Love Potion No. 9*, Chapter 23, Vol. 3)
First appearing on the market in 1962, this vintage three-wheeled truck was heavily customized by the N.I.T. Motor Club as their entrant in the Golden Hammer Competition.

M-Boy Type Oxygum (*The Fourth Goddess*, Chapter 68, Vol. 12)
Chewing gum that Peorth found in Urd's room while looking for the Love Seeds. In the original Japanese, this gum was known as *Pii Wan Zero*; it was a reference to the super-science chew that allowed Marine, the hero of the 1969–71 anime series *Kaitei Shonen Marine* ("Undersea Boy Marine") to breathe underwater. In the English-language dub, the show was called *Marine Boy*, and the gum was called "oxygum"—and now you understand.

Measure of a Man, The (Chapter 178, Vol. 28)
In the original Japanese, *Otoko no utsuwa*; Tamiya and Otaki sang this as a duet as the first (and by far, lowest-scoring) number performed during the N.I.T. Motor Club's Karaoke Contest.

Mensore (*Traveler*, Chapter 106, Vol. 18)
Saké manufactured by the Jigaa distillery from bitter cucumbers, which sounds intriguing. One of the cardboard boxes Keiichi was compelled to store during the "dorm renovation" incident was a case of Mensore, suggesting that his seniors are most fond of it.

Menzholatum (Chapter 140, Vol. 22)
A play on "Mentholatum," a mint-infused petroleum jelly used for therapeutic purposes. Originally invented in America by the Wichita, Kansas-based Yucca Company, Mentholatum, with its picture of the famous nineteenth-century nurse Florence Nightingale on the tin, has been popular in Japan since the 1920s, and the brand is in fact today owned by the Osaka-based Rohto Pharmaceutical Co. Urd apparently considers the picture on the tin irresistibly cute, a fact Mara used to her advantage. Urd, of course, likes to play nurse, and according to the Japanese editors of the *Encyclopedia*, she is "obsessed with little nurses." ➔ **Goddess Catcher**

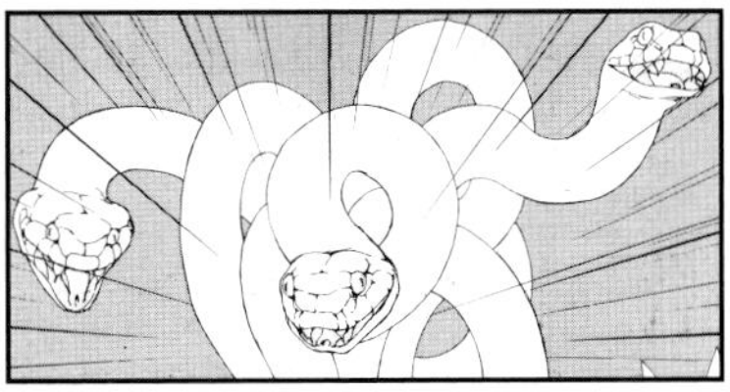

Midgard Serpent (*Terrible Master Urd*, Chapter 37, Vol. 6)
In the Norse religion, the Midgard Serpent was a snake beneath the oceans, so long that it encircled the entire planet. It was believed that during the apocalypse, it would surface to poison the earth and sky (Fritz Leiber's memorable short story "Myths My Great-Granddaughter Taught Me" imagined this as a prophecy of nuclear missile submarines). In *Oh My Goddess!*, the Midgard Serpent is the embodiment of the Ultimate Destruction Program Vaccine, and indeed rises into the sky against the Fenrir Wolf (albeit in the form of several giant, entwining snakes rather than just one), but is itself infected by the Ultimate Destruction Program. Note that *Midgard* was the Norse word for our world, the Earth, and that Tolkien's term "Middle-Earth" ultimately derives from it.

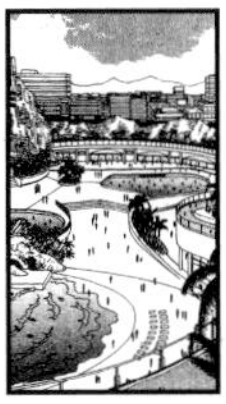

Mild Blue Nekomi (*The Fourth Goddess*, Chapter 69, Vol. 12)
Name of a local (hence "Nekomi") water park everyone went to on Keiichi and Peorth's "date." They all got in for free, using the tickets Belldandy had obtained from a liquor store (!). In the original English version of the manga, the park's name was given as "Aqua Blue," and Belldandy had won them from a radio station.

Millennium Blues (*Traveler*, Chapter 109, Vol. 18)
Single off Matthew Sweet's 1999 album *In Reverse*. The Schrödinger's Whale Keiichi meets becomes fond of Sweet after hearing this song, together with the singer's "Missing Time" off the 1997 album *Blue Sky on Mars*, on Keiichi's boom box (the original English version of *OMG!* Vol. 10 had Urd sing part of Sweet's "Hollow" and "Sick of Myself" during her karaoke battle with Mara). Matthew Sweet, himself something of a manga fan (he has Rumiko Takahashi's "Lum-chan" tattooed on his arm), was the first person to ever use anime in an MTV video, doing so for both his 1991 singles "Girlfriend" (which used clips from *Space Adventure Cobra*) and "I've Been Waiting" (which used *Urusei Yatsura*; Lum would also make cameos in his videos for 1993's "The Ugly Truth" and 1995's "Sick of Myself").

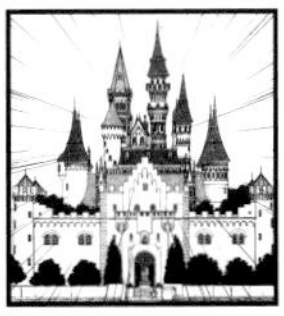

Mind Force Field (*Queen Sayoko*, Chapter 81, Vol. 14)
In the original Japanese, *nenjiba*; with the "power granted her by Mara, Sayoko's urge to dominate the N.I.T. campus as its "queen" became an actual force field strong enough to command obedience from anyone (even a goddess) entering its radius, through its emission of "will waves." ➔ **Skuld Will Wave Wall Shielded Ribbon Cable, Mark 1**

Minimum Rocket Punch (*Traveler*, Chapter 103, Vol. 17)
Low-powered version of the Rocket Punch attack that the Welcome Robot used to yank Banpei-kun's stop switch.

Mirror (*Wrong Number*, Chapter 1, Vol. 1)
Medium through which Belldandy can instantly transport herself through space; this will work regardless of the size of the mirror, and with mirrored surfaces. When she first met Keiichi, she naturally emerged from a mirror. ➔ **Television, Water**

Mishima, Sayoko (*Wrong Number*, Chapter 5, Vol. 1)
Rich, attractive, fashion-conscious, and aristocratic, Sayoko Mishima is your stereotypical female engineering student. When first introduced, Sayoko is a sophomore electronics major, and regarded herself as the *de facto* Campus Queen, only to later lose the title *de jure* to Belldandy in

Chapter 15. Her jealousy of Belldandy is so severe that even Mara is in awe of Sayoko's revengeful aura, yet Sayoko may be most jealous of the kind of love that Belldandy and Keiichi have together. She seems to drink a lot. There are a few mysteries surrounding Sayoko; in Chapter 44 she made, or rather, slurred the strange remark that a bar mate was "*one point two million yearsh* (sic) *too young*" to drink her under the table, although perhaps it's just an expression. Furthermore, the Japanese editors of the *Encyclopedia* remark about her that "Sayoko was a sophomore in Chapter 5, but a junior in Chapter 15, whereas in Chapter 15, Belldandy was still a sophomore. Does it mean Sayoko skipped a year, or that Belldandy was held back a year?" That they *were* both sophomores at the time is mentioned in both the English and Japanese versions of Chapter 5; whereas their class years were left out of the translation of Chapter 15. However, in the original Japanese of the scene where they're introduced on stage for the Campus Queen Contest (Vol. 2, pages 128–129) it did in fact say that Belldandy was a sophomore and Sayoko was a junior. Just another of *OMG!*'s cosmic mysteries. ➔ **Aoshima, Toshiyuki**

Mister Bester Tester (Beta) (*Childhood's End*, Chapter 78, Vol. 14)
A helmet that does not make Keiichi happy, as Skuld clamps it on his head to help him practice for his job interview at Wyvern. Mister Bester Tester (Beta) is itself, as its name implies, still under testing. It works by giving him electric shocks every time he gives the wrong answer. ➔ **Wyvern**

Miyamura, Yuko (Chapter 147, Vol. 23)
A go-for-broke investigative TV reporter, who dared cover the Inokuradai Race Circuit at night, despite the rumors it was h-h-haunted by a g-g-ghost. Her name may *sound* and her face may *look* like that of the actress who played Asuka Soryu Langley in *Evangelion*, but please do not think too much about it.

Monopolar Demon Personality (*The Devil in Miss Urd*, Chapter 63, Vol. 11)
Having both goddess and demon personalities originally within her, Urd enters into a dangerous monopolar state when the two become separated. With her ability to tap directly into Yggdrasil, Urd would become the most powerful demon ever; unfortunately, without her goddess personality to restrain it, the energies would eventually destroy Urd herself.

Moon Rocks (*The Queen of Vengeance*, Chapter 41, Vol. 6)
A potential alternate Alternative Energy Source (as it were) for the goddesses; Keiichi was given a hint to their efficacy through the oracles of the possessed Yuki Gomorrah. Keiichi at first despaired of being able to lay hands on any, but he then hit on the idea of synthesizing moon rocks in N.I.T.'s Materials Lab, based on their known composition of aluminum, calcium, titanium, etc.

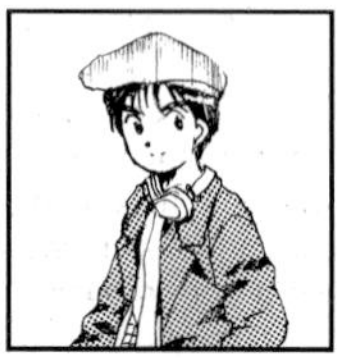

Morisato, Hotaru-no-suke (*Mara Strikes Back*, Chapter 48, Vol. 8)
Keiichi's grandfather. The old-fashioned way to write his name would have been with hyphens; so, Hotaru-no-suke. He was quite cool, having been both a pilot and a motorcyclist. They say girls used to go crazy for him when he was young. Urd's opinion on his photograph is that he was much better looking than Keiichi. One of Keiichi's early memories is flying a plane with Hotarunosuke. It is not known if he is still alive; evidence suggests if he is, he would be in his nineties. It is perhaps of some interest to note that Keiichi's father (and possibly Hotarunosuke's son), Keima, himself appears somewhat older than might be expected. ➔ **Honda, Chieko**

Morisato, Keiichi (*Wrong Number, Chapter 1*, Vol. 1)
Well, you know, our hero. The guy quite often inexplicably found in the time-space midst of girls ranging from cute to beautiful, and from human to goddess.

Morisato, Keima (Chapter 142, Vol. 23)
Do *not* use his full name; instead proceed directly to the listing for **Keima**.

Morisato, Megumi (*Wrong Number*, Chapter 8, Vol. 1)
Keiichi's perky younger sister, one year behind him in school. Also of a mechanical mien, she applied to Nekomi Tech without really informing Keiichi of her intentions first. She seems somewhat more mature when it comes to talking about relationships, although we've never seen any of her own.

Morisato Royal Smash Bomb (*Terrible Master Urd*, Chapter 38, Vol. 6)
Keiichi's "special attack" against the Lord of Terror in its Midgard Serpent form, which basically just consisted of him throwing himself at it. Note that in the original Japanese the attack was called *Morisato Gyokusai Bombaa*, literally "Morisato Honorable Death Bomber."

Morisato, Takano (Chapter 142, Vol. 23)
It is not known if the penalty for using her last (married) name would be as severe as with her husband Keima; nevertheless, do not risk it and instead go directly to the entry for **Takano**.

Most Distant Twins (*Mystery Child*, Chapter 101, Vol. 17)
The phrase used to describe the Doublets; evoking the idea that while their very souls are entangled in a contract ceremony, neither is allowed to retain a memory of the other's identity.

Motor Club Anthem (*Mara Strikes Back*, Chapter 48, Vol. 8)
Otaki sang this "old favorite" while doing karaoke at the Honda Inn; we heard only its opening strains of "*Risking our life on four wheels of fire/Onward we charge to--*"

Ms. Paku-Paku Bug Man (*Sympathy for the Devil*, Chapter 33, Vol. 5)
Referred to as "Mister Bug-Zapper" in the original English edition, this debugging device created by Skuld is susceptible to neutrinos—like the kind coming from Keiichi because, as it turns out, he has a quantum black hole inside him.

Mystery Circle (*The Queen of Vengeance*, Chapter 41, Vol. 6)
Also known as the "Campus Credulity Consortium," this is an N.I.T. club whose specialty appears to be forced fortune telling upon the unwary. In aid of this objective, their vice chairman straps her scrying table and sign display around her neck, thus allowing her to run after passerby who initially decline. ➔ **Gomorrah, Yuki**

N

Needle in a Haystack (*Ninja Master*, Chapter 53, Vol. 9)
Kodama's technique whereby she makes a show of discarding all of her many concealed weapons, in order to get close to the target with one holdout weapon. In the original Japanese, the technique was called *Hijutsu Sabaku no Suna*, literally "Secret Magic Desert Sand."

Neo Skuld Bomb (*Miss Keiichi*, Chapter 58, Vol. 10)
A new version of the Skuld Bomb, from which stubby cylinders protrude rather than the regular Skuld Bomb's U-tubes. We don't get to actually see it used, however—although Skuld does promise to one day do so on the captain of the Baseball Club.

Nekomi Aquarium (*The Fourth Goddess*, Chapter 69, Vol. 12)
Part of Keiichi and Peorth's "date," thanks to Belldandy, who got free tickets from a rice store (in the original English version of the manga, a supermarket raffle) so that everyone was able to tag along, and see the special exhibition "World o' Mollusks."

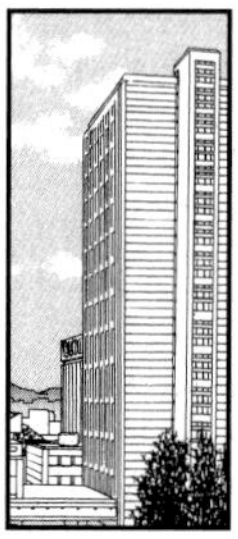

Nekomi Institute of Technology (*Wrong Number*, Chapter 1, Vol. 1)
In Japanese, *Nekomi Kodai*, AKA Nekomi Tech, or simply N.I.T. The engineering school many of the characters, including Keiichi, his sister, and (at least, on paper) Belldandy attend, and the setting for many of the stories in the *Oh My Goddess!* saga. Like WPI or Harvey Mudd, Nekomi Tech combines the best traditions of academics with hands-on chaos. *Nekomi* is written 猫, and means "cat," but it's also a homonym of *nekomi*, spelled 寝込み, that means "to surprise someone in their sleep"—fitting for a campus where anything may happen, at any moment, whether it's for credit or not.

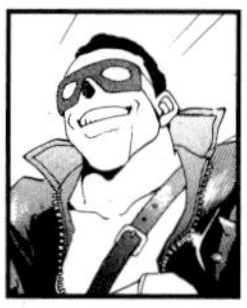

"Nice Middle" Yoshino (*Love Potion No. 9*, Chapter 21, Vol. 3)
The somewhat ambiguously named president of Nekomi Tech's S&M Club, which, frankly, Keiichi did not know they had. With the requisite whip coiled at his side, he holds court in the equipment storage room of the gym, a surprisingly amorous locale in campus manga. ➔ **Red-Haired Devil Nakano**

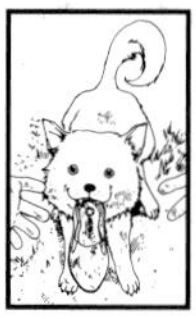

Nihonmaru (*Miss Keiichi*, Chapter 59, Vol. 10)
The name of the little dog Keiichi used to have when he was growing up, who died in an accident. *Nihonmaru* is a famous ship's name in Japan, although in the original English edition of the manga, the dog's name was "Kota," a private reference. It was because Nihonmaru still lived in Keiichi's heart that he

didn't want the stray pup Marone to come live at Tarikihongan.

Ninja Alarm Watch (*Ninja Master*, Chapter 53, Vol. 9)
Pocket watch carried by Kodama; on its outer face are the *kanji* for the twelve animals of the traditional Chinese zodiacal calendar, and on its inner face are those representing the guardian spirits of the four cardinal points. Naturally, being a ninja watch, its alarm has a silent vibration mode.

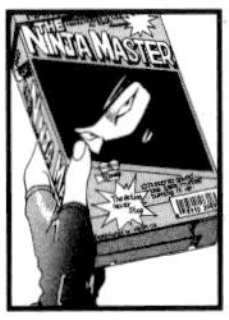
NINJA MASTER

Ninja Master (*Ninja Master*, Chapter 52, Vol. 8)
Name of a movie whose VHS box copy ("*The strongest warrior on Earth . . . the willpower to endure all adversity . . . eyes that pierce the darkness!*") apparently inspired Mara to use her powers to transform several rats into ninja to attack Belldandy's household. Being based on rats, they turned out to be fairly small ninja, yet they fully merited the tape sleeve's promise: "The action never stops." ➔ **Hikari, Kodama, Senrigan the Peeping Tomboy**

Ninpu Kamuri Gaiden (*Ninja Master*, Chapter 53, Vol. 9)
TV program that Kodama and Hikari ended up (successfully) fighting with Urd over to win viewing rights. A takeoff on *Ninpu Kamui Gaiden* ("Ninja Kamui: Side Story"), the 1969 anime based on Sanpei Shirato's influential manga that made the ninja not only an action hero, but a revolutionary guerilla. ➔ ***Holmes***

N.I.T. Baseball Club (*Miss Keiichi*, Chapter 58, Vol. 10)
Somewhat—as Rutger Hauer would say—unsportsmanlike campus organization that broke their verbal promise to Megumi's N.I.T. Women's Softball Club to share the practice grounds on Monday and Friday. As the latter only had four members, the captain of the Baseball Club maintained they weren't a legitimate team, and challenged them to a game to settle the issue—but Urd raised the stakes to having the winner take over the losing team. The captain agreed, because he'd always dreamed of having female gofers.

N.I.T. Four Wheels Club (*Love Potion No. 9*, Chapter 24, Vol. 4)
A rival club founded by Aoshima, apparently for no other reason than to destroy the Motor Club, and loot Belldandy from its wreckage. With Aoshima's filthy lucre behind it, the Four Wheels Club is able to afford not only the latest model cars, but the latest in model bunny girls to attract new members, whereas the Motor Club's idea of publicity, before Urd and Belldandy dropped by, was to stuff Keiichi into a moldy alligator suit. The Four Wheels Club went as far as to bulldoze the Motor Club's clubhouse, but the Motor Club won theirs in turn with their victory in the Economy Run.

N.I.T. Motor Club (*Leader of the Pack,* Chapter 10, Vol. 2)
Campus clubs are an important part of Japanese school life, and Keiichi has the honor to belong to one considered weird even by Nekomi Tech standards—the N.I.T. Motor Club. It is not known whether it had that reputation in the days of its first director, Chihiro Fujimi, who (according to the club's official history) first created the Motor Club by restructuring the "enfeebled and useless" Nekomi Tech Automobile Fan Club. It definitely acquired that reputation under the regime of Tamiya and Otaki, who took over after Chihiro graduated, and have continued to impose their colorful personalities on it despite first Keiichi Morisato and then Sora Hasegawa succeeding to the director's post. Belldandy has certainly supported the Motor Club in the past, although she maintained in Chapter 178, Vol. 28, that she's not a member (perhaps she meant that she's no longer a member?). Although the Motor Club mainly fools around with motorcycles, they have no objection to projects involving cars, trucks, or even airplanes, often salvaged or slapped together from parts they've got lying around. According to Tamiya, the club motto is "*Great deeds is done wit' no budget!*"

Noble Scarlet (*Queen Sayoko*, Chapter 79, Vol. 14)
Skuld's Angel; immature, as Skuld often is, but sweet as Skuld usually isn't. Prematurely manifested, Noble Scarlet returned to her egg, which Skuld wore around her neck from then on. During the fight against the Eater of Angels in Chapter 160, Vol. 25, Skuld finally learned the strength of heart required to have an angel, and Noble Scarlet returned to her at last.

Noise Silencing Shoes (*Sora Unchained*, Chapter 128, Vol. 20)
In the original Japanese, *Shoo'on Nikukyuu Shuuzu*—in the original English version, referred to as the Skuld "Neko Stealth Slippers" Version 2.0. Skuld donned these in hopes of sneaking up on the TV set and applying an electromagnetic lock on it during one of their Channel Fights. ➔ **High Sensitivity Sound Collection Sensor**

O

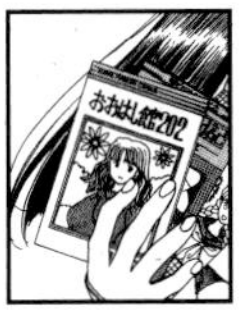

Ohashi Inn 202 (*The Fourth Goddess*, Chapter 69, Vol. 12)
Name of a shojo manga *tankobon* (graphic novel, as opposed to a magazine such as *Dobon*) Peorth read to research human romance customs. In the original English version of the manga, its title was given simply as *Love Stories*. ➔ ***Dobon***

Ohtaki, Etsushi (*Leader of the Pack*, Chapter 12, Vol. 2)
Not to be confused with the *other* Otaki, he is president of the Ushikubo University Motorcycle Club, to whom Tamiya wagered Belldandy on the outcome of a set of drag races. Known as "Snapping Turtle Etsushi," due to his reputation for not letting go of things.

Otaki (*Wrong Number,* Chapter 1, Vol. 1)
First name uncertain (some sources suggest it is "Aoyama," but unlike with Tamiya, the encyclopedia doesn't list one; see remarks under **Aoyama-sempai**). At the start of the story, he is codirector of the Motor Club, together with his best bud Tamiya. Female students consider him the weirdest guy in school, which, as Keiichi points out, is a considerable accomplishment. Habitually wears a black leather jacket with inside loops sewn in to carry tools, a necklace strung with hex nuts and washers, and a spark plug hanging from each ear. None of it is mere affectation; Otaki just likes to have them all handy for repairs. Dislikes dogs, likes cosplay (?), and has somewhat better luck with women than Tamiya, perhaps due to the fact that bizarre as he styles himself, he's more human and less humanoid. Affectionate nicknames used only with Tamiya include "Dai-chan" (from *dai*, an alternate reading for the *O* kanji in "Otaki"), "Takki," and, in the original English version of the manga, "Ottie."

Otakki Fried Chicken (*The Queen of Vengeance*, Chapter 44, Vol. 7)
Finger-lickin' good present Sayoko tried to give to Keiichi, after showing up drunk one night at Tarikihongan Temple. Instead she fell into his arms, cried, and passed out, but it came in handy the next morning when she used a drumstick to help retrieve Belldandy's hand-knit sweater from Yotaro. It is not known whether the name "Otakki" refers to an otaku (see the notes for 110.5 in *Oh My Goddess!* Vol. 1), but the tiny head on the "OFC" logo definitely resembles Sada's head more than that of the Colonel. ➔ **Sada**

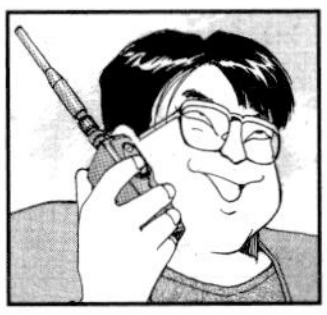

Otokichi (*Love Potion No. 9*, Chapter 21, Vol. 3)
Flunky of Sayoko, who directed Belldandy to the gym, to which Keiichi had been extraordinarily rendered by the S&M Club. Whatever ambush they had in mind, however, was spoiled by Belldandy's teleporting into the gym through a mirror, and Urd's volunteering herself to the evildoers as their impromptu dominatrix.

Ou Pyuru Kyuin (Chapter 174, Vol. 27)
The first Machiner to arrive at Whirlwind, needing its loose chain fixed. Ou is the temporarily detached nose gear of Pi Pu Pii Gaa. It seems to already know the "Lady Belldandy," as it calls her, and regards Keiichi as her servant, criticizing his pronunciation and perverted (from a Machiner's perspective) interest in the beauty of its body parts. Nevertheless, Ou likes Keiichi, regarding him as one of the few humans "who understands a machine's heart." ➔ **Pi Pu Pii Gaa**

Overcharge a Running Program (*The Fourth Goddess*, Chapter 67, Vol. 11)
In the original Japanese, *puroguramu jikkoo-chuu no yokoyari*, literally "interference during program execution." Peorth used this phrase to explain how Belldandy's attempt to magically retrieve Keiichi's printout ran out of control due to Urd and Skuld jumping in with their own spells while Belldandy's was running.

P

Pakdortamya X-20 Extract (*The Queen of Vengeance*, Chapter 43, Vol. 7)
One of Urd's many secret ingredients for her Ultra High-Grade Love Seeds (also referred to as a "love potion" in the original English version).

Panchira (*Love Potion No. 9*, Chapter 22, Vol. 3)
Meaning "a glimpse of panties," such voyeurism is only one of many behaviors in manga frowned upon by the law—although in manga, the more likely response is swift street justice. A practice dating back to Osamu Tezuka's *Astro Boy*, the skirt-flipping form favored by Urd was however popularized by Go Nagai in his scandalous 1968–72 *Shonen Jump* story *Harenchi Gakuen* ("Shameless School"), said to have been one of the first manga

ever burned by the Japanese PTA. The first time Urd tries this on Belldandy (to rally Keiichi's spirits in the Golden Hammer Race), it produces a gasp from the crowd and causes both Keiichi and his rival to drive into the safety barrier—despite the fact no panty was actually glimpsed, only Belldandy's black tights. Twenty-seven volumes later, Urd used her provisional first-class powers that could potentially destroy the Earth for the purpose of flipping Belldandy's skirt again. This time, *panchira* was in fact achieved, demonstrating that Keiichi's Happy Badge was working fine. Belldandy was prompted to utter the immortal line, "Keiichi? Is this . . . happiness?" ➔ **Happy Badge**

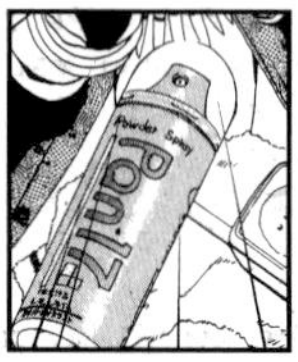

Pan 17 (*Love Potion Vol. 9*, Chapter 27, Vol. 4)
Brand name on a spray can Sayoko hurled at Mara when the latter appeared in her room; it is speculated this is a play on Ban's powder-fresh antiperspirant.

Parent-Child Showdown (Chapter 147, Vol. 23)
In the original Japanese, *Oyako Taiketsu*—although the name itself is not mentioned in the English version of the manga, this refers to the race on motorcycles Keima and Keiichi had on the road to the Inokuradai Campus. This was the ninety-eighth time parent and child had raced under varying circumstances; since the days of Keiichi's first bicycle, he had lost ninety-seven times.

Peorth Rose Storm Attack (*The Fourth Goddess*, Chapter 66, Vol. 11)
In the original Japanese, *higi bara no arashi*, or "Secret Weapon Rose Storm." Peorth's response to Keiichi's wish that she "please go home." A swirling mass of roses, of which Keiichi commented, "Yeoww! They're all prickly!!"

Peorth Wafting Rose Attack (*The Fourth Goddess*, Chapter 69, Vol. 12)
In the original Japanese, *higi bara no soyokaze*, or "Secret Weapon Rose Breeze." Peorth used this technique, which seems to involve distracting people by conjuring roses that drift gently past in the air, to grab Keiichi from Belldandy during their "group date." It didn't work.

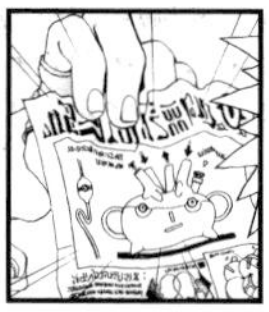

Personality Separation Precipitator (*The Devil in Miss Urd*, Chapter 61, Vol. 10)
An evil urn (Mara seems to like evil urns); an accursed, heretical artifact capable of the blasphemous act of separating Urd's divine and demonic natures. Mara got it through demonic mail order (in the original English version of the manga, the "Acme Novelty Supply Company"). ➔ **Separation of Goddess/Demon Personalities**

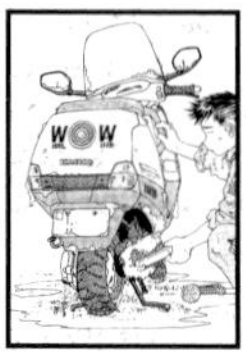

Piaggio Hexagon (Chapter 143, Vol. 23)
A contemporary Italian scooter manufactured by the Piaggio Corporation, whose line also includes the famous Vespa seen in the anime *FLCL*. One of several vehicles belonging to Whirlwind, Keiichi was obliged to clean it after losing a motor-assembly race with Keima organized by Chihiro, and then was promptly obliged to leap on it to chase Keima after Chihiro made the mistake of touching him.

Ping-Pong Match (*The Devil in Miss Urd*, Chapter 60, Vol. 10)
First of the three matches Urd and Mara fought against each other during their truce (from *actual* fighting) at the Daikokuya Inn. Mara won, despite Urd's boast of having "played Ping-Pong at countless tacky resorts around the universe." ➔ **Karaoke Match; Game Match**

Pi Pu Pii Gaa (Chapter 175, Vol. 27)
A graceful, VTOL-capable (vertical take-off and landing) jet plane Machiner, who came to pick up Ou Pyuru Kyuin, its nose gear, but missed the rendezvous. Having mechanical trouble, Pi was unable to land vertically, so Keiichi came up with a plan (based on a *Thunderbirds* episode) to have it land on an improvised runway, using his scooter to substitute for the missing nose wheel. ➔ **Ou Pyuru Kyuin**

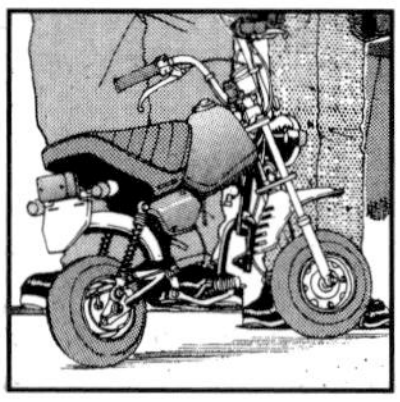

Pokke (*Miss Keiichi*, Chapter 56, Vol. 9)
Nickname for 50cc Yamaha minibike used as the foundation of the N.I.T. Motor Club's entry into the Hill Climb Race (the Mach Engine was kludged into its frame). *Pokke* is short for "pocket bike," and is a term very much in use today as well. ➔ **Mach Engine**

Polar Electric Shock Wave (*Miss Keiichi*, Chapter 54, Vol. 9)
In the original Japanese, *kyokuchi dengekiha*, meaning literally "polar region electric shock wave." Called the "Urd Ultra Lightning Strike" in the original English version. Urd attempts to lay her vengeance upon Skuld for scribing "BAKA" upon her face with this spell, but is halted by Belldandy.

Porsche 356 Speedster (*Sympathy for the Devil*, Chapter 29, Vol. 4)
This was the convertible variant, introduced in 1954, of the 356, the first Porsche production automobile. Mara turned Megumi into a Speedster; it is not known why she ended up in the form of that particular vehicle, but Keiichi remarked, "You're a lot better looking than the last time I saw you." Fortunately, when Megumi woke up herself the next day, she thought it had all been a dream.

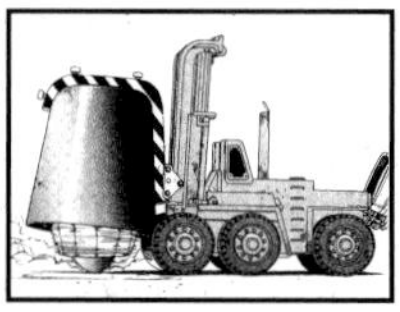

Pot Shaker Dragon (*The Queen of Vengeance*, Chapter 40, Vol. 6)
Megumi created this machine for the Robot Battle; it appears to be a sort of radio-controlled forklift with pinchers on the back, and a giant downward pail instead of a lift on the front. It was intended to collect a winning number of empty oil drums (the object of the Robot Battle), but Megumi found that Skuld's fast-rotating Hysteric Wheel #1 swiftly captured thirteen of the drums before Megumi could capture even one; it looked hopeless until Megumi hit on the novel tactic of simply capturing Hysteric Wheel. ➔ **Hysteric Wheel #1**

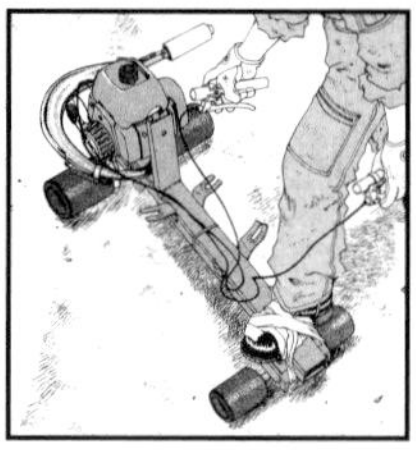

Power Board (*Sora Unchained*, Chapter 127, Vol. 20)
When his Racing Board's seat and handlebar struts snapped off in a crash, Keiichi kept going in the Director Race by holding the brake and gas grips by their cables, while balancing on the board's axle like a skateboard. Chihiro dubbed this kludge the "Power Board," and later claimed it was an "option" when she started selling Racing Boards retail.

Professor Kajigaya (*Queen Sayoko*, Chapter 81, Vol. 14)
Sayoko's thesis advisor. Sayoko uses her Mind Force Field powers to make him kneel and describe her dissertation in the most slavish terms, although later when the field vanishes, so does her dissertation.

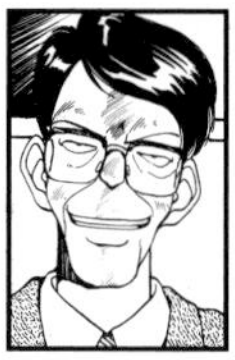

Professor Ozawa (*Wrong Number*, Chapter 4, Vol. 1)
Everyone remembers the cool instructors they had in school, those who inspire their pupils with a lifelong love of learning; Professor Ozawa is not that man. A martinet for attendance, Ozawa is the rival of the *genuinely* cool Professor Kakuta, whom he believes (falsely) is using Belldandy to steal his enrollment. His prying into her origins leads Belldandy to alter the N.I.T. records so that she is now marked as a legitimately enrolled "foreign exchange student."

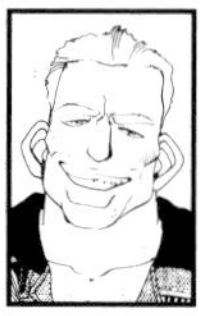

Proter, David (*Love Potion No. 9*, Chapter 22, Vol. 3)
The male half of the LAIT team, and Diana Lockheed's boyfriend (although, as is not uncommon, Keiichi's indomitable spirit makes her eyes wander just a bit). A beefy blond lummox in a sleeveless denim shirt with a "Laguna" patch (presumably for Laguna Seca, the famous racing track near Monterey, California), David finished third in the Daytona 500—a somewhat intimidating achievement to the amateur racers of the N.I.T. Motor Club. He seems to know Aoshima; did the latter arrange to have these ringers imported in his bid to get Belldandy?

Q

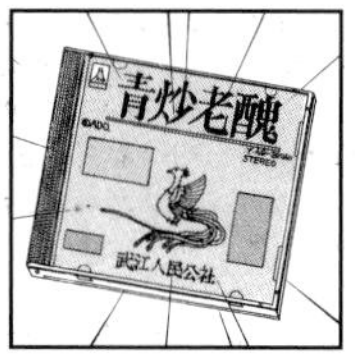
青炒老醜

Qing Chǎo Láo Chǒu (*Love Potion No. 9*, Chapter 27, Vol. 4)
Cryptically Chinese-named CD Sayoko bought the night before she met Mara; its mysterious nature is perhaps related to the fact that buying the CD is the *only* thing she remembers about that night. According to translator Deborah Hsu, the four characters themselves (called *hanzi*, rather than *kanji*, when used to write Chinese) don't appear to make much sense by themselves—they mean "green/youthful," "stir-fry," "old," and "ugly" (or in some cases, "scandalous") respectively. As these characters

don't seem to form a phrase in Japanese either, it is theorized the CD's title is an in-joke of some sort, which would not at all be out of character for the early volumes of *Oh My Goddess!* Note the line of six hanzi at the bottom of the CD cover has the more straightforward meaning "Wujiang People's Commune." ➔ **Demons CD**

Queen, The (*Hand in Hand*, Chapter 86, Vol. 15)
Not to be confused with the Campus Queen, this woman is an older Nekomi Institute of Technology student who rides a super-custom Yamaha TDM850, and whose particular joy in life is to always beat the thirtieth and last person in the race to attend Aerodynamics 101, taking the place of the straggler. She likes to compose poetry about this, and say queenly things such as "Receive thy crown!" and "Off with your head!"

R

Racing Board (*Sora Unchained*, Chapter 120, Vol. 19)
Under Article 26, Clause 5 of the N.I.T. Motor Club regulations (please see the section "Rules of the *Oh My Goddess!* Cosmos"), Chihiro decided that—as Sora Hasegawa couldn't ride a motorcycle—the Director Race would be done riding a charming little 40cc mini go-kart dubbed a "Racing Board." Chihiro's true intent in all this was for the Racing Boards to be seen in action by the entire student body along the campus route—thereby providing massive free publicity for Whirlwind's special sale of . . . Racing Boards.

Racing Kneeler (*The Phantom Racer*, Chapter 110, Vol. 18)
Slang (employed mostly outside North America) for a kind of sidecar used in motorbike racing; as the name implies, the racer's partner kneels rather than sits, allowing them more freedom of range to shift their body's position and weight according to moment-by-moment needs of the race. See **RS80 Tomboy** on page 181.

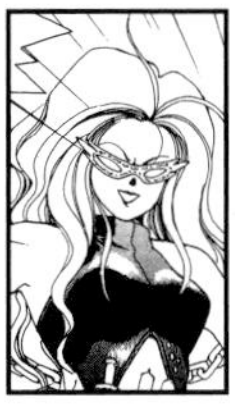

Red-Haired Devil Nakano (*Love Potion No. 9*, Chapter 21, Vol. 3)
Vice-president of Nekomi Tech's S&M Club. Equipped with syringe and candle, two of the "three sacred treasures," she wears the Harlequinade mask traditional in Japan for female practitioners. ➔ **"Nice Middle" Yoshino**

Regenerating (*Sympathy for the Devil*, Chapter 33, Vol. 5)
The goddesses are higher-dimensional beings, and in order to make themselves visible to people in three-dimensional space (i.e., on Earth), it is necessary for them to constantly "regenerate" their atomic structure. While the energy discharged in this process ordinarily disperses safely, in Keiichi's case, the energy from the goddess sisters built up, forming a vortex around him. ➔ **Singularity**

Remote Body Control (*Miss Keiichi*, Chapter 57, Vol. 9)
Taking advantage of the fact that Belldandy's sealing power is weakened when she is jealous, Urd used this magic spell on Keiichi in order to return Garm to the spirit realm. To be specific, Urd made Keiichi grope Shiho Sakakibara's bosom. ➔ **Jealousy Storm**

Ring and Bracelet (*Miss Keiichi*, Chapter 55, Vol. 9)
Gifts that Urd and Troubadour exchanged with each other back when they were first going out; Urd got the ring, and Troubadour, the bracelet. Urd was upset to see he still had it long after he abandoned her to chase the Golden Bush Warbler, as "that's breaking the rules," but they ended up deciding to keep them even after he ran off again in search of the bird . . . the bird that represents his quest as a man.

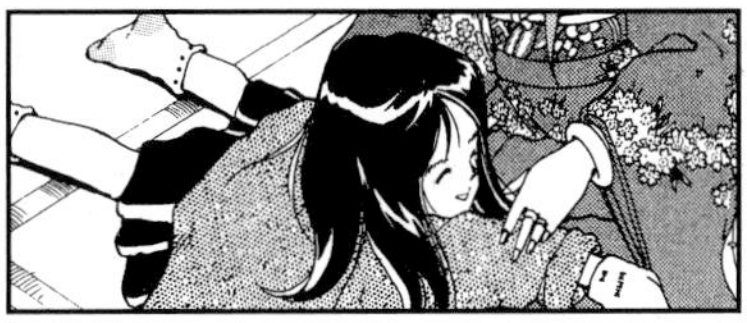

Risa-chan (*Final Exam*, Chapter 18, Vol. 3)
Name of a little girl living across from the Tarikihongan Temple. She referred to Belldandy as "Bell-Mama," a nickname which looked for a moment as if it was going to get Keiichi beaten up by Tamiya and Otaki, having jumped to some rapid conclusions. ➔ **Chobi, Life Sugoroku Special**

Robo-chan (*The Phantom Racer*, Chapter 117, Vol. 19)
Temporary nickname for the Welcome Robot. ➔ **Sigel**

Robot Battle (*The Queen of Vengeance*, Chapter 40, Vol. 6)
Impressed by the macho nature of Skuld and Megumi's rivalry (in reality, a one-sided feeling by Skuld), Tamiya and Otaki devised the Robot Battle event for them to settle the score (in reality, their motivation was to promote campuswide betting on the outcome for their financial benefit). ➔ **Hysteric Wheel #1, Pot Shaker Dragon**

Rock (*Sympathy for the Devil*, Chapter 28, Vol. 4)
One of Mara's weaknesses, as she tends to start performing an auto-irresistible dance whenever she hears rock music. Interestingly enough, the effect, or lack of same, it has on her can also be used to distinguish between fake rock and *real rock*. ➔ **Enka, Good-Luck Charms**

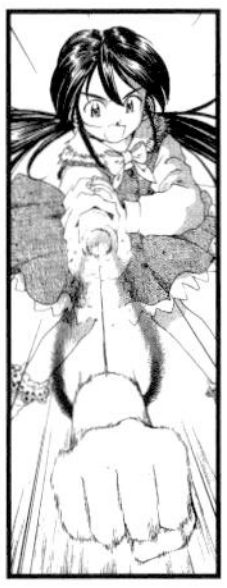

Rocket Punch (*Traveler*, Chapter 102, Vol. 17)
Skuld gave the Welcome Robot the ability to launch her fist off her arm like a harpoon as part of her general upgrade, regarding this feature as "basic robotics." The robot somehow knows this is a reference to the classic 1972 anime *Mazinger Z* (shown in the U.S. in the 1980s under the name *Tranzor Z*) whose eponymous robot hero had the original Rocket Punch as one of "his" many weapons . . . whereas his partner "female" robot, Aphrodite A, had only two—missiles whose warheads served as her breasts. ➔ **Breast Missiles, Emotion Circuit**

Rock of the Three Sisters (*Ninja Master*, Chapter 50, Vol. 8)
In the original Japanese, *Mitsugo Iwa*, or literally "Triplet Rock." On a vacation trip to the beach, Urd told Keiichi of this legendary rock offshore, a place where those who pledge their love beneath the full moon will be bound forever. It led to a very romantic quest by Keiichi, even though Urd "just made all that crap up."

Rom-In (*Terrible Master Urd*, Chapter 38, Vol. 6)
Name of a computer-related magazine through which Skuld claimed to understand the self-replicating virus function of the Ultimate Destruction Program. Urd still didn't get it.

Root Spell Formula (Chapter 133, Vol. 21)
The basic operating program underlying spells and enchantments in the *Oh My Goddess!* cosmos—analogous to a BIOS in a human computer system. There are both divine and demonic root spell formulae; the goddess sisters realized the reason they were unable to affect the spell that had turned Peorth into a kid was that it was running on a demonic root. ➔ **BIOS, Kid Peorth**

Runic Divination (*Hand in Hand*, Chapter 89, Vol. 15)
Although Belldandy makes mention of a "Goddess Rune" as far back as Chapter 56, Vol. 9, here is where we first see her casting fortunes by means of runes. Part of the Norse cultural influence found in the depiction of the *Oh My Goddess!* cosmos, runes were an alphabet used in ancient and medieval times by Scandinavian cultures (as well as others related to them), and were utilized for ordinary purposes as well as divination. There are several modern systems that claim to give a method for fortunetelling by means of runes, although it is debatable what connection they have to ancient Norse practices and beliefs.

Ryujin (*The Queen of Vengeance*, Chapter 42, Vol. 6)
Meaning "Dragon God," this is the brand of saké Yoshida buys at the local corner shop for Urd. The joke is that the real Ryujin is a limited-edition, seasonal microbrew made only in Tsurugashima (a city in Saitama Prefecture, which neighbors Tokyo), and if you want to buy it each year, you have to reserve in advance, with one bottle only per customer. ➔ ***Kintetsu (Kintaro Electric Railway) II***

S

Sada (*Wrong Number*, Chapter 2, Vol. 1)
An otaku (although technically an *anime mania*; please see the notes in Vol. 1 for 27.1) who briefly sheltered Belldandy and Keiichi after she inadvertently got him kicked out of his dorm.

Sadakichi Mikan (*Sympathy for the Devil*, Chapter 30, Vol. 4)
Untranslated brand name upon the crate Keiichi leaned his elbows on to mope about the envelope-stuffing job Tamiya had Belldandy and him do to raise money to build a new clubhouse (after the old was destroyed by the N.I.T. Four Wheels Club). A *mikan*, of course, is a kind of mandarin orange, whose empty crates and boxes seem ubiquitous as storage units in anime and manga.

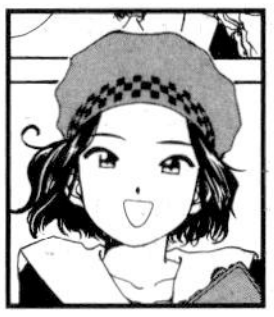

Sakakibara, Shiho (*Miss Keiichi*, Chapter 57, Vol. 9)
Introduced as a freshman electronics major, Sakakibara is adorable even by *OMG!* standards. Obsessed with performing exorcisms on

people, even if they're not possessed in the first place, or if her rites conjure up demons where none were present previously. ➔ **Garm, Kundali**

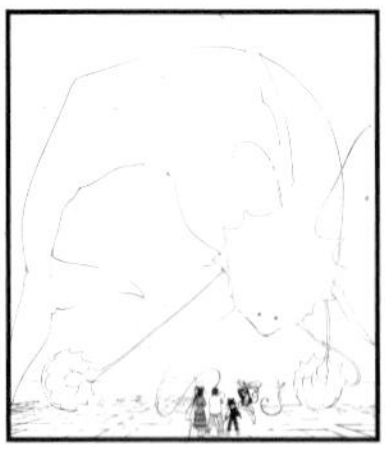

Schrödinger's Whale (*Traveler*, Chapter 108, Vol. 18)
A race of gigantic, floating creatures; so named for the physicist Erwin Schrödinger (1887–1961), famed for his study of quantum indeterminacy. By consciously manipulating its own quantum state, the "whale" is able to travel anywhere in time or space, or even between dimensions—but only for a limited time, or else its wave function collapses. Belldandy was very surprised to see one, as she had thought their species was extinct. The whale develops a crush on Keiichi, causing Belldandy to remark that it's always nice to be liked, "even by another boy." ➔ ***Millennium Blues***

Schwantz, Kevin (*The Fourth Goddess*, Chapter 66, Vol. 11)
Former motorcycle racer for Suzuki, Schwantz won the 1993 500cc World Championship. In the original manga, Keiichi is contemplating what he should wish of Peorth to make her go away, and considers "*Schwantz no zekken o 34 ni shite kudasai . . .*" meaning, "Give Schwantz the racing number 34." Since Kevin Schwantz's racing number was *already* 34 (it was so famously associated with him that the International Motorcycling Federation retired the number when Schwantz himself retired), it may be that Keiichi was indulging in a little absurdist humor, and the reason why in the original English version, the line was changed to "Get Kenny Roberts [himself a 500cc champion in the late 1970s—*ed.*] back racing motorcycles again."

Scroll of Golden Verse (*Miss Keiichi*, Chapter 55, Vol. 9)
Troubadour carries this magic scroll, whose sealing knot can only be untied by the tear of a goddess. He needs to open the scroll in order to summon the Golden Bush Warbler, but of course, he needs to play with Urd's emotions in order to open the scroll. ➔ **Troubadour**

Seal Mirror (*The Devil in Miss Urd*, Chapter 62, Vol. 10)
In the original Japanese, a *fuuinkyoo*; Skuld was trapped inside this miscellaneous magic item by the Demon Urd, who chortled that only she could unlock it—fortunately for Skuld, "she" included her *other* self as well—the Goddess Urd.

Sea Monkey (*Terrible Master Urd*, Chapter 37, Vol. 6)
The crew of this vessel looks familiar, as well they should, for the reference is a play on the *Sea Bat*, a submarine which—renamed the *Yamato* by its mutinous crew—becomes the central stage of Kaiji Kawaguchi's manga *The Silent Service*, a phenomenal bestseller in early-'90s Japan. Although Kawaguchi's epic of an alternate 2000 U.S. presidential race, *Eagle*, has been published in the United States, *The Silent Service* has never been—its 33-volume length poses a challenge for any publisher, and its assumption of Japan as a rising power seems itself now a product of an alternate history.

Self-Destruct Mode (*Traveler*, Chapter 103, Vol. 17)
Robo-chan (AKA the Welcome Robot), claimed to have such a mode, and activated its countdown sequence in protest of Skuld ordering her to try to like Banpei-kun. With one second to go, Skuld countermanded the order, and used the command override code ARDJ-5041.

Senbei (*Mara Strikes Back*, Chapter 45, Vol. 7)
Genie-like, New Romantic–dressed god of poverty and disaster that Mara had stashed in a *ramune* bottle (a type of soda bottle using a marble as part of its carbonation seal) and who emerges to do her bidding—namely, inflict poverty and disaster. Talks a little funny and somewhat of a moron, yet not entirely lacking in common sense—something useful to have if you're expected to follow orders from Mara. ➔ **Law of Conservation of Happiness**

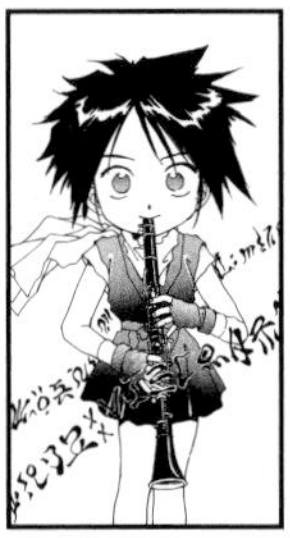

Senrigan the Peeping Tomboy (*Ninja Master*, Chapter 53, Vol. 9)
One of the three Ninja Masters that Mara created; original rat species unknown. Carries a clarinet by which she could summon a horde of equally tiny ninja from their clan, although apparently these were mere *ninja*, as opposed to a *ninja master* such as herself. *Senrigan* means "clairvoyance," and in the original Japanese, "peeping tom" is *nozomi*, which is pronounced the same (but spelled with different kanji), as *nozomi* meaning "hope," the fastest of the three train services on the famous Tokaido Shinkansen bullet train route between Tokyo and Osaka. ➔ **Hikari, Kodama**

Separation of Goddess/Demon Personalities (*The Devil in Miss Urd*, Chapter 61, Vol. 10)
As the name implies, this is the splitting into separate personalities of the goddess and demon natures entwined as one within Urd. Urd said it was an impossible task, even for the Almighty (does this imply it was tried at some point in the past?) yet Mara is able to do it, using the Personality Separation Precipitator.

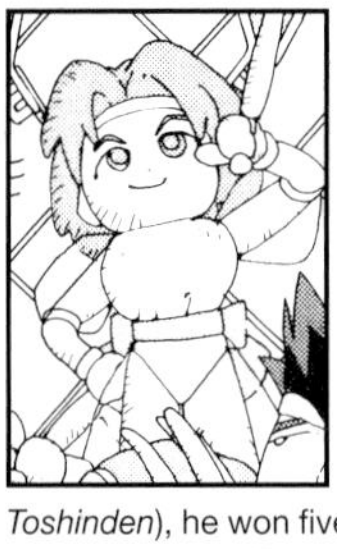

Seris (*Queen Sayoko*, Chapter 80, Vol. 14)
Name of the doll in the crane game machine Keiichi was trying to win while on an outing with Belldandy and Stringfellow. However, instead of the cute Seris (based on the cute "Ellis" from *Battle Arena Toshinden*), he won five non-cute Randers (based on the non-cute Rungo from the same game).

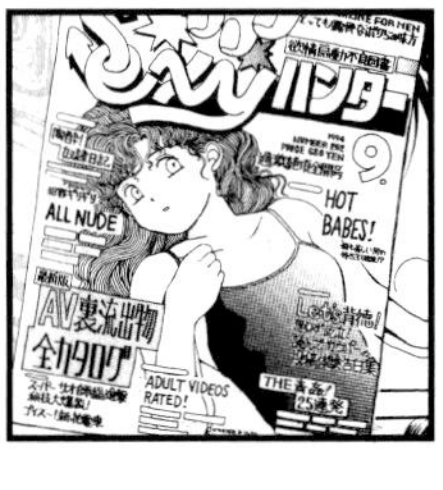
ALL NUDE
HOT BABES!
ADULT VIDEOS RATED!

Sexy Hunter (*The Fourth Goddess*, Chapter 72, Vol. 12)
An "adult interest" magazine Keiichi apparently forgot he had stashed in the back of the second drawer of his drafting desk; Peorth reminded him, in order to prove a point about his desires. Note that since this was a *different* hiding place from before, it suggests that either Keiichi moved it following the previous discovery, or Peorth moved it, in order that this "hint" might take him by surprise. ➔ ***Where Does Keiichi Hide His Dirty Magazines?***

Shinnentai (*Mara Strikes Back*, Chapter 48, Vol. 8)
When a person dies with a strong desire left unfulfilled, it may sometimes happen that the desire *itself* remains behind, taking on a physical shape that resembles the person, but is actually a *shinnentai*, or "manifestation of will," now existing only to carry out the lingering wish. Belldandy contrasts the "physical" shinnentai with the concept of a ghost, which, according to her, are not physical, but exist only as psychic images projected into the minds of those they haunt. ➔ **Honda, Chieko**

Shonen Dairugger (*Sympathy for the Devil*, Chapter 32, Vol. 5)
A monthly (manga?) magazine Keiichi was using to raise one side of his drawing board. Most likely a reference to the 1982–83 anime TV series *Kikou Kantai Dairugger XV*, much of which was later rewritten into the U.S. *Voltron* anime as the "Vehicle Voltron" segment.

Sigel (*The Phantom Racer*, Chapter 118, Vol. 19)
The Welcome Robot, aka Robo-chan, finally receives this proper name from Belldandy, after the struggle with Dr. Moreau convinces her that the robot deserves recognition as a living being; "Sigel" is a Norse rune interpreted by Belldandy as a sign of life. ➔ **Inanimate Spirits, Welcome Robot**

Singularity (*Sympathy for the Devil*, Chapter 32, Vol. 5)
In physics, a singularity refers to a situation where theory predicts that a rate of change in some process will increase without limit, or become infinite. The most well-known example of such a singularity are those that are believed to be within a black hole, where it is gravity that becomes infinite. Typically for Keiichi, one ended up forming inside his body, when the energy dispersed from the goddesses gradually built up around him, and, in concentrating, formed a vortex taking on the form of a stabilized quantum black hole. The tragedy of this explanation is it was actually far more complicated than that.

Skuld Bomb (*Sympathy for the Devil*, Chapter 32, Vol. 5)
Grenade-like . . . grenade, that's a trademark of the Third Goddess. It actually does resemble a modern grenade, with a fuse sticking out of a spherical body, but the distinctive thing about a Skuld Bomb are the multiple U-shaped tubes that protrude all around the sphere. Skuld seems to always have one handy, keeping them down her dress, where, as Urd would point out, she still has plenty of room. ➔ **Bundled Hand Grenades, Neo Skuld Bomb**

Skuld Comet Mark Two (*The Queen of Vengeance*, Chapter 44, Vol. 7)
Mini battery-powered spy satellite (deployed by a model rocket with orbital capacity!) Skuld launched to help search for Belldandy's missing hand-knit sweater. Also used it to discover an ice cream parlor she hadn't been to before.

Skuld Dolphin Gun (*The Fourth Goddess*, Chapter 69, Vol. 12)
The weapon Skuld used on Keiichi, whom she judged to be overly interested in how Belldandy looked in a swimsuit. It sounds menacing—well, actually, it doesn't—but it was just a dolphin-shaped water pistol. ➔ **Mild Blue Nekomi**

Skuld Labs (*Ninja Master*, Chapter 52, Vol. 8)
Skuld's private room at Tarikihongan, where she works on her gadgets of small-to-medium destruction. ➔ **Everybody's Tea Room, Keiichi's Shop, Urd's Room**

Skuld Magical Bomb (*Ninja Master*, Chapter 52, Vol. 8)
Tricked by Kodama into fighting with Urd (which admittedly doesn't take much doing), Skuld hurled this attack at her dear older sister. It's not clear how it differs from her usual Skuld Bomb, except that it seems to magically multiply itself, so that upon throwing, one grenade becomes four.

Skuld's Own Karaoke Scoring Machine (*The Devil in Miss Urd*, Chapter 60, Vol. 10)
Since the Daikokuya hot springs resort had a karaoke player, but no scoring machine, Skuld whipped one together by dismantling two of their tabletop video games. She left a note promising to return the parts, but no doubt encountered difficulties after Urd and Mara smashed her invention, offended at the way it insisted they kept trying.

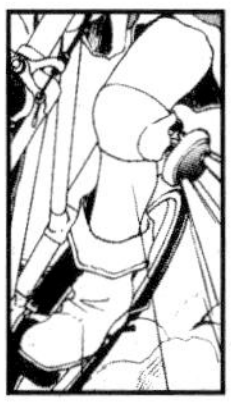

Skuld Special Active Balancer Knee-Pad (*Childhood's End*, Chapter 73, Vol. 13)
In the original Japanese, the *Sukurudo Tokusei Akutibu Purotekutaa*, or "Skuld's Own Active Protector"; trying to learn to ride a bicycle, Skuld wore this system of knee and elbow pads equipped with small rocket maneuvering jets designed to compensate with a counterburst if she started to lose balance. Skuld abandoned the gadget after it started to *over*-compensate.

Skuld Will Wave Wall Shielded Ribbon Cable, Mark 1 (*Queen Sayoko*, Chapter 81, Vol. 14)
Hair ribbon designed by Skuld, incorporating "anti-mind force metal" wires. Wearing it as protection is the only way to enter Queen Sayoko's Mind Force Field without being immediately overcome by a desire to obey her. Keiichi himself was almost overcome when he took the bow out of his hair for a moment, wishing only to retie it in a more manly headband configuration.

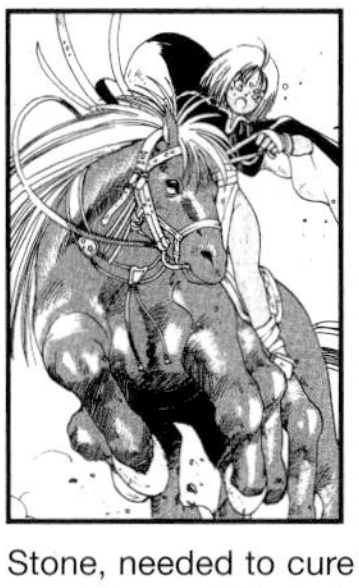

Sleipnir (*Leader of the Pack*, Chapter 14, Vol. 2)
In Norse belief, the god Odin, ruler of his pantheon, had a magical eight-legged horse named Sleipnir; similarly, in *Oh My Goddess!*, such a steed belongs to the Almighty. Urd once swiped it on a quest to obtain the Jade Dragon Stone, needed to cure Belldandy's illness—but spent the next three days just learning to control it, while someone else fetched the stone in the meantime. Belldandy uses this story to illustrate Urd's nature: tremendous passion, but a little short in the forethought department.

Softball Club (*Miss Keiichi*, Chapter 58, Vol. 10)
Megumi Morisato is the leader of this four-person club at N.I.T., together with fellow players Taira, Taka, and Junko. The head of the Baseball Club, Mitsuru Yamagata, stole their practice time, sneering that four people hardly made a legitimate team, but his real motivation was to break them up entirely, in hopes the four girls would join *his* club, as gofers.

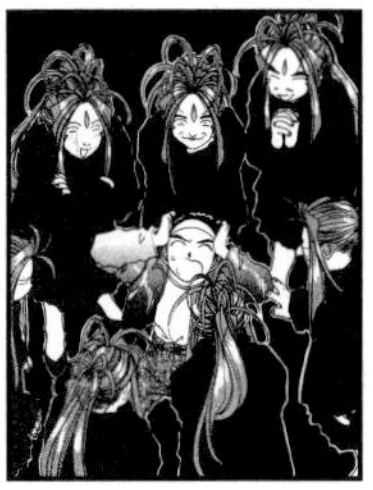

So Many Belldandies! (*Queen Sayoko*, Chapter 82, Vol. 14)
In Japanese, *Berudandii ga ippai!*—Keiichi's cry of despair at finding himself surrounded by cross-dressing decoys of Belldandy in Queen Sayoko's castle. In the original English version of the manga, he simply screamed *"Nooo!!"* ➔ **Mind Force Field**

Soup of a Jack o' Lantern (*The Queen of Vengeance*, Chapter 43, Vol. 7)
One of Urd's many secret ingredients for her Ultra High-Grade Love Seeds (also referred to as a "love potion" in the original English version). Even though we're giving you the recipe, don't try this at home.

Space Doubler (*Traveler*, Chapter 105, Vol. 18)
In the original Japanese, *kuukan daburaa*; known as the "Skuld Quantum Space Expander" in the original English edition of the manga. In fact, the gadget, designed by Skuld to expand their household storage area, can do far more than merely double it; it works by "borrowing" the future version of one's existing space, "thus making the perceived space bigger." For once, it wasn't her fault things went badly awry. ➔ **Infinite Tea Room**

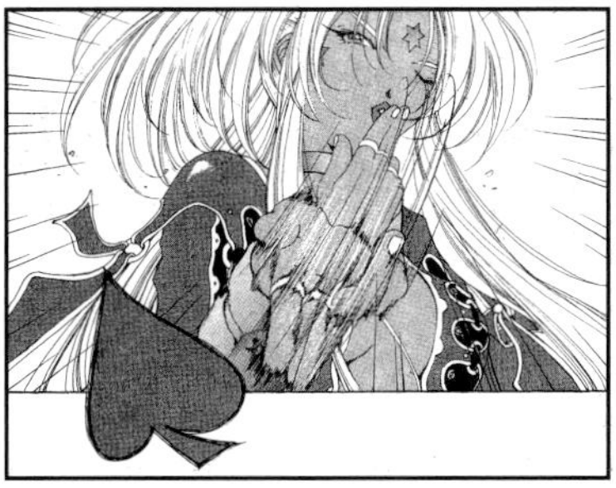

Spade Kiss Throw (Chapter 136, Vol. 22)
Punishment (?) Hild tried to inflict on Keiichi for questioning her honor; Belldandy deflected it with a Heart Kiss Throw. Although apparently not mentioned in the manga itself, the Spade Kiss could have turned Keiichi into an animal, had it hit him.

Spark of the Firefly (*Queen Sayoko*, Chapter 84, Vol. 15)
Urd used this spell to test the magical amplifying power inside Sayoko's castle. The version used in English would seem to work better for the joke, as the basic spell begins as a small point of light on Urd's finger, which then under the influence of the amplifier proceeds to jump away and ricochet down the hall causing havoc—and yet the basic spell's name in original Japanese, *keika rambu*, means literally, "wild dance firefly." Perhaps it was meant metaphorically?

Spear Mint (Chapter 155, Vol. 24)
One of Lind's twin binary angels; she has red eyes, and a single wing on the left-hand side of her body.

Standing Stalk in Tea (*Mara Strikes Back*, Chapter 45, Vol. 7)
A cup of maple leaf tea made by Belldandy (using the maple in their garden) turned out to have a stem (or stalk) of the leaf left in it, that floated upright in the cup. Belldandy thought she should have strained it better, but Keiichi explained that such a standing stalk was a traditional sign of good luck in Japan. Belldandy was able later to use this brew to exorcise Mara from the body of Megumi.

Step-On (*Ninja Master*, Chapter 51, Vol. 8)
Brand name of a seven-piece combination wrench set that caught Skuld's eye when she and Keiichi went out shopping; a play on the famous real-life Snap-On wrenches. As the set was 75,000 yen, Keiichi decided he would buy her just one instead.

Stringfellow Hawke (*Queen Sayoko*, Chapter 80, Vol. 14)
Chapter 80 was the first "speaking" appearance of the magical broom Stringfellow, although he was possibly the same broom seen back in Chapter 21. Able to fly due to its Maxwell's Demon Stone, Stringfellow also has the ability to speak and work his own minor magics; Urd, his apparent artificer, describes him as "maxed out" with enchantments. Being so, er, close to Belldandy, Stringfellow is smitten with her, but he turns out to have a roving eye. The broom is named for Stringfellow Hawke, the helicopter pilot hero of the 1984–87 TV series *Airwolf*—*hooki*, which means "broom," in Japanese, is also pronounced in a way similar to "Hawke." Hild brings this up in Vol. 28, and thus the name could be given as either "Stringfellow Broom" or "Stringfellow Hawke."

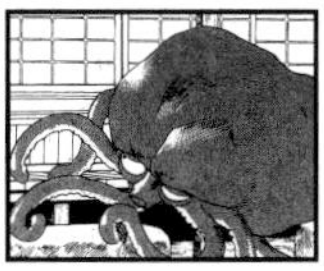

Sudaru (*Sympathy for the Devil*, Chapter 31, Vol. 5)
The nickname given to the giant Booster Demon formed by Urd from a fusion of five smaller ones. Although no longer the evil cephalopods they once were, their new unified incarnation is neither brighter, nor more fun to be around.

Sugar-Coated Confession Pill (*The Fourth Goddess*, Chapter 71, Vol. 12)
A pill formulated by Urd specifically to make the imbiber admit offenses; Belldandy agreed to take one because she couldn't remember how she had wronged Peorth. It didn't work, however, because the "offense" was only so in Peorth's eyes. By contrast, when Urd lobbed one into Skuld's mouth, she immediately began confessing to a long list of genuine misdeeds. In the original English version, the pill was known as "Sweet Project A."

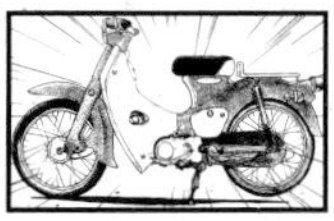

Supercub (*Leader of the Pack*, Chapter 12, Vol. 2)
First introduced in 1958, the Honda C100 Supercub is to motorbikes what the classic Volkswagen Beetle was to cars—cheap,

basic, and supremely successful (it is the best-selling motorcycle in history, with over fifty million made over the last half century). With a top speed of 70 km/h, however, Keiichi was a little surprised to find that the N.I.T. Motor Club intended him to win a *race* with one; little did he realize that his seniors had modified the 49cc base Supercub into a 1300cc monster funnybike—a life-threatening ride he deemed funny, "but not 'ha-ha' funny."

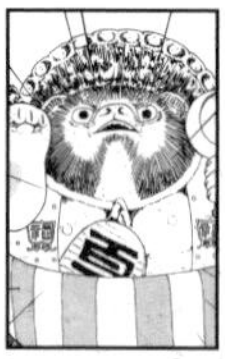

Super Combo Lucky God (*Sympathy for the Devil*, Chapter 30, Vol. 4)
In a bid to help the N.I.T. Motor Club make quick cash, Urd conjured the attributes of various traditional Japanese figures of good fortune—such as the mallet of the god Daikokuten, and the raised paw of the *maneki neko* (the "waving cat" statue often seen in Japanese stores) onto the body of a *tanuki* statue, itself a good-luck charm. It's not certain how well it actually worked, but Tamiya was so impressed he *did* offer Keiichi money to buy it.

Super Energy Infusion Machine Mark I (*Sympathy for the Devil*, Chapter 33, Vol. 5)
Ominous, gauge-bedecked, and valve-festooned, this is the contraption Skuld built to speed up the rotation of the singularity within Keiichi, causing it to deviate from its orbit, and hence become amenable to being "yanked out." It threw the breakers, and had to itself receive an emergency energy infusion from Urd's summoned lightning.

Super Sonic Strike (*Mara Strikes Back*, Chapter 45, Vol. 7)
Phrase uttered by Megumi's guardian Earth Spirit Third Class when—imprisoned within a stuffed doll—it nevertheless launched itself in attack against Mara, who was possessing Megumi's body. It probably has something to do with the doll's resemblance to a certain varmint video-game character.

Supreme Executive Committee (*Miss Keiichi*, Chapter 56, Vol. 9)
New, Illuminati-like level of government for the N.I.T. Motor Club created by Tamiya and Otaki for themselves, so that they could pass the position of Club Director on to Keiichi, now with all the responsibility, and none of the authority. In Chapter 70, Tamiya refers to it as the "Council of Elders."

System Down (*Terrible Master Urd*, Chapter 39, Vol. 6)
Condition incurred after the defeat of the Lord of Terror, when the Yggdrasil mainframe had to divert all its resources towards substituting for and reconstructing the Universal Superstring. As a side effect, all other heavenly contracts and duties were suspended, which might have meant Belldandy would have left Keiichi—were it not for the fact that besides her legal obligations to him, she also loved him.

T

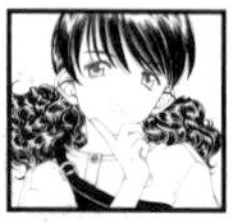

Takano (Chapter 142, Vol. 23)
Keiichi and Megumi's mysteriously youthful-appearing mother; as with Keima himself, their father insists they refer to Takano by her first name. Takano, unlike Keima (or her children), speaks with a country accent. According to the editorial staff of *Afternoon*, Takano is the character creator Kosuke Fujishima screams about because "it's difficult to draw her hair" (?).

Takeda Racing Thoroughbreds (*Childhood's End*, Chapter 78, Vol. 14)
Establishment where Keiichi's career-guidance office suggested he go work as a stable boy, on the grounds this was "something similar" to motorcycles. ➔ **Wyvern**

Takehiro (*Mystery Child*, Chapter 95, Vol. 16)
When Chihiro (who has little resistance to cute boys) asked Keiichi what the name of the mysterious kid accompanying him was, he blurted out "Takehiro," which surprised her as sounding "old-fashioned." The kid was later revealed to be the demon Velsper.

Tamiya, Toraichi (*Wrong Number*, Chapter 1, Vol. 1)
Otaki's best pal. Habitually found in an undershirt no matter the weather, the heavily muscled Tamiya is the former director of the N.I.T. Motor Club, and Keiichi's senior at the school, two facts he never lets Keiichi forget. Although a hulking, intimidating brute in appearance (and where Keiichi is concerned, in action), he is described as "pure of heart"—perhaps because his frequent scheming, swindling, and outright extortion of funds and materials is all for the benefit of the Motor Club, or at least, for the benefit of the Club's booze and snacks supply. And come to think of it, even though Tamiya is frequently gullible, impulsive, and outright dumb, he apparently *did* manage to graduate in less time than Keiichi. Note that Tamiya's first name "Toraichi"—which is also old fashioned, not to mention manly sounding—is never mentioned until Chapter 70. Affectionate nicknames used only by Otaki include "Den-chan" (from *den*, an alternate reading for the *ta* kanji in "Tamiya"), "Miya," and, in the original English version of the manga, "Tammy."

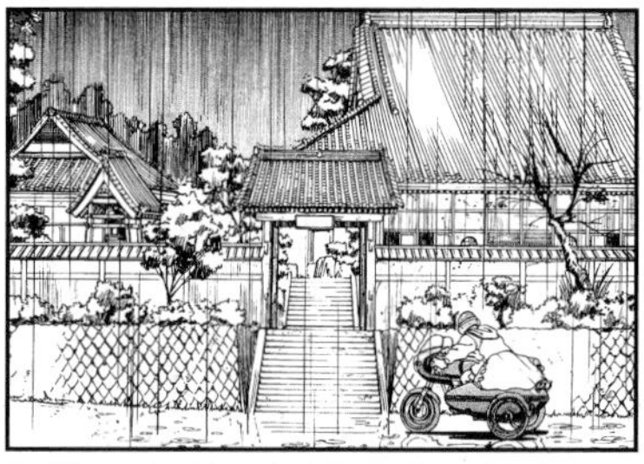

Tarikihongan Temple (*Wrong Number*, Chapter 3, Vol. 1)
Located at 3-4-106 Nekomi Ward, Nekomi City, Chiba Prefecture, Japan. The temple, run previously by the priest Koshian, is where Keiichi and Belldandy—together with her sisters and various occasional guests—have lived since the early days of the story. *Tarikihongan* is a Japanese four-character phrase that can be translated: "Relying on the strength of others to secure results." It is a reference to the *hongan*, or fulfilled vows of the Amida Buddha to secure the *tariki*, the power outside one's self (that is, from the oneness outside the personal ego), for the compassion and freedom of all sentient beings. Despite Koshian's "misunderstanding" that Belldandy, like the Amida Buddha, had achieved such enlightenment, Bell in fact seems to live this very philosophy—she is especially noted to have concern for the sentience and development of mechanical objects, as well as living creatures. ➔ **Koshian**

Television (*Leader of the Pack*, Chapter 14, Vol. 2)
Medium through which Urd can instantly transport herself through space; this will work regardless of the size or vintage of the television set. ➔ **Mirror, Water**

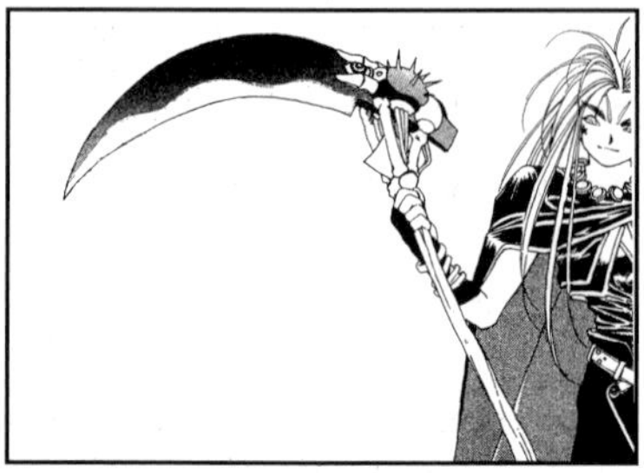

Ten-Dimensional Scythe (*Terrible Master Urd*, Chapter 39, Vol. 6)
Forged by a goddess (in this case Skuld, as she's good at building dangerous gadgets), a Ten-Dimensional Scythe is the only device capable of cutting the Universal Superstring—although since models differ as to whether the universe has ten, eleven, or twenty-six dimensions, *perhaps* it wouldn't have worked after all.

The Storms of Spring (*Traveler*, Chapter 103, Vol. 17)
In Japanese, *seishun no arashi*; Keiichi uttered this phrase in regard to the love-smitten Banpei-kun chasing after the Welcome Robot; *seishun* means the "springtime of life," or figuratively, "youth," as in how Kyosuke famously introduces himself in the classic 1980s anime and manga romance *Kimagure Orange Road*, *"Kasuga Kyosuke, seishun shitemasu!"* ("Kasuga Kyosuke, living in the springtime of my life!")

The Terrible Master (*Terrible Master Urd*, Chapter 35, Vol. 5)
Name written in English (in the original Japanese version of the manga as well) on the side of the giant, one-legged, massive-mace-and-morningstar-equipped robot conjured by Urd in her Lord of Terror mode. We are nevertheless assured by the Japanese editors that it is "not necessarily the real name of the robot," but the truth may never be known, as Belldandy destroyed it by the simple expedient of loosening its bolts.

Thousand-Ball Burning Fielding Training (*Miss Keiichi*, Chapter 58, Vol. 10)
In the original English version, called "Urd's Myriad Light-Speed Grounders"—another old-school method by which Urd proposed to improve Keiichi's baseball; when he pointed out it was too dark to see the rain of balls she was sending his way, Urd showed the name to be no metaphor, by setting them on fire. ➔ **Iron Ball Batting**

Three Laps around Town by Tricycle (*Childhood's End*, Chapter 73, Vol. 13)
The humiliating penalty Urd deems Skuld must perform, if she cannot learn to ride a bicycle. When Skuld does (after many skinned knees), she retorts that now *Urd* must try to ride a unicycle, and then say "I give up" one hundred times once she fails. A nonplussed Urd rides it easily.

Time Management Program (*Mystery Child*, Chapter 94, Vol. 16)
Software system within Yggdrasil, the heavenly computer responsible for maintaining the time-space continuum; when a malfunction developed in it, Urd and Skuld were summoned back to help work out the bugs.

Tomahawk Number One (*Miss Keiichi*, Chapter 58, Vol. 10)
The "vaguely disturbing bat" Skuld made to help the Softball Club win their game with the Baseball Club. Although it appears to be a Wiffle Ball bat (which no doubt amused the Baseball Club captain, who smirked about their rivals having brought a kid to play), the holes in the bat were in fact miniature jet engines. Sensors in the tip of the bat auto-track an incoming pitch, whereupon the engines fire in precise bursts to assure the barrel meets the ball. The Tomahawk Number One is a rare example of a Skuld invention that worked exactly as planned.

Torutoru-kun (*Miss Keiichi*, Chapter 58, Vol. 10)
Referred to simply as an "auto-tracking glove" in the original English version of the manga (although that is, of course, the glove's function), Torutoru-kun auto-tracks the ball to catch, just as the Tomahawk Number One does to hit it. Appropriately enough, there is also a screen capture tool for the Japanese version of Windows called "Torutoru-kun."

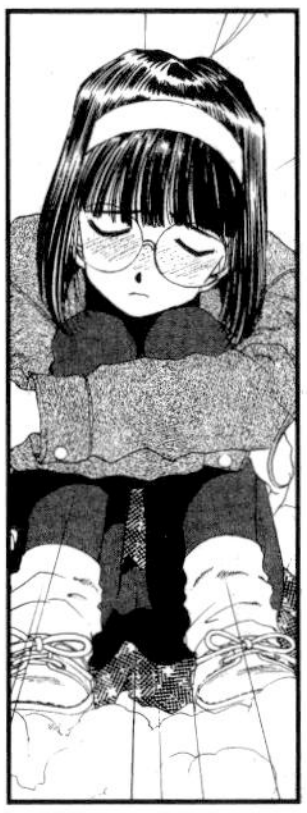

To You I Give All Joy (*Hand in Hand*, Chapter 90, Vol. 15)
Belldandy—after accidentally getting drunk on *Coca-Cola* at Whirlwind's opening party (much to Keiichi's surprise, it turns out to affect her like alcohol)—began invoking this phrase to magically correct people's unhappiness, with such effects as turning the short-statured Hasegawa into a giant. Due to the Law of Conservation of Happiness, this had the eventual effect of making misfortune fall upon Keiichi.

Treasure Map (*Childhood's End*, Chapter 77, Vol. 13)
Chihiro was able to motivate the N.I.T. Motor Club to clean the clubhouse with thoughts of the "treasure" they might turn up, but Keiichi actually *did* turn up a hidden treasure map. Tamiya and Otaki kept to themselves the facts that they had hidden it, yet could no longer remember where the treasure was—and came up with the idea to profit by this dilemma through selling copies of the map to their fellow students, leaving them the work of searching, while they prepared to pounce on whomever found it.

Triple Challenge of the Goddesses (*The Fourth Goddess*, Chapter 71, Vol. 12)
Peorth invoked this archaic conflict-resolution method in her *contretemps de coeur* with Belldandy. Please see the separate entry in "Rules of the *Oh My Goddess!* Cosmos" for more information.

Triple-S (Chapter 133, Vol. 21)
Short for the *Skuld Supah Stretchah*; in the original Japanese, the *Shinchoo Nobi Nobi Zetto-go*, or "Height Stretching Big Z." A contraption—essentially, a power-assisted rack—by which Skuld proposed to restore Kid Peorth to her original size. The Triple-S attempted to stretch Urd instead, who was neither pleased nor amused.

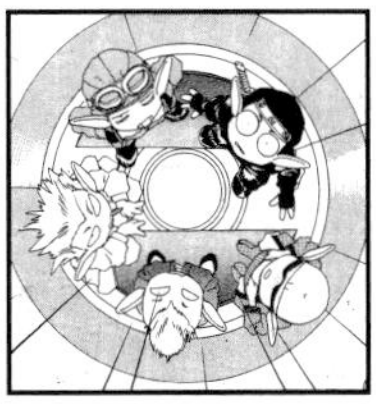

Trolls in the Engine! (*Sympathy for the Devil*, Chapter 30, Vol. 4)
In the original Japanese, *Enjin no naka no kobito!*—the gibbering, half-mad cry emitted by Keiichi when he realized Belldandy and Urd's references to small, mythological creatures powering their entry in the Economy Run were literal. The trolls briefly went on strike over the kerosene impurities in the fuel, but when Belldandy explained it was sabotage by "the big money men" (i.e., Aoshima), the working-class monsters, outraged, rose to the challenge. There were five of them for a 50 cc engine, so does that work out to 10 cc per dwarf?

Troubadour (*Love Potion No. 9*, Chapter 25, Vol. 4)
Urd's old boyfriend, a plum-tree spirit—first glimpsed in flashback in Chapter 25; his real name, Troubadour, is revealed when he returns to her life in Chapter 55. As befits his moniker, Troubadour carries about a lyre, upon which he performs impromptu odes of love, with fine instrumentals, and awful lyrics. His bardic powers are terrible in another sense, too, as he has been known to use them to conjure "buggy bugs" inside the bodies of rivals. Also the stuff of medieval romance is his questing nature—in this case, an eternal search for the golden bush warbler that even takes precedence over his love for Urd. All right, he's basically a bit of a flake.

U

Ugo Ugo Ruga (*Miss Keiichi*, Chapter 54, Vol. 9)
Urd asked Keiichi to record this show for her while she was away taking a remedial course in heaven. This show's name was mistakenly scrambled as *Ugo Ugo Rugo* in the unflopped English version of the manga—although the confusion came in part from the fact that even in the Japanese original, it was scrambled (perhaps for comedic effect) as *Uga Uga Rugo*. In any case, *Ugo Ugo Ruga* was a children's show on Japan's Fuji TV between 1992 and 1994 that attracted a cult following in part because of its music by Cornelius and Pizzicato Five, and its use of CG animation by Rodney Greenblat, who would later become known for his designs on *Parappa the Rapper*. Note that in the original English version of the manga, she asked him to record the admittedly contemporaneous *Beavis and Butt-head*. Uh-huh-huh-huh . . . that chick's cool.

Ultimate Destruction Program (*Terrible Master Urd*, Chapter 35, Vol. 5)
Well, the name pretty much sums it up. A sinister bit of self-aware software, long sealed away, it is the true power behind the figure known as the Lord of Terror—and the means through which he/she/it will destroy the universe. The password to activate it must be entered through the "terminal" of the urn of Mao Za Haxon. Not having a physical form, the viruslike Ultimate Destruction Program can exist and act through many hosts, including a goddess such as Urd, a monster such as the Fenrir Wolf, a human being such as Keiichi, or even a humble computer disk—although the last move was its undoing. ➔ **Lord of Terror, Urn of Mao Za Haxon**

Ultimate Destruction Program Vaccine (*Terrible Master Urd*, Chapter 37, Vol. 6)
Bestowed upon Skuld and Belldandy directly by the Almighty (who demanded they read the user's manual first) to help them save the earth from the, you guessed it, Ultimate Destruction Program. The vaccine takes the form of a flute that, when blown, summoned the endless Midgard Serpent to envelop Fenrir, the beast serving as host to the Lord of Terror. Unfortunately . . . ➔ **Fenrir Wolf, Midgard Serpent**

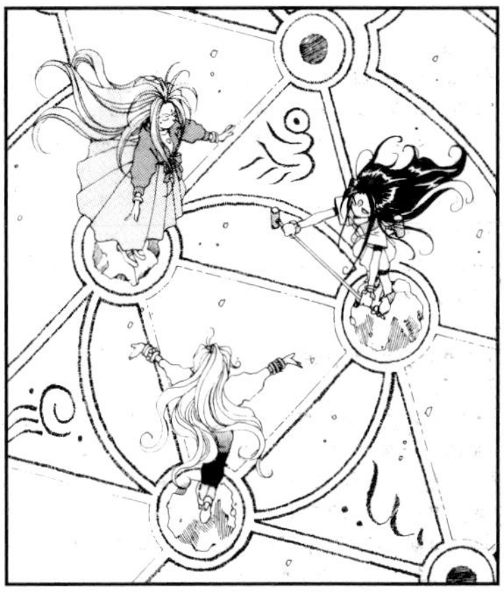

Ultimate Magical Warding Mandala (*Mara Strikes Back*, Chapter 47, Vol. 7)
Belldandy, Urd, and Skuld created this magic circle—apparently, the first time they ever cooperated on a project—in a scheme to prevent Urd from being forcibly repatriated to heaven by invoking Article 25, Section 16 (see "Rules of the *Oh My Goddess!* Cosmos" below). Using a mandala in this way was gravely illegal, so they maintained the ward was merely meant to keep out Mara, an excuse the Almighty graciously deigned to believe.

Ultra-Delivery Gun (*The Fourth Goddess*, Chapter 67, Vol. 11)
In the original Japanese, *tensoojuu* or "forwarding gun." Skuld's method to get Keiichi to class during the "Who's the Most Helpful Goddess?" contest. ➔ **Insta-Trans Spell, Interspatial Slide Technique**

Ultra High Grade Love Seed (*The Queen of Vengeance*, Chapter 43, Vol. 7)
Referred to as a "super deluxe love potion" in the English version of the manga, although it's technically a crystallized precipitate of such a potion. Because of accidental contamination by Skuld, however, the seeds, merely intended to make Belldandy amorous, instead turned her into a seething cauldron of desire.

Ultra Strength Vomit Pills (*Queen Sayoko*, Chapter 79, Vol. 14)
Urd went to find these bluntly named tablets after

Skuld childishly swallowed an angel's egg, but before she could administer them, the egg hatched inside Skuld, leading to a dilemma involving the immature angel, Noble Scarlet. ➔ **Noble Scarlet**

Universal Superstring (*Terrible Master Urd*, Chapter 38, Vol. 6)
Referred to in the original Japanese as the *uchuu no himo*, literally "space string"; it derives from the idea in physics that reality at its smallest scale is made up not of "point"-like particles, but "string"-like lengths, and the vibration of these strings through multidimensional space is what actually creates the matter and forces we can perceive. It is perhaps better called a model than a theory, as there is currently no way to test it—although that's perhaps fortunate, given that the Lord of Terror proposed to destroy the universe by cutting the string with the Ten-Dimensional Scythe. ➔ **Ten-Dimensional Scythe**

University President (*Wrong Number*, Chapter 4, Vol. 1)
Only seems to show up once, but he gave a critical early endorsement to Belldandy's presence at N.I.T. as a "foreign exchange student" (as claimed by Keiichi—Goddesses First-Class don't lie). The president seemed befuddled at the jealous Professor Ozawa's demand that Belldandy be expelled as a fraud, as she was "such a nice young lady."

Unlucky Star (*Leader of the Pack*, Chapter 12, Vol. 2)
According to Belldandy, just as individuals have lucky stars, so they have unlucky ones (Belldandy was able to perceive the passage of both during daytime, suggesting senses other than human). Although receiving good fortune from one's lucky star is said to be the result of prior actions, it is not known if prior actions are likewise responsible for getting bad fortune from the *unlucky* star, which Keiichi certainly did, in spades. Keiichi received a brief surcease from trouble when his lucky star eclipsed his unlucky one; however, the orbital track of his lucky star was closer to Earth than that of his unlucky star, and its orbital velocity was therefore faster; consequently, his eclipse of misfortune was short lived. The manga describes this as "elementary physics." The editor would feel guilty if he didn't note that, technically, the stars themselves don't pass overhead, so much as the Earth rotates to make it appear that they do, although perhaps any attempt at strict scientific accuracy is misplaced here. ⇔ **Lucky Star**

Until the End (Chapter 146, Vol. 23)
Response given by Belldandy to Keima when he asked if she would stay by Keiichi's side. Although given as "until the end" in the English version of the manga, in the original Japanese she said *inochi tsukirumade*, which means "until life concludes." Belldandy is presumably immortal (although it is unclear how much Keima perceives about her true nature), and she did not say specifically whether she meant Keiichi's life, her life, or their lives together, but her phrasing was not necessarily unusual, as the Japanese language often leaves out parts of a sentence where the meaning is understood—or is supposed to be understood—in context.

Urd's Room (*The Queen of Vengeance*, Chapter 42, Vol. 6)
Urd's private chamber at Tarikihongan, where she stores her potion ingredients and performs alchemical experiments. Note that the "Urd's Room" sign is on a small metal plate surrounded by a complex lattice of bent wire strung with charms, but we also see sometimes (for example, in Chapter 79) a different sign saying "Urd's Castle," that looks like a wooden carving of a woman with long hair (presumably, Urd) and flowers. ➔ **Everybody's Tea Room, Keiichi's Shop, Skuld Labs**

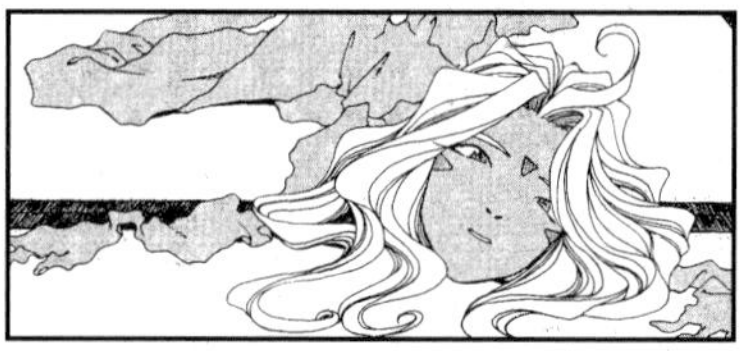

Urd's Skin (*The Devil in Miss Urd*, Chapter 64, Vol. 11)
Luscious, satiny, and brown—and not attached to the rest of Urd, for it was nothing *but* her hide, cloned by Mara, and then stretched by Skuld over a sort of mechanical bear trap. Such a decoy was necessary to capture the Demon Urd, and there was no time to clone a complete copy.

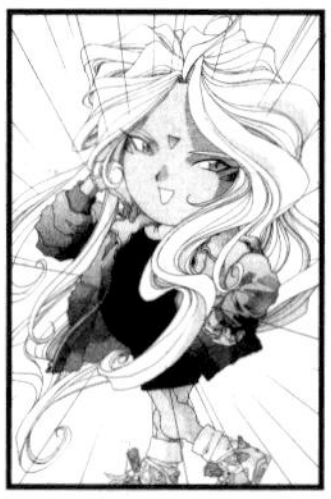

Urd's-Skin-Covered Banpei-kun (*The Devil in Miss Urd*, Chapter 65, Vol. 11)
Creepy but charming usage of the abovementioned pelt by Banpei-kun, who, wanting to go out without startling people at his robotic appearance, pulled the skin over his body, and then ransacked Keiichi's clothes drawer for apparel (the goddesses conjure theirs out of thin air). Belldandy, delighted at his initiative, felt that he would "blend right into the crowd." Actually, Banpei looked no less startling, yet spent his day doing good deeds about town, culminating in a fire rescue that finally burned the skin away. The *real* Urd was startled to later receive letters and gifts of thanks for her heroism . . . ➔ **Emotion Circuit**

Urd the Nightingale (*Queen Sayoko*, Chapter 82, Vol. 14)
Urd's stage name for the human version of *Virtua Fighter* she was drafted into playing within Sayoko's castle. The name in the original manga was *Howaitodoresu Enjeru Urudo*, meaning "White Dress [Japanese people write this loan phrase as a single word; it's often used to refer to a wedding dress] Angel Urd." As Urd's fighting outfit contains ambulance lights on her shoulders and red crosses on her boots, "Urd the Nightingale" in fact works as a play on Florence Nightingale, the nineteenth-century founder of modern nursing, who was often called an "angel in white." Of course, since Urd is here to issue beatings, she is announced as "the merciless angel of mercy." ➔ **Froghorn Leghorn**

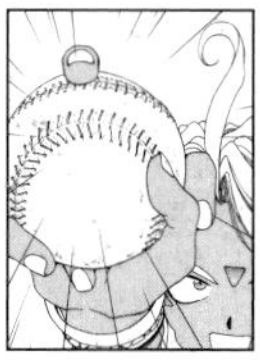

Urd Thunderbolt (*Miss Keiichi*, Chapter 58, Vol. 10)
Trick pitch thrown by Urd in the game against the Baseball Club—so fast, its flight cannot even be seen. The drawback is that this works by the ball never actually leaving her fingers.

Urn of Mao Za Haxon (*Terrible Master Urd*, Chapter 34, Vol. 5)
In the original Japanese, *Maoo Za Hakushon no Tsubo*; *tsubo* means "urn," whereas *maoo* is a word used to refer to the devil or Satan, and *hakushon* is the sound effect for a sneeze. This goofy-looking artifact was apparently found in a remote mountainous location by Mara, who believed it would summon the Lord of Terror (correct) to lend her power to destroy the goddesses (incorrect; Urd kept all the power to herself). Belldandy also is aware of the prophecy that the Lord of Terror shall return to Earth through such an urn, but wrongly assumes that destroying the urn will destroy the lord, when in fact the urn is designed to be destroyed by "a goddess of good and purity" as the final step of freeing the Ultimate Destruction Program within. ➔ **Lord of Terror, Ultimate Destruction Program**

Urudogen X (*Sympathy for the Devil*, Chapter 29, Vol. 4)
The remedy Urd prepared for Mara's memory loss, although Mara seemed to remember enough about Urd to flee in panic before it could be administered. Probably a play on *androgen*, which is the name for the chemicals (mostly hormones) that control masculine characteristics in animals; i.e., steroids are androgens.

Ushikubo University Motorcycle Club (*Leader of the Pack*, Chapter 12, Vol. 2)
Rival to the N.I.T. Motor Club; their race queens were not as attractive as Belldandy. Keiichi saved the club's honor, and possibly Belldandy's, by defeating them in the deciding round of a drag-race series, to which Tamiya and Otaki contributed generous portions of help and hindrance. ➔ **Ohtaki, Etsushi; Supercub**

V

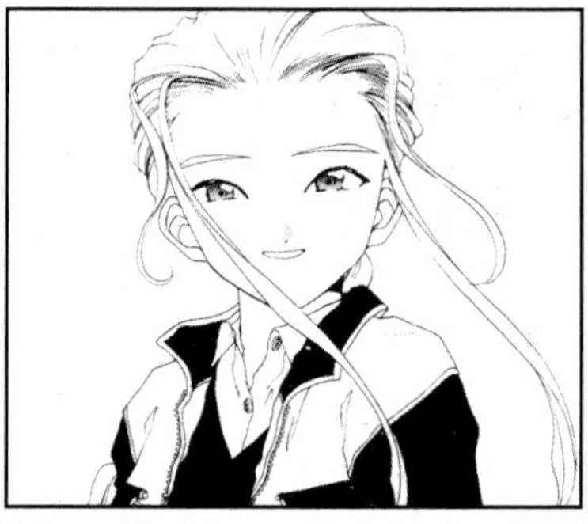

Velsper (First Incarnation) (*Mystery Child*, Chapter 94, Vol. 16)
Demon First Class. In his true form, he bore a four-pointed star on his forehead as his demon mark, but when introduced he had the appearance of a cute young human boy. Under the Doublet System (see "Rules of the *Oh My Goddess!* Cosmos"), Belldandy was chosen to be Velsper's "Most Distant Twin." Having fallen in love with her, and influenced by her belief that "somehow, I know we'll meet again," Velsper laid a curse on himself: in exchange for staying a child forever, he would retain his memories of his doublet's identity, something ordinarily forbidden. He was willing to hack Yggdrasil to stop time permanently in the universe just to be together with her, but ran up against a weak mortal with feelings as strong as his own—Keiichi. ➔ **Most Distant Twins**

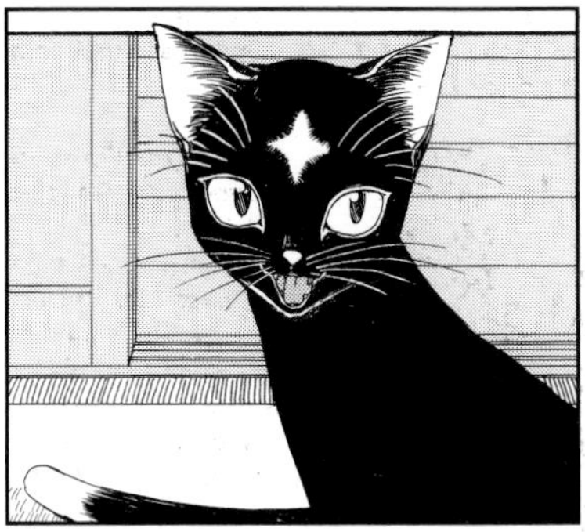

Velsper (Second Incarnation) (*Mystery Child*, Chapter 101, Vol. 17)
When Belldandy finally remembered his name and broke his curse, Velsper admitted his intrusion into Yggdrasil to his demonic superiors, and was sentenced to be reincarnated into a "level four life form," his powers stripped. After a black kitty cat showed up at Tarikihongan with a four-pointed white star on its head, Keiichi somehow sensed (although he had never seen the true form of the original Velsper) who it was. Belldandy seemed not to, yet named the "stray" Velsper. It wasn't until Chapter 171 that circumstances forced Velsper to reveal to Belldandy that he was a demon cat, supposedly traveling incognito to study Earth cats. Belldandy, of course, doesn't remember Velsper's first incarnation due to the rules of the Doublet System, but Velsper himself (although reincarnated into a kitten's body) remains Keiichi's romantic rival—now, on a somewhat less apocalyptic basis.

Velsper's Reserve Powers (Chapter 141, Vol. 22)
As the name implies, these are powers that Velsper managed to retain even when changed into his kitty-cat form. The first power wasn't identified as such in the English version of the manga, but was the Neko Beam he emitted in Chapter 141, Vol. 22; the second power was the electrical shock he delivered to Sigel in Chapter 185, Vol. 29. The "zeroeth" power, however, was perhaps displayed as far back as Chapter 133, when Velsper revealed to Keiichi, Urd, Peorth, and Skuld (but *not* Belldandy) that he'd used his old trick of laying a curse on himself in order to keep his memory, even into his second incarnation.

Virus Program (*Hand in Hand*, Chapter 91, Vol. 16)
Urd used this "program" to try to crash the spell routine that was keeping the hands of Belldandy and Keiichi stuck together. Oddly enough, it looked like a perfume tester. ➔ ***You Can't Let Go?***

W

Water (*Sympathy for the Devil*, Chapter 32, Vol. 5)
Medium through which Skuld can instantly transport herself through space; this will work regardless of the volume or temperature of the water available, although she naturally prefers it to be not *too* hot, the way a freshly brewed cup of tea is. ➔ **Mirror, Television**

Water Elemental Magic (*Hand in Hand*, Chapter 89, Vol. 15)
Skuld is associated with water elemental magic; it is not known whether it is coincidence that water is her transport medium, as her sisters' elemental magic lacks such a close correspondence. She built the α-707 magical amplifier in hopes of it enabling her to control her angel (actually, as typical with Skuld, it wasn't a mere "hope"—she believed with its help it would be a "snap"). When it went, predictably, out of control, it created a feedback loop that manifested itself as a cyclonic wall of water whipping around the amplifier, as well as Skuld and Keiichi. Only Urd's Fire Elemental Magic could break through it. ➔ **Fire Elemental Magic, Wind Elemental Magic**

Water Spirit (*The Fourth Goddess*, Chapter 69, Vol. 12)
Peorth plotted to become intimate with Keiichi through the old push-someone-into-the-pool-and-then-administer-mouth-to-mouth trick, but when Keiichi started thrashing about in the water, Belldandy commanded "*Dance, High Spirits of Water,*" causing all the water in the pool to swirl out, leaving Keiichi dry but Peorth flooded. It was then Belldandy who did mouth-to-mouth on the unconscious Peorth, explaining she had gotten a case of "water spirit poisoning," and was just trying to get some of them out of her body.

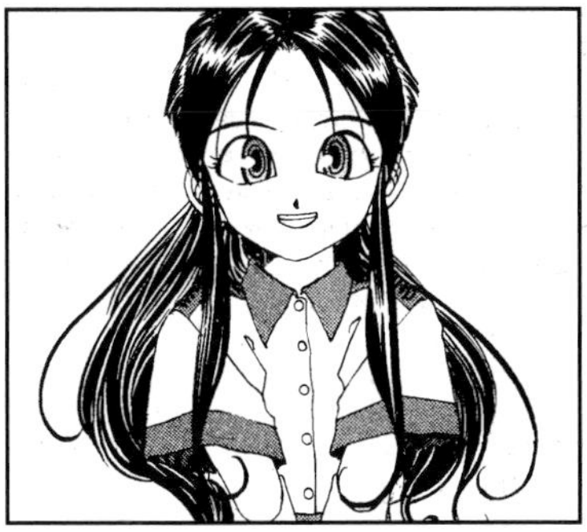

Welcome Robot (*Hand in Hand*, Chapter 92, Vol. 16)
A vintage, life-size mechanical doll of a young girl that Banpei-kun fell in love with at first sight; so named because her function was—in imitation of a traditional human greeter in a Japanese store—to repeatedly bow and speak the phrase *irasshaimase, maido arigato gozaimasu*, meaning "Welcome, and thank you each time" (that is, each time you patronize the establishment). Rescued from the junkyard by Chihiro, she was restored, and, eventually, at Banpei's request, upgraded considerably by Skuld. ➔ **Robo-chan, Sigel**

What a Man's Gotta Do (*Love Potion No. 9*, Chapter 26, Vol. 4)
In the original Japanese, *Otoko no Jingi*; the single Tamiya had planned to buy before falling under the spell of the Demons CD. *Jingi* is perhaps best known in the West from its use in the title of the famous 1970s series of yakuza films by Kinji Fukasaku, *Jingi Naki Tatakai*, "Battles Without Honor and Humanity," although *jingi* itself, "honor and humanity," derives from the classic Confucian virtues. By the way, have you noticed the common word in many of Tamiya's songs?

When Plants Attack (*Sora Unchained*, Chapter 128, Vol. 20)
Urd's favorite TV program, which she fought with Skuld over the right to watch in an elaborate battle stretching over two chapters. The original Japanese name of the show was *Hikyoo no Shokubutsu Shiriizu*, "Vegetation of Unexplored Regions Series." ➔ ***Amphibian Stalker***

Where Does Keiichi Hide His Dirty Magazines? (*The Devil in Miss Urd*, Chapter 63, Vol. 11)
In the original Japanese, *Keiichi no heya no ecchibon no kakushi basho?* The second question that the Goddess Urd and Demon Urd gave each other to try to prove which one was the real Urd, after the two were separated. Since *both* were Urd, of course, the exercise was pointless, except for the way it embarrassed Keiichi, revealed that Urd snoops through his stuff, and underlined a parallel fact to his platonic relationship with Belldandy. By the way, the answer is, "back of the third drawer in his bedroom desk."

Where Do You Keep the Togebo Shell? (*The Devil in Miss Urd*, Chapter 63, Vol. 11)
Referred to as "shell of Togebo" in the original English version of the manga; this was the first of two questions the Goddess Urd and Demon Urd gave to each other (see above). The answer is, "two down from the top right shelf, fourth from the left."

Whirlwind (*Childhood's End*, Chapter 78, Vol. 14)
Name of the bike shop Chihiro opened. Directed more toward motorcycle maniacs than the general public, it provides sales, repairs, tuning, and customization. Although Chihiro claims she chose the name to suggest "kicking up a storm in the biking world," she actually just got it from the British WWII fighter plane known as the Westland Whirlwind, which she ran across in a vintage aviation magazine. Keiichi (and sometimes Belldandy) has been working at Whirlwind ever since his graduation problems prevented him from accepting a job at Wyvern; Chihiro scooped him up with a "job opening" flyer designed especially for him.

Who's the Most Helpful Goddess? (*The Fourth Goddess*, Chapter 67, Vol. 11)
In the original Japanese, *Dare ga mottomo yaku ni tatsu megami ka?*—an impromptu contest Urd, Peorth, and Skuld decided to have that basically consisted of stalking Keiichi around campus, and immediately interpreting any problem he might have as a call to inflict bizarre techno-magical "solutions." Nobody won the contest.

Will of the Universe (*Sora Unchained*, Chapter 119, Vol. 19)
Belldandy used this phrase—in Japanese, *uchuu no ishi*—to explain why Sora Hasegawa, despite all opposition, kept winning all the *kujibiki* to decide who was to be the next N.I.T. Motor Club director. ➔ **Director Candy**

Wind Elemental Magic (*Hand in Hand*, Chapter 89, Vol. 15)
The elemental force associated with Belldandy. This force, enhanced by her angel, Holy Bell, has been made evident many times, in such magic as Belldandy's ability to create vortices (Vol. 3), her communion with birds (Vol. 11), her conjuring of a sprite to convey messages through the air (Vol. 23), and her mastery of flight (Vol. 29). Interestingly, Belldandy's powers are not limited to wind elemental magic, as indicated by her ability to command the Water Spirit in Vol. 12. ➔ **Fire Elemental Magic, Water Elemental Magic**

Wolf Rock (*Terrible Master Urd*, Chapter 37, Vol. 6)
The prophecy regarding this offshore rock is, "*At night, with the full moon shining and the surf*

roaring like a howl against its flanks, it truly evokes the wolf of its name . . . Gaze locked eternally on the heavens, the trapped beast seems to dream of the day it can again break free—to strike fear across the world." The prophecy was true, for Wolf Rock was in fact Fenrir.

Won't Have Mitts! (*Miss Keiichi*, Chapter 58, Vol. 10) A joke Urd tried in response to Belldandy's joke; it fell flat on her audience, yet Dark Horse Director of Asian Licensing Michael Gombos feels it was the better joke. What Urd said in the original Japanese, *mittomo nai*, could mean either that if they lose the game, it'll be disgraceful, or that they won't even be left with their mitts. In the original English version, Urd simply said, "She's right! We can't give up!" In the unflopped edition, it was rendered as "Yeah! So let's keep our mitts about us!" **➔ *Let's Have It Bat!***

World Inventions Journal (*Ninja Master*, Chapter 53, Vol. 9)
In Japanese, *Sekai Hatsumei Gijiroku*—in the original English version, the show title was given as *Beyond 3000*, a riff on the 1980s and '90s Australian show on future technology, *Beyond 2000*, which later aired in the United States. Skuld had previously planned to watch this show documenting great inventions at 5:30 p.m., and thus had to join the channel fight with Urd against Kodama and Hikari when the mini-ninja ended up hijacking the frequencies. **➔ *Holmes, Ninpu Kamuri Gaiden***

World of Elegance (*Hand in Hand*, Chapter 89, Vol. 15)
Urd's angel. Reflecting Urd's half-god/half-demon state, this angel's hair is divided black and white down the middle, with one white and one black wing. Urd was frightened of her for this very reason, as, growing up, she'd never quite believed she really was half demon. Confronted for the first time by World of Elegance, an angel that reflected the truth about her inner self, Urd screamed, "I never want to see you again!" and so the angel obeyed. When the crisis over Skuld's α-707 amplifier made it necessary for Urd to invoke her Fire Elemental Magic, and hence her angel, Belldandy revealed that her runic divination for Urd concluded with *berkana*, interpreted as "rebirth." Urd truly did want to face her angel again, and so summoned World of Elegance again at last. The reunion led Urd to empathize with Skuld's wish to summon her own angel, and she expressed hope to the unconscious Skuld that it would happen soon. To the *conscious* Skuld, of course, she rubbed in the fact that Urd now had an angel, while Skuld still didn't.

Wrd (*The Devil in Miss Urd*, Chapter 63, Vol. 11)
In the original Japanese version of the manga (and the new English version), Keiichi briefly pondered the idea of assigning the name "Wrd" to the other Urd. **➔ Separation of Goddess/Demon Personalities**

SEE YOU AGAIN NEXT YEAR...
...KEIICHI MORISATO!

Wyvern (*Childhood's End*, Chapter 78, Vol. 14)
Maker of after-market parts and complete customized motorcycles. Keiichi's former dormmate Imai got him an interview there, and the boss agreed to hire him after graduation once he saw the oil worked into the skin of his hands—evidence of Keiichi's true love of bikes. Unfortunately, Keiichi *didn't* graduate, having not realized he had to take a second foreign language to fulfill all his credit requirements.

X

There are no *X* entries, confirming it as truly a letter of mystery.

Y

Yamagata, Mitsuru (*Miss Keiichi*, Chapter 58, Vol. 10)
Captain of the Baseball Club, which he would definitely like some girls to join, although his open-mouthed raving about how they could serve him tea and towels helps to explain why none ever do. Secretly known as "Softball Mitsuru-chan" in his youth, he trusts to his childhood skills when playing Megumi's Softball Club according to that game's rules.

Yamano, Satoko (*Wrong Number*, Chapter 8, Vol. 1)
Considered one of the "top five babes on campus" at the time Otaki met her as a freshman, she looks sweet and innocent in much the same way Otaki doesn't. They were still together as of Vol. 3.

Yoshida, Shohei (*The Queen of Vengeance*, Chapter 42, Vol. 6)
A local schoolboy who fell in love with Urd during her brief, bittersweet kiddie idyll. See *Oh My Goddess! Colors*'s story "Urd's Fantastic Adventure" for full details (pages 039–068). **➔*Kintetsu (Kintaro Electric Railway) II***

Yotaro (*The Queen of Vengeance*, Chapter 44, Vol. 7)
The name of "that mutt from next door" who ran away with Belldandy's gift-wrapped hand-knit sweater in his mouth, under the mistaken impression it contained cookies.

You Can't Let Go? (*Hand in Hand*, Chapter 90, Vol. 15)
In the original Japanese, *Te ga torenaku natta?*—literally, "Can't part hands?"—Urd's comment when she perceived that Belldandy and Keiichi had become literally incapable of parting hands after Keiichi said having to ever let go of Belldandy's hand would be "the greatest unhappiness I could imagine"—to which Bell-chan uttered "*To You I Give All Joy,*" and finally passed out. **➔*To You I Give All Joy***

Yuufuin (Chapter 152, Vol. 24) Distant hot-springs resort, to which Keiichi and Belldandy won a four-day, three-night couples' trip. Chihiro insisted on coming along, but their congestion-and-car-troubled road trip never even makes it halfway there. Off a deserted back road, Belldandy brings a hot spring just big enough for the three of them to the surface, which Chihiro cheerfully dubs "Yuufuin Jr."

Z

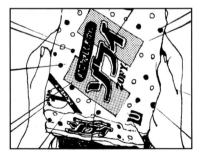

Zofi (*Ninja Master*, Chapter 51, Vol. 8)
Original Japanese name of the feminine hygiene product Keiichi bought for Skuld without being asked to when she seemed to be "acting funny." A play on the actual Japanese brand *Sofi*; you can see some commercials for it at http://www.unicharm.co.jp/sofy/cm/index.html. Known as *Feminine Moddess* in the original English edition. **➔ Kasugano Pharmacy**

THE *GODDESS!* GARAGE

女神用語の基礎知識　ガレージ拝見

A look at the vehicles owned by each character

Cars, bikes, brooms, and things that go! Just about everybody in *Oh My Goddess!* drives a vehicle of some sort, but more than that, many of the characters are gearheads who love to personally maintain, build, and customize their rides—whether mechanical or magical! Let's look at some of the different ways they get around, and what these modes of transport have to say about them.

BMW Rennsport with Sidecar

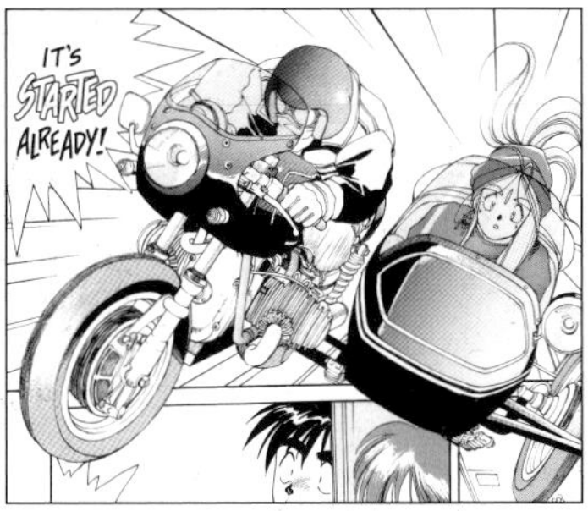
IT'S STARTED ALREADY!

Keiichi Morisato drives this famed 494cc, 48bhp bike, which dominated motorcycle racing in the sidecar class between 1954 and 1973. His particular sidecar arrangement is customized in the style of Oscar Liebmann, the master machinist for whom the American Historic Racing Motorcycle Association's Oscar Liebmann Trophy is named, awarded each year for the highest points earned on a BMW in road racing. Like his dad Keima, Keiichi rides a vintage bike. But the sidecar arrangement is symbolic of the partnership Belldandy has in his life (as seen also with the RS80 Tomboy on page 181). The very first chapter of *Oh My Goddess!* ended with the surprise revelation that Otaki had fixed the sidecar, enabling Keiichi and Belldandy to literally begin their new journeys together.

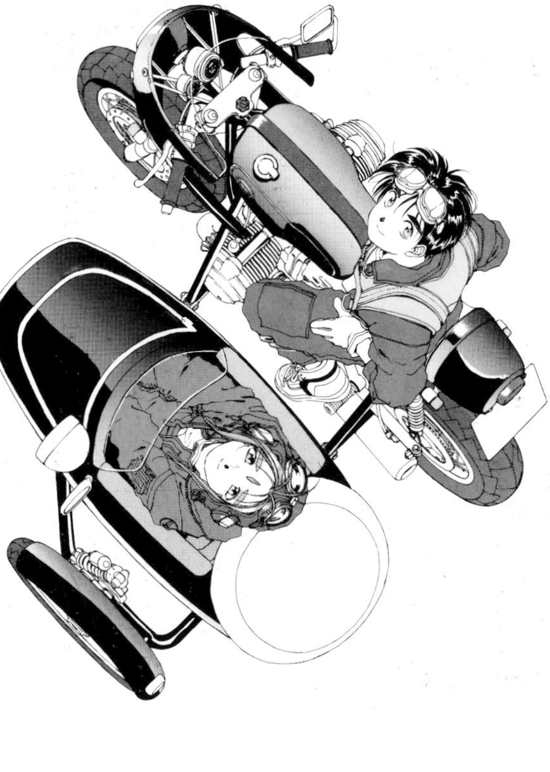

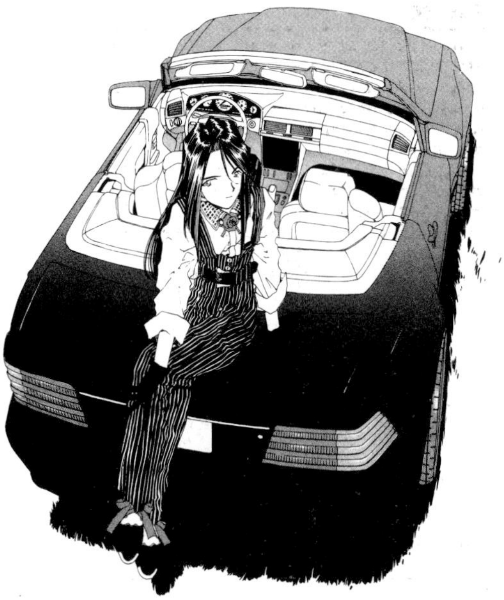

Mercedes-Benz AMG 500 SL

Sayoko Mishima drives this 5956cc, 381bhp imported roadster (note it doesn't have the right-hand drive of Japanese cars), a model that came on the market in 1989. The "SL" stands for "sport light," and the "AMG" signifies the craftsmanship of Aufrecht Melcher Großaspach, a company of ex-Mercedes mechanics who for decades modified their cars into high-performance versions (today it is a subsidiary of Daimler AG, the parent company of Mercedes). It's a car that seems to say "indeed!" (in Japanese, *ikanimo!*—an expression used by upper-class people) . . . and that's exactly why a girl like Sayoko wants to ride one. She used to have a BMW 535i, but her attempt to steal Keiichi away in it led the System Force to melt the engine.

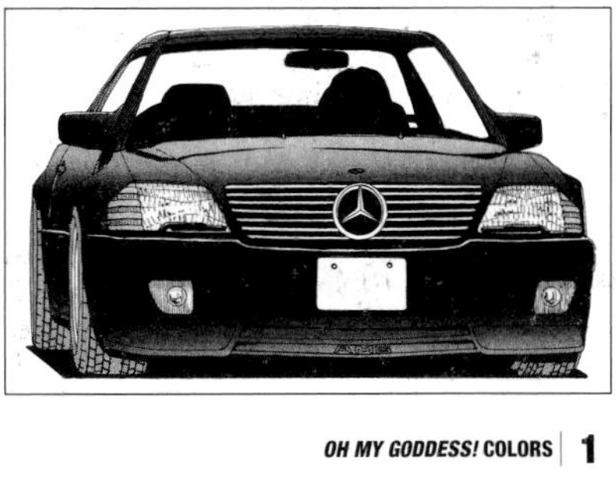

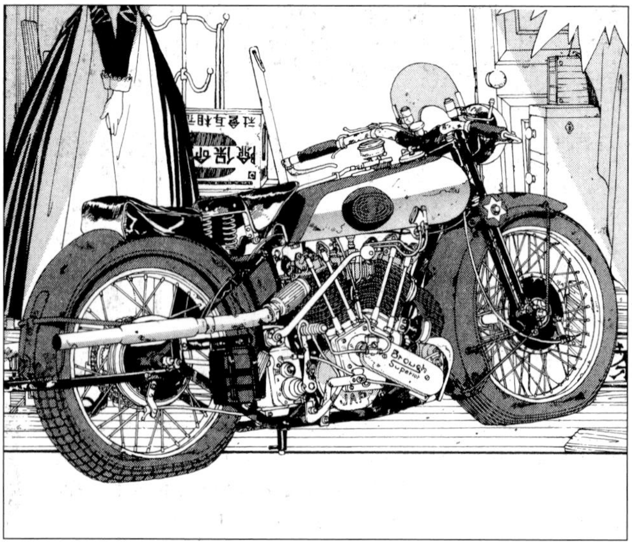

1930 Brough Superior SS100 Alpine Grand Sport

On a trip to the mysterious Honda Lodge, Keiichi discovered that his grandfather Hotaru-no-suke had left both this bike and an unfulfilled promise behind. The 998cc, 45bhp Brough Superior is itself the stuff of legend; T. E. Lawrence, the famous "Lawrence of Arabia," owned several, and in fact died riding one. Hotaru-no-suke's bike was one of 281 built with a JAP engine (nothing to do with Japan—it was named after the initials of its designer, John Alfred Prestwich) and well bore out Brough's slogan, "The Rolls-Royce of Motorcycles," as its £170 price tag was equivalent in 1930 to ¥520—at that time, more than five years' annual income for the average Japanese! Neither Keiichi nor his parents seem to be especially wealthy, so how his granddad came to have such an aristocrat's bike is one of *OMG!*'s minor mysteries. It was the perfect ride, however, for Keiichi to say goodbye to Chieko Honda, a girl from a more elegant age. Note "Brough" is pronounced *bruff*, and was named for its manufacturer, George Brough.

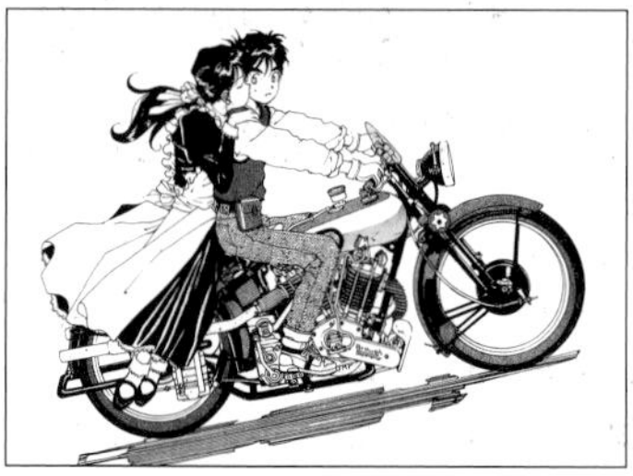

Fiat 500

Small, compact, and cute—much like its owner, Sora Hasegawa. The Fiat 500, manufactured between 1957 and 1975, was once a rival in Europe and Japan to the classic Volkswagen Beetle for cheap, practical transportation. At 499cc and a mere 22bhp, it's not the fastest hill climber on the Inokura Pass—perhaps because Sora doesn't have a supercharger installed, as Lupin III does in *his* Fiat 500 in the movie *The Castle of Cagliostro*, where it's driven in what may be anime's greatest car chase.

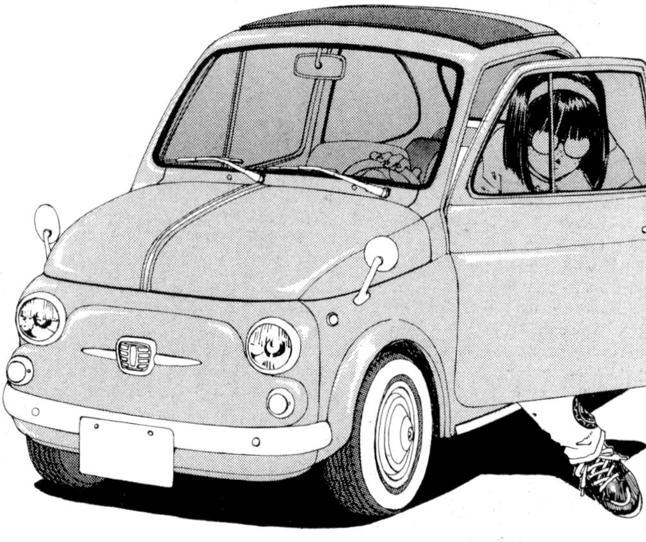

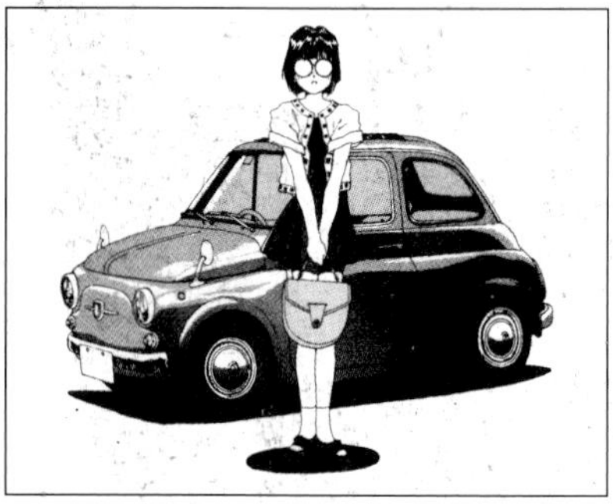

Suzuki GSX750 Modified Drag Racer

Toraichi Tamiya's bike, and therefore a dodgy monstrosity. This was in fact the same bike as the so-called "Honda Supercub" Keiichi had to ride in the "funnybike" division against Ushikubo University—funny, because the only actual Supercub parts still in it were the front rim and brake. It's equipped with a Suzuki GSX750 engine, overbored to 1300cc. Custom built for the drag race in Chapter 12, it literally only held together for the four hundred meters required, but it was rebuilt by Tamiya in time for Keiichi to borrow it to rescue Belldandy in Chapter 20 . . . although the Japanese editors of the *Encyclopedia* note that "due to safety aspects and traffic laws, this is conduct that cannot be imitated."

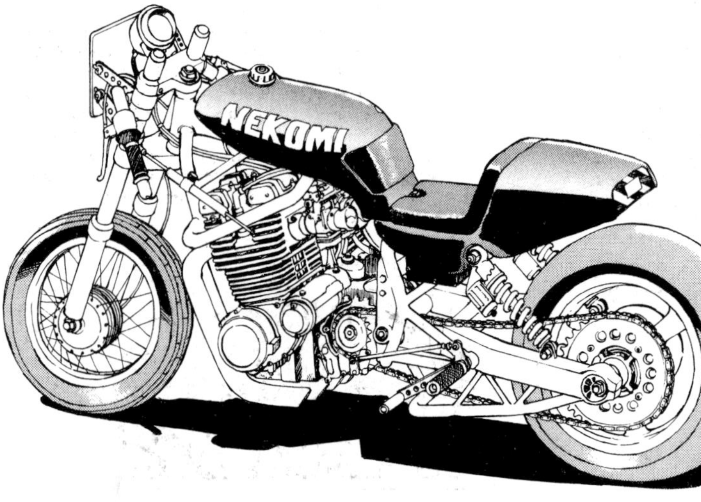
NEKOMI

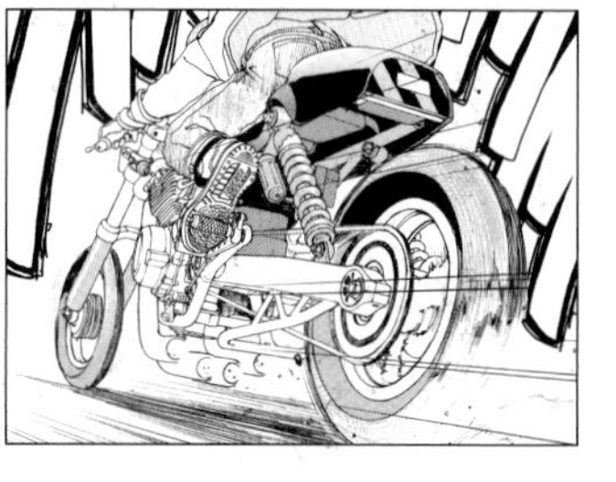

Krauser Domani SSi

Chihiro Fujimi makes her first appearance on this bike. Introduced to the market in 1989, and directed toward European and Japanese racing sales, the Domani is 987cc at 130bhp. Designed by Michael Krauser Motorradtechnik und Touren GmbH, a firm whose modifications of BMW bikes is comparable to AMG's historic role with Mercedes automobiles, the Domani uses a BMW K 1200 engine, but its innovation lies in the fact the sidecar and bike are part of the same frame, enabling a more aerodynamic shell for racing. Chihiro and Keiichi, both former directors of the N.I.T. Motor Club, could then also both be said to ride sidecar-equipped BMWs, but her approach is futuristic, whereas Keiichi's is vintage. Of course, she also seems to have more of what German engineers would term *das Kapital*.

Flying Broom

It's interesting to note Keiichi's doubts about Belldandy as a racer in Chapter 182, and then dropping his jaw at hearing she's a champion on the flying broom in Heaven. Despite having her as an actual racing partner on occasion, and watching her willingness to train Hasegawa to race, he seems flabbergasted. Is it simply that despite living together for years, Keiichi still doesn't really know that much about Belldandy? Or is it also that she's such a good partner in life with him that he couldn't picture her as a highly competitive person on her own? In any case, it perhaps helps to explain why Belldandy has always understood the Motor Club so well. And whereas her racing rival's broom, Glühende Herz, has won the demon championship eight times, Belldandy has won *as a rider* six times in Heaven—her handling of the anxiety-stricken Stringfellow suggests she wins her victories through personal skill and empathy with her "vehicle," not by simply having the best one.

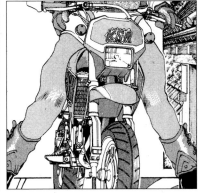

Kawasaki KSR-II

Megumi Morisato rides this stock little 80cc bike with a motocross design. In theory, it shouldn't have been able to beat the supercustomized Yamaha TDM 850 of "The Queen," and, in fact, Megumi would agree—the secret is that Megumi regards her bike as just a tool, which can only win with superior maintenance and riding on the part of the racer.

Kyushu J7W1 Shinden

The Shinden, or "Magnificent Lightning," was an experimental plane tested by its designer, Captain Masaoki Tsuruno of the Japanese Navy, in the final weeks of World War II. Intended as a high-speed interceptor to shoot down American B-29 bombers, it was never actually used in combat. The one known prototype is in storage at the U.S. National Air and Space Museum—but in *Oh My Goddess!*, the N.I.T. Motor Club discovers a second, hidden Shinden, buried beneath the ruins of their clubhouse (Nekomi Tech was built on the site of an old naval air station). Tamiya shows his usual mental flexibility by deciding it meets the definition of "motor vehicle," and his usual sadism by assigning Keiichi the role of its test pilot. The Shinden's offbeat configuration—with its canard design and propeller in back, known as a *pusher prop*—gave it an "alternate world" look that later inspired designs in such anime films as *Royal Space Force* and *The Sky Crawlers*.

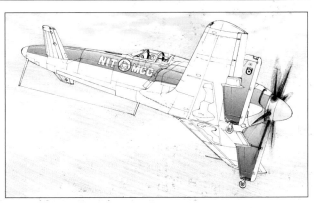

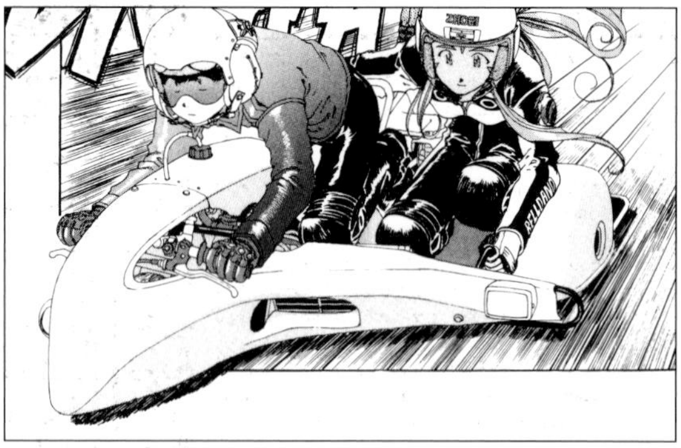

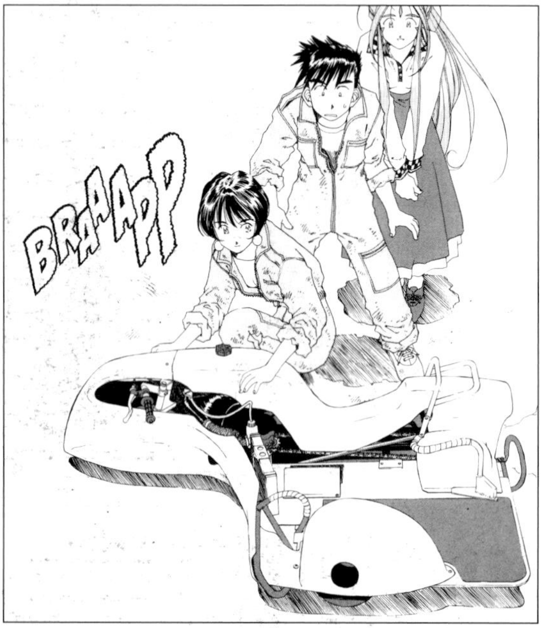
BRAAAPP

RS80 Tomboy

Reflecting Chihiro's (and the manga creator's) love of bikes and bike shops, the RS80 Tomboy is an ultra-sleek racing kneeler made by the real-life custom shop Cow Space, in Setagaya, Tokyo (www.visualware.co.jp/cowspace/). Using the same engine as a Kawasaki KX80, it's meant only for the track, and doesn't meet street registration standards—which didn't prevent Chihiro from buying it for its cuteness, or Keiichi and Belldandy riding it as a team (on a public road . . .).

Banpei-Kun (Two-Wheeled Mode)

Only a short time after Skuld first constructed him, and Belldandy gave him his "booster circuit," Banpei started to show signs of self-modification, culminating in a mode where he transformed into a sort of minibike—and out of devotion, used it to race to deliver Belldandy's lunch, even though this rapidly depleted all his power, and triggered his early loss of memory. Later Skuld would use a variant of this mode (with sub-helmet-mounted grips for her benefit) to ride around in—yet it was on such an outing that Banpei met the Welcome Robot, later using the mode to take her off on their first "date." Banpei-kun's free-wheeling mobility seems symbolic of something Skuld had to accept: that even though Banpei is her creation and helper, he also has a will of his own.

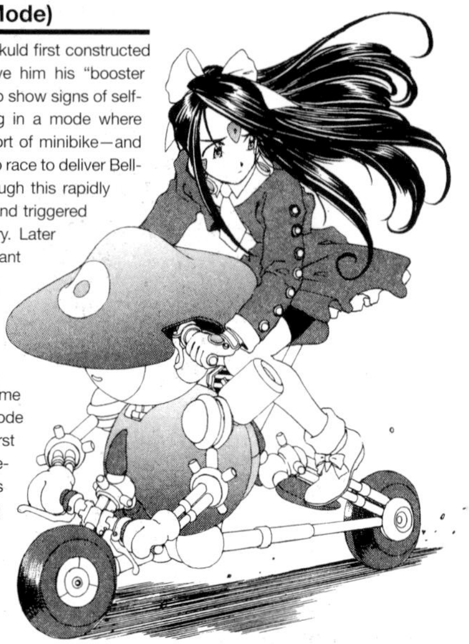

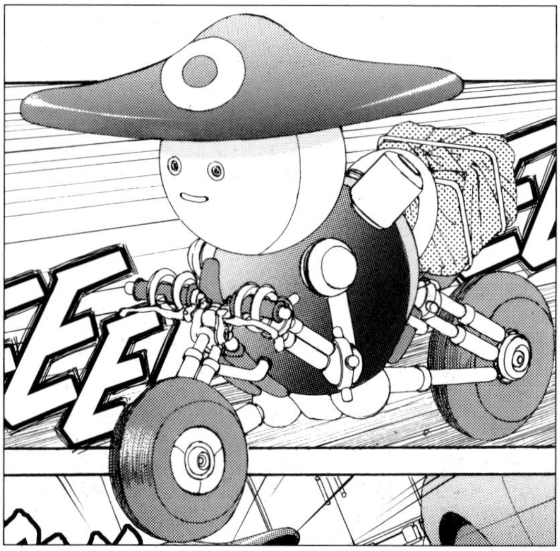

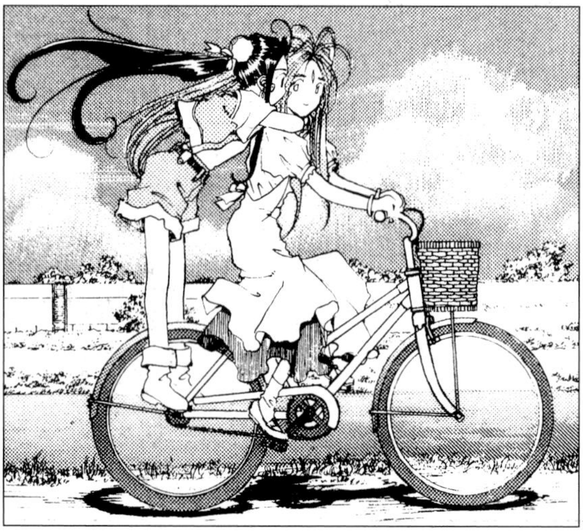

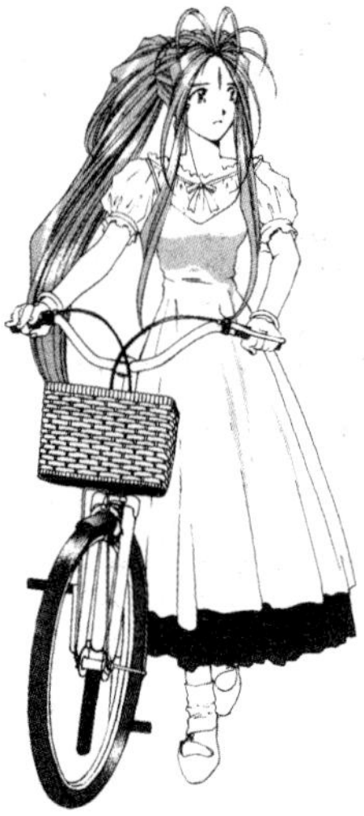

Belldandy's Shopping Special

Belldandy's personal ground transport, equipped with a wicker basket for groceries and a rear axle for little sisters to stand on (while learning to ride their own bikes). In Japan a bicycle like this is called a *mama-chari*, short for *mama charinko*, or "mama's bicycle." *Charinko* is a term used for utility (as opposed to racing or mountain) bikes, and combines the diminutive *ko* with the bell-jingling sound FX *charin*.

RULES OF THE *OH MY GODDESS!*
COSMOS
Fundamental knowledge of divine/infernal terminology

On Earth, we've got a lot of rules; it should perhaps be no surprise it turns out that the heavenly and demonic realms beyond our own have just as many! Without giving too much away, here's a look at some of what's been learned about the way the universe of *Oh My Goddess!* works.

1. THE SYSTEM

Yggdrasil (*Leader of the Pack*, Chapter 14, Vol. 2)

In the Norse religion, Yggdrasil was a titanic ash tree that formed the axis of the universe. In *Oh My Goddess!*, Yggdrasil serves the same role, but as a giant computer that maintains time and space throughout our plane of existence. Does this mean that existence itself isn't a self-sustaining phenomenon, but is in some sense virtual, a process that can be stopped or suspended? Was there an existence before Yggdrasil? What are the origins of Yggdrasil, and what does it mean for the demon-god conflict that Heaven is in charge of Yggdrasil?

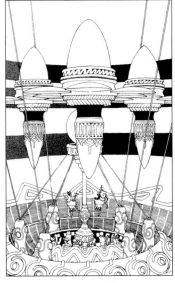

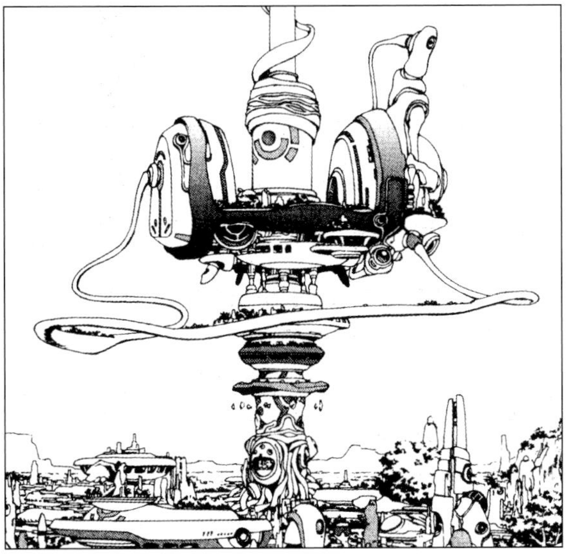

Special Access Information (*The Devil in Miss Urd*, Chapter 63, Vol. 11)

Special Access Information is data that, if divulged, is considered to pose a risk to the Heavenly Realm System. It is tagged with a special software lock that in turn triggers a protection program. This is what happened to Belldandy when she tried to warn Urd about the danger of her goddess and demon personalities remaining separate. As Mara herself broke a powerful taboo by effecting the split, it is not surprising the protection program rendered Belldandy mute on the subject; she literally was not allowed to speak of it.

2. LICENSES

Licensing System (*Leader of the Pack*, Chapter 14, Vol. 2)

Much like being a driver, you can't be a goddess without a license, and just like a driver's license, goddess licenses vary in what they permit the holder to do. Belldandy's license, for example, is that of a Goddess First-Class, Type 2, Unlimited. The "class" refers to the level of control and precision a goddess has over her power, not the level of power; Belldandy has said that Urd is more powerful than her, yet Urd, a Goddess Second-Class, has less control over her own power. The "type" refers to the purpose of the license; a type 2 license is for commercial work, as necessary for Belldandy's job at the Goddess Technical Help Line. Peorth, her professional rival, is also a type 2, but both Urd and Skuld have a type 1, noncommercial license, presumably because they're supposed to be back at their administrative jobs in Heaven rather than out here on Earth interacting with the public. Finally, "unlimited" means Belldandy may use as much of her power as she wishes (however, see **Containment Seal**, below).

License Suspension (*Terrible Master Urd*, Chapter 34, Vol. 5)

A goddess license carries responsibilities as well as rights, and there are penalties for ignoring them. A Goddess First-Class such as Belldandy is not permitted to lie at all, but that doesn't mean a Goddess Second-Class such as Urd can tell all the lies she wants; in fact, once Urd had piled up enough whoppers, tall tales, and misstatements, her license was suspended. Further use of goddess powers while under suspension is grounds for permanent revocation of the license . . .

Containment Seal (*Terrible Master Urd*, Chapter 36, Vol. 5)

As a sort of divine surge protector, goddesses carry a containment seal designed to restrict their maximum theoretical power. Each such seal is programmed to match the individual goddess's character, and in Belldandy's case, it takes the form of a ring in her left ear. Disengaging it without permission is a serious offense. During the period Belldandy removed her seal, her hair changed to a light color, and the appearance of her emblem program (see below) altered.

Emblem Program (*The Queen of Vengeance*, Chapter 41, Vol. 6)

The "essential functions" of the goddesses are maintained not only at a remote level by Yggdrasil, but also at a local level by their emblem programs—the marks on their foreheads. Urd's program has the emblem of the past; Belldandy's, of the present; and Skuld's, of the future, in keeping with their relative ages (and inspiration by the Norns of the Norse religion; please see *OMG!* Vol. 2, pages 182–183, for more details). When Yggdrasil went offline, the emblem programs could no longer sync, and Skuld started growing older, whereas Urd began growing younger. Note that Belldandy's emblem program ordinarily resembles a spindle, but during the period her containment seal was off, it changed to a sphere flanked by the two halves of the spindle, as if it had opened up to reveal it.

Forced Repatriation (*Mara Strikes Back*, Chapter 47, Vol. 7)

In order to punish someone who commits a serious violation in the earthly realm, there is a system of forced repatriation to the heavenly realm. Typically, a "forced repatriation gate" is opened by the Almighty for this purpose. The decision cannot be appealed, but when it was ordered down (or up, as the case may be) on Urd, Keiichi, interestingly, asked Belldandy what would happen if someone was *unable* to go back when a gate opens. In fact, Article 25, Section 16, of the goddess rules state that "should forced repatriation prove impossible at the scheduled time of said repatriation, the implementation of the decision shall be suspended." By building an Ultimate Magical Warding Mandala to guard against Mara, the goddess sisters were able to "accidentally" destroy the return gate; this side effect was purely coincidental, of course.

Remedial Course (*Miss Keiichi*, Chapter 54, Vol. 9)

In His mercy, the Almighty ordered Urd to take a remedial course at goddess school in order to help her get her license back much sooner. Belldandy had said in Chapter 47 that Urd's banning from Earth could last a hundred, or even a thousand, years; but the remedial course allows the ban period to be much shorter, by giving instruction through lectures, videos, and the use of a "spell simulator."

Earth Training License (*Miss Keiichi*, Chapter 54, Vol. 9)

Something like a "study-abroad visa" for goddesses, it enables them to stay on Earth for training purposes, even without a wish contract such as Belldandy's. The Almighty thought being on Earth was helping Skuld to mature, but He demanded she return temporarily to Heaven with Urd in order to formally receive this piece of paperwork.

License Expiration (*Traveler*, Chapter 105, Vol. 18)

Goddess licenses will expire after a certain period (even if no regulations have been broken), unless they are renewed. When Belldandy suddenly lost her powers, it turned out it was because she had forgotten her renewal date, and that it would take a week to process her papers to receive a new license. Unfortunately, this was also the week of the Infinite Tea Room incident . . .

3. WISHES AND CONTRACTS

Wishes (*Wrong Number*, Chapter 1, Vol. 1)

A summoned goddess is obliged to make one, and only one, wish of the summoner come true. Belldandy said the wish could be for anything, even the destruction of the world, although "we prefer to avoid doing business with that sort of customer." (The Japanese editors note "they try not to be summoned by a person that would wish for something like that.") Once a wish is formally registered in Heaven, it cannot be changed.

Double Contract (*The Fourth Goddess*, Chapter 66, Vol. 11)

The odds of a mortal contacting a goddess once (and receiving a wish contract thereby) are long; the idea that a mortal might do it *twice* are so long that there are apparently no rules to address the situation. This double-contract situation arose when Keiichi accidentally summoned Peorth to Earth; the problem from Peorth's perspective is that her professional pride demanded she stay until Keiichi spoke his "heart's desire" to her.

System Force (*Wrong Number*, Chapter 1, Vol. 1)

Wishes, once registered, are entered into the system in Heaven, and thus also acquire a force that makes sure they are carried out. Since what Keiichi asked of Belldandy ("be with me always") was open ended, it means the System Force worked to keep them together from then on. It might manifest as good fortune (such as Otaki unexpectedly fixing Keiichi's sidecar) or bad fortune (such as Sayoko's engine melting down).

Prohibition of Repatriation (*Leader of the Pack*, Chapter 14, Vol. 2)

This was the punishment Urd received for her antics causing Yggdrasil to crash; she was banned from Heaven until further notice (which she received in Chapter 47; see **Forced Repatriation** above).

4. LIFE

Moon Rocks (*The Queen of Vengeance*, Chapter 41, Vol. 6)

If cut off from Yggdrasil, and their alternative energy sources (see entry in the Encyclopedia section, page 153) become hard to obtain, there is a third option for the goddesses to receive power: from moon rocks. Interestingly, this seems to be due to their physical rather than any mystical properties; synthesized moon rocks proved to have power as well, although only to the degree their composition is accurate.

Bathing (*Hand in Hand*, Chapter 91, Vol. 16)

In order to purify their bodies, goddesses have to bathe once a day. The Japanese editors note, "even if she hasn't come in contact with Keiichi, Belldandy performs this ritual." Does this imply that contact with Keiichi makes Belldandy somehow impure?

Triple Challenge of the Goddesses (*The Fourth Goddess*, Chapter 71, Vol. 12)

When two goddesses have an irreconcilable difference between them, they have since ancient times resolved it through the Triple Challenge—which Peorth offered, and Belldandy accepted. In the first challenge, the rivals must each invoke their angels, and have them tickle each other; the goddess who laughs first (as the angels are linked to them) is the loser—in this case, Peorth. The second challenge is a game of whack-a-mole, which Belldandy lost, as the moles were too cute and she refused to whack them. The third challenge (and the only one Urd, the referee, liked) is the "pinpoint meteor strike," whereby the goddesses summon meteors from space towards a bulls-eye drawn in the earth. Both Peorth and Belldandy hit the center, but Belldandy a moment sooner, breaking the tie and making her the victor of the Triple Challenge.

5. SECURITY

Doublet System (*Mystery Child*, Chapter 98, Vol. 17)

The Doublet System is a form of hostage exchange, designed to prevent the battle between gods and demons over "market share" (i.e., contracts with humans) from escalating to lethal levels. At an early age, each god is paired with a demon, thereby becoming doublets—meaning that if one were to die, the other would die as well. The pairing contract also erases their memory of the event; therefore no god nor demon dares kill one of "the other side," for fear it might be their secret doublet. (See also **Most Distant Twins** in the Encyclopedia, page 167).

6. THE DEMON REALM

Nidhogg (Chapter 136, Vol. 22)

In the Norse religion, Nidhogg was the serpent which gnawed the roots of Yggdrasil; appropriately enough, it is the name of the demon realm's own operating system. Comparatively little is known about Nidhogg, yet it seems to perform some parallel functions to Yggdrasil; for example, just as wishes granted by goddesses are administered through Yggdrasil, Velsper's demonic curse of Peorth, making her child-sized, was administered through Nidhogg. Hild, CEO of the demon realm, has Nidhogg locked with her personal password. The fact that both Velsper and Mara have made reference to being Demons First-Class suggests a parallel licensing system as well.

Demon Central Court (*Mystery Child*, Chapter 101, Vol. 17)

Tribunal of the demon realm, of which thirteen members are seen in silhouette, with an additional speaker above them. It was this speaker who pronounced sentence on Velsper in Chapter 101 under Provision 1, Article 4 (below). Was it Hild? The silhouette appeared different . . .

Demon Realm Concordance Provision 1, Article 4 (*Mystery Child*, Chapter 101, Vol. 17)

Under their own laws, a demon is apparently forbidden from making an intrusion into Yggdrasil. Hild said in Chapter 135, "if she's talking about Yggdrasil, we *absolutely* made up for that!" which seemed to refer to the sentence handed down on Velsper: in his case, to be stripped of his demonic powers, and reincarnated as a "level four life form."

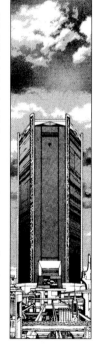

7. BONUS SECTION! RULES OF THE N.I.T. MOTOR CLUB

N.I.T. Motor Club Article 26 (*Sora Unchained*, Chapter 119, Vol. 19)

"Members designated by the director shall in principle be denied the right of refusal." Chihiro invoked this when Sora Hasegawa showed reluctance to accept then-current-director Keiichi's appointment of her to succeed him. The rule goes on to state, "However, right of refusal is granted if and only if said designee wins a race against the sitting director."

N.I.T. Motor Club Article 26, Clause 5 (*Sora Unchained*, Chapter 120, Vol. 20)

"The mode of competition shall be decided by the director emeritus." This actually wasn't part of the original Article 26, so Chihiro hastily scribbled it in with a ballpoint pen.

OH MY GODDESS!

Chapter Summaries and Conversion

GUIDE

This final section of *Oh My Goddess! Colors* gives summaries for the first 194 chapters of the series (still ongoing in Japan!)—all that was available from Dark Horse in English up through the end of 2008 (Vol. 30). That means there's new volumes out right now! ^_^

Unlike in North America, where most manga are published only as graphic novels, in Japan most manga first run one chapter at a time in an anthology magazine, and are only later collected as a graphic novel. So it is as well with *Oh My Goddess!*, whose original Japanese home is the monthly magazine *Afternoon*, published by Kodansha. A typical issue of *Afternoon* might be 1,000 (that's "one thousand") pages long, so as you can imagine, *Oh My Goddess!* has had plenty of neighbors over the years—and other *Afternoon* alumni published by Dark Horse have included *Blade of the Immortal*, *Eden*, *Gunsmith Cats* and *Gunsmith Cats Burst*, *Tanpenshu*, *Ohikkoshi*, *Shadow Star*, *Cannon God Exaxxion*, and *Seraphic Feather*. Other companies have published manga from *Afternoon*, too—the popular *Genshiken* also ran there between 2002 and 2006, for example. But *Oh My Goddess!* is still the flagship title of *Afternoon*, having run in almost every single issue of the magazine since the story began in November of 1988, and that's why this section breaks down *OMG!* by chapters rather than volumes.

For years (between 1994 and 2004, to be exact), Dark Horse also used to release the English version of *Oh My Goddess!* one chapter per month—but in the form of a monthly comic book. These chapters were all flopped for Western readers (as used to be the norm for all English-language manga). There were 112 issues of the *OMG!* monthly comic during those ten years, covering the first 127 chapters (some issues were double-sized). The monthly comics series didn't always publish the chapters in the order they appeared in Japan; however, when they were collected into graphic novels, it was in their correct Japanese order (with the exception of *1-555-Goddess*, as noted below). Now that you know *Oh My Goddess!* was once a monthly comics series, please do your best to forget it for the sake of this section, ^_^ where—in the hopes of greater clarity—we will discuss only the chapters as they appeared in the two different editions Dark Horse published them in: flopped (pre–July 2005) and unflopped (everything since then).

These chapter summaries, like the previous Encyclopedia section, are designed to serve both old readers and new. This is where the "Conversion Guide" aspect of these summaries comes into play—that is, converting between Dark Horse's old and new versions of *Oh My Goddess!*, to help you identify the chapters referenced in these summaries. The key point to bear in mind is that while both versions have the same chapters in the same order (with the obvious caveat that the old, flopped version went no further than Vol. 20), the two versions divvied up the chapters differently per volume. Basically, the old, flopped editions divvied up the chapters by story

arc, whereas the new, unflopped editions are based directly on the Japanese originals, which often end in the middle of a story arc. As you will see, during the first twenty volumes' worth of the manga, the only times the two editions started on the same chapter were with the first and thirteenth volumes of each series; otherwise, they always overlapped each other.

So in this guide, headings in boldface such as **Oh My Goddess!: Volume 1** indicate this is the starting point of one of the "new" unflopped volumes (again, even though as of spring 2009 only Vols.1–11 and Vols. 21–31 are out in "new" format, future volumes will follow this plan as well). Headings in *italics* such as *Wrong Number* indicate a starting point of one of the old, flopped volumes. Again, all of the old volumes had names such as *Wrong Number*, *Leader of the Pack*, *Final Exam*, etc., whereas the new ones only have numbers—so to hopefully reduce confusion, the old volumes will be listed only by their names (even though, in some printings, they had numbers on their spines as well).

Note that the old editions didn't include the chapter numbers, only the chapter titles, and in some cases, the chapter titles are translated differently between the old and new versions. In cases where there was a significant difference, the old-edition chapter title is given in parentheses. So, for example, Chapter 1's title name in the new version is "The Number You Have Dialed Is Incorrect," whereas in the old version it was "Wrong Number." Finally, the date given after the chapter name (in the case of Chapter 1, November 1988) is the date this story first appeared in *Afternoon* magazine. This may give you a sense of what was going on in society, technology, and culture at the time the story was drawn, and might help you get the most out of *OMG!*'s ever-changing references, in-jokes, and hairstyles.

Special note: There are two Dark Horse *Oh My Goddess!* graphic novels you may come across that don't fit in with the chapter breakdown described here. Both are in the flopped, old style. The first is *Adventures of the Mini-Goddesses*, which collected all of the *Mini-Goddess* strips available up through 2000 (and thus doesn't contain the more recent ones since the *Mini-Goddess* feature returned to *OMG!* in Vol. 24). These same strips are now appearing unflopped, of course, in the new editions, together with a few not previously published. The other *Oh My Goddess!* graphic novel that doesn't fit the breakdown is one entitled *1-555-Goddess*. This was an early (November 1996) edition designed to introduce more characters at once to new readers, so it contained Chapters 1, 14, 17, 18, 19, and 20, in that order.

Oh My Goddess! Volume 1

Wrong Number

Chapter 1: The Number You Have Dialed Is Incorrect (Wrong Number) November 1988—When underclassman Keiichi house-sits the dorm one Saturday night for his seniors at Nekomi Tech, the goddess Belldandy descends and grants his half-joking wish: "I want a goddess like you to be with me always!" They both promptly get kicked out of the dorm—it's males only.

Chapter 2: Lair of the Anime Mania (Into the Lair of the Anime Otaku) December 1988—Looking for a friend who would let Keiichi and Belldandy stay overnight, they end up at Sada's place. He's obsessed with the two-dimensional world of anime, and Belldandy tries to bring him back to reality, with questionable results.

Chapter 3: A Man's Home Is His . . . Temple? January 1989—While seeking shelter from the falling rain, Keiichi and Belldandy fall asleep under the eaves of Tarikihongan, a Buddhist temple. The priest takes her for an "enlightened one," and he leaves for India to further his training, leaving the temple in the care of the young couple.

Chapter 4: College Exchange Goddess February 1989—Belldandy accompanies Keiichi to school as a "foreign exchange student" and becomes very popular in Professor Kakuta's class. Jealous that people are abandoning his lectures, Professor Ozawa tries to find out who Belldandy really is.

Chapter 5: Those Whom Goddess Hath Joined Together, Let No Woman Put Asunder February 1989 (note: Chapters 4 and 5 appeared in the same issue of *Afternoon*)—The lovely and cruel Sayoko Mishima, previously the "Campus Queen," is the next person to feel envy at Belldandy's presence. Trying to split her up with Keiichi (despite the fact she previously wouldn't give him the time of day), Sayoko finds herself stymied by the System Force.

Chapter 6: Single Lens Psychic—The Prayer Answered (SLP Camera—Mission Accomplished!) March 1989—Learning about the thuggish yet shy upperclassman Otaki's feelings toward the cute young Satoko, Keiichi tries to play Cupid for them, with the help of Belldandy.

Chapter 7: Lullaby of Love April 1989—Keiichi puts some efforts into accelerating his relationship with Belldandy after realizing that it hasn't really gone anywhere, and gets a kiss on his sleeping cheek in exchange for a considerable amount of trouble.

Chapter 8: The Blossom in Bloom (The Megumi Problem) April 1989 (note: Chapters 7 and 8 appeared in the same issue of *Afternoon*)—Keiichi's younger sister Megumi visits, having been sent by their parents to stay with him while she studies for her college entrance exams. Megumi succeeds, but only afterwards informs them the college she was applying to was Nekomi Tech.

Leader of the Pack

Chapter 9: Apartment Hunting Blues May 1989—Keiichi and Belldandy look for an apartment that meets Megumi's detailed demands. They find one that seems too good to be true; maybe because there's a hostile earth spirit possessing it.

Oh My Goddess! Volume 2

Chapter 10: An Honest Match (Naked Victory) June 1989—After Keiichi gets his monthly living allowance confiscated by his seniors as a "donation" to the N.I.T. Motor Club, he tries to make it back with a modeling job, only to fall into another of Sayoko's schemes.

Chapter 11: This Life Is Wonderful (Let Flowers Bloom) July 1989—At Megumi's suggestion, Keiichi decides to take Belldandy out on a date to a seaside park. Seasickness, stumbling, and their first mutual-consent kiss!

Chapter 12: Love Is the Prize (Leader of the Pack) August 1989—To welcome new freshmen to the Motor Club, upperclassman Tamiya announces a race against rival Ushikubo University's Motor Club, without mentioning he promised them Belldandy if they win.

Chapter 13: System Force Down September 1989—The Motor Club takes its summer-break trip to the beach, getting a package deal with Sayoko's Art Club. Sayoko tries again to break up Belldandy and Keiichi, but the System Force that *should* be stopping her isn't working this time . . .

Chapter 14: Oh My Older Sister! (Sexy Sister) October 1989—Bell's "sophisticated" older sister Urd, administrator of Yggdrasil, the heavenly computer network, arrives at the temple residence, supposedly to recharge Belldandy's System Force. However, her true intention is to move the relationship along, even if she has to get physical with Keiichi . . .

Final Exam

Chapter 15: I'm the Campus Queen November 1989—Urd, temporarily trapped on Earth due to a violation of service terms (i.e., her constant lying), insists on entering both herself and Belldandy in the annual Campus Queen contest.

Chapter 16: What Belldandy Wants Most December 1989—A year has passed since Belldandy's arrival on Earth. To express his gratitude, Keiichi embarks on a rough week of extra part-time jobs in order to get enough money to buy her a ring.

Oh My Goddess! Volume 3

Chapter 17: Turkey with All the Trimmings January 1990—At a drawing, Keiichi wins two free tickets for dinner at a hotel. He looks forward to spending time alone with Belldandy, but there's a dress code—and there's Urd and Sayoko . . .

Chapter 18: Life's Just a Game of Sugoroku Roulette February 1990—Keiichi's seniors and friends gather at his place for New Year's Day. Rather than the traditional playing cards, they try their hand at a magical game of Life in which all your spinnings come true!

Chapter 19: Upon Close Examination (Final Exam) March 1990—Keiichi has one more exam to take and tries to study—but the session is disrupted by a night of revels with the Motor Club. Belldandy comes up with a plan to help Keiichi, without perhaps quite realizing how embarrassing it will be to him.

Chapter 20: Belldandy in Danger (Belldandy's Narrow Escape) May 1990 (there was no chapter in the April 1990 issue of *Afternoon*)—The slick, wealthy Toshiyuki Aoshima, Sayoko's cousin, starts attending Nekomi Tech and joins the Motor Club—in order to get close to Belldandy. Tampering with Keiichi's bike, he claims he's just going to give her a ride home . . .

Love Potion No. 9

Chapter 21: Exposing a Secret (The Secret's Out!) June 1990—Aoshima and Sayoko follow Belldandy around with a video camera in an attempt to spy out her true nature; fortunately, Sayoko won't believe the simple truth!

Chapter 22: Who Will Win the Champion Flag? (Winner Take All) July 1990—The Motor Club is about to participate in the First Golden Hammer Competition, an intercollegiate road rally. Belldandy and Keiichi run together in the coed preliminary, but Aoshima is waiting for them with his trademark dirty tricks in mind . . .

Chapter 23: What a Miracle August 1990—At the main event of the First Golden Hammer Competition, Keiichi has an American rival—a team from LAIT, the Los Angeles Institute of Technology! Featuring the famous moment where Keiichi actually gets to touch Belldandy's breast—for strictly magical purposes, of course.

Oh My Goddess! Volume 4

Chapter 24: The Flying Motor Club (On a Wing and a Prayer) December 1990—When Aoshima has the Motor Club's clubhouse bulldozed, the salvage effort uncovers a buried prototype of the Shinden, a push-prop plane from WWII. Keiichi, who knows a teeny, tiny bit about flying, is drafted into becoming its test pilot!

Chapter 25: Let's Take the Love Seeds (Love Potion No. 9) April 1990 (note:chapters 25 and 27-30 were collected in the Japanese [and unflopped English] volume 4 out of the order they ran in *Afternoon*)—Urd swallows her own love potion by mistake, and roams around campus declaring her passion for everyone she sees. Can Keiichi and Belldandy move fast enough to keep the damage under control?

Chapter 26: The Nemesis (The CD from Hell) September 1990—Demoness First-Class Unlimited Mara is accidentally (how else?) summoned forth by Tamiya. Her job as a demon is to make trouble for goddesses—most specifically, Bell and Urd.

Chapter 27: Mara's Counterattack (Mara Strikes Back!!) October 1990—Mara works through Sayoko—the only mortal as evil as she—to attack Belldandy, even as Bell and Urd try to figure out a way to send her back to the infernal realms.

Sympathy for the Devil

Chapter 28: Balance-Ball Amour (The Scales of Love) November 1990—Despite Keiichi being behind in his studies, Bell suggests it would be good for them both to get out of the house (or in their case, temple) . . . leaving them open targets for Mara's lethal brand of sorcerous high jinks.

Chapter 29: The Worst Day of a Demon (Sympathy for the Devil) February 1991—Megumi changes into a sporty little number . . . no, not an outfit: the demoness Mara polymorphs her into a Porsche 356! But after Mara steps on the good-luck charm Megumi left behind, she gets amnesia—and hence can't turn Megumi back . . .

Chapter 30: Engine o' Mystery (Mystical Engine) January 1991—Shivering in the cold wind (as their clubhouse remains destroyed) while their rivals, Aoshima's Four Wheels Club, chill in the lap of luxury, the Motor Club decides to face off against the enemy for the prize money of the Economy Run race. But how far can they get on one liter of gas?

Oh My Goddess! Volume 5

Chapter 31: Valentine Capriccio (Valentine Rhapsody) March 1991—When Belldandy hears that the Japanese Valentine's Day custom is for women to make homemade chocolate for the men in their lives, she vows to exceed her quota. Naturally, Urd and Mara insert their sticky selves into the mixing bowl . . .

Chapter 32: The Third Goddess April 1991—Bugs are everywhere at Tarikihongan—the rabbitlike magical bugs which usually plague the heavenly computer system, Yggdrasil. In hot pursuit is the system debugger, Urd and Belldandy's younger sister Skuld!

Chapter 33: The Goddesses' Greatest Danger (The Goddesses' Big Crisis) May 1991—Belldandy decides to go back to the heavens in order to save Keiichi from the danger caused by the bugs, but the effects of the infestation prevent her return. Skuld creates a debugging machine, which involves things that probably aren't dangerous, like a black hole and a fusion reactor.

Terrible Master Urd

Chapter 34: Urd Goes Wild (Urd Goes Berserk) June 1991—Previously merely banned from Heaven, Urd now finds out her Goddess License has been suspended by the Almighty—for fifty years! In despair, Urd is tempted to give in to her demonic side . . . and becomes the heir of the prophesied Lord of Terror!

Chapter 35: Terrible Master Urd (Urd's Terrible Master) July 1991—Urd's new project as the heir to the Lord of Terror is nothing fancy: destroy the universe, with the help of Mara, now a mere hapless flunky before such commanding malevolence. Can Skuld and Belldandy get Urd back to the happy days when she was merely reckless and negligent?

Chapter 36: The Ultimate Destruction Program August 1991—When the Almighty suggests that He himself must now strike Urd down, a desperate Bell risks her own license to save her older sister . . . not realizing she is falling into a trap that will only further the demonic Urd's wicked aims . . .

Oh My Goddess! Volume 6

Chapter 37: Urd Wakens the Wolf (Urd Calls Forth the Beast) September 1991—Urd gets the Ultimate Destruction Program activated and summons Fenrir. However, Fenrir shows his true colors and becomes wild, taking away Urd's energy. Belldandy and Skuld attempt to resolve this by using the Anti-Ultimate Destruction Program Vaccine, but . . .

Chapter 38: The Secret of the Lord of Terror October 1991—Urd is free from the Lord of Terror's spell at last. The Lord of Terror seems to have been defeated by the Midgard Serpent . . . until the King transfers into Keiichi!

Chapter 39: Confession November 1991—The Lord of Terror demands Skuld create a Ten-Dimensional Scythe to cut the universal superstring—but Belldandy's selfless courage leads to one last transfer, and his undoing.

The Queen of Vengeance

Chapter 40: Robot Battle (Robot Wars) December 1991—Megumi and Skuld run into each other when they both come to check up on Keiichi, and promptly get into a technical argument where honor can only be settled by . . . robot battle!

Chapter 41: The Trials of Morisato (The Trials of Morisato, Part 1) January 1992—The breakdown in the Yggdrasil system not only causes all three goddesses to lose energy, but Urd to get younger and Skuld to get older! But a divine revelation gives Keiichi an idea how to help; the only problem is, the idea involves *moon rocks* . . .

Chapter 42: Urd's Fantastic Adventure (The Trials of Morisato, Part 2) February 1992—Keiichi's artificial moon rock doesn't quite do the trick on Urd, but she finds that being kid sized is more interesting than she'd imagined when a young boy in the neighborhood falls for her.

Oh My Goddess! Volume 7

Chapter 43: Belldandy's Tempestuous Heart (The Trials of Morisato, Part 3) March 1992—To express her gratitude to Keiichi, Urd has made a crystallized love potion and gives it to Belldandy. The crystals, however, have been made with tampering from Skuld, leading to some most un-Belldandy-like behavior from Keiichi's favorite goddess.

Chapter 44: The Queen of Vengeance April 1992—Drunk as heck, Sayoko visits Keiichi in the middle of the night, and, the next morning, finds a hand-knit sweater that Belldandy has made for him as a present. Does she have it in her to make it disappear?

Mara Strikes Back

Chapter 45: The Man Who Invites Misfortune (Mister Unhappy) May 1992—Mara returns, with a new plan: first, sneak around undetected by possessing Megumi; then, in her body, call forth the genie Senbei—God of Poverty and Disaster! Can Belldandy protect Keiichi from this magical one-two punch?

Chapter 46: Thank You June 1992—To protect Tarikihongan from the present threat, Skuld creates Banpei-kun, an anti-Mara tactical strike robot. But Banpei creates two new problems: he tends to blow out the temple's fuses, and he's developed a mecha-attraction to Belldandy . . .

Chapter 47: Goodbye and Hello July 1992—The Yggdrasil System is finally back online, which means Urd has gotten back her full powers—but it also means she's ordered to report back to Heaven. Can her sisters and Keiichi block the recall on a divine technicality?

Oh My Goddess! Volume 8

Chapter 48: The Forgotten Promise August 1992—When Keiichi, Belldandy, Urd, and the Motor Club visit an old mountain resort, they're greeted by a beautiful young maid—only she's not young, nor even alive, but a manifest spirit who wants to hold Keiichi to a promise his *grandfather* made!

Chapter 49: Lunchbox with Love (The Lunchbox of Love) September 1992—Is the N.I.T. Motor Club's cutest member and worst cook, *meganekko* ("girl with glasses") Sora Hasegawa, really in love with Keiichi? Belldandy gives her expert lessons in home ec., but what truth does she sense?

Ninja Master

Chapter 50: Meet Me by the Seashore October 1992—At a beach retreat, Urd claims to Keiichi that a certain rock offshore has the power to seal eternal love for those who pledge under the full moon! That's just what Skuld feels she needs to prevent, but as Keiichi can't swim, can he even reach the rock in the first place?

Chapter 51: No, Sweetie (You're So Bad) November 1992—Skuld is confused emotionally with the outcome at the beach, while Keiichi mistakenly thinks she's got her first period! Will Urd's attempt at damage control just make things worse? Do you really have to ask?

Chapter 52: Ninja Master December 1992—Mara, thanks to an action movie on home video, discovers the secret concept of "ninja," and magically creates one, Kodama, to attack Tarikihongan. Having created her from a rat, however, Kodama isn't the world's *largest* ninja . . .

Oh My Goddess! Volume 9

Chapter 53: Law of the Ninja January 1993—Kodama, won over (as people tend to be) by the kindness of Belldandy, finds the others of her ninja clan coming to eliminate her as a traitor! Can even Bell-chan's compassion cover a swarm of little, tiny shadow warriors?

Miss Keiichi

Chapter 54: Together for Never February 1993—Keiichi is unexpectedly left alone with Belldandy, but a) he's nervous, and b) she's sick. When he taste tests some of Urd's magical medicines, hoping to cure her, Keiichi becomes somewhat gender ambiguous . . .

Chapter 55: Can't Stop Being Jealous (Jealous Love) March 1993—Urd's old boyfriend, the plum-tree spirit Troubadour, returns. Although wayward himself because of his questing nature, that doesn't mean he'll show any mercy to Keiichi if he finds out this person hanging around Urd really *is* a man!

Chapter 56: It's Lonely at the Top April 1993—With Tamiya and Otaki out sick, it falls to Keiichi to become acting club director and plan for a hill-climb race that his seniors forgot to register for, with a bike cobbled together from whatever junk they left lying around!

Chapter 57: Tainted Goddess (Fallen Angel) May 1993—Gorgeous freshman Shiho Sakakibara is attracted to Keiichi—or at least, the idea of exorcising the evil spirits she claims possesses him with her Thelemic magic—excuse me, "magick." The unflopped English version mistakenly called the chapter "Tainted God," which had the effect of losing the intended meaning—that Belldandy is shown to be "tainted" by jealousy.

Oh My Goddess! Volume 10

Chapter 58: Let's Have Fun (Play the Game) June 1993—When the N.I.T. Baseball Club tries to bully Megumi's Softball Club off the field, the goddesses (and Tamiya and Otaki, crudely disguised as the "Dynamite Baseball Brothers") come out swinging!

Chapter 59: Remember the Sad Times (Sorrow, Fear Not) July 1993—Megumi brings a stray puppy to Tarikihongan that everyone falls in love with—except, surprisingly, Keiichi, who doesn't want them to keep it. What's the truth behind his cold-hearted attitude?

The Devil in Miss Urd

Chapter 60: Karaoke Friend (Karaoke Hell) August 1993—Keiichi and the goddesses win a trip to a hot-springs resort—even though nobody can quite remember entering the contest. It turns out Mara is behind it, but do they have to fight, or can everyone have fun together?

Chapter 61: Urd Turns 100% Evil! (Evil Spirits: 200 Proof) September 1993—No sooner is their brief idyll over, then Urd is ambushed by Mara. Her sinister plan is to make a clone of Urd's (fabulous) body—then split off the demon part of Urd's soul and implant it in the copy!

Chapter 62: Skuld Strikes Back! October 1993—As seems to have happened before, Mara's attempt to use Urd's evil side for her own ends rapidly gets out of her control, as Urd, demon or goddess, is a) smarter, b) more powerful, and c) *far* more egotistical!

Oh My Goddess! Volume 11

Chapter 63: Goddess Urd Needed (The Battle for Urd) November 1993—As the good and evil Urd battle it out, Belldandy recognizes the cosmic danger of the struggle—but that same realization triggers a protection program that literally silences her!

Chapter 64: Fear Neither Light Nor Darkness (Shadow and Light) December 1993—The demonic Urd cannot endure the stresses upon her clone body anymore, and comes looking to capture the original body—the good Urd. The critical question Urd poses to Belldandy is, "Can any light exist without the darkness?"

Chapter 65: Urd Mode Is Gentle Mode (Superurd) January 1994—Banpei has managed to somehow restore his Emotion Circuit, and with it comes a flash of electronic inspiration as to what to do with the cloned Urd skin from last chapter. It sounds very creepy, but it's all in a good cause.

The Fourth Goddess

Chapter 66: Fourth Goddess . . . but Number One! (Fourth Time's a Charmer) February 1994—Keiichi accidentally calls Heaven again—this time, Belldandy's rival agency, and their representative Peorth descends to Earth. Keiichi informs her that he's "sort of full up on goddesses right now," but he says she will not leave until she gives him his heart's desire. But what is *that*?

Chapter 67: Are You Being Served? (I'll Do Anything for You) March 1994—Urd and Skuld, irritated by Peorth's refusal to leave, decide to challenge her to a "Who's the Most Helpful Goddess?" contest, full of dubious initiatives to help Keiichi in his daily tasks. Fortunately, Belldandy is there to clean up.

Oh My Goddess! Volume 12

Chapter 68: The Battle for Keiichi April 1994—Peorth accuses a flustered Belldandy of not giving Keiichi *everything* he wants, and intends to show up the competition by slipping him an "improved" version of Urd's Love Seeds. Rather than make him fall in love with Peorth, it makes Skuld (uh-oh) and Megumi (triple-double super-secret uh-oh) fall in love with *him*!

Chapter 69: Okay, This Is the Real Date (The Dating Game) May 1994—After stealing one of Skuld's shojo manga to see how humans date in the real world, Peorth invites Keiichi out to fulfill the sappy scenario, not realizing the other goddesses are coming along.

Chapter 70: When a Man Loves a Woman June 1994—Tamiya visits the Morisato household and falls in love with Peorth, although Belldandy thinks he's fallen in love with Urd, and Peorth thinks Tamiya has fallen in love with Keiichi. This will call for a very careful resolution if our protagonist wants to get out alive.

Chapter 71: Meeting a Goddess's Troubles Halfway (A Goddess Never Forgets) July 1994—Belldandy can't remember the thing she once did to make Peorth carry a grudge against her, and agrees to play the ancient Triple Challenge of the Goddesses against Peorth—for the prize of being reminded!

Chapter 72: What Men Really Want (Men Are from Earth, Goddesses Are from Yggdrasil) August 1994—Urd tells Keiichi he'd better find a way to get rid of Peorth before Belldandy experiences another Jealousy Storm. When he straight up *asks* Peorth about fulfilling his "heart's desire," it leads to a showdown over what it really *is*—and who's going to fulfill it.

Oh My Goddess! Volume 13

Childhood's End

Chapter 73: Mean Sister (Childhood's End) September 1994—Skuld, for all her mechanical acumen, cannot ride a bicycle—and can't figure out why Belldandy won't teach her. She runs out of the Morisato house and ends up meeting a boy, Sentaro, who helps her learn how.

Chapter 74: Crazy Little Thing Called Love October 1994—"A goddess's power is the power of love for others," says Belldandy, but Skuld using her own newfound power to fix the scratches on Sentaro's bike ends up making him upset. How is it tied to his feelings for Skuld?

Chapter 75: The Campus Queen Doesn't Trust Goddesses?! (The Queen and the Goddess) November 1994—Sayoko sees Belldandy teleporting through a mirror, yet doesn't believe she's a goddess when Bell tells her the simple truth. That's because she's been possessed by one of Urd's runaway critters—a parasite demon that devours the ability to trust!

Chapter 76: First Director of the Motor Club (Hail to the Chief) December 1994—Before Keiichi, before Tamiya and Otaki, the N.I.T. Motor Club was run by Chihiro Fujimi. And now she's returned, to test the fighting spirit of her successors in a minibike rally. But did she mention she's been a pro racer since graduation?

Chapter 77: Let's Go Feminine! (Forever Grrls) January 1995—Chihiro gets the gang to clean up the clubhouse by suggesting they might find forgotten treasure—but when they turn up an actual treasure map, it leads to something Chihiro would rather keep hidden!

Oh My Goddess! Volume 14

Chapter 78: Live to Work, Work to Live! February 1995—Keiichi's looking to line up a job after graduation, and his old club pal Imai has set him up with an interview. The goddess sisters are going to help him practice for it, but none of that's going to matter, for two reasons—one good, one *bad!*

Queen Sayoko

Chapter 79: I Want to Be a Goddess Who Looks Good in Scarlet (Pretty in Scarlet) March 1995—Skuld finally acquires an angelic companion, the underdeveloped Noble Scarlet, but the poor little angel, determined to prove she can help Skuld out, goes a bit too far when she tries to make her friendship with Sentaro a bit more romantic . . .

Chapter 80: The Goddess's Apprentice April 1995—Urd has loaned a fine piece of her magical craft to Belldandy: Stringfellow, a flying broom. But you can't be *that* close to Belldandy and not fall in love with her. Keiichi somewhat sympathizes, but can he and the broom be bros, or will rivalry prove the last straw?

Chapter 81: Call Me Queen! May 1995—Sayoko's desire to best Belldandy in the Campus Queen contest is so strong, it's detected by Mara, who grants her power—power to turn N.I.T. into a literal castle where *all* students must kneel and worship her—even Keiichi and the goddesses!

Chapter 82: And Then There Was One June 1995—With their heads protected by Skuld's anti-mind-force hair ribbons, Keiichi and the goddesses start to infiltrate the castle. But every campus club will obey Sayoko's command to capture them, from the chem lab to the dreaded Tea Fanciers!

Oh My Goddess! Volume 15

Chapter 83: Go after Sayoko! (Sayoko or Bust) July 1995—Belldandy is now a prisoner, but Keiichi finds Sora, who, freed from the mind control, helps him navigate the castle's booby traps. But Bell has already fallen into the clutches of the most depraved organization on campus; yes, you guessed it—the model builders!

Chapter 84: At Sayoko's Side August 1995—As Urd and Skuld, finding their magic strangely boosted, fight their way to Sayoko's throne room, Keiichi and Belldandy are already there. At the heart of Queen Sayoko's realm, one or the other of them must become her slave . . .

Chapter 85: Back Where You Belong September 1995—Mara shows herself as the power behind Sayoko's throne, and demands Sayoko use her power of command to banish Belldandy from Earth, telling her to go back where she belongs! There's something Mara didn't consider . . .

Hand in Hand

Chapter 86: Megumi vs. the Queen October 1995—Megumi, late and racing one day to the popular aerodynamics seminar held on N.I.T.'s satellite Inokuradai Campus, draws the attention of the Queen—no, not Sayoko, but the mystery rider who tests the last student to set off for class!

Chapter 87: The Secret of Speed November 1995—How did Megumi possibly beat the Queen on an ordinary stock bike? That's what the "Royalty of the Road" wants to know—but Megumi's only answer is to invite her to a race the next day, when she promises all will be revealed.

Chapter 88: Two Hearts Beat as One December 1995—The contest Megumi planned for the Queen isn't against herself—it's against Belldandy and Keiichi in his sidecar-equipped BMW. They would seem to have even less of a chance than Megumi did, but the Queen needs to learn their secret . . .

Chapter 89: Another Me January 1996—Skuld wants Noble Scarlet back, but Urd tells her she simply doesn't have the power to control it yet. Wait a minute, though: if Urd's so powerful, how come we never see *her* angel? Thanks to Skuld's latest invention going predictably wrong, Urd's going to have to summon her—even though she's afraid to meet her again!

Chapter 90: Never Let Go February 1996—Alcohol doesn't affect Belldandy. It's cola that makes her drunk! And when she has a little bit too much at the opening party of Chihiro's new garage, Whirlwind, Bell-chan does what she does best: dispense happiness. To everyone in town!

Oh My Goddess! Volume 16

Chapter 91: I Want to Hold Your Hand March 1996—When Belldandy wakes up, she finds her last gift of joy has led to her and Keiichi becoming literally inseparable, unable to let go of each other's hands. Skuld will understand the situation, right?

Chapter 92: Welcome! April 1996—Skuld notices that Banpei is acting strange, and is even keeping secrets from her—his maker! Belldandy's advice is to leave him be, but Skuld and Urd spy on him and discover he's fallen in love with a mechanical doll at the local store . . .

Chapter 93: The Sorrows of Banpei May 1996—Skuld tries to come to grips with the fact she'd been treating her creation like a thing without feelings. She decides to help bring Banpei and his love together . . . but the worn-out Welcome Robot has just been sent to the scrap yard!

Mystery Child

Chapter 94: The Boy Who Knows the Goddess (The Boy Who Could See Goddesses) June 1996—Peorth is hit by a surprise attack, and tries to mentally warn Belldandy of a danger facing the world. Meanwhile, a problem has occurred in the Time Management Program in the heavenly computer, Yggdrasil, and Urd and Skuld are called back to the heavens. Keiichi and Belldandy are alone at last . . . until a mysterious boy appears who claims to know Bell—but she doesn't remember *him*!

Chapter 95: Strange Things Are Happening (The Beginning of the End) July 1996—Belldandy still can't place the boy, but senses he's not really a human being. As he hangs out with them at Whirlwind, Keiichi starts to notice his watch is running slow . . . or other clocks are beginning to run fast . . . ?

Chapter 96: Memories of a Youth August 1996—Because of the time gap, Belldandy is spending more time asleep, and dreams of taking someone's hand, and being told there

is someone she has to meet. Realizing the boy's eyes are the same she glimpsed in the dream, she passes out—then the boy passes out, too . . .

Chapter 97: Return of the Fourth Goddess (Return of the Goddess) September 1996—In the Yggdrasil control room, Skuld discovers the heavenly computer has been hacked; someone has replaced its correct cosmic time synchronization file with a false one that's skewing time. Back on Earth, Keiichi sees reports of clock errors all over the country, and the boy reveals himself at last . . .

Oh My Goddess! Volume 17

Chapter 98: Light and Shadow October 1996—Peorth reappears just in time to save Keiichi from the mysterious boy, who now admits he is a demon. But time is beginning to slow to a stop, and the demon responsible for hacking the time system shows his power by rewinding Peorth's own time until she is a powerless child!

Chapter 99: The Truth about Doublets (The Trouble with Doublets) November 1996—Why is the demon boy doing all this? He and Belldandy are doublets. To prevent their rivalry from going too far, gods and demons have a kind of hostage exchange where each god is spiritually paired in their youth with a demon; after that, if one were to die, the other would die, too. But the memory of the exact pairing is erased from either party, so how is the boy so sure Belldandy is his doublet?

Chapter 100: Time without End, Hope without End December 1996—There are sixty seconds left now—to everything. Only if Belldandy remembers her doublet's real name can existence be saved, but there simply isn't enough *time* . . .

Chapter 101: Returned (Turn Back, Oh Time) January 1997—Urd, unable to slow the time program on Yggdrasil, had the insight to slow the clock speed of Yggdrasil itself. But it's only a temporary fix, and as Belldandy finally remembers everything about her and . . . Velsper, how will the cosmic crisis be resolved?

Traveler

Chapter 102: Come Walk with Me February 1997—Banpei asks Skuld to modify the Welcome Robot so they can take romantic walks together, but Skuld goes a bit further (as usual) and makes her able to speak, feel, and punch . . . Banpei, when he tries to embrace her.

Chapter 103: Getting to Know You March 1997—Skuld finds out she can't simply order the Welcome Robot to like Banpei, but Belldandy suggests she try to get to know him. But Banpei pursues a bit too eagerly, and the unbalanced Welcome Robot ends up falling into a dry well!

Chapter 104: Almost My Hero April 1997—Banpei heroically leaps down into the well to rescue the Welcome Robot, but feels he must commit a dubious act to recharge her. A miffed Skuld repairs them both, changing her order for the robot to like Banpei to a strong request to at least get along.

Oh My Goddess! Volume 18

Chapter 105: Expired Goddess License (Unlicensed Goddess) May 1997—Belldandy has forgotten to renew her goddess license, and will be unable to use magic for a week until the paperwork goes through. What a time for his Motor Club pals to show up, asking if they can keep "some stuff" at his place while the dorm is renovated . . .

Chapter 106: Wide, Wider, Widest June 1997—With no magic to use, Skuld's science seeks a solution with the amazing Space Doubler (actually, a cuber) that "borrows" space from the future. For once it's Keiichi's fault, not Skuld's, that the gadget goes awry—leaving him and Belldandy stranded in the center of an infinite tea-room floor!

Chapter 107: As Long as You're with Me July 1997—Keiichi and Belldandy are alone and Belldandy is powerless, yet they realize they're both together in good health, which is what's truly important in their relationship. Velsper, now their pet cat, shows up and leads them out through a clever if somewhat disheveled escape.

Chapter 108: Traveler August 1997—It'll be another three days before Bell gets her power back, and the tea room returns to normal—and Keiichi would have no reason to go back in there, were it not for the fact he left a textbook there! A sudden tentacle from inside returns it to him. Wait a minute . . .

Chapter 109: My Song Is Your Song (Missing Time) September 1997—The Schrödinger's Whale that has quantum-shifted into their infinite tea room (you see how complicated domestic life can get) likes Keiichi's taste in music, but he needs to get his giant self out of there before the batteries run out on the Space Doubler, seeing as how he's much bigger than the original room!

The Phantom Racer

Chapter 110: What's on the Mountain Pass? (The Ghost of the Pass) October 1997—Sora comes to Whirlwind and tells a g-g-ghost story—the story of the ghost rider she encountered on the Inokura Pass last night! When Megumi hears about it, she decides this calls for a race . . .

Chapter 111: Ghost Found (Sightings) November 1997—Riding out alone at night on the pass to challenge the ghost, Megumi's sharp maneuvers earn her no more than a glimpse—of a riderless bike! But did it really try to get her to drive off a cliff . . . ?

Chapter 112: Three Factors (Three of a Perfect Pair) December 1997—Keiichi and Belldandy show up in Chihiro's cute (but unregistered) racing side hack, determined to take up Megumi's battle against the ghost. For the first time, we hear the inner voice of the phantom bike, which is intrigued by their skill . . .

Oh My Goddess! Volume 19

Chapter 113: Welcome Back January 1998—Belldandy and Keiichi outrace the ghost with a daring move that raises the sidecar over the gutter. In defeat, it leaps again over the same cliff as before, but Belldandy realizes it's only trying to lead them to its true story . . . a story that lies within Chihiro's past.

Chapter 114: Meet Doctor Moreau!! February 1998—Dr. Koichi Morozumi is nicknamed "Dr. Moreau" by the students at N.I.T.—not because he wants to use horrific surgery to turn animals into men, but just because he's a mad scientist. Obsessed with developing a robot that can move like a human, he drafts Bell and Keiichi into being his lab assistants . . .

Chapter 115: Mankind's Dream Shattered (Android Dreams) March 1998—Dr. Morozumi visits the Morisato household and meets Banpei and the Welcome Robot. Overcome by scientific curiosity, he lifts up her skirt and is rocket-punched, but heavier is the blow when he learns that both were invented by Skuld, a mere child . . .

Chapter 116: The Trap of Doctor Moreau April 1998—Dr. Morozumi starts stalking the Welcome Robot, believing her scientific secrets must be unlocked by him for the benefit of all mankind. He says that he's kidnapped her "boyfriend," Banpei—a claim that makes her so mad, she comes to his lab to refute it . . . and falls into Dr. Morozumi's trap!

Chapter 117: Person or Machine? (Man? Machine?) May 1998—Morozumi's obsession sparks a talk between Keiichi and Belldandy on what it means to be a living being, even as Banpei, sensing the Welcome Robot's cry for help, blasts off toward N.I.T. to rescue her.

Chapter 118: The Sign of Life June 1998—The big showdown at the lab concludes with a thrashing (not from Belldandy) and a homily (from Belldandy) indicating that Dr. Morozumi should return to his prior mode of research. And at last the Welcome Robot receives a name: Sigel, from the Norse rune signifying life.

Sora Unchained

Chapter 119: Let's Elect the New Director! (I Choose You, Sora!) July 1998—At Belldandy's suggestion, Keiichi recommends Sora Hasegawa to succeed him as club director, although the other members object. Drawing random lots to decide, Sora wins every one, despite the fact *she* doesn't want the job either!

Chapter 120: Race Rules (The Shortcut to Winning) August 1998—A loophole in club rules says Hasegawa can turn the job down if she beats the current director (i.e., Keiichi) under rules set by the director emeritus (i.e., Chihiro). Chihiro chooses a mini-go-kart race as the contest, and assigns Belldandy as Sora's trainer . . .

Oh My Goddess! Volume 20

Chapter 121: The Doomed Director (The Director's Curse!) September 1998—Belldandy helps Hasegawa overcome her fear of speed and asks her why she doesn't want to lead the N.I.T. Motor Club. Reluctantly, Hasegawa tells Belldandy about her well-earned nickname—"Director of Death."

Chapter 122: Continued Special Training (Special Training) October 1998—In between his work hours, Keiichi fine-tunes his go-kart . . . while Urd cooks up something special in her test tube. Meanwhile, Hasegawa practices her turns . . . using the other club members as human traffic cones!

Chapter 123: Shall We Race Together? (Drive) November 1998—Hasegawa feels the rest of the club is working hard while she's training, but Belldandy convinces her that the driver's job is to drive—and it's precisely because everyone's working hard at their jobs, that she must, too.

Chapter 124: Keiichi's Distance, Hasegawa's Distance (Miles and Miles) December 1998—The race begins! The rules are that the racers each have to pass three checkpoints and get a stamp there—but the route they choose between the checkpoints is up to them. Keiichi takes an early lead, but as of checkpoint two, Hasegawa has caught up!

Chapter 125: The Race Gets Hot, a Goddess Gets Hotter! January 1999—Keiichi finds Hasegawa's shortcut course and follows her path . . . through one of the school buildings! She figures she's got him stopped by detouring through the women's locker room—but now's the time for Urd to administer her special surprise . . . to Keiichi!

Chapter 126: Kiss Off Course (Wrecked By a Kiss) February 1999—Thanks to Urd's Guts Accelerator, Keiichi becomes a steam-venting wild man, busting through the locker room and overtaking Hasegawa! But guts are one thing; smarts another, and Keiichi smashes up his go-kart . . .

Chapter 127: The Best Magic March 1999—With its seat and handlebar strut broken off, Keiichi straps his foot to the go-kart's axle in a desperate dash to the finish line. What will Hasegawa's decision be . . . and what was Chihiro's hidden agenda in designing the race . . . ?

Chapter 128: The Endless Battle, Part One April 1999—Urd and Skuld play Jenga over their favorite issue—who gets to watch what on television. But when Belldandy jumps in the game and wins handily, her sisters realize they'll have to take their fight to another level.

Chapter 129: The Endless Battle, Part Two May 1999—Urd figures the trick to beating Skuld is to create a whole bunch of *decoy* televisions, but fails to keep track of which one actually *is* real! Keiichi shows up with the gift of a second television so they can both watch what they want, but that's kind of missing the point with those two.

[Note: *Sora Unchained* was the last of the flopped editions of *Oh My Goddess!*—from this point, the story continued in its current, unflopped form, and the volumes have only numbers. *Sora Unchained* has the spine number "19/20" even though it is technically only the nineteenth volume in the flopped edition; the reason, as you can see from this conversion guide, is that it also contains all the chapters up to the end of the Japanese/unflopped Vol. 20. Since right after *Sora Unchained* comes *Oh My Goddess!* Vol. 21, there was a concern that if *Sora Unchained* were labeled only "19," readers would think chapters had been skipped in the transition between the two editions, when in fact *Sora Unchained* ends with Chapter 129 and Vol. 21 starts with Chapter 130.]

Oh My Goddess! Volume 21

Chapter 130: The Devil Inside June 1999—Hoping to get Velsper to restore her to her original size, Peorth comes to the Morisato household. She finds not only unkind laughs at her reduced circumstances, but also Velsper, who is now, of course, a cat.

Chapter 131: Go Your Own Way July 1999—Urd, much as she's amused by Peorth's state, hopes to show up the Yggdrasil techs who were unable to cure her by finding the solution. Can Belldandy sing the ultra-intricate incantation Urd devises?

Chapter 132: A Goddess Never Forgets August 1999—It turns out the problem is going to require more analysis from Urd and Skuld, and the others leave them to it and take off for the beach . . . where Keiichi and Peorth end up having a rather profound conversation.

Chapter 133: The Cat That Stretched September 1999—Peorth begins to suspect she's nothing but a guinea pig for Urd and Skuld's poorly tested "cures," but a chance conversation about computers with Chihiro gives Belldandy the key to helping Peorth.

Chapter 134: The Final Option October 1999—Velsper reveals to the gang—except, of course, Bell—that, although he was sentenced to reincarnation in this form, he enspelled himself to remember who he really was. He further tells them only Urd's *mother* can cure Peorth . . .

Chapter 135: She's a Devil Woman November 1999—. . . which is bound to cause complications, as Urd's mother is the dread Hild, CEO of the Demon Realm. But with all her immense power, restoring Peorth should be a snap. And surely the price will be fair and reasonable.

Oh My Goddess! Volume 22

Chapter 136: Let's Make a Deal December 1999—Urd politely turns down Hild's suggestion, but Hild agrees to help anyway, if Urd promises to owe her a "favor." Urd agrees, but only if the favor requires "nothing unbecoming to a goddess . . ."

Chapter 137: Sister Act January 2000—Hild enlists Urd to help sing the program—as it features parts for both goddess and demon—but tries to overwhelm her by tipping the song toward its demonic component. Fortunately, Urd has Belldandy and Skuld as backup . . .

Chapter 138: Maybe . . . ? February 2000—Peorth safely regains her original state, thanks to the quartet. Hild calls in the favor Urd owes her, but Urd refuses to honor it. The two part amid a less-than-conventional mother-daughter exchange of affection, but not before Velsper returns, with a surprise of his, or rather her, own.

Chapter 139: Wicked Game March 2000—Hild pays a visit to her erstwhile flunky, Mara, who flaunts her latest scheme to expand the Demon Realm's market share—a magical teapot simply known as "The Goddess Catcher."

Chapter 140: Morisato Residence, Rooms to Let April 2000—True to Mara's boasts, goddesses (and Chihiro) start falling into the teapot one by one, lured to kiss the image of that which they find most cute. Will anyone prove immune?

Chapter 141: Sparkle in Her Eyes May 2000—Everybody but Belldandy is in the pot . . . but then she has to spoil the fun by picking it up and washing it, the one thing that will release everyone within . . . including Chihiro, who has heard and seen everything.

Oh My Goddess! Volume 23

Chapter 142: Bell and Keiichi and the Terrible Guest June 2000—Megumi bursts into Whirlwind, with the ominous news that Keima, their father, is making an unexpected visit. Even though he doesn't want to shake hands, Chihiro finds herself impressed with this old man of mystery . . .

Chapter 143: Dad on the Run July 2000—Keima is pleased at his son's workplace, but when Chihiro makes the mistake of slapping him on the shoulder, he leaps onto his motorbike and roars away. Keiichi can only stop him by violating another taboo of Keima's . . . actually calling him "Father."

Chapter 144: Garden of the Goddesses August 2000—Keiichi decides now would be a good time to tell Keima he and Belldandy are living together—but he's already gone by himself to the Tarikihongan Temple! Surely he won't run into any strange *women* there, right?

Chapter 145: Dad in Hell September 2000—Keima's visit has already run afoul of Sigel, Banpei, and a swarm of dozens of mini-Banpei units that soon have Keima and the goddesses surrounded due to an ill-considered bit of programming by Skuld . . .

Chapter 146: Moment of Decision October 2000—Keiichi awakens from a vision of Belldandy to hear her singing by his side. They talk, and she tells him of her love for Keiichi. A woman named Takano shows up, however, and can tell right away Bell is the person Keiichi loves. How can she tell? Takano is Keiichi's *mother,* duh.

Chapter 147: Mother's Battle, Father's Battle November 2000—Takano wants Keiichi to prove himself by racing Keima, even though he's lost the last ninety-seven races with his dad! Fascinated by the fact Belldandy is the only woman besides his wife and daughter who can get close to Keiichi without him panicking, Takano insists Bell reveal who she really is . . . if Keiichi loses!

Chapter 148: Let's Dance! December 2000—While Takano teaches the other goddesses how to lose at mahjong, Keima and Keiichi race up the Inokuradai Circuit. Belldandy tags along in miniature form, noting that father's and son's styles are so similar, it's like their bikes are dancing . . .

Oh My Goddess! Volume 24

Chapter 149: Running Dialogue January 2001—A rock shatters Keiichi's headlamp, but even at night, he knows every inch of the course. Between his spooky skills and Belldandy's magic, however, he and Keima manage to put quite a scare into a TV crew looking for the "Ghost of the Pass."

Chapter 150: The Path of Belief February 2001—The TV producer's van, parked sideways across the road, means the lead in the race will be made by a split-second decision, as only one rider can get through the gap! Keiichi drops back, and . . .

Chapter 151: Prepared to Win, Prepared to Lose March 2001— . . . Keima makes it through, while Keiichi shoots behind the guardrail to crash into the brush—or so Keima assumes! Roaring out of the culvert on the next curve, Keiichi's right back on Keima's tail. He pulls even with his father at last . . . but he doesn't win.

Chapter 152: The Real You April 2001—Belldandy tries to keep her promise to tell Takano who she really is, but can't quite get it out. As a goodbye present, Keima gives the goddesses glass-feather pendants, sparking a strange vision . . . she didn't say who she was, but do Keiichi's parents understand anyway?

Chapter 153: The Hot Springs Episode June 2001 (there was no *OMG!* story in the May 2001 issue of *Afternoon*)—It turns out cheap Chihiro had tried to "repay" Keima for his earlier help with a raffle ticket for a stay at the Yuufuin Hot Springs Resort. But Takano gave it back to Keiichi, and it turns out . . . it won! *Road trip!*

Chapter 154: I Dub Thee, Yuufuin July 2001—Even though it's a ticket for a *couple,* Chihiro insists on tagging along, driving Bell and Keiichi there in her minicar. It's one problem after the other on Japan's crowded (and expensive) highways, until the last hair-brained shortcut by Chihiro gives Belldandy a chance to make a happy ending.

Chapter 155: Fighting Wings August 2001—The goddesses are having a tea party with their angels, when suddenly, after all this time, a new goddess descends: Lind, a stoic, no-nonsense warrior. She has come to put Tarikihongan Temple under quarantine, as the monster known as the Eater of Angels has escaped, and she suspects it's headed here . . .

Oh My Goddess! Volume 25

Chapter 156: Battle and Joy September 2001—Urd is the first victim of the Eater of Angels, and Peorth too falls soon thereafter, leaving them both comatose. Troubled by her inability to protect them, Lind talks about her profession with Belldandy.

Chapter 157: A Dance of Feathers October 2001—Lind and Belldandy point out to Skuld and Keiichi why trying to make decoy angels won't work, and that Peorth and Urd were forewarned, but still ambushed. But soon, so is Belldandy, and in Lind's presence. How can this be? Unless . . .

Chapter 158: The One-Winged Angel November 2001—Unless the Eater of Angels isn't roaming around somewhere for Lind to find—it's inside her, and she's been carrying it all along! Hild manifests herself (with Mara in tow), pleased that Lind has unwittingly carried out her plan: pull the angels out of the goddesses, so that she can then replace them with familiars under demonic control!

Chapter 159: Devil of a Plot December 2001—Lind rips the Eater of Angels out of her body—even though it still holds her angel Spear Mint—and, grabbing Skuld and Keiichi, escapes out onto the grounds of Tarikihongan to plan a counterattack. Meanwhile, Hild and Mara look forward to making Skuld summon her long-hidden angel Noble Scarlet—so Skuld, too, can be implanted with a familiar!

Chapter 160: What Times Demand January 2002—To keep the Eater of Angels from concentrating on a single target, Lind transfers her *other* Angel, Cool Mint . . . to Keiichi! A weakened Lind then urges the uncertain Skuld to call forth Noble Scarlet, and even at this moment of fear, it is a joyous reunion . . .

Chapter 161: Binary Wings February 2002—Keiichi, to Hild's astonishment, shows himself capable of carrying Cool Mint. But the dark mistress has her own secret weapon to reveal—Belldandy, projecting a powerful wave of demonic force from her implanted familiar!

Chapter 162: Goddess of the Ax March 2002—Then the field collapses, for something Hild did not foresee has happened—Belldandy has made the familiar angelic! Cool Mint

and Noble Scarlet, working together, free the other trapped angels from the Eater, as Lind charges in to strike!

Oh My Goddess! Volume 26

Chapter 163: Flight of the Fighting Wings April 2002—The Eater of Angels has gone berserk, and Hild and Mara decide to hightail it back to the realms below. Lind and Belldandy want to send the Eater there, as well. Ordinarily, it would be impossible, but . . .

Chapter 164: Pleasure and Duty May 2002—As Belldandy's new angel nevertheless has familiar blood, it gives her an opening to the demon world, and the goddess proposes to open a gate. Lind realizes then that Belldandy, too, is a warrior . . .

Chapter 165: With the Binary Angels June 2002—Skuld, Urd, and Peorth leap in to support Belldandy, using the power of their own angels, and the stubborn Eater of Angels finally departs. Now all they have to do is rebuild the shattered Tarikihongan Temple . . .

Chapter 166: To Call You Friend July 2002—Thanks to Keiichi, Lind has been able to see her twin angels meet at last, and realize she had been training in the wrong direction all these years. Keiichi points out it was hardly a waste, as the power she gained saved them all. Lind now realizes why Belldandy loves Keiichi . . . but she'll just have to settle—for calling him a friend.

Chapter 167: Inside Belldandy August 2002—Promising to come back on vacation, Lind has returned to Heaven. But there are unresolved issues left behind—most notably, the angelic familiar still inside Belldandy.

Chapter 168: Landscape with Angels September 2002—The rejection syndrome Belldandy is experiencing from the angelic familiar is causing disruptive effects all around . . . and now the familiar has found a new home inside Keiichi, who has become receptive to such beings since the fight with the Eater of Angels!

Chapter 169: What We Would Save October 2002—Belldandy is trying to calculate how to return the angelic familiar to its egg, as the burden is starting to sap both her and Keiichi's energy. Believing that Belldandy has hesitated too long to solve the crisis, the other goddesses conspire to put her under a seal!

Oh My Goddess! Volume 27

Chapter 170: The Great Earth Search November 2002—Borne on the familiar's wings, Keiichi flies off in sudden anguish, and Belldandy, breaking the seal, flies off after him. Skuld has an ambitious scheme by which the goddesses will literally search the entire planet for the two of them, but there's one flaw she hasn't considered.

Chapter 171: Kiss Me Goodbye January 2003 (there was no *OMG!* story in the December 2002 issue of *Afternoon*)—Keiichi's notion that a cooperative *demon* could be found to bear the familiar leads him and Urd to ask Velsper, and after suitable groveling, he agrees—but the transfer means two things: Velsper must admit he's a demon, and Keiichi must kiss Velsper!

Chapter 172: Shoot or Die! February 2003—Skuld and Urd's latest Channel Fight takes on the form of a rubber-band war, into which Peorth is drawn after her tai-yaki suffers collateral damage.

Chapter 173: Horseshoes and Handgrenades March 2003—The rubber-band war escalates into a three-way struggle that devastates the grounds and much of the structure of the Tarikihongan Temple. Belldandy makes them clean it all up.

Chapter 174: Is Here She? April 2003—While working late at Whirlwind, Keiichi and Belldandy receive a visit from a Machiner, a strange mechanical race, requesting the goddess's aid to fix a loose chain. But her spells don't work well on Machiners, so Keiichi does the repair, fascinated by their "beautiful parts," even if the Machiner thinks that makes him a peeping-tom freak.

Chapter 175: That Flying Entity May 2003—Another graceful Machiner is seen gliding above Whirlwind, and it turns out that the first one is part of its landing gear! Keiichi, taking inspiration from an old *Thunderbirds* episode, comes up with a plan for the flying entity to make a safe touchdown.

Chapter 176: Sign of Gratitude June 2003—Belldandy manages to use her magic indirectly to avert disaster at the last moment. In gratitude, the Machiners give Keiichi a wrench set . . . but not just any wrench set!

Oh My Goddess! Volume 28

Chapter 177: The Great Earth Search July 2003—Belldandy, infected by a magical Ahem Bug, comes down with laryngitis, for which both Urd and Peorth offer their treatments. What a time for Sora to show up, and request their help with the Motor Club recruitment drive!

Chapter 178: Those Who Guard and Those Who Plunder August 2003—The N.I.T. campus festival hasn't lost any of its madness since Keiichi was a student there . . . and Tamiya and Otaki are just as crazy if they think their karaoke tent is going to get people to join the club. Or are they?

Chapter 179: What I Can Do for You September 2003—Everyone's sticking around in hopes of winning the karaoke contest, and it's painful for Belldandy, who loves to sing.

She's about to finally get her voice back, but will bad old Mara use the impromptu campus concert for evil ends?

Chapter 180: The Polka-Dotted Cat and the Magic Broom October 2003—Velsper's having the same kind of problems bearing the angelic familiar that Belldandy had . . . and it's giving him unsightly spots to boot. Belldandy has the idea to ask Hild for help, and chases him down in a polite yet persistent fashion. Hild finally agrees to help—but on one condition . . .

Chapter 181: Fastest Broom, Greatest Race! November 2003—Belldandy must defeat Hild in a broom race, although Hild's "broom" is the mighty miscellaneous magic item, Glühende Herz. Even Stringfellow Hawke has heard of him, and is intimidated . . . until he remembers his partner is Belldandy!

Chapter 182: Courage and Trial December 2003—Keiichi is worried about Belldandy's safety . . . and the other goddesses are a little nonplussed that he doesn't know she's the six-time broom-racing champion in heaven. Hild has the faster broom, but on the neighborhood course, it's Bell who knows the territory . . .

Oh My Goddess! Volume 29

Chapter 183: The Barriers That Bind January 2004—As Keiichi and the goddesses watch via Skuld's sky-cam, the race roars down the culvert. A jet blast from Glühende Herz burns Stringfellow's straw . . . a dive into the river puts it out, but now he can't stabilize himself!

Chapter 184: Heaven and Hell February 2004—Overcoming his fear, Velsper asks the goddesses to work their magic and make his hair grow longer . . . and overcoming his distaste, Velsper asks Keiichi to knock him up into the air . . . where he merges with Stringfellow's damaged straw. Hild is a gracious loser, and says what must be done to fix the familiar . . .

Chapter 185: Beautiful Name March 2004—Namely, the familiar must be *named!* Velsper just wants to do so in peace and quiet, but Skuld and Urd insist on sharing in the joy. While out on a job for Whirlwind with Belldandy, Keiichi thinks about the importance of names—and then a certain black cat crosses his path!

Chapter 186: Wanted April 2004—Belldandy tries to put a stop to the chase, as the familiar must be named by sunset. Skuld and Urd claim they were just needed as witnesses, but Velsper points out goddess rules don't apply . . . to him. But what will be the name?

Chapter 187: The Path to a First-Class Goddess May 2004—Returning home, Urd gets a surprise: Peorth has just received word that Urd, long a Goddess Second-Class despite her power, has qualified for the First-Class test. But Belldandy will be her proctor!

Chapter 188: The Power of a First-Class Goddess June 2004—Having answered the initial question correctly, Belldandy provisionally unseals Urd's ability to use First-Class spells. Surely Urd will be okay with a sudden rush of near-limitless power? Surprisingly, yes.

Oh My Goddess! Volume 30

Chapter 189: Happy! Happy? July 2004—The final problem for Urd to solve is a bit of an essay question: how do you make Keiichi really happy? We see what really happened years ago, the first time Urd tried to take this test, and claimed to Belldandy she was rejected for being a liar. But *that* was a lie!

Chapter 190: The Herald of Happiness August 2004—Urd wakes up from a nightmare about her black and white selves being divided—and then realizing she's overslept for her exam, races off to follow Keiichi and Belldandy. But he'd rather find happiness on his own, thank you . . .

Chapter 191: Rain & Happiness, Cause & Effect September 2004—Urd makes it rain over Keiichi and Belldandy, causing them to seek shelter . . . in the doorway of a love hotel! He wonders if she's giving him a sign that it's time to take their relationship to another level . . .

Chapter 192: For Whose Sake a First-Class Goddess? October 2004—Urd has succeeded on the final question. But now that she's qualified to be a Goddess First-Class, she turns it down! The reason why is linked to why she lied to Bell so long ago . . . and why she feels the need to lie in the first place.

Chapter 193: Important Words November 2004—Peorth has never quite given up on Keiichi's personal life, and demands to know if he ever actually tells Belldandy that he loves her. The answer seems to be no, and the question throws him for a loop.

Chapter 194: Love Overflowing December 2004—Keiichi wonders exactly why it is so hard for him to tell Belldandy he loves her. Peorth decides to make him practice saying it to her over and over, sounding ever stronger . . . until the moment Belldandy walks in on them!

To be continued in future volumes of *Oh My Goddess!* . . . of course! And thank *you* all for making *OMG!* the longest-running English-language manga in history! Like a long-launched space probe, *Oh My Goddess!*, which first appeared from Dark Horse in 1994, is the oldest continuously running manga in the English-speaking world. The great majority of these stories were first licensed and adapted by Toren Smith, and those released since have continued to benefit from his superb choice of Dana Lewis as translator and Susie Lee as letterer. The editor would like therefore to dedicate the English-language edition of *Oh My Goddess! Colors* to those three people—as this work is essentially a record of their own.

ORIGINAL KODANSHA EDITION CREDITS:

CG COLORING SUPERVISORS
Kosuke Fujishima, Oujo Karei, Hajime Sato

PRODUCTION
Hiroyuki Yahiro, Satoru Mitagawa, SUBTLE, Hiro Koba, Kuki, and Kazuhisa Kuribara

TEXT CG PRODUCTION COLLABORATION
OLM Digital Corporation, Hiroshi "Space Dog" Yoshida, and Yumiko Shimada

COLLABORATION/WRITING
Go Momohara (Southern Peach House), Amaki Yabusei (Southern Peach House)

BINDING/DESIGN
Masashi Hisamochi (Stereo Graphics)

DARK HORSE EDITION CREDITS:

EDITOR
Carl Gustav Horn

TRANSLATORS
Douglas Varenas (text), Dana Lewis, Alan Gleason, and Toren Smith (color manga),
Dan Kanemitsu (Understanding *Oh My Goddess!* . . . In Eight Pages or Less!)

LETTERING AND TOUCH-UP
Susie Lee and Betty Dong with Tom2K

EDITORIAL ASSISTANTS
Rachel Miller and Annie Gullion

SPECIAL THANKS TO
Davey Estrada, Krystal Hennes, Michael Gombos, Tim Ervin, and Fred Gallagher

DESIGNER
Scott Cook

PUBLISHER
Mike Richardson

English-language version produced by Dark Horse Comics

OH MY GODDESS! COLORS

© 2009 by Kosuke Fujishima. All rights reserved. First published in Japan in 2001 by Kodansha Ltd., Tokyo. Publication rights for this English edition arranged through Kodansha Ltd. This English-language edition © 2009 by Dark Horse Comics, Inc. All other material © 2009 by Dark Horse Comics, Inc. All rights reserved. No portion of this publication may be reproduced, in any form or by any means, without the express written permission of Dark Horse Comics, Inc. Names, characters, places, and incidents featured in this publication are either the product of the author's imagination or are used fictitiously. Any resemblance to actual persons (living or dead), events, institutions, or locales, without satiric intent, is coincidental. Dark Horse Manga™ is a trademark of Dark Horse Comics, Inc. All rights reserved.

Published by
Dark Horse Manga
A division of Dark Horse Comics, Inc.
10956 SE Main Street
Milwaukie OR 97222
www.darkhorse.com

To find a comics shop in your area, call the Comic Shop Locator Service toll-free at 1-888-266-4226

First edition: April 2009
ISBN 978-1-59582-255-0

1 3 5 7 9 10 8 6 4 2
Printed in China

Publisher Mike Richardson • Executive Vice President Neil Hankerson • Chief Financial Officer Tom Weddle • Vice President of Publishing Randy Stradley • Vice President of Business Development Michael Martens • Vice President of Marketing, Sales, and Licensing Anita Nelson • Vice President of Product Development David Scroggy • Vice President of Information Technology Dale Lafountain • Director of Purchasing Darlene Vogel • General Counsel Ken Lizzi • Editorial Director Davey Estrada • Senior Managing Editor Scott Allie • Senior Books Editor, Dark Horse Books Chris Warner • Senior Books Editor, M Press/DH Press Robert Simpson • Executive Editor Diana Schutz • Director of Design and Production Cary Grazzini • Art Director Lia Ribacchi • Director of Scheduling Cara Niece

AFTERV

by *Megatokyo*'s Fre

D1290449

Sometimes, when browsing the remarkably extensive manga sections in my local bookstores, I think about how much has changed since I first became interested in manga back in the early '90s. There was no "manga" section back then, no shelves packed with a huge variety of translated, ready-to-read books. You could sometimes find translated and "flipped" titles in the "comics" section, but this usually required trips to well-stocked comic-book shops. After exhausting the rather limited selection of manga even the best comic shops could offer, your only alternative was to go directly to the source and find manga in its original, untranslated form.

I remember my first pilgrimage to a Japanese bookstore in New York City. I knew there was a lot of manga out there to discover (thanks to this newfangled "internet" thing), but it wasn't until I reached the second floor of that store that I realized how vast the sea of manga really was. Even with some foreknowledge of what to expect, I was overwhelmed by the sheer number of titles which I had never heard of before. I left the store several hours later with a big smile on my face, and two large and heavy bags full of books.

Now, there was one small problem with this: I can't read Japanese.

My efforts to learn Japanese over the years have been extensive and tragic. I was building a collection of books full of amazing art and engaging stories that I couldn't read. Since I am one of the chronically language impaired, "reading" manga usually involved poring over the art and ignoring the cryptic content of the dialogue bubbles. This might seem like an ineffective way to read a story (and it is), but it wasn't fruitless. Manga is an art form that relies on both text and art to communicate with the reader, but I have often been amazed how much the art can communicate on its own. The subtle play of emotions across a character's face, the complex rendering of a scene, the interplay of characters as they interact with each other . . . You might not know the details of what is going on, but you know what the characters are feeling.

While I may not have learned the Japanese language by studying manga, I did learn how to read the language of the art itself. I have been lucky enough to have the opportunity to put some of what I've learned to use in my own work. The artwork in the books I purchased that day has had an enormous impact on my artwork and my career over the past fifteen years.

Six of the books in those bags were the first six volumes of Kosuke Fujishima's *Aa! Megami-sama*.

It goes without saying that his artwork is beautiful. There is a flow to his lines, a delicate structure to his compositions that makes his work singularly amazing. His drawings are filled with amazing depth of detail that never overwhelms the overall composition, but adds pop to the characters few other manga artists can attain. His panels often contain little background, but this doesn't matter because the characters consume our attention. When he does direct our focus to more mundane, earthly things, from the springs on a cute plastic clothespin to the lovingly accurate detailing of a classic Brough Superior motorcycle, the care and attention to detail are remarkable. I could wax poetic for quite some time, but I'll spare you the ordeal. I'll let the artwork in this book speak for itself, much like it did to me in the years before Dark Horse took pity on us, releasing translated versions of *Aa! Megami-sama* to these shores . . . as *Oh My Goddess!*

There are four manga-ka that I list as my greatest influences. Fujishima-sensei is one of them. As any fanboy otaku-type knows, it is proper to refer to prominent manga creators as *sensei*, but in my case doing so is particularly appropriate. I have learned much from studying his work over the years. Given the difference of style and level of skill, it might be hard to see the influence that Fujishima-sensei has had on my work, but there is no question it is there, and my work is better for it.

Fred Gallagher is the artist and cocreator of Megatokyo, *the first three volumes of which are available from Dark Horse.* Megatokyo *is also published in Japanese by Kodansha, which is, of course, also the home of* Oh My Goddess! *itself. OMG! wasn't your typical manga on the U.S. market when it began here in 1994 . . . yet it has become the longest-running manga in English. In recent years,* Megatokyo *has become the most successful English-language graphic novel inspired by manga . . . and I think it's precisely because* Megatokyo *was the first such book to truly convey that balance of comedy and sensitivity in a relationship story that is what fans seek in a manga like* Oh My Goddess! *And for that reason, I couldn't think of a more appropriate person than Fred Gallagher to write the afterword to this edition of* Oh My Goddess! Colors, *a book which is for every English-speaking fan who has enjoyed and been inspired by Fujishima-sensei's work.* —ed.